Neighbors

NEIGHBORS

LIVING THE REVOLUTION
An Oral History of Contemporary Cuba

Oscar Lewis
Ruth M. Lewis
Susan M. Rigdon

UNIVERSITY OF ILLNOIS PRESS
Urbana   Chicago   London

In order to maintain the anonymity of the subjects of this study, the names of all informants, members of their families, their friends, and their neighbors have been changed. Places of birth, hometowns, details of work histories (but not salary or skill levels), as well as some streets, stores, hotels, and other public places, have also been changed. The names of historical figures and public officials have not been changed except in those cases in which a public figure or official had a personal relationship with one or more of the subjects in this study.

LIBRARY OF CONGRESS CATALOGING IN PUBLICATION DATA

Lewis, Oscar, 1914–1970.
  Living the revolution.

  Includes bibliographies.
  CONTENTS: v. 3. Neighbors.
  1. Cuba—Social conditions. 2. Cuba—Poor.
3. Cuba—Politics and government—1959- 4. Family—
Cuba—Case studies. I. Lewis, Ruth M., 1916-   joint
author. II. Rigdon, Susan M., 1943-   joint author.
III. Title.
HN203.5.L48   1977   309.1′7291′064   76-54878
ISBN 0-252-00641-0

Contents

PART III TEN YEARS OF REVOLUTION

PART IV THE CHILDREN

Preface [1]

THE GREAT SOCIAL UPHEAVAL that began with Castro's victory in 1959 brought large numbers of people of differing backgrounds to live together under radically new circumstances. To illustrate some of the personal consequences of this mass movement, especially the transfer of rural families to urban centers, we undertook this study of five unrelated families residing in a small apartment building at 411 Cristal Street, in the Havana suburb of Miramar. By examining, in the context of individual life stories, each family's day-to-day activities within the privacy of their homes, in their building, on their block, and in the neighborhood, we hoped to gain a more vivid image of life under the Revolution.

The five families offered contrasts racially and socioeconomically, as well as in their degree of "integration" or involvement in the Revolution. Three of the families were white, one was black, and one mulatto or, as they said, *indio*. Four families were from poor, rural, yet diverse, backgrounds and had settled in Havana only since the triumph of the Revolution; the members of the fifth family were middle-class and natives of the capital. All but the last family have had to make the difficult adjustment to urban life as well as to life under socialism. The level of education among the tenants ranged from illiteracy to college-preparatory school.

Field work for the Miramar study was begun in March, 1969, and was continued until June 25, 1970, a period coinciding with the government's all-out effort to mobilize the Cuban population for the 10-million-ton sugar-cane harvest goal set by Fidel Castro. In that "Year of Decisive Effort," with its shortages of goods and services, low priority for activities not connected with sugar production, and the unusually heavy work schedules, our research often seemed inappropriate. Nevertheless,

1. The study presented in this volume was part of a larger research project carried out by Oscar Lewis and his staff in Havana in 1969–70. For an account of the history and objectives of the research the reader is referred to the Foreward in *Four Men*, the initial volume in the series *Living the Revolution: An Oral History of Contemporary Cuba*.

most of the Miramar families we interviewed accepted us and offered their cooperation, for which we are greatly indebted to them.

In 1969 the interviewing of the five families was carried out largely by Rafael Rodríguez Castañeda and Olivia Hernández de Rodríguez, both of Mexico, and Claire Siegelbaum, of the United States. In 1970, work with some of the families was continued by Anadel Snyder de Domingo and Judith Ann Lewis, both North Americans. The interviewing of the parents was undertaken first, leaving for later the more difficult work with the children. Interviews with the latter were barely under way when the project was called to a halt, and we have little material to offer on this all-important aspect. The unexpected end of the project also accounts for the incompleteness of the neighborhood study and for much of the unevenness in length and depth of the life histories. These variations also reflected, to some degree, resistance on the part of two informants; both were very busy with their work, but one was also openly mistrustful.

This volume is based upon almost 5,000 pages of notes and transcribed interviews. A total of forty-one informants—members of the five families, their relatives, neighbors, and local schoolteachers—were interviewed. In addition to formal tape-recorded interviews, the staff made regular (usually daily) visits to the building, to talk to anyone who happened to be available. Occasionally one or two of the staff would be invited to a birthday party or family celebration, or, more rarely, to share a meal. These visits were later written up in the form of observations and comments. Two of the staff members spent an entire day in one household, taking turns observing and recording the activities and conversation of the family members from the time they awoke in the morning until they retired at night.

All work with the Cárdenas family (with the exception of two interviews with Pablo Fontanés by Oscar Lewis) was done by Rafael Rodríguez Castañeda and Olivia Hernández de Rodríguez between March and November, 1969. Eulalia Fontanés was interviewed eighteen times (663 pages in the original transcribed Spanish) and Armando Cárdenas twenty times (855 pages). Another 250 pages resulted from interviews with Lala's brother Diego (interviewed once), her father, Pablo Fontanés (four times), and her mother, Eulalia Torres (once). With fifty-nine additional pages of written observations on the family by the interviewers, the Spanish-language materials on the Cárdenas family totaled 1,827 pages.

Claire Siegelbaum interviewed the Pérez family between March and November, 1969, although visits to their home continued into May, 1970. Mercedes Millán was interviewed twelve times (323 pages); her daughter Merceditas, once (29 pages); and her mother, Alicia Moreno, once (16 pages). Juan Carlos Pérez was interviewed several times, but only one tape remained intact (34 transcribed pages); another was lost due to technical difficulties, but a written summary of the interview was available to us. Some of the material on the Pérez family, including a material-culture study, was confiscated by the government. The total amount of transcribed Spanish-language materials on this family, including eighty-seven pages of written observations, was 489 pages.

Work with the Rojas family was begun by Rodríguez and Hernández in April, 1969, and was continued by Judy Lewis from January to June, 1970. Sara Rojas was interviewed twenty-two times (871 pages); Eduardo Rojas, seven times (228 pages); Violeta, five times (137 pages); Ana Teresa, twice (36 pages); Bernardo, once (3 pages); and Euquerio Rojas, Eduardo's father, once (6 pages). A day study (232 pages) of the family was done by Rodríguez and Hernández, who also wrote an additional forty-one pages of observations and impressions, bringing the total amount of material to 1,554 pages.

The Labrada family was interviewed and observed between April, 1969, and March, 1970, by Rodríguez and Hernández, and by Anadel Snyder de Domingo. Leticia Manzanares was interviewed six times (198 pages), as was Domingo Labrada (261 pages); their daughter Lina, once (21 pages); and Domingo's brother Dámaso, four times (235 pages). An additional forty-six pages of impressions and observations brought the total to 761 pages.

Of the five families, the Hernández family study was the least developed; work with them was carried out by Rodríguez and Hernández between April and November, 1969. Lieutenant Hernández was suspicious of the project's motives and told his friend and neighbor Juan Carlos Pérez that he would not cooperate. The lieutenant was interviewed twice, however, resulting in 58 transcribed pages; his wife, Justa Díaz, four times (157 pages); their daughter Genoveva, twice (55 pages); and their daughter Florinda, once (16 pages). An additional twenty-five pages of observations brought the Spanish-language total to 321 pages.

In interviews with neighbors of the five families and with teachers in the neighborhood schools, Siegelbaum, Rodríguez, Hernández, and a Cuban assistant collected another 266 pages on the history of the block, the building, and the schools.

This book is divided into four parts, with an Introduction describing the setting of the study. In Part I, the adult informants discuss the changes that have come to the block and the neighborhood, some of their problems in adapting to their new lives, and the areas of conflict and cooperation among the families. Part II presents the life story of each husband and wife up to 1959, including childhood, family life, and marriage; the description of life in pre-Castro Cuba gives some basis for understanding the informants' present attitudes toward revolutionary institutions and the levels of their involvement in them. Part III presents life under the Revolution up to 1970, the impact of its

institutions upon the home and family, the sacrifices expected, the benefits offered, and what our informants think of these and of the future
for themselves and their children. Part IV consists of interviews with
three children from three different families, preceded by a brief account
of changes in the status of children and a description of the activities of
our young informants in school and at home.

Acknowledgments

IN ACKNOWLEDGING THE MANY obligations incurred in the long course of this project, we would like to thank the Ford Foundation for the original grant to do research in Cuba, and for a subsequent grant to write up the field data. We also thank the University of Illinois Graduate College Research Board and the Center for International Comparative Studies for additional financial support, and the university's Department of Anthropology for office space and other services. We are grateful to the Cuban Academy of Sciences for its early interest in the project and to the many Cuban citizens and government officials whose cooperation made the research possible.

Of the many people who worked on the materials for this volume, we would like first to thank Rafael Rodríguez Castañeda, Olivia Hernández de Rodríguez, Claire Siegelbaum, Anadel Snyder de Domingo, and Judith Ann Lewis for their field work in Miramar, Havana. We are grateful to Muna Muñoz Lee for translating the bulk of the data, and to Claudia Beck, Deborah Kolditz, and Nina Díaz-Peterson for other translations. For their organization of the Spanish interviews we thank Anadel Snyder, Deborah Kolditz, Judith Ann Lewis, Theodore McDonald, and Mary Anne Guerrero. We gratefully acknowledge Elizabeth Spence, Phoebe Stone, Judith Ann Lewis, Alice McMurray, Nina Díaz-Peterson, and Bernice B. Lieberman for their work on the preliminary organization and editing of the various English texts. Thanks are due to Lorraine Glennon, Barbara Anderson, and Shirley Lee for typing most of the manuscripts, and to Nina Díaz-Peterson and Janet Sobolewski for changing the original names to pseudonyms and for clerical work.

For their critical readings of large parts of the final manuscript and for helpful suggestions on all three volumes in this series, we are very grateful to Diane Levitt Gottheil, Susan Welch, and Alan J. Booth. We would especially like to express our deep gratitude to Fern M. Hartz, secretary to Oscar Lewis from 1959 to 1970 and to the Cuba research project since its inception. Finally, we wish to thank Elizabeth Dulany of the University of Illinois Press for her painstaking editing of the final manuscript.

Introduction

THE 400 BLOCK OF CRISTAL STREET, where the five families lived, is located in the *Zona Congelada de la Habana* or Frozen Zone of Havana, an area encompassing the middle- and upper-class suburbs of Miramar, Marianao, El Country Club, and parts of El Vedado. The zone was established by Castro after many of the well-to-do residents of Havana left Cuba. Emigrants were prohibited by law from taking with them their personal fortunes (or such part of them as were still in Cuba) or personal possessions of any significant value, and as a result, thousands of furnished houses and apartments reverted to the state.

Faced with the decision of what to do with the vacated homes, many of which were mansions and not practical as single-family dwellings, Castro decided against distributing them to individuals and families in need of housing. To use them in this way, he reasoned, would at best solve the housing problems of only a handful of families. It was decided, therefore, to make these suburbs into a zone that was "frozen" or closed to general residence. All suitable empty houses were to be used as schools, dormitories, or offices for the health, education, and welfare programs of the Revolution. Houses and apartments found unfit for government use were turned over to Urban Reform, the government office which administered all urban rental housing, and to the Frozen Zone's Housing office, to be leased as private residences on the basis of need.

The multi-purpose use of housing in Havana and the suburbs gave rise to a new type of mixed residential community. This, combined with the fact that the government had nationalized all businesses and rental property in the city and had subordinated urban development to agricultural investment and rural development, made life in the city radically different from what it had been in the past.

Many of the changes in Havana have stemmed from Fidel Castro's belief that the capital city was too large for a nation of Cuba's size and that its residents made excessive demands on the country's resources.[1]

1. Lee Lockwood, *Castro's Cuba, Cuba's Fidel* (New York: Vintage, 1969), pp. 104-5.

To Castro and the Twenty-sixth of July Movement,[2] Havana was a symbol of indulgence, exploitation, and privilege. During the first years of the new government, therefore, most construction of roads, schools, housing, and hospitals took place outside Havana Province. The state's program of urban housing was designed to keep just abreast of the growing population (although as of 1969 it had not been able to do this), and to provide new housing for those displaced by slum-clearance programs. Some of Havana's worst slums, including the shantytown Las Yaguas, were razed.

By the late 1960s, Havana was far from the city of privilege it once had been. The heavy downtown traffic, motor and pedestrian, had disappeared; nightclubs, shops and small businesses, many restaurants, concessions, and vendors had been "intervened" (nationalized) and shut down, or reopened on a part-time basis under state management. Tourism was, of course, greatly curtailed, especially after the United States broke off diplomatic relations with Cuba. Hotels, private clubs, and beaches were taken over by the National Institute of the Tourist Industry; clubs and beaches were opened to the public and hotel room rents were lowered by as much as $35 a day, making them available to large numbers of Cubans. The Havana Hilton, renamed the Habana Libre, was used to house foreign guests, government meetings, international conferences, and to provide classrooms for temporary schools set up to teach hygiene and basic domestic skills to country people.

The quiet, prosperous, all-white Havana suburb of Miramar underwent striking changes after being declared a Frozen Zone. Along with its pre-1959 residents, most of whom had been in business or the professions, the new population included heroes and leaders of the Revolution, foreign technicians, diplomatic personnel from capitalist and socialist countries, thousands of young students from rural homes, and other Cubans, black and white, of all socioeconomic backgrounds.

In 1960, schools, clinics, and rest homes were established in Miramar's larger vacated residences. The medium and smaller-sized homes became foreign embassies, administrative offices, and dormitories for boarding students on scholarships. The "Ana Betancourt Plan"[3] for training girls (mostly from poor, rural families) to teach primary and secondary school brought 8,000 girls on scholarships to Miramar. Single-family residences and apartments were assigned to visiting dignitaries, foreign technicians working on agricultural or industrial development programs, and diplomatic personnel. In one part of Miramar a small community was estab-

2. The revolutionary movement organized by Castro in 1955 to overthrow Batista. It took its name from the date of the attack on the Moncada garrison in Oriente in 1953, an event which marked the beginning of Castro's armed revolt against Batista. After the attack, Castro and the other survivors were captured and imprisoned.

3. Part of the Ministry of Education's larger "Plan for Advancement of Women."

lished for the families of counterrevolutionaries who were serving time in prison or on work farms. Brought to the city in 1965 at state expense, these families, once numbering 1,000 people, from rural Pinar del Río and Las Villas provinces, were to be "rehabilitated" and integrated into the Revolution while husbands, sons, and fathers underwent the same process in prison.[4]

For the old residents who remained in Miramar, personal lives were turned upside down. Their life-styles, which once embodied Cuban society's definition of success, became objects of contempt and examples of what not to be. Many of the families were divided by conflicting attitudes toward the new system, and relatives were separated from one another, perhaps permanently, through emigration. Those who remained in Cuba retained ownership of the homes they lived in, but some lost their businesses and large property holdings, and/or lucrative private legal or medical practices when they were nationalized. They were no longer able to hire domestic servants, nor to organize landowners' associations to maintain the appearance of the community, or a private police force to keep "undesirables" from entering the neighborhood. The "undesirables" had moved next door and had taken over the private beaches and clubs. The scholarship children played in the streets, parks, and yards, picked fruit from private gardens, and marched in formation past their homes, singing and shouting slogans of the Revolution as they went.

The Block

The changes that had come to the 400 block of Cristal Street were indicative of the transformation of Miramar. The block was just off Fifth Avenue, a broad boulevard with a median and promenade that served as a park. Fifth Avenue runs east-west just three blocks from the shoreline and is one of Havana's main thoroughfares. Cristal and many of the other residential side streets that intersected Fifth Avenue were not as carefully maintained and provided a contrast to the well-kept boulevard.

The houses on the 400 block of Cristal Street displayed a potpourri of architecture, from the two palatial mansions that stood on either side of the intersection with Fifth Avenue to the smaller traditional Spanish colonial and simple modernistic designs of the thirteen houses and three small apartment buildings which fronted on Cristal Street. The two mansions had large, ornate gardens with pools, fountains, and marble statues. These were clear exceptions to the more modest mood of Cristal Street but they were designed to blend into the architectural grandeur of Fifth Avenue. The other houses and apartment buildings had small

4. See Lockwood's description and photographs of this program in *Castro's Cuba, Cuba's Fidel*, pp. 261–80.

yards and gardens on lots separated by wire fences and masonry walls covered with flowering vines. The gardens of the one-family residences, which had the best-groomed lawns, typified Cuban landscaping, with free-form gardens containing native greenery, a variety of shrubs, cattails, and laurel plants, and exotic flowering trees. Even those lawns and gardens no longer tended had some flowers growing, the most common varieties being *crotos* and *malpacíficos.* Among the native trees growing on the block were palm, olive, lemon, coconut, avocado, mango, jasmine, papaya, and banana trees.

All the buildings on the block had been designed as private dwellings, but in 1969 the smaller of the two mansions, the former home of a sugar-mill owner, was a school in one of the scholarship programs, and the larger house had been converted into a home for the aged. On the lawn in front of the school, suspended between two palm trees, was a poster with a slogan for the 1970 harvest: "One *arroba*[5] more per man each day. Nothing nor anyone will ever be able to stop us."

Another house on the block was also being used as a school, and five others served as dormitories for scholarship students (one formerly used as a dormitory had been vacant since 1968). The dormitories housed eighty-eight scholarship students. These children and their house-mothers (all of whom were under twenty-five years of age) were not prepared to care adequately for the homes they had been assigned. Poor supervision of the children contributed to the rapid deterioration of the buildings. The paint was chipped and peeling, the lawns littered, the windows broken, and the garage doors of all five dormitories were missing. Paint was a very scarce commodity in Cuba and its use for residences had low priority.

The scholarship students participated in two different programs. The "Mayitos" were enrolled in the "May First Program," part of the "Fidel Plan" to bring educationally disadvantaged children from the country to Havana for schooling. The second program trained high school students to be physical education teachers. This program's dining hall, shared by students from neighboring blocks, was also located on the 400 block.

The nine private residences housed 105 people—sixty-three adults and forty-two children. Of the six one-family dwellings, three were occupied by their pre-1959 owners, one housed a Cuban couple teaching at the University, and two others were protocol houses. One of the apartment buildings housed the five families in this study; the other two housed a mixture of new Cuban residents, ten Soviet and Bulgarian technicians (six men and four women), and one pre-1959 resident. Four garages on the block were also being used as family dwellings.[6]

5. Twenty-five pounds.
6. Tenants occupying garages paid no rent.

Relations among the Neighbors

The block, with its combination of new and old Cuban residents, students, and foreigners, was not a united community. The old residents had little contact with their new neighbors. The students kept to themselves and usually restricted their friendships to those enrolled in the same scholarship plan. In addition, they had their own organizations and activities separate from neighborhood or block organizations. The foreigners sometimes stopped to greet their Cuban neighbors or to give candy to the children, but for the most part they lived apart and had no significant contact with them. The foreign technicians spent long hours on the job and socialized mostly among themselves. In addition, they and the diplomatic personnel shopped at different stores, were given a more lenient rationing system or none at all, and their children often attended special schools.

In the early days of transition, there was a more cordial (if superficial) relationship between the old families and the few new neighbors. Since many of the pre-1959 residents were elderly, they asked the neighbors to do favors or run errands for them. In return they drove the newcomers on errands, allowed them to use their telephones, and gave them food and other gifts. As one of the residents who had moved to the block in 1961 commented, "It was a matter of reciprocity. That was the kind of friendship we had, nothing very deep, just pleasant, neighborly relations."

Some of the new residents were less critical of the old residents who emigrated than they were of one another, explaining their departure in terms of health or family problems rather than as opposition to the Castro government. For whatever reasons, most of the residents on the block did emigrate, among them several physicians, tobacco-industry executives, an artist, owners of a lime kiln, cement factory, and salt mine, a number of North American businessmen, and two sugar magnates. Only five of the old homeowners on the 400 block of Cristal Street remained after 1961. They were Máximo Abay and his wife, Luminosa Muñoz, José Sabina, Clara Falcón, and Carmen Tamayo, all of whom were questioned by project interviewers about how their lives had changed since 1959.

Máximo Abay, sixty-seven, lived with his fifty-eight-year-old wife, Luminosa Muñoz, in her family's home across the street from the five families being studied. The couple had moved there at the time of their marriage in 1938, when the land on the other side of the street was a pasture.

Abay, a physician's son, had inherited a share in his family home and the income from his father's investments, and owned an electrical-supplies company with his wife's brother until it was nationalized. The

Abays had since lived on a pension and on additional income from a private retirement fund.

Luminosa Muñoz, who taught art for twenty-two years in an American school in Havana, was bedridden and dying of Parkinson's disease. She had only her husband to care for her, and he rarely went out because he could not leave her alone. Their son, an only child, was living in the United States, where he had been educated; four of Abay's sisters and brothers had also left Cuba for the United States.

Living as a semi-recluse, Abay no longer bought clothes or went to church or to social clubs such as the Casino Español, to which he had formerly belonged. He said, "I do the cooking and I read and I spend my days taking care of my wife. I guess you could say I feel alone because our son is out of the country."

The Abays' only visitors were two old friends, his neighbor José Sabina, and another friend from outside the neighborhood who came to visit Luminosa on Sundays.

Abay's sister handled his ration book and did the shopping, and an old family servant, a Jamaican woman, still came in several times a week to do the laundry. The Abays had little or no contact with other residents on the block. An apartment at the back of the house, once used by Luminosa as a studio, was assigned to a family whom Abay greeted on sight but did not know.

Abay said that his life had been changed completely by the Revolution. He could remember the block as a lovely, quiet place where everyone knew everyone else. "It was all family." Now at 5:30 in the morning he heard the sound of wake-up calls for the scholarship students. "It's not that they [the students] really bother us; it's just that it's a completely different kind of life than we were accustomed to."

Abay's friend, José Sabina, a seventy-one-year-old native of Spain, lived alone just three doors away. He had immigrated to Cuba in 1916 and since 1932 had served as representative of a Spanish business firm. Although no business had been transacted with the company since the 1962 missile crisis, he still went to his old office every morning. Sabina had lived in his four-bedroom house since it was built in 1940. He had two daughters, one married and living in Mexico and another going to school in the United States. In 1964 his wife left for Mexico to be with her grandchildren and did not return.

Sabina often visited his old friends the Abays and, less frequently, Clara Falcón, who lived across the street. His only other contact in the neighborhood was with an old family servant who lived in a room above the garage and helped take care of him. Sabina knew none of his new neighbors but resented them, especially the students, whom he tried to keep away by planting cactus in his front yard. His friend Abay was less hostile and had apparently taken in stride their raids on his fruit trees.

Clara Falcón was fifty-four years old and had lived in Miramar since she was ten. In 1952 she moved into a modern, concrete apartment building built by her mother. Señora Falcón and her husband, a physician, frequented the Miramar Club and a local businessmen's club, where men played dominoes into the morning hours and the private beaches opened for swimmers at 6:00 A.M. When the clubs were opened to the public in 1960, Señora Falcón and her husband stopped attending. In any case, they no longer had a car and the Miramar Club was too far away to visit without one.

In 1963 Señora Falcón was divorced and her ex-husband later went to the United States. She continued to live alone in her old apartment, a unit with nine rooms, including three bedrooms and three baths. She still shopped, out of habit, at her old grocery, rather than at the store where most of her neighbors shopped. Instead of going to downtown Havana, she bought clothing and other items at El Tesoro, the local shopping center. Señora Falcón lived on a 106-*peso*[7] monthly stipend from Urban Reform (compensation for nationalization of her apartment building) and the 60-*peso* monthly salary she received from her job as a receptionist at a neighborhood church.

Señora Falcón seldom went out and rarely visited her neighbors. She said she liked the new residents assigned to the two other apartments in her building. One was Sonia Suárez, a forty-eight-year-old woman who had fought in the Sierra Maestra and who was on leave from her job as manager of a rest home in order to finish secondary school. She lived with her son, his wife, and their two children. The apartment was in her name and she paid 33 *pesos* a month for rent.[8] Another of her married sons lived in one of Señora Falcón's garages. The other tenants were four women technicians, three Russians and one Bulgarian.[9]

Señora Falcón said she got along very well with all the people in her building. "I've never had any problems with anyone on the block and I certainly hope I never will. Usually all the neighbors help each other. For example, if a person needs to borrow something, they ask for it and someone gives it to them. Another thing is the use of a refrigerator. If anyone needs to keep something in my refrigerator, I don't mind."

Like most of the old residents, Señora Falcón was disappointed by the changing physical appearance of the neighborhood. "Before the Revolu-

---

7. Cuban currency was maintained by the Castro government at the pre-1959 rate of 1 *peso* = 1 U.S. dollar until 1974, when the rate was changed to 1.25 *pesos* = 1 U.S. dollar.

8. A rent ceiling of 10 percent of household income went into effect in May, 1961. Sonia's rent was based on her income of 106 *pesos* a month plus the salaries of her son and daughter-in-law.

9. Six other technicians from Russia and Bulgaria also lived on the block; they occupied two apartments in the building at 409. They were recent arrivals in Cuba and were specialists in hydraulic engineering, soldering, transportation, topography, petroleum, and sugar.

tion, the block was a lot neater. The owners here cared about the surroundings; there were people hired to keep the garbage out of the
streets and take care of the trees. . . . But now it's up to the people that
live here and they don't seem to have time."

Señora Falcón was confused by all the changes in her life, but she
attributed them to the breakup of her family and not to the Revolution.
"I don't know exactly what to say about what has changed. I've always
kept pretty much to myself, more so now because my life is so different,
but it doesn't have anything to do with the situation. If I still had my
family living here, perhaps things would have remained the same for
me."

Carmen Tamayo, seventy, lived on the corner of Cristal Street and
Seventh Avenue in a large house containing nine bedrooms, six baths,
two living rooms, two terraces, two kitchens, and two dining rooms. She
had had it built in 1952 for 60,000 *pesos*, in the hope that her son, who
was studying engineering in the United States, would return to Cuba.
But the son suffered a mental breakdown while still in school and was
interned in a mental hospital near Havana.

Señora Tamayo was a descendant of an old landed family of slave-
holders. Her uncle had fought with General Maceo in the War of Independence against the Spanish and both her father and grandfather were
members of the Academy of Sciences. Besides her home, Señora
Tamayo had owned property in Old Havana and El Vedado. After this
property was nationalized by the state, she received a pension of 200
pesos a month. She was not happy with her life under the Revolution and
if she had had the money would have gone with her son to the United
States to seek a cure for him.

Living with Señora Tamayo since 1952 was her former maid, Norma
Gutiérrez, Norma's husband (a personnel chief in Transportation who
earned 160 *pesos* a month), and their two children. Señora Gutiérrez said
she was proud of the Revolution and had been sympathetic to it from the
beginning. Her husband had fought in the Sierra and she had aided the
Rebels by storing armbands for them in Señora Tamayo's home, which
had been searched several times by Batista's police.

As an old resident of the block, Señora Gutiérrez was distressed by its
current condition, blaming it on the students, whom she called "the little
warriors." She had had problems with their rowdiness and on one occasion even called the police to restrain them. She was especially upset by
the lack of student supervision and by the neglected appearance of the
dormitories, which she believed reflected poorly on the Revolution.
"Whenever a foreign delegation comes and passes by this block, I sometimes say to myself, 'What will they think seeing the cans piled high with
trash that rises to the top of the bushes, and the whole block without a
single garage door!' This is a disaster, simply a disaster!"

Despite her concern, Señora Gutiérrez saw a new kind of neighborhood in the making. She pointed to the cooperation among the neighbors in lending each other food, or giving scarce items from their own allotments to children and the elderly, and to people with health problems or special diets. Neighbors were also learning a cooperative system of shopping to reduce the time spent standing in line. "We are all conscious," she said, "that we're living in a different age than before the Revolution. We realize we have to help each other. Today we live in a much closer understanding with our friends."

The fourteen new Cuban households were in fact not yet united, but as in most neighborhoods everywhere tended to be divided into small friendship groupings. However, the mass organizations functioning on the neighborhood and block levels were designed to foster a new sense of community through programs of collective action. One of these is the Committees for Defense of the Revolution,[10] whose base level of organization in urban areas is usually the city block.

The Committee on the 400 block of Cristal Street had had a very sketchy record since it was organized in 1964. In 1969 it was not meeting at all. This was due, in part, to disorganization at the CDR sectional level, the source of directives for many of the block Committee's activities. CDR organization and recruitment suffered throughout Cuba in 1969–70 due to the tremendous effort being made toward achievement of that year's 10-million-ton goal for the sugar-cane harvest. A more important reason, and one which was probably unique to the Frozen Zone, was the composition of the block itself. The eighty-eight students, ten foreign technicians, and two diplomatic families were not eligible for CDR membership. Discounting the four old residents, who did not participate, there were only fourteen households from which to draw active members. The small size of this group accentuated differences in personality, levels of education, political integration, and regional and urban-rural origins, further discouraging collective action.

One resident, who was herself apolitical, said, "This is a system of collective action but that's exactly what we don't have here. People are

10. The *Comités de Defensa de la Revolución* (CDR) were founded September 28, 1960. They are active in a broad range of programs including public health, education, political education, urban reform, sports and recreation, local administration, as well as in surveillance work against counterrevolutionary activities. The Committees' activities (organized as *frentes*, or fronts) include recruiting volunteers to work in agriculture, standing guard duty to prevent neighborhood vandalism as well as sabotage, administering vaccines and other injections, encouraging adult education, organizing study groups, and calling meetings to deal with problems that arise at the block level (e.g., noisy or disorderly conduct by residents, neighborhood clean-up, school attendance, organizing support for national campaigns, etc.). Membership in the CDR is open to all Cubans fourteen and older who are "willing to defend the Revolution."

still living only for themselves and that's not right." It seemed unlikely that the situation would change unless there were a merger of the local Committee with one from the neighboring block, or stronger direction from the sectional level, or a change in population composition which would give this Committee a larger, more solid base.

Community Services and Facilities

Miramar had not originally been planned for residents without private means of transportation, and in 1969 very few Cubans had cars. But good public transportation had been set up within the area and between Miramar, Havana, and the western suburbs. Two buses ran an east-west route from Old Havana, along Fifth Avenue through Miramar. One bus was an express and the other made many intermediate stops. A second bus route ran east-west along Third Avenue through Miramar, as far west as Marianao. The residents of the 400 block of Cristal Street were less than a block from the Fifth Avenue bus stop and only two blocks from the Third Avenue stop. A third route connecting Havana, El Vedado, and Miramar passed along Cristal Street. The Fifth Avenue buses were scheduled to run at five- to ten-minute intervals and the other two routes at half-hour intervals, although that schedule was not completely reliable. Bus fare was 5 *centavos*.

Among the five families studied, only one, the Pérezes, owned a car; another tenant, a lieutenant, used a police car to get to and from his work. Most of the other residents of the building and on the block used the bus service frequently.

The nearest shopping center, El Tesoro, was eleven blocks away from Cristal Street and was a stop on the Third Avenue bus line. El Tesoro contained a drugstore, barbershop, pizzeria, coffee bar, cafeteria, dime store, and the local outlet of the national repair service center. The nearest food store, the Minimax,[11] was five and a half blocks away from Cristal Street.

The children of the families on the block did not attend the same schools as the scholarship students. The two primary schools serving the

11. Minimax was the name of a former food-store chain; it is used synonymously with "supermarket." Cuban citizens were required to register at one neighborhood store of their choosing, where all food shopping had to be done. This requirement existed because most basic food items were rationed, and to facilitate the correct distribution of goods from the central warehouse, the state had to know the exact number of people who would shop at each store. Additions or deletions to the household ration book or changes in residence had to be reported to the Office for Control of Food Distribution.

Clothing and other goods could be purchased by Cubans at any store of their choice, provided the buyer had the ration coupon entitling him to purchase at that time. Each household was assigned a number and was entitled to buy only when that number came up, on certain days of the month. Number groups were posted in stores and announced over the radio. (See Appendix A.)

neighborhood families were located two blocks away in two adjacent, vacant houses that had been converted to classrooms, library, and administrative offices.[12] One was for children in preschool through second grade and the other for third- through sixth-graders. A basic secondary school was located six blocks away.

There were two other primary schools in the vicinity, one for children with special learning problems and one for adults studying the primary grades. All persons sixteen and over who were still at the primary-school level were referred to the adult-education night classes. Each school was limited to an enrollment of about forty students.

The neighborhood was served by a polyclinic on the 500 block of Cristal Street. Standards set by Cuba's Ministry of Public Health required each polyclinic to have on duty (for outpatient treatment) a gynecologist, dentist, pediatrician, epidemiologist, nurses, and one intern. The two primary schools had their own clinic to treat minor injuries or illnesses and administer injections and vaccinations. For inpatient treatment, neighborhood residents went to hospitals outside Miramar.

There were a variety of recreational facilities available in the neighborhood. The local Workers' Social Circle[13] was located in a former businessman's club. It had a pool and space for volleyball and other outdoor games. There were also rooms where indoor games such as chess and dominoes were played. The club had a food counter-service which offered a special Cuban malt soft drink, sandwiches, and cake. Some families went there to eat when their food allotments were exhausted; others went to attend the weekend dances and musical shows organized by the Social Circle.

Four blocks from Cristal Street was a small park that offered children a grassy play area. It was also the site of a *jardín infantil,* an open-air nursery school for children between the ages of eighteen months and five years. Another type of nursery school, the *círculo infantil,* which accepts children from the ages of forty-five days to five years, was located several blocks from the park. Only children of working mothers are accepted in the *círculos* and *jardines.* No child from the five families was enrolled in these day-care services because none of the women worked outside their homes.

A second park, about eight blocks east of the neighborhood, had a food concession where hot dogs and ice cream were sold, but it did not have a play area. There was another grassy play area one block away on the Fifth Avenue boulevard median, but this was not often used by the

12. See the Introduction to Part IV ("The Children") for a discussion of the neighborhood schools.

13. Community recreation centers organized under the jurisdiction of the Communal Services Front of the *Poder Local* (see Part I, n. 31).

neighborhood children, probably because of the traffic and the need for adult supervision.

In addition to the two food concessions already mentioned, and the cafeteria, pizzeria, and coffee bar at El Tesoro, there was one restaurant in the neighborhood, located seven blocks away on Fifth Avenue. It was a small shop serving only ice cream, cake, and other snack foods. Next door was a small grocery store.

Laundry and dry-cleaning delivery services were available, but they were slow and most families did laundry at home. The few families in the neighborhood who did send out their clothes used a service in El Vedado.

Public utilities were, of course, all under state management. For repair service of electrical wiring, plumbing, sewage, and drainage, residents called the appropriate public utility. Orders for cooking gas were also placed by phone; deliveries and responses to complaints might come within a day or might take a week or longer, depending on the number of personnel available. This varied with the harvest season, when many workers left their customary jobs to do agricultural labor.

There was regular garbage pick-up service, but the block continued to have a litter problem because the garbage cans did not have lids and trash was often blown about the street. Neighborhood clean-up campaigns, however, were frequently organized by the CDR, the local delegation of the Federation of Cuban Women,[14] or the Young Pioneers.[15] The Frozen Zone had a special maintenance service for the protocol houses.

The CDR office was located in the home of the block president, who lived in a garage next to the house on the corner of Cristal and Seventh Avenue. The Frozen Zone office, which was responsible for housing assignments in the area, was within easy walking distance. The nearest branch of Urban Reform was the central office at 0 and 23rd streets in El Vedado, about forty blocks away. The one church in the neighborhood was Roman Catholic.

The Apartment House

The building at 411 Cristal Street where the five families lived was a modern, white brick and concrete structure with no pretense to architec-

---

14. *Federación de Mujeres Cubanas* (FMC), a mass organization founded August 23, 1960, is open to all women fourteen years of age and older. Headed by Vilma Espín, a veteran of the Sierra del Cristal campaign and member of the Party's Central Committee, the Federation had 1,192,843 members in 1969 (46 percent of all women between fifteen and sixty-five). (*Granma Weekly Review,* Jan. 25, 1970, p. 5.) In 1975, 77 percent of all women fourteen and older were members of the Federation. (*Ibid.,* Aug. 31, 1975, p. 6.)

15. *Unión de Pioneros de Cuba* (UPC), an adjunct to the Union of Young Communists (UJC), open to all children from ages seven to fourteen.

tural style or beauty. The three-story building, originally designed for three luxury apartments, was built in the 1950s by a wealthy resident of El Country Club suburb as an investment rather than for personal use.

Dominating the front of the building were two garages with blank-looking pull-down doors that were generally kept shut. Adjoining the garages to the right and leading into the entrance hall was a small brick porch, open on two sides and reached by two low steps flanked by large brick planters, empty of flowers and usually containing trash. The porch overlooked a small unkempt lawn that extended from the sidewalk to a few feet back of the porch, where the building indented to form an L shape. A single banana tree grew on the lawn and the grass was patchy and often littered with papers. A curved paved path led from the front walk to the front door of the first-floor apartment. It was the only unit in the building with a private entrance on the street.

The first-floor unit, occupied by the Pérez family, had four bedrooms and two baths, a garage in the back with a servant's room and bath, and the only direct access to the backyard. In 1961 when the Pérezes moved in, the rent was 120 *pesos* a month. It had been substantially higher before the government-ordered rent reductions of early 1959.[16] By 1969 the Pérezes were paying just 26.43 *pesos* a month. The second- and third-floor units each had three bedrooms and two baths, and in 1960 rented for 105 *pesos* a month. When the Hernández family moved to the second-floor apartment in 1967, their rent payments were set at 19.50 *pesos* a month. The Labrada family, who had lived on the third floor since 1964, paid 9.21 *pesos*. Each of these apartments had one of the garages in the front of the building.

The two additional apartments in the building were created from the former servants' quarters and from one of the garages. The garage was entered by a door just inside the front entrance hall, at the rear of which were the stairs leading to the second and third floors. The stairwell received light during the day through a long glassed-in window that spanned the two stories. Several of the glass panes in this window and the front door were broken.

The servants' quarters, located over the garages between the second- and third-floor units, were two single rooms measuring 3 by 6 meters, each with a small bathroom. The two rooms were being used as a single dwelling by the Cárdenas family. One of the bathrooms had been converted into a kitchen. The entrance to the servants' quarters was on the

16. On March 10, 1959, the state ordered rents under 100 *pesos* reduced by 50 percent; rents from 100 to 200 *pesos* reduced by 40 percent; and rents in excess of 200 *pesos* reduced by 30 percent. The Urban Reform Law, adopted October 14, 1960, nationalized all urban *rental* housing and applied rents paid to the state toward the purchase price of the tenant's house or apartment. The period of amortization was determined by length of residence and condition of the housing. The 10-percent-of-income rent ceiling for all new and vacant units that went into effect in May, 1961, was the second stage of the law.

south side of the building through the service door, which was also the back entrance to the upstairs apartments. This door faced the narrow driveway that led to the Pérezes' garage and backyard, which they had fenced in for their private use. The rear of the driveway was also closed off with an iron grille fence that was kept locked.

The Families

The first of the present tenants to move into the building was Eulalia (Lala) Fontanés Torres,[17] who came in 1960 with the Dávila family, for whom she worked as a housemaid. She lived alone in the servants' quarters until her marriage to Armando Cárdenas, who then moved in with her. When Lala's employers left Cuba, she had a right to claim the entire second-floor apartment for her personal residence, but as Armando was earning only 74 *pesos* a month in the Army, the couple decided they could not afford it and turned it over to the state. They continued to live where they were, hoping to be assigned new housing. This was not forthcoming, however, and in 1969 they were still in the two small rooms with their four children, little Armando, age eight, Juan Pablo, seven, Germán, five, and Diego, four. One of Lala's brothers also lived with the family from time to time.

The little apartment was crowded with furniture, including a full-sized bed and dresser that had been given to Lala by her former employer when the family had left Cuba. Lala had another bed for which she had bought a mattress (a rationed item purchased for 11 *pesos*). In the living-dining room were a table, six chairs, a studio couch, and an ironing board. The board did not fold and apparently was never put away. Many of the family's pictures and frames, wall decorations, kitchen utensils, and dishes had been found by Lala in the vacated houses where she had worked as a cleaning woman in the first years after the Revolution.

Lala Fontanés, thirty-two, was born on a farm in Pinar del Río, the fourth of nine children. Her father farmed 2 *caballerías* (about 67 acres) which he rented from a U.S.-owned *central*.[18] The family was poor but never destitute. Lala worked at home and on the farm, attending school off and on between the ages of ten and seventeen. Disappointed over her broken engagement, she left home at nineteen to become the first in her family to work as a domestic.

Armando Cárdenas, thirty-two, was born in Oriente Province and lived with his parents and nine brothers and sisters in a two-room hut made of palm bark and *guano* leaves. His parents were landless, itinerant

17. In Cuba (and most Spanish-speaking countries), children take the surnames of both parents, with the father's name first. The mother's name is sometimes dropped. A woman does not give up her own name when she marries.

18. A sugar-mill complex, including the adjoining company-owned farms.

farm workers who barely earned enough for food; the entire family had to work during the coffee and tobacco harvests to support themselves. During the agricultural "dead" season, Armando's father did house-painting and odd jobs to support the family.

Of the ten adults presented in this study, Armando had the poorest, most deprived childhood. His diet consisted mainly of sweet potatoes and boiled cornmeal, and he suffered from malnutrition and parasites. Unable to attend school, he was illiterate until after the Revolution. In 1958 he joined the Rebels in the Sierra Maestra.

At the time of this study, Armando was a cafeteria manager earning 130 *pesos* a month after deductions, and was a member of the Cuban Communist Party. Lala had a laundry job at home, earning from 30 to 70 *pesos* a month.

Compared to the other couples in the building, Lala and Armando were the most "integrated" in the Revolution. Together they helped found the block CDR, which was named for Armando's cousin, a Playa Girón[19] martyr. In 1969 Lala was public-health officer for the Committee and was in charge of finances for the local delegation of the Federation of Cuban Women. In addition, she served as the block contact for the Department of State Security. She reported regularly to Department agents on the activities of all her neighbors on the block. Lala had also stood guard duty, done voluntary labor, and participated in a variety of other CDR and Federation projects.

Most of Armando's activities were carried out not in the neighborhood organizations but in his work center, Party sectional, and militia unit. These activities included long hours of unpaid overtime on his job, voluntary work in agriculture, guard duty, attending study groups, and helping in the political education of the employees under his supervision. In 1969 Armando volunteered to work in agriculture for two years on the Isle of Pines.[20]

The second of the five families, the Pérezes, moved to Cristal Street in April, 1961. Juan Carlos Pérez, Mercedes Millán, and their two children, Mercedes (or Merceditas), ten, and Eloy Tomás, three, were the only tenants in the building who were of middle-class origin. Juan Carlos was born in Havana in 1937, but was raised in Oriente Province in a small town named for his maternal grandfather. He was the eldest of three children. His father was in the produce business and gradually built up a very successful trade in the Havana market. Juan learned the business and worked in it all through his youth. In Oriente the family had also owned a farm valued at an estimated half-million *pesos*.

19. The beach in southern Las Villas Province where the Bay of Pigs invasion occurred on April 17, 1961.
20. Also known as the Isle of Youth.

Juan Pérez's family were nominal Roman Catholics, but he received his primary education at an American Friends school, which his parents considered better than the Roman Catholic or public schools. At fifteen Juan entered a college-preparatory school in Havana, where he was involved in the anti-Batista student movement and became a spokesman and leader at demonstrations and strikes. In 1955 he met Mercedes, when both were in their fourth year at the school.

Mercedes Millán, whose parents had emigrated from Spain, was born in Havana in 1937 and had lived her entire life in the city. Her father owned and operated a small delivery service which afforded the family a modest, comfortable livelihood. Mercedes had one sister, ten years older, who was living in Spain.

Mercedes received her primary education at Roman Catholic schools. After graduating from the preparatory school, she and Juan were married in both civil and Roman Catholic ceremonies. They were the only couple among these five families to have had a church wedding, a newspaper announcement of the occasion, and a honeymoon. Their home was furnished in typical middle-class style, with most of the basic household appliances, custom-made draperies, and sets of furniture for the living, dining, and bedrooms. They had a refrigerator, two air-conditioners, a fan, freezer, two-burner electric hot plate, television, radio, telephone, and phonograph, and a car.

Juan Pérez's various business enterprises were nationalized in 1961, after which he held a number of responsible jobs with government ministries. He had also completed one year of technical school by attending night classes. In 1969 he was a lower-level administrator in charge of the import and repair of certain types of small machinery. His salary was about 200 *pesos* a month, or 175 *pesos* after deductions. Mercedes had never held a job and was the only one of the five women in the building who did not add to the family income.

Juan was integrated in the Revolution and eager to advance in the system. A former member of the Union of Young Communists, he was active in his work center and militia unit and did voluntary labor. In 1969, at thirty-two, he was a candidate for Party membership but was not admitted at that time. Of all the adults in the building, Mercedes was the least integrated. She was a member of the Committee in name only, did not belong to the Federation, attended no meetings, and did no voluntary or productive labor.

In late 1963 the second- and third-floor apartments were given to the families of Bernardo Rojas and Domingo Labrada while the two men were serving with the Cuban Army in Algeria. The gifts were made by Raúl Castro in fulfillment of a government pledge to solve the housing problems of the families of men who volunteered for the overseas assignment.

The Rojas family arrived first, in January, 1964. Included in the housing contract, besides Bernardo, was his sister Sara, who moved in with her family and another brother. Thereafter, many different people within the family occupied the second-floor apartment and sometimes the garage as well.

All members of the Rojas family were born and raised in Oriente Province. Sara Rojas Tabares, thirty-four, grew up in a small rural community populated largely by her relatives. One of eleven children, she was raised on a small piece of land owned and farmed by her family. Her father also worked as a cart driver on the nearby Miranda *central*. Working on the farm, Sara attended school very irregularly and was barely literate. At fourteen she made a bad marriage in free union with an "outsider" who worked as a cane-cutter on the *central*. After six years Sara left him and moved in with her parents, taking her five children—Concha, Gerardo, Violeta, Hilario, and Estela—with her. She had not seen their father since.

Several years later, in 1959, Sara married, again in free union, Eduardo Rojas Raventos, a younger first cousin. Theirs is the only free-union marriage among the five couples. Eduardo, twenty-nine, was born on the Miranda *central*, where his father worked as a cane-cutter. Eduardo was the eldest of three children and had twelve half-brothers and sisters. Like his father, he worked as a farm laborer and cane-cutter and never attended school; he was completely illiterate when, in 1960, he joined the Army with three of Sara's brothers. In 1961 he was stationed at Camp Managua and Sara joined him in Havana. It was the first time either of them had lived in a large urban center and it was an experience for which they were ill prepared.

In 1967, three years after the family had moved to Miramar, Sara's brother Bernardo became involved with another woman and decided to leave his wife. He tried to arrange a housing trade which would give him two smaller apartments for his large one. His objective was apparently to provide separate housing for his wife and children so that after he re-married he could continue to see his sister's family without also having to see his ex-wife. However, Bernardo was outmaneuvered by Ricardo Hernández, the police lieutenant with whom he had arranged the trade; in exchange for his large, modern home, Bernardo received one tiny ramshackle apartment into which he eventually moved his wife and daughters. He went to live with his new wife, but Sara and her family were left unprovided for and ended up in the garage, a 3-by-6-meter room with inadequate ventilation, no toilet, and one cold-water tap. They had been living there for almost a year and a half at the time this study began.

Two of Sara's children by her first marriage, Violeta, fifteen, and Hilario, thirteen, lived in the garage with Eduardo, Sara, and their three daughters. Occasionally one of Sara's older children, or another relative, came to stay, and although there was an extreme shortage of space and beds, room was always found for them. The family had one three-quarter bed with spring and mattress, and one folding cot that Sara bought from a friend for 8.50 *pesos*. Their one mattress was put on the floor to make an extra bed. The bed, two wooden chairs, and a buffet had been given to Bernardo by Lieutenant Hernández. Other furnishings included two additional chairs, a small wooden table, a wardrobe, a trunk, and a two-burner kerosene stove. With the exception of the table, which Sara found in the street, all of the items had been given to the family.

Eduardo Rojas worked as a security guard in the Ministry of the Interior. His salary, after deductions, was 130 *pesos* a month, 30 *pesos* of which were given to help support two sons by another marriage. By doing laundry at home, Sara also had a small income, sometimes no more than 10 or 15 *pesos* a month.

Sara and Eduardo belonged to the block Committee but neither attended meetings. Both had stood guard duty, and Eduardo also did volunteer work in agriculture. Sara belonged to the Federation of Cuban Women but did not attend meetings or participate in any of its projects.

Domingo Labrada and Leticia Manzanares moved into the third-floor apartment in April, 1964. They shared it with their five children, Lina, fourteen, Andrea, twelve, Bárbara, ten, Tomás, seven, Ana Luz, two, and from time to time with Domingo's brother Dámaso or one of Leticia's brothers.

Domingo Labrada, forty, was born in 1929 in Limón, a barrio on the outskirts of Morón, Camaguey. He was the youngest of six children. His father was a railroad mechanic, and after his parents separated his mother worked as a cook and housekeeper. He quit school when he was fourteen and had the equivalent of a third- or fourth-grade education. Domingo held a number of part-time jobs but didn't have permanent, full-time work until after 1959.

Leticia Manzanares, thirty-one, one of nine children, was also born in Limón. Her parents, like Domingo's, separated when she was young. At twelve, after a fifth-grade education, she quit school to take a job as a live-in maid. Domingo was her first and only boyfriend; they were married in a civil ceremony in 1954.

Domingo worked in a company store on a *colonia*[21] until 1957, when he followed his family to Havana to look for work. In 1961 he joined the Army and volunteered for service in Algeria. He was demobilized in 1964 and eventually took a job as a taxi driver, his last full-time job. He developed an undiagnosed skin disease and was given a job classification

---

21. Sugar-cane farm; some were independently owned, others were company-owned but operated by tenant farmers.

of "diminished capacity" that authorized him to work half-time. His half-salary of 70 *pesos* a month was supplemented by Leticia's earnings as a laundress, which ranged from 50 to 100 *pesos* a month. In addition, the family received occasional help from Leticia's father and brothers, and from Domingo's father.

Expecting to receive furniture from the government, Domingo and Leticia gave away the few furnishings they owned before they moved to the new apartment. The new furniture was not forthcoming, but they gradually accumulated several beds and mattresses, a table, and a few chairs. The living room was almost bare, except for four wicker chairs that Domingo repaired after receiving them as a gift. There were several orange crate–type boxes which were used for stools and end tables; one of them held the family's phonograph. Straw was scattered over the tile floor and on the balconies for the pigeons and chickens that the Labradas raised to supplement their diet.

Neither Domingo nor Leticia was particularly sympathetic to the Castro government, but because they were basically apolitical they did not actively oppose it. Both belonged to the CDR, and Domingo at one time held a post, although he did none of the work that went with it. Leticia belonged to the Federation and had participated in a number of block and Federation projects, particularly the clean-up campaigns.

All the Labrada children except Tomás were baptized (as were the Peréz and three of the Cárdenas children). Leticia and Domingo also attended Mass occasionally and were actively involved in *santería,* an Afro-Cuban saint cult. Their religious affiliations were, they said, more important to them than membership in the Communist Party or any other aspirations in the present system. They were, however, quick to take advantage of opportunities available to them and their children.

The Hernández family was the last to move to the building. Ricardo Hernández and Justa Díaz arrived in September, 1967, with their six children—Genoveva, seventeen, Florinda, fifteen, Gabriela, fourteen, Reinaldo, eleven, Engracia, nine, Antonia, three. A seventh child, Justa, one and a half, was born in 1968.

Ricardo Hernández, thirty-seven, was born near Guantánamo, Oriente, the eighth of nine children. His father, who died when Ricardo was five, was a machinist in a sugar mill, and the family was well off in comparison to the poor farm families in the area. Ricardo left school in the second grade, and at thirteen went to work in his brother's grocery store. He also played semi-professional baseball. In 1951, when he was about seventeen, he married Justa in a civil ceremony.

Justa Díaz, thirty-five, was born into a very poor family of eleven children. Her father owned a small farm outside Guantánamo but lost it to a wealthy landowner before the Revolution. For a short time he worked in a brick factory and afterward as a day laborer. We do not know the number of years Justa attended school, but she was able to read and write.

Ricardo joined the Rebel underground in 1956 and in early 1958 joined the Second Front (under Raúl Castro) in the Sierra del Cristal, north of Guantánamo. During this time Justa helped smuggle supplies to the Rebel camps and hide Rebel soldiers from the police. At the triumph of the Revolution, Ricardo went to Havana with the Army. He joined the new police force and the family moved to Havana.

In 1965 Ricardo graduated from officers' training school with a lieutenant's commission and was admitted to the Party. In 1969 he was with the police in Havana but spent long periods doing agricultural labor. His salary was just under 200 *pesos* a month, or 166 *pesos* after deductions. Justa did laundry on consignment from the Ministry of the Revolutionary Armed Forces and earned from 30 to 50 *pesos* a month. The Hernándezes were the only family besides the Pérezes to own matching sets of furniture, a refrigerator, telephone, and television, and were the only family to have a sewing machine. They bought a set of bedroom furniture for 400 *pesos* in 1959 when they first came to Havana, and living- and dining-room furniture after moving to their present home. They were still paying for it in monthly installments of 6.75 *pesos*. The living-room furniture included a sofa, a coffee table, a few cane chairs, and a wooden rocker. They also had a kitchen table and chairs.

Ricardo had been totally involved with the Revolution since 1956 but, like the other working men in the building, did not participate in the neighborhood organizations. Although Justa identified completely with the Castro government, her participation since 1959 had been largely restricted to verbal support. She belonged to the CDR but had participated only by attending a few meetings and by standing guard duty. She did not join the local Federation delegation until 1969, after a project interviewer asked her about her membership. Justa was so tied down by her family and job that solely on those grounds it is not difficult to explain her lack of participation. She was expecting their eighth child in 1970.

Relations among the Families

In 1960 the apartment building at 411 Cristal Street had been occupied by three couples and their live-in servants, but by 1961 most of these tenants had left the country. The number of new tenants increased rapidly after that until in 1965–66 there were nearly fifty residents. Relatives of the Rojas family lived in one of the garages in front of the building, and relatives of Domingo Labrada lived in the other. The garage in back of the building was occupied by one of Juan Pérez's colleagues, who lived there with his wife, daughter, and mother-in-law.

front of the building, or not maintaining an apartment properly, (4) the use of garages as dwellings, (5) the 1967 housing exchange between the Hernández and Rojas families.

Arguments over these and other points resulted in members of families avoiding contact and refusing to speak to one another; parents prohibiting their children from playing with the children of one or more of the other families; reporting one another to the CDR, the police, the Frozen Zone office, the Party, and Public Health; excluding one another from parties and celebrations; and making public and private statements accusing one another of a broad range of offenses, such as uncleanliness, laziness, profanity, theft, and counterrevolutionary sentiments and actions.

Many of the problems that arose might have been more easily solved had there not been such fundamental resentments among the families, stemming in part from class bias, racism, urban-rural differences, and the misuse of political influence. Mercedes Millán, for example, was very conscious of her middle-class background and she strictly observed class and racial distinctions, seeing herself as apart from and above all her neighbors. She did have nominally friendly relationships with the two other white families (Hernández and Cárdenas), but she was hostile toward the two black families (Rojas and Labrada). Mercedes referred to Sara Rojas as "a person of very low culture" who was "only half civilized."

Mercedes denied being a racist, saying what she objected to was the "lack of breeding and culture" that she said was characteristic of everyone in the building. Domingo Labrada and Eduardo Rojas attributed Mercedes's dislike of them to racism, and Domingo added that both she and her husband had "delusions of grandeur." According to Mercedes, Leticia and Domingo felt persecuted by her only because they had a "racial inferiority complex."

Although almost all the tenants liked her husband, Juan Pérez, Mercedes Millán was one of the most disliked and roundly criticized individuals in the building. She was seen as someone against the present system, "still living the old life." Mercedes not only tried to keep herself and her children physically apart from the Rojas and Labrada families, but she also maintained a certain role distance between herself and Lala Fontanés, whom she first knew as a servant. Mercedes still referred to Lala with the familiar *tú*, while Lala addressed her with the respectful *usted*.

For her part, Lala seemed to do nothing to change the employer-servant nature of the relationship, and more often than not she sided with Mercedes in conflicts with the other families. Although Lala had not worked as a domestic since 1961, she continued to iron clothing for Mercedes, and Lala's sister Serafina Fontanés, who lived two doors away, once worked as a maid in the Pérez home.

By 1969 the building's population had fallen to thirty-three, cluding several relatives who visited for periods of varying duratic presence of so many tenants, a large number of them childre building designed for three families resulted in much wear and both the structure and the people.

Relations among the five families were affected by certain feat the building's structure and design: (1) the louvered windows, (: balconies, (3) shared front entrance, hall, and stairwell, (4) inac systems of plumbing and wiring which caused the use of wat electricity in one apartment to affect the supply in another.

Louvered windows cannot be tightly closed and conversations easily from one apartment to another, especially when voice raised. The second- and third-floor apartments' balconies, loca rectly over one another in the front and on the south side of the ing, also restricted the privacy of the tenants. At the same tir balconies permitted or encouraged some cross conversation, bant general socializing among the families. Three of the women Leticia, and Justa—did their laundry on these balconies—Merce hers on the ground-floor patio—and their conversations could e overheard. Much of the personal information each family had ab other, or about their neighbors' attitudes toward them, had been l in this way, by accidentally overhearing or by eavesdropping.

The front entrance of the building was used by the Rojas, La and Hernández families, and by anyone visiting the second- and floor apartments. There were sixteen people living on the upper and this caused considerable traffic past the inside entrance Rojases' garage-apartment. When it was hot and they needed to h; door ajar for ventilation, curious passersby greatly interfered wit privacy.

The shared front entrance increased the contacts among these families, particularly the Labrada and Rojas families, who som visited together on the little front porch. The more frequent (resulting from the common passageways was less welcome to som dents than to others, but Domingo Labrada was the only perso admitted using the back stairs to avoid meeting people he did n

Another place where neighbors often came in contact wit another was at the garden wall that separated the building's pr from the adjoining lot. The wall was low enough to sit on, ar tenants, as well as their neighbors on the block, used it as a place t and visit with one another.

Most of the quarreling among the families centered on disagree over: (1) the general maintenance of the building and grounds, (2) iness and "offensive" behavior by residents, (3) violations of the p health code, such as keeping chickens or rabbits, hanging launc

Justa Díaz also had some feelings of superiority toward her neighbors, although hers were not based on class feelings as were Mercedes's. Justa's attitude might be described as a type of elitism stemming from her revolutionary background. When responding to the interviewer's questions, she often began with "It's not that I feel I'm better than anyone else, but. . . ."

All the neighbors except Mercedes Millán and Juan Pérez expressed the deep-seated conviction that Justa and her husband obtained their apartment through a combination of political pull and tricks (i.e., taking advantage of Bernardo Rojas's country ways). Their antagonism was based not so much on concern for Sara Rojas and her family as on resentment, or in some cases perhaps jealousy, of anyone who used his political office to gain material advantage.

Lala Fontanés, as block security agent, was observing the lieutenant's activities for evidence that he was using his position as a police officer and Party member to acquire goods to which he would not normally be entitled. She had also accused Juan Pérez of using his administrative position to engage in black-market activities and had cooperated with government agents in an investigation of alleged thefts from Pérez's work center.

There was a kind of loose alliance between the Hernández and Pérez families, although not a real friendship. Mercedes defended the Hernándezes' role in the housing exchange and said the Rojas family lived in the garage only through the generosity of the lieutenant. However, Justa's outspoken and aggressive behavior and her use of profanity were anathema to Mercedes, while Justa found Mercedes's bourgeois ways and antirevolutionary sentiments repulsive. Despite this, they acted friendly toward one another and their children played together, the Hernández children moving freely in and out of the Pérez home. Ricardo and Juan had more frequent contact with one another than with any of the other men in the building; occasionally they would visit or drink together, and they planned a few joint family celebrations.

Although the other neighbors were quick to condemn Ricardo and Justa in the housing exchange, they were not supportive of Sara and Eduardo. For the most part they were critical and disapproving of the Rojases' life-style, which they regarded as rustic and outmoded. They complained about what they regarded as instability and violence in their family life, uncleanliness, and a general lack of interest in taking advantage of opportunities offered by the state. Leticia and Domingo were Sara's closest friends in the building, although she had a cordial if somewhat distant relationship with Lala. In general, Sara felt displaced and isolated living in Miramar, much as Mercedes felt being a neighbor to blacks and the poor.

While there were many conflicts among the families, there were some notable areas of cooperation. These included: (1) borrowing food, household items, and tools, and exchanging foods, (2) running errands, shopping or standing in line for one another, and informing each other of items available in the stores, (3) occasionally taking care of each other's children, (4) working together in block or neighborhood organizations, (5) sharing items of luxury or privilege, such as telephones, automobiles, refrigerators, and small appliances.

This type of cooperation existed not only among families in the building but among all Cuban neighbors on the block. In addition, there were some specialized services neighbors performed for one another. Sara Rojas, for instance, was a *curandera* or native healer, and had "stroked" children of all families in the building except the Pérez, as well as some of the neighbors on the block. Lala Fontanés, as public-health officer of the CDR, had been trained to administer vaccinations and injections and performed this service for everyone on the block (excluding students and foreigners).

In general, relations among the families were determined by the women since the men in the five families, with the exception of Domingo Labrada, were rarely home. The men tended to greet one another on sight, but there were no personal friendships among them, with the qualified exception of Juan Pérez and Ricardo Hernández. Juan and Armando Cárdenas once belonged to the same militia unit and traveled to and from volunteer work sites together; Eduardo Rojas and Domingo Labrada went drinking together on a few occasions. Lala Fontanés was the only person in the building on friendly terms with everyone, and she was used at times as a go-between, especially for the purpose of arranging food exchanges.

In the pages that follow, much space is given to the families' conflicts and quarrels, but it should be pointed out that apartment-house living was comparatively new to these families, as was living among non-relatives, especially those of differing backgrounds. In addition, 1969, the Year of Decisive Effort, was a particularly demanding time, and the occasional outbursts may have been reflecting, to a certain extent, the tension of that period. In any case, they flared and died quickly. No matter how strong the words or feelings, the protagonists soon recovered and went about their business as usual.

Most of the time the building was quiet, with men and school children away and mothers and younger children indoors. Later in the day, one or two of the women might go to the Minimax, together or separately, or sit outside to watch their children at play. The voices most frequently heard were those of Mercedes Millán calling to her son, or Justa Díaz scolding one of her daughters. A loud argument among the women or children in one of the households, the hallway, or the street was an occasional but by no means daily occurrence.

Part I of the Miramar study will present the residents' early impressions of the apartment building, of their neighbors, and of the block. It is also intended to portray the interaction of the five families as a group and the interpersonal relations of the various individuals. Because of the large number of people mentioned by the informants, we have chosen to omit some whose presence was marginal to the lives of the five families. Nevertheless there remains a very complicated, and sometimes confusing, network of personal relationships. However, the many individuals, their comings and goings, the counterpoint of gossip and conflicting versions of incidents are all part of what we are trying to portray: the ordinariness of daily life in an extraordinary time.

Neighbors

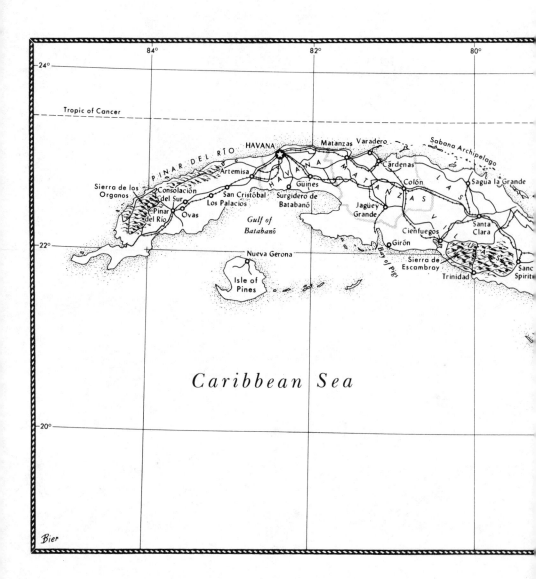

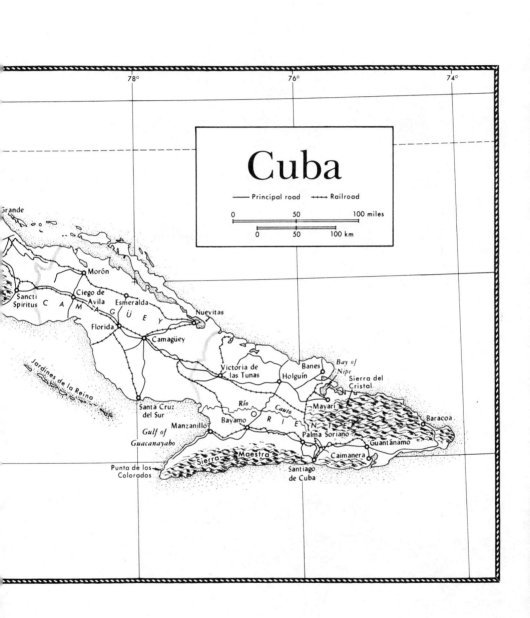

78°   76°   74°

Cuba

—— Principal road ++++ Railroad

0   50   100 miles
0   50   100 km

Grande

Morón

Ciego de
Sancti   Ávila   Esmeralda
Spiritus C A M A G Ü E Y   Nuevitas
Florida
Camagüey

Victoria de   Banes   Bay of
las Tunas   Holguín   Nipe
Sierra del
Cristal
Río   Cauto   Mayarí
Santa Cruz   O R I E N T E   Baracoa
del Sur   Bayamo
Manzanillo   Palma Soriano
Gulf of   Guantánamo
Guacanayabo   Caimanera
Sierra   Maestra
Punta de los   Santiago
Colorados   de Cuba

Jardines de la Reina

PART I

The Five Families

Moving to Miramar

EULALIA FONTANÉS:

I liked Miramar from the first. It used to be a zone where only the rich could live, where the husband and wife had their own private chauffeurs and went their own way, with a nursemaid to look after the children, a maid to clean the house, another to cook and serve the meals. The women of the family never did any housework. It was a quiet neighborhood, without heavy traffic. The only bus in that part of town was the one passing through Fifth and 20th.

This building was new and one of the prettiest on the block. It was quiet because there was only one family in each apartment. The front yard was beautiful, with flower borders all the way to the sidewalk— some kind of small red flower. A gardener took care of it every day.

The family I worked for, Evidio Carrera, his wife, Cristina, and their daughter, Tina, had the apartment on the second floor. We moved there in 1960, when Evidio decided to leave Artemisa[1] to take a job in Havana as an official in a government ministry. The apartment had three bedrooms, two for themselves and one for Tina. My room was on the back stair landing, between the second and third floors, and had a door independent of the apartment. I know they paid 105 *pesos* a month[2] for it because they once sent me to the landlord with the rent money. The apartment had an electric range and was complete in every way, except for furniture, curtains, and so on.

On the ground floor of the building lived a European diplomat, his wife and son, and their two maids. He and Evidio were on friendly terms, but they never visited us. On the floor above us lived an American couple who owned a big sugar-distributing company in Cuba. I believe they had a son and a daughter who used to come for visits from up North.

About two months after we moved here, the diplomat wanted to leave because Fidel had a disagreement with the ambassador from his country.

1. A city in the province of Pinar del Río.
2. After rent reduction (see Introduction, n. 16).

Evidio offered to assign him bodyguards but he said no, he preferred to leave. He took all his furniture with him—those were the early days of the Revolution when there was no problem about taking furniture out of Cuba.

And the next month the American couple left because the man's mother was ill and he wanted to see her again before she died. His wife sold or gave away all her furniture before leaving. She gave me a bed and left me the key to her servant's room. "Keep the key in case anything comes up and you need it," she told me. She was a warm, friendly person and wanted me to go North with them to take care of their granddaughter.

At that time Tina kept complaining that she didn't like Cuba, that there was no opportunity here. What she meant was there were no men for her to marry. Think of it—with so many men around she couldn't get one! It was because of her stuck-up ways, that's why. She was already thirty. Finally she decided to go back to New York to her former job at Bellevue Hospital. She was a doctor of pharmacy like her mother and had worked for years in her mother's drugstore in Artemisa. I went to the airport to say goodbye to her. Eventually she married an American up North.

After Tina left, Evidio got into some arguments because they took him off his post to make him minister of something or other. He refused to change posts, saying he was too old.

When the *doctora* watched Fidel on television, she'd cry and say, "You deceived me, Fidel. You said you'd never make Cuba communist. You deceived me!" She'd worked a lot for the Twenty-sixth of July Movement, giving them money and medicine. So she'd sit there looking at him and weeping.

"Ah, shut up now, Cristina," Evidio would scold. "Be quiet and forget it."

I moved into Tina's room, leaving the servant's room vacant. I told the *doctora* about my brother Pablo, who had no settled place to live. "Let him have one of the servants' rooms," she told me. "You may do as you please with those two rooms."

After the American couple and the foreign diplomat left, Mercedes, the wife of Juan Pérez, came around looking for an apartment. She came up to the *doctora*'s apartment and from that day on was friendly with us. She and Juan rented the diplomat's apartment and moved in, in April, 1961. At first Mercedes had three servants—a cook, a nursemaid for her little girl, and a housemaid to do the cleaning. Mercedes and I talked often because I had Evidio's phone upstairs and I'd take calls for her. She'd come and say hello to me but that was all.

One day Mercedes invited Evidio and the *doctora* to lunch. "Look," Evidio told her, "you've invited only me and my wife. If Lala can't go, we won't go either." And it's a fact that wherever they went, like to a good restaurant, they'd take me with them. They treated me like a daughter, not a servant. I slept in their apartment, I never wore a uniform, and I never called them *señora* and *caballero*. I addressed him as Evidio, his wife as *doctora,* and their daughter as Tina. That day Mercedes said, "All right, bring her along." But she didn't seat me at the table, she gave me my food in the kitchen. When we were back home, Evidio said, "I didn't like the way Mercedes treated you. She should have seated you at the table. If those people ever invite me again, I'll refuse."

"No, Evidio, don't take it that way," I said. "Why, I didn't even want to go in the first place."

"If you don't go, we don't go, and that's all there is to it," he said.

I knew my place, though, and I kept it. I never forgot that I was a servant in their house, and I always refused to sit with them in the dining room. The *doctora* would say, "But Lala, sit down with us," and I'd answer, "No, I'll eat later." In the kitchen we had a small table which I'd covered with a very pretty piece of oilcloth, and that's where I ate. Sometimes I'd put a tablecloth on it and Evidio and his wife would eat there with me.

When I moved here, the rich people didn't treat me like a servant either. Perhaps they thought I was the old couple's daughter because all the other servants around here—most of them were black—wore uniforms. In the afternoon I'd dress up and sit on the terrace just like Evidio and the *doctora.* Besides, wherever Evidio went he'd say, "Lala is one of our daughters." The *doctora* was naturally a bit fonder of her daughter, but she was terribly fond of me.

This block was full of people who lived well. It was full of doctors. You'd run into one no matter where you went. Clara Falcón's husband, Tito, was a doctor and he worked in a clinic in Vedado. Later, when I had my son, Tito came to the house to see him and prescribed medicines for him and everything.

Tito and Clara lived well. They had four maids, and in addition two men who helped out, plus a skinny *negrito* who did odd jobs like washing the cars. They had two cars and two garages.

Delfina and Georgina Soto were among the richest people here. They used to own four buildings in Miramar, and others in Old Havana and even in Varadero. Those little old women were rich, rich, rich! And yet, how miserly they were. You'd see them counting their money *centavo* by *centavo* when they paid for groceries at the Minimax, and they'd grumble about the prices. When they left Cuba in 1961, they gave the state a list of properties as long as your arm. I don't know how much money they left in the National Bank.

During the eight days before leaving Cuba, you used to have to move in with a friend or relative, unless you went to a hotel, because they made you move out of your house. So Georgina and Delfina spent the eight days with Clara Falcón. They went to Varadero and from there to Miami. They still write to Clara and they've also written to Mercedes and told her to give me and the kids their regards.

Georgina's son William was a priest. He was abroad but came back about two years ago and has been doing works of charity ever since. He used to come here often to play with the kids and he was very affectionate. In 1962 he baptized my two oldest boys, and now he wants to baptize my youngest.

On the other side of my building, in no. 413, Josefa Llera lived all alone. That woman never gave the time of day to anyone. She was very proud because her father had owned I don't know what all—a cigar factory, a cookware factory.... She never married because she didn't want to divide her inheritance. She had a house built in Marianao especially for her, and she was the boss. After her parents died, she turned in that house and kept this one.[3] She had four maids but kept only two.

A brother of hers lived on the other side of her house, but I hardly knew him because he left only four or five months after I moved here. His sister was his only relative in Cuba. His house stood empty for a year, then it was taken over as an embassy, and whenever a diplomat came to Cuba he'd live there.

Josefa wouldn't even say hello to me, but in 1966 or '67 she became friendly all of a sudden. She was on a very strict diet, see, and needed *malanga*[4] and other things, but they didn't give her any. I used to get lots of it, so I always shared with her—that's what made her get friendly. Then when her relatives sent her a package from the United States, she'd come over and bring presents for my children. She'd bring cornflakes, applesauce, and gelatin for my son, who often had stomach trouble. When the children's birthdays came around, she'd have a sweet made for them in her house, or she'd send over candy or money or something. When she left for Miami in 1968, she gave me a box of crackers and 25 *pesos* for the kids. I think they got her out so quickly because they wanted to give her house to some foreigners.

An old lady, Carmen Tamayo, lived on the corner in no. 419. She's still there and so is my friend Norma, who's worked for Carmen ever since she was thirteen. Norma's thirty-five now and practically a member of the family. The old lady treats her that way, too. Carmen's daughter and granddaughter lived in the upper story and Norma used to take care of the girls. They had other maids, but only Norma stayed on.

The people in no. 412 left for Miami before we had a chance to get really acquainted. They left because they didn't like communism—that's the reason people go. The only one remaining was Graciela, the maid,

3. Under the Urban Reform Law of 1960, a person retained ownership only of the home he or she occupied. Exceptions were made in certain cases.
4. A root vegetable favored by Cubans.

and they left her all the furniture. At the beginning of the Revolution people would take everything, but now you must leave everything behind. Clothes and things are taken out, sold, or given away. Graciela was moved when the house was taken over for scholarship students.

Máximo Abay lives in no. 408. When I came, he lived there with his wife and daughter, but six months later the daughter married a Spaniard and went to live in Mexico. The next year his wife asked for permission to visit her daughter for three months, but she's never come back. The old man is all alone now, except for his maid, Ramona, but he says he isn't going to leave Cuba because he has a good house and is comfortable in every way. If you so much as mention his family, he changes the subject. I don't blame him a bit, because his wife abandoned him when he was ill with ulcers.

About three months after Tina left, she wrote asking the *doctora* to go North because she was lonely. My husband, Armando, and I were already sweethearts then, and the *doctora* said that before she left she wanted to see me married to him so both of us could stay in the house with Evidio.

I told the *doctora* we were going to rent a place but she wouldn't hear of it. "How can you do that when we have rooms to spare right here?" she protested. "If you don't want to use your old room, move up into the apartment with us." But I told her that Armando and I wanted a place of our own, for the two of us. "A married couple should live by themselves," I told her. Then she said, "All right, take the servants' rooms for the two of you."

After our marriage, Armando stayed on at his job with the military police and I kept working for Evidio and the *doctora,* but Armando and I lived alone in the servants' rooms.

In June, when the *doctora* was about to leave, I'd say, "*Ay,* why must you leave when you're doing so well here?" She'd burst into tears and answer, "I must go because Fidel deceived me." But she wanted to go because she and Evidio quarreled all the time over a mistress he had in Pinar del Río. I never met her but the *doctora* told me all about the affair. So the *doctora* went up North and left Evidio.

She went by ship and I saw her off at the dock. Both she and Evidio cried that day. Then Evidio began to talk of going. He said he wanted to move back to Artemisa and tried to arrange an exchange of apartments with Fela, his secretary, who lived in Las Cañas. His idea was to move all his furniture to her apartment and leave it there for me when she moved into this apartment. But exchanges weren't permitted in that zone, even though Evidio and Fela were big shots in the government. Then Evidio made a written statement saying that another couple—Armando and I— were to stay on, living in that apartment, and that the place was mine. I was to keep the lease and present it when they came. Evidio left me the apartment keys and 400 *pesos*. Besides that, he paid all the household expenses, including the milk and electricity, for the next six months.

Then, one day he had lunch with me and said, "I'm going to Artemisa today, but I'll be back next week." I never saw him again. He left the country and never said goodbye to me. They say he left with the notary who married Armando and me. It seems that at my wedding[5] they made plans to leave in August on a launch out of Varadero.

Evidio went without permission from the government, but I sincerely believe his only reason for going was to join his wife and daughter. He never turned against the government, even when they took away his post. After he left, the government confiscated all the money they had in the bank, and everything else.

The apartment was mine but the rent was 105 *pesos* and how were we to pay that on Armando's 74 *pesos* a month? Armando said the two servants' rooms were plenty for us and went to explain our situation to Arturo Portillo, the man responsible for Urban Reform in our area. He'd been Armando's comrade in the Sierra. We told him we couldn't afford to keep the big apartment and that we wanted to be moved to a smaller place.[6] Arturo told us to stay in the servants' rooms until they found another place for us. Found another place! That was nine years ago and we're still here.

Then Aldita, who's the one in charge of Housing in Miramar-Siboney, took the remaining furniture from Evidio's apartment. I was supposed to have some of that furniture, but I was afraid to take it. Suppose later they were to say I'd stolen it? I could have taken the frigidaire, the TV set, the record player, and the radio, but like a fool I turned them in with the apartment.

Before Evidio left, he transferred his telephone to me. "*Muchacha*, have it installed in your room and you can keep it."

"What do I need a phone for?" I said.

I had a new job by then and I was away from home all day, so Juan Carlos Pérez, Mercedes's husband, came and asked me to give him the phone because he didn't have one. He said, "Look, Lala, you can make as many phone calls as you like from my place." I'm such a—I'd better not say the word—such a—something—fool, that I said, "Well, then all right, Juan."

That phone they have now is mine. When the black fellow came to disconnect the telephone he told me, "You sure are a dope, kid. Listen, all I had to do was attach a cable from there to here and you'd have had your phone. How could you give it away like that?"

5. May, 1961.

6. The rent ceiling for newly built and vacated housing units went into effect the month Armando and Lala were married. It is not clear whether this was known to them, whether the law applied since Lala was already living in the apartment, or whether they just did not want the expense and responsibility of maintaining such a large apartment.

Juan told me he didn't have a phone, but later on I saw another one in his kitchen. There was a shortage of telephones then, and it turned out Juan even had extensions in his apartment!

About a year later, they told all us tenants that we'd have to move out because this was to be declared a zone for scholarship students only. They gave me a paper saying I was to be at the Housing office at 2:00 in the afternoon. There they told us to look for another place. Armando and I looked everywhere and found an apartment in Almendares. It had two large bedrooms, a living-dining room, kitchen, a terrace in front, and another one in back. It was really a very good one.

A lady who lived in the building showed us her place and said, "That apartment will do fine for the two of you." She wrote down the address for us and we went to tell Aldita, who told us to wait for a call. We never went to see her again, because if you keep pestering them they say you're in too big a rush. So we just waited for word from her. And to this day we've been waiting!

Both the second- and third-floor apartments in my building were prepared for the scholarship students. Six or seven cots were put in the third-floor apartment; then they prepared the second floor but never moved anybody in there. The first students on the block were brought to no. 409, and about a week later they brought another bunch to 412—sixty or seventy girls in all. When those students arrived here, what an uproar!

Those girls changed the atmosphere. One of them sang on the third-floor terrace from the moment she got up. She sang well, too. Another, Eva Dulce, was very nice, and the Chinese girl was too. Later she wrote me from Santiago. All those girls are married by now. Every day they'd bring me some of whatever was prepared for lunch up there. They'd say to me, "Oh, don't bother to cook," and they'd bring me rice and chicken.

There were scholarship girls in the house next door, too, below Horacio's apartment. Then the girls were moved out and boys were brought in. The girls here fell in love with those boys and would slip down my stairs to see them. They'd tell the woman in charge, "We're going down to visit Lala," and they'd come down to talk with the boys. The woman would tell me not to let them in, but how could I do that? And they'd throw tomatoes at one another. One day the baby, Mandito, was lying on his cot and I found it filled with tomatoes that had fallen through the window. I went out and yelled at them and they came down, crying, because they were very fond of the baby.

The boys in 409 were nice kids and always asked permission before going down my back stairs. And they'd clean that staircase from top to bottom. I swear, the boys were a lot better than the girls! I was awfully fond of them.

The scholarship students stayed in those apartments from the beginning of 1962 to about the end of '63. After that, the house was left completely empty until the apartments were fixed up—windows and everything. Then one day Aldita came to tell me that two families would soon move into the upstairs apartments, that Raúl Castro had given them to Bernardo Rojas and Domingo Labrada for having fought in Algeria. That's why both Ana Teresa and Leticia, their wives, moved into their apartments at the same time.

Domingo's wife, Leticia, came over to clean the apartment . . . alone, or with another man, I don't remember. At that time I had a job and wasn't home much. All I know is that at 7:30 in the morning, when I left for work, she was already cleaning up the place. A few days later, my sister Serafina and I were sitting on the garden wall after work when Domingo arrived with their furniture, or rather their beds, because they had no furniture to speak of. Later, I gave her chairs from my apartment from time to time. She also has some very pretty little armchairs that she made herself.

Well, anyhow, Leticia moved in and at first she seemed like a real nice person. She never argued with anybody and stayed home all day long with her three little girls and Tomasito, all nice and quiet. But lately she's become quite nasty. What a tongue that woman has!

One day Armando was helping Ana Teresa clear a clogged drain, and he said, jokingly, "There must be a Negro stuck in that toilet." Leticia blew up because she took that comment seriously. My goodness, he didn't mean any more by it than if he'd said there was a white man stuck in the drain. She really told him off! Armando has quite a tongue too, so he gave her as good as he got, and they flung perfectly horrible insults at each other. It was quite a blowup, let me tell you!

The second-floor apartment had been repaired and thoroughly cleaned, too. It was spotless, like new. Then they gave it to Bernardo, Sara, and all those people, and afterward it was horrible.

Nardo was still in Algeria, so his sister Sara signed the contract. One day they showed up with everything they owned in one little truck—four or five cartons, one spring and mattress, but not even one bed. Sara came with all her kids, her sister-in-law Ana Teresa, two military men, and Ana Teresa's sister Peregrina, with a crowd of kids. A world of people moved in! I had my wash hanging up there and when I went up to gather the clothes, Ana Teresa snapped at me, "We've come here to live."

It was hell after that! There were twenty-seven of them in the apartment! The way they lived!

Their kitchen was terrible. I lived and died with my windows closed because of their smoke. And the dirt! They'd throw trash down into the street. If anybody happened to be crossing, *pam!* they'd fling the dirt right at them. It was unspeakable! The kids didn't shit in the bathroom but on the terrace, and then they'd throw the shit down into the street.

The outside drainpipes got clogged, and when it rained the water backed up there. You couldn't live. It was hell! Then they'd get drunk on alcohol from the grocery store and start throwing the empty bottles down the stairs.

Whoever they ran into in the street they'd bring home. Every day they'd bring someone new to stay. And the fighting... *vaya!* Besides, they were always on the road, going to Oriente and coming back.

One day, Juan, Mercedes's husband, said to them, "I want to show you my house so you'll see what it looks like." I was doing wash out on Mercedes's patio when Juan led those twenty-seven people to his place. Mercedes wasn't home. Juan had called only Nardo, but Ana Teresa followed with her filthy kids and Sara with all of hers. They all went trooping behind Juan. When they saw his beautiful apartment, they just stood there in amazement.

In the end, Ana Teresa, the owner of the apartment, quarreled with Sara, who was part-owner. First they quarreled about who should pay the electricity, so neither did. Then they gave Nardo the money for the electricity, but he kept it and didn't pay the bill either. It was then that I had my own light put on a separate connection. Finally, Armando called them over to explain things. After that they divided the bills and kept their mouths shut.

Each of the apartments in the building had a garage belonging to it. Ana Teresa's sister Peregrina lived in the garage with her four kids and husband, and later Ana Teresa and her two little girls and her mother moved into it too and left the apartment to Sara. They cooked on the little outside door ledge and slept on the floor because they didn't have any beds. At night they'd iron clothes on a folded bedspread on the floor at the entrance of the building. People would be going in and out and there they'd be, ironing. There used to be a faucet outside, but they pulled on it so much it broke and Juan had it shut off. They'd wash clothes on the porch, too, and hang them up to dry on lines crossed in front of Mercedes's house. She told them off any number of times.

And then the fights: "This is my house, not yours..." and so on. Ana Teresa's mother has the temper of a wild beast and is real pushy. One night they started fighting at 3:00 in the morning because Concha, Sara's daughter, had bought a bottle of alcohol at the Minimax and Nardo drank it. Then Nardo grabbed his belt and started hitting everybody with it, even Sara.

The noise woke everybody else on the block. I put my head out and then went back to bed. Armando wasn't home and I said, "I don't want to get in trouble with anybody." Nardo threw the bottle down onto the street and then water by the pailfuls because it seems they were also sorcerers. They threw water here, there, and everywhere.

We put in a complaint. How can you expect people to stand by and let somebody iron their clothes right in front of an apartment building? In no time at all someone from the Committee was here and we talked it over with her. I said, "This is the problem, Dora, the President passes by here, all sorts of people pass by, and can see them ironing out there. They've got no need to do that. They have a great big apartment upstairs." She told us, "Never mind, we'll see about that problem." Then she talked to them and everybody calmed down. Peregrina went to Oriente with all her kids and so did Sara. Ana Teresa stayed in the house.

There were other problems with the garages, too. Juan Carlos needed his garage for his car but he let Miguel, a friend of his from work, live in it for a while. Bernardo's garage was empty at the time so Juan Carlos had a talk with him. Bernardo had no motor for his water pump in his apartment and Juan Carlos said, "Look, *chico*, I'll install a motor for you if you'll lend me your garage." Bernardo agreed. But then Domingo Labrada's brother Dámaso was about to get married and asked for the garage.

Dámaso and Vitalia de Peña moved in, bringing with them a very pretty Empire bed, a stove with burners, a television, a refrigerator, a chest of drawers, and sheets. According to Vita, those things were Dámaso's from his first marriage. Vita was a slender little thing, with a very nice figure and lots of long, long hair. They lived there quietly and she was very nice and friendly. When my boy was sick, she gave him *malanga*. Then, when I had a hemorrhage, she went with me to the doctor and did all my housework. I'd say to her, "*Ay*, Vita, you've really got a sick taste, hitching up with that Negro." She'd laugh and say, "So what, kid? Such is life!"

One night two military men drove up in a jeep and took Dámaso away. Next day I asked Vita, "Where's Dámaso?"

"He's working," she said.

But Leticia, who can never keep anything to herself, told me, "No, he was arrested for stealing a TV set from his army unit." We couldn't intervene because it was a matter concerning the military.[7] Dámaso was sent to a prison farm for three years.

After Dámaso was taken away, Vita began to bring men to live in the garage. She went wild and used that place as a meeting place for her women friends and their lovers—black men, white men, even the Chinese butcher at the Minimax. Then Vita went to Oriente with Sara's brother Panchito, with whom she'd been living.

At the farm where Dámaso was, the prisoners got passes every month or two to go home for five days. The first time Dámaso came home, he found out everything, because Sara, who'd just come back from Oriente, piped up and said, right in front of Dámaso, "Do you know who I saw out there in Oriente? Vita and Panchito."

7. "We" refers to the CDR in which Lala was an officer.

When Dámaso got out of prison, he asked me, "Lala, what happened?" But how could I butt in and tell him? So I said, "Look, Domingo wants to talk with you." He went up there and Domingo explained everything to him. Then he came down and asked me for the ration book. So I handed him his ration book and he took it and left.

In the end, Vita moved all her things out of the garage and went to stay at her mother's house. Now Leticia says she won't let anybody else have their garage. She keeps chickens and other stuff there. Well, we'll see. They're the kind of people who like to have the building filled up.[8]

Once, when Leticia was mad at us, she came around asking me which of the two servants' rooms belonged to her apartment. "I believe the one on this side goes with that apartment," I told her. Then she made a big fuss because we live in that room and it wasn't included in her contract. So they went over to the Urban Reform main office and got a military man to come over to scare us and get us out of here. But it happened that the little Negro in charge of Urban Reform was an old friend and comrade of Armando's from the Sierra. When he saw Armando he said, "Eh, *muchacho*, so you're the one who lives up there! Look, Armando, this comrade brought me here but now I see that you and I are old friends."

Then Domingo told him, "Well, comrade, in spite of that, you were sent here to take action and you must take it." Domingo never fought in the Sierra. He's been a revolutionary only since the day of the Triumph, that 1st of January when he got into a uniform and claimed he'd been in combat. That's a lie; he never fought at all!

"Listen, you, what is it you want anyway?" the little Negro asked him.

"I want to get these people out," Domingo said.

"Well," Armando answered, "when anything comes up, we're supposed to ask Aldita about it. Let's go to the office here and see what she says."

So they went and Aldita told them that nobody had a right to interfere with us because she was the only one who had a say about such things. She explained that neither of the two servants' rooms was included in the contract and only when I moved out could anyone else have them.

Then Armando said we'd move immediately if they found us a place to live, otherwise we had to stay there. Where else could we go? And because of that Leticia said horrible things, really horrible things about us.

Later I went to the office to check up on it. They told me, "Relax, you've got nothing to be scared of. Aldita said you lived there and the place was yours." Then we went to the central Urban Reform Office, to

8. Vita's brother Daniel and his wife, Inés, had also been living in the garage and stayed there periodically after Vita left.

pay them to legalize our occupancy, but they said that wasn't permitted in the Frozen Zone.[9] We went back to Aldita and she told us, "Don't worry about it, *muchacha*, nobody is going to make you get out of there. If I don't tell you to get out, nobody else can."

We pay no rent but that's no advantage at all, because if we did, they'd give us papers and everything and we'd be able to make an exchange. Persons exchanging houses must exchange these papers. We have nothing to give in return. All we can show is the receipt for electricity, because that's the only bill we pay. We haven't even paid for water since the Revolution. So we simply have to wait until they move us elsewhere.

Nobody can get me out of here because I've lived in these two rooms ever since the family I worked for went away. I could have kept the whole big place on the second floor and I turned it in of my own free will. I used the apartment kitchen to cook in and the terrace for hanging the wash, that's all. After they took over the place for scholarship students, I'd sometimes use the refrigerator, but I never stayed in the apartment. Now I wish I'd kept it. We live well enough here but we're cramped for space.

MERCEDES MILLÁN:
After our marriage, my husband, Juan Carlos, and I lived in Vedado with my parents until the government began to give out lists of homes renting for more than 100 *pesos*. They unfroze those in the higher price ranges first, and since my husband could afford to pay a high rent, we went to Urban Reform to get a list of the vacant houses that were sealed.[10] We looked at a lot of houses but it was impossible to go inside them. We could only look around the barrio and judge the houses from the outside. We'd find out from the neighbors the number of rooms and other details.

I would have preferred Vedado to Miramar, but there was nothing on the Vedado list that suited us. The places were all big, but very old or in apartment buildings. There are too many people in apartment buildings; Juan wanted us to have a house of our own. He wanted a garage for the car, and I wanted a yard large enough for our daughter to play in. She was only one year old then. All the houses we saw in Vedado had two floors and I was afraid the baby might fall downstairs. I'd have to watch her all day long.

We finally chose this place because the building had only three apartments, one on each floor. At least that was better than one with thirty or forty apartments. At that time the people Lala worked for, Evidio Carrera and his wife, lived on the second floor, where Justa now lives. They were very nice, polite people, well educated too.

9. Presumably such papers were unavailable to Lala not because she lived in the Frozen Zone, but because no title deed existed for the servants' quarters.

10. Vacated homes were sealed by the Urban Reform Office to indicate they were being held in reserve for future allocation.

The day we looked at this place Evidio was at home alone. He let us look at his apartment because it was almost the same as the vacant one on the ground floor. The third-floor apartment was also vacant. We liked the floor plan, saw the private garage, the yard, the separate entrance, and decided to take it. They say that a European diplomat used to live in our apartment but I never met him. The apartment had been empty a long time and the grass had grown high around it. The building itself was better maintained at that time. In front, at the main entrance to the upper floors, there were fine plants that spilled over the sides of the planters. The entrance was always very clean.

Juan was in the militia and away on duty, so I signed the contract. Then I made a list of everything we already had and another of what we needed to get for the house. We bought all the kitchen utensils and the frigidaire, too, which we got through the classified section of the newspaper.

In January or February we talked to the man who was going to make our furniture, and to an interior decorator about the drapes. He calculated the amount of cloth necessary and went to the stores for samples. That was the way it used to be done. I'd already chosen the color of the furniture for our room, the baby's room, the parlor, and the dining room, so I chose drapes to match. I gave the decorator the money for the cloth, he had the drapes made and came and hung them himself. He charged 500 *pesos* for all his work.

After we painted the apartment we hung the curtains. The furniture was brought in gradually, as we bought it. By April all our things were here: Merceditas's crib, bureau, chair, bathinette, baby carriage, playpen, toys and clothing, our TV set, and the record player that we'd had at *mamá*'s house. Then we brought the bedclothes, tablecloths, ornaments, china, silver, goblets, pictures, and other things we'd bought or been given and had stored at *mamá*'s house. The only furniture we took to the new place from *mamá*'s, aside from the baby's, was the Hollywood bed that Juan and I slept on.

At first I had two live-in maids; one did the housework and the other cooked and washed clothes. It's such a big apartment, you see. Then one left and the other one did nothing but the cooking, so I sent the clothes out to be washed. I kept that maid until she got married. Then there were others but none lasted long.

We had the Carreras for neighbors only a short time before they left. They were always so polite and thoughtful. When the gas in my tank gave out and I had no fuel for cooking, they offered to send us our meals, or if we preferred, to let us use their kitchen. They also let us use their phone while we were waiting for one. And when they left, they had their phone transferred to us.

Lala got married on May 29, before the Carreras left. She invited us to the wedding in her hometown in Pinar del Río, but of course it was too far for us to go. The Carreras went—in fact, I think they paid all the wedding expenses. They were fond of Lala and treated her very well.

The next people to move into our building were scholarship students. They assign as many as possible to an apartment, sleeping on cots lined up one next to the other. Since these apartments have three bedrooms, there were fifteen or twenty children in them. They weren't right above us, but it was noisy, and sometimes they threw things. Oh well, the people who live up there now aren't students and *they* throw things and make a lot of noise, so maybe I shouldn't be too hard on the kids!

Shortly after we moved here, a young couple moved into our garage: Miguel Sardiñas, a man Juan knew from the market, and his wife, Leonora. They were about to get married and had no place to live, so Juan told Miguel they could live there temporarily, for two or three months. He wasn't Juan's employer or a close friend, only a mere acquaintance. Frankly, Juan didn't know him well enough to do him that kind of favor. But Juan is such a benefactor, the kind who'll give the shirt off his back. He's always doing favors for people. But at least Leonora wasn't the type of person Sara is. Leonora and Miguel were clean and neat. They weren't rich and didn't live in luxury or anything, but they had more or less what they needed—their bedroom set, tables, chairs, and the necessary number of beds.

Our garage is better than the others in the building because it has a small room and a bathroom attached. The garages in front of the building are just rooms with no toilets. Miguel got married and came to live there. Well, he didn't stay three months, but seven or eight years! His daughter was born there and his son. Then his mother-in-law moved in.

Miguel worked in food distribution as long as he lived here. Leonora worked in an office. We never charged them 1 *centavo* for rent. Why should we? We didn't need any extra money. In fact, we even let them have their electricity on our bill. But after a while they quarreled with us and accused us of trespassing. If I went through to hang clothes on the line, they objected. Merceditas would play in the backyard sometimes and Leonora complained that the noise woke up her children. One day when Merceditas was six, Leonora dragged her to our door and said, "This is the limit. This child insulted my mother and that's something I won't put up with."

Merceditas was sobbing hysterically and Juan was so angry at the child that he lost control and spanked her. He hardly ever does that. He may punish her by making her stand in a corner or by sending her to bed, but only rarely does he lay a hand on her.

I know Merceditas shouldn't have talked back to an older person because it's disrespectful, but after all, she was only a child. Leonora should have complained to me or else reproved the child, but not in such a rude way.

I'd never quarreled with those people before. I prefer to lose my rights than to have quarrels and problems. I always said hello when we met and I tried to keep Merceditas from playing in the backyard next to the garage. But from that day on, I never spoke to them again. After that they went around talking about us and put up a fence around the garage. Finally they moved away.[11]

SARA ROJAS:

When I first came to Havana,[12] I looked around at everything and thought, "Oh, how beautiful it all is!" I loved it. There's a big difference between the city and the country. In the country one walks in the dirt, but here in Havana everything is paved. Paved streets and sidewalks are such a good idea because your shoes don't get dirty and you can walk outside no matter how hard it's raining.

I brought my children Concha, Hilario, and Amanda Maria, and left Estelita, Gerardito, and Violeta with *mamá*. My husband, Eduardo, and my cousin Gloria met us at the railway terminal in Havana. We all stayed at Gloria's house, but it was a tight fit because she had several children of her own. We had to sleep in the parlor.

We needed a place of our own, so Gloria took us to an empty house with several rooms. We decided to break the seal that the government put on the doors of empty buildings. At 2:00 o'clock that very night, we broke the seal and moved in. But somebody from the block Committee saw us and right away they took us to the police station. When the guy there saw our shabby clothes I guess he was sorry for us because he gave us a letter to take to MINFAR.[13]

At MINFAR the comrade with us said, "Please give these comrades an occupation permit." Then, after Eduardo showed proof that we had no place to live, they gave us a letter and told us to look for a room or apartment with the MINFAR seal and when we found a place big enough for us, to break the seal and move in.

We found a room in Marianao, in a *solar*[14] that was only one story high and had a wide hall lined with rooms, one after another. In each room

11. Mercedes's husband, Juan Carlos Pérez, was very critical of the practice of permitting private garages to be used as apartments. Not only did he have a bad experience with his own garage but also with his mother's. A woman had moved into the rooms connected to the garage of his mother's house in La Vibora and had then refused to move out. He said he had suffered intimidation by a brother and three military friends of the woman and had to go to court before he got her to move. He was so upset by these two experiences that when a neighbor asked him to loan his garage to a sick relative, he refused, saying that he wasn't the Urban Reform Office.

12. In 1961.

13. *Ministerio de las Fuerzas Armadas Revolucionarias* (Ministry of the Revolutionary Armed Forces). Housing problems were usually handled through one's work center and Rojas was in the Army at that time.

14. A low-rent multiple-family structure, usually one story high, with one or more rows of single rooms or small apartments opening onto a central patio.

lived a married couple—eleven families in all. We were busy cleaning when a woman from the Committee showed up and made a fuss about it. We told her we hadn't broken in on our own but that we had a letter from MINFAR.

"That's all right, then," she said. "Tomorrow I'll see about filling in the blanks for your ration book."

That night we slept on the floor. Next morning the same woman comrade showed up and took me to MINCIN[15] to tend to the matter of the ration book. Then I went to the marketplace in Marianao and bought a big bed and a table with matching chairs. I also bought a small stove, a child's dresser, a kerosene burner, pots, pans, spoons, dishes— we equipped the house in no time at all. I got everything we needed. A lady next door lent us another bed, and since our electricity hadn't been connected yet, another neighbor gave us two candles.

I liked living there; we were real comfortable. The neighbors were very nice, the room was spacious, and the hall was big enough for the kids to play in. There was only one bathroom but all of us *compañeras* kept it spic and span because a number of little kids had to use it. Later, my brothers David, Pancho, and Bernardo, who were all in the Army, came to stay with us.

I had a very good friend, Olga, in Marianao. Olga took my kids to the park and spent a lot of time taking them places and keeping them amused. She looked after my kids as well as I did. She was very, very, very white but had no racial prejudice—at least she never showed any prejudice against me. She was always generous with help and advice. When I didn't have money, I didn't have to ask her; she herself would come over and offer me some. She had a refrigerator, and when she went to the butcher shop she'd pick up my meat for me and keep it till I needed it. She often helped me with the housework, and when she didn't, I'd drop in on her. After we sent the kids off to school, we'd sit chatting and watching TV.

We lived in Marianao two or three years. Then, while my husband was still stationed at Managua, my brother Bernardo was sent to Algeria, although at the time we didn't know where he was. He left his wife, Ana Teresa, and little girl, Melinda, in our charge because he himself had no idea where he was being sent.

Because Bernardo was in Algeria, Raúl gave him a present, a new apartment on the second story of this building. When Bernardo filled in the blanks before leaving, he put everything in my name. His salary was to be sent to me and everything. So when they gave him the apartment, they naturally put that in my name too.

I didn't want to move and neither did my husband. "We'd be taking a

15. *Ministerio de Comercio Interior* (Ministry of Domestic Trade).

big risk," he said. "In the end we might lose this house and that one." I was happy living in Marianao but I had to give up my place and move, because if not, Bernardo would lose his right to the apartment. The comrade said, "Your brother did this for your benefit and that apartment is roomy enough so that you can all live in it comfortably." But I think the real reason Bernardo did it was that he didn't want his wife, Ana Teresa, to be all alone because of her asthma.

Well, anyway, we moved to Miramar, to this building we're living in now—Ana Teresa with her daughter and me with all my family. I made all the arrangements for the move—the contract, the electricity, and everything because we were told to move in before my brother's return. Bernardo was the one in charge of the apartment but the contract was in both our names. My signature was in the contract, where it said, "Arranged by Sara Rojas." It said half the apartment was mine, to make up for the one in Marianao that I'd given up.

The only people living in the building then were Mercedes and her family on the ground floor and Lala and Armando in the servants' rooms. When we first arrived, I asked Mercedes to help me get the apartment door open because we didn't understand how the key worked.

Leticia and Domingo got their apartment the same way we got ours—as a gift from Raúl for going to Algeria. The first time they came to see the apartment, they cleaned it. Domingo walked down to ask Mercedes to close her shutters because they were going to scrub the floors and some water might drip through the open windows. They also came down to our apartment.

"Oh, so you're the ones who are going to move in there?" I said. "I want you to know that we're your friends." Two or three days later they moved in. Of course I was glad to have new neighbors because Lala and Mercedes stayed in their own homes most of the time.

EDUARDO ROJAS:

I was against moving from our room in Marianao to the Miramar apartment. I didn't want to lose my room only to have somebody say I was just an extra in the new place. And also, I didn't want to go because Sara's and Bernardo's brother, who has about six children, wanted to live with us in the new apartment. So did Ana Teresa's mother with all her children, five boys and three girls. I wasn't going there with such a mob because I'd lose the room I had. It was as big as this garage, and besides, it had a bathroom and everything. "So far as I'm concerned," I said, "the answer is no. I don't want any company. I just want to be left alone here in my little room. I'm fine here and so are my children."

The man who came with the document explained that if we didn't make the change, they wouldn't give Bernardo the house because Sara was the principal on the contract.

Everybody got on my tail, but I always told them I wasn't interested. They even came to talk to me at work. They'd been to see the apartment so they were pushing me. "Come on, Eduardo, you're going to miss out on a terrific house." I didn't bother to look at the place and I didn't plan on going.

After several days of this, I finally said to Sara, "Well, you go ahead and do what you like, but I'm not responsible for anything that happens. I'm going to move over there with you, but I never want to hear one word about it. Don't forget, we're losing our own house this way." I also told Sara that if all those people were going to live there, I wouldn't move.

Until I told her to go ahead, Sara hadn't done anything. She'd never do anything on her own. She simply wouldn't say anything. But as soon as I gave permission, things started moving. The man who first told us about the house said we had to move right away. He took Sara over to see the house and then to see Aldita, the woman in charge of the Housing office in the Frozen Zone, to draw up the contract.

I didn't do anything except go over to see the house, but when I did I felt pretty happy. It was a wonderful house, a knockout of a house! "This is really something!" I said to myself. I thought that now we'd be able to live well. But there was always a feeling in the back of my mind that something would go wrong. And it did.

So Sara and I went to live there with her children and ours. My brother Luis went with us too. Ana Teresa and her little girl moved in at the same time.

ANA TERESA RAVENTOS:
When Bernardo returned from Algeria, he was given the house in Miramar as a gift. We gave Sara and Eduardo a room because she was my husband's sister. But even though I was the mistress of the house, I couldn't say a thing, not a word, because everybody would jump on me. It was my own house but my sister-in-law wanted to be the mistress.

I'd been living in a room in La Asunción with my daughter, Bernardo's brother Fabiano, and his wife and daughter. Some of us slept on the floor and others on the bed.

The floor had holes, tremendous holes, in it. It was of mosaic tile and was never dry. The roof was a sort of cardboard and the rain would fall right into the very bed we were sleeping in, so that at night we didn't know what to do with ourselves. The room didn't have any toilet, so we used a potty and emptied it in a sewer ditch. One of the ditches passed right under the house, and when that overflowed it was terrible, let me tell you.

Just one room! Really, I felt embarrassed. We've always lived in the midst of all this hubbub, always. But I didn't want to come here because I was living in one place and Sara was living in another. I really didn't want to come. Wasn't I brave! I kept telling Sara, "Come on, *chica*, you go. I'm not moving from here. I'm not going anywhere." But they kept nagging and nagging at me until finally I came. Sara herself insisted on it. "Come on, let's go, Ana Teresa," she kept telling me. My mother told me, "Well, if it suits you, go. If you want to stay, stay. It would be better for you to stay here where you're living." That's what my mother told me, but what else could we do? When a man provides for you. . . .

Instead of putting us in the contract, Bernardo listed Sara and their brother David, who wasn't even on our ration book—he was stationed with the Army at La Cabaña. I didn't know anything about it. Listen, I was the mistress, but even if I hadn't had any right to it, the children he had with me did have a claim. He and I were married in court and people who doubt that are making a big mistake.

When I got to the Miramar apartment, Bernardo hadn't arrived yet. I came with my daughter Melinda, and nobody from my own family. From Bernardo's family there were his brother David and his woman, Panchito, Marcelina, Eduardo, Sara, and their children. All those people came to live with me—and from my own family, nobody. Eduardo's *mamá*, who's my aunt, did come to stay for a few days to have an operation. Since she didn't have any place to stay, she had to look to her family, isn't that right?

It was four or five days before Bernardo arrived. To tell the truth, when he'd left for Algeria he was a little on the thin side, but he came back nice and fat. We hardly knew him, he'd put on so much weight. He was really good-looking. He even had a beard. I couldn't pick him out. "This is Bernardo," they told me, and I said, "Oh no, that can't be Bernardo!" But Sara was hugging and kissing him and the others were coming at him, so I hugged and kissed him too. And all the things he brought!

The first night Bernardo spent at home, I slept in a bed. I think it might even have been Sara's. It was the end room that fell to me, and Sara's was in the front. And so Bernardo stayed with me that night. After that we were fine, nice and quiet, getting along well. He gave me some money and things, because now he had some, but I swear before that I had given a little money to the family when they needed it, chiefly to his mother and such. Not to my *mamá*; my *mamá* has never needed money or anything from him. She's been the one to help Bernardo.

SARA ROJAS:

I don't know but I've got a hunch that my sister-in-law had never lived in such a house in all her born days. I'd have to explain to her, "Look, Ana Teresa, here we have a special place to throw the garbage, a place to put the food scraps before throwing them in the garbage can." I even had to tell her, "Listen, kids aren't allowed to make *caca* all over the place. That's what we have two bathrooms for." But no, the kids would shit on the floor and she'd scrape it up and throw it away.

Another thing I had to tell her, "You've got to sweep all the trash off the floor before you douse it with water and mop it up. You aren't supposed to sweep water with trash in it down the drainspout. If you do, it gets stopped up, the water backs up, and our apartments get flooded." That happened many times. Juan Pérez, Mercedes's husband, came up to complain about it. The scraps of papers, the beans, all the stuff Ana Teresa washed down the drainspout, landed downstairs in the Pérezes' place, and, as he said, they have small children.

Another thing about Ana Teresa is her language. She's apt to speak kind of dirty. Most people paid no attention to her, but one day Juan Pérez came and complained to my brother about it. They talked just outside the apartment. Then my brother called Ana Teresa over and told her, "You better remember that this is the city, not the country."

Then Ana Teresa's relatives decided they wanted to move in with her. "Let's wait till Bernardo comes and let him decide," said I. "There simply isn't room for more people here." "All right," the girl said. And the next day she moved all her family—her *mamá*, her *papá*, and some kids—into the garage that was empty. They didn't live like Christians there, they just managed any old way. They cooked and ate outdoors and bathed in shorts at Mercedes's faucet as if this was a beach. They let the kids run around naked or in rags and the women sat immodestly and all that. They lived badly, country-style, only that isn't the style in the country anymore.

Imagine, living that way here! In the Frozen Zone no less, where people aren't supposed to make noise or pick fights or use swear words. If you live here, you've got to live like people.

I guess Aldita and the people who made the arrangements about the contract found out how those people were living because they called and asked me with whose permission I'd moved that bunch of people into the garage. They said I had to go over to their office and explain everything. I told them that *compañera* Ana Teresa was the one who'd broken the law by getting her relatives in there. Then they said I had to get them out immediately because those *compañeros* weren't living like people. Well, Bernardo was back from Algeria by then, so I turned the problem over to him. I told him, "You're the principal owner of the apartment so it's up to you to go talk with those people and resolve this problem. I've solved enough problems for you."

The patrol car came around and they drove Ana Teresa and my brother to the police station, but they didn't take me because they found nothing against me. There they gave the two of them a talking-to, telling Ana Teresa to quiet down and stop making such a rumpus. They told her I never interfered with anybody and it was plain to see that I was a noble-hearted person and that I never made any noise.

Then came the fight about the ration book. Out in the country I had a ration book of my own, but when I moved here they told me I had to put down my name in my brother's ration book. "I don't like that," I said. "I'm used to having my own ration book." But the girl from OFICODA[16] explained, "When two families live together, comrade, they must share one ration book." So I went back home and explained it to Bernardo and Ana Teresa. But she burst out, "Oh no, I don't want anybody else in my ration book!"

"Well, whether you like it or not, we'll have to put Sara in our book," Bernardo said, "because she can't live without a ration book, to say nothing of all those little kids of hers."

So what does Ana Teresa do but take off and fetch a patrolman! My brother, she, and I were there in the apartment. I didn't know what it was all about or why the patrolman was there. He took them to the police station with the contract, and they were told they had to put me down in their ration book because half the apartment belonged to me. "Just take a look at the contract—it's signed by her. Her signature is the one that counts there. You're trying to deny food to her children by refusing to have her in your ration book and that's no joke!"

After that, Ana Teresa holed up in one of the rooms and did her cooking and everything there. As for me, I kept on using the kitchen and I shopped for my own food. I have no idea how Ana Teresa lived. I never set foot in her room or in her bathroom, either. I simply refused to go where she was. What really got her goat was that I never talked back at all. She wasn't anything so wonderful that I should have to lower myself to her.

They say Ana Teresa cooked in the bathtub but I knew nothing about it. If I'd seen her doing such a thing, I'd have given her a talking-to. Anyway, if there's a stained bathtub in that apartment, it must be Ana Teresa's and my brother's because it isn't mine. For all I knew she cooked on the floor. I was just waiting for the day when the Ministry of Health would come to kick her out, because that sort of thing is against the rules, especially in a building like this one.

I had to disconnect the stove and heater because they used up more electricity than I could afford to pay. Sometimes Ana Teresa didn't have a match and she'd plug in the stove, though she must have known that every time you light one of those stoves, you spend a kilowatt. So I simply had it disconnected. Ana Teresa didn't get mad, because the stove gave off electric shocks from a length of cord and we were both afraid of it.

16. *Oficina de Control para la Distribución de Alimentos* (Office for Control of Food Distribution).

The electric company[17] said the apartment needed a whole new installation but that it would be a long time before they could get around to it.

I did most of my cooking on an electric hot plate after the stove was disconnected. I hardly used my little kerosene burner at all while I lived up there because I didn't want to get the ceiling all smoked up.

Then *mamá* got sick and I had to go home to Oriente for a while to take care of her. I returned to Havana all by myself. Eduardo stayed in Oriente for the sugar-cane harvest and I left the kids with him. I wanted to go back alone because I knew how I'd find the apartment.

I arrived at about 11:00 in the morning; the minute I opened the door the smell hit me. The place stank like the devil; it was enough to scare you. There were worms in the bathroom, the garbage, everywhere. There was dried shit all over the floor. An inspector from the Ministry of Health had already been there and filed terrible charges against them. Somebody told me they were even going to kick Ana Teresa out.

Four whole months I'd been in the country and in all that time that woman hadn't cleaned anything. I said to her, "If you can't clean up yourself, you might at least have paid somebody to come in and do it." Bernardo cleaned up whatever was most urgent and that's all.

I rested for three days after my return, then I really pitched into the job of cleaning and straightening up the place. I scrubbed the walls with a mixture of *Campeón* scouring powder, detergent, and wood ashes, up to the ceiling and down to the floor, and I washed off the window shutters with the same mixture. Fifteen whole days I had to work on it to get it clean, but when I was through the place shone. The kitchen walls were all tiled and so were those of the two bathrooms. The floors were of granite tiles. It was a real good apartment.

After I finished, a friend came to visit and said, "Oh, I see the apartment has been repainted." "No, just washed off," I told her. "It was shit that made this place look old and shabby. Now you can see how pretty it really is."

I had that place as clean and shining as a little golden cup. Everybody who went there asked me for a drink of water. Nobody would take the risk of drinking water in that place when Ana Teresa was in charge. "*Ay*, Sara," they'd say, "how nice the place looks!"

Ana Teresa got things dirty again just as fast as I could get them clean. I didn't complain; I simply went back a little later and cleaned it up again. It was the same with the steps outside. She never cleaned anything. You can go ask, neighbor by neighbor, if they ever saw Ana Teresa do any cleaning around here. They all complained because of the filth she threw down. Then Ana Teresa began to bring the police to the house and to annoy me in every way she could.

17. Consolidated Electric Enterprise.

EDUARDO ROJAS:

For the first few weeks things were fine in some ways, since we were beginning to live in comfort, but they weren't so great in other ways. In fact there were disagreements from the very first. The day after we moved, there was an argument because Ana Teresa's mother and one of my uncles both wanted our old room in Marianao. She got a seal for the door from her place of work and he got one from MINFAR, but that day the house was sealed by either the Defense Committee or Urban Reform, I don't remember which. Anyway, the two of them raised an awful rumpus about it. And in the end it was given to another woman.

Even before we moved to the new apartment, Ana Teresa was always griping because Bernardo's checks came addressed to Sara. I didn't mix into all this because I never interfere with their affairs. And finally one day Sara told them, "All right, you people take it. We don't need it. Just take it and do whatever you like with it."

Then they started fighting over the problem of Ana Teresa's mother and family moving in. Ana Teresa was always asking why they shouldn't have a right to live there. Well, *we* didn't take the right away from her. Aldita said that only the people included in the contract could live in the house, and if anybody else wanted to move in, he had to check it out with her. Sara told them Ana Teresa's family couldn't live in the house. So they moved into the garage, without notifying Aldita.

Bernardo came in March or April, about two months after we did. Both Sara and I welcomed him with open arms. We hadn't seen him for a long time. He only stayed a few days, long enough to say hello, before he went off to see his family in Oriente, because he hadn't seen them for ages. He didn't take Ana Teresa with him.

Sara and I first learned that he and Ana Teresa were on the outs when Bernardo and my brother Luis went out drinking together. The next day I asked Luis where they'd been. "Oh, tanking up with Bernardo and a plump chick," he said. A day later Bernardo came home and told me his story. "Yes, I was visiting a plump chick up there. I swept her off her feet," he said. That meant he'd slept with her. After that he began to visit there from time to time and finally went to live there for good. I think Bernardo's relation with his woman Catalina was the reason he wanted to get rid of the house and find another place for his wife.

All the time Bernardo was still living at home, I never said anything about it to Ana Teresa. I don't mix in such things, because I've had similar problems myself. If somebody butted in, I wouldn't like it at all.

Bernardo and Ana Teresa were a strange couple. They had their spells of getting along fine and their times of squabbling. They were always separating. They'd be apart for a few weeks and then come back together again. Since we were living in the same house, we couldn't help overhearing their fights. Ana Teresa and her mother were always kicking up a fuss. In fact, Ana Teresa's mother was behind most of the scenes. She'd get Ana Teresa worked up over nothing.

Those people are pretty low-down. They'd start a fight over the least thing. When Bernardo and Ana Teresa fought they'd call each other names, like "bitch" and "faggot" and a thousand more. It got so bad that I reported their bad language to Lala, who was president of the Committee. Lala said, "Yes, I've been hearing them myself." But she didn't lecture them or do anything else about it. If I were the head of a Committee and somebody called me about such a thing, I'd explain that they couldn't go on that way with so many children around.

Finally I went to Ana Teresa myself, but she just started arguing with me. I didn't want to get mixed up in their quarrels, so I just went off and let them wear themselves out shouting bad words at each other. I only fought with Ana Teresa a few times and that was over the ration books.

When Sara got into one of those quarrels, I didn't think it was my place to intervene. If a man had been fighting against her that would have been different. Sara's able to fend for herself against another woman. But when Ana Teresa said the house didn't belong to us but only to her and her children because she was married to Bernardo, I said, "Look here, don't talk that way. A lot of things may not be mine but one of these rooms here is mine, and that's that."

ANA TERESA RAVENTOS:

One day Eduardo brought another woman, called Pomposa, to the garage where my mother, father, and sisters were staying. When Sara saw her there, a free-for-all started between the two women. Sara was going to pounce on her, but they pulled them apart. It was a really low scene, but they didn't do any more than hit each other. Pomposa may have been the one who pulled a knife, but I think it was Eduardo. He kept saying, "Go ahead, get her! Get her!" wanting her to attack Sara. It was really something to watch him egging the two of them on.

Bernardo gave Sara an awful trouncing because she'd tangled with Eduardo and told him he was a no-good. How could she continue to live with him? Bernardo was mean because he'd been drinking. He hit her with his hand, not with a stick or anything. Sara cried so much she woke up the whole building. They must have heard her screams up in heaven. A group of people downstairs calmed him down but I went to my room in a hurry. Since we didn't have anybody to stick up for us, I yelled, "Sara, come here, bring the children over here."

I thought blood would flow, that Bernardo was going to kill us all, but he left. Later I told her to report him to the police. What could he have said? He was drunk as a skunk.

The next day he came and set things straight. He said, "Oh God, sister, it was the liquor that made me do those things to you," and Sara forgave him. He didn't leave bruises, but I heard Sara say that her body ached a lot. Things like this went on a few times because Bernardo was drinking too much then, and when drink went to his head he'd start beating his sister.

Now it seems like justice that Sara and Eduardo separated,[18] because I know she's the cause of Bernardo's separation from me. There was a woman called Vita living in the garage and she was a real tart, another hot number. Vita and Sara kept egging Bernardo on. They were always shoving that woman Catalina in his face. It was all because Sara wanted to be the mistress of the house. After all, Bernardo is *my* husband.

One day, when I was leaving Leticia's place, I saw Sara let Catalina in our apartment. I'd seen her before with her husband; she has seven children and none of them has the same father. When I saw that woman's face, I said, "This *compañera* here in this house?"

When I saw how things were going, I didn't make a move. I just kept my eye on things. But one day while my mother was at the Plaza de la Revolución, where Fidel speaks, she saw Bernardo strolling about with Catalina and Vita. So I said to myself, "Well, isn't that nice!"

When Bernardo came home and knocked on the bedroom door, I didn't let him in. I locked the door on him and he slept in Sara's room. The next day he came and opened the closet and took out his clothes. I didn't say anything. I kept quiet. He took the clothes and moved them to Sara's room. Then he went out and I couldn't tell him not to.

That day I went to the Club Obrero, and on the way back I saw Nardo and Catalina across the street. They had their arms around each other and were fooling around, but I didn't say anything. They came to the house and I didn't say a word to them, not a thing. They made a terrible scene because there was nothing left for them to do.

After that Bernardo didn't speak to me and didn't give me anything anymore. My children were having a bad time because of that, so I went to Leticia, the only friend I had left, to get a little food and such. She was the one who helped me while I was living there in the building. Then Bernardo left, and instead of giving me the money, he played a trick on me and gave it to his sister. Every time I went to ask Sara for the money, she'd say, "No, that money belongs to Bernardo and nobody can touch it until he comes."

"What's the matter with you, *chica?* Is he your husband or mine? Are you living with him or what? Tell me," I said. I didn't say anything stronger to her. Well, then Eduardo started to act like a shit too, to put it vulgarly, but I didn't pay any attention to him. I just wanted what was mine. Finally I got my nerve up and took all the money.

18. Sara and Eduardo were separated from 1964 to 1967, during which time he married, under civil law, and had two sons.

Bernardo was even worse than Eduardo, because when Eduardo went off with that girl he kept sending money to his children—he remembered them—but Bernardo never gives a thought to his children, except once when I sent him a telegram that the little girl was sick. As long as I was living in the building, Eduardo would come with that woman and bring Sara money. He'd call her or whistle, and she'd meet him on the sidewalk.

I'd always gotten along pretty well with Sara. But after what she did to me, I don't feel right about her anymore. I know that Sara and her daughter Violeta visited Bernardo's woman plenty of times and fought with her because she'd practically taken the food out of their mouths. That's something they never had to do with me. Not only that, when Violeta comes to visit me, I give her clothes, shoes, everything, even though I've hardly anything to wear myself. Sara caused me to suffer greatly in my own home but I was always good to her.

LETICIA MANZANARES:

When my husband, Domingo, was with the Cuban Army in Algeria, he wrote saying that I should go to Havana because a comrade's wife had gone there and the government had resolved her housing problem right away. I'd been living with my mother-in-law in Regla in a tiny wooden house and it was very crowded. There were twelve people living there. So I went to the High Command and asked for a place to live because my husband had been sent out of the country. They told me they'd let me know as soon as they could.

I went back to my home in Limón to wait for the High Command to find me an apartment. A week later the political instructor, who brought Domingo's salary every month, told Domingo's sister they had a place ready for me and she sent me a telegram. I packed all my stuff and rushed back to Havana.

When I first saw the apartment I was happy they were giving us such a good place. The best of it was that we could live by ourselves and be the bosses of our own home. But the apartment had no furniture and I had none of my own. So I said to them, "I want the apartment but you'll have to give me furniture too." They had furniture but didn't give me a thing, even though they promised. That's the way those people are. The apartment remained empty for about a month while I was waiting.

Domingo came home that same month[19] and we decided to sign the contract, because if we didn't move in soon we'd lose the apartment. There were lots of people in the same fix. The government gave thirty-five apartments in Miramar to the men who went to Algeria and many lost their places because they didn't move in right away for lack of furniture.

19. March, 1964.

The Army gave Domingo a month's leave, which we spent at the High Command trying to get them to resolve the furniture problem. Every single day we'd go there and they'd tell us to wait. We filled in a request the year before last and they still have it. We even wrote to Raúl and he sent word that we'd get the furniture, but they still haven't given us a thing.

That's injustice and I don't care who hears me say so. If Domingo had been a lieutenant or a captain he'd have gotten the furniture from them. I'd say that right to Fidel's face. In fact, if I'd gone to Fidel with the problem, he'd have made them give it to us. That's a good thing about this government—that Fidel and Raúl will solve your problems if you talk to them. You can also go to Celia Sánchez.[20] The trouble is, how are you going to get to them? Just as during the previous government it was hard to see Batista. Only powerful people can go straight to them. But it's true that to get a problem resolved right away, those are the three people to go to—Fidel, Raúl, or Celia.

The first night we spent in the apartment we all slept well, but the mattress was ruined from being put down on the floor. It was the only furnishing I owned. Little by little we bought the beds and everything else we have. My brother Tomás got four chairs for us where he works. Domingo put in the woven straw seats and backs and painted them. They brought them to the apartment and it was a great surprise for me to see how pretty they were and of what good quality. And it was all done free of charge. Our style of living has improved since we moved into this apartment. We're as well off as we can be, considering everything.

The first person I met when we moved here was Ana Teresa. There were always lots of people in her apartment and her door was always open. From the very first, we talked together. I invited her to my home and she invited me to theirs. We never quarreled. When I said, "Ana Teresa, let's wash the stairs," we'd wash them from top to bottom and scrub the walls and everything. Domingo always scrubbed the whole wall from our apartment down to the street door, every inch of it. Ana Teresa and Sara and all of us cleaned those stairs and Sara always cleaned the walls of her apartment. Every time a child shit on the stairs we'd throw a bucketful of water on it. These stairs were always wet, that's how often we washed them. As for Ana Teresa and Sara, they're country people and they may have been careless and sloppy at home but they were never as bad as some people say. Not a bit!

The first day we came here, we asked about the gas tanks that were outside Mercedes's apartment. But it seems she'd already taken a dislike

20. Celia Sánchez Manduley, a heroine of the Sierra Maestra campaign, one of six women on the Central Committee of the Cuban Communist Party, and Minister of the Presidency until 1976, when she was named Secretary of the newly appointed Council of State.

to us, because she didn't explain anything until she was good and ready. Mercedes is like that. She tries to act better than everybody else. At least that's the way she acted with the people on the second floor. But she can't treat me that way because I don't allow anybody to put on airs around me. Nobody is better than I am and they'd better not go thinking they are.

One day Mercedes called me to say that my kids had thrown paper down from the balcony. That's when I got good and mad at her and told her forty truths. I said, "You're dead wrong, kid, if you think you're worth more than anybody. This apartment was given to me, it wasn't lent or anything, so you can. . . ."

Mercedes's husband, Juan, is something else. He's a nice guy and we get along fine with him. When we stood guard, he'd talk with us out there. Every time he sees us he stops for a chat. He's very sociable, very different from her.

Lala always talked with me and acted friendly. She's the one who finally explained the gas tanks and Mercedes to me. We got along well from the very first, though we weren't as good friends then as we are now. I did have a problem with Lala and her husband once because they were taking their electric current from us. All those rooms and the garages get their electricity from my apartment and the middle apartment. One time I came back from spending a month in the country and my electricity had been cut off. "How can they cut off my light when I haven't been using it?" I thought. Well, it turned out that the electricity that was owing hadn't been used by us but by Lala. I went and had a talk with her and then they had a meter installed. After that, Lala and I never had any problems. That business of the electricity was the only argument we've ever had and it wasn't really an argument, only an explanation.

DOMINGO LABRADA:

My brother Dámaso and I returned from Algeria in March and we went directly to the High Command. An officer there said to me, "Look here, *chico,* we understand that your wife hasn't wanted to take the apartment that's been assigned to you. I advise you to go see the place for yourself and grab it, you hear? Don't waste any time."

Dámaso and I and Eladio, a friend who'd been in Algeria, went to see the apartment. A few days later they gave him a place too, on 6th Street.

When I opened the door of the apartment and looked in I only saw the parlor and the kitchen. I said, "Gentlemen, we'll have to gather up bricks like crazy to divide up this place. I can get at least four rooms out of this parlor!" I looked out the kitchen window at what I took to be another apartment across the way, but when I went to look at the bathroom I found two more bedrooms in back. "Hey look," I called to the others, "this is where most of the apartment is, back here!" Then

Dámaso and Eladio joined me and Eladio said, "*Compadre,*[21] you'd better run back to your wife and tell her to move in today, this minute!"

"I don't have to say anything to her," says I. "She'll move when I tell her to, furniture or no furniture! If they give us some, fine! If not, at least we'll be living here."

The truth is, I got real enthusiastic about the apartment the minute I saw it. For one thing, I didn't have a home. And then, when I saw this place. . . ! I've lived in comfortable houses before but never in my life in a place like this.

I went to the unit right away and talked with a friend of mine who was in Transportation. "I need you to take the truck over to my house tonight; we're moving."

When I talked to my wife about it, she objected; "Don't you agree to move in, old boy, not until they put furniture in the place."

"Look, let's move in right away so we can have a place of our own," I told her. "I saw the apartment and it's very good. Very, very good."

But Leticia said, "Let's at least wait until the furniture arrives. Comrade Larrazabal told me, "Don't go taking any old junk there because as soon as Raúl Castro signs, they'll give you all the furniture you need. They're going to give you a TV set and everything."

"Don't rely on Larrazabal," I said. "He's going to doublecross you. One of my comrades didn't move into the place they assigned him and they simply gave it to someone else."

And so we moved in, that very night, bringing nothing but the mattresses. I thought, "If it's the way they told Leticia, they won't wait two years or ten to give us all the furniture we need." I gave our bed to one of my aunts, my old lady kept the porch rockers, and we divided the few other things we had between them. Well, we put the mattresses on the floor and that's where we slept, and that night I said to myself, "This is magnificent! A fine apartment, *compadre!*"

Later, when my brother Dámaso needed a place to stay, I traded my garage for Bernardo's because his garage is better ventilated and has a closet. My brother and his wife, Vita, moved into the garage and gave me more trouble than if they'd moved right into my apartment. For one thing, the garage had no toilet, and they had to use ours.

Dámaso was in the Army and was assigned to a military unit in Marianao. His unit headquarters occupied a country house nearby where there was a TV set. Dámaso and another fellow took the TV over to the unit barracks but Vita asked him to bring the set home. Dámaso said no at first but she kept insisting. Being in love with her, he finally gave in. They made a big fuss at the unit and filled reams of paper about

21. *Compadre* and *comadre* are terms used by a child's parents and godparents in addressing or referring to each other.

it. In the end, Dámaso was arrested and jailed, first at La Cabaña and later on at a prison farm, for about a year and a half.

When Vita was all by herself in the garage, she carried on something awful. She stopped going to our house and started using the toilet in the house next door, where Horacio lives. She began to bring men to her place. She couldn't have behaved worse. If I should ever have the bad luck to be jailed—God forbid!—and while I was away my wife started laying on the makeup with a heavy hand. . . ! I mean, it's just too vulgar. I'm sure my wife would have her supper at 7:00 as usual, go right to bed, and fall asleep at once.

Vita's first husband, the one she was legally married to, was one of those who visited her. If you walked into the garage, you'd find the place full of men without their shirts on. She called them her "cousins," but I never saw one of those cousins as long as my brother was there. I saw all those things but kept my mouth shut. I simply wanted to get her out of the garage, and once she was out I would never, never let anyone else have it.

Vita had struck up a friendship with Bernardo's family and became very good friends with Sara. Then she made a play for Panchito, one of Sara's brothers, and began having relations with him. In the end, she went off with him to Oriente. All this while she was supposed to be living with my brother, who was in jail.

Altogether Dámaso spent almost two years in jail. While he was in La Cabaña, Vita would go to visit him but she'd never mention what she was doing. Instead, it was always, "Your brother did this and your brother did that." When his sentence was up, my brother arrived here one night and didn't even come up to say hello to me. "So that's the way it is!" I thought. "That woman has turned Dámaso against me somehow. Well, never mind, he'll come to me eventually."

By the next day I couldn't stand it anymore. I decided to wait until the two of them were together so I could talk to them both at the same time. At noon I went down while she was serving my brother's lunch. I told him, "A man who's a man doesn't go around spreading gossip; he says what he has to say right to people's faces. I wouldn't ever gossip about Vita behind her back, but now you're home, I'll have my say right to her face."

Then I told him everything she'd done while he was away: that she'd brought men to the garage, that she'd gotten involved with Panchito, that she'd hung photographs of herself and her first husband all over the walls of the garage. He just sat there as if he didn't give a damn and didn't say anything, but Vita started arguing with me.

My brother stopped speaking to me because of that. Days and days went by, and he kept on living in the garage with Vita but he still wouldn't speak to me. One day, while Dámaso was away at work, Vita

packed her things and went away. To this day I don't know what happened and I've never asked my brother about it. When he got home that
day, he called me over and said, "We're brothers and there's no quarrel
between us."

"No, and there never will be either," I agreed. "I'll always be the same.
Understand?"

It's more difficult now for a person to let someone live in his garage
because of the confusion over ration books. A law has been passed which
says a ration book can't be given to anyone living in a garage with no
bathroom or toilet. They send an inspector around to check on it before
they issue a ration book. Some people solve that problem by putting
down their names in the ration book of the family who lives in the house
or apartment to which it belongs. But after my brother moved out of my
garage, I made up my mind not to give it to anyone else.

JUSTA DÍAZ:

Four months after the Triumph I joined my husband in Havana. I
wanted to surprise him, so I didn't tell him I was coming. I set out by
train from Oriente with his mother and all the kids. A comrade told us
how to get here. When we got to Havana we went into the first police
station we saw and asked for Captain Reynaldo, who was from my
hometown. He told us where my husband's unit was and phoned him.

Like all the other comrades who came to Havana, I felt we were in a
new place and not civilized enough to be living in the capital. The government hadn't been installed yet and nobody knew what was going to
happen, because at that time the imperialists began to play all their
tricks. We didn't know what to think, or where and how we were going to
live—the thing that mattered was fighting off imperialism and trying to
figure out when and where it would attack us. All the comrades were in a
state of alert. Nobody had time to stop and say, "Hernández's wife arrived here with five kids; we've got to find a house for them!"

I took all our clothes and the boxes full of china and odds and ends
and went to my brother-in-law Felipe's apartment. My sister-in-law was
bowled over with surprise when I told her we were going to move in with
them.

When I saw how small her place was, I almost went out of my mind.
My problem is that I'm a very nervous person. To make things worse,
that apartment was so dark the electric light had to be kept on in the
daytime. It had windows but it was between two four-story buildings and
the electric fan had to be running all the time, even in winter, because it
had no kind of ventilation. The doctors have told my sister-in-law to
move because it's impossible to keep the children healthy in such a place.
She still lives there though and has to walk to the park to give her kids
some sun.

When I saw my husband I was overcome. And since I hadn't told him beforehand that I planned to come, I wasn't sure how he'd take it. He didn't for a minute suggest that I should go back to my mother's.

"*Caramba,*" he said, "I'd already sent off a letter asking you to come and bring the children even if you all had to stay at a hotel, because I couldn't keep on living like this much longer." It was hard on him to be without me. Poor man, he had to send his clothes to the laundry. He was used to the way I fixed his clothes, and at that time everybody was so overjoyed at the triumph of the Revolution and so full of plans about what they were going to do that you couldn't get anybody to do your laundry.

Felipe and my sister-in-law had nothing but the apartment they'd been given and a set of bedroom furniture they'd bought before my arrival. Later on she bought a table and four chairs. The apartment was so small there wasn't room for anything else. She had her own things one on top of another. We had a mattress that we put down in the parlor, and that's where the children slept. My husband and I slept on the floor and my mother-in-law on a small sofa. Sometimes my husband stayed at the unit.

I was fit to be tied, really on the point of losing my mind and rushing out into the street like a madwoman. I'd never lived in such a cramped, uncomfortable place. Never! My parents were far from being millionaires, but poor as they were, they owned the house they lived in.

I've worked all my life, and my homes have always been decorated nicely. I have a knack for that. I own little ornaments and good furniture. Hernández and I have always been hard workers. I've gone out to work as a cleaning woman, and washed and ironed mountains of clothes in my life. That way we managed to have nice things at home, by sacrificing and pinching and scraping.

I couldn't hope to stay on at Felipe's place permanently even if I'd wanted to. My intent was to get out of there as soon as we could find a place of our own. The children were always getting sick; when I saw them lie down on that mattress on the floor at night, my heart sank. We couldn't stop thinking about it. My husband keeps things to himself but I know he suffered. He's a good guy. "We must wait," he told me. "It isn't half as hard as when we were fighting in the Sierra and the whole Cuban people had to wait for our victory. If they waited, why shouldn't we?"

After about three months, I spoke to Hernández's chief, Comrade Ameijeiras.[22] Ameijeiras was annoyed at Hernández for not having gone to him before. "How could you let your children sleep on the floor all that time, Hernández?" But Ricardo is so reserved, he's ashamed to ask for anything. I'm just the opposite, always ready to speak up if necessary.

---

22. Efigenio Ameijeiras was Castro's first chief of police. He later became Vice-Minister of the Armed Forces, but in 1966, as part of a drive against corruption, he was removed from the Communist Party's Central Committee and imprisoned for "moral offenses."

I told him, "I'm not asking for luxuries but for something I need and am entitled to. I know where I stand."

I also talked to Captain Fulgencio, who'd been at the head of my husband's column, and he solved the problem for me at once. He said we could stay in a vacant house in Miramar until they found us a permanent place to live. When Ricardo found out, he said to the captain, "Well, all right, but remember, you were the ones who did this. I didn't ask for it."

I didn't have to pay rent, electricity, or anything—the government gave me all I needed. They sent a truck to move my things. It was an enormous house with twelve rooms. It was so big I felt afraid in it. Most of the rooms were empty because the government had taken out all the fine furniture. They gave us just enough furniture to make us comfortable. Since we now knew for sure that we were going to get a house soon, we bought a set of bedroom furniture costing 400 *pesos*. I started paying for it right away, 7 *pesos* a month, just as I'm now paying 6 *pesos* a month for furniture. I bought no other furniture until we moved to this place we live in now.

When they moved me to Miramar, I couldn't tell anybody in the world the address because it was right near Che Guevara's house. I'd see El Che drive out with his armed escort and I'd salute him. We lived in fear because Che was so careless with his life. When his bodyguards came hurrying after him, he'd say, "No no, stay where you are. I want to go out alone," and he'd drive off in his car. "El Che is a very trusting man," my husband would say. Why, living there I was afraid even for myself, and I told that to Aleida,[23] Che's wife. But nothing happened during all the time we lived there. Everything was calm and peaceful.

Aleida is a very able woman. You'll never see her wearing makeup and jewels or elegant clothes. She goes out wearing any old dress—that's what I call true socialism. She's like Vilma Espín[24] that way. The children spent a lot of time with the bodyguard and she'd often see us there. She was busy all the time but she'd stop and chat with us. She was very relaxed and natural, not the kind to clown around or raise her voice. And I want you to know that she was one of Fidel's very first followers.

El Che was a very intelligent, gentle, inoffensive person who never provoked anybody. He'd go out for a ride with Fidel, who is very, but very, daring. I've seen Fidel driving alone with his bodyguard nowhere in sight. If anybody wanted to kill him at such a moment...! One thing protected him though. The counterrevolutionaries knew that if some

23. Aleida March, Guevara's second wife.

24. Heroine of the Revolution's Second Front in the Sierra del Cristal, where she served (under the pseudonym Deborah) as political advisor to Raúl Castro, whom she later married. She is a founder and the current president of the Federation of Cuban Women, a member of the Central Committee of the Cuban Communist Party and of the Council of State, and a deputy from Santiago de Cuba to the National Assembly.

daring *gusano*[25] did such an evil deed, they'd simply be left with a more powerful man, Fidel's brother Raúl. He's very quick, you know; he can't be taken in. They're afraid of Raúl and that's why Fidel feels so safe.

We finally moved to this building two years ago.[26] This had been a fancy residential zone under the old government, but the Revolution put an end to all class privileges. Blacks as well as whites are allowed to live here now. Aside from that, I find little difference between the people who lived here before the Revolution and those who've come recently from other places.

Now and then Lala tells me about the people who used to live in my apartment, because she was their maid. When I moved in I said, "*Ay*, what a pigsty this place is!" And Lala told me, "You should have seen it before, it was really nice." She was shocked to see the state of the apartment, especially the kitchen and bathroom.

The kitchen had been a very good one with an American water heater and an electric stove. I didn't use the stove because it eats up a mortal amount of electricity, so we turned it over to the government. It was a wreck and we had one already. You'll never catch me using an electric stove and paying 30 or 40 *pesos* a month on the electric bill! Especially since I use up quite a lot of electricity on my job, ironing clothes. We analyzed all that and decided that the government should have those things to assign to somebody who could afford them. They belong to me, the Frozen Zone says, because they're included in my rent whether I have them or not, but why keep something I can't use?

25. Literally "worm," used in Cuba to refer to anyone who does not support the Revolution, from passive opponents to active counterrevolutionaries.

26. Justa and her husband, Lieutenant Ricardo Hernández, did not move directly to their present apartment from the house in Miramar. They lived for several years in Almendares, in an apartment they received through the armed forces. It was by exchanging this apartment for their present one that they were able to move in 1967.

The Exchange [27]

SARA ROJAS:
Ana Teresa didn't want to share the apartment with me because she's too selfish. That was the whole trouble. Then Bernardo got fed up and requested an exchange of apartments so he could live in peace. He wanted her to go live in one place and me in another and they started working on the exchange with Lieutenant Hernández while I was visiting my folks in Oriente. They didn't bother to tell me, much less to consult me.

I don't know how Bernardo and Lieutenant Hernández happened to get in touch with each other. My brother didn't know the lieutenant before—they weren't in the Army together or anything—but I guess Horacio must have brought them together to see whether they liked each other's apartments and wanted to exchange. Horacio lives across the way, in the Russians' building.[28] He used to work with Aldita at the business of moving people and exchanging apartments. At least that's what he says.

Later my brother told me he'd been trying to exchange our apartment for another one, but then he assured me that he'd given up the idea and I left it at that. He said he and Ana Teresa had decided to go to Oriente instead and would make out the contract in my name. I said, "That's all right with me, as long as I keep what's mine, because this apartment is mine."

The lieutenant came by one day when Bernardo was gone and asked me, "Are you Bernardo's sister?"

"Your servant," says I. And I offered him coffee and everything. "Bernardo isn't here," I explained. "He's out in the country visiting our old lady, who's sick." So he said goodbye and left.

When Bernardo came back from the country I told him, "A man in military uniform was here asking for you." I hadn't the least idea what it

27. September, 1967.
28. Two units of the apartment building next door (no. 409) were occupied by Russian and Bulgarian technicians.

was all about. Then I told him I wanted the contract for the apartment, but Bernardo said, "I don't have it here."

"Take care," I told him. "They could play some sort of trick on us."

Bernardo didn't suspect they'd deceive him shamelessly, but they did. I didn't know a thing about what they were doing then, but I dreamed that somebody had brought a goat to *mamá's compadre*, Oscar Balboa. "*Ay*, Oscar Balboa," I said, "this little *chivo* isn't going to be enough for so many people."

"Never mind," he said, "the big *chivo* is coming soon."

So what does that mean? *Chivo* is a goat but it also means to play a dirty trick on somebody. The dream was a warning that they were trying to trick me.

Maybe Horacio was trying to help, but he tangled it up more than ever. He and the lieutenant worked it by pretending they needed to know more about the place. They asked Bernardo to lend them the contract to study it, so Bernardo gave it to them. That's when they must have made the other contract, or God knows what. I sure don't know. Then, it seems, Bernardo told the lieutenant he no longer wanted the exchange. "But the contracts are already drawn up," the lieutenant said. They were already doctored is what he meant! "Show them to me," Bernardo demanded. And the lieutenant fairly threw them at him.

That night the lieutenant came over with the exchange documents in hand and said the deal didn't include me, that there was only one apartment and if we didn't move we'd go to jail. I repeated his words to Bernardo and what did he say? "I can't wear my pants like a man anymore!"

"Look," I told my brother, "this place is yours. If they should lock you up in jail a hundred times, it's still yours. You've got Raúl's letter, haven't you?"

Bernardo must still have that letter, and he had one from the Prime Minister of Cuba, Fidel Castro himself. But I was going to be out on the street! Where could I go? I kept worrying about my children and about the fact that I was pregnant. That night we didn't sleep at all—we were half dead with worry.

Next morning, Eduardo and my brother David went to the Party and saw a man there who told them we should stay put. "If the lieutenant goes ahead with the move, let us know," he said. "Neither he nor anyone else is allowed to push a family out of their home into the street."

My brother probably didn't know that there was only one apartment to be exchanged for the one we shared. What I don't understand is why Bernardo didn't check on that. It was his duty to make sure just what he was exchanging for. I asked him, "How come you just took his word for it when he told you there were two apartments? Why didn't you ask him to show you both of them?"

He didn't answer a word, not half a word. Then I said, "But look here, just exactly how did you make that exchange? I have my old contract where it says that I own half of it, and all the rest of the documents for the apartment. You know that if I should take that contract to the Party, they'd send you to jail—you and a few others."

Bernardo didn't say I had to move. On the contrary, he kept saying, "Sarita can't be left out in the street." But he didn't do a thing to prevent it. He simply bent his head and let matters take their course instead of keeping his head high. They kept on browbeating him and I guess he simply got scared of the lieutenant, because toward the last he wouldn't speak at all. Not one word.

There was nothing that could be done about it anymore because they'd already signed the contract. If it was a fake contract, I can't prove it. I simply don't know. Anyway, by the time they brought that contract to Bernardo, things had already been set in motion. In the new contract, my brother David, Bernardo, Ana Teresa, and the two little girls were the only ones mentioned. Eduardo and I and my children were left out of it.

I've sometimes suspected that Bernardo decided to make an exchange of apartments just to get rid of Ana Teresa, because at that time he hadn't completely separated from her yet but he was already involved with Catalina. The truth of it is that Bernardo was angry at Ana Teresa. She's a tricky customer; there's nothing she likes better than playing a dirty trick on somebody. The very day of the exchange she was getting ready to accuse him of trying to kill her *mamá*. According to her, Bernardo had threatened to chop off her *mamá*'s head, which was slander, pure and simple. Naturally, it made him mad to have her yelling such things at him loud enough for all the neighbors to hear.

I can't imagine how come Bernardo married Ana Teresa, and I don't know what went through his mind all that time when Ana Teresa was making so much trouble for everybody. I do know that he was annoyed with her then. As long as they were together, their life was one long quarrel. Whenever he called her attention to anything, she practically ate him alive. She'd go fetch her mother right away and her mother would shoot her mouth off at him. He really had a problem with such a wife.

It was for the children's sake that Bernardo put up with that woman as long as he did. But she never managed to dominate him—never. She's an Indian type, blacker than I am, with a broad nose and straight hair that she always wears cut like a boy's. She's kind of strange-looking. The truth is, there's nothing pretty about her. Nothing, not one feature.

In the last few days just before the exchange, Ana Teresa was like a wild beast, even worse than before. Aaahh, she was impossible. She'd quarrel with me all day long and make noise so my kids couldn't sleep. She'd sing stupid songs at the top of her voice until the neighbors complained of the noise. Ana Teresa said she could make all the noise she damn well pleased in her own house. But at least she did stop singing.

I, my brother Pancho, and Eduardo weren't getting along very well, trying to solve the problem. We had to go to Catalina's place to get Bernardo. We ran into the lieutenant on the way back and Eduardo and I really pitched into him. Eduardo called that man such names! They could really have arrested Eduardo except that what he said was all true, every last word.

Eduardo said to Bernardo, "Tell him the exchange is off. Tell him the place is yours and the exchange is off." The argument got good and hot. The lieutenant claimed that the agreement was between him and Nardo. Brazen, that's what he was.

Then Bernardo suggested we move to the garage, with no bathroom or anything. "Don't be a fool, let's stay right where we are," I told him. "No, no, no," the lieutenant insisted, "if you refuse to move, you're all going to jail."

When Eduardo heard that my brother Bernardo would go to jail. . . ! We didn't know what was what. We were clean out of our minds; we had nobody to tell us what to do. Eduardo was as much at sea as I. If he'd only been told by somebody, "Look, Eduardo, this is the way things are. Call your Party representative back. . . ." If the Party had at least given us some advice. . . . We were going crazy with worry and didn't know what to do.

Then Eduardo said to me, "Look, Sara, I'd be very sorry to see Bernardo go to jail because we refused to move. No matter what, he's a member of our family."

I didn't agree. I said, "Let him go to jail a hundred times if need be, *I'm* not going to let myself be put out in the street. I'm not going to give him that pleasure, or Ana Teresa either. Who helped me when I took the risk of breaking the MINFAR seal on that apartment at Marianao? Nobody! We made it our home by blood and fire without anybody's help. And when they all ran to us asking for *our* help, we gave them shelter and a bed to sleep in and food to eat—and nobody helped us then either. So now I'd cheerfully see Bernardo jailed a hundred times over rather than let myself be kicked out into the street."

Of course Bernardo couldn't have been sent to jail for the exchange—no money had changed hands or anything—but the lieutenant's threats terrified him. I'm telling you, that man got the apartment at gunpoint. I guess he thought he could scare Bernardo into going through the exchange. And so he did!

The lieutenant showed up on a Saturday when all the kids were home. He rudely burst in, threatening to send us all to jail. I felt terrible. My brother Pancho faced right up to him and said, "We went to the Party and they told us not to move out of here until they came."

"Then you'll all land in jail for going to bother the Party," the lieutenant yelled. "I'm a Party member too." And he pulled out his Party card.

Well, there he was in our apartment with all his things down below in the moving van and he was furious. "I didn't come here to sit outside and wait till you got good and ready to go!" he raged. "I've got all my furniture here and we've got to bring it up." He said to another comrade who was there with him, "Go and get two patrol cars."

So we waited for the patrol cars to come. After a while I asked, "When are they coming to arrest us?"

"Señora," said he, "I don't want to arrest you. All I want you to do is to move your furniture out of here."

"But where will *I* go if I take out my stuff?" I got into such a state of nerves! Never in my life had I been inside a patrol car or had to go to court or anything like that. I'd been brought up safe at home with no problems of that kind. When you aren't used to that kind of thing, the sight of a patrol car coming for you is a shock. Then too, I was pregnant and my nerves always act up when I'm that way. I simply got an attack of nerves.

"It's too late to fight back or to do anything about it," I thought. I took it for granted that all the patrolmen down below were his friends, members of the same unit or something. He brought them there to scare us. Eduardo and Pancho still faced right up to him, but nobody else made a move to help us; they simply kept quiet. Lala, who *was* the Committee then, stayed home.

The lieutenant started to move his things. He had several men helping him. The mattresses, beds, and refrigerator were hauled up to the terrace with ropes, and he and another comrade received them on the terrace and carried them inside.

After the lieutenant's stuff was moved in, they took Ana Teresa's things down and loaded them on the van. They took hers first because she was the one who was moving to the lieutenant's apartment. It's a tiny little place. You can't even say it has a bathroom because it doesn't drain. It has two bedrooms, a little parlor, a tiny kitchen, and a miniature porch, that's all.

Then they took our things down below, because every time we tried to argue he had just one answer: "I'll have you all in jail." I looked on without saying a word. My brother Bernardo, who was the one who could and who *should* have defended me to the very last, didn't say a word either, not even to ask where I was going to land after I was kicked out.

"Come here," we said to him, "explain to us, just what did you agree to do when you made the exchange? Did they give you money?"

But he just kept repeating, "This apartment is yours."

"Just what do you plan to do about me now?" I asked him. "Here I am pregnant. What are you going to do about it? Where are you going to send me? You'll have to conjure up a house out of thin air for me, I guess, because I don't have a home in Oriente anymore. I've been living in Havana seven years. What are you going to find for me?"

I'd made up my mind by then that if the case was brought to trial, I'd lose anyway. They probably would have told me, "This contract is legal, Señora. Your brother gave his word to exchange and everybody was in agreement. If it leaves you out in the street, that's not his problem."

"I shit on God!" I said. I was driven to say that dirty word. Who wouldn't if they found themselves thrown out like that?

All of this flashed through my mind in that instant. Then I began to carry things downstairs. The first thing I took out—or, rather, that Eduardo took out—was the food. I went up and down, up and down, several times, fetching and carrying things, and it seems that did me harm. I was about six months pregnant at the time and it must have harmed the baby.

Then, to make things worse, I had a fall. I was going upstairs to the bathroom when it happened. A comrade was carrying down a dresser but I didn't see him until he turned the corner, and I bumped against it. I was wearing high-heeled shoes and I lost my footing and fell over backward.

It wasn't a really bad fall. I sat down hard, that's all. At the moment I didn't feel the effect because my body was hot from so much exercise. I got up and went on upstairs to go to the bathroom, and then, all of a sudden, I got chills and felt sore all over. Eduardo opened up a cot right away. No sooner did I lie down than I was writhing with pain.

"I'd better take you to Maternity; it's probably some sort of trouble in your belly," Eduardo said. He asked one of the men there, "Would one of you please drive us over to Maternity? My wife is sick."

"Of course, hombre," they said. One of them drove us to the hospital right away, a fellow with an Indian complexion, very kind and gentle.

Eduardo was terribly upset when he saw me sick. "I'm not going to lose you just because of the trouble over the apartment," he said. "I'd sooner live out in the street." By that time all my belongings had been brought down and tossed outside. The door was open and people kept going in and out, in and out.

When we got to the hospital, I was all swollen and they admitted me right away. I had a nervous fit when I saw the blood. The doctor told me I should keep calm, follow the plan he'd made for me, and come back to see him in four days.

My brother had stayed behind in the apartment so the lieutenant and his family wouldn't move in, but by the time I got back they were already settled there. According to Eduardo, if my brother hadn't reacted the way he did, we'd still be living in that apartment. I'll say one thing for

Eduardo—he's afraid of nothing and nobody and that's the truth. He wasn't far from beating the hell out of the lieutenant. He would have, if I hadn't said to him, "Control your nerves a bit. Remember I'm pregnant." That's the only thing that held him back.

Some of the neighbors were also upset. Lala was sorry for me; we always did get along well with each other. And it was either Juan Pérez or Armando—I don't remember which—who said, "This is scandalous! Things can't go on like this. That woman can't be left out in the street, pregnant and with so many children. You've got to find a place for her." So the lieutenant decided we could stay in the garage until we found someplace else. When I got home that evening, all my furniture was in the garage.

I hadn't the slightest idea that we were going to be moved to this garage. How could I even imagine it when Vita, Dámaso, and Inés were already living here? Their things were still here—two beds, a big stove, a dresser with a mirror, a sideboard—the place was full of their furniture. But that's the way they resolved the problem: they moved Vita and Dámaso to the other garage and gave us this one. It was Vita's place, not mine or the lieutenant's, or any other damn person's, because as long as a family is living in a place, they can't be kicked out of it and into the street.

When I got back from the hospital, Inés, Vita's sister-in-law, was already busy cooking dinner outside on a little alcohol burner. I sent for the shots the doctor had prescribed to tranquilize me. Aside from that, I did nothing but cry and cry. I couldn't control what I felt, being sick and having to live in such a place from that day onward. My daughter Violeta was sobbing at the top of her lungs. Every time she heard somebody say that Eduardo was going to be arrested and sent to jail, she'd hang on to him and cry aloud. It was the strangest thing in the world. As for me, I couldn't eat or anything. I did nothing but cry.

I didn't say a word to anybody, I really didn't. I lay down and Lala came to give me my shot.[29] After she'd injected me she said, "Now Sara, my child, just try to keep calm and get some rest. It's up to the men to do something about this. Don't you interfere in any way. Lie down quietly, keep calm, and cover your ears if you have to. Don't even listen when they talk about it." But that first night in the garage, I felt so bad I couldn't sleep.

At first I wanted to die. Not just to die, but to put a gun to my chest and fire four bullets into my heart. Because the truth of the matter is that such things simply never happen to anyone else.

I thought of moving in with Ana Teresa, in the apartment the lieuten-

29. Administering injections and vaccinations was part of Lala Fontanés's job as CDR public-health officer.

ant had exchanged for ours, but my brother Bernardo said, "Oh no, the two of you would be forever fighting just as you did here!" So I gave up that idea. If my brother didn't want me in his new apartment, I wasn't going to insist. It wasn't out of respect for him, it was only that I thought he'd see to it that I got another place. He promised to and I believed him.

Neighbors told him, "You've got to find a place for her." But what nobody ever told me was to move right back into my old apartment and take possession of it the way the lieutenant had done to us. I finally lost hope when I saw how time went by and nothing was done. Sometimes I suspect that Bernardo knew perfectly well what the exchange was about and that he agreed to the arrangement knowing it would leave me homeless. Well, anyway, he's still my brother.

I looked and looked again into the four winds—although I was ashamed to, I looked everywhere for help, but I couldn't resolve my problem. If I should talk, a number of people would land in jail. If I should go to the Party with the contract and my ration book and explain the problem to them real well, even Bernardo might land in jail, because an exchange that leaves a family out in the street can't be permitted.

EDUARDO ROJAS:

When the housing exchange came I wasn't anybody. I wasn't working or anything. I'd been demobilized from the Army and I didn't belong to anything at all. Probably if I'd still been in my unit, I would have been able to make out. The *comandante* or somebody else there would have helped me.

This all happened when I was living with Pomposa, the girl I'd married in 1964. I didn't tell her anything about the exchange since she wasn't involved. We were breaking up anyway and I was living part of the time with Sara.

We knew the housing exchange was going to take place about fifteen days before it happened. They were beginning to talk among themselves about it and then Ana Teresa was always after me, nagging to see whether I'd agree. I agreed, all right, and I told them what I thought of them. I said to her, "I don't care one way or another about this. But one thing I do insist on. I don't want a large house, but I have to have a room to replace the one I let go. We're in the contract and it's a good thing we are. So now you know where we stand."

"Yes, you need a room, I know. All right, we'll find you a room," said Ana Teresa. But then Bernardo jumped at her. "I wish you'd shut up," he said. "You don't know anything about it and you've no reason to mix into it."

Sara and I were such trusting souls we thought we'd get a room or an apartment through the exchange. I was willing to take the room and let

Ana Teresa take the apartment, but it didn't turn out that way by a long shot.

Then the lieutenant came to tell us we had to get out by the next day. When I discovered how things stood I saw all this trouble coming on us. So I went to Catalina's home, found Bernardo, and brought him back. "Come on," I said, "we've got to settle things because we can't live in the street."

On our way back we met up with the lieutenant. "Listen here," I said to him, "what you people are doing to me isn't going through because I'm not staying out on the street." Then the lieutenant and I began to quarrel. I don't remember all we said there—a heap of things. I said to Bernardo, "You talk to him, since you're the one who's handling the affair." But Nardo didn't have a word to say. He had cold feet and was scared. I was really angry with him that day.

I said, "There's nothing for me to do but kill myself." Later I talked to Bernardo for a long time. "Your trouble," I told him, "is that you're not a man." I didn't feel like killing him, but at my age, if I tell someone he's not a man and he answers back, then we get in a fight. But what happened? I yelled one insult after another, and Nardo wouldn't say a word. He just bowed his head and stared at the ground. I had to let him be.

The next day when the lieutenant came with the van, Bernardo was sitting outside with his head down. The lieutenant came up to him and Bernardo said, "No, no, the exchange can't be carried out like this, because this is my family and I'm not going to leave them in the street."

The lieutenant answered, "The exchange has to go through, no matter what, and it's got to be now." That's exactly what he told us. So Bernardo shut up. Then they called us and said, "Take your stuff out of the upstairs now."

I said, "No, I'm not going to move it out. How can I? Where am I going to take it?" I didn't lose my temper but I was upset. Then the lieutenant said to the others, "Call and get them to send a car here." A car! I don't know how many police were already there. At least four.

Sara and the children began to cry and I started to argue with the lieutenant. That day I spoke back pretty strong. I said, "How can you think of putting us out on the street just to benefit yourself? Under the revolutionary government that just can't be, man! What you people are doing here is an abuse. Even under the dictatorship you never saw such a thing."

He hemmed and hawed, saying he knew I had children and this and that. Then he said, "You're afraid you'll be taken away and have to leave your children here and God knows where they'll end up." That was just what he said, giving me to understand that they were going to put me in jail and my children would be left to shift for themselves. But he had no reason. How the hell was he going to put me in jail without a reason? So I told him, "I'm ready to go wherever I must. You can kill me right now, if you want." I even got to the point of crying that day, I was so damn mad.

I found the housing contract in one of our boxes of clothes. It was drawn up in Sara's name. If that doesn't show that we had even more claim to the house than Nardo...! I picked it up and said, "Look, Sara, this contract is worth keeping." Then the lieutenant shouted, "No, no, that's no good anymore. Give it here!" And he grabbed it out of my hand and took it away. I don't know what he did with it. Most likely he threw it away or burned it. With that contract we could have gotten somewhere. All of our names were in it.

After that, I went with Sara's brother Pancho—he's in the Communist Youth[30]—to the Party office at MINFAR. We explained our problem and they told us this, that, and the other. When we got back we told the police we'd been to see the Party. Then the lieutenant took out a card and said, "All right, you're going to jail because you went and pestered the Party. I'm a Party member too." Sara kept after me and said, "No, no, stop that. Let it be." So, poor mug that I was, I just put up and shut up. But what the hell! Of course it's true he brought the whole gang of police and he might have shot me. What were we going to do?

They began to take our things out of the house, and we began to get things out too. We threw them out onto the ground. It didn't take us more than half an hour to move because we didn't have much—two beds, clothing, and other odds and ends. When one of the policemen saw me throwing things out of the windows during the moving, he said, "No, no, don't do that. This isn't an eviction or anything of that sort." The way I look at it, he was making fun of me, because, what the hell, if it wasn't an eviction, why did I have to get my things out of there?

After we moved everything out we just stood out there in the street until the lieutenant decided to move us into the garage. Vita's sister-in-law Inés was still living there on the day of the exchange, but she wasn't in at the moment, so the lock had to be broken.

The lieutenant called Domingo and told him he'd have to get his brother's things out. Domingo did, but Inés continued sleeping in the garage after we moved in. She didn't bother us. She had her bed in the back near the water pipe and we put our two nearer the door.

If the lieutenant hadn't given me the garage, I was really going to put on a show. I was ready to set up house right there on the street, put the children's beds on the sidewalk and let them sleep there, even if I stayed up all night watching over them. I wasn't going to leave unless they took me off in the police car. Where else would we have gone? If I'd stayed in the street I'd have gotten action. If an official car came along and saw me there, they'd be asking questions: "What the hell? What's this family

30. Unión de Jóvenes Comunistas (UJC).

doing here, with the little kids sleeping right here on the street?" That's why the lieutenant got scared and said, "Let's stick him in here, then things will be all right." His letting us use the garage set me back.

While we were moving into the garage, Sara began to have pains, so we had to go running to the hospital. The police took us there in their own car. When we got back Sara and I began to settle ourselves and talk things over. Sara was still feeling sick and I felt like a living corpse.

A few days later the lieutenant came to me and said, "Now let's see, how many children are there here?" We told him and he made notes on a paper. Then he said, "Well, now I have no more business with you people." Well, it's true he didn't have any more business. Just a little problem to solve, that's all. We were so sure he was working on the whole thing, we just let things ride. Now we've been here two years and the only thing he's done is fill out that application form.

After that he just strung us along day after day. He and the other one, Horacio, who was mixed up in the exchange too. In fact, he first spoke to Nardo about it. Oh yes! That Horacio was around every day saying, "Yes, yes, we're going to get things cleared up." He even spread a story that there was an apartment up the street that they were going to give us. I waited and waited and waited, then finally one day I asked him, "Well, are you finally going to get my problem straightened out or not?"

You know what the guy said? "Oh, I don't have anything to do with that." Well, that day I certainly told him a few things. I said, "The two of you are nothing but con men and crooks." That was a long time after the day of the exchange so I didn't use any strong language.

Then I went to Aldita to see if she knew anything about the exchange. I explained to her about the lieutenant and the garage and all. "No, no," she said, "I have nothing to do with that."

I couldn't tell whether that was true or not, but she must have known something because she's in charge of this whole zone. And another thing—when we went to the Party they asked us whether we'd gone to Urban Reform to try to get them to solve our problem. But since we didn't know about that, we said no. So the Party explained to us, "Look, if you've gone to Urban Reform you can't be out on the streets, because when there are two families in a house being exchanged, the Reform doesn't allow one family to take a house and leave the other on the street." Since they hadn't gone to Urban Reform, they must have gone to Aldita in the Frozen Zone office and nobody else. They arranged the whole thing among themselves over there.

I went to *Poder Local*[31] for help but they sent me to the Marianao

31. Introduced in 1966-67, *Poder Local* (Local Power) was the national agency for coordinating local government functions. It was designed to decentralize administrative decision-making so that localized problems could be solved at the local level. Its administrative base was the sectional level in urban areas and the *municipio* in rural areas. The

Planning Board,[32] who sent me back to *Poder Local*. I explained what had happened, but the *Poder Local* people said they couldn't do anything for me because their work was repairs and such. So I went to the Planning Board again and spoke to a girl there. "Look here," I said, "you sent me back to *Poder Local* and this is the second time they've sent me here. I'm not a football, even though you people are kicking me around like one."

Then one of the architects came and told me that there was no way the garage could be fixed up for housing and that we could expect a notice in the mail. The notice came, but nobody from there has come or done anything about our problem.

About a year later I wrote a letter to Celia.[33] A comrade typed it up for me. In it I asked for an investigation, for them to come and see how I was living and why. But I never received an answer and I don't know whether they've done anything about it or not.

Ana Teresa is still living in the lieutenant's old apartment. Her whole family is living with her—her mother and father, and her sister with five children, all of them. I wish you could see the place that lieutenant turned over to them. It's a crime! The apartment itself is falling apart. The bathroom is wrecked and you have to haul water to fill the tub. That guy pulled off highway robbery! In exchange for his worthless apartment, he got one with two baths, a living room, kitchen, three large bedrooms, two terraces—a world in itself. He probably saw that nobody would take the lemon he had, so he said to Nardo, "Look, you have to make the exchange or I'll lock you up." Let him swear to me that's not what happened.

Everybody in our family blamed Bernardo for making the exchange. His father, Inocencio, gave him a terrible dressing-down. Of course that was in Oriente and I was here, so I can't say what was said, but I know he really told Bernardo off.

---

base-level offices were run by committees of delegates from local units of government ministries, the Party, and the CDRs. Two CDR delegates were elected (apparently in public assemblies at the zone level) from each zone in the sectional to serve as intermediaries between municipal administration and the people. *Poder Local* had jurisdiction over seven administrative "fronts": commercial services, communal services, construction, economy, supplies, transportation, and organization. There was considerable overlap between these areas of responsibility and the "fronts" assigned to the CDRs, causing some rivalry between the agencies. (This description is based on Oscar Lewis's 1969 interviews with a *Poder Local* official and on David K. Booth, "Neighbourhood Committees and Popular Courts in the Social Transformation of Cuba" (unpublished dissertation, University of Surrey, 1973), pp. 56–57.) In 1974 the Cuban government was in the process of implementing a new administrative system, *Poder Popular* (People's Power), which will supersede the authority of *Poder Local*. Castro said the primary objective of the system is to control at the grass-roots level all production and service units that serve the community. (*Granma Weekly Review*, Aug. 4, 1974, p. 4.)

32. Same as JUCEI (see n. 40).

33. See n. 20.

Bernardo lived here for a month or two—right here in the garage. He quarreled with Catalina and wasn't seeing Ana Teresa at all by that time, so he came here. I'd have gotten lost if I'd done such a thing. Bernardo doesn't have any shame, or any pride. He and Catalina are in Oriente now.

ANA TERESA RAVENTOS:
Because Bernardo was the way he was, I didn't know anything about the exchange of houses until it happened. Bernardo didn't tell me what the house was like or explain anything. The day of the exchange the lieutenant showed me around, but I didn't think about what it meant. That was another mistake of mine. The lieutenant's wife told me that Sara and even Catalina had been there several times to divide up the rooms. In other words, I was the mistress of the house and they didn't leave me anything except air.

It wasn't right for me to have to exchange that house for this one, considering the condition my house was in and what I found here. I thought it would be in good condition but it's in pretty bad shape, especially the bathroom. The lieutenant left an armchair, a wardrobe, and a bed, and also three chairs. Bernardo made off with the chairs, though he didn't have any right to take them. But the armchair and bed are pretty good. In Miramar we'd been sleeping on the floor, right on the floor.

Since Bernardo left me, I've been living with my *mamá*. She's the one who gives me everything. She pays the rent, the light, and the rest. I don't know how much the rent is because it's discounted at her place of work. She works as a housemother in the scholarship program here. I stay at home with the children, though I'm going back to school now because I went only to the second grade.

I'm certainly sorry I changed houses and came to live in this one. It's in such bad shape. Even if he was in love or something, Bernardo shouldn't have done that. I've gone to the Urban Reform Office about it, to the one in Havana and to a hundred other places. I took a paper to the police station that explains the day and year we got married, who married us, and everything. I've also shown the contract to a lot of people who say it's no good. They've taken out their contracts and shown them to me and I've seen that they're different from mine. Instead of being in my name, the contract was put in the name of Bernardo Rojas, David Rojas, and then I'm down with the three little girls.

When Bernardo left me I was pregnant with my third daughter, Eugenia. I already had Melinda and Dorita. At present we aren't living as man and wife but we aren't divorced either. Bernardo doesn't give any money for his children, not a thing. He's even left all his jobs here and gone away, to keep from sending anything to the children. I've called him on the phone, but I still have to come back and fend for myself the best I can. He went off and I never heard a word from him. He hasn't

seen the girls since he took off for Oriente. He's at his family's house
with his woman, raising seven children who aren't his own.

I sent him a telegram that the little girl was sick, and when he came I
was really sweet to him. I had a pair of trousers someone gave me, and
some boots and underwear, and I gave them all to him. Then he went to
his sister's house, and when she saw him looking like a million dollars,
she said to him, "Hey, where did you get that glamour-boy look?" "Why,
Ana Teresa gave me the outfit." I'm still like a wife to him, and I do love
him, but it's impossible to expect him back. He's crazy, and I'm sick and
tired of waiting for him. It's nothing but a pipe dream.

EULALIA FONTANÉS:

The night the lieutenant came, I was sitting on the wall outside and I
heard him tell Sara that he'd arranged to exchange apartments and that
she, Sara, was out of it. At any rate, he and Horacio eliminated Sara from
the contract and the exchange was made. They moved Ana Teresa out
of here to Justa's house and moved Justa here. As for Sara, they simply
threw her out with her things in front of the building.

Panchito, Sara's brother, came over and talked to Armando, who was
the president of the Committee then. "Look," Armando told him, "go
over to the Party and tell them what's happened."

But the lieutenant told Panchito, "Listen, if you go to the Party I'll
have you arrested, because I'm a Party member."

Then I think Panchito went to the Communist Youth, of which
he was a member. They told him, "Look, it will mean three years
in jail for your brother Bernardo, then the lieutenant will have to
move out and you all can move right back in." But Sara wasn't going to
make any accusations against her brother. In the end, she was given the
garage. The lieutenant promised to get her a room but nothing has been
done. And ever since, the lieutenant's wife keeps needling Sara, telling
her, "This apartment is mine."

But exchanges are forbidden in this Frozen Zone, so how come that
exchange was made in the first place? I've heard that the deal hasn't
been completed yet, because Aldita refused to sign the final papers. If
that's true, Eduardo, Sara's husband, should get busy and find out how
come the place was taken away from them. If he personally went to Raúl,
special investigators would be sent. And if Raúl should come to ask, I'd
tell him quite frankly, "That comrade over there in the middle apartment has made use of his officer's rank." If it had been up to us we'd
have acted, but Sara and Eduardo got scared when they were told that
her brother could get jailed for it. As long as they don't take the first
step, we can't do a thing.

I'd like to see that problem resolved, because that woman Justa is so
mean. She has the temper of a wild beast. All the neighbors are wit-

nesses, so if we bring them before the People's Court,[34] all the neighbors will know what Justa and her husband are like.

I hope they give Sara someplace to live soon so they can seal that garage and we won't have to see anybody living there anymore. *Ay*, the place looks so ugly with clothes drying on lines strung up in front! It's vulgar, that's what it is.

ARMANDO CÁRDENAS:

I'm not sure whether or not I was already president of the CDR when Eduardo and Sara had to move out of the apartment. At any rate, the Committee wasn't actually functioning at that time. I mean, I was only a part-time president in the meetings and such, because of my job. One of the first motions I made was that another comrade should be put in charge of the Committee because I didn't have enough time. The sectional granted my request and turned over my tasks to Comrade Nicasio, who was carrying out CDR functions at my request at the time of the exchange.

Anyway, the fact that a fellow belongs to the CDR doesn't mean that he's got to go sticking his nose into his neighbor's family problems, and that's what the housing exchange and eviction was all about. That family was always quarreling and telling one another to get out. After a big quarrel, one or another of them would go to Oriente, but in the end they always came back.

As for that exchange deal, even if the government itself wanted a house, they wouldn't use such methods to get it. Take the case of the woman comrade living in this neighborhood, between Fifth and Seventh avenues. The government wants her apartment for foreigners but it's *her* apartment, so how do they go about it? They promise to move her to any place she likes. But if she doesn't like the place they find for her, they've got to let her stay where she is. They can't kick her out against her will.

I don't know how the lieutenant managed the deal, but they took Sara's name out of the contract. Nobody knows exactly what happened. I can't figure out why they couldn't get along with Sara and let her share the apartment. After all, Sara is Bernardo's sister and she wasn't hurting anything. Anyway, I don't think she could have been put out legally; only Urban Reform can take a contract away from somebody.

At that time I was working pretty hard, going from place to place, so I

34. The *Tribunales Populares* were neighborhood courts established in Havana on an experimental basis in 1966 to hear minor civil and criminal cases involving "antisocial behavior" (e.g., petty theft, drunkenness, disorderly conduct, juvenile delinquency, health and sanitation code violations). The Courts were empowered to impose sentences of up to 180 days' imprisonment. The cases were heard by a panel of three lay judges popularly elected in public assemblies at the neighborhood level, after nomination by the CDR or the Party. In 1974 the People's Courts were incorporated into Cuba's new judicial system. (*Granma Weekly Review*, Feb. 19, 1974, p. 3.)

didn't spend much time at home. But one day I came home and found that Sara had moved to the garage, and Ana Teresa had taken their furniture and moved away to a new apartment. They also told me that Juan Pérez had lent Sara his garage and said, "That family can't go on living in such a place."

Well, when I saw what was going on, I said to Sara's brother Panchito, "Look, the problem is that the lieutenant has threatened to arrest you people if you don't go through with the apartment exchange. You shouldn't buy that, see? You should go to the Party sectional, explain the problem, and ask them to intervene in the matter and do whatever has to be done." The lieutenant had pulled out his Party card and said, "I'm going to have you all arrested and sent to prison for daring to bother the Party with such trifles." I myself never heard him say that. But I do know a Party member has no right to use his Party card to threaten his neighbors like that. He shouldn't get away with it. Had I witnessed him threaten those people, I'd have complained to the Party myself. As a militant,[35] I have the authority to say to him, "No, you can't act that way."

But the problem is, I can't act on the basis of neighborhood gossip, only on what I myself see. I blame Sara's brother Bernardo for the whole mess because he allowed all those things to happen.

Sara has brought up their housing problem several times, and I've tried to hint about her duties. I try to make her see that she and her husband are going at it the wrong way. They don't know how to defend themselves, that's all.

When such things happen to me, they turn out differently because I know my rights and how to defend them—every citizen should. I'd simply stop paying rent until someone tried to throw us out. Then I'd tell Aldita about it and she'd say, "You leave those people alone." And as soon as they found out what they were up against, that's what they'd do, leave us alone.

Sara knows I'm a Party militant. She should have told us the whole thing at the beginning. If only she'd said, "Look, Armando, I've got a problem," I'd have tried to guide them and take them wherever they had to go. I myself would have taken charge of seeing their rights upheld. I've done as much for many comrades here.

Because I'm a militant, everybody living on this block, no matter who they are, has to pay attention to what I say. But Eduardo and Sara haven't spoken up about that business—neither to me nor to the CDR nor to anybody else. They keep it hidden from everybody and only discuss it between themselves.

In my opinion, Bernardo shouldn't have let his wife rule him that way.

35. A full Party member, as compared to an aspirant, or candidate for membership.

It was his duty to tell her, "Now listen, Sara is my sister and she's got a right to live here. If she were a bad woman, you'd have a right to quarrel with her and want her out of here. But it isn't as if she were out in the street looking for a man. Sara stays home with her children, and it's only right that she live here with us since we've got plenty of room for her and her family." But that wasn't Bernardo's attitude.

Juan did the right thing to intervene, offering the garage as he did. I'd have done the same thing. Juan was in charge of Revolutionary Instruction in the Committee, which means it was his duty to help Eduardo and Sara as he did. It was a beautiful action on his part, but no more than any militant of the CDR here was duty-bound to do if they could.

MERCEDES MILLÁN:
When Sara had the second-floor apartment they literally tore it to pieces. They lived in such a way. . . ! Really, you should see the way they left it! They used to cook with wood right in the kitchen sink. They tore down every last tile from the walls, destroyed the doors . . . they destroyed everything. It was horrible, horrible! That place was more like a hotel than a home—some left and others moved in to take their place.

Then Justa, who was living someplace else, arranged an exchange, which is the way such things are usually done now. Justa moved into Sara's brother's apartment and he and his family moved into Justa's house. But the sister-in-law didn't want Sara and her family living with them, so they stayed behind.

Justa's husband let them have the garage so they wouldn't be left out in the street. The garage goes with his apartment and he allowed them to stay there of his own free will. He was in no way obligated to do it. The understanding was that Sara should stay there only long enough to make arrangements to move to Oriente, where she has a home. But now there's no telling how long she and her family will stay here. Forever, I guess, unless the government gives her a house or a room or something.

They're living in perfectly horrible conditions—that garage doesn't even have a toilet! Justa's husband couldn't make them move if he wanted to, not after they've been living there two years, because there's a law that you can't kick people out into the street. But the fact remains that he was under no sort of obligation to let them move into that garage in the first place. He did it to help Sara.

That's how Sara got the garage. But when she had an apartment like ours with three bedrooms, living-dining room, kitchen, and a sink for the laundry, they'd spend the whole day downstairs. There was a water faucet outside in my garden and they used it so much they broke it. They'd wash their clothes out in the front yard and spread them out on the bushes to dry. They bathed those kids under the garden faucet and ate out there in the yard, holding their plates in their hands. They have twenty different kinds of trouble now, but the truth is, they lived exactly the same way before. Those people are only half civilized.

LETICIA MANZANARES:

It was fight, fight, fight, day in and day out, in Sara's apartment, until the housing exchange finally went through. Those people yelled at each other so much I thought the whole building would tumble down. Sara was always butting in between Bernardo and Ana Teresa, because she thought that if he married his other woman, Catalina, then she could keep the apartment. I'm telling you, if it hadn't been for Sara, they wouldn't have gone so far as to make an exchange, or not the way they did it anyhow. If they'd made an exchange it would have been for all of them to move together someplace else.

Horacio, who lives next door, worked in Aldita's office, and he pushed real hard for the exchange also. The lieutenant and Horacio would come here every single solitary day with the patrol car and I don't know what all. Well, when the deal actually went through, Sara was out in the street. She and Eduardo had thought that if Bernardo married that other woman it would be better for them, but what happened? They found themselves without a place to live! It was one horrible mess!

Mercedes's husband, Juan, said, "Well, we can't have that kind of spectacle out here. They can't stay outside." So Juan asked Domingo to exchange our garage with the one that belonged to the middle apartment so Sara could live in it. It was more suitable since it had a window and a door. We agreed and Sara moved into our old garage.

DOMINGO LABRADA:

All that quarreling between Ana Teresa and Sara came about because of Vita. She not only tried to turn my brother against me, but was also at fault in the business of exchanging Bernardo's apartment. It was brought on by her devious maneuverings. And she was also the one who fixed up Bernardo with Catalina, that woman he's living with now.

I think the lieutenant threatened Bernardo and his family to make them go through with the exchange. At least that's what I've heard, because the lieutenant was in the police force. He told them that the papers were already signed and that Nardo's family had to move out at once. The apartment the lieutenant was exchanging for theirs was falling apart and to this day *Poder Local* hasn't repaired it. When Ana Teresa saw it she exclaimed, "What kind of deal is this? I won't exchange my good apartment for this broken-down shack!"

"A deal's a deal," the lieutenant answered. "The papers are already signed."

Moving Sara to the garage was a crime, that's what it was! All I can say is that I hope the lieutenant's apartment goes to seed worse than the one he exchanged it for, and that it happens pretty damn soon. I think it will, because from my place I can see the door that opens on their terrace and they've already broken the place to pieces.

JUSTA DÍAZ:

It all started when Vita's sister-in-law Inés said to my husband, in the presence of the Party, "Say, lieutenant, I'm a woman alone, with no husband or children of my own, but Sara has four children and look at the way they're living. I wish you'd allow them to move into the garage with me."

Then my husband said to Sara, "Very well, since she makes the offer, you may live in the garage until a place is found for you." And that's the truth—I'll say that anywhere.

Sara was thankful to accept, let me tell you, and they got along beautifully at first. Sara used to say that she was fonder of that girl than of her own blood kin. Vita was also part of their gang. They used to quarrel and insult each other all the time. Any way you look at them, they're all the same. They were all out for Ana Teresa's head. Then, from the night to the morning, that beautiful friendship of Sara and Inés went *bang!* Because it so happened that that little blond was having a love affair. The way she lives is none of my business, but Leticia and Lala told me about her lover. They said she was a sore spot, but weren't they all?

Later Sara spread it over the whole barrio that she wanted Inés out of her house. She and Sara were about to come to blows, but then I went down and said, "Come up to my house, Inés." If she had hit Sara with that big belly . . . imagine! I think it was because of all those upsets that Sara lost the child. That woman went through you can't imagine what, with so many problems at that time. It was quarrel, quarrel all day long. But when they weren't fighting, they all went places together and, so to speak, ate from the same dish.

Sara and Inés kept on fighting until Sara finally went back to Oriente. Then people were saying that Eduardo wanted to live with Inés. That was another battle. Once, at 1:00 A.M., Inés came knocking on my door, asking me to take the little girls because Eduardo had gotten fresh with her while she was looking after them in the garage. I took Violeta and the five smaller girls into my house. Then, when Sara came back, everybody here said that Eduardo was a drunkard, a marijuana smoker, and everything bad you can think of. And they said he was so brazen that he even dared to live with Violeta, because they caught them giving twenty thousand shows in the garage.

One day Inés was sitting on the garden wall crying because she'd had a big quarrel with Sara and Eduardo and they told her she had to get out. Just then my husband came up the walk carrying a box of soft drinks. I was standing out on the porch and I never will forget that incident. She said, "Lieutenant, I was waiting for you because Sara says I have to go."

"Impossible!" said my husband. "They can't kick you out. You were living in that garage before Sara ever moved in there." I saw what happened the day they quarreled, but what do I care? It's none of my business, and anyway, that kind of thing went on here all the time.

People told us, "A patrolman has to come and quiet down those people about once every five minutes. They're always making scandals and quarreling." Well look, if you move someplace and get that impression of your neighbors, how can you be friends with them? After all that mess I was afraid they might get me involved in an even bigger one.

RICARDO HERNÁNDEZ (the lieutenant):

My only problem here is with those people I gave the garage to. They turned against me because they claim my apartment partly belongs to them. I made a deal with Bernardo, the man who used to live here, to exchange apartments. Since he had a smaller family, he went to my old place, which is smaller, and I moved in here. But when we made the deal, he had his sister's name taken out of the documents and her family kicked out in the street. So I let them have my garage until they found something more suitable. And when I saw how they were living, with only one chair and several rotting mattresses on the floor, I gave them some furniture of my own free will, because helping those in need is the revolutionary thing to do. But that wasn't in the contract. After they moved I gave them a set of dining-room furniture and told them, "Here, take this." I also left Bernardo some things in my old apartment—a bedroom set, an extra bed, and a living-room set.

But they've never understood my generosity. Their attitude is downright ungrateful. They've done twenty different things to upset us. They've quarreled with us, talked all sorts of foolishness. They go around in their underclothes with the garage door wide open knowing that I have daughters who are señoritas. And the way that woman's husband treats children! One day he ran out in the yard brandishing a gun at a group of children, mine among them. His only complaint was that the kids were playing out there.

Judging by the way that man acts, he's no revolutionary. If you terrorize children, who knows what scars that may leave on them. It's a revolutionary's first duty to be kind to children, because they're the ones who'll carry on and reap the fruits of our efforts.

SARA ROJAS:

In the beginning there were eleven of us living in the garage: four kids—Amanda María, Faustina, Hilario, Violeta—my oldest child Concha and her baby Aidita, Eduardo, me, Vita's sister-in-law Inés, and my two brothers, Panchito and David. Pancho was living here because this was near his place of work. He was working in FAR[36] and David was with

36. *Fuerzas Armadas Revolucionarias* (Revolutionary Armed Forces).

the Army at La Cabaña. They kept their ration books and everything here. They used their ration books for everything they needed; I only gave them a place to stay. If I hadn't done that for them, they'd have been out in the street.

It was a tight fit but they were my relatives, except for Inés. I'd met her at Vita de Peña's years ago. She was married to Vita's brother then but they got a divorce just about the time of the exchange. She'd been working at a lady's house and slept there. But then she got sick and the lady couldn't look after her. Well, I took the girl in with me because she had no other place to go. She'd lost both her parents and I was overcome with pity for that poor girl every time I saw her looking so ill.

I brought my daughter Concha from Oriente about four months after we'd moved here because she was ill and I wanted her to see a doctor here in Havana. She stayed with us almost a year. Her husband, Manolo, left her with us because I told him it took a while to get a turn with the doctor and I couldn't let her go back while she was still under treatment. Concha had a big belly at that time and things weren't going at all well with her. "Until her baby is born I can't send her back to you," I told Manolo.

We had lots of beds because Inés brought her own and shared it with Faustina. Violeta, my brother Pancho, and Hilario shared one bed. Violeta was only a little girl still ... well, she was about thirteen, but I knew Pancho would respect his niece. Besides, what else could we do? Later, David shared his bed with Pancho because they're both men. Violeta, Hilario, and Amanda shared another bed, and Eduardo and I had a bed to ourselves. We managed.

The five beds were practically on top of one another. One whole side of the garage was filled with beds, with only a tiny bit of floor space so we could get up in the morning and make coffee. After breakfast Concha and Inés took the beds apart, leaving out only one small bed and the big bed where Eduardo and I slept. Then the girls folded the sheets and put them in the wardrobe and we stored the beds outside in the hallway, under the stairs.

I had to cook on a little alcohol burner which I set on a chair or on the table. Well, it was actually just a tin can with alcohol, and I set a pan on top of it. It was difficult as hell. I was afraid all the time that a potful of hot food might spill over on one of the kids. One day when Concha and Inés were cooking on the table, a big pot of boiling soup actually did slide off the burner, but it simply slid onto the tabletop without spilling. Since I got the little enamel kerosene stove last year, cooking is no problem.[37]

About three days after we'd moved into the garage, the pipes burst and stinking black water poured out on the floor. It stank unbearably.

37. In late 1969 the Cuban government banned the use of alcohol for cooking because of the high incidence of accidents. Owners of alcohol stoves were encouraged to turn them in for kerosene stoves.

This started at about 4:00 in the morning and at that hour we had to get up and pour clean water over it. Then the drainpipes burst in two other places. Every day at daybreak water started pouring out of the wall. We put a board over it and hung a sack on top of that, but still the stink came through. It smelled like rotting mud; it was unbearable.

A few days later they came to fix the drainpipes out on the street, where they were on the point of bursting too. I asked the man who came to please cover up the spot here too, because we couldn't stand it anymore and we didn't know what to do about it.

The exchange was made during the summer and this place was like an oven. I'd raise the garage door real high and flop down on the bed to try to sleep as best I could, but the kids stayed outside, running around most of the night to get cool—until 2:00 or 3:00 in the morning. The front and side doors were left open because the heat was simply unbearable. Otherwise we'd have been roasted alive.

"I can't get enough air to breathe," the kids would complain. "Oh, *mami*, I can't take a breath."

"It's because of the drains, *muchachos*," I'd say. Then I'd put them all in the big bed and put up the mosquito net. I'd drape the coverlet over the mosquito net so they wouldn't smell the stink and I'd keep them there four or five hours. That calmed them down. Of course it was hotter under the tent I made, but at least that kept out the stink, which bothered them more.

You can't imagine how uncomfortable it is to live in a garage. Nobody can unless they've lived in one themselves. We have no comforts at all, not even a bathroom.

The first problem was where to take the kids when they had to go. Sometimes a neighbor would offer their bathroom, sometimes we'd use a public one.[38] What we sometimes do is throw the shit in the trash can, well wrapped, so that the garbage men will take it away when they come. Most of the time what we have to do is go into the closet to use the chamber pot, then throw the shit into the sink and wash it down with plenty of water. That's where I wash the clothes and dishes and everything, but where else can I throw out the shit? If only there was a deep ditch or hole of some kind to throw it in, but this is Havana, not the country. Nobody expects me to just throw it out in the street, I suppose.

When the hot weather comes, the sink smells to high heaven although I'm always washing it out with sand or *Campeón* or Fab. I keep it just as clean as I can. At night, before I go to bed, I stop up the drain with a piece of cardboard so as not to have to breathe in that smell.

Listen, we've been living here about two years and that's bad for our health. I mean, look, shit is the food you've digested that comes out

38. The closest public toilets were two and a half blocks away.

rotten, no? Your body can't dissolve it. And the stink that comes from it makes you sick. The time is bound to come when we can't stand it anymore.

The inside of the wall is green with dampness. We used to have heaps of cockroaches, but there aren't so many now. I've gotten rid of lots of them with Flit. We have mosquitoes too, sometimes. It's been raining so much the urns outside fill up with water, and when they overflow the earth gets soaked because there's no place the water can drain. Then my floor gets wet and the walls get fairly black with the dampness.

Living this way, we have to sleep with clothes on even when it's too hot to breathe. Sometimes Eduardo sweats like a horse, but he can't sleep naked because Violeta and Amanda María are big girls. He can't risk having them say, "Oh no, *papi*, you can't scold us because you strip naked right before our eyes." I look upon it as a duty never to show ourselves naked in front of the children. Terrible problems arise when people do that kind of thing—brothers making babies with their own sisters and all that. It happened back in Oriente. I cried when a girl there bore twins by her own brother. Imagine that! No, it's not right that boys and girls should sleep in the same room. It isn't customary in the country, and it's even more risky in town.

Then too, if Eduardo has to make water, Violeta and the rest of the girls have to go outside. Hilario and I can stay in, but it wouldn't be right for the girls to. I'm tired of living like this. I'm fed up!

My parents told me, "Sara, you can't go on living in that place. Your children are getting older. Violeta is a señorita, too." I don't know what to do. We can't allow the children to be raised like savages. And that's what we're living like—savages. Worse than savages—dogs!

It was only a short time ago, when I went back to Oriente, that Eduardo said, "I think I'm going to have to send the kids to my old folks' home because they're disgusted with this place." When they returned from a visit to Oriente last year, the kids were all mixed up. They didn't want to stay in the garage, they wanted to go back to Oriente.

I'm living much worse here than I would be back home in the country. In Oriente one can always add another room, even if the walls are of palm leaf. For me a palm-leaf house is ugly—worse than ugly, ridiculous—but at least it's a place to live. You can go get your own palm leaves or else buy them—they cost 2 or 3 *kilos*[39] each—and you can make a room for each of the children if you like. Then they can sleep naked or any way they please.

Not long after we moved in, Horacio called me and said, "We're going to move you within the next few days." According to him, they were

---

39. A kilo is equal to one *centavo*.

going to give us a room. We waited and waited but nothing happened. Finally I went to him and asked, "Look here, Horacio, just when during the next few days are you going to get a place for us?"

"Soon," he said; "better get your things packed right away."

So I packed everything up. Time and more time passed and still nothing. When I saw that months and months had gone by with no word about a place for us, I called Horacio again. And do you know what he told me? He said, "But I have nothing to do with it! I have orders to help you get a place to live, but my orders are only for one room, and one room isn't enough for all of you." And there the matter rested.

That's the dirtiest trick I ever heard of! I mean, he gave us—a whole family—his word and he knew in what horrible conditions we were living and how we came to live that way in the first place and he offered his help. Then when we asked him to make good on his promise, he calmly said it was none of his business. Don't I have a right to think he's a bastard who played a dirty trick on us?

After that, we went to *Poder Local* and asked the architect to build us a small bathroom here with a tub, a washbasin, and a toilet. But he said to do that, the garage would have to be enlarged, and then it would be right on the sidewalk. "It's too dangerous," he explained. "Suppose a car crashes into your wall? Besides, it would be too noisy for you to sleep at night—especially for the children, and some of the children are very small. Not only that, but new drainpipes would have to be laid right under your floor, which is much too damp as it is. And suppose the drains burst? Besides, if we build a room over the sidewalk, where will people walk?"

It's just impossible to fix this place. The architect said, "The only solution is to get them to move you to adequate housing. But we of *Poder Local* can't solve that sort of problem because it's not under our jurisdiction. All we can do is repair a place or maybe add a bathroom or something to it." And it's true, *Poder Local* is only for fixing up places. If you need cement or lumber they'll give it to you, but it isn't their job to get houses for people.

The lieutenant's wife, Justa, had been threatening Eduardo to kick us out. Eduardo was fed up so he called Horacio. He told him, "All right, Horacio, if you have nothing to do with the matter, at least tell me to whom I can go. Give us some hope or at least an explanation." He didn't fight or anything. That was the whole discussion.

I told Lala, "The lieutenant can kick us out whenever he likes. For him it will be like winning in the lottery without buying a ticket. I'm not afraid of anything anymore. I'd just as soon be in jail as out of it."

I don't know whether it was true that the lieutenant was going to kick us out—he's never told *me* that. But let him try if he thinks he has the authority to throw people out on the street. Just let him try! What does he think this is—a dictatorship?

After Eduardo called Horacio, I think he went to JUCEI.[40] About fifteen days later, I got a card in the mail from the Ceiba sectional of the CDR saying I should wait for the inspector to come by and see whether the place could be fixed up, and if it couldn't, then they'd transfer the card to Housing Control. When the inspector never showed up, I went there, pregnant as I was, but I didn't take the card myself because it couldn't be transferred until the inspector came. The trouble is that they have so many cases they haven't been able to send the inspector yet. Well, then with the problem of my belly, I didn't go back there or anywhere else and nothing more was done.

Not long ago Eduardo presented the problem at his work center. They're already taking steps to see if they can get us out of here. Well, we'll simply have to wait and see.

In a few days I have to go to Social Welfare[41] to see what they can do. I found out about it from my godson Leonel. I went to his house and he told me, "Godmother, I'm solving my problem through Social Welfare. They're giving away wooden houses for us to fix up. Go there and say you want them to investigate the place you live in. Then they'll ask you some questions, fill out some blanks, and tell you to go back the very next day."

When they ask me, "What do you want, comrade?" I'll say, "A little house, even if it's only a wooden shack of the worst-quality lumber, where my children can live." After I've made my request, I guess it's up to the Ministry to decide if they should send an inspector. If they do, they'll come here and investigate and give me a little wooden house. No matter how bad it is, I can fix it up.

I'm going to work that angle. If it means buying a bathtub and wash-basin for it, we'll buy them. Social Welfare will give me cement if I need it, or tarpaper to cover the house, if it's wood. Then I'll go to Housing Recovery, where they give you lumber to repair your house.[42] They themselves repair whatever defects the house may have. No matter how bad the house turns out to be, it will be a great improvement on this garage. At least we'll have a bit more room.

Well, let's see if they can solve our problem that way. From the day after tomorrow on, I'm really going to get busy and do something about finding us a place to live. Tomorrow I'm going to wash a few of the dirty clothes so the work doesn't pile up too much while I'm going the rounds.

40. *Juntas de Coordinación, Ejecución e Inspección* (Boards of Coordination, Execution and Inspection), a network of regional agencies which supervise implementation of state policy on provincial and local levels.

41. Although the *Ministerio de Bienestar Social* was abolished in 1961 and its functions divided among other government ministries, many Cubans still referred to any social service agency as *Bienestar Social*. In the following discussion Sara includes under this heading a number of agencies about which she is confused.

42. *Recuperación de Vivienda,* perhaps a confusion with *Recuperación de Bienes* (see Part III, n. 36); the agency for allocating supplies for housing repair was *Poder Local* (see n. 31).

If they ever give me a little house where my children will be comfortable, it will be the happiest day of my life. That's all the happiness I can ask for now. The thought of getting a decent place to live is always in my head. I'd be happy forever if they gave me a house.

I want my children to have plenty of room to play without bothering anybody, so the neighbors won't have to be always coming to me with complaints. The kids would be happy then and so would I. We're so cramped for space; when the kids aren't pestering me, they're pestering each other. If they're outside, I worry. Indoors, they either start fighting or playing games and I don't know which of those two annoys me more.

Hilario says to me, "If I go out to play in the street, you get mad at me; if I take a bit of wood and start drawing on it, you get mad; if I start playing with my bow and arrow, you get mad; if I lie down, you get mad. *Cristiana*, what do you want me to do?"

If I had a place to live where I didn't feel so cramped, they'd never again bother me. They say so themselves. They can't help pestering, the way we're living one on top of the other.

Since we moved into the garage Eduardo has changed an awful lot. He broods about the children's problems and sometimes lies awake all night. He'll spend the whole night tossing around and getting up to drink coffee. I ask him, "What thoughts do you have that keep you awake all night?"

"Who, me?" he answers. "Absolutely nothing. I have no problems at all."

"You must have a problem," I insist. "Why don't you tell me what it is? I know we have a housing problem and so on but nothing to keep a person awake all night."

"Leave me alone," he says. "I'm not sleepy, that's all."

And he spends the rest of the night smoking. Sometimes the coffee gives out and he'll get up to brew some more. But I don't think his depression has affected our relationship at all because he treats me the same as he ever did.

EDUARDO ROJAS:

The worst problem I have is living in this garage. I'm doing something now about getting a house but I'm not supposed to tell anybody about it. I'd been putting up with the situation, waiting for the lieutenant and Horacio to do something about it, but when I didn't see any way out I told my boss about it. He was interested in getting me out of this spot, so he came here one Sunday. Sara and the children were here but didn't meet him because he wouldn't come inside. He didn't ask me any questions then, not even how many beds we had, because I'd already told him there were seven of us living here. I also told him I had to put a mattress down on the floor for part of the family.

He told me, "Look, I'm going to give you a plan but don't tell anybody about it. Take pictures of the place, of your sleeping arrangements and all, then bring me the photographs. We'll draw up a letter and I'll take them right to Montané." Montané is the Minister of Communications.[43] I actually belong under the Ministry of the Interior but I'm working in Communications now because I'm guarding their installations.

My hope is that when the Minister sees my case, he'll say to himself, "If anything in the way of housing comes to Communications, this man has a really bad situation and we'll have to solve his problem." Or if not, they'll at least put me on the waiting list of the neediest. That's the way houses are given out, by work sector.

It never occurred to me to take pictures before because I thought you weren't supposed to do that. It's a great idea but I've been having a hard time getting the photos together. The only person in the neighborhood who might be able to take them for me is Nicasio, who's a photographer. I even mentioned it to him in passing. I didn't ask him definitely but just suggested that if I couldn't find anybody else maybe he could do it for me.

Sara says she thinks maybe our problem will be solved soon, but I don't know what's going on. It was a little less than a year ago that I wrote my letter to Celia asking for an investigation. But recently people have been coming here every once in a while. Someone wearing a military uniform with some sort of an emblem came when I wasn't home and asked Sara questions like, "Do you live here?" and this and that. Then he said, "I've already seen two other cases like this," and he called Aldita on the telephone. Later a woman came and asked whether Eduardo Rojas lived here, then another woman came who said she worked with Aldita. Violeta says she knows the last woman and that she's come around several times asking for me.

Right now I'm going off to the cane fields again. I don't know whether I'll be there forty-five days or three months. The last time I was there twenty-four days. When they tell me I should go to the cane I always go, no matter where they send me. I want to be right up to the mark so I can get our housing problem solved. You have to keep in good standing these days. If you're a slacker you're worthless and you don't have a chance of getting shit. But that isn't the only reason I always go. I'm not the kind of person who'd say, "I won't work because they haven't given me a house and solved my problems." I don't go around telling the whole world my worries. Some people might do that, but not me.

One day the Revolution will see what's going on. I'm talking about the leaders, the ones who take care of things—the Party and the other big

---

43. Jesús Montané Oropesa, in 1976 a member of the Central Committee and deputy from the Isle of Pines to the National Assembly. The present Minister of Communications is Pedro Guelmes González.

agencies. Fidel has said a hundred times that what existed here before was José looking for a way to live well while Pedro lived a dog's life. And worse still when it's a lieutenant. He's no revolutionary, no socialist, no anything! He only had to use his eyes to see there were three little children here. He should have thought it over and said to himself, "Damn, I can't do it. How can I shove these people into this lousy place just so I can live comfortably?" And I told him so to his face: "You're no revolutionary, pal. You're nothing."

The Neighbors

Eulalia Fontanés:
When I need help I go to my neighbors. They're always willing to help me. When my kids get sick, I call upon Juan at any hour of the day or night to drive us to the doctor. If Armando gets a call at 2:00 A.M. on Mercedes's phone, Juan gets up to get him. As for me, I help them too—anyone who calls me. When Mercedes was ill, I washed her children's clothes, and if she needed someone to help clean house, I'd help her.

I got along well with Ana Teresa when she lived here, but not with Sara. She was hard, but lately she's changed. She finally started talking to me, but at first...! When she ran into me or Leticia, she wouldn't even say hello. She says she acted that way because she didn't want to give us a chance to say anything to her about her brother Bernardo's wife or about his other woman. But goodness, we never gossip. I'm not interested in the way anybody else lives. I live on what my husband earns and not on what anybody else gives me. What other people do is none of my business.

Sara was mean, too. Once, when she lived up above, the drain was clogged, so I begged her as a favor to my two little children not to throw water down from her terrace into my apartment. But she heaved down more water on purpose. One day she shut off the main water tap so we couldn't get any water at all. Armando went up and said, "May I go in please, to look at the main tap?" And there it was, shut off, which they had no right to do.

Later on, Sara and Justa quarreled, in spite of the fact that Sara's children, especially Violeta, practically lived up in Justa's apartment. Concha, Sara's eldest daughter, was here then. They'd spend the whole day up there, and once, when Sara was in the hospital, Eduardo came home drunk and Concha and Violeta went to sleep in Justa's apartment.

Sara even did her wash up at Justa's place. I'm telling you, she lived and died there, but after they quarreled, Sara stayed in her garage and Justa in her apartment. As long as Sara was friends with Justa she didn't speak to us. After they quarreled, Leticia came right out and said to Sara, "So now you come around sniffing at our asses, eh Sara? Well, at this late date we're the ones who should refuse to speak to you."

Eduardo is very rude to us; he says hello and that's all. When Sara feels like it she speaks to us, and when she doesn't, she doesn't. When she was mad at me, I'd still call her and ask her to "stroke"[44] my children when they were sick, and whenever I didn't have anybody to leave the kids with, I'd ask Sara.

Sara doesn't get along with Leticia, and Leticia is against Sara and Justa, too. When they were invited to the Committee meetings, Leticia asked Armando, "Why did you invite the people in the middle apartment?" And Armando replied, "Because it's my duty as a Cuban and a revolutionary, whether the rest of you get along with Justa or not."

"I didn't go because they went," Leticia said. What if *I* didn't go to the meeting because so-and-so went? Then neither would Armando nor Serafina nor anybody else go, right? No, no, it was our duty to invite them.

Then Leticia griped about Justa's having a party. But Justa can do as she pleases in her own home. We loaned her some of our beer rations so she'd be able to buy beer for her party. It's none of my business what they do with their money. And what business is it of Leticia's whether or not Justa feeds her children? But she kept gossiping about it. What do I care?

Leticia never got along with Mercedes either. One day they quarreled about an *almácigo* plant that Mercedes had asked Cipriano, the gardener, to cut down. Why should Mercedes have that big bush there? But Leticia came rampaging out, saying nobody had a right to cut that bush down, and she told Mercedes off. Since then Leticia and Mercedes have never liked each other.

The arguments about the garden started when Leticia moved in. Leticia said that Mercedes was a busybody who thought the whole place belonged to her, and I don't know what all.

I said, "Now don't get mad at me, but the truth is the garden belongs to Mercedes because she's the one living on the ground floor. When the *doctora* and I lived upstairs, Mercedes was the one who paid the gardener and we had nothing to do with it."

Leticia got angrier than ever and raved like a madwoman. Then Mercedes told the gardener, "Look, Cipriano, this part of the yard is mine, so you tend that piece for me. I'll have nothing to do with the rest of it from now on."

I didn't like to see the place full of overgrown grass, so I said to Leticia, "You and I can pay 1 *peso* each to Cipriano to clean up the rest of the

44. A gentle stroking or passing of the hands over the painful area, a technique widely used by folk healers.

yard, too." But she objected, "Oh no, not me—I'm not going to pay any gardener!" In that case, why couldn't she just have kept her mouth shut and let Mercedes pay for keeping the yard nice, the way she always had? Afterward Mercedes had the yard cleaned, but I paid for having the grass cut on my part of it. Justa and Leticia each gave Cipriano 1 *peso*, but I think after a while Justa stopped paying her share. So then I said, "Look, Cipriano, I'll give you the 2 *pesos!*" So Cipriano comes and cleans up the whole yard and that's that.

Then Leticia started quarreling because Mercedes throws her trash out there in the front. She's got to, there's no other place for it. Even Cipriano puts all the trash, grass clippings, and so on out front. Where else can you throw it? It's got to be put outside. You can't make big piles of it and let it rot. But Leticia doesn't want anybody throwing anything out in front after she has it cleaned up.

Leticia and Mercedes quarrel about every little thing. I say, "*Ay*, Mercedes, but you shouldn't argue with her! And when Justa joins the quarrel, they all say terrible words, like "you blubber-lipped Negroes," within hearing of all the neighbors. Besides that, Leticia hates Justa's guts. She says that if she runs into Justa on the stairs, she's going to sock her.

One day a pipe from the water heater in Justa's kitchen sprang a leak. Concha went up to ask her about it and Justa explained about the burst pipe. Well, the water was leaking down into Sara's garage and Justa got into an argument with her. Justa yelled, "Come out, you dirty pig!" Sara doesn't usually get into arguments, but she, poor thing, had just had a baby and had to climb up on the bed to get out of the puddle. That day we helped her sweep the water out of the garage.

Leticia and Mercedes joined in the argument. They told Justa she was a bully. Justa said that the broken pipe wasn't her fault. Something like that isn't anybody's fault, but they had a terrible quarrel. At that time Horacio's sister was the Committee organizer. She lived in the next building, and she came over and joined the argument too.

Then they quarreled about gas. The gas had come for Justa but Leticia took it for herself, claiming that Justa had gotten Leticia's number for buying gas. Then Mercedes butted in—she always does when there's an argument.

I never interfere. I'm not trying to act holier-than-thou or anything, but I've never argued with anybody here. Armando says I shouldn't because nobody has ever interfered with us, and he's right.

Last Christmas Eve, Mercedes's husband and Leticia had a fight. It takes a lot to make Juan quarrel with anybody. As far as he's concerned, anything that anybody does is all right. I was in Oriente visiting Armando's home so I didn't hear Juan and Leticia, but I've been told about their quarrel. Leticia was washing the staircase as Juan left to go downtown. When he came back home, she was still hard at work and he remarked, "They're still throwing water down here." Leticia stuck her head out over the banister and said, "If you don't want me to throw water down there, put your wife's ass where it can catch the dirty water." And they started quarreling right there.

Mercedes is stuck-up as anything. She talks about others who once lived in a low barrio of Havana and how they start giving themselves airs because they moved into Miramar. One day her husband's uncle came to stay with them, but when he arrived Juan was out. I found out later that Mercedes sent Juan's relatives to eat at the club and later she brought them home and sat them at the kitchen table. Her little girl blurts out everything. She said, "*Mamá* told *papá* that the next time one of his relatives comes to stay, she's leaving home. She told them to go away but they stayed."

That's not the proper way to treat a relative. They shouldn't have to stay in a hotel when they come all the way from the country to visit, especially as Mercedes has such a very comfortable apartment! And yet, those people are so good, they sent her an enormous box of plantains and bananas.

Mercedes is lazy and hates to work. She doesn't like to cook or do anything. She doesn't even clean her own apartment! The place isn't dirty, but that's because nobody goes in except her and her little boy. Even the kid is out in the street most of the day. At 12:00 noon she gives him his lunch, then sends him out to play again. And she keeps all the rooms closed. I know because I used to help her clean.

I get along well with everybody. If Justa doesn't get along with me it's because she doesn't want to. She's got no reason—I've never done her any harm. One time I did call the Public Health people on her because she throws down shit through that drain. And rice and beans and dog turds besides. I told them, "Look, comrades, do you think those people are supposed to use the drain to throw out the waste of those rabbits they keep? And everything else besides?"

"No, Señora," they said. "We'll see about that right away." Then Public Health gave her twenty-four hours to get the rabbits out of there, so she got them all out. Afterward she talked, and how she talked! I kept my mouth shut so she wouldn't find out I was the one who'd complained.

Leticia and Mercedes have given lovely birthday parties for their children. When Leticia has a party all the blacks get together up there. She had a sort of dinner the other day and everybody was nice and quiet. She didn't invite any of us who live here, though she usually does. I've been to many of her parties.

I've also gone to some of Mercedes's parties. Sometimes I just send the kids, but Mercedes will come up to get me and Juan scolds because I won't go. It's just that I don't like parties. Justa has given only one party so far, to celebrate her daughter Florinda's fifteenth birthday. She didn't invite me. I don't remember whether anybody from this building went, perhaps Mercedes and Juan. Maybe Justa simply would rather not be friends with any of us.

Her husband is just as bad; he never says hello to anybody. I don't know how many times I've run into him out here and he never bothers to speak. They're the kind of people who are polite and friendly when they need you. When he needed to fix the water pump he'd always say "Hello, how are you?" very cordially, because I have the key to all the tools. "Could you let me have the key?" he'd ask, oh, so politely. Or "May I borrow the wrench, please?" Then the next day he'd pass me without a greeting.

Leticia is always friendly, but not Domingo. He has his days when he'll walk right by people without saying hello. One afternoon they had a *santería*[45] celebration in their apartment. What a noise they made! It really was a *fiesta de santos,* because the next day we could see the dead chickens out there. I don't know what those fiestas are like except that they kill chickens and suck their blood.

Next day Armando teased Leticia: "Listen, Leticia, if you want to ask St. Lazarus for something, you've got to strip to the skin."

"Is that true, Armando?" she asked.

"Yes, indeed it is," he said with a straight face. "In Oriente when the women give a St. Lazarus fiesta, they take off all their clothes and ask him for whatever they wish, and he always grants it."

Afterward Armando said to me, "I'll bet you anything that from now on, whenever Leticia has one of those sessions she's going to strip naked."

Not long ago, on the Day of the *Virgen de la Merced,* Leticia had a party up there. When she goes to Regla it's always connected with sorcery. She doesn't deny it, in fact she comes right out and says so herself. Domingo says that when he was in the Army he was a *santero.*[46] Leticia's brothers are also *santeros.* One of them was going to be elected to the Communist Youth and he refused because his religion forbade him to accept.

If Leticia brings me food, I take it because I'm not afraid of any of that stuff. I don't think Leticia is going to pull any dirty sorcery on me. I believe *santería* is simply a religion like any other. Of course they can work all sorts of evil on other people. For instance, I think that Leticia has worked some kind of sorcery on Justa, and Justa on Leticia. Justa believes in that too, especially in St. Lazarus. She keeps his statue well hidden because the lieutenant isn't permitted to have such things. I know because Leticia told me.

Mercedes believes in religion. Juan even had his Communist Youth card taken away because she had her little boy baptized. She simply went ahead and did it without considering the problems she was bringing on

45. An Afro-Cuban saint cult that combines Yoruban and Roman Catholic beliefs and traditions.
46. Priest-practitioner of the *santería* cult; also called *babalorisha.*

her husband. He wasn't supposed to allow that. Now he'll have to earn his card all over again.[47]

It isn't only the people in the building who help each other, it's our neighbors on the whole block. I used to be the one who lugged Sonia's groceries—she's my sister's mother-in-law—because everyone in her house had jobs. The other day Armando got sick and Alma and her husband, the new people who live in the garage of no. 409, drove him to the doctor.

Gisela, who used to live upstairs in no. 409, was a really good friend of mine. Her husband was the owner or the manager of a shoe factory. Before leaving Cuba she gave me a small set of shelves, little pillowcases for my son, clothes, and practically the whole layette she had for her little girl.

Gisela's maid Amalia was a very good *negrita*, sweet as they come. She stayed on when Gisela left. It used to be that when a family left, the servants didn't have to move but stayed right on in the house as if it were their own. Now the servants have to move out when the family leaves. Amalia had a fully furnished apartment with three bedrooms, a living room, dining room, and everything. They moved her three years ago to a good place in Guanabacoa, but they let her keep all the furniture.

In 1963 or '64, Clara Falcón's husband, Tito, presented a request to leave Cuba; then he got a divorce and married another woman. Clara was left all alone and did nothing but cry. She leads a sad life, working and knocking herself out. Before, she never had to do a thing. Not a thing! She has no need to work now, either, because she used to own the building she lives in and Urban Reform pays her 106 *pesos* a month and gives her the apartment rent-free. Such a good apartment too! She's got more than enough with only herself to support. Clara is a very good person. She had every luxury but she never snubbed me or anyone else either. She's always been as friendly and affectionate as she is now.

By the time I got to know my friend Norma well, she and Carmen Tamayo were living alone. Carmen had a VW and another small car, and on Sundays Norma would drive the old lady around, and I'd go with them. And sometimes she'd drive me home from the store. They sold that car about five years ago. It seems she couldn't get some of the parts. Things were already beginning to get scarce by then. Norma always got along fine in that job of hers, and whenever they got something in the house, she always gave some to my kids. I also help Norma whenever she needs it. When her son is ill, I shop for her food. And sometimes when

47. Juan Pérez left the Communist Youth because he was too old (thirty-two) to belong. He can be considered for Party membership but he cannot earn back his Youth card. There is no evidence that his children's baptism had anything to do with his ambiguous political position. Three of the Cárdenas children were baptized and it did not prevent Armando's admittance to either the Youth or the Party.

we run into each other at the Minimax, she'll ask me to bring her things home, so I do.

I've only gotten to know Luminosa and her husband, José Sabina, the old couple across the street, since we started the Committee and organized the block. I was the one who filled out the retirement-pay blanks for him because the request had to go through the CDR. I get the data on everyone now.

I'm friendly with Máximo Abay, who lives near them. I read the newspapers to him, and when I need lemons and oranges I go over to his house to get them. I just ask and he gives them to me.

This block used to be so pretty, with all the gardens nicely cared for. But it has changed for the worse. Our garden used to be beautiful, especially when Vita lived here. She planted a lot of flowers and trimmed and cleaned up the yard. It looked simply lovely. But now there's nothing, everything's falling apart. The yard across the street is all torn up, the one at 412 is a mess, and ours is finished. And the buildings! Number 417 has no more windows! It was destroyed by the scholarship students and the families who lived in it. Those houses used to be as pretty and well kept as the protocol houses and José Sabina's. The apartment buildings, the schools, and the home for the aged were also well cared for.

Our building used to be beautiful too. Now it's torn to pieces. The apartments aren't even the shadow of what they were. The cyclone shutters blew away about three years ago but Aldita had them fixed. Justa broke one of the two panes down by the entrance. She was mopping the floor and accidentally hit the glass with the end of the stick. Then she started throwing broken glass into the yard where the kids were playing. I was sitting on the wall and called all the kids to get out of the way of the glass. The next day, Justa's daughter Gabriela broke the other pane.

The reason for the tremendous change in the neighborhood is that now there's a lot of riffraff. You never used to see barefoot, much less naked, kids running around this neighborhood. And they didn't stay out in the street all day or make much noise. In fact, it was very rare that anybody made noise around here. Now people will keep up a conversation for two or three hours and drive you crazy, because you can't go to sleep with all the noise.

The other day I lay down to nap with my son Dieguito, but Mercedes and Justa started a conversation and it was impossible to sleep. How can anybody stand it! And they didn't even have anything interesting to say. Mercedes spoke only of not having this or that and Justa boasted about how *much* she has.

ARMANDO CÁRDENAS:

It seems to me since we're all living on the same block we should be one big family, like brothers and sisters to one another. When I have a pain, I have to ask my neighbors' help and they have to rush around to help me, right? And when they have a pain, it's up to me to find a way to help them. I can't turn my back on anyone who lives here. They might turn their backs on me, but that wouldn't make any difference—I'd still be ready to help them whenever they needed it. Above all, I'm a communist, and a communist can't bear a grudge or look down on anybody.

The lieutenant says he's a Party militant and I am too, which means there should be strong bonds uniting us. But I've never exchanged one word with him. Never in my life! We've had no dealings at all with each other. However, I've chatted with his wife and daughters. When she first moved here, she'd come over and we'd talk about all sorts of things. Lately, when I see her we say hello, but I hardly ever see her since she stopped visiting Lala. That happens often here.

I've been told that the lieutenant's wife uses all kinds of foul language, even around her own children. They say she sometimes makes a scene up there on the terrace, calling her kids damn fools and all that sort of thing. I'm the kind of guy who doesn't like to act on things he's only been told about. But if I ever hear her carrying on like that, I'll tell her, "Now look, comrade, stop and think who you are. Remember, your husband is a police officer, so it's improper for you to make a scandal out in public like this. That's no way for you to behave, and it could have very unpleasant consequences for you and your husband."

I won't take it sitting down the way the rest of them have done. And she'd better act respectful when I tell her, because if not, I'll go to her husband to make a complaint. I'll say, "Look here, comrade, there's a problem I must bring to your attention."

Of all our women neighbors, I find Mercedes the most pleasant and the easiest to get along with. We've never quarreled. I get along well with Leticia also, but Leticia got angry with me once, even though I was only doing my duty as a citizen. I wasn't a bit embarrassed about it, because I knew I was simply doing my duty.

This is what happened. There was a law that in this zone nothing could be moved from any of the apartments without a permit. So if I saw anybody on this block moving out a piece of furniture—a bed, a radio, or whatever—it was my duty as a revolutionary citizen to ask them to show me their permit. If they didn't have a permit, I'd escort them to the Committee, where they could get one. Otherwise, they simply couldn't move it out.

Anyhow, soon after Leticia came here, a certain family moved out of 418 and left a number of things in storage at Leticia's apartment. Well, about that time I had a birthday and my father-in-law came from Pinar del Río and brought a suckling pig that we roasted behind Juan's house. We were sitting down to eat when I saw a car stop in front of the building. Some people got out and went up to Leticia's place and started carrying down all sorts of furniture and stowing it in the car.

I'm the one who must be on the lookout here, so I went over to the driver and asked him, "Will you please show me your permit to move these things?"

"Oh, look, I don't have one."

"Well, until you do, you can't take those things out of here. Come to the station with me for just a moment." The chauffeur started protesting and said I didn't know anything. Then my friends Fabio and Juan joined me and we got in the car with the driver and drove over to the station, where I talked with the comrade in charge. There they made a record of the whole thing, how it had come about, where the family had stored the furniture, and how they had sent Emilio, the man driving the car, to gather up all the furniture, etc. Then the sergeant told them that until they brought a written permit they couldn't take anything, so Emilio went back to the lady's house to get it. After they gave him the paper, he got the furniture out. Later, Emilio said there weren't any hard feelings and told me to continue supper with my guests. So I went home and had supper.

Leticia got mad at me because I interfered. She called me about twenty thousand names—like "that skinny yellow-face," and "son-of-a-bitch," and a lot of other things too. All because she didn't like what I did. She was furious with me and Lala, and refused to speak to either of us.

Then when the Committee was about to be organized, a *compañera* came over and told me that I was the best one around to organize it. So I had to call on all the neighbors to ask if they wanted to join. Well, I went to Leticia's apartment too, and rang the doorbell. When she came to the door, I explained, "I've come to see if you and your family want to join the Committee we're organizing here." I spoke with her and Domingo and they thought it was a good thing and wanted to join.

After that, she started saying hello to Lala and me again. Sometimes I ask her, "Leticia, why did you get so mad at me that time? Did you think I took Emilio to the police just for the fun of it? Why were you so foolish about that business?" But she simply burst out laughing. After all, what can she say, eh? I was simply doing my duty. She herself might have done the same thing if she'd seen someone taking out a TV set. There was a reason for that ruling. There had been a lot of stealing, you see, and the permit was required to put a check on that.

I get along fine with all the neighborhood men—Juan, Domingo, Horacio, and all the rest. The only one I haven't met is the lieutenant, but I have no quarrel with him either. Juan and I often stop for a chat with each other. Besides, we both belong to the same militia unit and have done agricultural work in the same battalion. When we got leave to come to Havana to see our families, he and I used to drive over in the same car.

Eduardo was born in Oriente just like me, but he lived in one barrio and I in another. Sometimes we say hello when we meet, other times he passes right by me without a word or even a sign of greeting. Besides, when they lived upstairs in that apartment, there were so many of them it was impossible to tell which was which. I've come to recognize him only recently, because he's the only man in the garage. I've never been great friends with him because, heck, he's kind of crude. I think his drinking has got a lot to do with his outbursts of temper. Does that guy drink! Besides that, he never talks much with anyone. I don't think he and I have exchanged ten words in all the time we've known each other.

I don't talk much with Horacio because he's always rushing around— he's kind of crazy, you know—but when we do talk, it's always in a perfectly friendly fashion. I consider Horacio a friend and a comrade because he's a revolutionary too. He may have his insane moments, when he gets kind of confused and overexcited, but I think that's because his fighting in the Insurrection affected him.

Horacio is the type who sticks his nose into everything. He can't sort things out and put them together in one piece, if you know what I mean. He's very disorganized and he's a liar. Suppose I should mention to him that I needed a bedroom set. He'd say, "Don't worry, I'll take care of that for you." Well, like as not that would be a lie. He might put his mind on it, but then again, he might not stir a step. But with all his faults, he's a revolutionary. He'd be willing to die for the cause, but he simply can't get himself straightened out.

I know Horacio was arrested once, but I can't discuss it because we're not allowed to say anything about the people on our list who are investigated. We're absolutely forbidden to make the slightest comment on such matters. The order comes directly from the DSE.[48] The only thing I can say is that Lala is their direct contact with us here in the CDR. The people are specially chosen for the job and must be responsible. Many people can't be trusted as contacts because they'd blab about the questions that were asked and all the details of the investigation. That simply can't be allowed. All those discussions must remain secret because they investigate in many places.

The people come directly to us and must show us their identification from the Department. This is a signed authorization with the official seal, saying, "Please cooperate with comrade so-and-so and give him whatever information he asks for." Their identification must be authorized and signed by whoever is responsible for the particular zone where the investigation is to be carried out. Without such an official authorization, we can't receive anybody.

I'm very much against race prejudice. When Lala's sister Serafina was staying with us she took off with our neighbor, Rodolfo; he's Sonia's son.

---

48. *Dirección (General) de Seguridad del Estado* (Department of State Security).

Serafina's parents opposed the marriage because he's black, but I guess it was their opposition that decided Serafina to do it. I talked to Lala's parents about the business. I told them it didn't matter if Rodolfo had dark skin—he wasn't actually a full-blooded Negro, but even if he had been, it shouldn't make any difference—because he's a good guy and that's all that's important. Well, in the end they had to accept it. You know how it is.

To make the Revolution succeed, everybody must work together and understand how to behave with one another. For example, twice people have given birthday parties and have discriminated against some of the kids on the block by not inviting them. The right thing would be to invite them all, whether they're white, black, Chinese, or whatever. Invite those who go barefoot as well as those who can afford to wear shoes. They're all children, aren't they? To me everybody is equal.

Look, I'll be frank and name names. When Mercedes had a birthday party for her kids, Sara's kids weren't invited. Then there was another party at Serafina's and Sara's family was not invited, and neither was Justa's. Lala says her sister didn't invite Sara because they'd had a quarrel. But heck, that's no reason not to invite the children. That's the kind of problem I think shouldn't exist. I told Lala, "Don't ever give a party, because if you do you'll have to invite every last soul on the block and his cat, if need be!"

MERCEDES MILLÁN:
I'm very changeable. Sometimes I'm communicative and at other times I'm reserved. I'm a talker all right, but not the kind of person who makes lots of friends. I can talk with anybody, but it isn't easy for me to think of just anyone as a friend.

I haven't talked with Leticia, but I overhear some of her conversations with Lala. Lala goes to Leticia's house to wash clothes and they start gossiping. I'm always at home cleaning and looking after Eloy Tomás, so I hear everything they say. That's how, without talking to Leticia myself, I've gradually learned what kind of a person she is. Besides, you only have to look at how that woman lives and how they act.

Leticia's brother-in-law Dámaso and his wife, Vita, used to live in one of the two garages up front. Dámaso left—he was sent to jail, I think. They're that kind of people. He's black, even blacker than Domingo. Vita is white but a very low type. And her morals. . . ! But I didn't have any problem with her; we said hello and got along perfectly well. A lot of other people used to stay there too. They were arguing there all the time. One day they came to blows because Vita had taken off with another man. I think she went to Oriente with Sara's younger brother. It was scandalous, the way they yelled and fought. I could hear the noise so I understood what was going on.

That kind of confusion makes me nervous. I hate it. I simply can't stand it. If it's directed against me, I burst into tears. I can't help it, I'm just no good at quarreling with anybody. If the quarrel has nothing to do with me, I walk away.

Lala and Sara are on friendly terms with Leticia. Justa doesn't get along with any of them. I'm the only one in this building with whom Justa is on good terms. She says Lala talks too much. It seems that Lala and Leticia began to gossip about Justa's eldest daughter, Genoveva—they made up twenty stories about her and . . . well, they said the girl was trying to steal the husband of a woman in the Committee here. Justa told me they were saying that.

Justa tells me that the problems with Sara began when Justa started missing things from her clothesline on her terrace. First it would be socks, then it would be underpants, and so on until one day she caught Sara's daughter at it. That's when the quarrels began, according to Justa anyway. I don't know what Sara has to say about it. I have the impression they aren't on speaking terms anymore.

Of all the people living in this building, I've had the least contact with Sara. I greet her when we meet, but I've never had a conversation with her. You can't get to know people that way. Just "Hello, how are you?" and she answers, "Hello, how are you?" and then we might say a few words about the children or some such trifle and that's it. I know she's backward and has a very low level of culture, but aside from that, I can't say what she's like as a person.

I'm on friendly terms with Lala. She's very obliging and that's a fine thing in a neighbor. She does anything she can to help you. I've known her many years and we've never had a single disagreement in all that time. She gets along well with Leticia and Sara too. Lala has one grave defect, though—she's a terrible gossip. Not right to one's face—she wouldn't dare—but behind one's back. She makes up things, too. Some of her stories are true, but a lot of them are not. Still, she's respectful. She'd be quite incapable of insulting you to your face or quarreling or anything like that. We have a saying that "your nearest neighbor is your next of kin," and it's true. If something happens to you, you might die before your relatives could get to you or even know that anything was wrong.

Justa is altogether a different kind of person. She doesn't gossip or talk about you behind your back. Anything she has to say to you, she says right to your face. She's brusque, perhaps because of her background and lack of education. She's said horrible things to me. When she does that I ignore her. I say to her, "I'm not going to answer because the breeding you lack, I have in excess. I refuse to sink to your level. I'm not the kind of person who enjoys insulting other people or being insulted by them."

When she starts that kind of thing I get so upset I burst into tears. I'm not used to being spoken to like that. If you insult them back, there's simply no end to it. Justa actually enjoys those slinging matches because it's something she's seen and done all her life. She's rough and rude, but even so, she's a decent, obliging woman.

I only know Leticia and her husband well enough to greet as neighbors. Once, about four years ago, Serafina saw them carry a TV set out of the corner house, which was sealed, and take it to their own house. Lala told Armando and he spoke to Juan. It was Sunday, I remember, so Juan was home. Juan drove him over to the police station to make the accusation and a police car came over. They found Leticia alone at home with the children, so they didn't take her to the station. I don't know how it all ended—whether there was a trial or not. Lala told me they found more stolen goods in the house, but that's all I know.

Well, of course Leticia was angry, especially at Armando and Lala, who'd taken the leading part, and she stopped speaking to us all. She said all sorts of horrible things. Insults like "dirty white man" and obscene words I don't like to repeat. No matter where she met Armando, on the steps or anywhere, she'd yell twenty different insults at him.

Leticia kept telling Lala that she could have her kicked out any time she pleased because one of the rooms belonged to Leticia's apartment. But of course Lala can stay there until Urban Reform or the Frozen Zone office finds her another apartment.

Leticia went out of her way to be disagreeable about a plant I'd cut down. The whole bit of yard looked terrible because Sara's family was living there and had long since pulled down the plants in the planters and everything. It was nothing but bare earth and that scrawny-looking *almácigo* bush.

I learned later that Leticia and the others used that plant for home remedies. But honestly, the bush wasn't pulled out by the roots, simply cut back so it would put out leaves and grow into a prettier shape. Sara's family too, of all people, complained, but Leticia was the most insulting of all. She went around asking if I thought the whole building was mine or what? Oh yes, she also said she could afford to pay the gardener herself and didn't need anybody to go paying him to interfere with her part of the yard.

I heard her, so I went out and said, "Look, I was alone in this building so long—except for Lala in the servants' quarters—that I got used to having the gardener do the whole yard. I had no intention of annoying anybody and I don't think the whole building is mine." Then I said to the gardener, "Look, from now on just take care of this bit of yard from here to there. If the other tenants want the rest of the grass cut, let them do it. And if they don't, that's their business."

Leticia felt bad when I paid the gardener to fix up the whole front yard because those people have an inferiority complex. They thought I did it to humiliate them because they're poor. That's why she said she could pay a gardener herself any time she wanted one. Envious, that's what they are.

I believe that envy is the worst poison there is. It's the cause of all the evil in the world. There are always people who are better off than one's self, either financially or in some other way, but I don't envy anyone. That's why I live a happy life. Each of us should try to live the best we can and struggle to fulfill our aspirations, but in what way would it be to my neighbor's advantage if I were worse off than they? If they were to gain something, it would still be wrong of them to want to drag me down, but at least I could see the logic of it.

I don't speak to Leticia anymore. She goes her way and I go mine. When we run into each other, she keeps to one side and I to the other, that's all. But she keeps on blowing up trifles just to find an excuse to quarrel. She'll do anything to annoy me. Her husband too. They're always trying to provoke me.

Well, I'm just not that kind of person. Neither is *mamá*. I never saw such things in my home. I'd rather lose my rights than get into an argument. Let them think I'm an idiot or a coward if they like. That's what Leticia probably thinks—that I'm scared of her—when she talks so much and I don't answer. But I'm not afraid because I've done nothing to her. If I were a thief or a murderer in danger of being caught, I'd be afraid, but when somebody has a clear conscience like me, they don't have to be afraid of anybody.

A good person is someone who's sensitive and generous in his or her feelings. Someone who knows how to treat others and respect them. I remember that Benito Juárez,[49] the Mexican, said that peace is respect for the rights of others. I've always agreed with that. The other person's rights extend thus far—well, I can go that far and no further. When one person invades another's right, the result is discord.

I feel happy enough, though I can't say I enjoy having the kind of neighbors I do. I wish they were people I could be friendly with—not chummy, simply on good terms, with everybody keeping to his own house. I hate the resentment, the needling, the dirty looks they give me, and the way they exploit the most trivial things to provoke a quarrel. I can't stand a person like that Sara, who resents everything. But, well, what can one do?"[50]

49. President of Mexico 1858–60 (in Veracruz) and 1867–72.
50. Juan Pérez summarized his feelings toward the block and his neighbors in an untaped interview. He said he was seldom at home and didn't know all the tenants in his building by name, nor was he familiar with the other neighbors on the block. He apparently accepted his wife's perceptions of the neighbors, using the same adjectives and phrases as she to describe them, as well as her versions of incidents between the families. He was very negative about Leticia Manzanares and Domingo Labrada, and hostile toward

When we first saw this *reparto*,[51] the streets and yards were much better kept. The lawns were trimmed and the trash gathered and put in the cans on the sidewalk to be picked up every afternoon. The appearance of the block has changed a great deal. Everything is run-down and uncared for. The house across the street is a mess inside. The man there said the students tore the place apart. So many kids, you know, are much harder on a house than a family—some families, anyway.

Now when you walk down this block, you see the trash lying in heaps all over the place, and the garbage cans stay on the sidewalk for days because the truck doesn't come daily as it used to. People drop things on the sidewalk, too. I sweep it up when it's in front of my house. It isn't just strangers; sometimes the kids at Justa's house throw things, and the family in the garage throw things, and I know that Leticia litters my yard on purpose, and so does Domingo. I've seen them. Sometimes I've been out sweeping and trash falls on me from upstairs, so it's got to be on purpose.

It's horrible! The kids are out there on the terrace all day long. If they eat an orange or a banana, they throw out the peel; if they suck on sugar cane, they throw out the stalk. When they eat meat, they throw the bones into the garden. The people on both sides of the building do it, so the front yard is always filthy. The gardener quarrels with me about it and says I shouldn't allow them to do that. "Well, and what do you want me to do about it?" I ask him. "I can't control them."

None of that trash comes from my house, because if my kids toss down so much as a scrap of paper, I make them pick it up. I know my kids are bad and mischievous, but that's one thing they don't do. In the first place, they sit down at the table to eat. I keep after them not to walk around nibbling, because I don't like it. Those people have that habit; I used to object but by now I've lost all hope of their changing.

My daughter plays mostly with Justa's girls, Gabriela and Engracia, and with Isolina, Serafina's niece-in-law, who's here now. She used to

---

Lala Fontanés, accusing her of being gossipy and snoopy, "like everyone else in her family." Pérez consistently defended his wife's position in her relationships with other families in the building, saying that she was "not accustomed to living with such neighbors."

In his interview, Pérez suggested a relationship between the incidence of theft in the neighborhood and the new people who had moved to the block. He suspected that the thefts were committed by a "low-class" family who had lived in the garage of the house next door. He also suspected two of Sara Rojas's brothers and suggested that their residence on the block at the time the thefts occurred was more than a coincidence. He also expressed annoyance with the Rojas brothers because they had, on occasion, jumped over the garden wall and cut across his backyard to enter the side door of the apartment building. One night he saw them jumping over the wall just as he was coming home from work. Irritated because he had asked them several times not to take the shortcut, he pulled out his pistol and fired several shots over their heads "to frighten them."

51. A suburb or subdivision of a city.

play a lot with Lala's boys when there were no other children here, but as soon as girls moved into the building, she started playing with them. She's always liked playing with girls more than with boys. Sometimes when Sara's children are out there, she'll play with them. Eloy Tomás doesn't know how to play with other kids yet; he fights with everybody. But when they're out there, all the children go out and play together. Leticia's children too.

Most of the scholarship students are much too old to play with Eloy, who's three. But Rigoberto, who's ten, keeps coming over anyhow. He didn't go to school for about a week because somebody had stolen his only pair of shoes, or he lost them or something. I think he didn't even eat, because he says he wasn't permitted in the dining room without shoes. He said Sara gave him meals at her house but I don't know. He was out in the street all day long. One day he came here to watch television and fell asleep in the chair. He went back to the student house and rang the doorbell for a long time but nobody answered, so he finally let himself in through the back and went to bed. I guess he's going to school again because I saw him wearing tennis shoes the day before yesterday.

The girl in charge of the student house is only about sixteen. One day she called and called him and he didn't go for a long time. Later on I asked him, "Why don't you mind her?"

"Because when she calls me and I go, she pulls my ears and pinches me," he explained. I don't know how he behaves at the house. The girl claims he pays no attention at all to anybody and that he's unbearable, but in my house he's obedient and well-behaved.

I don't forbid my children to play with any other children because, after all, they aren't responsible for what their parents do. Leticia is the one who objects to her children playing with mine or coming in here. One day her little boy jumped over the garden wall and started to look at a program on our TV. She found out and beat him and the child screamed—it was horrible. I no longer invite her children in because I know their *mamá* will punish them. I say hello to the kids—I have nothing against them, even though I don't speak to their mother. When I have a party I invite everybody in the building except Leticia. I'm sorry to exclude her children, but I couldn't invite them without telling her.

Our most recent party was Eloy Tomás's birthday. Justa didn't send her little girls, not one of them. I don't know why because I reminded them at least twenty times. Lala's kids came and Serafina's and Sonia's two grandchildren and Normita, the one who lives on the corner of Seventh Avenue. I invited practically all the kids on the block.

Juan and I very rarely give a party for adults. We celebrate my saint's day sometimes, but we only invite our closest relatives, my parents, perhaps my mother-in-law or sister- or brother-in-law. We may get a cake and some soft drinks. If we have cake, I send a piece to each of the neighbors afterward, but I don't invite them because it isn't a party. If it were, I'd invite people from outside the family.

I don't think they've ever had a party at Sara's house—if they have, I wasn't invited. Lala always invites us when she has a party for her children. We were also invited to Justa's house a short time ago, when they celebrated Hernández's birthday. They had roast pork and beer. I went up, but stayed only a little while because it was really more a men's party—you know, drinking beer and so on. Horacio, the one who lives next door, went, and Juan too. There were mostly men, his comrades in the patrol and so on.

I've never had a long conversation with Armando, Lala's husband. He's very reserved and serious. I know him well enough to say hello, or when he's sick I ask him how he's getting along. I haven't ever talked much with Ricardo Hernández either. We've chatted briefly about the children or about some incident, but I've never had long conversations with him. He too seems rather reserved and uncommunicative. He does talk more with Juan, and now and then comes here to chat with him. But that's between men.

Juan is friendly with them all, but I believe he's friendliest with Armando and Ricardo Hernández. Both of them served in the Army and they're both involved in the Revolution, although I don't know anything about their revolutionary work.

I've been in Clara's house and in Sonia's, and also in Serafina's, but I don't consider any of them friends of mine. We're friendly neighbors, that's all. We say hello and do one another a favor if the occasion arises, and I might go to one of their parties if they invited me.

I used to be really friendly with Georgina and Delfina, who lived in no. 409. They were over sixty, older women who didn't work. One of them had a widow's pension and payments from Urban Reform and Agrarian Reform. I went to their home only when necessary, if my telephone was out of order, or, on certain occasions, to offer condolences. They came to see me when my son was born, and I always invited them when I had a children's party. They were very fond of children and always came. If several days went by without our seeing each other, they'd call me to ask how I was or I'd call them. We'd let each other know if anything came to the Minimax or when the mineral-water man came around. It was a matter of reciprocity. Nothing very deep, just pleasant neighborly relations.

I was on quite friendly terms with a family from the United Arab Republic—because of the kids. Their three little girls and Merceditas played together all the time. We visited sometimes and always invited each other for the children's birthdays. They left last year.

The corner house is Carmen Tamayo's. When I meet her, we talk and that's all. She has nothing to do so when she gets hold of you she talks your ear off. I think she's a little touched in the head because she tells you the same story twenty times over. The person I'm most friendly with in that house is Normita, but even with her, days and days go by without our having any conversation. When we do talk, it's about the children and household matters.

Actually I spend my life inside my own house and I don't know much about what goes on outside. I may run over to somebody's house for a moment when I have some specific reason for going, but not for a real, sit-down visit. I'm always too rushed for that.

SARA ROJAS:

The first week or two after they moved here, the lieutenant and his wife, Justa, acted very friendly. The lieutenant came to see me and said, "A way must be found to move you out soon. This can't keep on for long because you have so many children." And when he saw my kids, he'd ask them how I was doing because he noticed I wasn't in good health. The kids would answer, "She doesn't feel well." And he'd ask the people around how I was, and would drop in to see me.

I didn't see Justa at all on the day they moved in or the next day either. Then on the third day, she came down to call on me. She never talked about the exchange, and she said she knew nothing of the arrangements because it was her husband who'd been in charge of the whole thing. That much we did discuss. One day she asked me, "Have you always lived down here in this garage?"

"No," said I, "I used to live up where you live now." That was five or six days after they'd moved in and she acted as if she knew nothing about it. "*Chica*," I said, "you know perfectly well that I was the owner of that apartment you have now. And owning it is precisely what landed me where you see me."

"Oh, don't worry about that," she said, "they'll find a place for you right away. They surely aren't going to leave you stuck here."

I didn't answer. Why should she pretend she didn't know how I came to be living in the garage? I only said these few words: "All the harm people do in this life they pay for sooner or later. I've never interfered with anybody or harmed anybody, but I'll get even somehow." I didn't speak angrily or anything. Then she changed the subject and has never tried to bring it up again.

I was friendly with Justa because she helped me. Besides, a neighbor is a neighbor, and anyway, she's not to blame for that exchange business. Heck, I wasn't going to turn my face away and refuse to speak to her when what happened wasn't her fault in the least.

At first I'd forbidden my kids to go up to Justa's or play with her children, but later I thought, "Oh well, they're just kids," so I told them it was all right. Violeta and Concha would go there to chat with Justa's daughters, Genoveva and Florinda. My other son, Gerardo, who was away on a scholarship, would also visit there when he was home. When my kids had to go to the Minimax for me, they'd stop by and ask if Justa wanted them to bring her anything.

I myself never went to the lieutenant's house. Justa didn't come to my place much either, but we'd sit outside and talk. We always stood guard in the neighborhood together because that's the way the turns fell. We didn't have a profound friendship or anything like that, but we got along very well with each other. And then, all of a sudden that woman changed. After we'd spent about two months getting friendly, she insulted me, and it was all because of some quarrel our kids had.

Afterward I asked Concha what it was all about. "Florinda shit on my mother," Concha said, "and I wasn't going to just stand there and let anybody say such a thing, because you're sacred to me, and besides, you never interfere with anybody."

I guess Justa was spoiling for a fight anyway and took advantage of that falling-out between the girls to break off the friendship with us. I don't intend to be friends with her ever again. It seems to me that if you're friends with somebody you shouldn't come raging at them because your kids quarrel. I mean, butting in on a kid's quarrel is as foolish as butting in on a quarrel between a married couple. I simply don't know how Justa's mind works. If she'd hauled off and slapped both girls, mine and hers, I wouldn't have minded. But she came rampaging down just about ready to eat me alive. She knocked on my door with a mop stick, crying at the top of her voice, "Come out, you dirty bitch!"

Eduardo was out at the moment, so I was all alone, washing clothes. I was recovering from the stillbirth of the baby born after the exchange of apartments. I was supposed to stay calm, so I said to her, "Señora, don't come here trying to pick a fight with me. I never interfere with anybody but I've gotten back my strength now and I'm not about to swallow any of your garbage, you hear? So just pipe down and stop provoking me."

Concha wanted to open the door and have it out with her, but I didn't allow it. Justa knocked on my door a long time, fit to break it down, but she finally got tired and went away. She made that show because she knew I was sick and weaker than a cat.

Then, I don't know what happened, I swear by my mother I don't, the lieutenant interfered and threatened to kick us out of the garage—for no reason except that fight the kids had gotten into. He said to me, "If your kids keep on misbehaving, I'm going to kick you all out of the garage."

"Kick me out any time you like," I answered. "I can't promise to keep kids from fighting, because as you well know, children do fight and the next minute they're fast friends again. Grown people shouldn't interfere in children's quarrels."

The next day Eduardo stayed home from work—he was working as a guard, same as now—to go talk to the lieutenant. Eduardo was sitting on the front step in plain sight of anyone who passed, and the lieutenant went by without saying a word to him. Nothing! He simply stopped speaking to us. Then Horacio called on him and told him he couldn't kick me out or abuse me with words either.

Justa was the one who started the trouble and she did it to make me move from the garage because she needed it. It must have been that because I can't imagine what she could have against me personally. I didn't do anything to her—I didn't even know her. God knows what it was! It couldn't have been that she had racial prejudice because her family is "backward" too. Don't go believing she's white or anything like it—she's a faded black, that's all. She *looks* white enough, sure, but I don't believe for a minute that she is. I've seen lots of her relatives and some look white but others are colored. Anyhow, if she had racial prejudice, she wouldn't have married the lieutenant, who's *jabao*—you know, mulatto. His skin is light enough, but he has bad hair so I really don't see how she could be a racist.

Justa has never made any racist remarks to me, not even when she insults me, but she's called me a pig. I can't see that she's got any right to call me "pig." From all accounts, she's a worse pig than I am. Why, for all that, she's got a big apartment instead of being crowded into a small place the way we are now, and she doesn't keep it clean. At least that's what everybody says—I wouldn't know because I've never in my life set foot in that woman's home. Clean or dirty, it's none of my business anyway. I couldn't care less. I'm only repeating what I've heard.

Justa got into the habit of throwing all her garbage down here. One day when I was feeling real sick, she dumped her garbage down right after I'd finished cleaning up. Then she said, "Don't pick it up, just leave it there." Eduardo finally lost his patience and quarreled with her, and she said horrible things to him. She said to him, "For all your 'gun,' I'm not scared of you!"

"No, indeed, Señora, why should you be? I'm a nobody," he answered. "But let me tell you one thing, watch that loud mouth of yours and stop being so insolent to people, because it isn't doing you a bit of good."

Eduardo hates loudmouths like her. He's quiet and peaceful, and he hates noise and quarrels. He says, "You know there's nothing I hate like a woman who speaks dirty." He says a woman who's dirty-mouthed is dead as far as he's concerned. When Justa is off on one of her tirades, Eduardo says to me, "Close that door, I don't want to hear."

How can a married woman with small children—girls, some of them—who are in school, speak in such an insolent way? She's simply teaching her little girls to use the same foul language. Lately she seems to have quieted down—ever since the foreigners moved in next door—but before, it used to be "balls" this and "balls" that, day in and day out, in a voice that carried right inside our place. You should hear the way all the neighbors talked about her then! You know, that kind of language had never been heard in this zone before she moved in. This is a scholarship zone! She was very, very mistaken if she thought that kind of language would go over big here.

Someone from the Committee heard Justa one day and said they were waiting for an opportunity to explain to her that she couldn't talk like that. They were even planning to hold a meeting to force her to use decent language, but then the foreigners moved into no. 413 and she calmed down considerably, so they let the matter rest.

After the day Justa insulted me and Eduardo, I said to Nicasio, the Committee president, "I will not stand guard with that woman anymore." She wouldn't speak to me for a long time.

Not long ago, one of Justa's little girls got sick to her stomach and Justa came down to beg me to stroke the child and make her well. I'm so goodhearted I went right up and did it. I'd never gone into the apartment since they'd been living there. Never. I hadn't even knocked on the door and stood outside to tell her something. I call to any of them I see to ask if any mail for me has been left at their place or something like that, but I don't go up myself.

EDUARDO ROJAS:

I don't pay attention to the affairs of the lieutenant and his wife. One thing I do know is she doesn't respect him. She's always telling him "balls this" and "balls that." She says anything to him that passes through her mind, and in front of the children, too. She's said it in front of us, or where we could hear it anyway. She has more problems with the neighbors than anybody here. When she first came she was on speaking terms with us. But what the hell! She's a filthy person, speaking plainly. She's got a foul tongue in her head, spouting one bad word after another. In the house or on the street, no matter. An insolent, dirty woman. Everybody around here knows how she talks.

Her first brush was with Leticia, and we heard them bickering all the time. And then later on it was with us. Practically every day she'd have words with Sara. She was always saying, "You people have to move from here." One day when I was here she was sweeping down the stairs and she left a heap of rubbish near our door. Then I got annoyed and said to Sara, "Look, you leave that trash right where it is. Don't clean it up." And right away the lieutenant's wife came down and jumped on me.

Then I told her a thing or two. That day I even used words like "prick." "Look here," I said, "I've already had too much abuse at the hands of you two. I'm not going to put up with any more of your gutter shit. I don't care what I do now. You may be a lieutenant's wife and all, but you can kiss my ass, you old bag." I said all that to her. And she began to fight and yell I don't know what all. Oh yes, she asked why I had a revolver. "What revolver?" I said. "I'm not threatening anybody with a revolver, nothing like that."

I think Leticia is the only friend Sara has in the building. Sara talks to a whole lot of people in the neighborhood, but I doubt that they're really friends. Being on speaking terms isn't the same as being friends.

Leticia and Domingo seem to get along fine. They've never had any trouble around here, at least none I've ever seen. They're sending their children to school and the kids never miss a day. I think they're going about their education the right way.

I haven't seen much of Armando and Lala. But they're good people, they're all right. They don't bother anybody else or anything. I've only been to their house twice, once when I went to complain about Ana Teresa's bad language and another time when I took Lala a paper, a notice from Public Health to the Defense Committee.

My kids get along well with Lala's and Leticia's children. They're even friendly with the lieutenant's family. They were always visiting them. It got to such a point that I put a stop to it. If it were up to the kids, they'd practically live there.

Mercedes is still living the old life. You can tell she's a racist. I've heard the husband's a nice guy to talk to but I don't care for that woman. I'd say she's arrogant and stand-offish. Mercedes has her own crowd and seems sociable with them, but she can't be sociable with the neighbors. She just had a party and I guess it was a good one. I don't know whether we were invited, but nobody said anything about it to me. I wouldn't have gone even if we'd been invited. She doesn't have anything to do with me or with Sara, but I wouldn't want to associate with her either. She's never done anything to me but her ways put me off.

It's odd but her husband seems different. I've watched him around here but I've never had the chance to meet him. We don't even greet each other, and I've never been to their house, so I'm talking about things I've just seen from the outside.

The neighbors here exchange things and I think it's a good idea. It's better than selling things. I don't know what exchanges we're making now, but we used to trade milk and canned fruit for root vegetables. Recently Sara traded cigarettes to a neighbor down the street for canned fruit. A couple of weeks ago I couldn't get any cigarettes so I traded two or three cans of milk for some. I made that exchange because I needed the cigarettes at the time. But usually Sara makes the exchanges we need. I don't mix into her deals.

The last time I tried to help Sara make a bargain was when she sent me to exchange a lady's wristwatch for one of Armando's watches. That morning I'd stood in line for a man's watch at El Tesoro department store. I had no. 36 and they passed me into the store, but by the time my number was up they'd run out of men's watches, and tough luck for us.

Naturally I was annoyed. So when I got to the counter I asked Sara what she thought about buying a woman's watch and trading it for something else later. "Take it," she said, and so I did. We ended up with practically nothing, only the lady's wristwatch and an alarm clock. The watch cost 70 *pesos* and the clock, 10. I didn't have to save long because my last fifteen days' pay was 99 *pesos*.

I came back home in a grumpy mood. But Sara said she thought Armando had two men's watches and maybe he'd exchange one. Lala was there and she went up and asked him. They sent for me right away and I went up to their place. I was there for about half an hour. When I saw the watch, I didn't really like its looks, but after all I needed a watch.

Another thing I didn't like was that Armando invented a whole story about the thing. He handed me an old piece of junk and said, "This is the watch I have to exchange because I'm going to try to trade the other for a pair of trousers." I felt like asking him to let me take it to Sara so she could give her OK, but I felt funny doing that. So I said all right. Then, on top of everything else, Armando took the little band off and put on an old one.

When I showed it to Sara, she said, "No, no, this isn't the watch I meant. Don't be a fool. This isn't worth 30 *pesos* even." She was mad. She said Armando has a new watch but that he gave me his old one, since I didn't know. It was Sara's watch, so I couldn't argue with her about taking it back. But I was embarrassed and I told her, "All right, you take it back then. It's yours. Do what you like with it."

I guess I was a little put out. Of course I saw that I'd been taken. From the very beginning I wondered. But I told Hilario, "Here, take this up to Lala and tell her that Sara didn't agree. This watch belongs to her and she doesn't want to trade it." So he took it up and they sent back ours.

I'm the one that got stung. The trouble is I can't face Armando now. He's going to say, "What an insect, backing out like that after making the trade."

I don't know where any of my neighbors work, except the lieutenant of course. He gets a good salary and his wife takes in washing, too. I think I earn the smallest salary in the building. I'm not sure but it seems that way. Armando and I are the small earners, I guess, and Armando must get a hundred and some *pesos,* but maybe in the end he has less than I do.

In Domingo's house they have two working in the family so they must have a large income. They say he's sick with a disease. I don't know what it might be. It would be nice to be like Domingo and stay at home sick for months on end without working. Under this government the sick ones get along fine and have an easy life. If the doctor gives you a certificate saying you're sick, who's going to deny it? Some people aren't really sick, just slackers, but the government doesn't get after them at all. Domingo could be like that. I don't know if he is or not. I haven't known him very long, only since we moved into the garage. When we lived upstairs we used to greet each other but that's about all. Now we get together and chat and have a few drinks. But we aren't what you could call friends, not really. We're acquaintances and neighbors, but no more than that.

SARA ROJAS:

If I had a nice place to live here I'd like to stay, because I really have no problems with my neighbors. I've known the people for many years and that makes quite a difference. It's hard to move someplace where you know nobody. And my children get along well with everybody here. If they do something they shouldn't, the neighbors scold them or slap them if necessary. I have no objection when my kids deserve it. All the neighbors know I don't approve of naughtiness either.

Leticia, Lala, and I will often go to the Minimax together and help each other bring home the bundles, or we'll take turns shopping for each other's rations. When I have to fetch a can of kerosene or milk from the Minimax, I ask Lala's sister Serafina for the loan of her shopping cart, and she always lets me have it. I send Hilario to ask for the cart, because Serafina and Rodolfo have been nice to him from the time he was little.

I've lent Leticia things. When she runs out of rice, I let her have some of mine, and if I run out of it, I borrow some from her until my quota comes. Milk too, but it's not a gift. What we borrow from each other we pay back. Those things must be paid back; they come out of our rations.

I'm the *curandera* here. I know a bit about rubbing a pain away, curing indigestion and such. People ask for my help, and since I know I can cure them, I give it. I go to Lala's when she needs me to cure one of her kids, and I've also cured Leticia's mother and her husband by stroking them. I've done that favor for all of them.

Nothing has changed between us—nothing. I've been just as friendly with my neighbors since the move to the garage as before. I speak with Lala and Leticia as much as I ever did and with Mercedes, too. I've never had any trouble with any of them. The only woman I don't get along with is Justa.

Mercedes and I have always gotten along exactly as we do now—our acquaintance goes no further than saying hello to each other when we meet. If a letter or telegram comes for her when she isn't here, I sign for her and slip it under the door. Or if her son is doing some mischief or something I think is wrong, I call out to her, "Mercedes, Eloyitos is out in the street!" or eating dirt, or climbing up someplace dangerous, or whatever. Then she'll say, "Oh, thanks for telling me, Sara," and that's all.

I don't visit Mercedes because she's never invited me in or said, "Why don't you come around to see me sometime, Sara." Not that I'd go even if she invited me. I've never, never, never in my life set foot in Mercedes's house. I've never so much as stood in the doorway there. I don't even know where in the apartment the kitchen or bathrooms are, or the bedrooms or anything. I know where the parlor is because when they give a party they open the shutters and then I can look inside, but that's all.

I know nothing at all about her life except that maybe her family has been rich from way back because she used to have a maid, and when people have employees, well. . . .

Mercedes has always been a homebody. When she had a maid and didn't have to go shopping herself, she never went out at all except now and then for a drive in her car. Only somebody who has domestic help can do that. It's only lately that she's begun to go out a little oftener. Now we sometimes hear her calling her little boy, "Eloyitos, Eloyitos." But before, she didn't make a sound that could be heard beyond the walls of her apartment. I'm telling you I never heard her.

Mercedes's husband, Juan Carlos, is a fine person. He's always pleasant and never interferes with anybody. I've never heard him raise his voice. When they talk, nothing is ever overheard out here. I have no idea whether they ever quarrel with each other or how they live, because nobody can tell what's going on inside their apartment. All I know is that they've always been polite to me.

With Lala, too, I get along now as well as I ever did. We've always been neighborly and helpful but we've never been in the habit of dropping in on each other just to chat. When she needed something I had, I always gave her some and she'd do the same for me. If I want something, I feel free to go to her and say, "Could you lend me such-and-such, Lala?" But as for visiting each other—no. She comes here only when she needs me to do something for her or lend her one of my kids because hers are in school. She'll say, for instance, "Is Hilario here? Can he come up to shine some shoes for me?"

Lala did visit me a little oftener when I was living upstairs because I told her, "Lala, if you have no place to do your wash, you're welcome to use my laundry sink. You may come here to wash every single day if you like." So she accepted and would do her wash and hang it up to dry at my place. Every time she came to do her laundry, she'd brew coffee and bring some for me and we'd chat while we worked. Nothing personal, only about what the Committee was supposed to do, how it worked— things like that. I never told her any of my intimate thoughts or feelings. Not her or anybody else here either. I'm not that close to any of the people in this place! I don't know what they're really like or what's in their hearts.

I don't believe Lala has ever worked, outside of running the CDR. Perhaps she did, but I always saw her here looking after her children. I don't know anything about the job Armando had then, or before or after. I have no idea how much money he earns either. I know nothing about the earning of anybody here except my husband. I don't know what kind of job Domingo has. In fact, I don't know whether he has a job at all.

My friendship with Leticia started when we went to call on her at the time she moved in. We'd visit back and forth, not like with Lala. Leticia is always busy and has been that way as long as I've known her. She's quick as fire, that little bug is. She doesn't stand still long enough for a fly to land on her. When she isn't ironing, she's washing or cleaning up her place. She keeps it nice all by herself with not a soul to help her. But during all the time of the exchange and the illness with my pregnancy, Leticia didn't do a thing for me. Vita and Catalina, Bernardo's new wife, washed and ironed for me, brought me food, and offered to share their homes with us if we were out on the street. But Leticia and Domingo never did a thing for me. They never said, "Sara, you're welcome to come to our place." I've nothing to be grateful to Leticia for.

But I'm rather fond of her because at least she never tried to quarrel with me—nor I with her, for that matter. I don't know whether she's fond of me, too, because I can't read her heart. In any case, she's never helped me.

Something happened to make Leticia turn against me all of a sudden—I honestly don't know what. It wasn't my fault that my brother took up with Vita, the wife of Leticia's brother-in-law Dámaso. Listen, I consider myself a *negra,* you know what I mean, but I'd never go to bed with a man like Dámaso. I don't like men who are darker than me. Dámaso is black as black can be. He's black, black, black, but he's a good guy in spite of it. Vita is a blond though—she's white on both sides of her family. My brother Panchito's skin is lighter than Dámaso's and he has hair just like mine. People can be mulattoes and have good hair and that's the way it is in my family. We aren't Negroes, we're Indians.

I simply paid no attention to the change in Leticia. As things have turned out, I'm grateful that she never did me a favor. If she had, and then got mad at me the next day, she'd have probably thrown it up to me. When she calls me to stroke her children, I go there, but not because I owe her anything.

LETICIA MANZANARES:

If I know that someone has problems, I go out of my way to help them. I'm trying to stop doing that because sometimes I get into a lot of trouble by butting in. It used to be that if I knew someone wanted to trade something, I'd take the burden on my shoulders of finding a person to exchange it with. Sometimes I helped so many people I could hardly keep up with it, yet I'd still take on more worries. What problems I got myself into because of that! Domingo and I were always quarreling about it. Nowadays when I hear people complain about something I pretend not to notice. It pains me not to be able to help somebody—that's the way I am, I really suffer—but one simply can't be too tender-hearted. The way things are now we all have the same problems.

People still haven't awakened to the fact that we're living under a system of collective action. They're still living only for themselves and that's not right. If I have something I don't need but another person does—well, that gives me the opportunity to be of service, right? I could easily give it to him or exchange it for something else. But there are many people who'll do nothing of the sort. Under this system, we should all realize that everybody is equal and we should share among ourselves. If someone doesn't like it, they can go elsewhere. I'm not leaving, so I must find a way to help those who are all screwed up. As for the rest, if they plan to stay here and lead such selfish lives, they're going to find themselves in a bad way.

The only person I've bartered things with in this building is Mercedes, and I didn't make the trade directly because we aren't on friendly terms. She sent Lala to see if I'd take 1 pound of rice for two cans of milk and I said no, that wasn't enough, I wanted 2 pounds for three cans of milk. Mercedes didn't need rice—they don't eat much of it and always have some left over. Or maybe she gets more than the ration. God only knows. Then another time, she and I exchanged six cans of milk for 4 pounds of rice, and once nine cans for 6 pounds of rice.

After that, I never traded with her again. Now I only exchange with one woman, who gives me one for one: she needs milk more than rice, so I let her have four cans of condensed milk for 4 pounds of rice. One for one, that's what I call a fair exchange. With Mercedes I was the loser, but I did it because everybody exchanged at that rate at first.

When Lala needs something, I let her have it, and when I need something, she gives it to me, but that's not an exchange. I very rarely bother Sara; mostly Lala and I ask each other for whatever we're short of and don't worry about paying it back. Between Lala and me, when we say "lend me" we mean "give me." Most of the time it's a gift, except for coffee. That we pay back when it comes to the store. Why should we pay back things as long as the other one has plenty?

Most of the time Lala asks for eggs or sugar, and now and then milk. She often lends me rice or gives me lard. Lala and I have done other favors for each other numerous times. If I can bring her stuff from the grocery store, I'll do it, and if she can bring mine, she will.

When Ana Teresa and the rest of those people were living in the middle apartment, they were forever asking for things. When it wasn't salt they wanted, it was sugar, when it wasn't lard, it was alcohol for their stove. They asked Lala for all sorts of stuff too. I don't know whether it was Sara or Ana Teresa who did it, because they all lived together and they'd send one of the kids. I think they simply have the bad habit of asking for things, because it isn't possible that they could have run out of this or that so often. But we got along all right with them . . . it's better to be on friendly terms with one's neighbors.

It seems there have been a lot of quarrels in this building. Sara and Ana Teresa fought with Mercedes all the time. She'd call them pigs and say they threw dirty water and garbage down into her place, then they'd say two or three things to her, but when it was over they'd be on speaking terms again. Me, I'm not like that. From the very first day I saw what Mercedes was like, so I never made friends with her.

The lieutenant's wife, Justa, fought with everybody in the apartment building. Right now Mercedes is the only person she's on good terms with. When I was on friendly terms with Justa, she and I did a few small favors for each other. For instance, if I brewed coffee in the afternoon, I'd send her some and she'd send me some in the morning. And our kids would run errands for both of us. She told me I was welcome to keep meat in her refrigerator, but I only used it once. After about a month I noticed that she'd kind of draw back when I spoke to her, but I didn't know what was wrong until somebody told me it was some kind of mix-up over something I said about Sara and Inés living in the garage.

One day Justa's little girl hit our daughter Andrea, so Domingo and I went there and we had a real set-to. I said to her, "My goodness, when somebody tells you I've said something to offend you, come ask me about it instead of sulking. I don't enjoy talking to people who act as if they wish I wasn't there. No indeed, that won't do. If only you'd told me what was bothering you."

I've got my own policy for dealing with people. If I quarrel with someone, they're dead for me. So I said to myself, "Very well then, Justa's dead as far as I'm concerned." After that, I simply had nothing to do with her. That's the way I am.

Right after the exchange went through, Sara and Justa were chummy as all get-out and Sara hardly gave me the time of day. Even though she'd known me first and I'd done her plenty of favors, she'd hardly speak to me because she wanted to be friends with Justa. Sara told me she was afraid Justa would think she was gossiping with me about her because Justa and I weren't speaking. When Sara and I met, we'd say hello and that was it. As for me, my conscience was clear so why should I care?

Then one day Sara's daughter Concha showed up at my place and I said, "Eh, what miracle brings you here?"

"*Ay,*" she says, "that Justa is so neurotic, she won't speak to us and she's been saying things and. . . ."

"Don't come to me with gossip," says I. "Up to now you people have been going to her place and you never thought of dropping in to call on me. You wouldn't even speak to me. Well, you're welcome to come here whenever you please but I won't listen to any gossip, get it? I don't care if she kicked you out or what she did." Justa was standing right there at the time and must have heard me say those things.

After that, Concha and all her folks went at Justa tooth and nail. Sara would bang on Justa's door and say they were going to throw her down and roll her on the ground and do this and that and the other thing. I don't know what set them against her.

I never had any quarrel with Sara—we always got along fine. When we moved here, her little girl Faustina wasn't even a year old. At that time Sara was separated from Eduardo so the child ate with us and everything. She'd stay at our place all day long. Every day Sara would run upstairs looking for her, and there she'd be, sitting in front of our locked door, waiting for us to open it. Why, she even called Domingo *papá!* She's a spoiled brat now, but when she was tiny she was real sweet and affectionate with us.

People here act real friendly to your face but then they go and talk behind your back. That's not what I call being a friend. A friend is someone who'll stick out his neck for you any time. Out in Limón—that's where my real friends are, friends who've known my mother and all—friendship is a sacrament. That's the way we were brought up.

Lala is one of my few friends in Havana. I have a lot of acquaintances here, but few friends. When my laundry job got to be too much for me to do alone, I asked Lala if she wanted to go shares with me. "Sure I'll do it, as long as Armando doesn't find out," she said. And she's been helping me ever since.

A good friend of mine used to live next door in the apartment that Horacio has now. She and her folks were good people. As soon as we moved here they told me I was free to keep my family's meat in their refrigerator. She said I shouldn't be ashamed to ask for anything I needed. "We're neighbors," she said, "and that's what neighbors are for, to help each other." We got to be friends right away and it was as if we'd been friends all our lives! They've even come to visit me since they moved away, and they scold me for not going over to see them.

They had to move because Horacio wanted their apartment. He made them give it to him. That's the way things work here. When somebody is stronger than you they'll snatch your very food away and give it to someone else. Horacio fought tooth and nail for that place so they gave it to him and his wife. That apartment had been left to my friend five years ago by the people who lived there before her. She only paid 22 *pesos* a month rent on it. They moved her to Regla, where the plumbing leaked at night and made puddles all over. It was a disaster! Now she's living on Milagros Street in Havana.

I used to give lots of parties, but for the past year it's been difficult to get liquor and beer, so I've just given up. The time I gave a party for our daughter Bárbara's baptism, I invited everybody in the building except

Mercedes. Domingo went to Justa's house to invite her little girls, but Justa refused, saying they didn't have the right clothes and I don't know what all. I guess she thought it was going to be something real fancy. I invited Sara, too. I've got photos of her and everybody else who was at that party. Mercedes never said anything about not being invited.

Mercedes gives parties, but she doesn't invite everybody in the building the way I do. She only invites Lala and Justa. She never, never invited Sara. She only likes to have rich people in her house, not anybody who's poor.

Her husband, Juan, is something else again. He calls the kids over to play and to watch TV in his apartment. When they gave a party for their little boy, Juan invited Sara's kids. I don't know whether Sara let them go. She might accept an invitation from him, but not from Mercedes. Sara herself didn't go and neither did Justa. Justa never lets her kids go either, I don't know why.

I think Justa gave a party once, a fifteenth birthday party for one of her daughters. I heard a lot of noise and people drinking but I'm not sure it was a party. Nobody from the building was invited except Mercedes's daughter. Justa doesn't get along with people so she doesn't invite them. Lala has given birthday parties too, but she generally invites everybody.

Domingo Labrada:

I felt that the move to Miramar was like starting life anew, but it's turned out just the opposite. I just don't feel satisfied about my neighbors here. Listen, there's nothing worse in this life than to know that people are looking askance at you. I'm country born and bred and I guess people like me are always wary of neighbors in the city. In the country it's the custom to walk right into a neighbor's house and then you can't get away, that's how hospitable the people are. They insist, "Stay and have supper with us," or "Don't go home yet, they won't expect you so early," and so on.

When I first came to Havana I lived in Regla, and the people there were more like country people. You were safe making friends because there's more harmony among the people there. But here in Miramar that warmth between neighbors doesn't exist. People don't get along as well or visit each other as often. I really miss that country friendliness. It's something I feel deep in my soul.

My wife and I both like to socialize, but from the very first day we moved to this apartment we've had trouble with the neighbors. The first neighbor I talked to after moving in was Mercedes. I asked her if she knew where the gas tank for our apartment was. She didn't bother to answer. Well, the fact is she simply didn't want to tell me. The gas tank is right next to her door and she'd been standing beside it all the time I was talking to her.

"It's unbelievable," I thought, "that at this late date, with all the progress made by the Revolution, there should still be people like that!" Mercedes has the same attitude people had in the old times. She feels she deserves the best of everything and that everybody has to kowtow to her.

I said to my wife that day, "The woman downstairs is a racist. It seems she doesn't like the idea of our moving here. We'll have to measure our words whenever we speak to that lady, to avoid quarrels."

Well, that's how everything started. Since then, I never talk to her unless it's absolutely necessary, and when I do, I watch my words. No matter what you talk about with that woman, she manages to get rude about it—always! You try to talk politely with her and her answer is a kick in the ass.

The grounds of this building belong to Mercedes and Juan, but we pay the gardener to cut the grass in front of our garage. The day my brother Dámaso and his wife moved into the garage, Mercedes told the gardener she was no longer responsible for that bit of lawn. While Dámaso lived there, Vita paid the gardener, but after they left, Leticia arranged for the gardener to do that piece.

Since Mercedes and Juan fenced in the backyard I have to ask her to open the gate every time the man from the gas company comes with a delivery. If she wanted to put an iron grille around the place to keep the kids out, she should have had a latch put on the gate and left it unlocked so that any adult who needed to could get in.

One time I'd been without gas three days, and it so happened that when the gas man arrived, Mercedes had gone out, leaving the gate padlocked. The gas man put his key in the lock and it sprang open, but when I told Mercedes about it later she got mad. So I said, "Look, when Juan comes home, I'm going to ask him to take that fence down and move it back."

"You're fresh, that's what!" she answered. "Fresh and uppity!"

I turned around, *bam, bam,* and left without another word.

There's a drainpipe in my porch which empties water down into Mercedes's place, so I put a stopper in it. Never since I moved here have I emptied water down on her place. I know the quarrels she had with Sara and Ana Teresa about that, so I'm careful to avoid it. I take the trouble to sweep the water up in a dustpan and empty it into a bucket. I hate to argue, especially with women.

I've never heard Mercedes say one word or do one thing that would show her to be a revolutionary. But the only way to know how good a revolutionary someone is is to belong to the same associations they do. Mercedes belongs to the Federation of Cuban Women,[52] but that in itself doesn't prove a thing. I, being a man, can't belong, and only another

---

52. Mercedes Millán was not a member of the Federation.

Federation member could tell whether or not Mercedes is a revolutionary.

Her husband, Juan Carlos, is a real decent guy. He really knows how to treat people. I don't know him any too well, but when we meet, we say, "Hello, how are you?" I can talk with him better than I can with his wife. Yet recently when I was standing out in the yard—I'd let my chickens out to peck in the grass for a while—he didn't say hello to me or I to him.

I know that Juan has an important job but I'm not sure what he does. I don't know whether he's a Party member or whether he's even a revolutionary. How can I know anything about a neighbor's life when we don't see much of each other and our wives aren't friends? Juan belongs to the CDR just as I do, but anybody can join that. I might be a *gusano*, but nobody could say no to me if I wanted to join the CDR.

I used to be head of Vigilance for the CDR and it was my duty to assign the turns for standing guard on this block. One night when I had assigned a turn to Juan, he failed to show up to relieve me. One just can't judge anybody else's revolutionary attitudes—no, not unless you know that person's life thoroughly.

Juan and Mercedes have delusions of grandeur. They used to have servants and all that—not that I ever saw them, but I heard that they had a maid who quit because she couldn't put up with Mercedes's ways. Mercedes won't even let her kids play with ours. When her kids do go out to play, she starts yelling at them because she's afraid they might lose one of those toys the other kids don't have. The other day she made a scene about a marble her little boy had lost. Imagine making a fuss about such a trifle!

Bernardo and his wife, Ana Teresa, lived like country people who'd never before had a house with certain comforts. That's only natural, but they were clean. They had a pile of kids running around naked and so on, but as for the rest, I have no reason to complain. The only defect those people had was that they drank quantities of liquor. Ana Teresa's *papá,* who lived in the garage, drank floods.

Relatives quarrel, there's nothing new about that, and I'd be lying if I said there was never a yes or a no among Nardo's relatives. They simply couldn't live together in peace because they didn't adapt to one another as family members should.

But I have no complaints about the way either Ana Teresa or Sara treated me. They were both nice people, very friendly and cordial. Leticia got along with Ana Teresa as long as she lived here, and she still gets along with Sara. I also got along with Eduardo and Bernardo. We've met them at parties a number of times and had drinks together. In fact, Nardo's relatives are the only people in the building we've been together with socially.

Eduardo is not a Party member but he was in the armed forces just like me, that much I know. He works as a night watchman I think. He also does volunteer productive work and works in the sugar harvest, but I don't know how integrated he is.

I know Lala's husband, Armando, just well enough to say, "Hello, how are you?" but we don't stop to chat. I've always tried to win my neighbors over gradually, but Armando is not what you'd call a sociable fellow. Being sociable with your neighbors is one of the best ways of winning them over, but with Armando it won't work. He's the kind who doesn't enjoy parties or anything like that. When we have a party, Lala comes in one door and goes out the other because she can't push Armando into coming.

I know a lot about Armando's revolutionary attitudes because Leticia and I see a lot of Lala. While she washes clothes here, she chats with Leticia and I hear their conversations. Armando used to be with INIT,[53] I believe, but I don't know where that is. And he's supposed to be a Party member, but I can't tell for sure because not even Lala has mentioned it to us. Armando is integrated all right. I know that he's gone out to do productive work, to harvest sugar cane, and that he's now working on the Isle of Pines.

Soon after they moved here, the lieutenant's wife, Justa, and my wife became great friends. I warned Leticia that the friendship wasn't good for her. "If somebody who's just moved in keeps after you all the time, you should stop and try to analyze things because that's being a bit too forward. A friendship needs time to develop."

Well, I was right. It turned out just as I said. Leticia was neglecting her friendships with other neighbors because of Justa, and that's just what Justa was trying to make her do. When Justa came to visit, she'd walk all through our apartment, but I've never set foot inside Justa's home. She acted very fond of Leticia—it was "negra" this and "negra" that. As for Leticia, whenever she cooked anything extra nice, she'd send a dish of it to Justa.

Then Justa made friends with Mercedes and right away she started gossiping about us. One day when Leticia was talking to Mercedes, objecting to something or other, Justa plunged into the discussion defending Mercedes. Justa decided to change friends, that's all. After that, she and my wife weren't on speaking terms. Well, that's their business and I'm not interested in women's quarrels, but one day, as I went upstairs, Justa was standing by the door. I said hello to her and she slammed the door in my face. Now whenever I go out and see her standing in the stairway, I return to my apartment and go out the back way. I do that because I was raised very differently. I can't pass by someone I'm acquainted with without saying hello.

Let me tell you something—if a man's wife insults me, I don't feel that her husband has automatically insulted me too. I swallow the insult like a

---

53. *Instituto Nacional de la Industria Turística* (National Institute of the Tourist Industry).

man and think, "That woman is a dirty bitch." But I keep my mouth shut, and when I chance to meet the husband, I say hello to him as if nothing had happened. Well, that's what I've done in this case.

I say hello to the lieutenant but I've never made friends with him. I don't spring on a new neighbor with my tongue hanging out, all eager to make friends with him. One sees more and more of people and gradually gets to know them and then decides whether to be friends or not. I don't know a thing about the lieutenant's life or about his attitude toward the Revolution or anything else. He must be integrated because he's in the armed forces, but I don't know whether he's in the Party. He used to work in a police patrol, but I don't know what kind of work he's doing now.

In this whole building there are only three families you can rely on in case of need: Armando's, Eduardo's, and mine. I don't mean that we've gone out to give aid to anybody in particular, but we've gone out to work on the street and so on. The Sunday before last we cleaned this part of the block and everybody helped except Mercedes and the lieutenant's family. Juan Carlos came out for a while, but only looked on while we worked. He did help us fix the water faucet in front of the building, but that was for his own convenience.

About my other neighbors on this block there's very little I can say. I know no more than what I can see from my window or find out from the little contact I have with them. I did get to know Horacio pretty well after he moved next door to no. 409. He'd been living in the Frozen Zone and working with Aldita before that, but he and Aldita quarreled and she wanted him to move away.

Horacio is in the habit of boasting about his role in the Revolution; he manages to bring that subject up no matter what you're talking about. Well, frankly, I'm an open-minded guy willing to admire others and proud of knowing somebody who's done something for the Revolution. But Horacio would boast to my *papá* and he'd simply steal away the old man's attention.

One day he began with his usual refrain, "I, as a builder of the Revolution. . . ." I broke in and told him that was enough "builder-of-the-Revolution" business. I said, "You keep harping on that, but let me tell you, I feel I'm as much a builder of the Revolution as you are. I abandoned my family and went to Algeria, leaving my daughter when she was a babe in arms. I went to a foreign country to risk my life for my fatherland, and yet I don't go around boasting about it. I never mention it to anybody because the past no longer exists. You were a builder of the Revolution. All right. Fine. Now forget it, and give the rest of us a chance to forget it too."

Horacio got mad over that. We had an argument and for a few days he wouldn't speak to me, but I never brought up the subject again.

Besides Horacio, I've also visited Sonia's family, in no. 407, and Serafina, who lives in the garage belonging to that house. When I visit Sonia, I always sit on the porch. I've never been inside the house. I have on occasion offered to help Sonia's son, just as he's offered to help me, but neither of us has ever accepted the other's offer.

One day he was driving a small car when somebody hit it. I knew he didn't have a driver's license, so I went over at once and offered to say that I was driving the car at the time of the accident. "No no, don't worry. It's all settled," he told me. He'd had a talk with the driver of the other car. The police weren't called so there was no problem.

I went to no. 416[54] once, about two years ago when an official from the police came out here looking for a Committee member to go check on the place. I don't know why they made the search, but I was the one chosen to go. The only thing they found there was a trunk full of letters dating from 1928 to the present, several transistor radios, and some boat motors that belonged to the man's son, who's in the United States now. He was very fond of sailing and used to have several motorboats. At the time of the Triumph he'd turned his motorboats over to the government and had given them notice that he didn't need the motors, but nobody ever came around for them. The only thing the police took were the letters. The search didn't get those people into any trouble—they're still living there. I talked to the man afterward to explain that I'd gone simply to represent the Committee. He wasn't annoyed at me, but he isn't my friend either.

I've spoken to the man who lives in no. 408.[55] I even asked to borrow his monkey wrench to repair the water pump. He seems to be a swell guy from the way he acted, but I've never visited there. I don't even know what kind of work he does.

I can't say that my neighbors in this block or this building are my friends, or even my acquaintances for that matter. Somebody isn't an acquaintance just because we exchange greetings and live on the same block or in the same building. It takes a lot of socializing for two people to really get acquainted with one another. To us Cubans, the word "friend" carries a lot of meaning. If you say that somebody is your friend, you're saying that he's very, very close to you, almost closer than a brother.

On the first birthday of my youngest child, Ana Luz, we gave a swell party and invited all the neighbors on this block, every single one of them except for Mercedes and her family. I went personally to Justa's house to invite her family to the party, but she wouldn't even come to the door. I talked to the eldest daughter and told her to ask her mother if the kids at least could come. But Justa still refused, so I gave up and went

54. The home of Máximo Abay.
55. José Sabina.

home. About a month later, one of Justa's daughters had a birthday party and they sent the eldest girl to borrow our records. If they'd come to my house to invite me to the party I would have gone out of courtesy, even if only long enough to say, "I have to rush off." My temperament, my breeding, or whatever you call it, wouldn't allow me to snub them. But we didn't receive an invitation and I didn't loan them my records.

All the other kids on the block came to our party, including the kids of the Chilean family who lived next door and the Arab children who lived on the other side. Serafina came with her children and so did Lala. Armando was like a flying fish, staying just for a minute. He doesn't like parties, but he did us the courtesy of coming. Eduardo came later on, at night, because that's when we started serving drinks for the grownups. Besides our neighbors and relatives, we had my comrades at work and their families. There were as many guests as there are trees in the forest.

I was working full-time then and was able to get six crates of beer from my work center. I also got some from Matanzas. I had a good connection in the beer warehouse there, and I'd been buying some whenever I could and saving it up for a long time. I'd accumulated five crates of beer that way. Altogether I had about thirteen crates, plus four or five crates of soft drinks. At that time, the Minimax had a supply of Casals brandy; I mixed it with other stuff that made it taste like anise liqueur. I made liters and liters of it. We had plenty of drinks all right. I still had about six crates of beer left after the party.

I ordered a special cake. It was a wedding cake, longer than the table, simply enormous. At that time the cake problem wasn't as bad as it is now. You could still go into a confectioner's shop and order one prepared as you liked.

You need a permit to give a party, so I asked the military for a permit and it was good up to midnight. I got another permit from civil authorities that was good until 4:00 in the morning. I had to go to the Ministry of Education for that because this is a scholarship zone and the party was to run from Saturday afternoon until the early hours of Sunday. Saturday and Sunday are days of rest for scholarship students, you see. That's why I took the trouble of getting an additional permit and taking it to the military police to have it stamped.

In spite of all my trouble, two patrol cars parked in front of our building at 10:00 P.M. The police came up to the door and asked to see my permit. When I showed it to them, they said everything was all right. At 11:30 the police were back, but they were different men. When they came to the door and asked for my permit again, I said, "Tell me, chico, is there any trouble here in Havana at this moment?"

"Why do you ask?"

"Because here you are, asking for my permit, when two other patrol cars just left. The policemen even had a couple of beers with us."

"Well, *chico,* the problem is that the phone over at the station keeps ringing and every time it's one or another of your neighbors complaining about this party. I bet there's one of them on the phone complaining right this minute."

That's the trouble with having neighbors you don't get along with. It was Mercedes who was phoning again and again, insisting that the police stop our party. I know because the police told me, and besides, they were the only ones who had a phone at that time.

Well, the party went on. I'd borrowed an enormous record player from a friend and we kept it going good and loud all the time. The record player had an amplifier and a girl was singing along with the music. The house was full. A little after midnight, no less than five patrol cars drove up and parked in front of the building. They planned to arrest every single guest at the party besides me and my family.

They asked for my permit again. They told me that it was only good until midnight and that it was already 12:45. Then I went inside and came out with the other permit. I'd made sure to have all the right permits I needed because I knew damn well what was going to happen. I knew practically down to the last detail what trouble I was due for, so I took every precaution to be within the law.

The last group of policemen left just as the others had done. They realized somebody had been playing games with them, having them send patrol cars out again and again when there was nothing they could do about it. I invited the policemen in for a drink, but they refused, though a few of the officers accepted soft drinks. The one who was heading the group asked me to turn down the record player when it got to be 1:30, and I assured him I would. I told him, "I've already thought of that myself because it's a bit loud. But it's early yet and everybody is still up, you hear?"

And so they were. The scholarship students were all outside. I'd invited the woman in charge of them to come up to the party, but she refused because she said if she went, the girls would want to come too.

About 3:00 in the morning I turned off the record and four of us guys sat around competing with each other to see who could drink the most. The last of the guests left about 5:00 in the morning. That's the kind of party I like.

Frankly speaking, there's been a tremendous change in this block since the time I moved here. In some ways it's changed for the better, in other ways for the worse. The trees look exactly as they did when we moved here, although a year ago the electric-light company did cut down some that interfered with the electric wires. There's a defect in the street lighting in this area—some days it works and some days it doesn't. Sometimes the streetlights are off until midnight, and then they'll light up all of a sudden. Then there's also the problem of the kids who often break the light bulbs.

Many of the neighbors we had here in Miramar when we arrived in 1964 have moved away, and their places have been taken by foreigners and scholarship students. I've always respected scholarship students more than other students because they are, as we say in the Army, subjected to a chief, and that's something I like. They have discipline. It doesn't bother me to see the students marching down the street like an infantry platoon. On the contrary, I like it.

Even though I absolutely accept the scholarship students, I've never established any kind of relationship with them because that's something that could bring problems. If those kids start feeling too much at home in our yard, in no time at all they'll wander into the building and get into people's apartments. Then, when somebody loses a ring or something, who will they blame? One of the scholarship girls, of course. That's one of the reasons I don't want my kids to get chummy with those kids, because what *one* does, *all* pay for.

Those scholarship students live like soldiers down to the last detail, even to snatching other people's things. There's a kid there, Rigoberto, who comes to visit us and takes things without asking for them. He walks in without knocking or ringing the doorbell and opens the oven and helps himself to a hunk of bread. The other day he ate some canned fruit. Why, once he went to Sara's house and ate their dinner! He filled a plate from the pot on the stove and ate it all. Leticia is sorry for him and keeps giving him things. I told her to quit spoiling him or he'll be acting here the way he acts at Sara's. But she only laughs.

I said to Rigoberto, "I don't want to see you in my house ever again!" But he kept coming all the same. It's a problem for me. I've gotten to be my age without anybody ever having accused me of stealing so much as a safety pin, and I want my kids to be able to say the same thing when they grow up. So whenever I see them at the student house across the street, I call them home.

Before the scholarship students were moved into no. 412 it was occupied by the wives of political prisoners from the country who were jailed for taking part in the uprisings in Camaguey, Santa Clara, and so on. There were over a thousand of them here, all of them poor country women. The government decided that since it locked up the men of those families, it should support their wives, not just because they'd starve to death if they were left alone in the country, but as an example to the people of Cuba. Those women's husbands, every single one of them, had committed a political lapse. They were caught trying to block the way of the Revolution, and yet the government gathered up all their families and supported them during the whole time the men were in jail. Not only that—they even gave the men passes to go visit their wives. If it had been one of the governments we used to have, the prisoners would have been roughed up or killed, if need be, and their families abandoned.

The women in no. 412 used to come over to talk with us and we made friends with one of them. According to what she told us, she was very well treated and had no problems in that place. Her only complaint was that she hadn't been given a place to live in the same section of the country where she'd lived before.

When the women were living here, they spent their time sitting outside and the place was alive with their noise. Gosh, the block was gayer then. Nowadays, the neighbors keep more to themselves.

RICARDO HERNÁNDEZ (the lieutenant):

I haven't had much opportunity to get acquainted with my neighbors because I'm hardly ever at home. I've just come back from over a year's work in the country. I know the foreigners on the block by sight and we say hello when we meet, but I have few friends here. For me a friend is something like a brother. Of course, we Cubans should all be like brothers to one another but there are certain things that make friendship difficult.

On September 28, CDR day, I visited the men in the neighborhood who are in the military, but it was the first time. I don't even know who the CDR president is for this block, though I do know some of the members. I've gone to only three of the meetings—I didn't have the time to go to others and I haven't been given any post because I wouldn't be able to carry out its functions.

I've also visited both Horacio and Juan. Horacio fought with me in the Sierra and I consider him a friend. We weren't in the same camp, but we'd run into each other every now and then.

I don't know whether Juan and Mercedes are revolutionaries. Whatever they may be, they're a whole lot quieter than the rest of them. Juan is a very obliging comrade, very obliging indeed. Whenever anybody here is sick, he takes my wife in his car to get medicine or whatever is needed. But his wife still has traces of past mentality. She gives herself away all the time without realizing it. They had money before, you see, and could live as they liked, openly. Now she has to adjust to a situation where everybody must share equally, so she can't have all the things she had before. Sometimes she forgets and lets some remark slip which shows a real revolutionary that she still has ties with the past. She'll have to try to eliminate these attitudes. Whenever I go to her house, I take every opportunity to speak about the Revolution and communism.

The last time I went there was on my birthday. Since Juan and I always drink together, I went down and he helped me slaughter a pig in the morning. Then we drank beer at his apartment before I went back up to my place. That night we had a party and finished off the whole pig and plenty of beer. Juan's family, Horacio's family, and the new couple who just moved in next door all came to my party.

That day Juan's wife said, "You're certainly splurging on beer." "Yes," said I. "One can always get beer as long as one pays the regular price for it. I went down to OFICODA and explained that it was my birthday and I got several cartons at 40 *centavos* a bottle. Next time I want to get some, though, I'll have to pay the price all Cubans pay for it—60 *centavos*."

The thing is, Juan's wife plans to throw a party and she wants to get the beer at 40 *centavos* each. Well, she can't, that's all, except to celebrate a birthday or some other special occasion. If you go to a Social Circle or anyplace else, you must pay 60 *centavos* for beer just like everybody.

We usually have parties at home to celebrate my birthday or the birthday of one of the girls. For those we get a cake, soft drinks, and so on. And usually we have an end-of-the-year party but this year that won't come until July.[56] I'm going to celebrate the end of this year at the sugar *central* where we're cutting cane. When we sew up that last bag of sugar, we're going to celebrate the triumph. After that, we can have as many fiestas as we like!

JUSTA DÍAZ:

I like to get along with my neighbors. I'm very tolerant of them, and let me tell you, living on the second floor as we do, we have to put up with a lot more than any of the others. At first I was on good terms with Leticia, Lala, and Mercedes. We always said "Good day" when we met, and "How are you?" Then Leticia and I became friends. My trouble with her and with Lala came about because I'm a very frank and truthful person.

Leticia and Inés, a blond girl who lived at Sara's, were very close. Inés came to me one day and said, "Leticia told me you said I'm going around with Conrado, a delinquent, an escaped convict." And I, innocent as a babe unborn!

"Wait a minute, I'm not that kind," I told her. I asked Leticia about it right in front of Inés.

"Who, me?" Leticia protested. "May all my children drop dead!"

"Look here," I told Leticia, "I've only lived in this place about a month, but you might as well know that I'll face up to you or anybody else if I have to. I'd just as soon slap someone's face if I must. You've no call to get me mixed up in such goings-on when I've never in my life said anything about Inés. I don't even know all the people involved." Then Leticia began to cry and tremble and I said to her, "Listen, *chica*, if this is a sample of your friendship, I want none of it. You acted so friendly with

---

56. Celebration of the year's end was officially deferred to July, 1970, when it was expected the sugar-cane harvest would end in the achievement of the 10-million-ton goal.

Inés and went everywhere with her and now look!" That's when I stopped being friends with Leticia.

Sara and I used to get along very well. It was her daughter Concha who made trouble between us. After Concha came, Sara and I both kind of withdrew, but before that, they used to be in and out of my house all the time. They practically lived here. I shared with them the way families in the country do. Sara's a poor soul, but in my opinion she's better than that whole bunch. All she can do is try and preserve peace and quiet.

I haven't had quarrels or conflicts of any kind with any of my other neighbors. All I did was call to order a couple of loose-tongued gossips, including Lala. I didn't make a scandal. Afterward I was on speaking terms with Lala again because I saw that she wanted to talk with me. I took good care not to let her involve me in anything, though. Whenever she started talking about somebody, I'd break in with, "I must go away now, I have so many things to do!" After a while she seemed to catch on.

When I first moved here, it was agreed that Leticia, Lala, and I would pay 1 *peso* each to the gardener to take care of the bit of lawn in front of the garage. The part in front of the buildings belongs to Mercedes alone - and she pays for that and also for part of the back. Rightly, though, the whole front yard belongs to all the tenants in the building, and it's our duty to keep the whole place neat. I've heard certain people yaketty-yakking about it but all I know is that I only paid 1 *peso* twice because nobody ever came around to bother me about it again.

"Oh well, it's their funeral," I said. Then I stopped to think, "Why should I spend my money anyway on that tiny patch of ground? What's the point when Mercedes, Lala, and Leticia are already paying?" It isn't the money, you understand. I wouldn't mind paying, but he's their gardener, not mine, because they were all living in this building for years and years before I moved in. So it's up to them to pay him for keeping the yard neat. It always looks a mess.

Sometimes we have problems with the water supply here, I don't know why. Lala claims that my water consumption doesn't affect the flow of water in her house but it does; that's a proven fact, even the Ministry says so. If Lala and I happen to open our faucets at the same time, we both get a smaller stream of water. The same thing is true for Leticia's apartment. If Lala should decide to let all her faucets run until the tank is empty, we wouldn't get a drop of water.

If someone turns off the master tap, and then I turn on my pump without knowing the water's been cut off, it burns out the pump's motor, as happened to me once. Whoever decides to cut off the water should tell the neighbors beforehand. Those motors belong to the state, and if one breaks down and the state has no parts to repair it, we're screwed up. Then everybody in the whole building has to fetch and carry water for several days until the state comes and installs a new motor.

Our water tank is on top of the building, but Mercedes's is inside our apartment. There are days when Mercedes's tank overflows into my bathroom and bedrooms. That's bad planning and it's the builder's fault. Juan should look into the problem because that waste of water hurts them, and it sets my nerves on edge. Sometimes I fix it up with a bit of wire, but then I forget to take it off until I hear Mercedes complain, "*Ay,* I'm all out of water!" Sometimes I'm even embarrassed to think that maybe she believes I put that wire there so she won't have any water. I tell her, "Oh, I put that wire there so the tank won't overflow in my house." Imagine what happens when the people who live in these two apartments don't get along!

Whenever a problem arises about the construction of a house or the plumbing or anything, you can go check with Urban Reform because they keep all the blueprints on file. But people are reluctant because it's embarrassing to ask for the blueprints. And getting something fixed takes a number of days and *pesos.* For instance, my bathroom doesn't have a drain in the floor, so when the water tank overflows, or when I clean the floors, I have to sweep the water out through the terrace because there's no other outlet. Embarrassing as it is to admit, I only clean the bathroom floor once a week, and do you know where I have to throw the dirty water? Right into Mercedes's patio. How else could I get it out? Still, it should be done considerately, after asking permission from the people below. Mercedes says, "Don't be embarrassed about it; I know it's because of the way this place is built. All these houses are the same that way."

One day Mercedes called me over and said, "Look, I don't object to your throwing out the water, please understand, but this is full of pigeon shit and feathers." Was I embarrassed! I understand all right. Leticia is the one with pigeons, and she throws her dirty water on my clean wash. But I arm myself with patience, gather up all the clothes, and wash them out again.

I try not to get involved in arguments or quarrels, but there are times when I feel like telling Leticia a few home truths because she drives me clean out of my mind. Yet in spite of everything, I wouldn't for the world inform on her for keeping chickens and pigeons. The other day a man from Public Health came around asking and I told him, "I know nothing about it. I spend my life inside my house." I wouldn't have had the courage to speak up. I just couldn't do it, even though somebody went and informed about four rabbits I was keeping here. I don't know who did it because everyone tells on one another. We always cleaned up the rabbit shit on the terrace. They didn't stink or anything, but there was really no room for them anyway.

After the man from Public Health left, Genoveva said, "So what are you going to do if they come back and see all the chickens and pigeons those people keep in the garage?"

"I'll just tell him that everybody lives in his own house and every man is king in his home. What business is it of mine anyway?"

Someone from Public Health also came here once to tell us we couldn't hang clothes on the front porch because that was a habit of the past. "It looks very ugly," the man said. "This is the Frozen Zone and we're already progressing beyond that." It's against the law so I've never in my life hung clothes there, though it's a nice sunny place, and when it rains the porch stays dry. Sara still hangs her clothes out in front of the garage because she has no other place.

One day the Ministry of Public Health took her wash down and piled it up in front of Mercedes's door thinking it was hers. When Mercedes came home, I had to laugh! But they really didn't have a right to come in here without our leave. The place doesn't belong to them. If I go into someone's courtyard to pick a flower, I have to knock first. I couldn't barge in simply because I felt like it, could I? No indeed. What kind of manners would that be?

Another problem we have here is the electricity. Sometimes when Mercedes's light goes off, Lala's does too. Or if the electricity is turned off upstairs or in the garage, then mine goes. Who can understand such a thing when every apartment has its own meter?

And the ironing is another thing. Now I won't say that it's Lala's fault, because she had a meter put in for her place, independent of the others. She irons just the way we all do, yet her electricity bill is only 1.30 *pesos* a month, and she even has a radio. We examined the accounts for this building, all of us together, to try and figure it all out. I've paid 15 *pesos* for the last four months. The man from the electric-light company told me I couldn't possibly use as much electricity as my meter showed. We were charged for something owing from way back by the people who used to live here before us, for something in advance, and I don't know what all. Nobody can make head or tail of those accounts, but they all got paid by none other than Ricardo Hernández, because the meter was put in his name.

Mercedes has an air-conditioner, a TV, a frigidaire, a freezer, an electric iron, and an electric hot plate, which she uses when she runs out of gas. Sometimes she borrows her mother's electric blender for seven or eight days. And with all that consumption of electricity, she says that never in her life did she pay more than 13 *pesos!* And it's true because the company checked up on her canceled bills. In hot weather Mercedes keeps her air-conditioner on day and night, the rest of the time she keeps it on from 8:00 A.M. Just think how much electricity an air-conditioner uses up!

Just once Leticia had to pay 11 *pesos* for electricity and she was furious. And here am I, paying over 11 *pesos* without knowing why. This time when I paid my bill, I said to the man, "Look here, *chico*, I'm tired of living only to pay light and rent. My husband's salary isn't that big."

I've been taking in laundry for the state for a long time and never have I done as little ironing as I'm doing right now. I used to wash for six or seven soldiers and I'd get thirty or forty white shirts and thirty or forty pairs of pants at one time—not nine like now. And besides all that ironing, I had a radio and a refrigerator, yet I only had to pay 5 or 6 *pesos* for electricity.

The company still hasn't solved my problem. They changed my meter right away but the new meter marks the same as the old. So now they say the whole thing has to be torn up. Every day that passes I understand this business less.

You see, this whole building was made for one large, rich family to live in. Different families, I mean, upstairs and downstairs, but all close relatives. It isn't the state's fault that this house was built this way and it isn't our fault.

There used to be some people living around here who didn't agree with the new government. There were two sisters, little old ladies who were very Catholic. They were respectable, well-bred people, and they didn't like fuss or quarrels or loud noises. I don't know how they decided who to make friends with—maybe it was all a matter of money—but the fact is, they were right friendly with those colored people upstairs. They even invited them to their parties. They got along with Mercedes, Lala, and Horacio, too. As for me, when we chanced to meet somewhere they always greeted me politely. But I never saw them visit anybody outside their own class.

I used to enjoy seeing the sisters dressed up every afternoon and sitting on their little porch with their fans fluttering in their hands, their prayer books and rosaries always by them. After they had read for a while they'd say their beads, then they'd go back in and you'd see no more of them till the following day.

They left in February, 1968. I guess they felt lonely, because I often heard them talk about how they had no relatives here, except that one had a son who's a priest. Mercedes told me there was also a daughter who lived up North. I don't know whether they left because of the Revolution or what, but I heard they didn't want to die alone.

I'll say this for them—they helped others. I often saw them call Sara's children over to give them food and ice. One day they called Ana Teresa and asked her to bring her little girls over. They took the children's measurements and made dresses for them before they left. I often saw them sewing for people. So it seems they didn't go North because they were against the Revolution. Those who knew them say they left quantities of food behind when they went, so it's clear that they weren't poverty-stricken either. They got along well with everybody. Anyone could see they were kind, decent old souls.

A single lady and her maid used to live next door in no. 413. They left the year we moved here, so I don't know much about them. The señorita had her TV inside the house, but she used to sit on the porch, right outside the door, to watch the programs. There was a lovely dog there, very plump and pretty. I love animals so I often used to stand there watching him. I'd say to Hernández, "She's going to think I'm spying on her." But it was that lovely roly-poly dog I was watching. Sometimes I exchanged greetings with the old lady, and I was quite friendly with her maid, Dalia, who's still around.

I don't know whether the señorita worked for a living, but I never saw her go out to work anywhere. Lala and Mercedes were on friendly terms with her, and sometimes Lala would get their ration book from the maid and shop for them. The lady visited José Sabina and Carmen Tamayo and went out for drives in the car with them. They were all upper-class people and on very friendly terms.

Sabina has money; he still has a good house and drives around in his own fine car. The people who go there in their big cars with their little shopping bags are real high-class, like from before the triumph of the Revolution. They seem to be relatives of his. I've never seen any people of our class visit there, though some of the people on this block are on friendly terms with them. I've seen the old man talking with the militia women when they were cleaning up the street, and so on.

I have no idea what goes on inside his house. Since I've been living here, I've never had a chance to peek inside because they never use the front door. I don't believe even the gardener has ever had a glimpse of the inside of the house from the front. People are always stealing things from the front lawn so I guess the old guy is in a panic for fear they'll steal something from inside.

Only the old guy and his maid live there and there's a lot of gossip about them. The maid is a fat old woman who's always criticizing everybody and complaining that the kids out on the sidewalk bother her. She's been his maid practically all her life. I don't know whether she belongs to the past or the present, if you know what I mean. But Serafina and Lala, at least, get along with her fine. As for him, it's plain to see that he can't possibly favor the Revolution. He's too set in the old ways. The other day two scholarship students—not little boys, young men—passed by and tore a twig off the flame tree in the street, and that old fellow said things to them that shouldn't be said to any man. We were standing at the doorway and Hernández said to me, "If that old guy ever dared say those things to me... !"

"You'd ignore it just as they did," I told him. "Because any of you could kill him with one blow."

"I wouldn't do that, but I'd sure like to knock that arrogance out of his head."

Once my neighbor Alma and I were standing outside when Sabina drove up. We saw him leap out of his car and rush at Sara's son Hilario, who was killing lizards with his slingshot. He grabbed the boy and called him delinquent and I don't know what all. The boy was scared, see, for fear we'd go tell his mother, but I stood aside and didn't interfere.

Then Alma said to me, "Listen, Justa, I'm going to give you a piece of advice. I've told my children not to go near that place. The other day that old guy got hold of your Reinaldo, and if you'd heard the things he said you'd have come right out and insulted him. Look, I'm as frank as I am ugly, and if that old man said to one of my kids what he said to your son, I'd knock him into a cocked hat, that I would!"

He has no children of his own at home, but it seems to me any older person should talk gently to a child. He could have said, "Look, love, please don't spoil the plants. I haven't got long to live myself, but after I'm gone they should still be here for you to enjoy." He should talk to them in terms of the Revolution, no? That way the kids would obey him, I think.

Some Chileans, a married couple with two children, used to live in the apartment building next door. I think the husband was a technician. Lala got along very well with them because they were cut out of the same cloth. The Chilean woman is kind of uppity, though, as a lot of them are. She thought she was the only one who had the right to keep her radio turned on high and do as she pleased. One night Mercedes turned on her TV at 10:30 and that woman came over to tell her that her TV was too loud and was keeping her awake. Mercedes and Juan felt insulted. Another time she called Horacio a peasant. She told him to turn down his radio because "*guajiros*[57] like him" were used to such loud noises but she wasn't.

She never interfered with me, though, because I told her what's what early in the game. The way I see it, you've got to speak up for yourself and tell off that kind of a neighbor before they start interfering with you. Standing right here on the porch I said, "If you interfere with me, I'll show you what's good. You should be proud to be here even if your husband did come to help us as a technician. You're here because the Cubans offered you their sincere friendship, so why are you so rude to us and to our children?"

I was told later that she was stuck-up, the kind who goes through life with her nose high in the air. Her husband and children weren't like that when she wasn't home. Her mother-in-law went out of her way to greet the neighbors politely, but with her daughter-in-law around she didn't dare. Imagine!

Her children played only with those she allowed them to play with—with nobody, in fact. They couldn't go near Sara's children because she

57. Cuban peasants; the word is sometimes used derogatorily to mean a rustic.

thought they were ill-bred and ragged. Several times she chased them away, saying they were dirty and couldn't associate with her children. She was the kind who bawled out a child instead of explaining things to him.

Toward the end of her stay, she got Lala to do her laundry and they became friendly with each other. She left not long ago, then some other foreigners moved in there—Russians or Hungarians, I don't know which. You'd hardly know they're there, they're that quiet. Sometimes you see them and they greet you, but it seems they work very hard and are really decent people.

The first foreigners to live on the block were Sergei, the Russian, and another older man. They were very nice people and awfully fond of children. Those Russians made friends with everybody here. Sergei was very fond of my daughter Antonia. When he got home from work, he'd call her over and throw candy down to her. He always said, "When I have to go, I'll just leave. I won't say goodbye to any of you because that would make me feel too sad. I hate to leave you all. When I'm back home in Russia, I'll think of you often."

Horacio is a good neighbor. He works in the Ministry of Labor—I always see him going there in a car. I know he's a soldier, a combatant, just as my husband was. The two of them fought together. He's lived in no. 409 ever since I moved to this block. His family is from my hometown, and after we found that out we began to say hello when we met, but I never visited them at home. Recently he got married and invited me to the wedding, but I couldn't go because Hernández was away doing farm work.

Horacio's wife teaches in a night school for women. She's a machine technician. We're on friendly enough terms, passing a few remarks when we run into each other, but we've never had a real conversation so I know nothing about her life or she about mine. She's a very agreeable, well-bred person, and very hardworking, too.

My closest friends here are Mercedes and now Alma, a light-skinned woman who moved into no. 409. Her husband is a relative of mine but for a long time neither of us knew it. They're very nice people. He's well liked at his work center, too. Alma never quarrels with anybody, she's always calm and easygoing. I'm not a close friend of her husband's but she and I are great friends. "We're practically as close as relatives already," I tell her. "Your nearest neighbor is your relative." That's just lovely, let me tell you!

The block used to be badly organized. People were always quarreling and the patrolman had to intervene all the time. But it's changed for the better over the past two years. Things are more peaceful.

After 7:00 at night, Miramar streets are dark as a wolf's mouth. All those trees and bushes make it worse. They should get rid of all those plants. In the darkness it's very easy for a burglar to go into any building and then slip away again. And when one single light burns out, the darkness is really terrible, and they're out more than they're on. You have to think twice before so much as going out to the porch. Sometimes I won't even go as far as the Club Obrero for a *maltina*.

Littering is one of our main problems here. I never litter. I just help clean it up as a service to the rest of the people here. They're the ones that litter. I clean the stairway and five minutes later it's dirty again. Sure, I know people have to go up and down, but clean, considerate people don't let their children tramp up and down another person's stairs all day long. I've put the problem to them twenty thousand times and suggested that everybody should take care of the surroundings, and if somebody dirties another person's part, let him clean it up. But my steps are always the dirty ones, no matter how often I sweep and mop them, because that's where all the kids congregate to play. I can't chase away anybody's kids.

My daughter Genoveva was appointed to do something about the garbage problem and to see that the street was kept clean. As her mother and fellow Committee member, I helped her go around and talk with the neighbors and advise them to get lids for their garbage cans. We told them not to throw any kind of trash on the ground and to let us know two or three days ahead of time when they were going to cut down or trim a plant so we could have a truck sent around to pick up the branches. That's the way they did it on my block in Almendares and it was always clean.

Well, do you know what happened? When we got the meetings organized, people came to them all right, but everybody started saying we were the last to move here and we already acted as though we owned the Frozen Zone. I said to Rodolfo, "Look, if this is the way it's going to be, I want you to relieve Genoveva of this duty immediately! She's a young girl and I won't let her be involved in this kind of free-for-all. All we've been trying to do is organize this properly. We can't do our work if this is the way people react. They're all gossiping about us, and if this keeps on we'll end up quarreling. If you don't like our methods, then tell us what methods you do like."

And there the matter rested. That was our way of doing things from the very first, ever since we moved here. The other day they finally got around to picking up the trash and even started burning it, but I couldn't care less.

The Committee has given orders that people should have medium-sized garbage cans with lids. But you can't leave your garbage can down in the street after it's emptied because if you do, the next car that comes along will cart it away.

Two years ago the hardware stores were selling uncovered drums to be used as garbage containers—open drums out in the street, overflowing with garbage, and everybody breathing in those germs. That's where the gastroenteritis and all sorts of serious illnesses come from. Even inside the houses we get the germs from those open containers. But you can't explain that to everybody because they wouldn't understand what you were driving at. They just think you want to show you're cleaner than they are.

I was still living in Almendares when they started selling those drums, and at that time I bought one for 3 *pesos*. When I moved here I didn't bring it. Somebody took my next-door neighbor's drum so I left her mine, thinking that the hardware store over here would call us block by block to buy drums. That's something the Committee should do. It's their duty to see that the block is kept clean and they're the ones who should bring up the matter. But as anyone can see, we've got a do-nothing Committee on our block.

Since I've lived on this block, my milk has been stolen twice. I believe Mercedes has been left without milk a couple of times too. It used to be delivered at 5:00 in the morning. The milkman left it on the doorstep, and at that hour it couldn't have been in anybody's way. I always took mine in before anybody else was up. It isn't the milkman's fault; distribution's been functioning smoothly for ages. It's the people around here.

If Lala has three liters of milk out in the street and Mercedes one, and the people down in the garage and those upstairs get milk, why should it be mine that's always stolen? That's what started me thinking, and I've come to a conclusion. If it were somebody from outside, they'd make a clean sweep and walk off with everybody's milk, not just with mine. Alma, who lives next door, says, "You've sure been unlucky having your milk stolen twice. In all the years I've lived here nobody has stolen mine even once." See what I mean? I say that it's somebody right here on the block who takes it. An outsider wouldn't know that I was a revolutionary, either. I speak up everywhere and tell everybody that I'm a revolutionary and the counterrevolutionaries steal our milk to sabotage the Revolution. There are many other revolutionaries living around here, but the only one wearing a uniform is Lieutenant Hernández. When I say that, he laughs.

It's a sad thing to get up in the morning and find your milk gone. I'd be incapable of playing such a mean trick on anybody. Oh well . . . it takes all sorts to make a world. Now the milkman knocks on my door and gives me the milk and I hand him the empty bottles.

It isn't just the milk that gets taken in this place. Mercedes, Alma, and I have all lost other things. Not just once either; every little while something disappears. One day Alma had to go to the doctor and she asked me to keep an eye on her clothesline from my window. But I was busy around the house and the kids were running around down below. So when nobody was looking they swiped three pairs of white socks and two new pairs of panties. When she got back and saw her things gone, she said to me, "Do you think I'll ever feel safe leaving things out there again?" Then she burst into tears. "I'm left with only one pair that I knitted myself and made off with the only three pairs I'm entitled to buy." Then I gave her a pair of white socks.

"So now we aren't the only ones whose things get stolen," I thought. But Lala has left panties and all sorts of things down there and she says nobody has ever stolen anything from her. All I know is that I myself have had stockings and panties disappear from the line, but I couldn't tell you whether it's Lala or Leticia that takes them. Mercedes has hung out clothes back there too, and they've stolen lots of things, including some of Juan's undershirts. She said, "Well, that's really made my day! But who cares? After all, compared to other things I've had stolen from me—record players and all sorts of things—they didn't take anything valuable." It must be one of the neighbors, because nobody is going to come in from outside just to snitch a few pairs of socks or a brassiere.

When we lived in Almendares, I saw a woman tried by a People's Court in Marianao for stealing a man's shirt. There was a great scandal and the woman was brought to trial and found guilty. How shameful! How embarrassing! She stole the shirt, no? But it was her husband who was sent to jail—he got three months—although he didn't steal anything. Everybody said, "The court has made a mistake. What happened is that two women bought shirts in the same place." The husband had a shirt just like the one stolen because that's the way shirts used to come—in big lots, all looking exactly alike. But the woman who brought the complaint proved the shirt was stolen because she'd mended it and the stitches showed. Listen, we lost ourselves fast afterward! You see, those people were neighbors of ours.

To my knowledge, things have been stolen from our building three times. But such strange robberies! Listen, a thief is a specialist in stealing. He steals only what he needs, but whoever steals from us in this building snatches up whatever he happens to see unguarded. The only things they've taken from me lately are a purse, a sponge cake, and a bottle of milk.

I told Hernández, "We'll have to put a good lock on the door. If not, somebody's going to break in some day and tear the place apart. And I'll tell you one thing, I'll never open that door to anybody, not unless you happen to be home. I'm not going to risk having somebody kill me and all the children." It was then that we fixed the door lock.

Not long ago, Rodolfo, Serafina's husband, came here to get the police patrol's phone number. He wanted to call them because he'd been robbed—in broad daylight, too. It was only 1:00 o'clock in the afternoon and Serafina was home and everything. He said they'd stolen two radios, some clothes, perfume, and all sorts of things. Unfortunately, the thief is a socialist—he stole Russian perfume but didn't touch the American perfume. You can see how carefully we analyzed everything. They stole again, but I don't know what they took—a radio or an electric iron or a camera or some such thing.

The Russians who live across the street were robbed too. The Russian woman heard the burglar in the kitchen but she thought it must be her husband, back from guard duty. Then she heard the door slam and thought, "That man must be nuts!" Those were the words she used because she was embarrassed to say what she really thought. But Hernández understood and told her, "Don't be embarrassed, we know that it's a Russian custom to drink heavily." She drinks as much as her husband does. It's a cold climate in their country so they get used to drinking and can't stop even where it's warm.

Then she said, "But I looked out and saw a colored man leaving the house with a lot of my things. I saw the truck take off and just then the patrol car drove up."

Hernández was returning from a Party meeting and a patrolman was driving him home in the patrol car when the Russian woman, who speaks very good Spanish, stopped them. They analyzed it all on the spot and came to the conclusion that the burglar is somebody from the same block who has the stealing habit. He stole two bedspreads, their radios, a hot plate, an air-conditioner, an electric fan, and an electric iron.

We're going to fight this "rifle in hand as if we were going into battle," as our leader, Fidel himself, has said. One way is by standing guard on our block, but when we do guard duty in the street we should stand under a tree so nobody can see us. The trouble is that a thief can take cover in the darkness just as easily as we can. Luckily, the police patrol makes its rounds here at all hours, everywhere—day and night, night and day.

Some people here can go to sleep at night completely relaxed, but I can't, and when they do guard duty, if they don't see anyone around sometimes they go back home to bed. But not me. You can go all over the Frozen Zone and ask how it was when Justa Díaz and Sara Rojas had guard duty and see if they don't have our papers all in order, with the hour we signed in and out. If the people whose duty it was to relieve us didn't bother to get up, we'd go to their houses and knock on their doors until we roused them. After that, it was their responsibility, not ours.

One night when Sara and I were on guard, I said, "We were supposed to be on guard until 2:00 A.M. and it's already 3:00, and here we are, both of us with our big bellies...." The Chilean woman was supposed to relieve us so Sara went to get her. That woman came out like a fury, shouting that this was no hour to wake her up, that she should be assigned special hours for standing guard. "Special or not," said Sara, "this is the hour assigned to you. It says so right here on this bit of paper."

After that we went home to bed and the next day the Chilean made quite a show. So then I told the man from the Committee, "Next time you assign somebody to relieve us, choose somebody a bit more conscientious. We don't want any problems." After my baby was born and Sara lost her belly with a miscarriage, we didn't stand guard any longer and nobody else did either. But about a month ago, I think, they were going around asking people to volunteer.

The kids from the scholarship students' houses make plenty of trouble around here. They were very well-behaved at first. They were always in class when they were supposed to be because María, a girl who recently graduated as a teacher, ruled those kids with a strong hand. She kept strict discipline there. You should have seen the place in her time, always clean and neat. The problems started two or three months ago when she left.

Just recently, I returned home and found Rigoberto and two other scholarship kids in Sara's garage. I called their housemother;[58] She had nothing to do with this but I happen to be acquainted with her, no? "Well, *chica*," I said to her, "this kind of thing is a blot on the Revolution. What's the problem with this boy, Rigoberto? He's a disgrace to the whole block. I wish you'd tell me everything about him."

"He never goes to class," she said, "or to the dining room, either. And do you know what that brat has gone and done? He's lost his shoes so we'll send him back home. There are kids here whose shoes have worn out and they've gone to school wearing torn shoes and even bedroom slippers because they want to do their duty. But that boy is simply not interested in studying and he doesn't want to stay here. We know because we've read every letter he's written to his mother, and we've sent them to the Ministry of Education. Rigoberto is only ten but he has a grown man's mentality."

People seeing that boy wandering around will say, "Look at the way Fidel's scholarship students wander alone all over the place. The neighbors have to give the poor hungry child bread." Get it? Are the people who give him bread being conscientious? It hurts me, because those kids have the best of everything. We never eat a bit of ham or other things so that the school children may have all that good food. I don't remember the last time I was able to buy a piece of ham, but sometimes when my son Reinaldo comes from school, he brings me a ham sandwich and says, "*Ay, mima,* I brought you this to eat because I know how things are with you. In the boardinghouse we have plenty of ham." If you hear anyone say the students go hungry, all you've got to do is to take him to the directors. They can show him the vouchers for all the food bought for the scholarship students.

"Well, *chica,*" I said, "things can't keep on like this. Just imagine what

58. Cubans refer to these young women as *tías* (aunts).

the government is going to think of us if we revolutionaries don't put a stop to this right away."

She said they'd already brought the problem before the Ministry of Education and nothing had been done. "You know, that doesn't sound right to me," I told her. "I'm going to call a patrol for you, with your consent."

If you have any complaint you call the Public Order patrol of the Ministry of Education and tell them your problem. I haven't called them before because I don't want to speak up and maybe make trouble for the lady in charge. She's sacrificing herself by taking care of three scholarship houses because there's a shortage of teachers. More children have entered school this year and the people in charge of the student houses are young. So when we see a wrongheaded child like that, we try to help him.

"I'd be real proud of you if you called and had all those kids picked up, because I feel for the Revolution too." That's what the little colored housemother told me.

Aside from Rigoberto, there were three more, including Ivan. He's the other one who's setting everything at sixes and sevens here. I'm told they're tired of moving him to other student houses, bringing him back, and taking him away again. I went over to the boys and told them, "I don't want anybody here. Beat it or I'll call the patrol right away." And I said, "Ivan, you're the leader of this little gang and you know how it is—from here you go to a work farm." Then I went upstairs and made the call. If you call the Ministry of Education about anything having to do with a student boardinghouse, they'll put your call through right away. Having my daughters on scholarships, I already knew that.

At around noon, a patrolman came with a tall young colored woman from the student home. She talked to Rigoberto very sweetly: "Come here, love." They kept glancing at me but I just stood there as if I didn't know a thing about it. "Tell the lady why you keep running away. You must pay attention and answer anything she asks you. Just tell her what you told us."

The young colored woman said, "Come on, *chico*, we won't do anything to you. We only want to talk with you." She spoke to Rigoberto for a while with all the girl scholarship students watching them, looking scared. Then she said to him, "Well, dear, in a few hours you'll have new clothes and shoes. Then what will be your excuse for not going to school? And don't go throwing your new things away. We know that's what you did with your shoes. We have proof of it. And why did you? Don't you want to stay in the boardinghouse? What kind of work does your *mamá* do? Why do you say they don't give you any food here? You're not a revolutionary because a good revolutionary doesn't tell lies."

The kid just stood there. Then I said to him, "I don't want you coming around here anymore because you might tell even worse lies and destroy somebody."

A few days later, Alma called me to come outside. "Take a look at Rigoberto." There he was with new tennis shoes and socks and very, very clean. "Hey, what happened to you?" I asked him.

"Nothing. I just came from school and I'm sitting here waiting for them to call me to stand in line for lunch." Very quiet, very decent.

Then I said, "I'm going to find out whether you're telling the truth." I guess that scared him because I haven't seen him around since. Even if he came, we couldn't receive him in the house. As they told me, "If he runs away from his teachers it's up to all of you, as neighbors and conscientious revolutionaries, to force him to go back to the student house, because he's only a child.

We shall see whether things will improve at the students' house now that the housemothers have received their orientation and know what they have to do. If it doesn't work out, they'll have to take other action, because things can't keep on this way. It affects the fatherland. As a revolutionary, a Cuban, and a patriot, I think it's a disgrace!

PART II

Backgrounds

Eulalia Fontanés

I was born in the Maternity Hospital in the city of Artemisa, Pinar del Río, on October 11, 1937. *Mamá* came in from the country to give birth and stayed in the hospital three days before returning home. Everybody went wild over me, the first girl after three boys in a row—Pablo, Mario, and René.

My godmother, *mamá*'s younger sister, was a seamstress and made all my baby dresses. They dressed me well and I was always *papá*'s favorite. He says I'm very like his mother. She died when I was still a baby, so I never knew her. I was small and scrawny and at six months I got very sick with pyelitis. *Mamá* nursed me until I was one year old.

Papá, Pablo Fontanés, was a country man. His father had been a cane-cutter and died when *papá* was very little. His mother raised him alone. *Papá*'s only sister, Lilia, lived well after she married because her husband earned 12 *pesos* a day as chief of ovens at the sugar mill.

Papá's farm was across the road from my mother's parents' place. He paid 90-odd *pesos'* rent a year for 2 *caballerías*. But *mamá*'s folks were better off than *papá*'s. Her father worked in the cane and also owned about 6 *caballerías* of land. He had twelve children who all worked on the farm as long as they were single. With what they earned, each bought his own little farm later.

Papá and *mamá* were engaged for eight years before they saved up enough money to get married. They say *papá* was wild in his youth—he was like fire—but he settled down after they were married. He must have been about twenty-seven then and *mamá* was no spring chicken either.

The first house I remember was the one in which *papá* and *mamá* got married. It was in a *batey*[1] planted with bananas and plantains, yucca and maize. The houses were scattered over a clearing bounded by a line of trees. Our small front yard was planted with yucca and had a curving pathway to the road. The house itself was large, longer than it was wide,

1. Settlement for workers at a sugar mill or *central*.

with a front porch, a parlor, two bedrooms, a dining room, and a kitchen made of palm leaf. The floors were of packed earth and we cooked with wood in a square, wooden, earth-filled stove.

Mamá had furniture when she got married, but by the time I was old enough to notice, it had all fallen apart. We sat on stools and the three older boys slept on cots made of jute sacks, stretched like hammocks on a framework of wood. The girls—Beatríz, Pilar, Serafina, and I—slept together on a big bed. The youngest children, Diego and Isabel, slept in a cradle hung from the ceiling, and *papá* and *mamá* had a bed to themselves. *Mamá* made the mattresses out of hemp straw. We were rather crowded with so many of us sleeping in only two rooms. But I never in my life saw *papá* caressing *mamá*. Kissing, yes, but I don't imagine they had any difficulty having relations because *mamá* kept on getting pregnant.

As children, we never ate with our parents. We were served our dinner first, then *papá* and *mamá* ate theirs. As each of us grew up, *papá* admitted us to the table. For breakfast we had *café con leche* and bread or crackers. Lunch was cornmeal and milk, and for dinner we had a vegetable stew with beans and rice.

We owned only one cow, which Grandma had given us for milk. We ate meat once a week and *mamá* would kill a chicken now and then. We never ate fish. I remember lots of rice—the grains were the tiniest you ever saw and full of black seeds. *Mamá* would set us to picking over the rice in the morning, and sometimes at 2:00 o'clock we were still sorting the good grains we were to eat that night. It was very poor-quality rice, sticking together after it was cooked, but at least we never went to bed hungry. We had hard times, sure, but we always managed because we had a fairly big piece of land.

Our parents had a lot of trouble keeping us decently clothed. There were a lot of nicely dressed little girls in our neighborhood, but we had nothing except one uniform, one pair of tennis shoes apiece for school, and a pair of shoes and a dress to wear when we went visiting on Sunday. At home we kids wore beat-up clothes and went barefoot. *Papá*, being the only wage-earner, couldn't possibly buy us nine pairs of shoes.

In December, when everybody bought something new to wear for Christmas, Grandma and Uncle Cosmé gave each of us a new dress or shirt and a pair of shoes. As far back as I can remember, *mamá*'s family helped us a lot because she kept having one baby after another.

My mother's brothers adore us to this day. They're like fathers to me. When they come to Havana, they call on us right away, and if I don't go to see them when I'm in the country, they're offended. We played a lot with the cousins living nearest to us. Sundays, we all went to Grandma's house and played ball, hide-and-seek, any of those games. *Mamá* made dolls for us and I loved to play house with them, marking out the rooms with stones on the ground.

Our cousins on *papá*'s side were awfully stuck-up. When we went to the sugar mill, they snubbed us because we were country girls and didn't dress well. They always sent us their cast-off clothes, which upset *papá* so much he wouldn't let us wear them. *Mamá* said we should keep them so as not to offend Aunt Lilia, but *mamá* never visited her. Aunt Lilia came only once a year, when *papá* invited her to eat roast suckling pig.

Aunt Lilia treated us like strangers when we children visited her. She didn't bother to go to church when my brother René was baptized, though he's her godson. When I came to Havana and started working, I visited Aunt Lilia and those cousins a few times, and they fawned all over me. It was "Lala this" and "Lala that," so I stopped going. In that way I do bear a grudge. They used to treat me like dirt under their feet, so why should they pretend to be so friendly all of a sudden? And then, when Aunt Lilia was leaving Cuba, she wanted to give *papá* everything she owned but he refused it.

I have pleasant memories of my *mamá*'s *mamá*. I loved her better than anybody when I was a child. She was always kind and affectionate. Her hair was completely white, and early each morning she'd come to our house to have *mamá* shampoo it. If she stayed away for one day, *mamá* missed her. When Grandma wanted one of us to help in her house or if she wanted to give us something, she'd come over to fetch us. *Mamá* made us go, whether we wanted to or not. Sometimes Grandma would come for one of us to help her carry eggs to sell at the sugar mill. I never went—I was already in love and didn't want to be seen in public with a basket of eggs. I should say not!

Grandma never worked because Uncle José and his wife, Margarita, lived with her. Margarita did all the housework. When we went there, we'd do whatever else there was to be done so Grandma could take it easy in a rocking chair beside a big window. As she grew older she became a bit bad-tempered—she'd get mad and cuss at us—but she was really good.

In 1948 a cyclone passed through the province of Pinar del Río. Very few houses were left standing—ours was flattened too. When we felt the house shaking, we went outside and lay down under some carts. We wrapped ourselves up to keep warm as best we could, in sacks or whatever was handy. After the cyclone was over, *papá* knocked a hole in the corner of the house and we all crept inside. When my uncles came, they thought we were all dead.

We stayed at Grandma's for about two months while *papá* built a new house for us, this time entirely of roof tiles and cement. *Papá* also made a palm-leaf hurricane shelter sunk deep in the earth. Then he said, "Now if there's another cyclone, we won't have any trouble."

The road in front of our house was unpaved and full of stepping-stones and large holes. The neighbors got together with the owner of the quarry to rebuild it. Every afternoon *papá*, my older brothers, and all the able-bodied men in the neighborhood worked on the road. They paved the stretch from the sugar mill to the grocery store.

The sugar mill was in a metal building as big as a city block. It had three towers and a zinc roof covered with aluminum paint. Inside, it had all the machinery needed to grind the different types of sugar cane and to turn the molasses into sugar. The molasses vat was in a round building with a pointed top, but the sugar warehouse was rectangular. Huge scales were rolled from place to place by pulleys. Iron hooks lifted large loads of cane from the carts and weighed them in mid-air, then unloaded them.

The blacks who worked at the sugar mill were as dirty as a bunch of pigs. There were always a lot of them living near us, in big barracks built in a circle. There was a dormitory for the employees who stayed all night, and an alley where the cooler continually dripped the hot, dirty water from the mill. Then there were the grocery store, the clothing store, the butcher shop, and the post office. In the center, between the mill and the cafeteria, was the park belonging to the sugar mill, then the church, some of the employees' houses, and another restaurant. Across the way was the Red Cross, the ball park, and another large dormitory. The manager of the mill had a big, beautiful white house made of concrete. The townspeople used to have their houses on the road to the nearest village, Las Mangas, though their land was somewhere else. Now small prefabricated houses for the sugar-mill employees have been built there.

Everybody was either a sugar-mill employee or a peasant. The *guajiros* lived more comfortably than the mill workers because they planted their own vegetables and didn't depend on the grocery store. But the townspeople dressed better than the country people, who were always dirty, with patched, mended pants and filthy old hats. The country kids ran around barefoot and some of the smaller boys didn't even wear pants.

Mamá wanted us to learn to do everything well so we wouldn't be useless lumps when we got married. I began to cook and wash clothes when I was seven. I stood on a wooden crate to reach the washtub that *mamá* kept in a shack. As I washed each piece, my sister Beatríz would wring it out and drop it into a tin basin. That way we both helped our old lady. *Mamá* boiled the clothes in a big tin over a wood fire in the yard. We girls never did that or the ironing because they were dangerous jobs. *Mamá* used flatirons heated on hot coals.

When we were ten or twelve years old, *mamá* took in laundry from her brothers and from strangers, too. *Mamá*'s brothers were single and lived with Grandma. They'd pay us 1 *peso* for each shirt and pair of pants. Some weeks we washed as many as fifteen pairs of pants.

We girls helped *mamá* draw water from the well in the morning and in the afternoon *papá* and the boys would draw some more. *Mamá* wouldn't allow us to get water alone because the well was very deep. *Papá* dug that well right by the house and it belonged to us alone. Every family had its own well.

A little later, we older ones—my brother, Beatríz, and I—started helping *papá* on the farm. He'd rouse us early in the morning to dig the holes to plant sugar cane. After the cane sprouted, *papá* would put manure on it and we'd spade around the stalks. I helped cut the cane, peel it, and load it onto carts, working side by side with my brothers. That was the part I enjoyed most because it was the most comfortable job—all I had to do was sit in the cart sucking cane. René's shirt front would get stiff as cardboard from the sugar-cane juice that dried on it. I also planted tubers, spaded the ground, and weeded the yucca, corn, and bean plants. I know what really hard work is, so nobody can come boasting to me about that. When we were through working, *mamá* would set out a big washtub and we'd get in and splash around while she bathed us. When we were older, we bathed inside the house. Later, *mamá* would sit us all down to do our homework. I began school when I was ten or eleven.

Papá never got as far as the sixth grade, but he's a man who gives a lot of thought to things. All of *mamá*'s brothers and sisters completed the sixth grade because the school was so near their home and her mother was a teacher's assistant. Later my aunt took over the job of assistant and *mamá* got a job as school janitor.

School was a big wooden barn of a house with a tile roof and a cement floor. We had only one teacher, a tall black woman, who was very good and respectable. I was very fond of her. There were fifty or sixty students, from first to sixth grade, all together in one classroom. We sat on benches, chairs, and even on the tables—wherever we could get a seat. How could we be expected to learn anything that way? Sometimes we were stuck in the same grade for two or three years. By age twelve I'd completed only the third grade. But in those days children were taught more in school—grammar, arithmetic, and a lot of Cuban history.

The girls wore pleated blue jumpers and white blouses, the boys wore blue pants and white shirts. *Papá* bought us enough cloth for one or two uniforms each and *mamá* made them. When some parents couldn't afford to buy their child a uniform, the rest contributed money for the cloth and one of the mothers made it. Only children like us went to that school. The rich sent their kids to a better school at the sugar mill, or else to boarding school in Havana. I never played with any rich children.

Most of us country kids had to help our parents, and we went to school only when we weren't needed at home. I hardly ever attended because there was a lot of work at home, especially during the last three months of *mamá*'s pregnancies. In school I was a dope and always copied from the other children.

My best friend was Jaquelina, a little Negro girl who lived near us. Practically all our neighbors were blacks but very, very well-bred. When I didn't understand something, Jaquelina would explain it to me, and when she didn't understand, I'd explain it to her.

Country parents never talked with the teachers about their children's grades or behavior in school. They only went to meetings about school repairs or when they were called upon to contribute to a school party. *Papá* was president of the parents' association and he wore himself out explaining to the other parents why they should go to meetings.

I stayed in school until the age of seventeen but I never finished the sixth grade. I knew how to read and write and my parents figured that was plenty for poor people. So they took Pablo, René, Beatríz, and me out of school and kept us home to work. Mario was allowed to stay in school because he was a very studious boy.

When I was about ten, my sister Pilar died of some kind of parasite which the doctors said got into her intestines. *Papá* was so poor and people there didn't know about such things, so by the time they decided to take my sister to a doctor, it was too late. None of us kids went to the wake in Aunt Lilia's house. I guess *mamá* thought we were too little and was afraid it would shock us.

Mamá knows more than the devil about home remedies. She learned all her medical lore from my grandma, who was a *curandera*. Grandma would even pass her hands over women with big bellies. She'd pass her fingers gently here and there until she found the place that hurt and then she'd pray for them to get well. She could cure anything, and *mamá* can too. *Mamá* makes the sign of the cross several times over the patient while she says the children's prayer of San Luis Beltrán. That cures the evil eye and suchlike.

Mamá grows all sorts of medicinal herbs in tin cans. She uses American basil to cure worms, camomile for the stomach, rosemary syrup for aches and pains as well as for liver complaints. She makes linden-flower tea which she gives, along with an aspirin, to everyone when they feel bad. It's supposed to be good for the nerves and for menstrual cramps. For earaches, *mamá* pours rue juice into the ear. When we got an upset stomach, she'd give us guava or a puree of green plantain and that drove the infection right out of our systems. Doctors say children get diarrhea from being given so many cures, one on top of the other, but now they prescribe tetracycline and twenty more things that do nothing but tear up a child's stomach.

Mamá used the red incense flower to drive misfortune out of the house, and sage to sweeten the air. Sage leaves in coffee also give great relief. You place two leaves in the form of a cross at the bottom of the cup, pour coffee on top, and then drink it.

When I was thirteen my first period came, and then I began to use makeup and let my hair grow long. I must have been fourteen or fifteen when I realized I was pretty. I was always looking in the small square mirror that *mamá* had on the wall. The other girls started urging me to use lipstick and I did, but I was ashamed to let *papá* and *mamá* see me with painted lips. Now I never use makeup, not even powder, unless I'm going out somewhere.

In the city, a girl's fifteenth birthday is a very special occasion celebrated with a big party, but in the country we weren't in the habit of celebrating birthdays, so my fifteenth went by like any other day in the year. I never had presents for the Day of the Three Kings, either. Never, not even once, because it wasn't customary in the country. The only one of us who ever got Three Kings' Day presents was Isabel, my youngest sister. I never felt deprived because I'd never heard of that custom. Our big celebration was December 24. When Grandma was alive, we all celebrated at her house and everybody brought things for the fiesta. After her death we gathered at our house.

My first sweetheart, Arturo Pérez, was about twenty, several years older than I. He was the son of José Pérez, the richest man in the neighborhood, a cheat and a miser who grabbed everything for himself. Whenever he liked a little farm belonging to some poor man, he'd tell the owner, "You can't keep that land because you can't take proper care of it," and then he'd grab it for himself. Arturo worked as a dairyman on his father's farm. His mother had died in childbirth.

We were neighbors and they'd come over to our house to play dominoes. Arturo and I would sit and talk at the same table where the others were playing. We saw each other daily but never alone because I wasn't allowed to go out. We were sweethearts in secret for three years. We kissed but that's as far as we went. He always respected me.

When I was about nineteen, Arturo got mad at *papá* and stopped coming to our house. He had asked *papá* for my hand in marriage and *papá* refused to "give him entry" because he knew Arturo had a mistress and that I'd be unhappy if I married him. I told Arturo to insist but he refused to ask again.

"I'm going to Artemisa to work," I told him. "And as soon as I find a good man, I'm going to marry him."

"We shall see which of us gets married first, you or me," he retorted. I wept a lot when we broke up and I was unhappy for a whole week afterward.

At that time, around 1958, my Uncle Raúl met a woman doctor of pharmacy who was looking for a maid. Nobody in my family had ever been a servant before, but I decided to take the job to help out my parents. Besides, I wanted to forget Arturo. *Papá* didn't like the idea of my going to Artemisa, but I convinced him we must have more money to buy the things we needed. I was tired of living in the country anyway.

From the time I opened my eyes until I was nineteen, I'd been stuck out there. When I left, I vowed I'd never go back again. I said I'd marry a garbage collector before I married a *guajiro*.

When I arrived in Artemisa, I went first to my uncle's house. He owned a grocery store—this was still during the dictatorship—and that night my Aunt Edenia took me over to the *doctora*'s house. The *doctora*, Cristina Delgado, was in her forties, a woman of high rank and very rich. She had an enormous income from her drugstore and owned the whole block. Her house was made entirely of cement and in the back there was a large terrace where she had her tea.

We talked and she told me, "You'll like it here with me. There will just be the two of us alone." Her husband, Evidio Carrera, was a political exile in New York because he belonged to the Twenty-sixth of July Movement and had to get out of Cuba. Their daughter Tina, who was about twenty-eight years old at that time, was also in New York, working as a pharmacist in Bellevue Hospital.

I started working for the *doctora* the very next morning. She explained how she wanted lunch prepared, then gave me some tablecloths to iron. "I'll teach you to iron," she said. With all the loads of clothes I'd ironed at home, I could have given *her* lessons!

I helped the *doctora* in the pharmacy too, because she was all alone there. I cleaned up, waited on customers, and filled bottles of pills. I liked working in the drugstore, and when the *doctora* was on night duty, all alone with me, she'd read the prescriptions aloud and tell me where to find the ingredients. "I'll teach you to prepare this so when you have to do it you'll know how," she said.

The *doctora* kept in close touch with the people in the Twenty-sixth of July Movement, and since I was new, she was afraid I might give her away. She asked me if I'd like to join the Revolution, but I was very young and knew nothing about such things. *Papá* had been a candidate for councilman for Batista's party, but the truth is I knew very little of what was going on. I was interested in my work and nothing more. The revolutionary in my family was my brother Mario. He was well educated, and when Fidel first went up to the Sierra, Mario said he was going to win.

At the end of 1958, the *doctora* went North to spend the New Year holidays with her husband and daughter—that's where the triumph of the Revolution found her. The couple who'd stayed to take charge of the drugstore were away too. I was alone with the lady next door.

At 10:00 o'clock on the morning of January 2, 1959, some men from the Twenty-sixth of July came to the door and ordered me to open the drugstore. I didn't want to and told them I couldn't because I didn't know anything about medicines.

"We'll get a pharmacist to work here temporarily until yours returns. But you must open because those medicines are needed."

"All right," I said, "but remember, you're responsible for whatever happens." The couple came back that afternoon and were in charge until the *doctora* returned with Evidio and Tina a few weeks later. Evidio started to work at once with different organizations in Pinar del Río and also in the drugstore.

The store opened at 8:00, so Evidio liked to breakfast at about 7:00. The *doctora* usually ate a little later, though never after 7:30. Some days they breakfasted together. The daughter got up at 10:00, and after she had breakfast I did all the dishes, started cooking lunch, and then cleaned the house. Sometimes I breakfasted sitting down, sometimes standing up. It made no difference to me. Anyway, all I ever have for breakfast is milk. They urged me to eat what they did but I didn't like it, and besides, I was in a hurry to get things done.

I served their midday dinner at 12:00 and went back to my housework. They never ate a real meal in the evening, just *café con leche* or a little steak with mashed *malanga*, light things like that. Evidio liked a glass of *café con leche* and a piece of toast with ham—we still had ham in Cuba then.

I finished my day's work at 9:00 or so, but usually didn't go to bed until 11:00 or 12:00 because I loved to watch television. Nobody in the family watched it, so I had their set all to myself. When Tina was home, she'd sometimes sit and watch TV with me, but she was a bit stuck-up. Tina and I had an argument once. I told her there were no servants anymore, because since the triumph of the Revolution we were all equal. "I used to be your maid," I said, "but now that we're equals I'm something like your sister."

"I refuse to argue with you, Lala," she said, and flounced off to bed.

I have no complaints about the family. They treated me really well and paid me 25 *pesos* a month, out of which I sent 10 to *mami*. At Christmas they doubled my salary and then I kept 25 *pesos* and sent the other 25 to *mamá*. But the work was too hard and I never went to bed. Now and then, on Sundays or at night when I was through with the housework, I'd go visit Aunt Edenia, because she lived right around the corner. By 11:00 I'd be back home.

In 1960 Evidio was given a government post in Havana, with a salary of about 500 *pesos* a month. Before accepting, he said he couldn't commute from his home in Artemisa every day and asked them to get him a house in Havana. The *doctora* didn't want to move at all, but they arranged to have Evidio's cousin take over their drugstore and live in their house. Tina wanted to go to Havana, but I told them I wasn't going because I was tired of working as a servant and wanted to go back home.

The *doctora* said to me, "Ah, Lala, if you don't go with us, we won't go to Havana at all." Then she burst into tears and cried for a long time.

My real objection to Havana was that it seemed awfully far away from home and *mamá*. I didn't know anybody there. Only my brother Pablo was in Havana, working in a cement factory. He was single and earned about 10 *pesos* a day, but he had no home of his own. Sometimes he stayed at a hotel, other times with relatives. Before making my decision, I talked it over with *mamá*. She said, "Don't ask me, do whatever you prefer." So I decided, "All right, I'll go to Havana so I can help Pablo."

We moved from Artemisa to Havana in June, 1960. We got a beautiful house in Vedado, but they said it was too large and that washing so many windows would be too hard for me. Evidio worked in Old Havana but he wanted to live in a quiet neighborhood, so his secretary, Fela, told them to look in Miramar. They all went out driving around that section, to look for a small apartment. They had three cars: a Chevrolet belonging to the government, a Peugeot that was Evidio's, and a blue Ford Tina had brought with her from New York.

The *doctora* and Evidio finally found a vacant place in this building. An American woman lived on the floor above and she showed them her apartment, which was the same as the other one. They liked it and went to see the landlord, who lived in El Country Club. He rode back with them and let them see the place and they took it.

I didn't much like Havana, though I stayed on. I had no friends in Miramar. The only person I knew or ever went anywhere with was a girl who worked nearby. Otherwise I'd ask my brother Pablo to take me places, because I didn't know my way around the city. I couldn't take one single step by myself.

I'll never forget the day I met Armando—November 4, 1960. I was walking down the street on my way to Berenguela's, the *doctora*'s friend who was teaching me the sixth grade. As I turned the corner I found myself face to face with Armando. He was wearing a military uniform and was with a friend. I'd never met either of them before but I liked Armando as soon as I saw him. He said to me, "Look, I came with this friend whose sweetheart lives near here." I went on to school, and when I came out, there was Armando. "I was waiting to take you home," he said, using the familar *tú*.

"All right," I answered. As he walked me home, he asked me where I came from and I asked him the same. His conversation pleased me too, so we went on chatting until we reached my building, then we stood in front awhile longer. The *doctora* walked up and the three of us talked. Then Armando said, "I'll come by to see you tomorrow," and I answered "All right."

"Who is that boy?" the *doctora* asked after he'd left.

"I met him around here and we talked for a while," I said.

"Be careful about boys you meet out in the street," she warned me. "If he's interested in you, ask him to visit you at home."

Armando came to see me the next day, and again on Thursday and

Friday. On Friday he said, "I'm coming to see you on Sunday." He always wore his army uniform because he was stationed at a military police base.

On Sunday he arrived at 2:00 in the afternoon, dressed in civilian clothes. He took me to the Havana Woods, which is a park, and saw me home at 4:00 in the afternoon because he had to return to his base. When he said goodbye he told me, "I can't come tomorrow because I have to stand guard, but I'll see you on Tuesday." We were still only friends but were beginning to fall in love. For me it was love at first sight.

About a week after we met, as we were strolling down 12th Street on the way to my tutor's, Armando told me he was in love and wanted to marry me. My teacher was absent that day, so we strolled around, but not for long, because Berenguela was bound to mention to the *doctora* that there had been no class that night. Besides, it bothered me that Armando was so affectionate in public, kissing and caressing me right in the street.

The next time he came, I said, "Armando, the *doctora* and Evidio told me to ask you up to our place."

"Well, I won't go," said he. "If you like, we can talk down here, but I'm not going to go up there." He never did; he was too embarrassed. One night Evidio invited him upstairs and said that was as much my home as my parents' house was. Armando said, "Yes, yes, I'll go up someday." But he never did. I'd meet him out front and we'd sit on the wall to talk. It was still November when we became sweethearts.

I saw Armando Saturday nights and Sundays, because during the week he went to school to learn to read and write. He was completely illiterate. When he'd first come to Havana he couldn't sign his name— they had to take his fingerprints instead.

Armando's family is from Oriente, near Bayamo, right next to the Sierra Maestra. They're country folk but they don't have a farm—his old man hires out and his sons help him. They have a small plot of land, a yard with their cottage in the middle, and that's all. My folks were twenty times better off than his. My house was made of cement, but Armando's was made of palm leaves.

A month after we met, Armando went to the country to visit his mother and took along a snapshot of the two of us together. He had another sweetheart back home called Cora, and he consulted his parents about his problem. He told them, "Get Cora's photograph. Now look, which of these two women do you like best?"

"I prefer Cora," his mother said.

When he returned to Havana toward the end of December, he said to me, "Know what? *Mamá* thinks I should marry Cora."

"All right," said I. "Go marry her and leave me in peace. After all, I haven't lost anything."

But he said, "No, you're the one I'm going to marry. I want the woman I like, not the one my parents like." Ever since then, I can neither chew nor swallow Armando's old lady.

Our engagement was very short. In January, 1961, we went with my brother Pablo to spend a few days with my parents. I introduced Armando to my family and he talked with my parents for a while—to ask for my hand, I thought. On the bus returning to Havana Sunday morning, I said, "Did you ask for my hand, Armando?"

"Who, me? Why no! What for? That isn't necessary. The next time I go there it will be for our wedding." And so it was. He never did ask my parents' consent.

Armando wanted to get married in February, but I said no, we should wait a little longer to get to know each other better. He said, "No. I'm going to get everything ready and start buying things we'll need."

"All right," I said.

In April he said, "Let's try to get married this month." But then came the attack on the FAR[2] and the invasion at Girón. We couldn't get married then, so he said, "All right, let's see if we can get married in May."

At the time of Playa Girón, Armando phoned to say he'd probably be sent. I heard no more from him for almost a week. When it was all over, the dead were brought back and a wake was held for them at the University of Havana. Armando was in the military police and had been assigned to stand in the honor guard. He and his comrades went without sleep for about three days for that. They were about to drop from exhaustion and had to prop themselves up with their rifles, but they marched in formation in front of the coffins from the University to the cemetery of Colón.

The military police often didn't get any sleep. When a certain diplomat died abroad, for example, his body was brought to Cuba and an honor guard met the coffin at the airport. Evidio, the *doctora,* and I watched it on TV, and right off, the first person the camera focused on was Armando as he stooped to pick up the coffin. "Look at him!" I said, "There he is!" They showed four of them lifting the coffin and carrying it out. They always put Armando and Guzman in front because they were the two tallest. In that conspicuous position, they want somebody with style and dash.

The military police were chosen for their build and good looks, because they're always in the public eye. For instance, if a foreign president comes to Cuba, the military police have to be there to receive him. And each time they were given brand-new olive-green uniforms, the really good gabardine kind that used to come from the United States. And they

2. The airport of the Revolutionary Armed Forces on the outskirts of Havana was bombed by Cuban-marked American planes on April 15, 1961, two days before the Bay of Pigs invasion at Playa Girón.

were issued beautiful boots, not like the Russian boots that come now. It was a really beautiful uniform. Armando still has the long white gauntlets.

I was the one who had to tell *papá* that Armando and I were getting married. He made no objections. The only thing he asked was that we have the wedding on Wednesday, May 31, which is his birthday. We wanted to get married on Saturday, May 27, because Armando had been given eight days' leave, and if we married on Saturday we'd have two extra days together. Armando took the papers to a notary but he forgot the required bachelor's certificate, so we had to postpone the wedding until Monday, May 29.

Armando earned only 74 *pesos* a month with the military police and was paying to have a house built for his mother. So I began buying things for our marriage with the money I'd saved. Everything was still un-rationed in 1961 and there was still loads of stuff in the stores. The *doctora* took me in her car to all the shops and bought me lots of clothes. I bought Armando underclothes and things for the house, but not kitchen equipment because I cooked in Evidio's apartment. When the *doctora* left, she gave me a lot of things—glasses, dishes, pots and pans. She gave me Tina's bedroom set and said, "Take this and you won't have to spend 400 or 500 *pesos* on a new one." I consulted with Armando and he said, "Fine, take it; the fewer expenses we have the better." I'm still using that set.

I spent over a hundred *pesos* on my wedding clothes. The *doctora* and I made my wedding dress. I bought some beautiful nylon organza and we made a blouse with lace and embroidered tiny flowers on it. The neckline was high, as is suitable for a bride, and it had a tiny collar and close-fitting sleeves. The skirt was of some blue material the *doctora* had brought me from the North. It had large polka dots and a lovely satiny sheen. Everyone thought the wedding dress was so pretty they didn't want me to ever take it off.

We left for home at about 11:00 on Sunday morning. *Mamá* fixed up a bed in the parlor for Armando and he stayed in my house that night. Evidio and the *doctora* arrived on Monday, in time for noonday dinner. They came in their Peugeot, with the chauffeur, Varona, driving. *Mamá* prepared roast suckling pig, rice and beans, yucca, and tamales. We invited our whole family, but Armando didn't invite his. "Aren't you even going to invite your *mamá* to the wedding?" I asked.

"No," he said. "Why should they come? They don't even have decent clothes to wear." That's him all over—he blurts out the truth.

Armando has never liked anything to do with the church, so we got married right there at home at 6:00 in the evening. Evidio was one of the witnesses at the wedding. The *doctora* brought a beautiful wedding cake and sandwiches and good liquor. *Papá* bought the beer. There was an abundance of things because it was at the beginning of the Revolution.

I chose to marry at home so that my old *novio* Arturo Pérez would see that I was getting married. I didn't want him to think I'd simply taken off with Armando. My brother-in-law Mongo told Arturo soon afterward, and that very night Arturo took off with his mulatto mistress. He has two children now. When I go to the country I often see him. He speaks to me and I say hello to him, as friendly as ever, but what there was between us is dead and buried.

Armando and I stayed until about 10:00 at night, and when we left they threw rice at us. We returned to Miramar in Evidio's car. We didn't go to a hotel or anything but spent our wedding night at home. I'd fixed up my room very nicely. Next day we got up around noon.

I was a virgin and was afraid on my wedding night because I had no idea what it was going to be like. The next day I awoke all torn up. Of course I didn't blame Armando—it wasn't his fault. I went and got milk and made toast upstairs and we had breakfast by ourselves. Then we went back to bed and didn't go out until about 9:00 at night. I was embarrassed and didn't want to be seen by the *doctora* and Evidio. "Suppose they notice something?" I thought. We ate in a restaurant, went to the movies, and came back home about 3:00 in the morning.

That week we went out to eat and to the movies every night. On Wednesday we went to Pinar del Río for my father's birthday. We returned to Havana on Friday because Saturday was the last day of Armando's leave. When he left for the base I couldn't console myself. I was very much in love with him and felt happy and joyous to be his wife. He was madly in love too and said, "If all marriages are like this, I'd like to get married every day!"

On Saturday afternoon I was alone, cleaning Evidio's house, when all of a sudden there was Armando! "Do you know what they did, *muchacha?*" said he. "They extended my pass until Monday at 6:00 A.M.!" So I finished cleaning and then we went out together.

That month Armando came home every night. The captain allowed him to slip away unseen and he left at 3:00 in the morning to be back in camp in time for roll call. They never caught him. We went to eat wherever we pleased—we ate a lot of chicken—and then we'd go to the movies. Everything was lovely. One time they held a dance at El Chaplin Theater. It was the only party we'd ever gone to together.

Armando never wanted to dance. He hates to be in a crowd, he's very shy, and everything embarrasses him. I was sorry for him, thinking, "It's because he doesn't know how to read or write." I love dancing, but I didn't dance that night because Armando was in uniform.

I kept on working for Evidio and the *doctora,* and Armando stayed on in the military police, learning to read and write. When he missed a class, I'd teach him at home. I was able to give him quite a bit of help. He'd get desperate because he wanted to learn and couldn't. It's difficult for a grown person, especially when they know nothing to start with. But I'd say, "Take it easy. These things have to be done slowly."

After the *doctora* and Evidio left Cuba, I worked for the Frozen Zone Housing office, cleaning and doing laundry for foreigners. I earned 60 *pesos* a month plus lunch and dinner. All of us who'd been servants in Miramar were employed that way. I also had to pick up the clothes, but they provided the soap, starch, and everything. Sometimes I washed as many as thirty sheets and earned 200 *pesos* a month. For ironing that pile, one of the Russians paid me 12 or 15 *pesos* a week, and the others, 8 or 10 *pesos* each. Aside from the pay, they gave me rice, coffee, canned meat, and a heap of other presents. It was a good thing for me, but it was barbarously hard work, especially since I was already pregnant with Armandito. Sometimes I wonder how I can stand up at all after having worked so hard then.

I got pregnant right away, on my wedding night. I had a very bad belly and vomited all the time from sheer nervousness. I couldn't eat and probably didn't weigh more than 50 pounds at the time. I felt destroyed. But Armando was madly happy. He made bets with all his friends that the baby would be a boy. We went out to buy things for him—that's why Mando's so spoiled now, because I spent my pregnancy gadding about for him.

Mando was born prematurely on December 27, 1961, a seven-month baby, weighing only 4¾ pounds. How I suffered to see him come into the world so little and skinny! They had to give him special infants' formula during the first few days and I also nursed him. That baby was the joy of my life because I'd wanted a boy from the very first. I lived only for my son. I didn't worry so much anymore what my husband did out in the street.

In April, 1962, when Mando was just over three months old, we visited my mother-in-law in Oriente for a week. Armando was embarrassed to show me his home and family. His mother went around barefoot and her grandchildren went naked, the girls with their little bottoms out in the air and their bellies swollen with parasites. The beds had no mattresses and all the water had to be fetched from the river. The house was one of those straw huts sunk deep in the ground and practically falling down. While we were there, Armando built another house with a cement floor and a palm-leaf-thatched kitchen.

I had a lot of trouble during the week we stayed there, because the baby was small and soiled his diapers often. Armando's sisters would take the diapers down to the river and wash them for me. But his mother was jealous. Whenever Armando came over and kissed me before going out anywhere, she looked grim. And when we sat together, that old woman would sit near us giving me dirty looks. I'd always prepared

Armando's bath and bathed together with him, but she told me not to. She said, "*Ay*, Mando, prepare your own bath and bathe by yourself." But Armando would fill a big tub with water and say, "Lala and I are going to bathe together."

Oriente mothers say that Matanzas and Havana women steal their sons from them. And there's something to that. Almost all the men who came down from the Sierra married Matanzas or Havana women because they're so much more affectionate than the Oriente women. In Oriente, when a man marries he leaves his wife shut up in his parents' home while he goes chasing other women. That's why their houses are always chock full of people. Here in Havana, when a man marries he sticks to his wife. Husbands may have affairs on the side but they don't carry on like the men of Oriente. Armando was a bit like that himself, but little by little I've set him straight. It was awfully hard on me. How I cried!

Armando's mother's interference has caused trouble and divorce for all his brothers, especially Raúl. One day I said to her, "Look, I'm going to speak frankly. The trouble here is that you encourage Raúl in his ways. You should give him a good talking-to and say, "Raúl, you're a married man. You've got no business chasing after other women." Instead she pampered him, serving his dinner ahead of time and ironing his clothes so he could dress up to go see his mistress.

One day I got hold of Raúl and said to him, "You're downright brazen. Every single day you take off to enjoy yourself. Listen, if Armando should ever treat me the way you treat your wife, I'd leave him at once. A wife is not a slave."

"Oh, sure," said he, "I know you've got Armando under your thumb."

"That's where you're mistaken," says I. "Armando and nobody else wears the pants at home."

It was in his mother's home that I found out Armando had another woman. She was Cora, his former sweetheart from Matanzas. He'd gotten her pregnant and she'd had an abortion and everything. Armando told the whole story to his family. I was in another room changing the baby's diaper when I overheard him say, "Did you know that last night before coming here, I was with her?" And so forth and so on.

Then I heard his mother say, "You know very well I wanted you to marry that girl. I like her much better than this one." She encouraged Armando, too! She's the worst go-between you ever saw. I can't stand the woman! Listen, I don't trust her or anybody else. Thank God my parents are still alive and well off. And if I have to I can work and do all right alone.

I was very stand-offish with Armando during the rest of our visit, but I didn't say anything about the conversation I'd heard. When we got back home, I waited and kept my mouth shut, because I never discuss my problems, not even with my relatives. Besides, if I'd told *mamá* she'd have

said, "Don't worry about it, that's the way men are." Or she'd have said I
was lying. And if I'd told his mother, whose side do you think she was
going to take? My sister Fina had come to help me with the baby—I was
closest to her, but I didn't tell her anything either.

At that time Armando was working as a bodyguard for a government
minister, and he'd say to me, "I have to stand guard tonight." Then he'd
spend the night with Cora.

One night he came home with a lipstick-stained shirt. When I saw his
collar I said, "So, you've been with another woman!"

He swore he hadn't done anything. "You're making it up," he said. "So
now you've started picking fights with me!" We had a big quarrel about
it. I told him he had no need for another woman when he had a wife who
gave him everything. And he answered, "I can have another woman if I
want to!"

"Is that so? Well, I won't go anywhere with you as long as you have that
woman." When he got into bed, I got up and said, "No, no, go to that
other woman and leave me in peace."

One night, to test him, I said, "I went to get you last night, but you
weren't there. You must have been with somebody because you didn't
come home."

"Very well," he said, "if you want to know, I was out with a woman."

Armando is hard; he lives for himself alone and won't let anybody
scold him. I often told him to get out. "I can get a job anywhere, and the
child is mine." He'd go, then come back and say, "I'm not getting out of
here." He finally promised to break up with her. I said, "Well, all right,"
and left it at that. But then he'd come home with lipstick stains on his
shirt again.

That's when I really put my foot down. "You've got to choose," I said.
"Either you stay with the baby and me or you go to her for good. But
remember that if you go to her, you'll never see either your son or me.
And you can't come back to these rooms because they belong to me." But
he said he didn't want to go, that he'd stay with me and the baby. He was
crazy about Mando.

I had a job at that time and was able to place Mando in a *círculo*[3] while I
worked. Besides, I could have gone home because *papá* is better off now.
Of course, it pained me to think of my son growing up without his
father. When I told Armando these things, he promised at once to leave
Cora and he changed his ways completely after that.

3. The *círculos infantiles* or nursery schools are part of a nationwide child-care program
under the jurisdiction of the Women's Federation since 1961. The *círculos* accept children
from age forty-five days up to five years. The service, intended primarily for working
mothers, has been free since January, 1967. In 1969 there were 44,245 children enrolled in
364 *círculos,* with thirty additional *círculos* under construction. (Figures quoted by Clemen-
tina Serra, former national director of the *círculos infantiles,* in *Granma,* July 4, 1969, p. 3.)

Then she wrote to him and enclosed two snapshots of herself, trying to make him go back to her. I got hold of the letter and read it. Something had gone wrong with her period; she thought she was going to have a baby again. She even sent her cousins to Armando. When he asked me about taking that letter, I denied it. But I told him I had proof which I could present, if necessary, so nobody could say I was slandering them.

You know, Fidel is ... I don't know how to put it into words, but he cares more for wives and children than for husbands. According to the law, if Armando ever abandoned me, they'd take away his salary and give it to me to feed the children as long as I didn't remarry. So walking out on me would have been pretty tough on him, see? I'd have to go to the Party with the proof to sink him. But I swear by my four children, I'd never have done it. I simply discussed the matter in private with him. I threatened him, but inside, it hurt. I never cried in front of him, because that would have been lowering myself.

I kept on having relations with Armando, and when I didn't get my period, I realized I was pregnant again. About that time Armando was transferred to the Isle of Pines. Then he broke up with Cora because he was having an affair with still another woman on the Isle. That was in the summer of 1962.

I stayed in Havana with my sister Serafina and Mandito and kept on working for the Frozen Zone. I'd get up at 6:00 in the morning, eat my breakfast, give the baby his milk, and then leave him and Fina asleep. Cleaning houses was very hard—bending over, carrying pails of water, scrubbing floors, and so on. When I got back home, all I did was take a bath, spend a little time with the baby, and eat whatever Fina had prepared for dinner. When I told Aldita I was going to quit, she said, "All right, but after you have your baby, come back." But then Armando didn't want me to.

Juan Pablo was born on December 30, 1962. Mando hadn't started walking yet, so now I had two babes in arms. Fina got a job with a Russian woman and worked there until she married.

The children were baptized when Mando was a bit over a year old. I didn't want to baptize them with Armando away on the Isle, but he himself preferred not to go to church or to mingle with the guests. So he told me, "Baptize them. Do as you like with them."

Miguel and Leonora, who lived in Juan and Mercedes's garage, had a one-year-old daughter, Lourdes. I told Leonora, "I'm going to have a talk with the padre about baptizing my kids."

"Well, look," Leonora said. "Let me go too, and we can baptize all three at the same time."

I dressed my kids and we all walked to the church. I asked *mamá* and *papá* to be godparents of one of the boys and Armando's *mamá* to be godmother of Juan Pablo. She refused—she hated to be called *comadre*, she said—so I asked my sister Isabel and my brother Diego. They couldn't come either, I forget why, so Serafina and a boy called Manolo acted as godparents instead.

We photographed the children in the church with the padre after the ceremony. When we got home at about 6:00 o'clock, we held the baptismal fiesta jointly but I paid all the expenses. Armando didn't like liquor to be served because, he says, people come only to drink and have a good time at another's expense. I let people drink if there's a bottle of something in the house, but I couldn't take advantage of Armando's absence to do something he disapproved of, so I didn't allow drinking and it spoiled everything for me.

After Juan Pablo, I didn't want to have more children and Armando used condoms for six months. Then he said we should try for a girl, and soon I was pregnant again. With two children and expecting a third, our money didn't go very far, so I started taking in laundry and Fina also helped us out. She earned 40 *pesos* cleaning and gave me 20.

In March, 1964, my third son, Germancito, was born. My obstetrician was a woman doctor. I practically lived in the hospital with that baby because he was always sick with vomiting and diarrhea. I decided to baptize him to see if that would make him well, but I didn't have a party because he was so ill. His godparents were my brother René and Serafina. Armando didn't oppose the baptism because he could see that the baby hadn't improved at all under the doctor's care. And you know what? The baby *did* get well after he was baptized!

I told Armando I didn't want any more children after Germancito, but again he asked me to try for a girl. He was wild to have a daughter. If I so much as looked at Armando's underdrawers on the clothesline, I'd get pregnant. There isn't more than a year's difference in age between Germancito and my fourth boy, Dieguito. But after he was born and baptized, I said, "Never again!"

It was too much. I couldn't leave the house, ever. Our armchairs were all beat up because the kids sat there for hours on end. They made me a playpen for Germancito but he wouldn't stay in it long. It wasn't only the strain of taking care of four small children—pregnancy itself wears you out. I've become a dried-up, skinny old woman, not to speak of the number of teeth I've lost. A belly will ruin your teeth. Serafina is just the same; her molars have fallen apart, in spite of the fact that the first thing they do when you get pregnant is send you to the dentist.

After Armando became a militant in the Youth, he told me if I should have another child he wouldn't allow it to be baptized. When he told me that, I decided never to have another child. Besides, with five children I'd be tied down to the house again. Who'd go out and run errands for me? Who'd get the groceries? I sure can't count on Armando. Anyway, though Fidel said at first that Cuban women should have lots of children, later he had to change that, saying, "There's not enough milk for so many children." Armando doesn't want any more children either, because by now we have enough to know that he's a father and I'm a mother.

So what with one thing and another, after Dieguito was born I decided the only thing for me was to put in the ring. I went to the doctor and he told me, "Come back on the forty-first day, after your period." During the forty days' wait, we used Chinese contraceptives, but those were very harmful to both of us. Armando got a lot of little blisters and I got an itch.

When I went to have the ring inserted, a Russian doctor was teaching a Cuban gynecologist how to insert it. That day I was wearing a wide skirt, so they asked me to take just my pants off in front of them. "No, no," said the Russian doctor, "don't embarrass her." He helped me get up on the table, and I pulled the sheet over me. "Don't cover yourself so much, we can't see you that way," he said. My period had ended that day and I was still spotting. "That's good," the doctor said. Sometimes it happens that a woman is already pregnant when she gets the ring and then she says it's no good.

I was embarrassed while the ring was being inserted because a lot of doctors walked in and out of the room. The doctor explained to each of them how to insert it. Finally, the woman at the door said, "I won't let anybody else in because they're embarrassing her." She locked the door and refused to open it again. The doctors were mad, but I *was* embarrassed.

They said I wasn't to have relations with my husband for five days, then I had to go back and get three shots. After that the doctor tells you, "All right, now it's not rationed!" and everybody laughs.

After my ring was inserted, I used to go every month to have it checked, but then I stopped going. Two years ago I had a hemorrhage and they say my ring fell out, but I haven't gone back. I don't take any precautions at all and I haven't gotten pregnant. I haven't had any problems nor missed my period even once. I know that as soon as I miss one period, I should run to the doctor. If I tell him, "My ring fell out and now I'm pregnant," they're sure to perform an abortion.

If a woman decides to have more children after having worn the ring, they simply remove it, clean her out, and she can get pregnant. If you get pregnant with the ring in place, you can have an abortion. Some women use that as an excuse because it's a crime to have an abortion unless a woman tells a doctor that she lost her ring.[4] They keep a tight control over such things now.

4. According to Elizabeth Sutherland, as of 1967 abortion was also legal and performed free of charge for any woman reporting to a hospital before the second month of pregnancy. (*The Youngest Revolution* (New York: Dial Press, 1969), p. 178.) Of course, if this time

I'm against women's liberation. Ever since that business came up, you see women going around with men all over the place. It's a disgrace, the things that are going on. Strong measures will have to be taken. If you go in the park at night, you find a bunch of guys and girls sitting on benches, kissing and pawing and doing all sorts of things. Before, at least there were houses where men and women could go and do such things in private.

The girls now walk around naked; when they sit down in the bus they show their bottoms. In the street, they give me a sort of sidelong look as if they despised me. Girls talk back to their mothers and the mothers don't say a word of reproof to them. My sisters and I weren't raised that way and I wouldn't want it for a daughter of mine either. If I had a daughter, I'd keep her locked up at home all the time.

There's a girl down the block who goes around smoking in the street with her skirts up to *here,* and she has two sweethearts at the same time. Serafina saw her standing with one of them. They were in each other's arms, but Fina thought they were doing something more than that. She told me that the girl's mother beat her up but good, on the mouth, on the eyes—all over.

It isn't only the young girls, even some of the married women have lovers and disgraceful little secrets of their own. Take that government minister who lives near here. He's having an affair with a Russian woman, even though he's married and has children. I myself have seen him come to fetch her, because she lives in the same building as my sister. If someone high up does such things, what can you expect of people of low rank?

I don't know whether such goings-on are a result of the times we live in or whether it's a fashion or what. All I know is that, whatever the reason may be, women are behaving disgracefully. It isn't liberation, it's downright shamelessness! Women have become shameless and our youth depraved. The government will simply have to take the situation in hand.

During the October crisis, I was terrified because Armando was on the Isle of Pines, surrounded by the sea. If it were invaded, I'd never see him again. I was pregnant with Juan Pablo at that time and still working, so I had to leave Mandito with my sister. My greatest fear wasn't for Ar-

---

limit were strictly observed most women would have had a very difficult time qualifying for the operation. Official policy on birth control was not clearly defined in 1970, and from the experiences of our informants we would conclude that the availability of abortions and birth-control devices depended to a large extent on the attitudes of the individual doctor and the persistence of the woman in her demands. In 1976, Carl T. Rowan, on a trip to Cuba, reported that abortion was available on demand and that in 1975 there were 64 abortions for every 100 live births. (*Chicago Daily News,* Dec. 15, 1976, p. 8.)

mando or for me but for the baby. He was still so small, and if something happened, we'd all have to go and fight. If we got killed, we got killed. I've never in my life been so scared. I didn't have a radio then but people said we were surrounded by ships and so forth. At first Armando called me from the Isle, but soon all communications were cut off. There were no airplanes either, so we didn't know anything about him or he about us.

Later, when Juan Pablo was about eleven months old, I went alone to the Isle of Pines to visit Armando. I sent for *mamá* and left the children with her because I hadn't seen Armando in three months. It was the first time I'd ever been in an airplane. I left for the airport early because so many people went and they had to examine the parcels. Prisoners were kept on the Isle of Pines then, and their wives went to visit them there.

As I was going down the steps of the plane at the small Isle of Pines airport, I saw Armando hiding behind a column, as a joke. I was carrying a small suitcase, cosmetic case, and several parcels. After they looked through my suitcase, we gathered up everything and took a drive along a very pretty palm-bordered road to the hotel. They wouldn't let me in the hotel because I had no identification. The manager explained that many prostitutes were there, especially when a ship came in, and that I needed a card from the Women's Federation or my place of work to be admitted into the hotel. The only identification card I owned was the hospital card, which I'd left with Fina in case the children got sick. The CDR didn't exist at that time[5] and I hadn't yet joined the Federation.

The Isle of Pines was run along terribly strict lines in 1963. Though Armando showed them his military identification card, I had to go to the police station. There Armando explained my problem to a police lieutenant or captain who was in his undershirt and without shoes. They asked for my name, address, parents' names, my place of birth, and my work. He wrote out a slip of paper for me and we returned to the hotel, where they gave us a small room. It was festival time and all the large rooms were taken.

Some comrades from Havana were staying at the same hotel with their wives. The boys would buy beer for all of us because Armando was wearing his uniform and couldn't buy it. We'd go to town and stroll around or go to a restaurant to eat a typical dish of the Isle, bonito, a fish they cook in oil with tomatoes. We'd also take the first shift in the hotel dining room to eat fried beef.

About a week later, I returned to Havana and went with Fina, *mamá,* and the kids to stay at my parents' house. I was there only a few days when Armando sent for me. He was in Havana. I left the children with

5. The Committees for Defense of the Revolution were founded September 28, 1960, but Lala's block CDR was not organized until 1964.

mamá and went. Armando told me, "I've asked for my discharge so I can stay here." I said, "Oh, I'm so glad! Now we can be together again."

I never urged him to get out of the Army. On the contrary, I preferred to have him there because it meant less work and less fuss and bother for me. I mean, of course I'd rather have him with us all the time because that's very important for the children, but if it's impossible, what can one do? One must adjust to the situation. What would be the point of making a big to-do about it when you know he's got to go anyway? Besides, here in Cuba there are many married couples who have to live apart. So I'd think, "Why should I embitter my life by refusing to accept things as they are?"

They discharged him in November, 1963, and sent him to Havana without pay and without a job. All he had was a letter. If he didn't find a job, he could always return to the Army. I wrote to *mamá* that I'd leave the children with her until Armando got a job, because there they'd never lack food or milk or anything.

Armando registered at the Ministry of Labor and through them he was called to MINCON.[6] He began to work in construction, laboring with pick and shovel under the hot sun. He was paid by the hour and earned according to how much he did. There were times when he left at 5:00 in the morning to work in Varadero and came back home at 8:00 that night. "It's hard," he'd say to me, "but I've got to earn money somehow."

In January, 1964, INIT called Armando for a job as dishwasher in a cafeteria. He was undecided about accepting the job, but I said to him, "Go there. At least you'll be working more comfortably. Besides, you'll have a steady salary." So he accepted it and gave his job at MINCON to my brother Diego, who'd just come to Havana looking for work. His wages were 89.35 *pesos* a month for eight hours of work a day. He worked until 3:00 in the afternoon and always brought home things for the kids to eat—rice, fritters, pudding. Then he'd go out to buy the groceries.

Later they sent him to a school of cookery. They paid him the same wages until he completed the course. I think he was in the school for six months—he graduated and everything. He's a good cook. After he graduated, his wages were gradually increased to 106 *pesos*. It took him a fairly long time to get to that level, but at least things improved little by little.

Armando didn't work long as a cook because the heat affected his stomach. The doctor prescribed a special diet for him—*malanga*, chicken, and milk. For a whole year he could eat nothing else because he had the beginnings of an ulcer. When he got sick, they transferred him to a job as assistant manager of an ice cream parlor in Old Havana. The

6. *Ministerio de Construcción* (Ministry of Construction).

workday there was eight hours and he got the same salary. After two
years they made him manager of two cafeterias. He now earns 160 *pesos*,
which, after the deductions, comes to 130. As manager he had nothing
to do except keep the accounts. Of his six years with INIT, he's been a
cafeteria or restaurant manager for at least four.

Armando is a strange fellow. Sometimes I ask myself why I ever married him and I can't explain it. I've been a lively, happy person ever since
I was a girl. I like to be on friendly terms with everybody, but Armando
doesn't. I wish he had a happy temperament like me, and liked parties,
going places, dancing. On Saturdays he comes home, takes a bath, and
goes out alone to a movie. I never say anything to him about it; why
should I embitter my life? In no time at all I'd become bitter about things
in general.

It's difficult for Armando to talk to people. When my brother comes
here, Armando hardly says a word to him beyond "Hello, Diego." Then
Diego says hello, and that's all the conversation between them. Other
times, after they're both in bed, one of them will start telling about this or
that and then both will talk.

Whenever I suggest that we go visit somebody, Armando says, "When
I'm in the mood we can go." He simply doesn't enjoy going out to see
people, nor does he like to be forever barging into other people's homes.
The only one on this block he ever visits is Serafina.

Armando never even goes to visit his family. More than six years have
passed since he's seen his mother. I urge him to visit his *mamá* but he says
why should he go there when he knows they're all right. The last time he
went to see them was when Mando was small.

I've never asked Armando to take me places, either when we were
newlyweds or now. When we go out, he himself invites me. He likes to go
out all right but we don't go much now because the buses are so bad and
going with four kids is too much trouble. Sometimes we all go to the
movies or to a park.

All in all, my folks in the country live better now. Before the Revolution, *papá* owned the house they live in and the farm it was on; he rented
a second farm that he had to sublet to eight or nine people in order to
pay the rent. After the Revolution when the Agrarian Reform[7] was
beginning, they made him the owner of that land. The former owners

7. The first Agrarian Reform Law, adopted May 17, 1959, prohibited private farms
larger than 400 hectares (approximately 988 acres). The expropriated lands were to be
distributed among former tenant farmers and sharecroppers, but during 1961 and 1962
most of the land was organized into state farms. The second reform law, enacted in
October, 1963, prohibited private farms larger than 67 hectares (about 5 *caballerías*, or 167
acres). The remaining privately owned farms (including those of Lala's father and uncles)
were incorporated into the National Association of Small Farmers (*Asociación Nacional de
Agricultores Pequeños*, or ANAP) under the National Institute of Agrarian Reform (*Instituto
Nacional de Reforma Agraria*, or INRA). INRA has been responsible for all major agricul-

tried to buy it back from him, but *papá* refused to sell, saying that the government had given it to him. Now he doesn't have to pay rent and has kept both farms for himself.[8] *Papá* has always been a hardworking man. The doctor told him it's time to quit because he has asthma, but *papá* says he's young yet and he's got to work.

My parents still have no electricity because there's no transformer in that part of Pinar del Río. They use kerosene lanterns, gas lamps, and candles. The company would have to bring the lines from quite far away and then install transformers. There's a state farm nearby that has electricity, but the dairy farm, which is the main part, doesn't.

In the country there are more things than there used to be. Before, we didn't have any plantains or bananas planted on our place; now we have a grove of them. We never used to plant rice at home either. Now it's necessary to grow rice because the ration isn't nearly enough for *papá*, *mamá*, and my brother René. This is the last year *papá* will plant rice, because they're going to stop him. From now on he won't plant black beans, red kidney beans, *malanga*, or corn either. In a socialist country there can't be any private producers, so next year all those things go to the state.

We used to eat the animals we raised on the farm; we never sold any of them. The fruits we grew were also eaten at home. Now, sometimes *mamá* exchanges farm products for something she needs, like a pair of shoes or a length of cloth. If you need a couple of chickens, all you've got to do is take a dress length to *mamá* and she'll gladly exchange the chickens for it. She doesn't exchange with her relatives, of course. When I need something, I ask for it and she gives it to me.

None of *mamá*'s relatives left Cuba. They all live and work in the country as before. The Revolution hasn't affected them at all. Some of my uncles on *mamá*'s side are doing well because the government hasn't taken their property. Only farms of more than 5 *caballerías* are taken. Uncle Raúl, who had more money than the others, added to his land regularly, so now the government has taken the whole thing. They still haven't taken Uncle Cosmé's farm, La Joya, which is more than 5 *caballerías*, though he tried to turn it over to them. They want to buy it but Uncle Cosmé says no, he wants to give it to them. He doesn't need the money, he says, he just wants to work.

---

tural and marketing functions since its establishment in 1959. (Carmelo Mesa-Lago, "Economic Policies and Growth," in Mesa-Lago, ed., *Revolutionary Change in Cuba* (Pittsburgh: University of Pittsburgh Press, 1971), pp. 282–83.)

8. Although Señor Fontanés received title to his farm for life he did not control utilization of the land or sale of the crops. The cane planted on his land was harvested by brigades of government workers. Señor Fontanés said he supervised maintenance on the farm, milked his dairy cows, and planted vegetables during the dead season. The only legal market for his milk, vegetables, livestock, and poultry was INRA. Señor Fontanés could divest himself of the farm only through sale to INRA.

They say that my grandma's farm is the inheritance of all her children, though there is no inheritance in Cuba anymore.[9] The sons are the ones who work the farm, and out of the money it earns they pay all the expenses and then divide the rest equally among their sisters. Every year, at the end of the sugar-cane harvest, they divide the profits.

My uncle Adelfo held many government posts when he was in charge of ANAP, but all he did was destroy it. He fell like a plague on the poor *guajiros,* took away their land, their pigs, and lots of other things, until they kicked him out. Now, after working so long for the government, he's turned against it. But his three sons are all integrated.

One son, Cornelio, is blondish, tall, a real cute kid, but he's been a thief ever since he was a child. He's seventeen or eighteen years old and entered military service at the time of the fifth call.[10] He worked in an FAR warehouse loading trucks and was caught stealing. He wasn't the only one arrested; they got seventy-two in all, every one of them in the military.

Cornelio and another boy were the ringleaders. They were given longer sentences; the others got from six months to ten years. Everything they stole, Cornelio took to his house. They really dug their own graves, because a woman from the CDR saw them and wrote down the license number of the truck. Then the people from the Committee phoned the unit and the information was spread around. The authorities allowed them to steal all they wanted for quite a while before moving in on them.

The Department investigators say that even millionaires don't have their houses equipped like that one. They had electric lights, record players, radios, an electric iron, and electric fans. They also had a chest of drawers with a big mirror, lots of cloth used only to make pants for militia officers, and two pairs of gloves meant for Fidel himself or, anyhow, somebody big in the government.

One of the girls in the family who was soon to be married had lots of Georgette crepe for dresses. They also had army sheets, coverlets, and sweaters. Can you believe that right in the middle of the Revolution any bride could have over twenty bedsheets for her new home? How could she have all those sheets and thirty towels when you can only get two with

9. Land titles granted to small farmers are only transferable to heirs who cultivate the land. Surviving spouses and children can inherit private residences (providing they do not already have another house or apartment), furnishings, and personal effects. Inheritance is regulated by Cuba's new Constitution.

10. Military service was made compulsory in 1962, and there is an annual conscription. The peak draft years are sixteen to twenty-seven, although all Cubans are subject to call-up until the age of forty-five, and most men demobilized from the services are enlisted in the militia until that age. Many young people elect to fulfill their military obligation by enlisting in paramilitary productive labor units within the Army of Working Youth (see Part II, n. 63).

your ration book? They haven't given out sheets since my sister Isabel got married two years ago. They found fifteen bedspreads stamped "Revolutionary Army" in the house and she had a kind of blanket only the armed forces get. They also turned up a lot of old money no longer in circulation, and a solid-gold watch.

The prosecution asked for a sentence of fifteen years, but in the end Cornelio got twelve years in jail plus three in military service. Armando says it was lucky for him they found nothing worse or they'd have tried him as a counterrevolutionary. In that case, he'd have gotten thirty years or the death penalty.

They're *gusanos*, the lot of them! I raised those kids when they were little. Now that they're grown men, they kiss me whenever we meet, but I don't like to go there. As soon as I do, they start whining, "*Ay*, there's nothing to eat in the house!"

"Well, suppose there isn't," I think, "just shut up and do something about it!" Those people had nothing before the Revolution either, so they've got no right to complain now.

The only revolutionary is their son Alfredo, who took the oath for five years of military service. After that, he'll go to officers' school. When he goes home on a pass he always quarrels with the rest. "You're selfish," he tells them. "You want to have more things than anybody."

All my other relatives are real revolutionaries. They're all good people but some of my cousins are *jabaos*, that is, they have coarse, kinky hair. I don't know who they took after. They say they were born with kinky hair because their parents are twice first cousins, and when cousins marry, something always comes out in the children. There are some others distantly related to them whose children were also born with kinky hair. They get that from their father's side of the family. They couldn't have gotten it from *mamá*'s family because all of us have good hair.

All my uncles are very well off, but Uncle Lázaro always speaks ill of the Revolution. They visit us and bring vegetables to *mamá*, but it's plain to see that they're not in favor of the Revolution. Maybe their sons who are working with tractors are revolutionary. Lázaro and Aunt Verónica turned their whole sugar-cane farm over to the government so as not to have to work. They said they were too old. Their son Lemuel was a *casquito*[11] and so was the other brother. At the beginning of the Revolution the two of them got out of Cuba in a small boat and were picked up by an American ship and taken to the United States.

Uncle Roberto used to keep a grocery store in his own house for his workers. Those poor people spent their whole year's wages in food before payday and Roberto got rich off them and bought lots of land. It's a

11. A derogatory term of reference for the special forces recruited by Batista to fight the Rebels. The name, literally "little cap," comes from the type of military headgear worn by the special forces.

mean thing to do and he's as mean as they come. He won't even come out from behind the counter to say hello. He has enough money to live on and even to leave to each of his children.

The store is now a people's store and the government left him a small plot of land. He manages the store, so he still fills his pocket. If, for example, he was sent a shipment of fifty bedsheets, he'd hide three or four and sell them to the poor people who used to work for him. They were assigned to his store, so they still buy there. They haven't put an end to his racket yet. I know because my sister Isabel tells me that his girls have boxes full of panties. Well, all you can get legally are just two little pairs at a time. And when his daughters Clemencia and Eglantina got married, he gave them tremendous weddings. Now his children are all revolutionaries.

All my brothers and sisters adore one another and are united even though we're scattered far and wide. My brother José lives in Las Mangas and works with *papá* on the farm. René lives at home but works on Uncle Cosmé's dairy farm. René spent eight months in jail for killing a heifer that Uncle Cosmé had ordered killed because it had a broken leg. René is out now but has to report to the authorities every month for five years.[12] All for killing a heifer! Some people kill them on the sly and nothing happens to them.

My other brothers left home—Diego is in Havana with his wife, Patricia, and Mario is the manager of a state dairy farm. Of my brothers, he's the only woman-chaser. Ah, Mario! They say he's like fire and takes after *papá*. He's a real revolutionary; we call him "the advocate of the poor." He got to the ninth grade and knows a lot. When he was manager of the state farm he knew every least little thing the animals ate. He argued once with Che Guevara from 6:00 P.M. to 1:00 A.M., about a women's work farm nearby where there was a lot of prostitution. El Che said they couldn't take the women away and my brother insisted that they couldn't allow such goings-on on an agricultural farm.

My sister Beatríz is married and lives near home, but Isabel is in Camaguey. Serafina is the one I see most because she lives right down the street. In December, 1965, we found out that she was living with our neighbor Rodolfo, Sonia's son. Rodolfo was in the military and Fina still worked for the Soviet woman. On New Year's Eve Serafina came home crying because of a quarrel with Rodolfo. I went to Rodolfo and he said, "Why no, there's been no trouble between us. We simply don't get along with each other so we decided to break up." Serafina doesn't like to confide in anybody, so I asked my sister Isabel, who was spending New

12. Under a law passed in 1963, any person convicted of the unauthorized slaughter of an animal can receive up to five years in prison.

Year's with us. "I don't know anything about it," Isabel answered. About midnight Fina said, "Lend me your suitcase; I'm going to Pinar del Río tomorrow. I'll drag myself home in my sorrow."

At daybreak she left to catch the bus that goes to the terminal, without telling me anything about her condition. I awoke when I heard her slam the door. We all got up and then Isabel told us, "Don't tell me you didn't know that Serafina is one month pregnant!"

I said, "No, I didn't know it, but if that's true, Serafina certainly can't go home."

Armando rushed out and caught her just as she was boarding the bus. He made her get down and told her angrily, "You're going right back home with me. I'm the one who'll settle this matter with Rodolfo. If he doesn't accept you willingly, he'll have to accept you by force. He can't do this to us." Fina came back, weeping.

That day Armando and Diego had to go to the Plaza de la Revolución to commemorate the anniversary of the Triumph. Before leaving, Armando said to me, "Don't let Fina leave this house!"

Rodolfo's sister Paz came to explain that her mother, Sonia, had gone to spend the holidays with her family in Oriente. "But," she said, "when she returns, she'll settle this problem." Guido, Rodolfo's brother, said, "Rodolfo can't do that to Serafina. He's got to marry her. Especially since our two families are such good friends. If those people push the matter, Rodolfo is going to land in jail."

Guido told Rodolfo, "Look, you must take the responsibility for Fina. She was a señorita living at home when you got involved with her, so now that you've gotten her pregnant, you must marry her."

"Sure, I know. I'm not blind," Rodolfo said. "Of course I'll marry her." That afternoon he came to talk with me. "I'm awfully sorry for what I did, Lala." And he said to Armando, "I'm going to marry Serafina. Let the old man know and ask him to come."

Diego sent a telegram to *papá* and he came that same afternoon. "What's going on that you send for me in such a hurry?" he said. I didn't dare tell him, because Fina had been staying with me and I expected a scolding. Diego told him everything and *papá* was furious with Rodolfo. He didn't blame me at all, though he refused to stay for lunch, saying, "No, I'm going back home at once."

"But *papá*," I objected, "aren't you going to go see Fina?"

"That brazen hussy? I should say not!" he replied, and he left.

About a week later Rodolfo said to me, "Tell the old man to get Fina's birth certificate for me. Fina and I are going to get married." *Papá* got it for them but Fina and Rodolfo kept on postponing the wedding.

When she was three months pregnant, Serafina lost her baby. She was alone in Sonia's house and she says she slipped and fell, but I think she provoked the miscarriage because the afterbirth stayed inside and got infected. Sonia took her to a doctor, but he said there was nothing wrong with her. A week later she hemorrhaged. She was seriously ill and delirious and I left the kids with Leonora and took her to the Calixto García Hospital.

I was terribly upset to see my sister so desperately ill. Nobody at home knew about it. I phoned Rodolfo at his military unit, then I phoned his sister. I also phoned my family, around 4:00 o'clock, and at about 11:00 *mamá,* Isabel, René, and *papá* arrived in Havana.

Papá didn't want to see her. I said to him, "Look, what's done is done. She's terribly ill now and we should all stand by her. So please don't refuse." But *papá* was still angry and didn't go to the hospital. Instead, he went back home at daybreak with René. *Mamá* and Isabel stayed with me.

The next day Serafina was in critical condition. I stayed in the hospital that day from 9:00 in the morning on, without breakfast, because I couldn't eat seeing Fina in such a state. Rodolfo behaved very well, driving to the hospital in a military truck at all hours of the day and donating blood. Later on the whole military unit offered to donate blood.

The doctor interviewed me, because at that time abortions were strictly forbidden. Nowadays a doctor will give you an abortion if you want it, but it was illegal then. Rodolfo and the woman to whom he'd taken Fina were liable for jail terms. I told the doctor I didn't know anything about it. I've never spoken about it to Fina. I was sorry for her, poor thing.

Since then things have gone well for her. Rodolfo is a good husband. He loves her, and his whole family is very fond of her too. She and Rodolfo lived at Sonia's house for about three years. Then about a year ago, Clara, the lady who used to own the building they live in, gave her the garage. Fina still worked for the Soviet woman, who paid her 40 *pesos,* and Rodolfo's brother Guido gave her 10 *pesos* a month for her personal expenses.

My sister Isabel was married on September 30, 1967, which fell on a Saturday. They phoned me a week before to tell me. Armando and I planned to go to the wedding and stay over until Sunday. I was going to take two of the kids with me and leave two with Fina, who couldn't go because her son Rodolfito was only five months old. But on Saturday, around 10:00 in the morning, Armando called me from work to say we couldn't go because he'd been assigned guard duty at his militia unit. "All right, then I'll go alone," said I. But he objected, "Oh no, if I can't go, neither can you!"

I don't cry easily but I cried that day. After we'd made all the arrangements, why couldn't he have said to them, "I can't stand guard next

Saturday, I've got to go somewhere"? I couldn't even phone my folks because they live out in the country. I took the kids out for a snack at the ten-cent store and then I stood in line to buy some clothing.

Armando got home about 3:00 in the afternoon and said, "You've got to get my dinner ready." At 6:00 I said to him, "You'd better eat out at the Club Obrero tonight." He didn't get to eat that night until after his guard duty was over. After that, we didn't speak to each other for a week. I'd serve his dinner and he'd eat and go out again, without either of us saying a word. He tried to make up with me several times, but I didn't want to.

Then Guido saw that we were mad at each other and said, "Armando, why didn't you let Lala go to the wedding even if you couldn't go?" He also told Armando that he could never in his life find another woman who always stayed home like me. So we were reconciled. I don't get angry easily, it simply isn't in me, but there are times when I have to get serious with Armando.

I know that whenever I want to go home all I have to do is pack my things and go. He'll say, "Don't leave me alone," and I'll tell him, "Why shouldn't I? You go wherever you please and leave us all alone. The kids and I never go anywhere." Now *mamá* wants to take Juan Pablo and Mandito to stay with her during their vacation. One of these days I'll take off and go there myself to have a good time with my folks. Armando won't say anything except that he'll have no place to eat while I'm away.

"Eat in a restaurant or cook your own meals," I'll tell him. He's a very good cook.

Recently I spent three days in Pinar del Río and he missed me. When we got back he told me he couldn't stand being alone. He'd go to sleep so as not to feel anything. He's just so used to having us around.

Armando is really a strange character, damn him! He thinks only of himself; nobody else exists. When he gets mad, he comes home late and then I won't speak to him. He comes in, takes off his clothes, and flops face down on the bed. But he's affectionate with me when he feels like it, I'll admit. He always calls me *mamá*. He calls me Lala only in front of other people. I'd rather he called me *mamá* because I hate to be called by my own name. We've called each other *mamá* and *papá* affectionately ever since we got married, even before we had children.

I used to be affectionate with him but now I simply don't feel like it. I show affection to anybody I'm fond of, but Armando doesn't. He's reserved, like most people from Oriente. He keeps his feelings hidden. What upsets me is his indifference. Sometimes he's so detached with the children that I can't help reproving him. "What's wrong with you, Armando, aren't you fond of your own children?"

The way he is, I don't know why I haven't left him. But I've changed. If I find out he's up to his old tricks again, I won't remain with him one minute longer. I love Armando more than myself but I've had enough. I can't bear more fooling around. Let him go his way and leave me alone and simply send money for the children every month. I'm young and I know how to work. I'll go to the Party sectional or the Federation and they'll give me a job at once. I can sew, and it wouldn't be hard to place me in a workshop and my children in boarding school. That way I can support myself and then I won't grow bitter.

Armando has no reason to complain about me. He depends on me a lot. I've always run the house and managed his money. He gives me 50 *pesos* every fifteen days for household expenses and he saves the rest. I spend that money as I see fit. He never argues with me about what I spend. Before, when he was in the Army, he'd hand me his entire paycheck. Some women can't go buy groceries until their husbands come home and give them money, but not me. I get what's due to me and when it's gone, it's gone. Now he has to keep some money for himself because he's got to ride the bus to work.

We have a bit of money saved up—almost 300 *pesos*—toward the price of a frigidaire. I also have 50 *pesos* put away in a purse. That's where I save what I earn doing Mercedes's laundry, and every time Diego gives me 10 *pesos,* so we have money to spare in case the kids get sick or we need anything. After all, what do we spend money on except food? And what food can we buy anyway?

I wish Armando would take more responsibility for doing things around the house, but he's never here. Sometimes he'll straighten up a bit or dust the shelves and so on. But I had to get a man to install the kitchen. Before that, I cooked in Evidio's kitchen. When the sink fell, I got a man to fix it—for 25 *pesos.* Sometimes when the light goes, I have to get Guido or Rodolfo to fix it. When it rains, the overhead lamp globes fill up with water and those two men pour it out for me. Armando won't do it, or if he takes out the globes to pour the water out, he won't replace them, so I say, "Never mind, I'd rather fix them myself."

He's like that because of the strange way he's been brought up, without love for his home. He could see the house falling down on top of him and not move a finger to fix it. He's very neat, though, and hates to see things out of place. He straightens out the bureau drawers and all that. When he sees something dirty, he'll say something about it at once, but all he really cares about is that I should have his dinner ready early.

He wants me to do everything for him. When *mamá* comes, he doesn't like to have her even put his food on the table. And he doesn't want anyone else to wash or iron his clothes because he likes the way I do it. When somebody else irons his clothes, he notices right away and says, "You didn't iron this yourself, Lala." I mend his shirts and sew on buttons but he always mends his socks himself.

When Armando and the children get sick, I take care of them myself at home. I'm like *mamá*: as long as I can cure them with home remedies, I don't go running to doctors. The doctor prescribes benadryl or ephedrine for a cold, but I prefer a good glass of lemonade.

When chicken pox and mumps were going around, everybody got chicken pox except me. Armando, Diego, the four kids, all sick at the same time—I thought I'd go mad! Armando was desperate—he spent all his time sitting in the corner of the sofa complaining, "*Ay*, it burns, it itches, I'm dying, I've got to take a bath!" I took Diego to the doctor because he got rubeola along with the chicken pox, but the rest got along fine at home.

I used to buy the children's shoes, but now Armando does, and their clothes, too. He buys everything, even my clothes. I have a pair of very pretty jersey panties with lace that he picked out himself. He knew the woman who ran the dress shop. Lately, I go shopping because he doesn't have the time any longer. He likes to have us all well dressed when we go somewhere, that's why we never go out at all.

Armando takes good care of the children. When they're alone, the children treat him like a playmate and he encourages them by playing and dancing with them. "They'll lose all respect for you," I tell him. But he answers, "Not a bit! Let's test it. Yell at them the way you do and tell them to sit still." And it's true, they don't respect me. I can't understand why not, I spank them often enough.

Armando has his own way of managing them. He'll tell them to sit down and they obey him. But when Armando threatens to punish them, they call out, "*Mami, papi*'s going to spank us," so that I'll intervene.

I punish my children by forbidding them to go downstairs to play. When I tell them, "If you don't eat all your dinner you can't go down," they'll polish off everything on their plates. If they don't behave, I make them get into pajamas and go to bed, then I take their shoes away because they won't go out barefoot.

In my time we children were whipped with rope; nowadays children are hit with soft leather belts. I've whipped my kids because there are certain things I won't permit. I never spank them out in the street though. If they act up, I wait until we get home before spanking them. One day Mando did something out in the street—I can't remember what it was—and when we got home I made him put on his pajamas. Then I hit him with the strap until Armando told me to stop. I've never had to spank any of them since, only scold them.

The same thing happened last year with Juan Pablo. We were watching TV at Sonia's house when he smashed a vase of hers. I was embarrassed to death. I whaled the daylights out of him when he got back home. Afterward I brought Sonia a lovely vase that my mother-in-law had given me. I was so ashamed I haven't been in Sonia's place since.

Armando adores Mando, but he loves Dieguito even more, because that little one knows how to get around him. He and Mandito are the most affectionate of my children. Mando kisses me when he comes in and he kisses me every day before going to school. Juan Pablo is more stand-offish. If I want to kiss him, I've got to go to him. Germancito is even less affectionate and more stubborn. If he says he wants something a certain way, it's got to be done that way.

When Armando doesn't come home to sleep, the children ask about it. Sometimes he gets home after they're in bed and leaves before they're up, so they ask whether he slept at home or not. I think it's important for children to see their father every day, to grow fonder of him and to know that he's their father. At this age the father is more important than the mother. They don't respect me but if they so much as see Armando, they behave themselves.

Armando was away for three months at a school for Party members—it would have been longer if they'd wanted him to be a Party official. After he finished school, he would have had more political activities and more responsibility at work, but he volunteered to go to the Isle of Pines to do agricultural work. I found out about it when I overheard him saying to a friend, "They've just told me I must go to the Isle for two years." When his friend left, he said to me, "We had a meeting at 3:00 o'clock this afternoon and we were told we have to go to the Isle for two years." I didn't believe him because they've said that so many times and he never went. Then one morning Armando phoned and said, "You know what? They've just given me orders to go."

I wasn't feeling well because the whole business made me nervous, and besides, I was having my period. I was simply going crazy. Then when he got home that afternoon, he said to me, "If I can get somebody to wash my clothes there, I'll send them to her."

"Now look," I said, "you bring your clothes here and I'll wash them. If you come home on three days' leave, that's plenty of time for me to wash and iron enough clothes to last you months." He has about eight khaki pants, not counting the olive-green ones, and on top of all that, he'll get two more full changes there. He has heaps of shirts, too.

So I said to him, "You've got no need to go looking for another woman to do your laundry. And look, I'm giving you fair warning, if you take up with another woman there, I'm through with you for good. From that day forward you needn't bother to come home again, or send any money for the children, either. I've put up with enough already and I've had a hard life. It isn't as if I were the kind of woman who spent her life at the movies, or went without you, or spent all my time sitting in a chair at home waiting for everything to be given to me. Oh no, kid, I've sacrificed myself taking in laundry to help you out. I do big loads of wash for other people and iron heaps of clothes. I'm not going to put up with your making love to other women out on the Isle while I slave away at home. So if you're planning to do anything like that, you know what to expect. I'm warning you. The minute you take up with another woman there, I'll know about it."

"Don't worry," said he, "I'm not going to take up with any woman there. Besides, you know what would happen to me if they caught me doing anything like that now that I'm a militant."

"No, no, don't try to throw dust in my eyes," I answered. "I know you too well. Militant or not, you've always had women on the side." I came right out and told him in so many words. Whenever he was having an affair, he never gave me a hint. But he told my brother all about his affairs and I found out by hiding and listening.

I don't believe he chose to go to the Isle again because he thought it would be easier to have another woman there. No, I'm sure he really meant it when he said he wanted to go to help the Revolution, and that he wasn't helping it at all here. But even so, I simply don't trust him. The Party didn't want to send him; they said he was needed here in Havana. It was Armando himself who insisted on going.

The truth is I've suffered a lot because of Armando. But he's settled down. The Party helped a lot in that, because the Communist Youth and Party members are forbidden to have affairs. Of course, forbidden or not, there are cases.... I know some officials who do. If someone high up does such things, what can you expect of people of low rank?

I wouldn't be surprised if Fidel himself had his little affairs. He needn't pretend that he can get along without women—we all know better than that. He's sure to have something going on. But anyway, when a man is made a militant, he's not allowed to have more than one woman. In that sense, the Revolution is helping women and children more than men. For instance, while Armando is working out on the Isle, the Party sees to it that I get his entire paycheck. It's sent directly to me.

Armando left for the Isle around 5:30 on a Sunday morning. Only three men from his sectional went, and he was one of them. It came out in the paper that altogether only 53 had gone when 105 were supposed to go.

The night before he left, we went to bed around 12:30, because Armando was putting his things in order. We didn't have relations that night because I had my period. So he went away without doing anything and he really needs it, I know. He told me he'd wait until he came home on leave. Well, I'll believe him, for the time being. But just let me find out that he's got another woman out on the Isle and he'll never darken this doorway again.

It's hard for Armando to go away, because he gets very nervous. He's got a nerve ailment now and has to take permanganate pills to control himself. I'm used to his going away and I know more or less how he's going to react. He didn't even wake me up, but I heard him in the bathroom. Then, when I saw him dressing, I asked, "Don't you want your breakfast, Armando?"

"No, no, I'm not hungry, don't get up," he said. "I don't want any breakfast." He went to the kitchen to get a glass of milk and I was right behind him, but he kept turning away from me. He didn't like me hanging around, so while he was putting his things in order, I boiled milk and washed the dishes. In all that time he wouldn't look at me.

Then he picked up his suitcase and said, "Let's go down." I hugged and kissed him but he turned his back on me right away and hurried off. I stood by the open window, watching him, but he never once looked back.

Now that I'm all alone, I miss him a lot. At first I didn't sleep a wink. I kept getting up and going back to bed and getting up again. I don't know why I was so nervous. Diego and Germancito began sleeping with me and it seemed that it was Armando there beside me. One night I dreamed I saw Armando in the bathroom, then I woke up startled. It seemed as if I'd really seen him. Then I dozed off again and, half asleep like that, I seemed to hear him putting his key into the keyhole. He has a whole bunch of keys and makes a lot of noise. I thought somebody really was trying to get in, so I got up and turned on the light. It was like that all night long; I'd doze off and wake up scared.

I always feel like that the first few days after Armando goes away. Later I get used to it—until he comes home on a five-day pass. Then, when he leaves, I go through the same thing all over again. Armando tells me that if he can get leave to sleep away from the camp and stay with me every night, he wants me to go to the Isle to live. But not otherwise, because there's no point in my going if we can't be together there. But I want to see the Isle again no matter what, so if I don't go this year, I'll go next year.

Armando Cárdenas

I was born in a barrio called Santa Ana, near Bayamo, Oriente. Santa Ana is very small, just a few huts with two or three little grocery stores and one café. We lived on a broad mesa where there were five houses altogether, counting ours. Our house was built of palm leaves and palm bark. It had two rooms, and a kitchen in a small, separate hut connected to the house by a passageway. There was no toilet or latrine because we were out in the country. Our drinking water came from a well, and we washed our clothes in a brook a kilometer from the house.

I lived with my mother, Maida Pardo, my father, Armando Cárdenas, and my sisters and brothers. Ana María, the eldest, died, but the rest are still living. Elena is the eldest now, then María Luz, María Nieves, me, and Luis. The younger ones, Juan, Raúl, Amparo, and Lazlo, were born in Las Marías, Oriente. The place we lived in wasn't ours. The other houses stood on their own land; only *papá* had to work other men's land for wages. We had to depend on other people's willingness to sell us the things they grew. Sometimes we didn't even have the money to buy them.

Before I was born my old man had been in the Army, the Navy, and the police force. Once he was stationed in Havana and that was the only time he was ever out of the province of Oriente. Aside from that, I don't know a thing about my old man's past. *Papá*'s stint with the Army was the best time of his life, but he left a short time before qualifying for retirement. It was during Machado's[13] regime—my old man turned against him and was kicked out of the Army. That's when *papá* went back to farm work in Santa Ana.

We were so poor there were days when we didn't eat. I remember my old lady sitting on the doorstep with us children clinging to her, waiting for our old man to bring home the *factura*.[14] There was nothing on the

13. General Gerardo Machado, President of Cuba 1925–33.
14. An invoice or itemized listing of groceries bought on credit at the company store and charged against the farm worker's earnings at the end of the harvest season.

stove but an iron pot with a few sweet potatoes boiling, skin and all, without a bit of lard or oil, the way you cook them for pigs. The groceries *papá* was able to buy on credit lasted only one week, and after the food was gone we had to go without eating all day long, or even two or three days with only plain boiled sweet potatoes or cornmeal. It was a sad thing and it happened to us often.

We never ate breakfast, just a cup of black coffee in the morning. We never had any milk to drink. I remember my old lady giving the younger children the breast until they were two or three years old, so I guess maybe she did the same for me. I didn't get into the habit of drinking milk until I was in the Army. Our lunch was boiled sweet potatoes or boiled cornmeal. In the evening our big meal was a bit of rice with beans. That was the most we could hope for in those days.

Mamá usually managed to give us at least one meal, because mothers always manage somehow. When there was rice, she'd often make some kind of soup in the morning and serve the rice for our evening meal. She'd buy eggs in the neighborhood for 2 or 3 *centavos* each, but we didn't eat them regularly. We ate chicken when we had it—to have chicken with rice was a festive occasion for us. We never managed to raise any chickens, because if we did happen to have one and there was nothing else in the house, into the pot it would go. *Mamá* would make it last two or three days. I don't remember ever eating beef as a child, but I guess maybe I did now and then, probably when somebody killed a cow or an ox and gave my old lady a few scraps. There isn't the remotest possibility that she ever bought any.

We weren't in the habit of eating dessert or fruit compotes. Heck no! I never even heard the word "compote" until I came to live in Havana. We didn't have any fresh fruit either, because they didn't grow much fruit out that way. There was a lot of fruit where my uncles lived—mangoes, oranges, and so on—but it was a whole day's journey on horseback each way.

Our problem was that we had no land to work and no way of making a living. Things were so bad for us that my folks migrated from place to place in search of a way to better their situation. I was almost eight when we moved from Santa Ana. We took along everything we owned, loading the mules with pots and pans and beds. First we went to Bayamo, where we stayed a few days with Aunt Carlota. She was *papá*'s oldest sister but she was more like his mother because she raised him. She adored *papá* and loved us dearly for his sake. I remember that those were good days, although she was miserably poor. She was a sweet little old lady and treated us with so much affection. You know how it is—a child responds to affection, like a puppy.

Papá's half-sister, Aunt Regla, lived behind Aunt Carlota's house. They got along well because Aunt Regla was poor too. We didn't stay with her because she simply couldn't take us in. She had to do laundry to support her own children, so how could she have possibly offered us hospitality?

Papá's brother, Uncle Eladio, lived near Carlota and Regla. He worked hard at his candy stand to support his wife and children. He sold *prú*, a kind of soft drink, homemade coconut candy, and other kinds of candy. The only relative who was pretty well off was Uncle Andrés, another of *papá*'s brothers. He owned an enormous grocery store. How he made enough money to start it I couldn't tell you, because before that he was as poor as the rest of us.

When my folks were comfortably off, Uncle Andrés lived with them, because he was so poor he didn't even have a place to drop dead in. *Papá* gave him food, and pocket money too, because Andrés didn't have a thing. But when *papá* left the Army and went to him for help, Andrés turned against him. Andrés helped very little, and not with very good grace. He'd give *papá* food from his grocery store, but only small scraps of this and that.

Uncle Andrés and his wife, Natividad, had a daughter and a son, but I remember seeing them only once. My old man didn't like to go to their house because they acted like aristocrats. They looked down on their poor relations and refused to have anything to do with them. After we moved away from Bayamo, I didn't see Uncle Andrés again until the triumph of the Revolution.

From Bayamo we moved to Dos Palmas to ask my grandpa, Mario Cárdenas, for help. My parents took María Luz, María Nieves, Luis, and me, but Elena remained with Aunt Carlota. My folks decided to see how it would work out in Dos Palmas before making a definite move, and they left most of their things in Bayamo.

Grandpa's farm was in Dos Palmas, but he lived in a grand, well-furnished house in Bayamo. My old lady says that Grandpa had promised to give *papá* a piece of land after he'd worked on the farm for a while. Grandpa himself told *papá* to come to Dos Palmas. If he hadn't, my old lady would never have gone. But he didn't treat *papá* kindly. We lived in an old house that he let *papá* use. It was a typical house, surrounded by stones, rotting trees, and snakes. Grandpa paid *papá* very little and didn't help him at all. That was the dirtiest trick in the world. There didn't seem to be any real love and understanding between my father and his old man. They simply didn't get along with each other. I don't know what it was that kept them apart.

It wasn't only with *papá* and *mamá* that Grandpa was so selfish. He treated some of his other children the same way. But he let Uncle Lalo run the farm and he was the one who paid the others. Grandpa could have helped *papá* if he'd wanted to. He was pleasant to *papá,* but what good did that do? What's the point of being pleasant and polite to somebody if you wouldn't hand him a change of clothes, no matter how ragged he was?

It seems he wanted all he could get for himself, even if his children starved. I can't understand that. After all, what does a father want money for, if not to be able to leave it to his children when he dies? Or, if he sees one of them in need, to be able to lend a helping hand? It seems to me that if a father owns a farm, he should share it with all his children, but Grandpa gave his money to Uncle Lalo and his favorite people. *They* could have what they needed.

In spite of everything, my old man and Grandpa Mario never quarreled, because my old man doesn't quarrel with anybody, not even when they start a quarrel with him. Even if you didn't talk to him, he'd talk to you.

When *mamá* saw how we didn't get anything and were starving to death for lack of work, she sent word to Aunt Carlota not to send our beds or anything, because we were going back. My old lady didn't get belligerent about it, but she's always blamed Grandpa for promising *papá* a piece of land to work and then not keeping his word.

My old lady had to work pretty hard on Grandpa's farm. She harvested coffee from the beginning to the end of the season to get enough money for us to leave. She had to buy us clothes and tennis shoes so we'd have decent clothes to travel in. To get to the store the old lady had to walk practically all day long, because the only way to go was on foot. There were no cars in that zone, only beasts of burden.

We left Dos Palmas at night in a torrential rain, riding a neighbor's team of mules. We rode at night because it was cooler. I was mounted on one of the mules, slippery with rain, and I fell off. They were crossing the river and when I screamed they turned back to pick me up. In spite of the swollen rivers and the slippery slopes, we arrived at Palma Soriano, where the railroad station was located.

We went to the house of some people we knew, to bathe and change our clothes for the rest of the trip. Then we took the train to Bayamo and that time we stayed at Grandma Matilde's house. Uncle Claudio, *mamá*'s brother, lived there too, with his wife, Luisa. My mother's *papá* died before I was born. Grandma Matilde was very sweet and affectionate with all of us. She always helped *mamá* as much as she could. When my old lady went to see her, Grandma would give her chickens or two or three pigeons. When her sow lightened, she'd give *mamá* a little sow. None of those sows ever lived to have piglets of their own because *mamá* always had to slaughter them when things got bad. Uncle Martín helped too. He was a barber and had saved a bit of money.

From Bayamo we went back to Santa Ana. We kept wandering over highways and byways for almost a year trying to find a place to make a living. We'd have given anything for a piece of land, even if only yucca and sweet potatoes would grow on it. At least we could have lived on that. But we had nothing. It was desperation that drove my folks on, looking for somebody to give them a piece of land.

At that time, one of *mamá*'s brothers, Uncle Juan, owned a bit of land in Las Marías. He was a small farmer but had saved enough to buy himself that little piece of land. Well, Grandma Matilde explained *mamá*'s problem to him: "Look, Maida's so badly off, she's going to come here."

I guess Grandma harped on the subject until my uncle gave in, so *mamá* finally got her bit of land. *Mamá* and Uncle Martín bought five *varas*—that's about 50 square meters—for 20 *pesos*. Grandma gave *mamá* the money to buy it. I was nine years old then.

We finally settled down in Las Marías. Uncle Juan had already started building when we bought the lot, because he'd planned to open a small grocery store there. We stayed with Aunt Evelina until he finished building our house.

Most houses had only two very small bedrooms. In our house, you stepped right into the parlor and there was one bedroom on either side. The parlor had no windows because it was right in the middle, but the bedrooms did. The kitchen was covered with palm fronds and had two doors on opposite sides. The kitchens always had a window to let the air in and the smoke out. The sink was under the window and had a vent to the outside, to let the dirty water out.

A palm house soon looks run-down even when the roof doesn't leak, which it usually does. When that happens you must pile more palm on top, and so on. I never saw the kind of inside roof that's called a ceiling until I came to Havana.

In our kitchen there was a table, scarred and falling apart at the joints. The stove was the earthen kind, about waist-high, with four iron grills to hold the pots. I also remember two chairs with the seats and backs missing. In the parlor we had two very poor-quality benches. That was all the furniture we had. In one corner there was a water jar and in the other corner, a cabinet. There we kept enamel plates, spoons, some glasses and pitchers, and a few things like that.

Our beds had wooden headboards and frames and flat wire springs. There were three beds, counting one that I bought much later, after I started working. To pay for that bed, I worked three days on a piece of land owned by a guy called Ubaldo, the lottery-ticket seller. Actually, all I got was the wooden frame. We didn't have any mattresses—we used cotton quilts instead. *Mamá* used to lay sacks on the springs, under the cotton quilt.

We managed all right with those beds; the girls slept in one bed and all of us boys in another. When Juan was born, he slept with *mamá* and *papá* until he was three or four—there usually was a little child sleeping with my parents because there was no crib—then he moved to the boys' bed. By that time I was sleeping in the parlor in a hammock made of sacks.

For light, we made a *candil* from a condensed milk tin filled with gasoline. We'd put a flannel rag in it and light it. We had two like that made from sardine cans, and another that looked like an old-fashioned gas lamp.

There were very few trees along the road to the house because they'd leveled the place with a steamroller, so it had an awfully bare look—not at all a pretty landscape. If only it had been a cattle farm with trees growing on it! But there was nothing around the house except cornfields, and the corn was so high you could see nothing beyond it. There was a line of *maya* plants, too—what we called "rat's pineapple" because of its long, spiky leaves. I remember that a rosebush and *adelfas* grew in our front yard, but we didn't have even one little fruit tree.

From the left side of the house you could see the town grocery store, and from the right, my cousin Melchor's house. Aunt Evelina and Uncle Rafael lived about 4 or 5 kilometers away. They aren't very close to our family, but Aunt Evelina was nice to us and came to visit whenever she went to the store for food.

About 150 meters away from our house, the road went straight through a hollow. When *papá* was coming home down the slope we could see him some distance away before he got to the house. We could see as far as a little brook and a farm with a palm grove. The grove was cut down bit by bit because palm trees were sold for building houses.

When it rains hard in Las Marías, the place floods and then it's nothing but black mud, the kind that sticks to your feet. The worst of it was that our food was soon gone and we starved, because we were shut up in the house. I remember one season when it rained for fifteen days, and the corn loaded on the carts sprouted right through the sacks. The supplies at the grocery store were exhausted because the carters couldn't cross the flooded rivers; the oxen kicked their yokes trying to pull the carts out of the mud. It was a nightmare—nobody could come in or get out.

Nowadays, the rivers have new dams to prevent those troubles, but at that time the Contramaestre River would back up, flooding an enormous field almost 2,000 meters long. They called it "the graveyard" because the carcasses of drowned animals were thrown there for the river to carry away. Where the Cauto and Contramaestre rivers pour their waters into the sea, living animals and whole families were swept to hell in the floods.

There were many Chinese living in town near the river and a lot of them drowned. They were very poor and built shacks by the riverside so they could grow their own vegetables. That's about all they had to eat. The Chinese are tightfisted, that's true, and they like to save their money, but they're not the kind of people who quarrel with their neighbors. They get along well with everyone.

There was only one school anywhere near us, in Cerro Gordo. The schoolteacher taught for pay and my parents couldn't afford that, so none of us kids went to school. The only ones who could afford it were those who had some kind of good connection or owned a piece of land. The children whose families had to struggle to just stay alive started working at an early age. Besides, we couldn't go to school because we didn't have decent pants or shoes. Having shoes was important; in that school they only accepted the children of fairly well-to-do parents.

At home I always went barefoot, wearing shoes only to go out. I remember going to El Paso de Palmas, to a store that my old man was painting. It really wasn't a town but just a small group of houses. When I appeared, a girl said, "Look at him! So big—and barefoot!" I don't remember being ashamed or embarrassed or trying to hide or anything. But my old man had heard too, and he seemed to mind because he bought me a pair of *espadrilles* that had rubber soles and canvas uppers. After that, they started buying me that type of shoe. I'd wear them until they fell apart. That embarrassed me terribly.

Later I made friends with some boys who lived next door to us, and one day one of them said to me, "Hell, Armando, stop wearing canvas shoes. Buy yourself a pair of work shoes. A fellow who wears *espadrilles* is dirt poor all his life." They kept after me until I finally bought a pair of leather shoes with money I'd earned working on a neighbor's farm. I don't remember how much they cost because I was illiterate at the time. All I know is they seemed like the best shoes in the world.

As a child I wore overalls and flour-sack shirts. *Mamá* made knickers for me from large, thick flour sacks. My old lady says that she once made me a pair of short pants but I refused to wear them. After that, she made me long overalls. I often wore pants with two patches behind and two in front. We had to wear our clothes as long as they'd hold together. By the time we discarded a pair of pants, they looked like one of the patchwork sheets my old lady made. Nowadays, if a pair of pants gets wrinkled I set them aside. If I have to wear them again, I will, but only if I really must. And I'll seldom wear a pair of pants that's been mended.

My old man dressed the same as us boys. Sometimes he'd go out with pants almost falling down with the weight of the patches. His shirt was all patched and ragged too, and he wore an ancient straw hat. My sisters dressed in cheap, simple clothes, like all poor people. *Mamá* dressed the same way, because they bought cloth by the yard and made all their dresses from the same goods and in the same style.

My old man didn't work in the village. If any odd job turned up anywhere, he'd be there to do it. Many days he'd return home empty-handed after looking around all day for a job. When he did find work, he'd stay away a week or two, or even a whole month. He wasn't paid in money but with slips of paper that were good for a certain amount of food at the grocery store. Usually, whoever owned a large farm also owned a grocery store. That was the way they did business. So if you worked for a landowner and needed to buy something, you had to buy it at his grocery store because the credit slip wasn't good anywhere else. The landowner had a thief in charge of his store who would sell short, knocking off an ounce from the weight here and there. So the landowner robbed you twice: once at work, and again at the store.

When *papá* came home, he'd bring a sack of food for us. He'd buy rice, sugar, coffee, dried salted codfish, which was used a lot in those times, tomatoes, a kind of very salty meat called *mabinga*,[15] and root vegetables. Sometimes he couldn't get any work. The dead season here was truly a time of death—people really did starve.

Then my old man started housepainting, because in those times you had to get along one way or another. He got a job painting a hospital in La Venta de Casanova, and afterward looked for a job painting in another town some distance away. But when he got there the job was almost finished. After a time he quit painting and went back to farm work.

My old lady had to sew for a living, even though she had no training for the job. She'd cut out a dress with the cloth draped over the client's shoulders, then sew it on a rickety, queer old machine, the kind you turn by hand. She worked until her eyes were red and watery from the strain, just to buy us a bit of food. Sometimes my sisters helped her, sewing things by hand. We boys helped too, by turning the crank of the sewing machine. When there wasn't much sewing, my old lady worked out in the fields of the farms nearby. María Luz and María Nieves worked in the fields with her.

Elena would spend days on end at my uncle's house in Bayamo. My old folks kept her there as long as possible because they had no place for her and we were all hungry as hell. Later on, some relative helped Elena get a job as a servant in Santiago. She was the only one of my sisters who ever worked like that. She always sent money to the old lady. Later, the family moved from Santiago to Havana and brought Elena with them.

When I got big enough, I'd do a little work around the house, but never sweeping or anything like that. Nobody ever asked me to do housework. Sometimes we went out with the old lady and helped her. Other times, we stayed at home and brought her a piece of sweet potato at noon.

We'd also carry water cans on our shoulders and gather dried palm leaves for firewood. We fairly cleaned the place of palm leaves and *yaguas*,[16] and there was a time when we had to split the trunks of the palms to use for cooking fuel. Then we had to go farther afield to gather firewood. We simply had to have it, so we'd get it wherever we could, even from somebody's private property if necessary.

15. A type of jerked beef.
16. The bark of the royal palm.

There was some pastureland nearby belonging to a certain Dr. Galiano, but poor people didn't have a chance of gathering firewood there. He had two men, Abelardo and El Negro, looking after that land. They'd chase away any trespassers, running after them, cursing and trying to hit them. But my old lady decided to get in there and gather firewood no matter what. She's always been brave. She got together some women from the neighborhood and told them, "On such-and-such a day we're going to gather firewood on Dr. Galiano's place."

They all went, and, as usual, Abelardo came raging at them, but my old lady didn't run away. She stood firm and waited for him. "You people don't need those dry sticks," she told them. "You don't cook with wood. Let us take them. It's all right to tell everybody to be careful of the fences, not to break or bend the wire, but there's no need to offend people the way you do."

We were very badly off in Las Marías, almost as much as we were in Santa Ana. You have to live through such things and feel them in your heart to know what it's like.

I don't remember ever having been taken to a doctor or having a physical exam until I joined the Army. I'd get feverish colds and that sort of thing, but they never took me to the doctor. Even now, when I run a temperature or something, I keep going without taking any medicine, just as if nothing were the matter.

My old lady didn't have any special knowledge about curing, but she knows how to treat a flesh wound. She always had either iodine or mercurochrome for our cuts and scratches, but she never kept any pain-killers. She didn't keep alcohol, either. Sometimes she had hydrogen peroxide at home, and if she didn't, she'd borrow it from a neighbor. She'd buy *Mejoral*[17] or Alka-Seltzer in the grocery store. My uncle kept a medicine cabinet and usually had all those things handy, but we couldn't afford that.

Once, when I was twelve or thirteen, I got indigestion from eating bad corn. Whenever I ate corn, something would stick inside my stomach and I'd start throwing up. This time my sister had to pick me up, big as I was, and carry me piggyback uphill to the house of a woman called "Biliosa" Maldonado. After I got home, they gave me a laxative. Boy, do I hate laxatives! I can hardly bear to take castor oil, cod-liver oil, or any of that stuff. They had to force it down my throat. My old lady has always been a strong woman, toughened by hard work. My sisters held my hand while the old lady dug her knee into my belly and forced my mouth open. Listen, if the only way to cure a cold was with cod-liver oil, I wouldn't get well. I'd rather have an injection!

My old lady used to give me a syrup called *guira* honey, which Grandma made and kept in a big bottle. They'd force me to take two or

17. A type of aspirin.

three tablespoonfuls for indigestion. When I got the measles in Oriente they gave me corn water. They'd soak an ear of corn and give me the water to drink. And I was shut up in the house a number of days to keep me from infecting others and protect me from drafts. At that time I'd never been vaccinated against anything. I got the mumps and the chicken pox after I was married.

One time I got worms. When I had a bowel movement, the worms would hang halfway out of me and would have to be pulled out with a piece of paper. It scared me to see such a long animal come out of my gut—each worm was about 30 centimeters long and looked exactly like an earthworm. They used to treat intestinal parasites with a kind of syrup sold at the stores.

Many children in Oriente died for lack of medical care. There was a hospital in La Venta de Casanova built by the local people and financed by the government. Even if the hospital had been twice its size, it still wouldn't have been big enough, because it was the only one serving a very large area. People flocked there whenever they had to see a doctor, and the clinics were always chock full.

My cousin, Conrado Ramírez Pardo, died of tuberculosis when he was twelve or thirteen. He was a weak, sickly child and his parents took good care of him, because they lived well. Cousin Conrado was well fed, but he died all the same. We spent a whole night at his wake.

In Oriente it's customary to lay out the corpse on a bed, then transfer it to the coffin as soon as it's brought to the house. They light candles and sometimes cut plantain leaves and put a candle on top of each leaf. Then they raise the corpse—I don't know how—with the feet down and the head up, and stick flowers all around the edge. The relatives bring the flowers—any kind, like carnations or wild flowers.

People don't pray at wakes. The relatives cry and you drop a few tears, offering condolences to the family. As soon as you arrive, you go up to them and say, "I'm with you in your sorrow." You say a few more sentimental words, walk up to see the corpse, and go out as soon as you can to join the other guests.

Outside you talk and joke and laugh with the others. It's almost like a party. They'll kill a pig or a calf to feed the guests, and also offer cheese, coffee, and cigarettes to keep them awake. Otherwise, people would fall asleep right in front of the corpse they're supposed to be watching. Besides, wakes last the whole night and people would get awfully hungry if they weren't fed. That's the way wakes used to be in the country, but I don't know what they're like now there, or here in Havana.

One time when Grandma was almost dying, a spiritist told her she should have some *despojos* to be cured. A *despojo* is done by making the sign of the cross over the person. Grandma wanted it, but *mamá* refused to go along with her because she doesn't believe in such stuff. Grandma believes in God but I don't know what she calls her religion. Whatever it is, she's a devout believer. I think the *Virgen de la Caridad*[18] was the saint of her devotion. Grandma was also the only one who believed in witch-craft. My old man doesn't believe in anything, not even himself, and *mamá* is just the same.

Some of my aunts and uncles didn't share Grandma's beliefs, but others, like Uncle Rafael, are religious fanatics. He had statues of St. Michael and the *Virgen de la Caridad,* and a picture of the Sacred Heart of Jesus. His house is full of saints' images, and yet he'll shit on God just as he shits before the saints, which goes to show how strange people can be.

As a child I played with my cousins, the children of Uncle Rafael. I never had any toys or got presents on the Day of the Three Kings. Marbles was the game I played most, but I was a pretty poor player and always lost. We made slingshots out of two garters tied to a piece of shoe leather. I wasn't a good shot either, but one of my brothers-in-law was a real tiger with a slingshot and could bring down birds.

It was customary in the country for boys and girls to play the "Little Blind Hen," a game in which one of the players is blindfolded. At night we'd play hide-and-seek. We used to play house, too, and a little girl called Cuca always said that I was her husband. I'd laugh whenever she said that. We'd get inside a little house and lie down together on a sack, and then she'd play around . . . you know what I mean. We'd do naughty things. Our parents allowed us to play. How were they to know we'd do such things?

My parents never talked to me about masturbation, but I guess they must have known about it. And let me tell you, if anybody ever tells you that he's never masturbated, he's lying. Girls do it too, but I never found that out until I moved to Havana. I forget exactly how old I was when I started, but I used to hide to do it about once a week or so. Masturbation really saps a fellow's strength. Doing it once wears you out almost as much as laying a woman five times. It really destroys the organism, and besides, it's habit-forming.

I have a cousin, Goyo, who we used to catch masturbating all the time. We sure teased him about it. We called him "the Haymaker." Every chance he got, he'd masturbate—at work or anywhere. He'd also have intercourse with mares. The rest of us did too. Sometimes when we went bathing in the river, we'd round up the mares for that. The boys screwed mares, she-goats, ewes, and heifers. My cousin's parents owned mares and cattle and such, so they had plenty of opportunity to do it. I couldn't do it except by getting onto somebody else's property to catch an animal. I've screwed mares, goats, and heifers, but not dogs, because they said

18. The "compassionate Virgin" and patron saint of Cuba, enshrined in Cobre, a mining town near Santiago de Cuba.

that bitches had some disease. Some of the boys would turn it into a kind of competition, but whenever I did it, I went off by myself. I've always been very reserved about such things.

My friendship with the Ibáñez boys started with a practical joke. One day I was on horseback, riding pretty fast, and the Ibáñez boys scared my horse. The horse reared, threw me, and the milk bottle I was carrying was broken in the fall. The next day I hid in some bushes and yelled at Fabio, one of the brothers, who was riding by on a pinto horse. The horse shied and threw Fabio. I came out of the bushes and said, "Now I'm even with you guys."

As a boy, I never disliked anybody; I don't even remember finding anyone disagreeable. I got to like the Ibáñez family real well, and they liked me too. There were seven boys and three girls. Even old Hipólito, their *papá,* became real fond of me. He loved me like a son. I was equally friendly with all, but the ones that my brother Luis and I went around with were those nearest our own age: Lorenzo, Baltasar, Pancho, and Fabio.

Hipólito's house was very near ours. We'd walk along a path that cuts through my Uncle Rafael's farm and we'd be right on Hipólito's land. Their house was made of palm leaves with an earthen floor, but later they built themselves a chalet-style house of zinc, although it had an earthen floor too. They also built a tank to catch rainwater. They did all that before the Revolution. The house was enormous, much larger than ours, and they were a lot better off than we were. They owned a lot of land, most of it planted in oranges. They picked from 30,000 to 50,000 oranges in a single harvest.

Sometimes I'd spend the day at Hipólito's place. I even ate and slept there. I'd go out with his boys to work in the fields—it was just to lend a hand, I didn't work for wages. I did all sorts of work—gathering corn for his animals, picking oranges at harvest time. He gave me lots of free oranges to take home. They also gave me coriander leaves. The plants grew wild in the shade of the orange trees. The work would last four or five days at a stretch, and then there'd be lots of days without having to work at all, so we'd spend the time playing baseball. I was thirteen or fourteen years old at that time.

My old lady and Hipólito's wife were friends too, but old Hipólito Ibáñez hardly got along with anybody. He and Uncle Rafael were forever quarreling. They'd quarrel about the land and about each other's animals crossing over from one farm to the next. I guess there's hardly a small farmer in Oriente who hasn't fought with his neighbors about straying animals. Hipólito always owned more animals than Uncle Rafael. He had two or three cows, one or two yokes of oxen, and some horses. Uncle Rafael owned only one cow, one ox, and one small mare. More than once Hipólito and Rafael were at the point of attacking each other with their machetes. They'd also go to court about it. That didn't affect my friendship with Ibáñez, though, and Uncle Rafael never quarreled with us about it either.

On Christmas Eve the Ibáñez boys invited me to their supper so I'd eat there. *Mamá* didn't object or get jealous on that account, because we never celebrated Christmas at my house. She knew where I was and that was her main concern. We never celebrated any of our saints' days or birthdays either. Now the family kills a suckling pig every year for Christmas Eve.

There are families here in Cuba who mistreated their children and beat them so often that the children ended up leaving home. Those things didn't happen in my home though. Hipólito was real tough with his sons, but he had to be because it was the only way to handle that squad of boys. They were the restless type and liked to wander around, but Hipólito always brought them back. If he had let those boys do as they wished, they'd all be out on the loose.

My old man hardly ever scolded us because he worked away from home, so it was up to *mamá*. My mother treated us well. She was firm; she had to be to keep the eight of us from going astray. Listen, if she told me to pick up two cans and go to the river for water, I'd pick them up and go out in a hurry. If I didn't, I'd really get it. She'd take a stick to me.

Mamá had a strong character and taught me a great deal. She'd spank us with a belt or whip, but never so hard as to make us want to leave. She also punished us by making us sit in a corner or on a stool until she was good and ready to let us get up. I never did anything to deserve a severe scolding, and *mamá* was always very sweet to me. Once I got whipped unjustly on account of my brother Luis. But I had to shut up and take it because if I'd protested, my old lady would have spanked me harder.

My old man spanked me once, but he hardly ever laid a hand on any of us. The most he's ever done is slap us. And he never tried to slap more than once. If he missed, he didn't try to strike a second time. The old lady was the rough one. *Was,* I say, because now the younger kids can do as they please. It makes me laugh to see the way she is with them. I think, "Man, who would ever believe this! You should have known the old lady before!" She'll say to my youngest brother, Lazlo, "Go out to the yard," and he'll answer, "*You* go if you want to!" If any of us older ones had dared to say that, wow!

The older sister we respected most was María Nieves, though we two quarreled a lot. She had a very strong character too, just like my old lady. She liked to be respected and she'd hit us often. When she gave me an order and I delayed in obeying, she'd slap me. She was that way with everybody. She has children of her own now and she treats them exactly the same way.

My old man would stay as long as fifteen days in Santa Rita when he had a painting job there. Sometimes he'd stay a week—depending. It was so far away he couldn't come home every day. When he did, he usually came home drunk, because he loved his liquor. While he was working, he'd drink every day he could. I don't know how he managed to combine drink and work, but there was an abundance of liquor then and it was cheap. A bottle of Bacardi rum cost about 35 *centavos* and he drank only rum.

Whenever we saw *papá* coming up the path we'd start yelling, "Hey, Asshole! Here comes Asshole!" That was our nickname for him. *Mamá* called him Red—nobody called him by his right name. I remember seeing him stagger up the path and cross the brook—he seldom rode a horse—and we'd all run as fast as we could to meet him, yelling "Asshole, Asshole!" We were overjoyed to see him because he always brought candy. That was one good thing about him.

Papá laughs a lot when he drinks. He doesn't pick fights because he's a peaceful drunk. He gets sort of dumb and dazed. As soon as he got home, he'd flop on the bed face up, and in a minute he'd be dead to the world. Then we'd jump on the bed and search his pockets. The old lady would take the money and we'd pull out the candy. What a hullabaloo!

Papá started drinking long before he and the old lady got married, but drunk as he was, he always got home. Later on, he started falling down in the street and going to sleep right where he fell. Sometimes his money was stolen while he lay in a drunken stupor. Once my cousin found him passed out by the edge of the road and took him home.

One time the old man went to Santa Rita to get some money that was due him, for work he'd done. Well, he drank to forget his troubles and went into a hotel to sleep. That dinky little old hotel was no better than a cave of wild beasts. They stole a pair of brand-new shoes that he'd just bought, and left a dirty, worn-out pair instead. He was ashamed to come back with torn shoes, so he left them to be fixed at a shoe-repair shop. *Papá* stayed away three days until his shoes were fixed, because he knew the old lady would kick up a terrific fuss if he showed up with old shoes.

Another time he stayed away for five days. We waited and waited, and finally a neighbor told the old lady, "I saw Red drinking in Contramaestre." There were always a lot of ruffians in Contramaestre, the lowest types in the countryside, the ones who didn't want to work and make an honest living. That was their haven, and they lived by stealing, by blackmail, and by twenty other dirty tricks. I was big by then so the old lady sent me out to fetch *papá* home.

Contramaestre was quite a long walk from our barrio. Once there, I went from bar to bar trying to find the old man. I finally ran into him sitting with a guy, the kind who lives off poor men, getting them to pay him for playing a tune on his guitar.

I stood in the doorway of the bar feeling as if the sky had fallen on my head. It was *our* money that fellow was getting from the old man. And on top of that, the poor fool was paying for everybody's drinks.

I stood there at the door looking straight at *papá*. He looked back at me, but I could tell that he hadn't the foggiest idea who I was. I wanted to beat up the guitarist.

I said to my old man, "You've got to come home now!"

"Come on, Red, let's go," said the man with the guitar. "Let's get out of here and go drink somewhere else."

"Oh no you don't! He's going home with me," I said.

"And who are you to take him away?"

"I'm his son," I answered.

That shut him up. If anybody had tried to interfere, I'd have started a battle in that place. Then I said, "One moment! Where's the parcel with my father's clothes?" And *papá* asked the bartender to bring it to him.

The old man tried to get tough with me but I spoke to him firmly, not as a son speaks to a father. I grabbed hold of his arm and made him get out of that place. He broke into tears but I was firm and made him keep on walking ahead of me all the way home. I guess he was afraid of the tongue-lashing the old lady was going to give him. And why shouldn't she? She was perfectly right to get angry about his drunkenness and the way he threw money around. Once he started, he drank up every *centavo* he had in his pockets.

As soon as we arrived home, he jumped headfirst into bed. Later the old lady started scolding. I told her, "He didn't want to come, *mamá*. I had to force him."

They'd exchanged his clothes parcel for another one, but *papá* came out ahead because the clothes were better than the ones he'd had. His were work clothes all stained with paint, and the ones he got were of good quality.

As we grew older and started working, things at home began to improve. When the old man couldn't earn money, we earned some and gave it to *mamá*. And when I didn't have any work, I could get a credit slip for 5 *pesos'* worth of food at the grocery store, and that was a help too.

I was eleven when I started working, but I don't remember who I worked for first, or how much I got paid. Sometimes I'd work a full month for the same person, but sooner or later the job would be finished and I'd go work somewhere else. Nowadays there's more work than there are hands to do it, but before the Revolution work was scarce. You had to go out and beg people to give you a job.

Once I went to work at a place where the owner wanted to pay me less than he paid the grown men. I said, "I work like a man and I expect to be paid like one. Give me what I've earned up to now; I'm quitting." So he paid me and I quit.

Another guy paid only 25 *centavos* a day, plus lunch and dinner. He owned about 3 or 4 *caballerías*, the most difficult land I've ever worked in my life. He was the only man I knew who gave the workers both lunch and dinner, although there were many others who'd give you breakfast. Rafael, my uncle, gave his workers breakfast and lunch and paid them 1.50 *pesos* a day. Another gave lunch and breakfast and paid 1 *peso*. Some paid only 1 *peso* and didn't give any meals. The farmer's wife cooked the meals for the workers because there weren't very many—two or three usually. The workers were all known to the family; they were never strangers.

For corn harvesting, the pay scale was determined by the size of the container. There were two different sizes of sacks: the smaller one paid 25 *centavos* full, and the larger paid 40 *centavos*. If you picked eight sackfuls of the larger size, you earned 3.20 *pesos*. If you filled four small sacks, you made 1 *peso*. I could pick eight or ten small sackfuls a day.

Sometimes it was beastly hard work because the cornfield was bad, but other times you were lucky and the corn grew well and bore large ears. On good land we filled our sacks quickly. When the picking was over they'd pay you, in addition to what you were allowed to pick out in the grocery store. When I was the only one working at home, as often happened, I had to give all I earned for the family's support.

Once we started working for wages, Fabio Ibáñez, my brother, and I went to ask for work as cane-cutters at the sugar-cane farm belonging to a man named Yiyo. Yiyo's *colonia* was about 10 or 12 kilometers from home. He told us to talk with the head manager. "You boys are minors, but I'm going to give you a note so you can work. I happen to know they're shorthanded right now."

When they needed extra workers badly they'd hire minors, but otherwise they wouldn't give you a thing. We made the trip to Yiyo's on foot, getting up at midnight to start out. We'd get there early in the morning, and we were able to work the whole day. You didn't get paid by the hour for that kind of work, but rather according to the amount of cane you cut. My brother Luis, Fabio and José Ibáñez, and I worked as a group because we'd agreed to share the pay equally among us. We slept with a crowd of people in old barracks at the *colonia,* and we bathed in a creek which was practically stagnant because of the slow current. Ugh, how it stank!

They'd give us a credit slip to use at the grocery store and we'd take the food and cook it at the barracks. We brought our own pots and pans and took turns cooking for the whole group. One time we all got diarrhea because we didn't know how to cook beans. One day, while working, I suggested, "Let's stop and drink some coffee." And then I simply passed out cold! When I came to, the other boys said, "You were talking and all of a sudden you fell down."

Shortly after, the sugar-cane plantation caught on fire. I don't know whether it was accidental or on purpose, but the cane had to be cut in a hurry. While we were cutting the burned cane, I fainted again. We were loading it on a cart and that's the last I remember. Both times I fainted from lack of nourishment.

Our main problem was that we didn't earn enough to buy our food. After working there five or six days, I said to my brother, "Listen, we'll never earn enough money here to do us any good. Let's get as much as we can with the credit slip and clear out before we starve to death." We still had 10 or 12 *pesos'* worth of credit left on our slip, so we spent it all on food and went back home.

In the midst of so much poverty, the best place to earn one's food was in the Sierra, picking coffee. I think the coffee harvest lasted from July to the end of November. We'd lock up the house in Las Marías and the whole family would spend the entire harvest in the Sierra. Since it was steady work, we'd take cooking utensils and so on. We didn't take beds or hammocks though, only the bedclothes.

At 7:00 in the morning we'd catch the jeep in Contramaestre. The road wound up and down hills and was so bad that the trip to the coffee plantation took five or six hours. When we arrived at the assigned farm we'd get settled. They had barracks for single men, and others divided into rooms for the men who took their wives there. Large families like ours were given separate houses.

We were given a fairly large house on top of a very high hill. It was pretty much like our own house, built of palm leaves with floors of packed earth. The beds were wooden and the mattresses were made of straw or banana leaves. We men slept in hammocks.

Papá, mamá, my brother Luis, and I set out very early to get to work on time, especially when the work site was far off, as often happened. Nieves stayed in the house caring for the little ones. You could see long lines of people struggling up and down the hills during the coffee harvest. There'd be 300, 400, or even 500 people climbing the hills, walking under the trees, talking and singing as they worked.

In the Sierra the sun always comes out late. First the sun's rays hit the tall shade trees that protect the plantings, later it filters down through to the coffee bushes. Because of that, it takes a long time for the dew to dry out. Some of the coffee plants are quite tall and you have to get underneath to pick the berries, so you get soaked with dew. We'd wait, sometimes until 7:00 or a bit later, to pick the coffee dry.

The foremen lived on the coffee plantations permanently. They were supposed to watch to see that the coffee was gathered without breaking the branches of the plants. When they got to know a person and trusted him not to do anything wrong, they'd say, "You go and pick coffee in such-and-such a place." Then they'd forget all about you, because they knew you didn't have to be watched every minute. They already knew our family and trusted us, especially *mamá.* They knew we never caused any problems and didn't have to be watched every minute.

Some workers picked green coffee berries together with the ripe ones. When that happened, the overseers would make them pick out all the green berries at the drying grounds. It was really something to watch them! The rest of the workers would gossip about it when that happened. A worker who picked green berries lost prestige with the rest of the coffee pickers. That never happened to anyone in my family.

The overseers liked to have a trustworthy family like ours working together. They'd assign a patch of land to the whole family and leave them alone to work. Earnings varied according to the quality of the land. Sometimes we got assigned a bad plot of land where we could only pick five or six cans in one day. Other times we got good land and picked twenty or thirty cans. My old lady would stay in the house toward the end of the harvest, when there wasn't much coffee left to pick.

My old lady picked the most coffee, then I, then my brother Luis. My old man picked the least because he's a slow worker. He can't help it. He didn't dawdle, he just worked slowly. My old lady knew exactly what he was like.

As we filled each can, we'd empty it into a sack and my old man would carry it over to the drying grounds to be measured. We usually filled about three or four large sacks a day. The number of tins of coffee that came out of each sack depended on the size of the sack . . . and that's where the robbery took place. Wherever we stuck our heads, we'd get robbed. The metal cans they used to measure the coffee were 1½ times larger than the cans we used while picking. That way, they measured your picking short and cheated you out of the earnings for a large part of your work. They paid at the rate of 45 *centavos* a canful, with no difference in pay for different qualities of coffee. They'd get us coming and going. When we got paid for our work, the earnings went right back to the owner. Robbery, that's what it was! The guy in charge of the store was the owner's son-in-law, so you can imagine. He was no better than a thief.

We ate better when we worked in the Sierra. My old lady cooked the lunch we carried out to the fields. It was usually rice and beans, roasted or boiled sweet potatoes, and codfish dressed with oil, tomato sauce, or with fresh tomatoes on the side. Although we ate much better on the coffee farms, that wasn't the reason we went. There were people who came from as far away as Camaguey, and lots of Haitians from Florida. It wasn't that they, or even we, enjoyed going so far from home. We went because poverty drove us anywhere we could find work.

It was the custom in the Sierra Maestra to give big fiestas when the coffee harvest was over. The fiestas were held in the *bateyes*. At that time, some men had women they'd take there to do business with. They'd build some palm-leaf shacks at the edge of the festival grounds and put beds in them. The other men would go there and pay to stay with the women.

Those women were prostitutes, just like the ones in Havana, except that each had a pimp she went around with. The man didn't love the woman; he only traveled with her to drum up business. As long as the harvest was in full swing, they'd carry on their business discreetly, but as soon as it was over and the harvest festival began, they'd come out in the open, right on the festival grounds, for all to see.

I remember paying 1 *peso* to have a woman in the *batey*. She was the first woman I ever had sexual contact with. I was about fifteen or so. She was called Rosa and I remember clearly how pretty and slender she was. It was a pity that she should be in that business, because one man would go in as soon as another one came out. She'd be at it all night long! It was terrible.

When the coffee harvest was over, we returned to Las Marías and looked for other work. I worked most for Uncle Rafael, because his fields were right in front of our house and he'd fetch me whenever he needed something done. I learned to do all sorts of farm work—plowing, planting corn, cutting sugar cane, or gathering corn. Uncle Rafael treated me like a day laborer, so he didn't mind my working for somebody else. After all, I was my own master, wasn't I? Uncle Rafael treated his own sons like day laborers too, because he'd thrown them out of the house.

When we were hard up at home and short of food, one of us would go to Uncle Rafael. He'd lend us money and we'd pay him back with work. We'd also go over to Cándido Ruiz, who owned a grocery store, and say, "Hey, we need a credit slip for your store." He'd give it to us and we'd get food from his store and pay him back by working. There was nothing we could pawn. We had no furniture. We'd never have pawned the sewing machine because my old lady could earn a bit of money with it.

One workday in the country is just like another. Before going to bed, we'd play awhile at home or at my uncle's house, or we'd listen to Leonardo Moncada's adventures on the radio. Leonardo Moncada defended the poor and attacked injustice. It was a lovely program and very popular. It started before the Revolution, but ran for years afterward. In fact, it ended only a short time ago, when they started the "Copper Arrow" series.

After listening to the radio, I'd visit relatives or one of the neighbors who lived nearby. We'd drink coffee and chat awhile. Sometimes we'd go as far as Uncle Alfredo Sánchez's house, which was quite a distance from ours. By the time we returned home, it would be 10:00 or 11:00 at night. Then I'd hang up my hammock and undress. I used to sleep in my undershorts, covered with one of my old lady's patchwork sheets. On cold nights I'd pile jute sacks on top of the sheet because we had no blankets.

If I was going to work the next day, all the arrangements would have been made ahead of time, so I knew exactly where I'd be going. If I was going to work for Uncle Rafael, I got up at 5:30 since he lived so close to us. My old man or my old lady would wake me at that hour. I've always been quick to wake up and jump out of bed, no matter how early I'm called. I've never had a beard, so I'd cut the few little hairs on my chin instead of shaving. My old lady always made coffee or reheated it for us to drink before we went out. Then we'd cross over to Uncle Rafael's house.

Uncle Rafael had rigged up a gong with a metal disc from a tractor, and he hung it from a tree with a piece of wire. In the morning he'd strike it, *pan, pan, pan,* and we all knew we were to report to work. When we arrived we usually found that his wife had gotten up early to prepare coffee and so on for us. We'd have our breakfast and then we'd get right down to work hoeing, weeding, or whatever had to be done. My uncle acted as overseer and most of the hired help was from the neighborhood. Around 9:00 or 10:00 in the morning, my aunt would always bring us another breakfast out to the fields. Then we'd look for a shady place and sit down to eat. Sometimes she'd bring sweet potatoes cooked with lard and a slice of pork, an omelet, or scrambled eggs. She also brought coffee and milk. We'd take fifteen or twenty minutes to eat breakfast and then go back to work. Around 11:00 or 11:30 either my uncle or his wife would pass around cans of water for us to dip out a drink.

We'd go to the house for lunch and all sit around the table to eat. Rafael usually had from four to seven men working there. Sometimes he'd serve rice and codfish cooked together. Other times, it would be codfish in sauce served with white rice on the side and boiled sweet potatoes, fried eggs, etc. We'd eat our lunch and stay there until 1:00 in the afternoon, when we'd go back to work.

While working we talked about baseball and things like that. At that time the big teams were those from Almendares, Havana, Marianao, and Cienfuegos. I was a Havana fan and some of the other guys were for Almendares or Cienfuegos. When our favorite team won, it was exciting. We knew the results of the ball games because my uncle had a battery radio. We didn't talk about women because we seldom went to "The Tunnel," the whores' barrio. "The Tunnel" was only seven or eight huts clustered around a bar. After we got older some of the fellows went, but I never did. I wasn't scared, I just never thought of it.

At quitting time, 5:00 or 5:30 in the afternoon, we went home, where each of us hung his spade on its own hook. When it wasn't in use, each tool had a special place. If there was enough water in the house, we'd wash up. If there wasn't, we'd take a can and go to the river to fetch some ourselves. I usually took a piece of soap, slung a towel over my shoulder, and went down to bathe in the creek. On very cold days I'd just wash my hands and arms and feet, change into clean clothes, and listen to the latest episode of whatever series I was following on the radio. After eating, I'd go to bed.

We didn't work on Sundays. When I got older, people began going to parties every Friday, Saturday, and Sunday. It was a torture having so many parties to go to. I didn't know how to dance—I didn't learn until after I moved to Havana—so I went to watch and have a few drinks. The music was usually provided by a record player and you were supposed to pay 5 *centavos* for every dance. A guy would go around the dance floor to collect the money. The girls were always from the neighborhood because those were decent, respectable parties.

In the country when you asked a girl to dance, another fellow could cut in and dance with her. There were many rude fellows who wouldn't take no for an answer. If you refused, they'd hit you. They were ignorant fellows from out of town who were afraid of losing their women. Then the fight would start, and guys would be rushing out and mounting their horses to get away. Such things don't happen anymore. Now you can go anyplace and people go out of their way to be pleasant, but back in those times they'd start terrible fights over anything.

There was another kind of party where you paid at the door or you bought a ticket ahead of time. We'd pay 1 *peso* to get in and not have to pay anything else all night long. Those parties—there'd be two or three a month—took place in gaming joints, and there were gambling tables for cards, roulette, billiards, craps, and that sort of thing. I'd go only to watch because I felt no inclination to play.

The places were always full of soldiers. A soldier would say to the fellow who ran the business, "Give me some money to gamble with," and the man would have to give him 6 or 10 *pesos* to keep him playing. Or else the owner would say, "You've got to get up and go now." And that would start a fight. They had some fights, believe me! Sometimes people were killed.

In the country it was unusual to give a party that didn't end in a fight. Somebody was bound to lose his temper sooner or later. Everybody drank, and toward morning they'd begin to feel the beer and rum. People would fight and throw bottles and stones and hit out with sticks. I'd stand quite far away to watch. The Ibáñez boys and I would go to parties and other places together. Until I was thirteen or fourteen I had to have my old lady's permission to go anywhere. She dominated us boys and made all the decisions. Nowadays any boy living in the country can go to the movies or go out alone. But I'd never been to the movies until I moved to Havana.

I never bought lottery tickets, but my old man always bought a piece of one, and every once in a while he'd win something. He also played the *bolita*[19] numbers, and what luck he had! His lucky number was four—the cat—but he never bet much, so he never won more than 3 or 4 *pesos*. He never bet on cockfights or played craps, and he and *mamá* didn't own any

19. Illegal lottery.

cards or dominoes. My old man's only amusement was getting drunk, then sleeping it off. *Mamá* always stayed home and he would too, to talk with her.

Once I was given a fine fighting cock. One time I was away for three days working on a farm, and when I returned my little fighting cock was nowhere to be found. Knowing my old lady, I looked in the garbage can and there I found my cock's feathers.

"Look, my cock is dead," I said.

"Yes, I killed it," she answered.

What could I do? I was a big boy already, thirteen or fourteen, and I understood that they were hungry and had nothing else to eat, so I couldn't even get mad. The other cock fought and won several fights, but mine had to go into the pot. It was more important to eat. I didn't go around betting on cockfights so maybe I'd never have gained any profit or enjoyment out of that little cock anyway. But somebody else might have entered it in a fight, or maybe somebody would have offered to buy it.

When I was almost grown, I saved my money until I was able to buy a little mare of my own, to ride to work. In those days a horse was something you could buy like anything else. Not like now, when you've really got to have dough to buy one. A little filly like that one would cost 100 or 200 *pesos* today. I bought it for only a little over 30 *pesos*. I got paid a little more than 1 *peso* a day for my work and I had to give some of that to my family, so it took a long time for me to get it together.

A horse was a good thing to own, to ride to work and so on, but it didn't impress the women at all. They admired the son of a man who owned a grocery store, or a farm, or someone like that. But the filly was very useful to us. We'd ride her down to fetch water, loading the tins on her back. We'd ride her to our relatives' houses and come back with vegetables, cuts of pork, chickens, and all sorts of things our uncles and aunts gave us.

There were always people who'd steal a horse that wasn't being watched, but it never happened to me. It was customary to brand animals with an iron, but I didn't brand mine. I took good care of my little filly. I'd bathe her and bring her food and always gather corn to give her at midday. If I was working someplace where there was no water, I'd ride her down to the river and let her drink.

I only had one sweetheart in Oriente. I was about eighteen then. Her name was Ana, and if she had another name, I don't remember it because we were sweethearts for only a few days. I forget how I approached Ana—I just saw her and liked her. The truth is I don't remember how I courted her. When the Revolution started, I couldn't go to see her anymore.

For a while I was in love with a girl named Rosaura, who lived near my house, but I never dared tell her how I felt. I worried that if I did, she'd say I didn't know how to court a girl. I never court a woman unless I'm pretty sure she likes me, because otherwise it's a mess. I'm a bit shy that way, so before I approach a woman, it has to be a sure thing. I never did manage to get up my courage to tell Rosaura.

The first thing I heard of a rebellion was when Moncada was attacked.[20] I heard people saying that a man called Fidel Castro had led the attack and several people were killed. The news spread all over Cuba, even into the country. It penetrated the remotest corners. People were surprised that such a small group of armed men would have dared attack the Moncada. To do such a thing was to invite death. What they were actually trying to do, of course, was show the Cuban people that it was possible to fight a powerful army. Later, people said there were rebels in the Sierra, but I never heard anybody call them bandits or say anything against Fidel.

To tell you the truth, I don't know how I got involved in the Twenty-sixth of July Movement. I did it without realizing it. I had no pressing reason to join—nobody was persecuting me or anything. Nobody ever asked me if I wanted to participate. I met the group and gradually became part of it. I felt good in it. I've been a rebel all my life. Any man who tried to take what was mine was in for trouble. I'll defend my rights against anybody, no matter who he is. I had my ideals, too, but if there had been no Revolution, I'd still be back home.

I started working for the Revolution by collecting arms and carrying out different assignments. We'd leave our homes at night as if we were going to visit somebody, and set out for an unknown destination. The man assigned the task would be told who had weapons for the Movement. He'd go there, knock on the door, and ask for them. I got more enthusiastic about the work and more involved as time went on. I was searched once as I crossed a bridge outside Contramaestre. I'd gone there for my old lady to buy some white flour sacks at the clothing store. As I was crossing, two guards signaled me to halt. "What are you carrying in that parcel?" they asked.

"Open it and see for yourselves," I answered, handing it over.

They opened it and said, "Say, how do we know you don't want these little sacks for the Rebels?"

I was already involved with the Rebels, but I answered, cool as you please, "I don't know any of those people, and besides, I wouldn't lend myself to such a thing."

20. On July 26, 1953, Fidel Castro led a group of 111 men and 2 women in an attack on the Moncada garrison in Santiago de Cuba, Oriente, with support actions against the Palace of Justice and the Civil Hospital. The latter two attacks, led by Raúl Castro and Abel Santamaría respectively, were successful, but the Rebels were unable to capture the main target, the Moncada garrison. Abel Santamaría was among over sixty Rebels who were killed, most of them after having been captured. Among those imprisoned were Fidel and Raúl Castro, Haydée Santamaría (sister of Abel), and Melba Hernández.

"Go on," they said. So I went on and had no further trouble with them. Even so, I decided, "I won't ever go again to Contramaestre, not even if driven there at gunpoint!"

We kept in touch with the Movement by listening to *Radio Rebelde* every night at 11:00 o'clock. We listened to the broadcast in a grocery store where they had a battery radio. It was impossible to get good reception of *Radio Rebelde* programs because the station was difficult to find on the dial. When we did get it, we could often only hear the voice but not make out the words. The broadcasters began with the announcer Violeta Casal giving a code word like "Blue Indian," "Apache Indian," "Frank País,"[21] etc. People used to listen to those broadcasts with the radio turned down low, especially us, because we were allied with the cause. Others listened out of mere curiosity, and still others, the spies in the government's service, took every opportunity to seek us out and accuse us. If they found you, you were beaten.

There were many people connected with our group, but we didn't know one another. They were all small farmers or men who worked on someone else's land. The very first underground activity I participated in was going to Mangos de Baraguá to get food for the Rebels from the warehouses of a stooge in the Batista government. When we arrived, some comrades went to his house and the rest of us scattered around town and cut telephone lines, electrical wires, and everything else. When the comrades asked the man to open the warehouse he refused, so they broke down the door and entered. That group was led by my brother-in-law, Cuco Fabregas.

We had two jeeps and we split into two groups. Shortly after we started, Captain Gerardo Paloma, a Movement leader in our region, showed up with his people. He talked things over with Bertico Ramírez, my group leader, and, well, they agreed to share the haul. Besides food, we loaded the jeeps with hammocks, shoes, and clothes.

The same day the Rebels took three spies prisoner. They were sent to Almeida's[22] command in La Lata, a tiny village of seven or eight houses. If the leaders decided that they'd committed some kind of crime, they

21. Francisco País García, a former student leader and schoolteacher, who became the Twenty-sixth of July Movement's chief organizer in Santiago de Cuba, Oriente. País planned the armed uprising in Santiago at the time of the *Granma* landing (see n. 22) in 1956. In July, 1957, at the age of twenty-three, he was shot down by police in Santiago (his seventeen-year-old brother had already been killed by police). País is one of the most loved and respected of all the Revolution's martyrs.

22. Comandante Juan Almeida Bosque, a veteran of the Moncada attack, was also aboard the launch *Granma*, which brought Fidel Castro and eighty other members of the Twenty-sixth of July Movement to Cuba from exile in Mexico. The *Granma* landed on Las Coloradas Beach in southern Oriente on December 2, 1956. The twelve survivors of the landing went to the Sierra Maestra and became the nucleus of the Rebel Army. Almeida is now a member of the Political Bureau of the Central Committee of the Communist Party of Cuba, First Secretary of Oriente's provincial Committee, and a vice-president of the Council of State.

had to pay for it. If it was decided to free them, they were kept only a few days. I don't know what the punishment was, whether they put them to work or what.

One day our leader, Bertico Ramírez, told us our time had come to join the Rebels. It was only then that my parents found out I was a member of the Twenty-sixth of July Movement. I was in the underground for such a short time they never knew about it. They never asked me any questions about where I went or anything.

When I told my folks I was leaving to join the Rebels, I forget what my old man said, but my old lady burst into tears and told me, "You must be crazy to think of such a thing." To my old man she said, "How can you allow this boy to go like that? You must be insane!"

My old man was neither for nor against the Rebels, because he had his own ideas. But *papá*'s ideas have always been more or less revolutionary. He was against Machado's dictatorship because of the injustices and abuses that were committed. He'd always been the kind of person who's in opposition. His friends were like that too. There was Navarro, for example, who was a communist. My old man read books and pamphlets that Navarro loaned him. So *papá* already had some communist ideas.

The last time I worked in the country, I was going around with my cousins "reserving," as we say there. That means we were hired by the day. One evening, as we finished working at Ciro Delgado's place, I said to my cousin Sergio, "This is the last time I'm going to reserve here." And that was the day I became a Rebel.[23]

I took an old hammock and a sheet, slung them over my shoulder, and went. I didn't walk along the open road, I cut through the cornfields. When I left I felt a great joy. At last I was entering into a truly useful undertaking, so I didn't take danger or anything else into account. I'd already gambled with my life working in the underground. I had participated in several raids, unarmed, running the risk that a patrol would catch me. I was taking a stand with the Revolution and I realized that at any moment I might have to face Batista's Army. I had no way of knowing whether I'd survive or be killed. Nobody could spare a thought for their families at such a time.

When I went to the Sierra, the only things I left behind were clothes and my little mare. They kept her at home until after the Revolution, then my old lady sold her. Each of my brothers had bought a horse by then, so a little old mare was of no use to them. I'd had only one sweetheart, so I didn't leave any love tokens behind—a ring, medal, or watch. Heck, I'd never owned a watch in my life!

The clothes I left at home really didn't amount to much. There was only one pair of good shoes—black with pointed toes—that I wore when I dressed up to go out. That was the first pair of dressy shoes I ever

23. Early in 1958.

owned and I bought them myself. I had four or five pairs of sturdy khaki pants and I don't remember how many shorts or undershorts, but I didn't leave any undershirts because I never wore them. I believe I only had one pair of socks, the 25-*centavo* kind, and a small white hat. I also left behind my tools—a machete and a hoe. My old lady sold my shoes, clothes, and the machete after I went away.

Two of my cousins joined the Rebels, but they weren't with me. Fabio Ibáñez was in my group. He was my true comrade and closest friend. Those three were the only fellows I knew who went to the Sierra.

My cousin's house was near our point of departure. We gathered there and walked along the mountains of Altagracia until we got to the camp. It was situated in a valley at a place called La Cita, surrounded by very high mountains, so it could be easily defended. There were different kinds of camps down in the valley—about five in all.

My group had about fifty men, but later we were divided. Some of the comrades from that first camp were selected for training in a school at Minas del Frío, where Che Guevara was supposed to be. Our site was well defended and we kept the place well patroled. Different orders would come down from above, but our main task was to guard the road so the enemy couldn't pass through to the other front. Groups of us under Comandante Almeida would patrol different sections of the road, or go to the Second Front at Sierra del Cristal, or go to town to get supplies. I remember I had to stand guard on my very first day at camp.

When Fidel attacked Guisa, Batista's forces left town and we entered. Among those who entered were Comandante Guillermo García,[24] Comandante Abel Palomil, and our direct commander, Captain Leyva. He got his orders from Abel and transmitted them to us. We entered the town at night, but they didn't allow us to attack the district military barracks, though we should have.

I only took part in one raid, in San Germán. Our plan was for one group to take all the horses and donkeys from the army barracks' stables, while our group stood ready to come to their defense if necessary. Fabio Ibáñez was part of our group but he wasn't beside me. Captain Omar García, who was on the hill outside Santiago de Cuba, sent us two comrades carrying automatic weapons to reinforce our group. Their weapons were more powerful than anything we carried. All we had was revolvers and some 12 mm. rifles.

Someone must have tipped off the enemy, or else we were careless and showed ourselves. Whatever it was, they surprised us before we got there. We approached the town by country roads, but they waited in ambush and we had to make a dash for it. The leader of the group,

24. Guillermo García Frías, known as the first peasant to join Castro in the Sierra campaign, is now a member of the Political Bureau of the Central Committee, and a vice-president of the Council of Ministers and the Council of State.

Tomás Ramírez, signaled us to retreat to the sugar-cane fields and to make a stand there, but we misunderstood him. We thought he'd ordered us to retreat, period.

I fired my revolver at them four or five times, then I turned tail and ran. What could we have done with our measly little revolvers when they were all armed with rifles? The shots whistled by me just like in a movie! Some of the men stayed and fought back, including one who had an automatic weapon. The enemy concentrated their fire on them, because the rest of us disbanded and ran. In that skirmish we shot a police constable, and one cop was killed in a fall down a ravine.

Many could have been killed, because we ran through the cane fields instead of beating an orderly retreat. We ran so fast we sent off sparks! I have no idea how much ground we covered, but we ran for a long time. Later on, the rest of the men appeared and we all went back to camp together. One of the guys showed up with one eye practically hanging out. We had to take him to the command hospital.

We stayed in the valley camp only twenty-some days before going up to the Sierra. The enemy had discovered our camp so we moved early one morning, before sunrise. The new campsite was almost a two-day walk from the first one. In the valley camp we sometimes had to sleep out in the open air, but usually we could take shelter under a roof. We ate whatever we could find, sometimes only sweet potatoes. We scrounged around for anything edible. In the beginning we hardly ever went hungry because we went out to get supplies. Half was for us and the other half was taken to Almeida's command. We managed all right until we went up to the Sierra. There it was different. But hell, I went hungry more often as a kid than I ever did in the Sierra.

We didn't have uniforms yet so we wore whatever we had, usually very bad-quality bell-bottomed khaki pants stolen from Batista's Army. Otherwise we wore regular work clothes with a red armband and work boots. I never went barefoot there. I also wore a cap. I didn't have a beard because I've never had much hair on my chin.

I often ran a fever up in the Sierra, but simply disregarded those things and went on as usual. I was never wounded or hurt in an accident or anything like that.

What I remember most about the Sierra is getting there. The mountain paths were steep and rough, and from there we went out to do whatever task we were assigned. Our main duties were getting food or guarding a stretch of road. Some days we simply stayed in camp or just stood guard.

One day a group of thirty or forty of us went to set up an ambush. We stayed there on the hill until dawn, waiting, but the Army didn't pass by, so we finally went back to camp. That night I had to stand guard and I fell asleep on duty. It was terribly embarrassing, the very worst error I'd ever made. It endangered the lives of everyone at the camp.

Actually it wasn't all my fault. I said to another comrade, "I'm awfully sleepy. I'm going to lie down and rest right here for a little while. You stand guard, will you?" But the other guy, instead of standing guard for me, went looking for a friend. Then the two of them took away my rifle, leaving me there unarmed. After that, some other comrades woke me up and asked me where my rifle was. Imagine playing a dirty trick like that on me!

My punishment was to stand guard unarmed with that same fellow. I got back at him though. I said, "All right, if the enemy comes, you'll have to fight them off alone. It's your problem, not mine, because you're armed and I'm not. Nobody in the world can make me come out and fight when I'm unarmed."

There were times when I was downright bored, mainly because the man who led our group wasn't very dynamic, and his lack of enthusiasm made the rest of us apathetic too. Now I realize that he didn't have the courage to seek out the enemy.

I went to visit my home only once after I went up to the Sierra. I went down with a guy called Lolo who had also been given leave to visit his folks. When I got home, everybody was overjoyed. Everybody in the barrio was very cordial to me. "Hey, Armando, so you're a Rebel, eh?" they'd say. By that time, many people from our zone had joined the Rebels.

We had leave only long enough to go to our homes, say hello to the old folks, and deliver messages to relatives of our comrades. I had arrived home early in the morning and left to return to camp that same evening. It was a whole day's walk away, uphill and downhill.

In late 1958 the Batista Army left Contramaestre undefended and we simply walked in. We wanted to attack the army barracks there, but Captain Leyva ordered us to leave it alone. Instead, we went hunting for a stool pigeon, a guy named Chacón. There were several barbers in our group, so we went into town looking trim and no one suspected we'd been camping with the Rebels. We knew full well who all the spies were. We went to Chacón's house, revolvers in hand, but he was gone. He'd left as soon as we entered the town and was never again seen around there. In the end, he was caught in Havana three or four days after the triumph of the Revolution.

We left town about 3:00 in the morning. After that, Bertico Ramírez and some others went to the BANFAIC,[25] where the Batista Army had been, and took all the typewriters there and a whole lot of other stuff. They had some problems on account of the army typewriters. They

---

25. *Banco de Fomento Agrícola y Industrial de Cuba* (Agricultural and Industrial Development Bank of Cuba).

shouldn't have taken any of those things. Bertico Ramírez really got into hot water because of that. Almeida ordered him to appear up in the Sierra and really told him off. "Who said you could go there?" Almeida began. Luckily for me, I hadn't gone so I wasn't involved in it.

Back in camp the next day, we heard that the Rebels had entered Contramaestre and that a tremendous number of people were running away through the streets and along the rivers. The markets were loaded with shoes, and Guillermo García took as many as he could and set fire to the rest.

I saw Fidel for the first time after the battle of Guisa, when we went down to the América *central*. It was just before the Triumph and everyone came down from the mountains and gathered on the plains. We saw him as we passed through Palma. A number of comrades who'd been sent on missions to the Sierra had already described him to me. I didn't feel anything in particular when I saw him. I felt I was equal to him and the rest of the leaders. He was the *comandante*, sure, but we were all in it together. I never saw Camilo,[26] but I met Che later when he was president of the National Bank,[27] where I was a guard.

When the Revolution triumphed, we were in the district of Palma Soriano. A group of us were sent there to organize small camps on the plain to protect the country people in case Batista's Army went there. When we arrived, everything had already been taken. So we went home, some to Santiago, some to Holguín, and so on. Then they organized the caravan to Havana and people started joining it. I went back to my hometown.

The triumph of the Revolution was something I'd been waiting for. I didn't know we were going to become a socialist country, but all of us knew that it was the common people, the workers, who were fighting. I never stopped to think what was going to happen. I planned to go back home and live there as I always had before I joined the Rebels. I had no intention of staying in the Army or of going to Havana.

Those days after the Triumph were happy ones. Everyone was overjoyed to see me back home safe and sound—the old lady, my old man, my brothers and sisters. The neighbors came to my house and asked me how it had been and I don't know what all. There wasn't much I could tell them at that time though, because I didn't know the right arguments

26. Comandante Camilo Cienfuegos Gorriaran was a *Granma* survivor and the only Rebel leader who rivaled Fidel Castro in popularity. Cienfuegos played an important role in the Sierra Maestra and Santa Clara campaigns and, with Che Guevara, led the Army into Havana on January 5, 1959. He was chief of staff when he died in a plane crash at sea on October 29, 1959.

27. Guevara was appointed president of the Cuban National Bank in November, 1959. In 1960 he was named Minister of Industry.

yet. One thing that struck me was the way the neighborhood girls, who'd never paid attention to me before, now came to visit and wish me well.

My family also treated me differently after I returned from the Sierra. It seemed as if they admired me now. Before, I was always being ordered around, but after I returned it was quite different. I mean, they didn't treat me as they had when I was nothing but one more person to get the food or fetch the water. It was as if they realized I'd gone through a certain process and had risked my life. So I won the admiration of my own family and the people in the barrio, something I'd never even thought of in the mountains.

Otherwise, nobody made a big fuss. Today when men return from fighting somewhere, they're given a tremendous welcome. Where we lived there was no celebration of the Triumph. Those people weren't involved in such things.

I didn't feel a bit tired or worn after the Sierra, but I spent that month going around the barrio without working. One day a group of us were bathing in a pond when someone said, "You fellows are a bunch of dopes. Everybody else is going to the big cities—Havana, Santiago—and here you are, stuck out in the country. You fought in the Sierra and now you should go to Havana to reap the rewards of your dedication to the revolutionary cause." That's what gave me and Fabio Ibáñez the idea of going to Havana and trying our luck. There simply was no future for us in the country.

In February Fabio and I went to Bayamo with my old man to arrange for our trip to Havana. I didn't know anybody but relatives in Bayamo, and I didn't even know their addresses. *Papá* went along to help me find an old Sierra comrade who dealt with the personnel that had scattered after the Triumph.

When *papá* and I got home, I told my old lady, "I'm going to Havana tomorrow with Lieutenant Cabal Montenegro." That's the way we did things, without any fuss. She wasn't the kind to go around sniffling and protesting when she had to say goodbye. I packed my things and left, and that was that.

Lieutenant Montenegro drove Fabio and me to Havana. We arrived at the Camp Managua entrance on February 5, 1959. There they put us in another car and took us to headquarters, where Montenegro introduced us and filled out some forms for us. That was when I became a soldier, and I've been one from that day to this.[28]

Montenegro took us for a medical checkup. After the examination we were taken to an X-ray unit. At first I was really scared. "Suppose that thing gives me an electric shock?" I thought. But then I noticed that the fellows ahead of me all came out safe and sound, so I stopped worrying.

28. Cárdenas was mustered out of the FAR in 1963, but he is a member of the militia.

They made laboratory tests and later told me I had some kind of intestinal parasite—an amoeba. They prescribed medicine for it, but the first dose upset my stomach so badly that I said, "Heck no! I won't take one more spoonful of this stuff!" Well, when they ran new tests later I had no more parasites.

I was never paid while I was with the Rebels. But shortly after I arrived in Havana, they decided to give some money to all of us who'd been in the Rebellion, so we could get along for a while until we got jobs. The married ones got 45 or 50 *pesos* and the single ones about 30. Was I surprised when they gave me 30 *pesos!* "What's this!" I thought. I'd never thought of money when I joined.

I'd heard a lot about Havana before I came. I knew that in the capital city there wasn't even a little mountain or ground cover. I'd think, "Isn't that something, *caballero*. What an amazing place it must be—the strangest place in the world!" I wondered how I'd walk down those streets with the cars rushing by! I'd never seen a street like that. Now, walking along the streets of Havana is the most natural thing in the world for me.

What impressed me most about downtown Havana was so many people living so close to one another. And the tall buildings! I'd never seen such big buildings in my life! When I go to any small town now, the houses seem so tiny! Everything looks small and strange. Every time I saw the enormous buildings here, like the Habana Libre Hotel[29] and the Focsa,[30] I'd think, "Look at that! What a great thing that is, *caballero!*" Once I got lost in the Habana Libre because I couldn't find the same door I'd come in by!

At that time we didn't know how to find our way around in Havana. I still couldn't read, so the street signs were of no help. I used to ask the comrades at Camp Managua, "Say, can you read? You can? Fine. Let's go to Havana." Then we'd slip out of camp and go to town. I can more or less find my way around Havana now but not too well at that.

We usually went to places where they had a bar. Sometimes we'd go in for a drink—a beer or something. Then we'd dance a bit. We'd go on that way, from place to place, until we got to the prostitutes' barrios. Prostitution existed in Cuba then and I was always going to brothels and such places. Captains, lieutenants, and everybody would go to the low districts. Whenever we got a pass, Saturday through Sunday, we'd get together and go there to get some relief.

Pila, a barrio near the Plaza, was the worst in town. In Pila you'd walk down the street, look around, and pick the woman you liked best. I'd walk around the whole barrio looking over what was offered. The

29. Formerly the Havana Hilton. It has thirty-two stories.
30. A high-rise *propriedad horizontal* or cooperative apartment house in Vedado.

women were no good at all but the price was right, 1.50 *pesos* to lie with one of them. We couldn't afford the better whores in La Victoria and Pajarito, where it was 3, 4, or as much as 5 *pesos* a throw. In Colón they charged 2 *pesos* or 2.50, but we didn't go there because there were always fights.

Whenever I went to one of those houses for a certain girl and found some other guy ahead of me, waiting for the same girl, it bothered me no end. If someone else's turn came after me, I didn't care at all. Often, after having a girl upstairs, I'd go right downstairs and lay one of the Italian women. In fact, when I went to that place I usually had three or four women the same night. It really was something!

When FAR organized the schools in Camp Managua, my barracks was assigned to one of them. Every company—tank, artillery, and infantry—had its own school. I was in the Infantry school. A captain and several lieutenants who'd been in Batista's Army were chosen to head the school.

There we spent our days learning to march, and we learned the parts and structure of the rifles. Of course we'd used weapons before and could take them apart and put them together again, but we didn't know the names of the parts. They'd tell me, "This is called the trigger," and I knew that, but when they said, "This is the pin" or something, I'd forget it in a few days. Illiterate as I was, how could I be expected to learn? They taught all of us illiterates reading and writing in a big classroom, but it didn't do much good, because in 1959 we were mostly interested in going out and having a good time. I don't think I went to that class more than three times.

We'd go to the shooting range and then do exercises in a big straw hut. We had all kinds of sports there—boxing, soccer, volleyball. After playing hard, we'd run out and bathe. They had enormous bathrooms there and they kept them very clean.

All those camp activities were good, but the truth is, I didn't like military school. What I did like was the strict discipline and the lessons in personal grooming. We had to make up our beds nice and smooth, without a wrinkle. I'd never learned to make a bed before. I didn't even know that you used a bottom sheet.

Very shortly after we entered school they gave us some clothes. We each had a locker with a key and had to keep it in perfect order. They taught me where to keep my socks and handkerchiefs, where to hang up my shirts and put away my shoes, and where to keep my gun and that sort of thing. We were each given a pair of slippers, too. Once a week an officer would inspect the whole company, and unless everything was perfect they took away your weekend pass.

There was one enormous mess hall. The kitchen was modern and we were well fed. We got lots of milk, chicken, rice and beans, and, every once in a while, beef. There was an abundance of everything. Of course the situation was different then, but even now, in spite of the shortages, there's plenty of good food in army mess halls. In military camps there's an enormously long waiting line in front of the mess hall. There was a ticket system and we were checked at the door as we went in. They'd call us to meals by companies and by schools.

Crazy situations sometimes arose in the mess hall. Some of the comrades from the Sierra were no better than animals—they'd fight and kill each other. Suppose you said something one of them didn't like. He'd pull out his gun and as soon shoot you dead as look at you. I saw a man shot and killed in Managua, but I don't know exactly why. The killer was sent to prison. Aside from such incidents, though, most fellows got along well with one another. But there wasn't the friendly spirit between comrades and the strict discipline that we have now.

In April they began trying to sift out the undesirables. After the triumph of the Revolution many guys who hadn't so much as thrown a pebble to help win had infiltrated the caravan on the road between Oriente and Havana. They weren't against the Revolution, but those men weren't trustworthy and might have turned against us at any time. Things were pretty disorganized. Guys who disliked school simply didn't go to classes. Anybody could leave the Army by just walking out of camp; nobody worried about it. Every time they called roll, at least a couple of people were missing.

In the first elimination, they made us all line up and go into an office. They made a rule that you must have at least one comrade in camp who could swear that you'd really been involved in the revolutionary struggle. If there was nobody present who could identify you, you'd say, "Well look, ask comrade so-and-so. He was with me in the Sierra and can identify me." Then they'd tell you to go get him so he could say you were telling the truth.

There was nobody in camp who'd known when I participated in the Rebellion. Fabio Ibáñez, who could have vouched for me, was in another company. The only one I could go to was Captain Leyva, the commander-in-chief of Managua. So I went to his office and told him my problem. "Don't worry. Leave it to me," he said.

The first process of sifting out was very effective. The second elimination was carried out by Comandante Juan Almeida. That took place on April 14, 1959. They ordered the whole company to stand at attention in front of their beds, because Comandante Almeida was going to call the roll and eliminate anybody who didn't belong there. He walked up to each of us in turn and asked, "Under whom did you fight? Where were you? What weapon did you use? In what area did you fight?" Under such questioning, it would have been very hard for anybody to lie convincingly.

He came up to me and asked, "Who were you with?"

"Humberto Ramírez."

"Under whose orders?"

"Captain Leyva's, who got his orders from you."

"What type of weapon were you using at the end of the war?"

"A Springfield."

"Where did you get it?"

"It was issued to me in the troop." Those arms were captured and then distributed. After he'd finished interrogating me he said, "Step over this way." Then he went on to the next man.

That interrogation was for the purpose of choosing personnel for different assignments. I was picked for the Military Hospital. Almeida said to us, "You fellows are going there to work. I don't want any of you coming to me to say you don't want to work. If you do I'll boot you in the ass and kick you the hell out of here. You've got to work at that hospital, see? I don't want any of you sent back for lack of discipline."

At that time I didn't understand his words. Now I know that he meant we were being sent there to be tested.

Juan Almeida was a comrade who got along with all the rest of the men, one more soldier among soldiers. I thought he was a swell guy who treated us real well. Then he went through military school and, because of his rank, had to take on greater responsibilities. That's the way it should be. Now he's a militant comrade of the Party. But in spite of all that, he's still the same pleasant, unassuming guy he always was, not only with the soldiers under him and his Party comrades, but with all the Cuban people. Anyone who wishes to see him about any problem is given every attention. I haven't seen him since 1963.

In April the thirty-five of us who were sent to work at the Military Hospital were given physicals. Five comrades were rejected, but after hearing their story, Almeida sent word to the hospital that they were to be sent back to Camp Managua. "I'm willing to accept them all. When those comrades went to the Sierra to fight, nobody asked if they had flat feet, lame arms, or a blind eye. Every one of them was gladly accepted then." So the matter was dropped and those comrades were allowed to return to Camp Managua.

In the hospital we were assigned to different departments. I was given a long white smock and a white cap and put to work in the operating room. One of my duties was to help wind gauze and surgical thread. Another duty was to fetch patients and wheel them to the operating room. I also helped carry in the anaesthesia containers. Another comrade and I gathered up the bloodstained clothes used during the operation and took them to the laundry. The other comrade knew how to work all the equipment we had to handle—the sterilizing machine and so on—but I didn't. At that time I didn't even know how to read.

When they found out I was illiterate, they ordered me out of there immediately. "Look, Armando," they said. "You can't work in here if you can't read or write. There are lots of switches that you aren't supposed to touch, and how are you to know, if you can't read? You might touch the wrong button and accidentally kill a patient!"

I hated being transferred, because I liked the comrades there and felt at home with them. Besides, I could have learned from the experience. But I was sent to the fifth floor, the officers' ward, to clean up. I mopped the floors and helped the patients there. Some of them were in very bad condition.

I worked on the fifth floor for only a short time. Then I was transferred to the hospital garrison or Guard Corps. We'd take turns standing guard at the entrance, or beside the elevator or places like that. There were always one or two guards stationed at the elevator to check passes and make sure that anybody who went up left his weapon in a special place. There were a lot of guards, because wounded prisoners from Batista's Army were in that hospital too.

Among the comrades hospitalized were some soldiers suffering from war psychosis. They belonged to the military units stationed at Minas del Frío. It turned out I was the only person in the Military Hospital who knew how to get to Minas del Frío, so I was assigned to accompany the first of those comrades there. I was given the bus tickets plus money for expenses along the way. In addition to the time it took to get the comrade to his home, I was given a five-day pass to visit my own folks.

Many of the soldiers in Havana made up stories about a sick relative so they could go home, or else they'd run away from camp. But I didn't play any of those tricks. I knew that my day to go home would come, and it did. I hadn't seen my family in four months. I'd heard from them through my cousins, who went back and forth between Havana and Oriente. They didn't expect any letters from me, because they knew I couldn't read or write. I'd have been embarrassed to ask anybody to write a letter for me.

I was very happy to be going home and anxious to see my folks. When I arrived they went mad with joy. The first one I saw was Amparo, the youngest girl. She called, "Here comes Mando!" Everybody ran out to greet me. My old lady had tears streaming down her face, and Grandma wept too. *Mamá* hugged me tight and I was very moved, but I managed to keep my feelings inside. My eyes stung with tears but I held them back. I haven't broken down and wept since I was a little boy. It was a great moment for me and a tremendous welcome.

Naturally they prepared a big feast with all kinds of special dishes. Chickens and pigs were killed and they gave me the best of whatever they had.

My old man was away at Dos Ríos, caring for a very famous Canadian breeding bull called Rockefeller. One of my brothers went to Dos Ríos at once to tell *papá* the news. He'd left at daybreak that morning, but when he got the news he hurried back home.

My old man doesn't drink much anymore because there's no hard liquor to be had except a small bottle on Christmas and other holidays. He drinks it but rum is what he likes. Drunks in the country drink raw alcohol now but he doesn't.

Fifteen days later I had to make another trip to Minas del Frío, so I got to visit my folks again. The second time I got a big reception too, though they had to improvise the dinner because they hadn't expected me back again so soon. I didn't take any presents for the old lady, just candy and such trifles, which I always bring her.

On my return to Oriente for those two visits, I didn't see any changes. Everything was just as it had always been. Things didn't begin to change until 1960. Until then we lived on that same tiny plot of land without taking away or adding to it. That all changed when I began helping out my old lady.

When I started in the Army, I was earning 75 *pesos* a month. Every month when I got paid I'd keep 20 *pesos* for myself and send the rest to my folks so they could build a new house. My old lady sent me word that a cousin of ours who owned a bit of land next to us was selling it. I asked her how much it cost and then sent her the money to buy it. She got it for a little over 30 *pesos* because my cousin wasn't doing anything with it.

So they added that 40 meters of land to the 50 we originally had and were able to build a larger house. That's the one they live in now. My old lady hired a guy in the neighborhood who built houses. The woods nearby were being cleared at that time, and my folks bought the wood cheaply. After that they bought cement. My folks got a lot of pleasure out of seeing the cement delivered there and made into the floors. They'd never in their lives had a cement floor or a wooden roof. The new house has a good kitchen and a latrine, too. It's much more spacious and there's still a bit of land left over at one side.

We got some new furniture—new stools and a center table. I sent water glasses, spoons, and all sorts of tableware from Havana, because it was difficult for my old lady to buy them in the country. Little by little they got the house fixed up with the help of my brothers and me.

When the Marine Infantry Corps disbanded, they wanted to replace us with the ex-marines and make us go back to mopping floors in the hospital. Many of my comrades in the Guard Corps accepted, but Mario Blanco and I refused to be transferred. We had cooperated in all the assignments before that, but we weren't about to be kicked out in order to make room for someone else!

I can't really explain how it worked, but it seems to me there was some kind of favoritism shown to friends of those in the director's office, especially the head of Personnel. The officers from Camaguey also favored their friends from back home. When one of them went to the Military Hospital looking for work, he'd be hired immediately. Comrades from different places would flock there; men whose revolutionary history, if any, we knew nothing about would enlist with no trouble at all. It was easy for anybody to walk into the hospital, join the Army, and be put to work at once. I'm not saying they didn't deserve to get a job, because many of them probably did. But they were inducted without anybody taking the trouble to analyze their good and bad qualities, to see if they were really fit to be soldiers. That was one of the things that disgusted me and, more than anything else, led me to quit my job at the hospital.

There had also been a problem about the Army not wanting to pay our wages. We didn't get paid for two months because they wanted to start paying us on the 15th. The first paycheck we got was for 150 *pesos* and it more or less covered the amount owed us for those two months. That was the first pay we'd received since the 30 *pesos* we got for having fought in the Sierra.

The people in the director's office at the hospital did what they damn well pleased. There were three officers giving orders, and one civilian. In the end, every one of them was kicked out. Leal, the civilian, is dead now, but what a son-of-a-bitch he was. He was responsible for the cleaning assignments. When he told us to mop the floors, we said, "Send the Marine Corps to do the cleaning jobs and keep us in the garrison."

"Well then, go to work in the dining room," he told us, and we said, "Well, all right."

So we went to the dining room in the morning, serving our comrades at the table. After the meal we gathered up the dishes and took them to be washed. We only worked like that one morning, and then they sent for us. They had the idea that we should be mopping floors, and that's what they wanted us to do.

Leal came to us and said, "Comrades, Lieutenant Valdés says you must go back to mopping floors."

"We won't go!" Mario repeated.

We faced up to Leal, yessir!

He threatened, "If you don't, I'll send you to the military police."

"Send us anywhere you like," I retorted.

"How about the military police at Minas del Frío?"

"Anyplace you like, but we're not going to mop floors!"

"All right, come along with me to the director's office."

So we went to the director's office and waited outside while they fiddled around with a lot of papers and wrote a letter. When the officer who took us there came out with the letter, I said to him, "Look here, you've written a letter and how do I know what's in it? You locked yourselves in there and wrote whatever you pleased. How do we know you haven't accused us of things we never said or did? I'm warning you, an investigating officer is going to come and find out what's going on here. Things aren't going to go on this way."

"Never mind all that, come along to G-3," he said curtly.

We got into a jeep and were driven to G-3, to Comandante Sergio del Valle.[31] After I'd had my say, he told us, "Go back to the hospital, turn in your gear, and then come back."

So we went back and turned in all the state property we had, including our revolvers and rifles. Then we packed our own clothes and went back to G-3. There we were ordered to report to Ciudad Libertad,[32] to the headquarters of Company 22, where Hubert Matos's men were sent after he was arrested.

The Hubert Matos affair[33] had already happened by that time. Matos had been the Rebel head man in Camaguey, and it was his idea to make himself the strong man there. When Matos realized Fidel had found out, he tried to start an army rebellion in Camaguey. Raúl Castro himself had to go and take a hand in the matter, but the only leader they allowed inside was Camilo. I don't know what they were up to, but Camilo arrested Hubert Matos and most of the officers with him. The regular soldiers weren't arrested because they weren't responsible for the officers' actions. They were transferred to Company 22, and other troops replaced them in Camaguey.

Mario and I didn't like being transferred to a group of ex-counterrevolutionaries, not one bit! Lots of the men of the 22nd were old comrades of mine whom I hadn't seen in years. It was pretty damn uncomfortable to meet them again and hear that they'd been with Matos in Camaguey. I was annoyed at having been plunged into such a situation, and I was uneasy, too.

Despite their reputations, those comrades hadn't turned counter-revolutionary at all. They knew perfectly well what the Revolution was doing for them. It was mostly the officers who sided with Hubert Matos. The soldiers had to go wherever they were sent, just like me. They'd been assigned there and that was that.

After the transfer everybody was expecting Camilo to talk with them, but then Camilo was killed. So Juan Almeida and Sergio del Valle came

31. Dr. Sergio del Valle Jiménez replaced Che Guevara as physician to the Rebels in the Sierra Maestra when Guevara became a column commander. Del Valle later became commander-in-chief of the Air Force, Army chief of staff, and is now Minister of the Interior and a member of the Political Bureau and of the Council of State.

32. Formerly Campo Columbia, military headquarters of the Cuban Army since 1902. After the Revolution it became Campo Libertad, but by 1961, when the group of buildings were transferred from the Army to the Ministry of Education and converted into schools, it was known as Ciudad Libertad (Liberty City).

33. Major Hubert Matos resigned as military governor of Camaguey in 1959, protesting the appointment of Raúl Castro as Minister of Defense. Fourteen officers from his command resigned with him. Camilo Cienfuegos replaced Matos as military governor. Matos charged that Raúl was directing (behind Fidel's back) a conspiracy to infiltrate the revolutionary leadership with communists. Matos was tried by tribunal in Havana in December, 1959, on the charge of "uncertain, anti-patriotic and anti-revolutionary conduct." He received a twenty-year sentence and was still imprisoned in La Cabaña in 1974. (Hugh Thomas, Cuba: The Pursuit of Freedom (New York: Harper and Row, 1971), pp. 1244–56.)

to talk instead. We sat on army cots while Almeida talked. "Look here, boys," he said, "we're the balls, see? You've got to respect us. We won't stand for any shit . . . ," and so forth and so on. That's the way he talked that day, but Almeida always uses tough words like that. Among his comrades he'll use really obscene language.

That day he told us what had happened to Hubert Matos. And he announced that the comrades in the troop were to be given a month's pass and round-trip fare to visit their families. They were going to start studying when they returned to camp and he wanted them fresh and rested.

I whispered to Mario, "He doesn't mean you or me. There's nothing for us in this deal. We don't have a month's holiday coming because we weren't part of this. Listen, when Almeida and Sergio del Valle come out, let's grab them and ask how we fit in."

When the talk was over, I hurried over to Almeida and said to him, "Comandante, we weren't involved in the Hubert Matos business, but we're in that troop now because we were transferred here from the Military Hospital. We have nothing to do with Hubert Matos's men."

"No, no, no, you've got nothing to do with that," Almeida agreed. "You don't go on that month's leave."

Comandante Sergio del Valle told us to go around to G-3 to find out what we were supposed to do. We spent the next ten days being excess personnel without a fixed assignment. We'd go in and out of camp as we pleased. Nobody objected. Hubert Matos's people had already gone away on their month's leave. So there we were, idling our time away.

"We've simply got to find some way to make them see," I kept telling Mario. They wouldn't let us into G-3, so I'd stand out in front chatting with the sentry while Mario sneaked in to pester G-3 into transferring us. He'd tell them how we weren't doing anything useful there. We drove those guys crazy!

Finally they got fed up and said to Mario, "Go to the military police at La Cabaña. We'll phone ahead and ask them to transfer you and your friend there." We packed in a hurry and went to La Cabaña.

In La Cabaña I was assigned to guard a place called "The Cat's Post" behind the prison. It was a narrow, ugly, uncomfortable place full of trees and underbrush which kept the sunshine out. On the fifth day Corporal Inocencio Maldonado, who'd been my comrade in the Sierra, showed up. He'd come to La Cabaña to recruit men for Urrutia's[34]

34. Judge Manuel Urrutia Lleó, first President of the new Republic, was in office from January to July, 1959. As a provincial judge in Oriente, he had refused to sentence 100 Fidelistas accused of insurrection. As early as November, 1957, he had been selected by Fidel Castro as provisional president for the government-in-exile in Miami. Urrutia's short term of office was marked by many clashes with Castro, particularly over the Agrarian Reform Law and the growing influence of communists in the new government. Urrutia offered his resignation for the fourth time after Castro made a speech accusing him of being a traitor. The resignation was accepted and Dr. Osvaldo Dorticós Torrado was immediately chosen to replace him.

bodyguard. When he saw me he hurried over, saying, "Well, I'll be damned, Armando! Why don't you come along with me and join the bodyguard?"

So that's how four of us transferred to the special bodyguard—José, Pedro, whom we called "the Dead Man"—he's now in the Ministry of the Interior—Crazy Osorio, and me. There were two others, Abel, who'd been in Che's bodyguard, and another guy from Matanzas. We all got along like brothers.

Even though Urrutia was no longer the President of Cuba, he still needed a bodyguard. If not, the counterrevolutionaries might have killed him simply to accuse the Revolution of doing it. I didn't keep up with events so I don't know why Urrutia resigned, but that's what we were told. I only know there were problems and Fidel made a speech on the radio, saying he was resigning as Prime Minister. When Osvaldo Dorticós took over as President, everything calmed down. Then they assigned national police force members as Urrutia's bodyguard. His life was protected both at home and out in the streets.

Urrutia wasn't under house arrest. On the contrary, he was given every freedom. He could go anywhere, any time he pleased, and we went along to protect him. He lived in the Biltmore district. When he was home, we remained outside with the policemen. I'd stay on duty two full days, then another comrade would relieve me and I'd get an eight-day rest.

I received special military police training and knew how to protect the life of an important man. When we stopped for a red light, I'd take a good look at all the cars that drew up beside us, and I was alert to any movement made by the people within them. I was always alert because it was my responsibility to make sure that nothing happened to him. Whenever he went to visit his old lady, I was on the lookout outside the house.

Urrutia treated us very well. He was a well-bred, amiable man—why should I deny it? He may have betrayed the Revolution but he was decent to us; he was a scholar, after all, and knew how to treat people. His wife was very nice too. She chatted with us whenever she went anywhere in the car. She'd scold Urrutia sometimes, because when he drove himself he was apt to get a bit careless, like one time he ran through a red light.

At first they served our meals in the family dining room and we'd sit at the table with him, his wife, and two sons. The policemen had six-hour turns, so they went back to the unit to eat, or got their own meals somewhere else. I ate with the family three or four times, but I'd get up from the table still feeling hungry, because I was ashamed to act greedy in front of them. I didn't want them to say, "That fellow sure makes a pig of himself."

Sometimes relatives or family friends would come to call, and they'd sit around the dining table talking. By then I'd gotten over the embarrassment of eating with the immediate family, but when all those other people came, I felt uncomfortable. I saw them surround the table and sit down. They talked among themselves but everyone's eyes were on me. My embarrassment prevented me from eating properly, no matter how hard I tried.

I made up my mind that I wouldn't eat with the family anymore. "If I get caught eating in a crowd like this two or three times, I'll starve to death, because I won't be able to eat anything," I said to myself. Soon afterward I told Urrutia, "Look, Doctor, I don't like to eat where there are a lot of other people. I'd rather eat alone, because that way I can pick up a piece of chicken or steak in my hands and really eat."

He replied, "That's quite all right, Armando. Whenever you're hungry, simply go to the kitchen and ask Pura to serve you dinner so you can eat alone. We'll let her know that it's all right."

Pura, the cook, was a real nice, young girl, very warm and friendly. After that, she always served my meals at the kitchen table. At breakfast I'd really get into my bread and butter and *café con leche.* Then, when I was hungry, I'd go back to the kitchen and ask, "Pura, is dinner ready?" I'd go in and I'd eat all by myself. I enjoyed my food more that way.

After a time the bodyguard was disbanded. They kept the police guard at his house, but I don't know how long that lasted. The rest of us were brought back to La Cabaña.

Shortly afterward, Comandante Almeida, Captain Arsenio Carbonell, and another *comandante* went to La Cabaña. Each company stood in formation in front of its own barracks while they picked out the taller men. They'd look a company over, then point at you and say, "All right, step out of line and come up front." I was one of those picked. Inocencio Maldonado thought the taller ones were to be sent away somewhere, so he crouched down and they passed over him. Brigades of soldiers were being organized to plant trees—pines and so on—at Pinar del Río and to build houses for people out in the country. Four of the men from the bodyguard were sent to different places to plant pines or build houses, so our group was broken up and scattered. Only Faustino Díaz and I were chosen to stay in the military police. They organized a battalion of the PMR[35] in the chief of staff's office under Captain Carbonell, who got his orders directly from Almeida.

They picked the tallest because the military police were supposed to stand out in any activity in which they participated. They were also supposed to maintain the strictest discipline at all times. There were fifty or sixty of us sent to the Fifth District. Then some of those in Security were left with us and the rest were transferred to different departments. Our group in the battalion specialized in honor guards, escort duty,

35. *Policía Militar Revolucionaria* (Revolutionary Military Police).

parades, and other military ceremonies. Whenever a prominent person died, we attended the funeral and provided the military honors. As a military policeman I always had to be neat, without so much as one button of my jacket undone. My cap sat straight on my head, leaving exactly four finger-breadths of forehead clear. If I stopped another soldier in the street to call his attention to something he might be doing wrong, he had to salute me as an officer. Out in the street, as a military policeman I was the highest authority, and he had to do as I said.

Along with the national police, the military police were the ones who patrolled the population, keeping the soldiers in line. I patrolled the prostitutes' barrios of Marianao. Usually a patrol consisted of four men—a corporal and three soldiers—plus the driver. We started on patrol from the Jaimanitas base at 7:00 or 8:00 at night and went into all the clubs and cabarets of the barrio. We'd head straight for the men's room, because lots of soldiers hid in there as soon as they saw the patrol coming. Usually we were through by 2:00 or 3:00 in the morning, but some nights we had to stay out till daybreak. I never had problems because we were always fully armed, each carrying a loaded carbine and a pistol.

Pity the soldier who was caught drinking! We'd call him aside so no one would notice, and say, "Look here, *compañero*, you know this is improper behavior. We soldiers can't go around making a show of ourselves like that. Now look, we've got orders to arrest any soldier found drinking, but it looks bad to arrest a comrade. We've got an officer who's responsible for all the night patrols in every zone and he's out on patrol himself. What will he think if he passes by? He'll wonder what kind of job we're doing. So look, why don't you cooperate with us? Stop drinking and go home."

We never once arrested anybody for drinking, because our corporal was a drunk himself. Of course he didn't drink in uniform, only in civilian clothes. As for myself, I didn't drink at all, so I was the one sent into the bars to talk with any *compañeros* there. We were usually lucky and they left when we told them to. But in the bad barrios like Pila, Colón, and San Isidro, you'd really have to arrest people, because they'd fight with you. Some of the military police didn't have the ability to talk with them in a nice, comradely way.

The military police also guarded all the prisons, and in the spring of 1960 we were reassigned to the garrison at El Príncipe, which was in our jurisdiction. I was responsible for the cleaning. Every day I'd sign out two prisoners and help them clean up their cells. After they finished I'd check their work, then I'd take them out to walk around the camp. At 5:00 or 6:00 in the evening I'd get them back to jail and sign them in.

I stayed in El Príncipe only five days. On the fifth day a comrade told me, "Know what? I think Captain Carbonell is coming over to select some personnel for the May Day parade because the men they have don't know how to march."

Carbonell brought his personnel, relieved all the sentries, and ordered both groups to march around to see who marched best. Our group had more experience than anybody else, so naturally we marched the best. Not only that, we knew what to do at every kind of ceremony. In the end, they picked only twenty or thirty of us from over a hundred men in the garrison. We were issued new boots and uniforms.

Captain Germán, an American,[36] trained us for the May Day parade. He'd taught us before, too, when we were in the Fifth District. They told us that the national police, the Navy, the militia, and the military police would all march as representatives of the armed forces. I got my feet all blistered from marching in new boots. For two whole days we did nothing but train for the May Day parade.

When we arrived at Circo Plaza on the day of the parade, I found that the orders had been changed. We weren't going to march after all, but protect those who did. After all that training and practice for the parade, they stuck us in back of the grandstand! We stayed there from 10:00 that night until 10:00 the following night, watching over the most important points of the plaza, where Fidel was going to be. One guy was stationed as far away as the Martí monument. Between us and the other security forces we had the whole place covered.

I was stationed about 5 meters behind Fidel's place in the grandstand. Only the high-ranking personnel—the entire Council of Ministers and the President—were allowed to stay there. The invited visitors were on the steps. We had to watch over them all. Fidel talked that day, but I didn't catch one single word because I was too busy watching whatever had to be watched.

When Fidel came down from the grandstand I was there; he passed by me like a gust of wind. I remember thinking, "Hey—" when he came out. Before I'd finished the thought "—here he comes," he was already gone. That's Fidel's way. As soon as he's through making a speech, he gets into his car and *zzzzt!*, he's disappeared.

A man usually has his women, and I never was without some little girl friend here in Havana. I had some sweethearts for seven or eight days, others for only a day or so. The girl would say yes and give me her address. Then we'd exchange two or three kisses that same night. After that I'd disappear for good and never show up at the address she gave me.

36. Captain Herman Marks, an American from Milwaukee who trained Rebel troops, served as an assistant to Che Guevara and as chief of security at La Cabaña fortress. (Marks is discussed by Ruby Hart Phillips in *The Cuban Dilemma* (New York: Ivan Obolensky, 1962), pp. 64–65.)

I never went to bed with any of my sweethearts. Once a man does that, he's got to accept responsibilities. I'd give the girl a kiss or two and a feel here and there, but I was careful not to go too far. I was their boyfriend but never their lover. For sex I went to older women living alone.

It wasn't long before I found a real sweetheart in Havana. Even my love life speeded up because of the Revolution! I saw her first in the amusement park and I began to pay her compliments. "What a pretty little thing! Just look at that baby doll!" Things like that. She responded with a smile so I knew she liked me.

Her name was María del Carmen Pacheco and she was thirteen. We met again in the amusement park and kept on seeing each other until we became sweethearts. She told me I'd have to talk with her *mamá* because her *papá* was dead. María del Carmen's mother was crazy about me! She gladly gave me permission to see her daughter. After that, I visited the girl at home and met the rest of her family.

María del Carmen and I broke up because she had a domineering temperament. Frankly, I knew she and I would never get along because she wanted to do what she darn well pleased. She was disrespectful to her mother and quarreled with her sister. As I got to know her better, I found out her faults and decided that I'd always have problems with her. Besides, she was only a kid!

One day she got angry because she saw me at the amusement park riding the "Octopus" with Fabio Ibáñez's sweetheart. She took off the ring I'd given her and threw it at me. Well, I'm not the kind of guy who waits for somebody to insult him twice. I walked out on her and that was that.

My second sweetheart in Havana was Irma Ochoa, who lived on Acosta. Fabio introduced her to me because he was engaged to Irma's sister Goya. I could see that Irma had taken to me right away because she smiled. Fabio said to me, "Go to it, boy!"

When we went out on the street, I walked beside the little one—she was only fifteen—and started to make a play for her. I'm not exactly a whiz at that kind of thing, but I did my best. The first thing I said to her was that I'd liked her from the first moment I saw her, and I hoped we could mean something to each other. Irma's old lady, her aunt, and one of her cousins had come along too.

We went to a dance hall in Managua. I'd never tried to dance before, but I was in love. I even danced a Spanish paso doble with the little one that night. I don't know how I managed; I simply looked at the others and tried to do as they did.

We became sweethearts at that dance. For the next ten or twelve days we argued about whether or not I should ask for her hand in marriage. I wanted to speak to her folks right away, but she didn't want to. They more or less knew what was going on. The old man said he hoped I wouldn't get his daughter into trouble and so on. The old lady simply adored me. She said, "I don't have any objections to your being Irma's sweetheart." It was wonderful how fond the old lady was of me.

I'd been on my best behavior with them since they first met me so they knew what kind of a fellow I was. The old lady would bring me coffee and everything! Nothing was too good for me. When the little one came out, the old folks would leave us alone. I never went out alone with Irma though; her old lady always went along. The only chance I got to kiss Irma a bit was at the movies, when the old lady got very absorbed in the picture or dozed off. And when we said goodbye on her front porch I'd give Irma a single respectful little kiss.

While I was Irma's sweetheart, I had another—a little dark girl—and Irma caught us together one time. She made a big scene and burst into tears. Well, we made up in the end, but the episode made her mother very uncomfortable, because that girl had a temper like a wild beast!

Meanwhile, I was getting everything ready for my marriage with Irma. I bought a stove and all those things. Irma's old man, a construction worker, had added a story on top of his house and built an outside staircase so we'd have a private entrance.

Listen, she was the only woman I'd ever given real presents to, and I really went all out with expensive stuff from Havana shops: bottles of perfume worth 20 or 30 *pesos* each, powder, and a lovely pair of earrings. I personally bought her shoes, stockings, dresses, bras, practically everything she wore, because her *papá* was too poor to give her what she needed. I never had any money left over for myself after sending part of my salary to my old lady and spending the rest on Irma.

I got disgusted with the girl when we went to Oriente one time. That's when I began to realize she was rather weak. I thought, "If I marry her and then have to go live in the country, she isn't going to have the strength to work the way a woman has to there." They didn't allow her to do anything at her house. She didn't know how to wash, iron, or anything. She didn't even know how to read.

Taking all those things into account, I thought, "This is going to be a tragedy, like in the movies. These days in Cuba, everybody must know how to do everything." What I needed was what I've got now, a grown woman who can do whatever has to be done, even climb a palm tree if necessary.

But that wasn't all. I knew Irma and my old lady simply wouldn't mix, and somebody who doesn't get along with my old lady will never get along with me. Besides that, Irma was quarrelsome and disrespectful to her mother, so she was bound to be disrespectful to me and my old lady. What with one thing and another, I was getting disgusted with the whole business. I thought the whole thing over and decided, "If I marry Irma I'm going to be left holding the thin end of the stick."

One day when I arrived at her home, I saw her old boyfriend Lorenzo coming out of the bedroom, shirtless, with his hair soaking wet. He was still a friend of Irma's family and visited them now and then. "I was in there taking a bath," he explained to me. "I came here to change my clothes."

Well, there wasn't anyone else in the house but him and Irma, so I thought, "Damn it, what's going on here? Something funny, sure as hell! I'm screwed if I let anybody make a fool of me!"

I didn't say anything at that moment, but as soon as Lorenzo left, I asked Irma to explain. "He simply came here and told me he was going to take a bath," she said. Hardly an explanation to satisfy me. It was an excuse I could have accepted only if her brother or sister or one of her parents had been in the house with them.

After that I no longer trusted her. "What am I doing here anyway?" I thought. A man's got to act like a man, and no man would accept such a story. Even giving them the benefit of the doubt, it was still very wrong.

I had a talk with Irma's parents and told them I was breaking up with her. They had to accept my decision. Her father said I was perfectly right and he scolded Irma. I simply walked out and left her everything I'd bought for our marriage—bedspreads, pots and pans, and lots of kitchen utensils. I'm still on friendly terms with the family and I visit them every so often.

Cora was from Matanzas, but she worked here in Havana and lived with one of her aunts. I met her in 1959, when I was guarding Urrutia's house in the Biltmore district. Cora worked as a nursemaid for one of the families living there. I'd broken up with Irma by then so Cora and I became sweethearts, and after a while we started leading a marital life together. When she was free on Saturday afternoons, she'd meet me somewhere and we'd spend the night in a hotel. She'd always come to me, no matter where I was. She really loved me.

I was the first man Cora ever went to bed with, the first one that ever did anything to her. As we Cubans say, I was the first one to split her *moroco*. She was my woman and I intended to take off with her, but then her parents started fooling around. If it hadn't been for them, Cora and not Lala would be my wife today, because Cora was a very nice kid.

Lala and I met one night when I was out with a comrade named Jesús. He had a little woman in Miramar, and one day he said, "Hey, Armando, I want you to meet the woman I've got over there." So I went with him.

While I was waiting on the street, I saw Lala pass by, but it didn't occur to me to talk to her. Then we went over to a truck where they were loading furniture. I asked to see their permit to transfer furniture from one place to another, because I concerned myself with all those things. They showed me their permit, so Jesús and I left them in peace. I was still standing there at 11:00 when Lala passed by again. I said to Jesús, "I'm going to chase that girl." So I followed and caught up with her.

I said something to her and she stopped short. "Look," she said, "I'm not in the habit of stopping in the street to talk with just any man who passes by." Then I began to court her. I forget what I said, but we talked about this and that. After a while she said to me, "I've got to go before the family I work for starts wondering why I'm late."

"May I see you home?" I asked.

She said yes, so I accompanied her home. I stood outside and watched her go upstairs, but we'd already set a date to meet again.

I saw Lala two or three days later and we kept seeing each other. I was quite attracted to her. Soon I was urging her to be my sweetheart, but she said, "No, not yet, it's too soon."

"Ah, come on, say yes!" I insisted. Until one day she told me, "Come around later and I'll say yes."

Since I didn't have anyone to wash my clothes in Havana, Lala asked the *doctora* for permission to do my laundry at her house. She'd bring my clothes to Jaimanitas, because while we were at school we weren't allowed out. We got passes only on Saturday afternoons and had to be back by midnight Sunday.

Cora and I were still sweethearts then, so I'd visit her first and then I'd go to Miramar to visit Lala. When we went to the movies or anywhere, Lala's brother Pablo would go along too. He slept in the servant's room in the house where she worked. One Saturday she took me to meet her folks in Pinar del Río.

That year[37] I got permission to go to Oriente for Christmas, to spend the holidays with my old lady. I had marriage in mind then, so I took a snapshot of both my sweethearts to Oriente and consulted my old lady. I hadn't proposed to either girl before that. I said, "Look, *mamá*, these are my two sweethearts. I've known Cora longer than Lala, and I'm living with her. I intended to propose to Cora. If she accepts, I'll marry her. Understand? If she says no, then I'll marry my second sweetheart, Lala. I plan to send Cora a telegram asking her to come here from Matanzas if she wants to marry me."

I didn't know about Urban Reform then or how to go about getting a room where I could keep my wife. So I thought, "I'll marry Cora and send her to live with my folks in Oriente. That way I can see her whenever I'm free." My mother agreed to the idea since she knew I didn't have a place of my own.

I sent Cora a letter but she answered, "Let's wait until I have time to ask my parents and see what they say."

"Well," I said, "why the hell should I have to go asking her folks' permission to marry her at this late date? Why should I humbly ask them, 'Do you like me?'" She and I were already sweethearts, so what the

37. 1960.

hell difference did it make whether her folks liked me or not? It was for her to decide.

I was on guard duty at the Ministry of the Treasury when they phoned to tell me that Cora had taken poison. I asked for leave to go immediately and ran all the way to her aunt's house. "She's alive," her aunt told me, "but they had to take her to the hospital." It was too late to see her that evening, but the next day I went to see her.

We talked and I gave her some money and told her to ask for more whenever she needed it. "Money's no problem, understand?" I said. I faced up to the situation, but then she told me that her trouble was a difficult pregnancy and not poisoning. The doctor had asked her if she was married and whether she'd missed her period and she'd said no.

"Now wait a minute," I objected, "if you deny your symptoms, you might die of this. If you don't tell the doctor, you'll get him all confused and he won't know what to do."

Cora followed my advice and told the doctor. He had her transferred at once to the Workers' Maternity Ward, where they prescribed treatment for her. She told her parents the following day. The old lady hadn't even suspected it.

"Don't worry," I told her. "That's my problem and I'll shoulder it. She's pregnant and the child is mine, so I'll take care of her." I really loved her.

But the old lady said, "She'll have to have an abortion."

"Oh no, she's not going to get rid of that baby. I won't allow it."

That night, when I went back to Cora's house, she told me her old lady insisted on her having an abortion. Cora didn't want to. "They took me to the house of a woman who does abortions," she told me. "But I don't want an abortion."

"All you've got to do," I advised, "is pretend you want to go through with it. Tell that woman to take the money your parents pay her and let them *think* she's done the abortion, but not do it. If you get rid of the baby, that's the last you'll see of me. I want you with the baby, not without."

She cried and cried, and swore she wanted the child too. But then, as she told me later, they took her to the abortionist's house and gave her a shot to sleep. Then, with her unconscious, they took the baby.

The trouble was that everybody in her family butted in, not only her parents, but her aunts too. When they made her abort . . . well, I resigned myself. What else was there to do?

After having given up the idea of marrying Cora, I decided to propose to Lala. I'd already met Lala's parents. So I said to her, "Look, I want to marry you, but if you agree, it's got to be right away. Otherwise, I might lose interest and not marry you at all." I came right out and told her that, in those very words. I said, "Get all the papers ready, because if not, I won't get married after all." So she got all her papers, I got mine, and we got married. That was in May, 1961.

Lala and I married in Pinar del Río. Our relationship was a good one. We had a short courtship, but my wedding is still a pleasant memory for me. I liked the idea of having a wife, a woman who was to be the mother of my children. As for the wedding itself, I don't remember it in detail; I was confused to find myself among so many people. I didn't even know how to sign my name then, and I can't remember what I did when the time came to sign the papers. I'd slept with a lot of women already, so my wedding night wasn't a great occasion for me.

When we were first married, Lala continued to work. She quit later, when I was transferred to the Isle of Pines in July, 1962. She didn't look for another job, so I was the only one working then. I went all over trying to get one thing and another for the house, but I couldn't find much. Things were scarce and expensive and our budget was pretty tight. The 75 *pesos* a month I earned in the Army then didn't go far, and getting married is an expensive proposition.

What we most urgently needed was kitchen utensils. We had no furniture to speak of either. As for clothes, that wasn't a big problem, nor was food either. At that time there were no ration books. A grocery store at the base gave us credit tickets to buy food; we paid for it at the end of the month.

Within seven months my first child, Mando, was born. He was premature, and they had to put him in an incubator. I waited around the hospital until Lala had the baby, then I came back home. I didn't even wait to see the child that night.

My *mamá* came to stay with us to take care of Lala and the baby. We didn't have a coat or anything for him, so the next day I had to go to Havana to buy one. I can't say much about little Mando. The truth is I can't remember what he was like when he was small. I've never been one to go wild with joy at having a child. I was happy, sure, but I wasn't out of my wits with joy or anything.

While serving with the military police at Jaimanitas I was sent to a school for illiterates. I wanted nothing so much as to learn to read and write. I'd stand at a bus stop wondering, "Where the hell is that bus going?" and I'd see how easily the other people could read the signs. I had my first reading classes at Camp Managua in 1959, but I wasn't able to learn anything. Where I really got a good start on learning was at Jaimanitas, early in 1961. All the comrades who didn't know how to read or write were given classes, not by army teachers but by civilian teachers from outside.

Our orders from staff headquarters were that as long as we attended school we couldn't go out except on weekends. They even sent special guards over so we wouldn't have to interrupt our schooling for sentry duty.

I forget how many comrades there were in school, but there were even officers learning to read and write, side by side with the rest of us. It was no trouble for me to learn. Time was the only problem. In three months I learned all it was possible to learn in such a short period. I more or less understood what I was reading, and by the end of the course I could read aloud pretty well, without stammering or stopping at every syllable. Another thing I learned was how to sign my name to a check. Before that, I had to be fingerprinted. I was no longer illiterate. In the years since, I've kept on studying, bit by bit. If I'd been able to study each grade completely, as one is supposed to, and taken my examinations normally, I'd have reached the pre-university level by now. As it was, I had to interrupt my studies often because of the number of foreigners the government invited to Cuba.

The problem was that the government always chose the comrades with the most military bearing for the parades held in honor of the visitors. The soldiers taking part in such ceremonies must master the different kinds of turns. Without precision and coordination, the whole thing looks ugly and awkward. Besides appearing on television, they're photographed for the papers. I'm proud that I was always chosen to participate in the parades for special occasions.

The first honor guard in which I took part was for Manuel Bisbé, the diplomat who died in an airplane crash.[38] The day his body arrived in Havana we went to the University, where it lay in state. We stayed there until the funeral, which took place at about 10:00 the following morning.

I was kind of jittery, but it wasn't the dead man that made me nervous, it was the crowd. I didn't know anything about it and I was scared to death I'd do something wrong and make a fool of myself in front of all those people. It was terrible to think that I might make a mistake while rendering final honors to a fallen comrade. Later on I learned about the discipline of an honor guard, how to manipulate the coffin with the corpse in it, how to carry it, and what military honors had to be rendered.

The honor guard for Bisbé consisted of the six of us, six comrades from the Council of Ministers, and six from the Cuban Diplomatic Corps. I'm clever about finding a good spot for myself, but that was my first time and I failed. I ended up out in front where the spotlights hurt my eyes. Usually the turns for an honor guard were only fifteen minutes. Then one group was relieved by another. But that day our group had to

38. The former *Ortodoxo* (see n. 57) politician appointed by Castro as Cuban ambassador to the United Nations; he was killed in March, 1961.

stay on guard about half an hour. They took so many photographs, one after another, that they didn't take the spotlights off us for even a minute. I was so blinded I couldn't see where I was going. I saw stars and I walked unsteadily. If there had been stairs, I'd have crashed down them, sure as hell.

Lots of people recognized my pictures in the papers. I felt proud because they were taken while I was rendering honors to a revolutionary. It was the last thing we could do for him, and it was a pleasure to be a participant in his final guard.

We also rendered military honors at the University to the men who fell in the attack on the FAR airport.[39] An invasion was feared at that time so we went around armed all the time. At the base we'd go to school rifle in hand, in case of an enemy landing in our zone.

The attack on the airport took place on the morning of April 15. Some say it happened at 5:00, others say 7:00. All I know is that because of the heat, we were sleeping in palm-leaf huts on the beach outside the barracks. The officer on guard, Reinaldo Vaquero, was sleeping right beside me. We were awakened by the *put-put-put* of the machine guns and the noise of the explosion. We saw the enemy planes because the airport was quite near us.

Comrade Reinaldo dashed out with one shoe on and the other one in his hand, to take his place at the front of the unit. We all hurried to pick up our weapons and get into battle formation. We knew the enemy was bombing but at that moment we didn't know exactly where. We learned afterward it was the FAR airport. By noon our orders had arrived. We were to present ourselves at the Military Hospital to stand honor guard for those who'd fallen at the FAR. They put the corpses—there were seven or eight of them—in a hospital refrigerator that was usually used for autopsies. We stood guard in the hospital chapel until the hearses arrived with the coffins. Then we went over to the room with the refrigerators and helped take out the corpses and put them in the coffins.

The day after the attack at Playa Girón, when the first of the fallen reached Havana, we started working on the burial of all the dead. They were buried with full military honors. I wasn't acquainted with any of the comrades I helped bury. The only one I knew a little was Miguel Fonseca Costa, who married my cousin Ana. Miguel left her with a baby when he died. Later I named my block CDR after him, to honor his memory.

In those days I didn't feel a thing when I had to take part in an honor guard. I mean, sure, I had a kind of feeling for the mothers weeping for their sons, when they cried aloud, "My son, I'll never see you again!" And I had some feeling for the sisters and brothers, too. Besides, those dead men were either comrades of mine whom I'd never see again, or

39. See n. 2.

whom I never had the honor of meeting. Sometimes it happened while I was in an honor guard that some loving relative who lived far away would appear. They'd just have heard about the death of the fallen comrade, and when they came in weeping, everybody would crowd around to offer their condolences. I'd be moved too. But, I mean, heck, I was so used to being around the dead all the time that it no longer made any impression on me. Standing beside a corpse affected me no more than standing beside a stick.

When you're in an honor guard, you have to stand very straight and stiff. I've gone to as many as four funerals in one day, and I guess the tension affected me because I started getting very bad headaches. The doctor forbade me to stand guard. "You can be a pallbearer, though," he added. So they transferred me to that kind of work.

As I remember, there were twenty-five comrades in each group that accompanied the fallen comrades to be buried, plus four pallbearers. At first we took turns being pallbearers, but after a while the job was always assigned to the same man. So whenever there was a funeral, I went as a pallbearer. I also helped the officer in charge of the platoon. Since I already knew all about the ceremony, he had me give instructions to the boys who were still weak on the ritual.

After the whole business at Playa Girón, the relatives of those men who'd been buried at the battle site wanted the bodies transferred to Havana. The government transferred them either to the soldiers' crypt in the Colón cemetery, or to individual crypts.

Some of the corpses were transferred after having been buried ten or twelve days. We were the ones who had to take them out. By that time they were already in a state of decomposition. The last corpse we reburied was about one month after Playa Girón. The stink of that one was horrible, so bad that the people who attended the wake went outside in the fresh air because they couldn't bear the smell. The boys on guard complained they couldn't stand it either.

I said to the guy in charge of the platoon, "Let me go see how it is. I'll tell you whether or not they can stand it." Of all the men, I was the one who'd specialized the most in stink. I'd dealt with so many corpses that it was easy for me to tell whether or not there was a smell. As a pallbearer, I didn't have to go inside until it was time to leave for the cemetery, but I went in anyway to see if it was possible to stand guard there.

Well, the boys were right. The corpse stank to high heaven! Imagine, it was so rotten that a kind of yellow, sticky-looking liquid seeped out of the coffin. I went out and told them, "It's true. It's impossible to stand guard in there. The stink is horrible." They knew if I said so it was true, so the Public Health doctor ordered them to suspend the honor guard and they sprinkled chloroform over the room to drive away the stink. By that time everybody was outside.

Then they ordered the pallbearers to take out the corpse. We lifted off the flag—ugh!—and folded it. One of us couldn't stand the smell—it made him want to vomit—so they took him out. Finally the rest of us lifted the coffin and carried it outside. When I put my hands under the coffin, they got all wet and sticky with the slimy yellow stuff dripping from it.

We placed the coffin on the caisson, draped the flag over the coffin again, and the platoon formed. We carried out the military ceremony and followed the corpse to the graveyard, which was very near. At the entrance, the four of us carried the coffin, with our hands all sticky, over to the crypt, where they had a niche prepared. The only thing to do was to drop the corpse in and get away as fast as possible. We fixed the pulleys around the box and the bugle played taps until it reached the bottom. We had to stand at attention the whole time. The three volleys were fired, the coffin was covered up, and we retired at once.

Near the graveyard we stopped to wash our hands in a stream, but we couldn't wash away the stink, so we had to take gasoline from the jeep to get rid of it. It was one helluva job, but I carried it off with no reaction at all.

It was only after I left the Army that I started getting upset stomachs. Ever since, when I hear people talk about some things—like when they say, "Somebody was killed in such-and-such a place and the corpse looked thus-and-so," it affects my nerves.

When Yuri Gagarin came to visit Cuba, on July 24, 1961, we received him in the midst of a rainstorm. Water and more water poured down on us as we stood at attention and presented arms, while the band played their national hymn and ours. Then they raised both flags, and the President, Fidel, and Raúl reviewed the troops.

I felt terribly proud to take part in the reception of our government's guest. The ceremoney was beautiful and it was our chance to show all our fancy parade steps with the public looking on. Nobody could say they saw any hint of nerves in any of us. It was child's play to us, because we knew the routine so thoroughly.

Besides Yuri Gagarin, I also received Sékou Touré and Sukarno. One is the President of Guinea and the other is the President of Indonesia, but I'm not sure which is which. We had the same kind of ceremony for them, but at least it didn't rain again.

In late 1961 I was assigned to the bodyguard of the Minister of Justice. There were always a national policeman and a military policeman guarding the minister's house. We were supposed to protect him when he went out, but he didn't like having the military police tagging along after him, so we always stayed behind. Since he lived near my home, I didn't have to take a bus but just went to work on foot. Every day we worked rotating six-hour turns in three shifts. The minister was a very nice man, a good boss, and a serious-minded comrade.

I was a member of the military police until sometime around the beginning of 1962, when it was disbanded. I was neither glad nor sorry; it was an order from the High Command so it had to be carried out, and that was all. I kept on earning the same salary as before. The only change was that I was transferred from the military police to the combat forces. Lala didn't say anything about the change. After all, how could she have an opinion on the matter?

A group from my division was mobilized to relieve the personnel on the Isle of Pines, which was done every six months. Eighty-two of us went. We rode in cars as far as Batabanó, where we took a ferry to the Isle. That was my first boat trip and it went off fine. I didn't get seasick at all.

We arrived at the Isle on the morning of July 25, 1962. There were a number of army cars waiting for us and they drove to Nueva Gerona through the worst mud you ever saw. It had rained hard just before we arrived and the cars kept getting stuck in mudholes all along the way. At the base, the head of Artillery showed us our quarters and issued us weapons. The fellows we were relieving got into the trucks that had brought us there and returned to Havana.

The camp quarters was a prefabricated house with bunk beds inside. The kitchen was about a kilometer and a half down the road; to get there we had to cross creeks and mudholes. It couldn't have been more badly placed, so we improvised a stove out of a few bricks and an iron grill, and some tables and benches out of old boards. We never went back to eat at the old kitchen. The decision to build a new one was made by the comrades in the platoons, together with the political comrades. We bent all our efforts toward making our home away from home as comfortable as possible.

There was a creek bed just below the camp with a small, badly built house beside it, which we decided to remodel as an office for the lieutenant and the second-in-command. In addition, we built a smaller house for food supplies and for a classroom for the self-improvement courses and lectures that were part of our military training. The classroom had benches and a blackboard, and two of the comrades got together and painted a great big mural that was very pretty. The mural showed Lenin and Marx, as well as Fidel, our present leaders, and lots of martyrs. There was also a rising sun and a portion of countryside lighted by the sun's rays, with flowers and all.

At first there wasn't any electricity in camp and we used kerosene lamps. Then we got together and pooled our money to buy electrical wire—because the Army couldn't afford to do it—to bring electricity from "Shanghai," the nearest barrio. A comrade who knew electricity planned the project and the whole unit worked on it.

"Shanghai" used to be the whores' barrio on the Isle of Pines. But there were some perfectly honest, decent families living there in a few small apartments and houses. There were also the families of some prisoners who were serving out their sentences by working.

I worked on all stages of our camp projects, helping with all sorts of jobs. First I cleared away underbrush and cut down trees. We used the tree trunks as foundations for the houses we built. We split palm trees, stripped off the bark, and took out the insides to line the houses with palm planks. We cleared the ground around the unit, cut the grass with machetes, and carried loads of gravel to be scattered over the site. We even put up a fence at the end of camp.

In spite of all the work we did, we didn't interrupt our schooling. While one group studied, another worked. We got up at 6:00 A.M. and at 7:00 formed ranks for roll call. After that we had breakfast—*café con leche* and bread. Then we scattered to different classrooms according to what each group was studying. If it was "Reading and Discussion," we'd read the newspaper and discuss the international news. If it was "Political Instruction" or "Ethics," the classes were based on textbooks. There weren't any professional teachers, but some of the comrades had had a lot of schooling, so they taught the rest. Unfortunately, I've forgotten everything I learned there.

I was able to visit my family four times a month. I left the Isle by boat several times, but toward the end of my tour I came and went by plane. It was difficult to get a seat because they were reserved for visitors to the prisoners on the Isle. At that time you could get a lot of unrationed stuff on the Isle, so I'd buy Lala stockings, panties, and once even a pair of shoes, just before I went on leave.

Sometimes everybody was confined to quarters and no leaves were granted, and I'd go for fifteen days straight without leaving camp at all. I wouldn't even go to the town on the Isle. I always felt happy to see my family after being away for such long stretches of time.

I saw Cora twice when I came to Havana on leave. She was attending a school for revolutionary training in Santiago de las Vegas and had written to me, giving me her address. That's why I went to visit her, even though I was married. I didn't sleep with her then. I simply called on her before going back to the Isle, but I slept with her twice after that. I'd met Cora in 1959, so our affair lasted quite a long time. But I didn't chase her, she came after me.

I was in Havana seeing a doctor about my headaches when Fidel gave the alarm and combat orders for the October crisis. After hearing that, I asked my doctor for permission to join my platoon. She agreed, but gave me a letter saying I should return for treatment after the whole business was over. I was on one of the last boats that made the run to the Isle. Lots of people rushed to the Isle that day. Besides all the soldiers returning to their units, there was a team of doctors sent there from Havana. Soon afterward all boat and plane trips were suspended until the end of the crisis, and we were isolated. That's why the Isle of Pines must have large reserves against any emergency that may arise.

I don't know much about what happened outside the Isle during the crisis because we didn't have a radio. All land and sea communications were suspended, except shortwave radio. We got no outside news at all; we just followed orders. We did hear Fidel's speech over a civilian's radio, but that was our only outside information.

People say there were missiles here in Cuba. I don't know whether that's true or not. All I know is I didn't see any missiles. But we came pretty close to war about it. Nikita talked with Kennedy and then somebody from the Soviet Union, Anastas Mikoyan I think, came to Cuba and talked with our leaders. Things started calming down and finally some sort of agreement was reached. I don't know what the agreement was. All I know is that things got pretty tough before the crisis was over.

Lala visited me at the Isle of Pines a year later, in October, 1963, just before I was demobilized. When your wife or any of your relatives came to visit you on the Isle, you didn't ask leave directly from the chief of the squadron, but went to the lieutenant instead. Then the lieutenant spoke with the chief of the squadron, who was a captain, and he gave you a pass to stay in town for five to ten days. They gave me five days' leave.

I waited for Lala at the airport. It had been a long time since we'd last seen each other and I was so happy I kissed and hugged her. Then I hired a car to drive us to town, where we looked for a room in one of the lodging houses. But first we had to go to the police station, which was run by the Navy, show our identification, and prove that Lala was my wife. They didn't serve meals at the house, so we went out to eat. We took walks and went to the one movie theater. While we strolled, we'd chat about things in Havana, how the kids were doing, and so on. There wasn't much else to do on the Isle.

The local authorities checked all the hotel and guest-house books every day to make sure everyone was registered. That way they could prevent any infiltration of prostitutes. There weren't any of them left on the Isle. In fact, there were so few women that some comrades weren't able to have intercourse. I can't swear that if they came across a man who was willing, they wouldn't touch him in some way. If anybody did, they wouldn't have come to tell me about it. Hell, I wouldn't be the right guy to tell that kind of story to! My relationship with my comrades was always sober and respectful. Luckily I never had any problems, like working next to a homosexual. That kind of thing wasn't permitted in the Army.

We had a homosexual once who was the paymaster at La Cabaña. I think he bothered one of the comrades in the department and that's how they caught on to him. I was on duty at staff headquarters and I happened to be in the office at the very moment they took him away. The chief of the Military Police Battalion dishonorably discharged him right then and there. That was the only incident of that kind while I was in the Army.

Some of the fellows on the Isle struck up friendships with divorced women and widows from the contingents of women sent there to work, but if a guy had a woman to screw, he had to protect that property like crazy. If he lost her he was sunk, because he didn't have much of a chance to get another one as long as he was there. It's a terrible place that way.

Things were so tough out on the Isle of Pines that if I had run across a mare there, I might have gotten my relief that way. Fat chance! I never even caught sight of one. In case of need you aren't choosy, so you grab the first animal you can find. If I had a choice, I guess I'd choose a sow. That's not so dangerous as a mare, which might kick you and break a bone or something. There are animals that struggle when you pin them down, because when you come right down to it, an animal is pretty much like a woman. An animal has a reaction kind of like a woman's orgasm; I don't say that a mare reacts exactly like a woman, you understand, but there are animals that do.

It never happened to me but I've been told that with an animal you can feel almost as much pleasure as with a woman. I don't know the explanation for that, whether it's desire or what. I can't tell you for sure which females are best among the animals, because it's been a long time since I've had to seek out an animal—not since the triumph of the Revolution.

Right now, many married people on the Isle of Pines simply control themselves and abstain from sex as long as they're away from home. I can't tell you how, but I myself have abstained, and if I can do it, they can too. After all, I can't claim to be either more saintly or less highly sexed than anyone else.

I'm not the kind of guy who will, as we say vulgarly, "give a woman the stick" three or four times a day, because a fellow who does it that often is going to land in the graveyard. I keep my wife on a once-a-day diet and that's the way it is. If I can't do it one day, I simply don't. But as long as it's up, I do whatever I get the chance to.

I've put up with bad times and not doing anything when there was no help for it, and I know there are some comrades who do the same thing. However, there are some guys, even married guys, who play with themselves when they can't do anything else. I never did that though, because I realized it weakens a man terribly. If a fellow is working hard, day in and day out, and on top of that masturbates, he'll die of exhaustion.

There's a law I read about on the back of the certificate FAR gave me, stating that after you'd been x length of time in the Army, you could choose whether you wanted to be transferred, stay where you were, or be demobilized. Well, when my time was up I chose to be demobilized. It was my own decision, made of my own free will.

I was demobilized in November, 1963, after being stationed on the Isle for just over a year. I left with nothing but the clothes I had on. There was no ceremony or anything; you just got on the boat and that was that.

When I went back to Havana, I got busy right away looking for a job. First I registered with the Labor Census. Then I went to an office run by the Army for demobilized comrades. They put your name on a list and looked for a job for you through the armed forces. I also went to the Ministry of Labor to fill out some forms there.

I got a construction job with MINCON, but I was there only a few months before I was transferred. A telegram came from the Ministry of Labor telling me to go to the INIT office. I started working at INIT in January, 1964. My first job was in a workers' dining hall, as a dishwasher. I was promoted almost immediately, and after three months my superiors, who'd noticed my outstanding work performance, selected me to go to cooking school. I started the cooking course in August and by November, 1964, I was a master chef.

When the master chef at the dining hall left, I was the logical person to take his place, because I was his assistant. That's when they gave me a salary raise, from 89.25 to 106.94 *pesos* a month.

I got my revolutionary training after I was nominated as a candidate for union leader and representative to the Labor Justice Council.[40] For the elections, they set up a ballot box and handed out cards with the names of all the candidates printed on them. You were supposed to mark your card with an *x* beside the name of the candidate you preferred. Then, on voting day, everybody went to count the votes. I was new in INIT, so practically nobody knew me there. Most of the candidates elected as Labor Justice judges were well known INIT comrades. Only the people who knew me voted for me, so I got a total of only a little over sixty votes, but even so I was elected union leader.

In the dining hall I had an assistant, a young fellow called Sergio Gutiérrez. He worked like a lion in school and never cut class because he was paid for going. I can't say he didn't work at his job too, but his

40. The *Consejo de Justicia Laboral,* or *Consejos de Trabajo,* were established at the enterprise level and consisted of five members elected by the workers. Members were required to have a socialist attitude toward work, be disciplined, and have a good work record with no instance of absenteeism. The Councils handled violations of labor discipline: tardiness, absenteeism, disobedience, negligence, lack of respect for superiors, physical offenses, damage to equipment, fraud, and robbery. Decisions of the Councils could be appealed to the Regional Appeal Commissions and, at the highest level, the National Revision Commission. The manager of an enterprise could, under the law, impose disciplinary sanctions without hearings by the local Council. And the Ministry of Labor could dismiss members of local Labor Councils, recall cases being heard, deny appeals procedures, or annul a Council decision. (Roberto E. Hernández and Carmelo Mesa-Lago, "Labor Organization and Wages," in Mesa Lago, ed., *Revolutionary Change in Cuba,* pp. 221–22.)

attitude was terribly negative. He said all sorts of foolish things and wasn't really for the Revolution, because he did nothing to help it. He quit the minute he completed his eight hours of work because he couldn't see the progress brought about by the Revolution. From his very first day on the job, he started protesting about lots of different things, starting with the food. He did nothing but gripe the livelong day. He said he was being punished for a mistake he'd made in his previous work center. He claimed they'd done him an injustice by accusing him of stealing.

He'd been working at an athletic field on Consulado Street, which is in a bad area. You've got to run for it when you find yourself in that part of town. People will offer to sell you different things illegally and then leave without giving you what you bought, and things like that.

Well, Sergio claimed he'd overcharged a customer at the bar. Then he tried to correct the sales slip, but the manager caught him and accused him of stealing. He had Sergio arrested right there and sent to the DTI.[41] Sergio claimed that what had happened to him could have happened to anybody. From the way he told it, I think his story was true, but of course one never knows. A guy will hardly ever tell such things the way they really happened.

Well, they sent him to El Príncipe, but he was in jail only a short time. They took him to trial and sentenced him to house arrest and made him work as a dishwasher and kitchen helper for a year. That's how he came to work with us. At first he worked very well, but he kept talking about his problem and blaming it on the Revolution. That wasn't right. If he was punished unfairly, it was the fault of the guy who'd played that dirty trick on him.

People usually criticize the organizational defects in their place of work, because naturally they have more opportunity to see the deficiencies there than anywhere else. Sometimes certain comrades don't blame the people who are really responsible for those errors, and instead blame them on the Revolution. We all know perfectly well that certain individuals aren't functioning as they should, and they commit errors.

When they took away Sergio's achievement rewards, he remarked in front of me, "Now I won't go to school anymore!"

"So you went to school only for money?" I said. "Now look, that's not right."

He didn't say a word, but he did quit going to school. He simply wasn't committed to anything. I was never paid any cash prizes at that time because only the managers and those going to school at night got the awards.

41. *Departamento Técnico de Investigaciones* (Department of Technical Investigation), the subdivision of the Department of Public Order responsible for criminal investigations.

After I was elected union leader I practically talked Sergio Gutiérrez's ears off trying to persuade him to join the CDR at the work center. He resisted joining because he said people would kid him about it. "What do you care whether they kid you or not?" I argued. "What have such people got to do with you anyway? If your ideals lead you to join the CDR, you should join." I kept after him until he finally gave in and joined.

Sergio worked with me for nearly a year as a kitchen helper. As we worked we'd have long conversations, until little by little he started trusting me and accepting my orientation. Gradually I led him to the right path and he became a true revolutionary comrade.

One time, some comrades came to the dining hall to get volunteers to work in the cane fields. They held an assembly and asked who was willing to go. I raised my hand, but I was the only cook there. Sergio wanted to go with me. When I volunteered, he said, "If you go, I'm going too, Armando."

But then the union committee conferred with us and it was decided that I couldn't go. "We can't spare you," the manager said. "That would leave us without a cook, and it would be very difficult to get a substitute." The union committee said the union leaders couldn't go because there would be no one to work for the union local. So in the end, Sergio volunteered to work in the cane fields until the end of the harvest. He worked six whole months without even one pass to come see his children in Havana or anything! He's volunteered for every sugar-cane harvest since. He's gone to work on the *Cordón de la Habana*[42] and also on the INIT farm. I'm telling you, that guy has really improved in a fantastic way!

I was doing well on the job but I think working with a petroleum stove gave me stomach trouble. I've always had trouble with vomiting and diarrhea and I guess in 1965, when I was a cook, it affected my sympathetic nervous system, which brought on the whole problem.

I'm a guy who has to sit down to dinner at 6:00 sharp. If I don't, I get an upset stomach. When I get out of a meeting at 5:30, I rush to catch a bus. Then the bus shakes me up on the way home, which makes me feel even more anxious and upset. As soon as I get home after such an ordeal, I hurry to the bathroom. When I get out, I want my place to be set and my food served. I'll sit down at the table and in five minutes I'm through. I've been told that it's bad for me to wolf my food down like that, but what can I do?

I went for a medical checkup and was assigned a woman doctor. First they X-rayed me and made all sorts of tests, and they told me, "Look, there's nothing wrong with you." Then I myself said, "Look, Doctor, don't waste your time making more tests. My problem is nerves."

42. The cultivated greenbelt that encircled Havana.

Well, that very day the doctor gave me a letter to a psychiatrist, a woman. She told me to draw birds, plants, and lots of things. "Look, I can't draw anything," I protested. "Never mind," she said. "Simply draw whatever you like." Then I drew a tree, a man, and a woman. The woman had a dress on and I painted all the little ornaments and details of her dress—all sorts of little things. I couldn't help laughing as I drew all that stuff.

After I finished drawing, the doctor took out a bunch of cards and started showing them to me. "What do you see there?" she asked. There were ten or twelve cards, all different shapes in different colors, but they were disfigured, and none of them really looked very much like anything. You're supposed to say this looked like a man's legs, that looked like a hand, some looked like a dog's head, and there was one like a pig's leg. They show you all that stuff to test whether you're right in the head. Then she showed me a certain card and I could only say, "Oh!"

"What does that look like?" she asked me. I simply couldn't tell her what it looked like to me. It was too embarrassing to say such a thing to a woman. To me, it looked like the inside of a woman's genital. It seemed disrespectful to say such a thing to a *compañera*. I was wrong though. I should have told her, because that's what she was there for—to be told such things. But heck, I wasn't crazy or anything, and it was too damn embarrassing.

My trouble is I've become cowardly. I feel afraid and have complexes. I never had any such nervous problem in the Army. There are still times when I'll rush fearlessly into any kind of situation. But now some days I feel jittery in the morning, in the afternoon, and at night. I feel restless inside, a sort of desperation, as if something were about to start aching. I don't know if anyone can understand what I mean. It's as if I were going to fall or go crazy.

When I was a kid I used to have lots of nightmares. I often dreamed of flying or falling down a precipice. I still dream about all sorts of things, but I don't have nightmares anymore. I dream of having intercourse with women, but never in a house of ill fame; rather, they come to my house. I dream of fighting, too, especially shooting. In the dream I feel very old. I never get scared though, even when I dream that I'm trying to shoot, but my revolver won't work. I simply wake up at once.

I didn't go back to a psychiatrist for a year. But the doctor had given me a certificate saying I couldn't work in a kitchen anymore because of stomach trouble. After that INIT looked around for another job for me.

In late 1965 I was made manager of the El Castillo ice cream parlor that had just opened. I told Duran, the head of Personnel at the regional office of INIT, that I didn't want to be manager because I didn't know enough for that kind of job—my cultural level was too low. Then Duran spoke with the director of the regional office, Comrade Rosales. "Look," Duran said, "I have a young fellow here who doesn't have much schooling, but let's take him anyway and put him to work with a comrade who knows more and has the patience to teach him. He's a good managerial prospect."

Well, Rosales sent for me and we talked. He told me that I should accept the job as manager. Duran said, "Look, Armando, we require a manager to be honest and to be revolutionary. You're both. If any problem comes up, call on any comrade here in the regional and we'll help you."

Then they told me, "We're going to send you to El Castillo with Comrade Carlos Figueredo. You can count on him to help you." Between him and Director Rosales, they talked me into accepting the job.

When you start a new job, somebody's got to show you the ropes, so Carlos went through the accounts, the orders, and all the papers with me, explaining, "Look, this is done thus-and-so."

I wish I could explain just how good Comrade Carlos Figueredo is. He's like a father to all of us workers. The truth is I haven't found many comrades who can match him. He really understands things and thinks more or less the way I do, though he wasn't a militant, only a manager.

Since there was no one who specialized in syrups, Carlos and I made the syrups ourselves. After a time Carlos left the task to me, because I improved so much I did it better than he. It wasn't really my job, but there was no one else to do it. I also took over the cash register on Saturdays because the manager gave Friday off to the night cashier and Saturday off to the daytime cashier. Since Carlos lived near work, he always took the Friday-night turn and left me the Saturday-morning one. That way I could rest up and go to school.

Carlos did the paperwork, while I did all those other things. Once Carlos, the janitor, and the cashier were all sick and absent from work at the same time. I had to take over the whole job of managing the place, doing all their work to boot. I'd get home in the early hours of the morning, and by 7:00 I had to be back there opening up the place. I often fell asleep at the cashier's desk. My problem was to stay awake so I wouldn't press the wrong key on the cash register and mark more money than really went in. I spent a whole week like that. Lala never raised any objections. She knew I had to take over until my comrades got well.

I'm free and willing to go anywhere the Revolution sends me at any time, and I know that if Lala and I should be sent to work away from Havana, the Revolution would give us leave every year or two to visit our families.

My whole family is in Oriente, but I've been gone as long as four years at a time without visiting them. Our life in Havana is very different from the life my parents led. I have a steady job and I make plenty of money to feed my kids. All Lala has to do is tell me when she needs to go shopping. Under our former system of government, my parents had a hard, sad struggle to raise us. We were always in a tight fix and our situation was critical up to the triumph of the Revolution. Now nobody lies awake thinking, "How am I going to get through tomorrow? Where will I find work for the day? Will I find work at all?" That kind of thing doesn't happen anymore.

My parents' situation has changed greatly. Before the Revolution my old lady lived in a palm-wood hut and never had any cement floors like now. When I was a kid, we could never afford to buy a radio, but the last time I visited they had three. Each of my sisters had her own—the portable kind that work with batteries, because there's no electricity there yet. My old lady's greatest wish before the Revolution was to own a decent sewing machine. Well, now she's got a good imported one. It isn't an electric machine or a Singer and it doesn't have its own stand, but it's a good modern model.

It gives me great satisfaction to see that my father is no longer living in miserable poverty and doesn't have to work as hard as he used to. He must be about sixty-five years old now, and can't be expected to achieve more than he already has. He still does farm work, but it's not like the old days when he couldn't eat if he didn't work. They show him a lot of consideration on the job and assigned him to a brigade of women so he wouldn't strain himself. He earns 2 or 3 *pesos,* then goes back home and rests.

Mamá is still strong but doesn't have such a quick temper now. My grandmother is over eighty and keeps on going to spiritist centers. She keeps urging me to go too. When I went to say goodbye to her the last time I was home she said to me, "God be with you, my child." But I said, "Let God be with whomever he pleases, I'm going by myself, Grandmother!"

As for my brothers, the only spirits they believe in are the distilled kind. Yeah, drinking is their only religion, but that doesn't mean they're not revolutionary. I'm proud of my brothers and sisters because they're all ready to go forward with the Revolution. Two of them, Juan and Luis, make a greater effort than the rest of us because they're young yet. Right now they're working in the kitchen at the sugar mill, but they could do more to help in the Revolution.

It's hard to say whether in my family my brother Raúl or I benefited most from the Revolution. Raúl started going to school at the time of the Triumph. From the fourth grade he was skipped to the sixth. When the teacher shortage occurred, tests were sent to Santiago to find students who were good teacher material. Well, Raúl scored on the sixth-grade level, so they sent him to a teachers' school where he graduated without any problem. Then he entered the Frank País Brigade as a teacher. After a time in the Brigade, they sent him to the lowlands. He started as a teacher there, but was appointed to a regional education committee in some municipality, and now he's a municipal inspector.

Getting to be a municipal inspector was a giant step forward for Raúl; he wouldn't have been given that opportunity before the Revolution. Whenever there's a meeting to plan something for the barrio or pass any resolution, Raúl is called right there with the older people, Party militants, and even though he's just a young kid, he gets chosen to take the minutes and to phrase resolutions.

The rest of my brothers and sisters haven't benefited nearly as much as Raúl and I have. They simply don't have the right approach to things. Now that everybody has the chance to study and get ahead, they don't take the opportunity the way any right-minded person should.

I went to visit my sister María Luz when I was home in 1968. She lives in the Sierra, a long way from my folks, so Juan, Raúl, and I left early in the morning and arrived at her house around 5:00 in the evening. Her house is on the very crest of a hill and we were only about 5 meters away when they first saw us. We sure took them by surprise! It had been about four years since I'd seen my sister last. She grabbed me and hugged and kissed me. So did my brother-in-law Napoleón and my little nieces. All of them seemed in good health and spirits.

Napoleón is a pretty sloppy individual who likes his liquor and goes around barefoot. He's the kind of guy who doesn't like to be tied down to one place—a bum, in other words. But one good thing I can say about him is that he's a loner. And I was happy to see that he was making an effort to lead a better life by cutting himself off from the hell-raisers who lived in the *batey* belonging to the cooperative farm. Napoleón built himself a new little house away from the community. It has earthen floors and a palm-thatched roof. He was even raising a few chickens and so on. When I'd last seen that family, they hardly had a rag to cover their backs. Now they had decent clothes and shoes, and a real bed, which is something no one used to have around there.

Looking down at the *batey*, I could see over a hundred houses, which is an enormous community for the Sierra, and I couldn't help noticing the kind of people who lived there. I cataloged the area right away and said, "This place is no good." Everybody there spent their lives playing *bolita* numbers and gambling. They cheated, too. Suppose you played a *bolita* number and won the prize. They'd tell you that you hadn't won at all and refuse to pay. There were even guys who'd demand money by force. If they saw you had money, they'd show up some night and try to force it out of you. Yes, armed robbery was what it was.

The reason why there were so many troublemakers in the community was because they worked on a quota system. Say, for instance, that one day's work quota on the cooperative was three rows, for which they were paid 3.60 *pesos*. Well, suppose you did six rows in one day, you'd still be paid the standard daily wage. The extra rows would be counted toward your next day's quota. And any worker doubling the daily quota would have the next day off. So the men would go to work three days a week and the rest of the time they'd loaf and play *bolita* numbers. I'd never have set such work quotas because they created a minimum ceiling for the workers' production.[43] If the workers were paid according to the amount of work, they wouldn't spend their time gambling.

The Sierra is one place where the Revolution hasn't brought progress. It's exactly as it was when I first saw it—a place where no policeman dared set foot. Well, I don't mean there's been no progress; there have been land reforms, of course, and road repairs too, but what I mean is that the bad people who used to live in the Sierra are still there and they're the ones who are holding up progress. Why, the union leader who's supposed to enforce the law is the main *bolita* agent there! It's not that any of those people are against the Revolution, but, well, they don't adapt to it either. They don't realize they should stay put in one place and work hard to make a living because things don't fall from heaven.

Whenever I went to the Sierra, I met with difficulties because of individuals who weren't committed to the Revolution. There are guys there who've made a business of buying *alcoholito* in Havana for 16 *centavos* and taking it to the Sierra, where they sell it for 13 *pesos*. *Alcoholito* is made by heating alcohol and something else over a flame to reduce it, then they mix in sour oranges and lemons or some other stuff to flavor it. When I was visiting Oriente, my brothers told me about a guy named Nacho who did that.

"Is that right?" I said. "Well, I'm going to keep an eye on him until I catch him at his little game. His *papá* will answer for everything he's doing." Those were my very words. I've got a hunch that Nacho's family never did anything for the Revolution. Even now he takes the easy way to make a living, coming to Havana, enjoying himself here for a few days, buying a bit of merchandise cheaply, and selling it back home for more than the legal price.

Well, I've decided to stop him next time I go there. I'm not out to destroy him—a revolutionary should never do that to anybody—I'm simply going to try to help him, to lead him away from his evil path and bring him to the right path. My duty as a revolutionary is to catch him in the act, then talk with him and advise him to stop dealing in contraband. It wouldn't do a bit of good to have him thrown headfirst into jail without first giving him a chance to reform. That wouldn't be right. People should always be given a chance to reform.

On the way home I faced another difficulty—the transportation problem at one of the main crossroads. There I found that the drivers of the Sierra buses drove wherever they damn pleased. For instance, a driver

43. See Castro's report to the First Party Congress for a discussion of the failure of this policy and the shift in 1970 to the practice of using output rate to determine salary level. Castro estimated that by 1976, 20 percent of all workers received salaries on a piecework or yield basis, resulting in an "increase of productivity per man-shift...." (*Granma Weekly Review*, Jan. 4, 1976, p. 5.)

who was supposed to take the Los Baños route would take whichever route he wanted.

I told the driver, "Now look, if I get into this bus, you better keep to your regular route. People are waiting for a bus at the crossroads, and if you go by Los Negros, they'll be waiting a long time. It isn't right to just leave those people standing there and never show up." But he made all kinds of excuses and even gave me the finger. Then the driver said, "There isn't a thing you can do about it."

"I can't, eh?" I said. "I sure as hell *can* do something about it! Nobody can give me the finger and get away with it! Just you wait! If I catch anyone driving outside of his route I'll see him sent to the kitchen to peel potatoes! Or get him fired from his job with this bus line! Just you wait and see if I can't get this straightened out!"

I really told those bus drivers off. I laid down the law all by myself, even though surrounded by counterrevolutionaries and all those others who aren't counterrevolutionaries but who don't support the Revolution either. And if anybody had tried to stop me, there'd have been trouble.

Lala and I have no real problems in our marriage. We've had arguments now and then, like when I get home late from work because I've had to stay for a meeting. All married couples have their little tiffs, but I draw the line at a certain point. We never refuse to speak to each other. Lala's never stopped speaking to me on account of my affairs, for instance. Sure, she argues and makes a scene, and if she happens to be right, I keep my mouth shut and let her talk, because I figure she'll talk herself out sooner or later. But our quarrels never go any further than that.

We've never hit each other either. She better not try to hit me, because the day she does, that will be the last she ever sees of me. People shouldn't lose control of themselves like that. That's the way it is, and that's all. I won't put up with any disrespect from my wife. Hell no! Just let her try it, that's all! If she ever refused to speak to me, I'd divorce her and that would be the end of it.

Most women probably wouldn't think me very attractive. I'm tall and skinny. I've got bushy eyebrows and am really kind of homely. Not what you'd call downright ugly, but sure as hell not what you'd call handsome either. I'm no monster, but I'm ugly, sure enough. I'm not going into the details about what's ugly about my mug because I might sound as though I had a complex or something.

Despite all that, I've had my good times and have gone to bed with about twenty women. I've got the luck of the ugly, as the saying has it. I've fallen for a lot of girls, since my first little sweetheart in Oriente. But as for falling really in love and wanting to marry, I only loved Irma, Cora, and my wife. The others were only passing things, with no strength of love to bind me to them. I've tried to behave as a good revolutionary should, but any woman who puts herself within my reach I'd grab, because I don't claim to have the morals of a saint as far as women are concerned.

I'm bringing up my children pretty much the same way I was brought up. When I was a kid, my old lady gave orders because *papá* was away most of the time. Now that I have kids of my own, Lala gives the orders. After all, the mother is supposed to be with the kids all the time. I've never spent much time with them. I don't even remember their birthdays. For most of their lives I've been going here and there and staying away for long periods of time. Even when I worked in Havana, they barely caught sight of me during the day, so they're used to getting along without me. That's why they don't miss me when I'm away.

I don't believe my presence at home is terribly important for the children. If I went away and didn't tell them where, that would be different. As long as I'm doing my revolutionary duty, they should know that it's up to their mother to be with them.

I've never spoken to my children about my functions as a revolutionary. Little kids only think about their play. Perhaps, when they're older and can understand, I'll explain the kind of things I do, and why I'm a revolutionary. Anyhow, I'm sure their mother will talk to them about all those things.

I hope my children turn out to be revolutionaries just like me. Not everybody is alike, so it's quite possible that one of them may turn out differently. But I'm pretty sure they'll be good revolutionaries. I can tell from the things they say. For instance, one boy said, "I want to go to the Camilo Cienfuegos School."[44] Well, since that school bears the name of a revolutionary hero it tells you something if a kid wants to study there. It means he wants to go someplace where he'll learn discipline and be given a good example. It also means he wants to defend his fatherland.

A boy can go from the Camilo Cienfuegos School to an aviation school or to work in agriculture. Or he might decide to study for the Merchant Marine or become a technician in an army laboratory. From there he might go to work in a civilian laboratory. But one day they'll tell you they want to be a doctor, and the next day they might say they want to be a bicycle racer. It's too early to really know how the kids will turn out.

44. A system of military-preparatory schools for students from ten to sixteen years of age. Located in all six provinces, Camilo Cienfuegos Schools offer the basic secondary curriculum plus a program of military training, sports, and political instruction. The most outstanding "Camilitos," as the students are known, have the opportunity to attend a military academy after graduation. (See *Area Handbook for Cuba* (Washington, D.C.: Government Printing Office, 1971), pp. 448–49.)

Mercedes Millán

My childhood and adolescence were wonderful. I never had any problems at home. My *papá* was a working man and wasn't rich, but he supported us. He couldn't afford a mansion with a swimming pool or an automobile, but those are luxuries. I never lacked anything. My folks loved me and gave me everything I ever thought of wanting. I could go to the beach, the movies, or other places whenever I liked. Oh, I couldn't have made a trip to Europe, say, but that would have been opulence. Only the rich could do that.

My first home was in a poor neighborhood in the center of Havana, with modest houses and small apartments, some with only one room. It wasn't a barrio of indigents, but poor, humble working people lived there. There were slight economic differences—some people had better houses or furniture, and a few even had cars. Our house had a very small living-dining room, two bedrooms, a bath, and a kitchen. There was a little strip of yard running the length of the house.

In the morning the men would be off to work, the children to school, and the housewives to shop for food. The commercial district was just a few blocks away, on Belascoain Street. It had many stores—hardware, clothing, lingerie, everything. Every day *mamá* went to the grocery store on the corner and to a butcher shop four blocks away.

Papá owned a delivery truck. He worked mostly in Havana, but once in a while he made a two-day or three-day trip to other towns. He was self-employed and didn't keep regular hours, or take vacations either. At that time a working man or white-collar worker had to have a month's vacation by law, but there was no one to give *papá* a paid vacation.

My parents had a different sort of childhood than I had. Both were from peasant families and grew up in villages in Spain. Most of the peasants, although they weren't rich, owned their land. *Papá*'s family owned land too, and he worked on it from the time he was a child, milking the cows and helping with the farm chores. Here in Cuba practically none of the farmers owned land.

Mamá's family also owned land in Spain—and had cows and sheep, too—but I don't know how much. They grew wheat and potatoes. They lived in the upper story of their house because the ground floor was the barn. It was a large family but only four are still alive: *mamá*, who was the youngest, her sister Matilde, who lives here, another sister in Spain, and one brother.

Mamá has only a vague memory of her father—he went to Venezuela when she was only two or three years old. As far as I know, Grandfather didn't abandon my grandmother; he simply left, hoping to improve his situation. But in America everything went wrong for him. When he did return to Spain, Grandmother had been dead for years and years and *mamá* was in Cuba. They never saw each other again. Grandfather died shortly after his return. We got the news when I was a small child.

My grandmother was a good woman in every sense of the word. She never remarried or anything. She stayed on alone, working the land and rearing her children. She was very badly off and had to sell most of her land to feed herself and her children. People took advantage of her and paid much less than the going price.

Mamá has a photo of her mother, sent after *mamá* had lived in Cuba many years. In Spain, older women drape themselves in black from head to foot, which made my grandmother look terribly old. *Papá's* mother was a peasant too, and was just as dedicated to her children, her home, and her husband. She worked the land—it's customary in Spain for women to work side by side with their husbands. Of course some tasks were only for men, but women did a large share of the planting and harvesting. It's only recently that Cuban women have participated in agricultural labor, but in Spain they've always done so.

Even *mamá*, who was the youngest, gleaned the wheat and did other farm chores now and then, though usually she sewed and kept house. Her childhood was hard, but they never went hungry, or naked, or barefoot. She came to Cuba on a ship when she was fifteen or sixteen. Her brother Jesús, who's now back in Spain, lived in Cuba then. I guess he put the idea of emigrating into her head.

In Cuba *mamá* began to work in a dress shop. Her life has been a hard one, always working, managing on whatever she earned. *Papá* was also very young when he came to Cuba in 1923, seventeen or eighteen I think. He came partly to escape conscription, partly to make his fortune in America. That was the idea, but he had a hard time, at least at first. Imagine what it's like to arrive in a foreign country without a *centavo!*

Papá's first job here was in a warehouse. I guess he did whatever he was told to do—clean the place, run errands, and so on. He was young, new in the country, ignorant of Cuban ways, so I imagine they took advantage of him. He slept right there in the warehouse. He worked at different jobs and later on drove a truck. He began a small delivery business of his own, with two trucks. When somebody needed a truck they'd call him, agree on a price, and he'd do the work. He was his own boss then. Now it's different.

Papá has always been scrupulously honest. He doesn't like to fail anybody or to owe money. When times were bad under Machado, *papá* sold a truck to pay his bills, keeping one for his work. Later on, he gave up his business and got a job as an upholsterer until he was able to go into the delivery business again.

Mamá, it seems, lived nearby and sometimes went to his place to use the telephone. That's how they met. They married in 1926, and my sister Socorro, who's ten years older than I, was born within a year. She's now forty-two, so my parents were married forty-three years ago. After she married, *mamá* never again went out to work. At home, yes, but not outside. By the time I was born, *papá*'s financial problems were over.

I was born in 1937 in the Hijas de Galicia Hospital and was baptized when I was about six months old. *Mamá*'s sister Matilde is my godmother and Rufino García Pabón, an old friend of *papá*'s, is my godfather. He was affectionate and gave me money when I was a kid. He lives in Havana, near *papá,* and I still see him.

I don't remember much about my sister when she was a child. We must have some things in common, because after all, we *are* sisters, but on the whole we're very different. By the time I was old enough to notice other people's personalities, she was no longer a child. Ten years is a big difference. When I was small we didn't play much together, but we always got along well without quarreling. I was the baby of the family so I suppose she went out of her way to please me.

Mamá says I was a very mischievous and restless kid. Now, when I complain about my own children, she tells me, "What have you got to gripe about? You were just like them."

I played with the children who lived in our building. They were a year or two younger than I. We girls would play house with our dolls. We had doll houses and little stoves and all kinds of toy kitchen utensils. We'd take the dolls to the doctor and for walks. We'd dress and undress them, bathe them, and so on. When we played with the boys, the games were more active. We'd play hide-and-seek, or we'd pretend we had a theater and we'd sing, dance, or recite poems. One of the boys would be master of ceremonies and announce the performers. You know what terrific imaginations children have! Sometimes we played school, too.

On the Day of the Three Kings, January 6, we always received toys. In those times parents made sure that children really believed in the Three Kings. On the great day I'd get up at the crack of dawn. The night before I'd be so excited sometimes my parents would have to give me soothing herb teas to calm my nerves. Every year I wrote two letters to the Three Kings—one for my parents and one for Brígida, *mamá*'s best friend. Whatever I asked them to leave me at Brígida's house, I'd get. They left me even more than I asked for. It was lovely.

Brígida lived just around the corner from us. I called her Gida because when I began to talk I couldn't pronounce her name properly. She always introduced me as her niece, though everybody knew we weren't really related. She had her quirks, but she spoiled me a lot more than *mamá* ever did. When *mamá* scolded me, Gida would always come to my defense and cover up for me.

Brígida was a secretary to a factory manager. She kept up with everything I did from the time I was very small. She even helped me with my homework. When I was older, she was as interested in me as ever. We often went shopping together and she'd urge me to buy myself this or that. We shared everything. She'd drop in to see me every day after lunch, before going back to work.

Brígida's *papá* was a tobacco worker in the Partagás factory. They weren't rich, only middle-class, but they lived well. Their apartment was tiny but they had a television, radio, record player, electric mixer, and toaster—all the appliances that could add to their entertainment or comfort. Brígida dressed very well indeed. After the Revolution, even with rationing she still managed to dress attractively.

I went to church with *mamá* occasionally when I was little. I made my First Communion before I was seven and was confirmed at ten or eleven. At thirteen or fourteen I began to go to Sunday Mass with my friends. I'd go with a neighbor of mine, Elena, who's now in the United States, or with Cacha, *papá*'s goddaughter, or Carmen, *mamá*'s goddaughter.

Both *papá* and *mamá* are believers, though they're not devout. They're just like me, letting years go by without attending church. *Mamá* goes sometimes when they hold Mass for the Dead, or to a funeral Mass for a friend. She'd like to go every Sunday, but she doesn't have the time or doesn't feel well. *Papá* never went to Mass, but he believes too. After all, that's the way they were brought up.

My family usually celebrated Christmas Eve by gathering at one of our relatives' homes for midnight supper. On my birthday *mamá* would buy me a cake and candles, and the family's most intimate friends would bring me gifts. It wasn't a big party, but refreshments were always served—cake, small sandwiches, soft drinks. My saint's day was celebrated the same way.

I wasn't quite four when I started kindergarten in a public school across the street from my house. I was eager to go and didn't cry or anything, not even the first day. The teachers were delighted. I had long, curly hair and they were very fond of me. *Mamá* told me that when I was absent, they'd send an older pupil to my home to find out whether I was sick.

After kindergarten I went to another school. It wasn't a nun's school but it was extremely religious, with very antiquated teaching methods. I lost a lot of time praying—before going to the classroom as well as the rosary at noon—and we had many religion classes.

I believe in God, but I don't believe in mixing religion with education. *Mamá* was very dissatisfied with the school, so when I was about to enter upper second grade, she transferred me to the Estrellas School. There I learned to read and write almost at once, *mamá* says. Both schools were private; only poor children went to public school. Naturally, private schools were of different categories. The ones in the highest category were very expensive. In my school they taught very well and the director was a famous educator.

I wasn't exactly wild about school, but I didn't rebel or refuse to study. *Mamá* says I was mischievous at home, but in school I behaved myself, except for talking. I'd get punished for that by being told to stand in a corner or remain an hour or two after class. I got good marks with no trouble and was always promoted. I believe I was a better student than my sister, who quit school after sixth grade. I tried to teach her English, but she didn't want to learn. I'd say to her, "Study this lesson and do this exercise." She wouldn't do a thing. No matter how mad I got, she still refused to study.

After school I'd bathe and change, then study until dinner time. All the homework had to be copied neatly in a notebook. I might play a little while after that, then eat dinner and go to bed.

Before the Revolution, you went to an institute or took a commercial course after completing the sixth grade. The *bachillerato,* which is more or less equivalent to what they call high school in the United States, took five years. In the last year of *bachillerato,* you chose to specialize in science or in liberal arts, depending on the career you planned to study. Now the school system is different; after primary school there's basic secondary school, and after that, pre-university.

My parents let me choose my own career. In fact, they didn't even insist that I study for the *bachillerato.* That was my own decision. I could have taken a commercial course, it made no difference to them. They did encourage me to go on studying, though, because they said a well-educated person can get along in life better.

I decided to get my *bachillerato* in the Havana Institute. At that time, I intended to go on to the University to study pharmacy. But I found I didn't like chemistry one bit so I decided to study law. I have so many pleasant memories of my student days. I think it's the best time of one's life. A student has no real worries and nothing to think about except studying. Sometimes I didn't do well in an examination or I got tense from studying, but we had fun, too.

At the time I went to the Havana Institute I was much thinner than I am now. I looked very good and I liked to dress well and fix myself up. I'd keep up with the latest fashions as much as I could afford to. I wanted my purse and shoes and dress to go together, and to have pretty jewelry—all the things women like, especially when they're young.

I always had lots of clothes that *mamá* sewed. Sometimes I shopped with her for the cloth, sometimes she chose it herself. I bought many blouses ready-made but not dresses, because my hips are so broad in proportion to my torso.

I loved to go places. I even went to Varadero[45] sometimes, on excursions on Saturday and Sunday. A group of friends would hire a bus and take food or buy it there. We'd share the expenses of the bus and a room or two in a guest house for changing our clothes. Even if twenty people went along it was no problem, we simply took turns dressing. We all knew one another so we weren't worried about stealing. When you go to Varadero now, you can't find anyplace to spend the night. It isn't as easy as it was before.

Papá, mamá, my sister, and I belonged to a Spanish club, a mutual-aid society that met monthly in the Centro Asturiano. When one of the members got sick, the others would visit him and give him money or whatever he needed. The society was always having fiestas and lotteries to raise money, and businessmen would donate things to be raffled off. *Mamá* and I belonged to the Ladies' Committee. The committee members were very friendly and visited each other on their saints' days and exchanged gifts.

St. James is the patron saint of my parents' village in Spain, so every year on his day, or the closest Sunday, there'd be a free banquet for the members in the gardens of the Polar brewery. It was a large field with trees, nicely decorated for the party. They had a kitchen where the food was cooked. The menu was elaborate: first they served vermouth, then ham and cheese appetizers, next fish, usually with almond dressing, then rice with chicken—half a chicken each—bread, dessert, coffee, and cigarettes and beer. The Polar Company provided all the beer free. Practically every Spanish club had an annual banquet like that. Dinner was served at midday and an orchestra played for dancing at 6:00 or 7:00 in the evening. Oh, how I loved those banquets!

The Revolution put an end to all that. The club still exists, but the banquets are forbidden—there isn't enough food for that kind of thing. The last banquet took place in 1960, I think. The club is quite dispersed by now, for many of the members have left Cuba. *Papá* still goes there; he's the treasurer. I'm a member too, but I never have time to go. Besides, there's nothing going on except the mutual-aid thing. It's so different now; it's lost its flavor.

To celebrate my fifteenth birthday we had a party at the clubhouse ballroom of the Laundry Workers' Association. *Papá* arranged it through friends of his who were members. The clubhouse was built by the workers themselves. The Laundry Workers' ballroom was a large room and we invited about 200 people. We had a buffet with small sandwiches, crabmeat, and little pastries, and beer and soft drinks. We

45. A popular beach and resort area in Matanzas Province.

danced to a record player and I had a special ballerina-length dress of blue nylon tulle and lace with a very full skirt made for the occasion.

That was in 1952, the year Batista came to power. On the day he took over, I got up as usual to go to the Institute, then I heard the neighbors saying that schools were closed because Batista had carried out a coup d'etat. That's all. I didn't realize it was important. Nobody was interested in politics at home. I don't even remember hearing about the attack on the Moncada the following year. Even *papá*, a man and head of the family, wasn't interested in politics. Of course, like anybody else, he made an occasional remark about the news. But he lived for his work and his home, that's all. As for *mamá*, she was even less interested in politics.

I stopped studying, not because *papá* wasn't able or willing to pay for my education but because I decided to get married. I wasn't looking for any particular type of husband as long as he was responsible, a hard worker, and so on. I mean, naturally I couldn't fall in love with an irresponsible man who wouldn't work or study. What kind of a future would I have had with a man like that? And of course I never would have fallen in love with a drunkard or a gambler or anyone like that. But within those limits, my only requirement for my husband was that I be in love with him.

I met Juan Carlos at the Institute during our fourth year. We were simply schoolmates. In the fifth year we talked together about school work or maybe about some movie we'd both seen. I was so distant he thought I was engaged to someone else. I was a very proper young girl, always with two or three girl friends, never alone. I was no *pepilla*, the kind of young girl who goes out with one boy after another.

Then, in December, Juan Carlos invited the whole class to his sister Diana's fifteenth birthday party. He noticed that I didn't go with a boy. If I'd been engaged, I'd naturally have gone to the party with my fiancé. After that Juan Carlos made an effort to be with me. If a group of us went to the library, he joined us. And so, little by little, we got to be friends.

One day he invited me to a dance. That was in February, when the carnival[46] was celebrated in Havana. I was in the parade, on a float for Bacardi rum. All the firms selling or making beer, cognac, cigars, and just about everything else had pretty floats decorated with flowers and paper and girls in costume. A boy we knew who worked at Bacardi asked *papá* to let me ride on their float. At first *papá* wouldn't hear of it, but this boy persuaded him. The float was decorated with a large globe of the world and five girls representing a country on each continent. I was dressed in a Spanish costume representing all of Europe. Then there was

46. The Mardi Gras celebration before Lent.

a fat papier-mâché waiter carrying a tray with a bottle of Bacardi rum on it. The idea of the float was that the rum was sold all over the world.

There were five Sundays of carnival, the first in Havana, the others in nearby towns, and we went on the float to all of them. Juan Carlos still hadn't spoken to me of love, but we'd become a great deal friendlier and I was beginning to realize what an effect I was having on him. He went to the carnival with Blanca, a close friend of mine and a girl he'd known for years in Oriente. This gave him a chance to talk with me, although Blanca's *mamá* and my *mamá* went along too. The Bacardi firm had a station wagon to drive the girls and their *mamás* or whoever chaperoned them.

One day in May, 1956, we went with Blanca and another boy to dance at the Bambú, a cabaret that no longer exists. We were chaperoned by our *mamás*. It was there that Juan Carlos made a formal declaration of love. He told me he was in love with me and asked if I loved him. I said yes and that was it.

Before the Revolution Juan's family lived well. His father was a small *latifundista*.[47] He also had a stall in the Mercado Unico,[48] where he sold oranges. He made a lot of money that way. *Papá* didn't make as much; all he had was his truck.

In 1955 we'd moved to the apartment where *papá* and *mamá* still live. It was bigger than our other one and the rent was higher, too. I shared a room with my sister until she married, but we each had our own bed. The furniture was more or less presentable, not broken or anything, and we had a good stove, but it was all on a modest scale, no? We weren't rich like Juan Carlos's family.

It was around that time that I began to be more interested in politics. The students at the Institute held demonstrations against Batista's government. We suddenly realized that young revolutionary students were being tortured by Batista's police. We were accustomed to governments stealing and to violence between politicians and to promises that were never carried out, but . . . well, that was normal. Torturing young people was something else again. Repression was widespread. Just about everybody knew about the Rebels and how they were treated, though it wasn't in the newspapers.

Sometimes there were strikes and protests at the Institute. When the university students went on strike, the Institute would strike too, as a gesture of solidarity. Juan Carlos was one of the leaders at the Institute and he helped direct the strikes and the whole opposition to the government. At that time he and I were not yet engaged, but I knew he was involved with the strikes.

47. Owner of a *latifundia*, an agricultural complex.
48. A large central market in Havana.

Everyone was talking about the fighting and the rebellion and the crimes against the Cuban people. I was always against those abuses. Nobody with the slightest human feeling can condone torture and murder. Such things are beyond politics. My family criticized the tyranny, but they weren't directly connected with either the Batista regime or the revolutionaries. As older people, my parents were always advising Juan to be careful and not look for trouble because he too could be arrested and tortured.

The director of the Institute had Juan arrested to scare him and stop him from agitating and organizing strikes. The description and license number of his car were circulated among the police and they arrested him two or three times but let him go when he was found unarmed. They didn't really know what he was up to, but they had a pretty good idea, no?

We hadn't fixed a date for our wedding because we intended to enroll together in the Law School. But just as we both completed the *bachillerato* in 1956, the University was closed down. By then the problem of the Batista dictatorship had become really serious. The University would be opened and three days later they'd have to close it again because the students were on a rampage. Finally it was shut down indefinitely and remained closed through 1957 and 1958. It wasn't reopened until 1959, after the triumph of the Revolution.

By that time I had no intention of going back to school. I was married and pregnant with Merceditas, and once a woman has a husband and a child, she'd need tremendous willpower and peace and quiet to begin studying again. Some women can, but I'm not up to it. No, no, no! So I didn't go on and neither did Juan Carlos. After finishing the *bachillerato*, we both quit.

What I did was study typing and shorthand in English and Spanish at the Ruston Academy. I also completed a correspondence course in English, but I'm forgetting English for lack of practice.

Juan has always had a lot of ability and initiative. In fact, he began to work with his father while still in school because he never liked to ask for money. His father paid him a salary and with that Juan paid his own expenses. He always had money.

After he finished school he worked full-time and soon became independent of his father and got his own produce stand at the market. He sold retail and his father sold wholesale. They got practically all their oranges from Oriente, in trailer trucks, paying the transportation costs besides the cost of the fruit, which they then resold.

Juan Carlos had to be at the market by 1:00 A.M. He'd stay there until about noon, then go home, take a bath, have his lunch, and lie down to sleep. He'd sleep all afternoon. Around 9:00 he'd come to my house and visit with me until 10:00 or 10:30. Then he'd go home to nap before it was time to get up again. He'd visit me about three or four times a week, especially on Saturdays and Sundays, though he had to work those days too. That's the way the market is. It was very profitable work but you had to slave at it.

Once I went to see Juan Carlos at the market. It was an awful place. The workers there were a class of people with no breeding at all. You heard all sorts of dirty words and there were women of the evil life all over the place. The truth is, it was full of low, crude, rough people. Not all were bad, but all were low-class and foul-mouthed. Juan says he grew up in the marketplace and learned to struggle and face up to life there.

It didn't bother me that Juan worked there; that was his own affair. He liked it, so it wouldn't have been right to nag him about it. I did feel he worked terribly hard and I kept after him to get more sleep. Why, sometimes I'd even call him and tell him, "Never mind coming over. Get some rest."

We decided to get married in April, 1958. We rented an apartment, selected our furniture, and bought the rest of the household things— bedclothes, towels, china, and so on. Then Juan's grandfather died. We postponed our wedding because his whole family was so saddened and simply not in the mood for a celebration. We gave up the apartment. It meant losing the deposit and the first month's rent that we'd paid in advance, but we said, "All right, we lose the money. That doesn't matter." We didn't fix a new wedding date right away and I thought, "Here's my chance for a December wedding!" I'd always dreamed of being married in December.

By the end of June, Juan began to insist that we get married in July. "But that's too soon," I objected. It wasn't as hard to find a place then as it is now, but it wasn't easy either. I didn't want to just grab the first vacant apartment that was offered. "It's too much to look for an apartment and buy the furniture and do a million other things in less than one month," I complained. And then, too, we were being married in church and you always need more things for that—wedding dress, going-away dress. . . .

"Never mind," Juan told me. "Just see about your clothes, the church, and the lawyer. When we get back from our honeymoon, we can stay at a hotel and take two or three months to find an apartment and furnish it."

So we forgot about the apartment for the time being and concentrated on getting ready for the wedding.

At that time Juan was working underground for the Revolution and I knew it. He never told me, but I knew his opinions and I caught on. I'm not an idiot. He was even going to participate in the attack on the Presidential Palace in 1957,[49] but the *compañero* who was supposed to contact

49. In March, 1957, a group of about eighty men attacked the Presidential Palace in Havana in an attempt to assassinate Batista. Most of the attackers were members of the *Directorio Revolucionario*, a university student group organized by José Antonio Echeverría. The rebels were able to penetrate the Palace but could not find their way to Batista's living

him didn't. Otherwise he'd have been there, and maybe now he'd be a dead hero, because lots of people died in that attack.

In April, 1958, Juan went to Mexico and stayed five days. He told me he was going for a short vacation but I knew it was something else. Those were things he couldn't talk about, so I wasn't going to pester him to tell me. Of course my heart was right in my mouth the whole time. It could have gone pretty badly for him—not in Mexico, but after he got back. Afterward he told me he'd gone to talk with the members of an expeditionary force that planned to land in Cuba. He was sent by the Revolution as an envoy.

We were married in July, first in a civil ceremony and two days later in church. On the day of the civil ceremony Juan was told the police were looking for him. During the ceremony he wasn't his normal self. "What's the matter?" I asked him.

"Oh, I don't know. Nothing." But right afterward he explained. A *compañero* who'd been taken prisoner had talked and named Juan and others. Another *compañero* told him, "Look, kid, get lost, vanish. They're looking for you."

"Then let's go away together," I said. "After all, we're legally married." We weren't married in church yet, but in the eyes of the law our marriage was valid. We'd already arranged to go to Mexico and all the wedding invitations were out, so Juan said, "If they get me they get me, that's all."

Fortunately no one came to arrest him. I guess the police force was kept too busy getting ready for July 26. That's the anniversary of the attack on the Moncada, and there were always bombs and demonstrations then. The wedding was even reported in the newspapers; there was nothing secret about it. How could there be after so many people had been invited?

Juan married in church to please *mamá* and me, and because it was a pretty ceremony, as he said, but not because he believed in it. He never did, and neither did his *papá*. It has nothing to do with being a communist, either. Even when they were anticommunist—because communism here was considered the limit—they were already atheists. That's the way they were brought up, in spite of the fact that Juan's grandmother—may she rest in peace—and his mother were both devout Catholics, the kind who always went to Mass and kept statues of the saints in the house and put flowers and candles before them.

---

quarters. In a simultaneous attack the students took over Havana Radio, and Echeverría mistakenly broadcast the announcement of Batista's death. Shortly afterward Echeverría was fatally shot by police. An estimated thirty-five rebels and five Batista policemen were killed in the attack. The Castro forces were already involved in the Sierra campaign and were not a part of the *Directorio* action. Castro later criticized the attack as "a useless expenditure of blood." (Thomas, *Cuba: The Pursuit of Freedom*, p. 930. See also pp. 925 ff.)

We had no wedding reception, not because of the police but because Juan's grandfather had died so recently. One would have been ashamed to have a large reception when the bridegroom's family was in mourning. And if you have a small, intimate reception, you always offend someone who isn't invited. We were between the sword and the wall, so we decided not to have any reception at all. After the wedding ceremony we went home, changed our clothes, and went to spend the night at the Havana Hilton, which is now the Habana Libre.

Juan had been my only sweetheart. I never had sexual relations with him or anybody else before I got married. Here in Cuba it's taken for granted that a decent woman has no sexual experience before marriage. There are women who live free lives and don't care what they do. I don't mean prostitutes, but divorced women and so on, who go out with a man and do other things with him. But I don't like that. I've heard that in the United States people don't think it matters one way or the other. Perhaps here things will change, but so far that's looked down on. It's only logical that a woman should be a virgin when she marries. It's normal that sexual relations should come after marriage, not before.

I imagine that Juan must have had his experiences before we married. He's never told me and I haven't asked him. I wouldn't like to have him talk about such things with me, but he was twenty when we married and I don't believe there's a man in the world who reaches the age of twenty without ever having had sexual relations.

On my wedding night I felt very nervous, as every bride naturally does. It's only logical. I knew what was going to happen, but one always feels a bit nervous. Besides, there was the agitation of the wedding itself, not to mention the fact that I knew the police were looking for Juan.

Everything had been explained to me before, of course. Not by *mamá* but by my sister. *Mamá* had told me all about menstruation before I got it at eleven, but the things of marriage were easier to discuss with a sister. I don't like to talk about those things, not even with women friends. I'm very modest that way. The things that happen between husband and wife are private.

We didn't leave the hotel until it was time to go to the airport the next morning. One day later the police went to Juan's house to arrest him, carrying newspaper clippings and a large graduation photograph to identify him. They searched all over the house and also his place of work. His father wrote and told Juan to take as long a vacation as he liked, because he wasn't needed at work. That was the agreed signal, so Juan would know the police were aware that he was in Mexico and were watching for him to come back.

We were in Mexico from July, 1958, to January, 1959, after the triumph of the Revolution. Our stay was relatively short, only six months, but we had no way of knowing when and if Batista would fall.

Oh, we thought that in the long run the Revolution had to be victorious, but how could we be sure? Our worst problem in Mexico was not knowing when we could return to Cuba.

Aside from that uncertainty, my husband suffered, knowing that others were fighting while he was idle in Mexico. It was agony to him. He spent all his time talking with other Cuban exiles, trying to figure out how they could organize an expedition to return secretly to Cuba. I understood that he felt it was his duty as a Cuban to defend his fatherland, but I couldn't help worrying, "Suppose he does go and something happens to him?"

Economically we had no problem in Mexico. We'd taken some money along and my father-in-law sent us more as long as we stayed. Thanks to him we always had enough. The money my father-in-law sent was not a gift, it was Juan's. My husband was only twenty, but he already had a business of his own, which was run by his employees and supervised by his father while he was away.

There was a small community of Cuban exiles in Mexico in 1958. Some of the exiles weren't . . . well, as lucky as we were about having enough money. Several of them had lunch and dinner at my house. They were very badly off.

There's so much poverty in Mexico—just a few rich people, everybody else is poor. The middle class is very small. I don't know how it is now, but that's the way it was then. Even in Mexico City you'd see Indians, dirty and barefoot, and on the same street elegantly dressed people and late-model cars and modern buildings. There were rich and poor people in Cuba, too, but we also had a large middle class, at least in Havana. You saw women factory workers and office clerks, mere employees, well dressed with high-heeled shoes and fashionable, matching purses and beauty-parlor hairdos. You did see a few poorly dressed people and some ragged, barefoot children, but not like in Mexico.

Mamá and my mother-in-law came to Mexico to visit us. My mother-in-law had to leave soon because her mother was sick, but we persuaded *mamá* to stay with us longer. In December she'd already reserved her passage for January 11. Then, on January 1, when we heard about the triumph of the Revolution, we reserved passage for the 11th with her.

Practically all the Cuban exiles returned to Cuba before we did. For the first few days after the Triumph, the government sent airplanes to bring the exiles back to Cuba free of charge. However, to fly back on them you had to wait in the airport, perhaps for hours, since there was no way of knowing when the plane would arrive. Then, when it arrived, an avalanche of people tried to board it. We returned on the Mexican airlines, so we didn't take the seat of some other Cuban who might not have had the money for his return trip.

We were so happy to be back that we were standing at the door when the plane landed. The stewardess asked us to sit down and fasten our safety belts, but we were too anxious to get home. We practically went wild, my husband and I, in the last few moments on the plane. When they opened the door we were the first ones out. It was a very emotional moment. We hadn't been away so very long, but we'd been homesick. Besides, we were so happy about the triumph of the Revolution.

Havana was full of olive-green uniforms, long hair, and beards. Everywhere you could sense people's joy. We'd missed the first few days of the Triumph, but it was still a tremendous sight. The whole population of Havana seemed to be out on the streets.

Mamá insisted we stay with her, even if we were a bit crowded, while we looked for an apartment. We were still there at the time of the Urban Reform Law, when they froze all the apartments, so then we couldn't move. We stayed with *mamá* two years, from January, 1959, to April, 1961.

My daughter was born in November, 1959. We'd taken it for granted that our firstborn would be a boy. Most men want their first child to be a boy. That's what I wanted too, because a man has more authority and it seemed to me that if the eldest was a boy and the youngest a girl, he could take care of her if we should die. A younger sister can always count on her brother's protection. But the baby was a girl and everybody took it very well. We were so enchanted with her that we didn't even remember what we'd wanted. We hadn't even thought of a girl's name. "What shall we call her?" we asked. *Mamá* said, "Name her after you." I hadn't intended to name my daughter after me, but I couldn't think of any other name I liked.

Before the baby I'd had only Juan to think about, but he never objected when I had to neglect him to attend her. Besides, we had sexual relations throughout my pregnancy and resumed them forty days after the birth.

I wanted to baptize our baby but Juan didn't. We had quite a conflict. "I have as much right as you do to decide," I told him. He got tired of arguing about it and finally agreed, just so I'd stop pestering him. He even went to the church for the ceremony, but I practically had to drag him there.

I asked Brígida to be the baby's godmother. A godmother is supposed to take the mother's place if she dies or gets sick, but, well, I don't think anybody really thinks of that when they choose a godmother for their child. I didn't. I simply chose somebody I knew would be fond of the child and pay attention to her. Brígida lived for Merceditas. She'd take her out, buy presents for her ... she was devoted to her.

I chose my husband's brother Cándido for godfather. I didn't want to hog the whole business, so I said, "The godfather shall be a relative of

Juan's." Juan and Cándido always got along well with each other in spite
of the fact that my husband is about eight years older. Juan was practically a second father to him; Cándido asked his advice about everything.

Our biggest problem at the time of Merceditas's birth was *mamá*'s
apartment. It was too small for five people. It has a parlor, two bedrooms, bath, dining room, kitchen, and a tiny patio. We had two rooms
but they weren't very big. All we had was a Hollywood bed, not even a
bedroom set. We used the bureaus I'd had when I was single. But of
course we had to buy the baby a crib, a bureau, a bathinette, a baby
carriage, and a playpen. With so many things there was hardly room to
walk, but even so, we stayed for over a year after she was born.

My husband and my parents have always liked each other. They feel
he's the son they never had. He still goes there for lunch. Juan and I
have always wanted my parents to live with us. When we first moved,
Juan would say to me, "Don't worry. They'll soon come to live with us,
you'll see! They're going to feel lonely and come here. The house is big;
there's plenty of room for them." But no, they haven't changed their
minds. It's too far, they say. They're used to living in the center of
Havana and don't like our *reparto, papá* especially. He's spent a lifetime
with his trucks and his work and won't leave them now. And it's true that
living in this neighborhood is very different from living there in Havana.
In the center of Havana there are more buses and other means of transportation. Here we depend on one or two buses to get anywhere.

Now and then *mamá* and *papá* will come and spend a day or two, or a
weekend. If not, we go there. Naturally we don't sleep overnight because
there isn't room for all of us, but we often stay for lunch and dinner. It's
no trouble for us to come home at night in our car.

In 1966, after my son Eloyitos was born, we moved back to my parents'
house again for six months. The two children and I had colds that hung
on and on, and the doctor said this place—the apartment we have
now—was too humid and we should go elsewhere. When summer came,
we got better and came back home.

I feel very close to my parents and they still help me in every way they
can. Of course their financial situation has changed. Not long ago the
government took over *papá*'s business.[50] The truck still belongs to my
father and he pays the taxes and expenses, but he doesn't set the price. It
works like this. Suppose the load is worth 50 *pesos. Papá* gets the 50 *pesos*
from the customer and hands it over to the dispatcher, together with the
booking order. The dispatcher takes 10 percent for the government and
makes out a check for the balance to *papá*, who then cashes it at the bank.

I think it was a year ago in January when they started rationing
gasoline. All delivery trucks were transferred to the Le Coubre dock.

50. In March, 1968, approximately 55,000 small businesses were "intervened" and
closed down by the government as part of a new "revolutionary offensive"; some were
reopened under state management.

Whenever somebody needs a truck, they go there and request it. Each truck has a number and is sent out by turns.

Papá keeps on working though he really has no need to, because, after all, it's only for him and *mamá* now. But he likes to work. He's the kind of person who simply can't be idle. Until very recently *papá* had never had a vacation in his life. When we go to Varadero we nag him to take a week or fifteen days off. This year he refused to go—that's the way he is. No matter how *mamá* and I scold him, he sometimes takes a Sunday shift and works until 9:00 at night.

"Why should you do such a thing?" we ask him. "How many children are you supporting now, pray? You're an old man. You're in good health, thank God, but think of your age and all the years you've worked, lifting and lugging things." His work is really hard but nobody can tear him away from it.

Papá is very affectionate. He's a wonderful father. I'm proud of *mamá*, too, but it seems to me that a good father is much rarer than a good mother. A woman is usually motherly by nature. On the other hand, it's common to find men who, although they're not bad, simply don't care much for their homes and children. They live a life of their own and would never, under any circumstances, sacrifice themselves for their children. I see that other fathers are not like mine, and that's the truth. He has lived for his children, and right now, with my sister in Spain, he lives for me and his grandchildren.

Juan's mother lives in La Víbora, but his father lives in Oriente. They separated at the time of the first Agrarian Reform Law. He decided to let his overseer go and to look after the land himself. The next reform came and everybody having more than 5 *caballerías* of land lost it all.[51] They kept him on as administrator of his former land. Then he was a worker, just like my *papá*. Later he quit, because of the responsibility and because he got sick. But he stayed on in Oriente. He says he's never going to live in Havana again.

The disagreement between my parents-in-law arose when he wanted her to move to Oriente with him. She agreed to go, but they owned the house they lived in, and their other children, Cándido and Diana, were both single and still students, so she wanted to get them settled before she left. That made my father-in-law mad. They quarreled and he left. Now she lives in the house with her father, her son Cándido, and his wife, Digna. My sister-in-law Diana lives across the street in her grandparents' house.

I've always gotten along with my mother-in-law. We've never had any arguments, much less quarrels. She's always helped me out. If I need anything, she tries to get it for me. Of course we've never lived together, and I guess that makes a difference. We talk on the phone every day. If I

51. See n. 7.

don't call her she calls me—always, always. She tells me all the news about the family and asks about us. If I have something they need, I share it with them and vice versa. She comes to visit, too, but not often, because she has a house to look after as well as Diana's little girl. Diana works and the child is in a *círculo*. My mother-in-law has to get her granddaughter at 5:00 in the evening, and after that she's in complete charge of the child.

We don't see much of Diana because she works barbarously hard at the Labor Ministry. She's there from morning till night and has both lunch and dinner at the office. Diana is horribly integrated in the Revolution. She even goes to do productive labor in the country for days at a time, so we don't really have any chance to see her. Sometimes when she can escape for a minute—if she has to go out on an errand relating to her work—she'll drop in to say hello. But that's seldom; she's super hardworking.

First she worked as an industrial engineer in an enterprise under the Ministry of Domestic Trade. After that she was transferred to the Ministry of Industry, and finally to the Ministry of Labor. In 1964 or 1965 she spent six months in East Germany as a commercial attaché. She was already engaged and got married soon after her return to Cuba.

Diana is a very gay, happy person, always joking and laughing, although she has a quick temper, too. She loves parties. Like my husband, she's always doing something. She and Juan quarrel now and then—they're too much alike not to. It's what I call a "storm in a glass of water" because their quarrels blow over right away. They'll argue heatedly about something and then it's over. It's impossible for two such quick-tempered people not to clash now and then.

Cándido is twenty-four years old now and is a professor at the University, but he's also still studying. He married in May last year and his wife, Digna Bada, is expecting their first child soon. She's a nursery-school teacher. They're cousins three or four times removed.

Cándido visits us, but not very often. Once in a while he, his wife, Juan, and I go to the movies or out to eat. We get together rarely though, because everybody's busy. Cándido and Juan are very much alike physically, but there's a great difference in temperament. Cándido is rather passive and sleeps a lot; Juan is active, always doing something. When he's home on vacation or on Saturdays, he's fixing the car or repairing something. Only now and then will he sit still for a while to watch TV.

Juan's relatives have all been nice to me from the first, attentive and affectionate, but naturally I can't feel as close to them as to my own parents, or even to Brígida, with whom I had such close ties. Juan has such a big family and most of them are still in Cuba. As for mine, my sister Socorro left after she divorced her husband, and I've never even met many of my relatives because they've lived in Spain all their lives.

My sister didn't agree with the new government, but that's not why she left Cuba. She was upset about the divorce and felt disoriented and a failure. She said she wanted to go away, to see if a change would help her.

Socorro's husband loved her but his great defect was that he drank too much and spent his money as soon as he earned it. My sister, following *mamá*'s advice, talked to him to see if he'd change. He made many promises, but he kept on drinking and accused her of being domineering and spying on him. Things went from bad to worse; they had many debts and lost their home and had to move into a rooming house.

My sister finally became convinced that he'd never change. She couldn't even think of having children. What security or stability could she have given them? He wasn't a bad person, but his vice was stronger than he was and she filed for divorce.

When Socorro left Cuba it cut me to the soul. But I'd have been quite incapable of telling her to stay. Everyone is the captain of his own destiny. Once someone makes a decision, I wouldn't for the world try to talk him out of it. If that was what my sister wanted, it seemed to me I should resign myself to being without her.

Socorro is remarried now and she says her husband is a wonderful man. We write, though not very often, and she sends me photos of their child. They're very well off—she has a house of her own and everything she needs.

My two best girlhood friends, Carmen and Cacha, and a few others I knew, left Cuba after the triumph of the Revolution. Now I have very few real friends, that is, friends to the fullest extent of the word, as I understand it. Before I call someone a friend, I must have studied her character, her personality, and be convinced that they're compatible with mine. I choose my friends carefully. When I meet people, I don't right away feel as if I'd known them all my life and tell them intimate things about myself. I have lots of acquaintances, yes, but very few friends.

Last year Brígida, who'd been my great friend all my life, left Cuba. It was hard for me. How could it be otherwise? We were almost as close as relatives. She didn't go for political reasons but for the sake of her only brother, who'd gone to Miami long before the Revolution. When diplomatic relations were broken, Brígida and her mother couldn't visit him anymore. Her *mamá* was very old, around eighty, and she became ill. Brígida filed a request to leave because she knew her brother wanted their *mamá* to live out her last days beside him. But you know how long it takes—she waited over two years to go—and her *mamá* died before the permit arrived.

Having to leave all alone made it even sadder for Brígida, but she'd already resigned her job, and if she'd stayed in Cuba she'd have had to work as a farm laborer or factory worker or something like that. Besides, if she'd stayed her brother would have been angry with her—she had no excuse for remaining after her mother died. So she sacrificed herself for her brother, that's what it amounts to. But, well, it can't be helped.

Brígida has been up there almost two years; she's well and has everything she needs, but she still hasn't adapted. She writes us every week and in all her letters she tells us she's very homesick. Sending things to Cuba is forbidden, because I know that if it weren't, she'd have sent us things that are scarce here, especially medicines. She suffers, knowing that she can't.

We all miss her a great deal, especially me. She was very close to us. Merceditas remembers her because Brígida did so much for her. When I show my daughter photographs of Brígida, she says, "I'd like to go up there to give her a kiss and then come right back." Sometimes any little thing will remind her of her godmother, but then she goes back to play and forgets about her. Children don't feel things the way adults do.

Like *mamá,* I live exclusively for my family. I try above all to be a good wife and a good mother. A good wife looks after her husband and children, takes care of everything about the house, keeps the house clean and everything neat and orderly. She gives her husband his dinner when he gets home, takes care of him when he's sick, and does the same for her children. Juan is a good husband, too. He's concerned about his home and his children and is close to them. And he brings home the money we need, instead of spending it with his friends or drinking it up.

My husband has been faithful to me, at least so far as I know. If he were unfaithful I don't know what I'd do. I don't even want to think about it. I haven't been through that and I hope I never will. I'd feel so bad about it, so betrayed. But I trust him absolutely; he's never been a woman-chaser. Oh, when we were sweethearts, I know he had two or three girl friends at the Institute. Perhaps he had women, too—it's only logical that a young man should. But since we married I've never had any cause for complaint. He can come home late any time, and if he says to me that he was at a meeting or anyplace else, I believe him. I don't go around investigating.

I trust my husband, that's essential to marriage. If there's no trust, there's nothing left to the marriage. I don't think Juan and I could go on together that way. It would be a very bad thing. A woman should be faithful, but so should a man. I've never heard of any law that says the husband is allowed to be unfaithful. No, what the Civil Law stipulates is the husband and wife should be mutually faithful.

Juan is the one who gives the orders in our family, and that's the way it should be, since he's the man. Suppose it's a matter of going someplace. If Juan asks me, "Can you go out?" I say, "Sure, let's go." But suppose I'm the one who feels like going out and he doesn't? Well, we simply don't go out. It isn't that he's dictatorial—far from it—but he wears the pants in the family. He decides if we'll buy something or if something has to be fixed. I make him responsible for it—it's something I'll simply not take charge of. In a way, it's easier and more comfortable for me to let him do it. In that sense, I lean on him.

Both of us agree that children must be punished, but the truth is that I'm the one who usually hits them. He plays with them a lot and very, very rarely spanks them. Sometimes I'll slap Merceditas hard on her arm, but I don't beat her. I hit Eloy on the buttocks, or I punish him by having him sit for a time. Of course I don't demand as much from Eloyitos or punish him as hard as I do Merceditas—after all, he's three and she's ten. Their *papá* sometimes sends them to bed as a punishment. Sometimes I talk and talk and they pay no attention, but their father only has to say one word and they fly to obey him. In spite of everything, they respect him a lot.

Juan doesn't interfere with my decisions about the house or the children. I'm the boss at home. It's my duty not only to take care of them, but also to teach them how to behave, because that's as much a part of loving as feeding, bathing, and dressing them. I want them both to be courteous; you don't get anywhere being rude and rough. A good person is honest, sensitive, generous, kind, and respectful of other people's rights. You should know how far you can go. If you're nice and polite, you always get what you want.

Merceditas helps with the housework only when she feels like it, as I did for my *mamá*. Occasionally she'll say, "*Ay, mami,* I'm going to wash the dishes for you." Or she'll say, "I'm going to wash my panties." She hasn't progressed in school as much as she should, partly because of the constant change of teachers and partly because she's lazy.[52] She's an intelligent child—I can see she has a good grasp of what she's taught—but I have to keep after her all the time. It's much easier to play than to study. She's never failed a grade, but she's not a ten-point student. That's the highest grade in our system. In fact she's a mediocre student. I keep telling her that the most important thing for her to do is study. When she needs it I help her with her lessons, and sometimes Juan does too.

Juan and I both agree that school is very important. We really want Merceditas to get good grades. When she does, we always reward her. We can't offer to buy her a toy or a dress, with rationing and all, but we take her on an outing, to the movies, or to dinner somewhere. When she got the highest marks in her class and was a vanguard student, we took her on a vacation. Actually we've taken her on vacation every year, but as an incentive to make her study we threatened not to take her to Varadero if she failed or got low marks. It worked, too. Her grades were excellent this year.

Juan has his ways and I have mine. We don't interfere with one

52. A report on Merceditas's school work, and that of the other children living in the apartment building, is contained in Part IV.

another. I'm more drastic. He has a quick temper and often exchanges insults with people, but he soon forgets all about it. I don't have his temper, but I don't forget injuries. I harbor resentments. My way is to be someone's friend unconditionally and to help them any time they need me. But if I stop being their friend, then that's that. It's over.

Naturally I like to be liked, to feel that people think I'm an agreeable person, but I don't go around wondering, "Am I agreeable to this person or not?" If someone likes me, fine! If they don't, bad luck. I don't consider myself perfect—far from it. I'm too critical, for one thing, and too hot-tempered. Perhaps I need more daring, more initiative, and a calmer temper. Sometimes I think I should try to be a different kind of person, but other times I think, "Oh well, I am as I am, and there's no point trying to change now." It's very difficult to change oneself.

Juan Carlos Pérez

I was born in Havana in 1937. My father had a small business in the market selling produce he brought from the country. We lived in a building on a corner near the market, where the streetcars used to run. *Papá* liked to take me to a Spanish restaurant and bar, to see his friends. I was the pet of the place. They'd pass me from hand to hand, entertaining me. They gave me fried bananas and fussed over me and taught me to say dirty words. As a result, when I was a little boy my language was a bit raw.

I was still very young when a hurricane caused a produce shortage and my father lost everything. He couldn't make enough to support the family even though we lived the life of the poor, very simply, with no luxuries. So he took us back to Bada, Oriente, to live with my grandparents. *Papá* was so broke he only had bus fare for *mamá* and me; he made the trip in the boxcar of a train with a friend of his.

Have you ever seen those towns in western movies with the railroad tracks running down the center and the houses lined up on each side? Well, Bada is a town like that. At that time, it must have had 300 or 400 inhabitants and seventy or eighty houses. Eight or ten families were relatives of ours and we had other relatives on farms nearby.

The frame house we lived in was exactly opposite the railroad tracks on the outskirts of town. The house had a living room, dining room, two or three bedrooms, and a kitchen, with a large patio in the back where my father kept two or three horses. The floors were made of wood planks and were built about a meter off the ground because of the heavy rainfall and groundswells. All the houses there have zinc roofs with eaves to drain off the rain into a cistern. We had a water-storage system because the well water is too salty.

My father continued his produce business in Bada, buying fruit and vegetables from the peasants and shipping them by rail to Havana, Guines, Pinar del Río, and Sagua la Grande. Everyone in the area was economically dependent on produce. The town of Bada was the storage and distribution center. The farmers would get attached to certain buyers in town, like my father, because of their manner or their honesty, and would sell only to them.

I must have been about four years old when my sister Diana was born—my mother had her at home—and about eight when my brother Cándido was born. I was the eldest grandchild and my grandmother, may she rest in peace, spoiled me. I was her pet. My grandma was a very fat woman with a wonderful disposition, very appealing and sociable. She was affectionate with everybody, but even when she had other grandchildren she preferred me. She didn't show a lot of favoritism, but to her I was always the most intelligent, the best in every way. She bought me all the toys that came into town—balls, bats, pistols. Even when I didn't want something, she'd still buy it for me.

My mother's side of the family was very Catholic. My father's side were the kind of Catholics who say, "I'm Catholic, Apostolic, and Roman," but never really observe their religion. This might have caused some arguments between my parents, but not very serious ones. My mother joked about it. She'd say, "You know, Flavio's an atheist," because my father was always running down the clergy.

I was pressured to go to Mass and catechism as long as we lived in Bada. It wasn't that we children were interested in the religious instruction—at that age nobody knows what he really wants—but it was a way of getting together. We liked to play afterward and the priest would give us little holy pictures, sweets, and all that.

I began school when I was six or seven. We learned the usual things taught in the elementary grades. It was practically a family school, located in the dining room of a private home, with two young girls as teachers. I just crossed the railroad tracks and there I was right at school. The atmosphere was homelike—no great scholastic discipline, just five or six youngsters seated around a table, some more advanced than others. The teacher would sit in the center and attend to each in turn. We began our studies with the primer. It had the alphabet and all, but it always began with the word "Christ." It went "CHRIST, A, B, C, D, E, F. . . ." You had to say "Christ" first before the alphabet! I began in the second grade and passed into the third as the semester ended. Then I skipped a grade, going from fourth to fifth.

We moved from Bada when I was nine, mainly because we were growing up and they wanted to give all three of us an education. By that time my father's economic situation was much sounder and we were able to live in a rented house in Banes. I didn't go to a Catholic school there but one sponsored by some American Protestant religion. It was called the Friends. I think *papá* was responsible for my going to the Friends, but my mother didn't oppose it because it was a good school. I believe I had good preparation in my school at Bada, but I didn't begin to feel the idea of obligation until I began school in Banes.

Every Friday when classes were over for the week, I'd take the bus and spend Saturday and Sunday in Bada. The trip took about an hour. I almost always went to one of my grandmothers', but whichever house I visited, there was always a room for me.

Later my father bought a little farm jointly with his father, and then I'd go there weekends and ride horseback, help load up the cows, or ride herd.[53] Once my father bought some cattle from a farmer who'd sold them because he had no pasture for them to graze on. I'll never forget that scene when we went to fetch them. Those cows were terrible, as thin as rails. They looked as though they were ready to drop in their tracks. It was 12 kilometers back but we walked them so slowly not one died on the way.

My father had pastureland with good grass, and three months later those same cattle were as fat as they could be, just bursting with health. I learned a lot about my *papá*'s work, and as time passed I participated in it more and more. I felt very close to my father and was always interested in what he did.

I finished primary school through the sixth grade, and continued at the Friends High School doing the first and second year of my *bachillerato*. Then my family moved to Havana from Banes in July, 1953, during the summer vacation. Shortly after the move here, the attack on the Moncada fortress took place.

Everything was a bit agitated in that day and age, in the sense that fear always existed. It wasn't so much fear of house searches in themselves, especially if one had nothing to hide, but the climate of anxiety was always with us because my father had been against the tyranny from the moment Batista staged the coup. We were disappointed that the attack on the Moncada hadn't been victorious. Now people look at it as a stimulus for others to follow in the path of armed struggle, but at the time all of us felt it was a moral defeat.

Not long after we moved to Havana I had my sixteenth birthday. I began to attend the Havana Institute, where tuition was free. That and the La Víbora Institute had the reputation of being the best high schools, of having better teachers, better discipline, and the most serious student bodies. My third year of *bachillerato* was more or less a year of adaptation, since it was a new kind of environment.

The Institute was a change for the better because I felt freer, more liberated. It was manlier than to be in a school run by priests and such. For another thing, being in a public school meant you could find all sorts

53. Pérez did not state the exact size of the farm, but said (in a conversation that was not taped) that it was worth half a million *pesos*. In addition to raising cattle, his father had orange groves. He sold his oranges, as well as fruit he bought from neighboring farms, in the Mercado Unico in Havana. His business was very successful; a market stall he bought for 21,000 *pesos* in 1953 paid for itself within a year.

of people—good, bad, indifferent, poor, rich—everything. That's one of the things that made me feel freer and more comfortable. And there was the new life in Havana.

I made friends right away and by the time I was in fourth year I felt as though I practically owned the school. My adjustment was complete. At that time nobody had ever thought of a student organization at the Institute, and we took direct part in setting one up. It wasn't officially permitted, but we held meetings secretly. I was president of the Student Association and we were in all the actions and strikes.

I think my interest in politics was the result of my father's opposition to the Batista regime. I was always involved in my father's activities and I considered him a good guide and example. At the Institute I had the opportunity to take the lead and it was there I began political action of my own. I didn't let my father know about all of these activities because he was a bit strict about such things. He wasn't really opposed to them, but he didn't give me the green light either. He pretended not to notice that I was involved.

I can't remember all the details of how I got to be president of the Student Association, but it began with the setting up of a Botany Club, whose members planted trees and otherwise aided in the development of botanical things. After I was elected president of this club, I turned it to political channels. Later, other comrades from other classes formed similar associations.

The major political aim at that time, for me at any rate, was to fight against the dictatorship, against Batista. It was very dangerous, of course. Our direct activity was distributing secret propaganda, placing homemade bombs, and expressing our solidarity every time the police killed a comrade. The University of Havana was always involved in these activities and would send out calls for a particular action, then we'd back them up.

The first bomb I ever placed was in the chemistry laboratory at my own school. Somebody had to do it, so I did. They weren't very powerful explosives and didn't do much damage, but they made a good loud noise and everybody knew that a bomb had gone off. Later we had a group in charge of causing trouble for the government. I was the one who got jailed, though the others were planting most of the bombs. We created a great impression in the school. Once we staged a strike and a large body of *compañeros* teamed up with us. Some students were indifferent to most of our activities, but when we called a strike, that was something else.

As part of the strike I closed the school library, and the principal and vice-principal came to convince me to break the strike or call it off. First they threatened to speak to my parents, and I told them I was old enough to deal with my own problems. "Well then, we're going to expel you from the Institute," they said. I told them they couldn't, and we argued back and forth. They took me to the office, where they continued to threaten me.

They tried to get me to back down by taking me before the whole teaching staff, about fourteen teachers. I was the only student. The rest of my *compañeros* were waiting outside for the results. Inside we talked over the strike. The principal took some letters with Russian stamps on them out of a bureau drawer, laid them on the desk, and said, "To give you a good idea of what the Student Association really is, here are letters from the Soviet Union to the Student Association of this Institute. This is communist propaganda, and here it says a strike should be staged on such-and-such a date." To this day I don't know whether he was lying or telling the truth.

I said, "Look, I've called this strike not because the Russians told me to but because today we commemorate the first anniversary of Rubén Batista's death, just as we might the death of any comrade." Rubén, who came from Oriente, was the first student martyr.[54] Some of the teachers threatened to call the police, others tried to dissuade me by saying, "You're all good students and shouldn't get mixed up in these political things."

At that time there was a fine group of fellows, a nucleus ready for anything. The number of real activists—those of us who were front and center, who would fight the police, throw stones, and do whatever had to be done—amounted to about fifteen or twenty. We were quite a bunch of daredevils.

Once we called a strike for a Monday, but we sent out the call several days beforehand. "Monday there will be a strike to commemorate the death of a comrade." There was going to be a rally at the University so we said we'd call a strike and then go to take part in the university demonstration. But a problem came up. The word got around and that day the Institute was surrounded by police cars on every side, waiting for us. So we made a cordon around the police, and as students arrived we told them the meeting would take place at a park four or five blocks away because we couldn't enter the school. We staged our protest in the park, made all our speeches, and then announced, "Well now, everybody to the University on his own, because we can't stage a march. If we do, the police will break it up."

After I spoke—I was almost always the one who spoke publicly and agitated—we went to the University. We entered from the back and were at the top of the hill and there were José Antonio Echeverría, Fruc-

54. Rubén Batista Rubio, a twenty-one-year-old student of architecture at the University of Havana, was killed on February 13, 1953, when police fired indiscriminately into a crowd of students participating in a demonstration sponsored by the Federation of University Students.

tuoso,[55] and several other future martyrs of the Revolution. I don't remember who we were commemorating that day, but I do recall that José Antonio had a cracked skull with a great white patch on one side of his head, and I think he had a partial cast on one arm, too. These were from the beating he'd gotten at the last demonstration. Then Fructuoso and several other *compañeros* spoke. We had over 2,000 people up there, students from the University and those of us who'd come from the institutes. We felt fine because the University had autonomy and the police couldn't enter.

We were gathered at the head of the steps in the big square where the "Alma Mater" is. If you look down from the front of the campus there you see San Lázaro Street. That whole area was swarming with uniformed police—a great hive of blue figures. Every once in a while the police cars would pass and we'd call out all the insults we could think of, from "sons-of-a-bad-mother" to "sons-of-bitches" and "faggots." We threw paint cans down on them and rolled cans filled with earth down the hill. They thought it was dynamite and scattered in every direction. We were really having fun. We'd push anything that would burn down the hill—an old can with burning alcohol, for example—and watch them take to their heels. All this time we were yelling insults, having a ball.

Then Fructuoso spoke up. There were still about 2,000 of us gathered in the square. "Well, now we're going down the stairs," he said. "We're going to show them what we can do with only our bare fists." I wasn't too pleased with that idea, us with our bare fists and the police with pistols and rifles, but I felt it was my obligation to go, first of all because I represented the group from our Institute, and also because I'm not the type to back down. It was a question of honor, even though I didn't agree with fighting on those terms—bare fists against firearms. No thanks!

But down we went. I even went in the first ranks along with Fructuoso and the others. We all linked arms along the row and marched down the stairs that way. I learned from that experience that the worst thing you can do is to look back, because we started with 2,000 at the top of the stairs and by the time we reached the bottom, not a hundred were still marching. People kept dropping behind and others dropped out all along the stairway, but I was in it up to my neck and there was nothing to do but go on.

We reached the street and walked about a block when the police started toward us, a whole flock of them like a blue cloud. We kept on going, and when there were only 80 or 100 meters between us, shots began to come from behind us and the police began to fire into our

55. Fructuoso Rodríguez, deputy to Echeverría in the university student group *Directorio Revolucionario*. He survived the 1957 attack on the Presidential Palace but was killed by police the following month after he and three others had been betrayed by a fellow student.

ranks. Machine-gun, pistol, and rifle fire was all about, and we were caught in the crossfire.

Now this time we had some of Prío's[56] people with us. Prío was an ex-President we had here in Cuba, one of the many who stole what he could from the rest of us. When anybody said "Prío's people" we thought of gangsters and delinquents, and we considered our movement clean. It was a slur to be called "Prío's people," like being called a communist, or even worse.

Just as the shooting began, one boy came running down the hill yelling, "Fructuoso, Fructuoso!" I was right there at Fructuoso's side so I heard everything. "Prío's people are going to shoot back," he told us. So Fructuoso ordered us all to scatter and run. We were between two fires, and we gladly broke ranks and took off.

That day two comrades from my Institute were wounded. One received two gunshot wounds although he was hit by a single bullet. We picked up his jacket afterward and it had four perforations in it. That was my greatest experience with demonstrations. The others I attended were smaller, less active, and we stayed up on the university campus and didn't try to go into the streets.

I know several of those *compañeros* from the Institute and see them sporadically, especially the ones who are still on our side. Jaime Cedeño was the vice-president of our underground association. He was the son of a well-to-do family, people of good social position. His father had a television-repair business and also another business—possibly television sales, something like that. At that time I knew he belonged to the Socialist Youth. I came from a family of *Ortodoxos*[57] and my sympathies were more on their side. But Jaime and I had a lot in common; we worked together and were great companions. We used to study together, sometimes way past midnight when we had examinations. Today he's a Party official and the director of a cattle-feed plant in Pinar del Río. We see each other about once a year and scarcely even have time to talk over old times.

Another member of the group, Gómez Lago, was brave and tough, fiery, and a great *compañero*. He turned against the Revolution shortly after it took power and is serving a sentence of twenty years, I think it is. He wouldn't accept rehabilitation even though we tried to persuade him.

Yiyo Formoso also had a problem. I think he's in prison too, but to tell the truth I haven't seen him since. Emeterio Martínez Roig was another brave friend. As a matter of fact, Emeterio had made the contacts for two of us to participate in the attack on the Presidential Palace. We knew

---

56. Carlos Prío Socorrás, President of Cuba 1948–52, who was overthrown by Batista.

57. The Cuban People's Party, formed in 1947 by Senator Eduardo Chibás from a group of dissidents within the *Auténticos* (Authentic Revolutionary Movement), the party of President Grau San Martín. Fidel Castro was affiliated with the *Ortodoxos,* but the Twenty-sixth of July Movement itself was organized independently of the party.

only that it was going to be an armed action. We didn't know where or when, and we never even dreamed it would be against the Palace. So one night we went to his house, where he had a little room with a separate entrance to the street. We waited there until 3:00 or 4:00 in the morning, when we finally fell asleep. We put ourselves on call, so to speak, waiting for them to come for us as planned, to go to a farm for target practice preparatory to the armed action, but they never came.

And sure enough, a few days later came the attack on the Palace. I really felt bad at not having been there along with the rest of my *compañeros*. We almost got the chance but it fell through. It may have been because we were so young. That was in 1957, and I'd just finished my *bachillerato* in 1956.

The Institute was closed in 1957 and 1958, at least so far as I remember, but even so Emeterio and I and several other *compañeros* kept in touch and participated in all sorts of activities. Then about three or four months after the Revolution took power I heard that Emeterio was back at the Institute to finish his *bachillerato*. I was working in the market then and didn't go back to school.

At the beginning of the Revolution a lot of people thought the change was nothing more than "out you go and I'll take your place," and that the same old gangsterism and thievery were going to continue. Emeterio had this tendency toward gangsterism. There remained certain elements with a sort of Masferrerist[58] philosophy who were harming the Revolution. Later they were eliminated completely because such people couldn't do anything. Anyway, I found Emeterio showing off in his post as an officer of the Student Association, with a sinecure in the municipal government, doing nothing but tote a pistol and that sort of thing.

I didn't like this and I told him, "Look, I think you've made a mistake and you don't understand what's going on." That was in March or April—I'd just gotten back from Mexico in January. I happened to run into him two or three times after that, and he continued his old-style politicking.

Sure enough, when the attack on Playa Girón came, in April of 1961, Emeterio was one of those captured here in Havana as an accomplice of the invading mercenaries. The version I heard—although I've never confirmed it—was that he was one of the chiefs here in Havana, waiting to be notified in case the mercenaries were victorious. He'd become a counterrevolutionary and is now serving a sentence of twenty years.

So of that group I was closest to, three took the wrong road and three

58. Rolando Masferrer was widely regarded as a gangster, and that is how he is said to have (privately) characterized himself and his political colleagues. (Thomas, *The Pursuit of Freedom*, p. 769.) Before becoming a senator during the second Batista dictatorship, Masferrer had, in the thirties, fought against Franco in Spain, and in the forties had been the leader of a militant communist university student group. He reversed his position in 1944 when he founded the *Movimiento Socialista Revolucionario* (MSR) as an anticommunist action group.

have stayed with the Revolution. Of course they don't have top posts or anything, but they're doing important work.

While Juan Pérez was a student at the Havana Institute, he worked for his father in the Mercado Unico. He attended classes from 2:00 to 6:00 P.M. and worked at the market from 1:00 to 7:00 A.M. Eventually he took over part of his father's market stall and expanded his own business to include the sale of other kinds of fruit and vegetables. By his initiative, Pérez's monthly income increased from the 60 pesos his father paid him to as much as 200.

Shortly after starting his own business, Pérez had a dispute with his father, who had sold Juan's produce wholesale to a friend at a time when the retail price was at its peak. Pérez quit in anger and enrolled in a training program for insurance salesmen. He gave that up quickly and went without work for a month until his father, tired of the long hours, offered him 20 percent of all profits to go back to work for him. Pérez did return and again began to expand his part of the business, this time by entering into a partnership with his god-father. In 1957 they first rented and then bought a market stall, using 20,000 pesos of their own money and 9,000 borrowed from friends and from a bank. In this new partnership, Pérez earned from 300 to 500 pesos a month.

In 1960 Pérez invested in three tractors which he bought from a friend in Oriente and then rented out for use in road and highway construction. He also entered into a second partnership with another friend and two uncles, to buy a 30-ton van truck for 27,000 pesos. By 1961 his income had risen to 800 pesos a month.

In 1961, when the Castro government began "intervention" or nationalization of land and business, Pérez lost his market stall and his tractors. He was not compensated by the state for the stall, but he received 15,000 pesos for the tractors. In 1963 the government also "intervened" his van truck and paid him an additional 15,000 pesos. His father lost most of his land in the first Agrarian Reform and would have lost the rest in the second reform, so he turned it over to the state beforehand. He was made "interventor" or supervisor of his farm and of several others.

Juan Pérez became an employee of the state in 1961. At this time his income dropped from 800 to 180 pesos a month. His first job was to oversee the sale and distribution of fruit in the Mercado Unico. Nationalization of the market was a tremendous task because it affected 4,000 small vendors. It was especially difficult, according to Pérez, because the vendors were "people of a very low cultural level." It is much easier, he insisted, to nationalize telephone and electric companies, because the workers are more skilled and better organized. However, Pérez spoke proudly of the Havana market after nationalization. In the old Mercado Unico, he said, corruption was common and prostitution and the sale of marijuana were widespread. Now there are workers' homes there with little plaques that say "Aqui vive una familia decente." *("A respectable family lives here.")*

Sara Rojas

We were born on *papá*'s farm, all eleven of us,[59] in a place called Monte dos Leguas, in Oriente. *Papá*'s house was made of wood and palm leaves, with a tin roof. The two bedrooms had packed-earth floors. Attached to the kitchen there was a small storeroom for the harvest, and behind it a long terrace with a yard where a few palm trees grew. In front there was a garden with fruit trees—orange, grapefruit, and coconut—which made the entrance look like a little forest.

Our house stood on a spot of level ground through which a brook flowed. All around it the land sloped up—not into real hills, just hillocks with gentle slopes, one after another. A wooded hill made the front of our house dark with its shade, but after *papá* cleared it for planting, everything looked so bright. And you could see so far—even as far as the next farm below ours. It was beautiful, and it looked even more beautiful after *papá* planted plantains and *malanga*. It was such a happy-looking place!

I was a biggish girl—old enough to take notice—at the time my *papá* and my grandfather cleared that slope. The underbrush went first. *Papá* always burned it in the morning when the wind blows right. Oh, what a delicious smell of burnt earth! I loved to go up there after the burning, just to breathe it in. Then they took an ax to the tree trunks because of the tangle of vines and bushes. Afterward they'd carry those trunks down and heap them up where they were easy to get at for firewood, or they'd make it into charcoal. We made good use of those trees.

The farmland was planted in bananas and plantains, yucca, sweet potatoes, *malanga*, maize, beans, rice, yams, coffee . . . well, just about everything. *Papá* owned two yokes of oxen, three cows, hens, pigs—a whole lot of animals.

I don't know whether everybody in the country feels like this—maybe I was just born that way—but I find country air delicious. It was so wonderfully cool. When a strong breeze blew, you could see the

---

59. This number does not include Gloria, a foster child, or the youngest, Amanda Luz, who was born after Sara left home.

branches sway, and it was sweet to hear the leaves murmur at night. It's a pleasure to go to sleep with the fresh country breeze blowing through the house the way it does—through every chink in the wooden walls. Even on the sunniest days there's always a breeze to cool you off.

Monte dos Leguas used to be very different from the way it is now. The mountains that once were so thickly wooded are bare. Those mountains once produced everything, but land gets tired just as we do. The water goes too. Ponds dry up and so do rivers. A time comes when you put seeds in the ground and nothing comes up. Last year when I was home, I reminded my father of how beautiful everything used to be and he told me, "Everything must go in the course of time. You know that."

In Monte dos Leguas everybody is a relative of mine—those who aren't aunts or uncles are cousins. Next to my parents' farm is the farm of Margarita Tabares, whom we called "the Widow." She was the wife of Pedro Tabares, my great-grandfather on my mother's side. Next to that is the farm of one of my cousins, and so it goes. There are small farms within the larger ones, and little shacks piled on top of one another. The Widow gave each of her children a bit of land to build a house on, plant fruits, and raise animals. They're all married and have their homes on the farm just below my parents.

My maternal grandparents were originally from near Palma Soriano, but they left the farm to the old folks, and my grandpa, Pancho Tabares, bought a farm in Monte dos Leguas. Then he brought Grandma Camelia to live there, and there they raised their family. Their only two children were *mamá* and Uncle Héctor.

I know nothing about my grandmother's young days, and even less about my grandfather's. *Mamá* says that he loved parties and riding horses, but that his real passion was cockfighting. There's a photograph of my grandparents taken on their wedding day. It doesn't look at all the way I remember them. They were a couple of kids then! I don't know how old Grandma was when she married, but I believe Grandpa Pancho was seventeen. Grandma died so long ago that I can't recall her features, but the picture shows her as a *mulata*—a little Moor just like me—with a long mane of hair, round cheeks, tall, and quite good-looking. She was a strong, healthy woman.

Grandma Camelia was a midwife and mothered the whole town. A doctor sent her some books about women's problems and many's the baby she delivered. She was in full charge as long as the labor was normal. She also cured indigestion and distributed medicines and herbs. People from places nobody ever heard of would show up at Grandma's door asking for medicines. Everybody trusted her. She had godchildren in every family in town. Wherever she went, most of the people she met greeted her as *madrina* [60] or *comadre*.

60. Godmother.

I loved Grandma Camelia as much as I loved my own *mamá*, perhaps more. Her house was right next door to ours and we children were more with her than with *mamá*. We slept at our parents', but we ate our meals with Grandma and were bathed and ordered around by her. She took us for herself alone; she was everything to us. Naturally all of us children thought she was our real mother. That old lady was worth *pesos*—yes indeed, she was worth millions.

That's not to say that *mamá* didn't take care of us children. She did, and she was always nice to us. But imagine, we always called her Violeta and my grandmother *mami*. *Mamá* took it for granted that Grandma would always be around to help her look after us, and having that help suddenly taken away was one more blow she suffered when Grandma died. *Mamá* was not yet twenty-eight then, and Grandma was young also—forty-three or fifty-three, I forget which. I never knew her as an old woman.

Mamá was like a child; she didn't look old enough to have the children she had. She was Grandma's only girl-child, and whenever Grandma talked to her, it reminded me of the way a mother talks to her suckling baby. Grandma cherished that daughter of hers like her very eyes. Anything *mamá* wanted, Grandma would give her. If *mamá* took a notion to sleep awhile beside her, Grandma would tuck her in like a child. I'll never forget how Grandma whispered *mamá*'s name again and again on her deathbed. Every time she said "Violeta" it sounded like her last breath escaping in a sigh.

After Grandma died, *mamá* explained to us that *she* was our mother.

Papá's folks were townspeople from San Luis. *Papá* was born there and there his mother died, leaving Grandfather Martín Rojas a widower with four motherless children. God only knows what toil and trouble he must have had raising them. Finally he hitched up with Luisa Noda, who raised *papá* and was a second mother to him even though she had children of her own.

I have no less than thirty-four aunts and uncles on *papá*'s side of the family, but there are some I've never met. There were so many of them and Grandfather Martín's farm was so small—much smaller than my *mamá*'s father's—that his children had to scatter to find a place to live. Some moved up into the mountains, others went to different towns, including two who live in Soledad. Most of them lived so far away it was impossible for us to go visit them.

Papá and *mamá* met there in Monte dos Leguas because their parents were *compadres* and visited each other often. It seems that the grocery store was near *mamá*'s house, and one day she saw *papá* pushing his cart to the store. She innocently asked him, "Shall I save some coffee for you this afternoon?" That very day *papá* went to see *mamá*'s parents and told them he was in love with their daughter. They answered that they knew he was a man of good character and that he had their permission to enter their home as their daughter's suitor. So he kept on visiting her until they fell in love and got married.

I've been told that my parents' wedding was the most beautiful in the world. *Mamá* wore a wedding dress in the latest style of the time and a little white hat with a rose on it. Everybody says that such a wedding will never again be seen in the barrio—so much to drink, such quantities of roast pig, such a crowd of guests...!

Mamá was thirteen when they were married and *papá* was seventeen. *Papá* was very handsome—an Indian with a high-bridged nose. *Mamá* was beautiful too. That Doña Violeta Tabares looked like a doll, people always said. She was small and plump, with big fat legs. That does a lot for a woman's appearance, at least that's what everyone says. *Papá* is quite well preserved, but poor *mamá* is so skinny and wrinkled now, and her hair has thinned so much.

It's nearly fifty years they've been together and in all those years not a cross word has passed between them. They're as happy as a couple of kids. They both still enjoy parties—yes indeed, they're always the first to arrive. They won't even wait for the truck to pick them up. And when the band strikes up, they always have the first dance together. Oh, it's beautiful! I'm proud to see how much my little old parents love each other.

When *papá* and *mamá* got married, they built their house on Grandpa Pancho's land. Later my Uncle Héctor built his house on the farm too, and lived there with his wife, Asunción, and my cousin Piedad. Uncle Héctor was a cane-cutter; during the dead season he worked in the valley. He and Uncle Euquerio, *papá*'s eldest brother, are the uncles I've been closest to. Uncle Euquerio is the father of my husband, Eduardo. He lived in *chucho* 9,[61] which was not very near, but he always came to our house. I knew his second wife well because she was Eduardo's *mamá*. Uncle Euquerio liked nothing better than a fight. He was tough and mean as they come. He'd get drunk and pick quarrels and get arrested. *Papá* was always the one who got him out of jail. He spoke up for Euquerio and was very fond of him because Euquerio was his eldest brother. Uncle Euquerio's too old to fight now. He's retired and settled down with his children.

My grandparents were better off than my parents. Their farm was fairly large and produced well. They had a lot of cattle, too. Grandpa

61. A *chucho* was a small settlement along a *central*'s rail system, where cut cane was loaded from carts or wagons onto rail freight cars. The residents were employees of the *central*. Chucho 9 was one of many loading sites on the American-owned Miranda *central* (now the Julio Antonio Mella *central*).

Pancho achieved all that by himself through hard work and buying a little land here and there. *Mamá* and Uncle Héctor were brought up quite differently from us because, after all, they were only two. At home we were eleven and the only wage-earner was *papá*, so we had a harder time of it.

Papá worked as a cart driver on the Miranda *central*. All of us had to help out on the farm because he didn't have time to look after it by himself. When I was little, the girls in the family worked like men because we had no brothers yet, except for little Fabio, who was no good for anything. My eldest sister, Agustina, assigned the chores.

We got up at daybreak and went down to the cattle corral to fetch the charcoal or firewood for breakfast. The wood was often wet, and then what trouble we had getting the fire lighted!

We all helped—one would fetch firewood, another would carry water, and so on. We, the eldest, would hoe the corn and beans. That's the hardest chore of all for a child because you have to work under the hot sun. At 11:00 o'clock we'd go back to the house to eat the lunch Grandma had cooked for us, and then we'd rest awhile. Afterward we'd go to get the calves, feed the pigs, and gather cane for the cattle. At harvest time, when there wasn't much cane, we'd rake the cane fields to gather fodder.

Besides the farm work, we swept, washed dishes, washed and ironed clothes, ran to the store on errands, and looked after the smaller children. All day long we worked—they sure made full use of us!

I enjoyed moving the animals from pasture to pasture, gathering firewood, and all the rest of it. I was strong and healthy so I liked being active and did my work well. There was no sadness in my life. I was a joyous child because I never thought about anything. All I knew was that I had my breakfast, lunch, and dinner every day without fail. I didn't know where the food came from, but that wasn't my problem. The important thing was that it was there.

When my parents went shopping, they always bought things for whoever needed them most at the time. Maybe I was awfully childish, but whenever *mamá* brought me a new dress or pair of shoes, I felt it was the happiest, most beautiful day that ever was. I'd be too excited to eat. I'd run around showing everybody my new things. I'd visit my relatives and dance for them to show off my new shoes.

In the country you can really enjoy yourself. I loved riding horseback. *Papá* set aside a colt for us. The animal had never felt a rope around him and we had a number of falls before we could teach him, but I loved every minute of it. I loved going to the grocery store, because it was too far to walk and it gave me a chance for a gallop. I was always the one to take the reins, because Agustina was such a scaredy-cat.

Sewing was my chief delight. Back there in the country I sewed for everyone, not only my sisters and brothers but the neighbors too. I can cut a blouse, a skirt, a mosquito net—just show me a design and I can copy it. I learned by myself, starting when I was about eight. The first thing I made was a doll's dress. It was so well cut that at first Grandma couldn't believe I'd really made it, but then, for at least a month, she showed it to every visitor. Every time she got a piece of yard goods she'd give it to me, and I kept hard at work on her little sewing machine day after day. When Grandma lay dying she said to *mamá*, "Take care of this little one, she's got a good head on her shoulders. And when I'm gone, give her my sewing machine so she can learn. Don't go letting anyone else use it."

Papá never allowed us to listen to grown people's conversation. No indeed! When visitors came, the children were expected to go wherever their parents sent them, without passing in front of anybody, because that was an ill-bred thing to do. We were supposed to go play outside or keep busy sweeping, washing dishes, or doing just anything, as long as it kept us out of the grownups' way.

Old people are well treated and highly respected back home. Teen-agers never felt that they'd reached a time of life when they could defy their parents, or act more rebellious than before. Any time a child is disrespectful to an older person, that person complains to the child's father and the child gets punished. Old age must be respected and that's that. In my barrio everybody addresses older people formally as *usted*. When I meet any of my older relatives—an uncle, say, or my grandfather—after a long time away, I always kiss them on the cheek. That's one thing that hasn't changed at all; no matter how long I'm away, when I go back I find everyone as respectful to their elders as they ever were.

Sometimes we had to be punished, of course, because brothers and sisters are apt to fight. We girls would also quarrel with Fabio because, being a boy, he thought he could order us around. Once while we were fighting, the chickens got into the garden and ate the flowers off the bean plants. *Mamá* told us, "What you've allowed to go to waste is food that was meant to fill your own bellies someday."

The very next day *mamá* told us, "Remember the little pig out there. By 10:00 or 11:00 the sun in that spot gets too hot for him." But we were absorbed in our games—we were such little kids, after all. I was eight and Fabio seven. When *mamá* got home at noon, she found the pig dead and already beginning to rot in the heat, so it had to be thrown away. It died of sunstroke without even a squeal, and we hadn't given a thought to it after *mamá* left.

Mamá didn't spank us. She simply said, "Come here and look at the pig." *Ay*, dear God, we wanted to die ourselves! Fabio and I burst into tears because an animal had died through our carelessness. Every time I remembered that little pig, I'd think, "I'll drop just anything I'm doing to go take care of the animals." I love animals. If I raise a chicken myself and feed it with my own hands, I can't eat the little thing unless my need is very great.

When I was a child, I didn't know what death was, or war either. I didn't realize you needed money to buy food at the store, much less how you have to sacrifice to get that money. My only sorrows were the death of some little animals, not being allowed to play sometimes when I wanted to, and the times I was afraid *papá* might punish me. Later on I found out that we all had to die. It was *mamá* who told us, "We're not born to grow again the way plants grow from their own seeds. We're born to die."

When Grandma took to her bed with her last illness, I didn't realize what was happening. I noticed she'd taken to staying in bed all day long, that's all. We were in the habit of asking for her blessing every morning, but when she got sick she wouldn't let us kiss her. Later on they explained to us that she had tuberculosis. She didn't spit blood or anything, but she got thinner and paler—she simply dried up. Her illness lasted thirteen months.

Grandma's relatives in Palma Soriano were sent for. Two of the men came to run errands and three of the women to help with the housework and wash the sheets. Grandma had always been very clean, and in her last illness she insisted that all her clothes and bedclothes, blankets and all, be changed daily, and that everything taken off the bed be immediately washed and boiled. They did that for her until the day she died. I could see her brothers and sisters scrubbing the walls with brushes dipped in Fab, because she'd ordered everything cleaned and scrubbed, and I wondered, "Why are they doing all that housecleaning? What's it for?"

Grandma told Grandpa Pancho, "Get everything ready for my funeral because I haven't got long to live. Buy me a coffin, candles, a new dress and stockings to be buried in, sheets, if the ones we have aren't good enough, and whatever is needed for the wake. Buy them and put them away so they'll be ready when the time comes. But show them to me before you put them away."

Her burial dress was a long white one with pink embroidery. The embroidery was very flat and delicate—you could hardly distinguish it from the material of the dress. I remember every detail. I also saw the coffin; it was put away in a small room next to the kitchen. I caught a glimpse of it one day when my uncle opened the door. It was covered with lilac velvet. My sister Agustina was with me and said, "Oh look! That's the kind of box they put dead people in." I was panic-stricken, and didn't dare go into the kitchen after that.

About an hour before she died, Grandma told *papá*, "Inocencio, bring all my grandchildren to me." She also sent for Grandpa, Grandpa's father, and for María, a very old Jamaican woman who was a good friend of hers. When we were all gathered around her bed, Grandma said, "I've sent for you to tell you that my time has come to be put in the ground. My one wish is that you all get along with one another and live in peace after I'm gone, as you have while I lived. Live united and take good care of my little grandchildren and of my son and daughter, because they're all I leave behind on earth. I'm going to my rest."

One by one we filed past her to say goodbye, just as if she were about to set off on a trip, and she gave us each her blessing. Then she said, "*Ay,* dear God," crossed her arms on her breast, closed her eyes, and died.

As they led us children out of Grandma's room, we could hear the cries and lamentations of her brothers and sisters and relatives and friends. Everybody wept over her death. *Mamá* got one fit after another. They had to keep giving her linden-flower tea and some kind of stuff to smell. My grandpa went crazy from the moment he saw the death agony begin. They took him over to *papá*'s house and put him in a little room we had there. He tore off his clothes and tore his skin with his fingernails. He was raving mad; they had to tie him up. If he was let loose for a moment, he'd grab a knife or machete and start cutting holes in the floor. He didn't know about the wake or anything—he lost all sense of where he was.

Grandma died at 3:00 in the afternoon and it was 7:00 before anybody thought of taking us children back home. We were all together in the parlor with no idea where we were supposed to go, because *mamá* was like a madwoman. *Papá* didn't know what he was doing either. There we sat, screaming our heads off, waiting for somebody to tell us what to do.

Grandma was laid out in her bed and dressed by her son and one of her sisters, who then got a heart attack and had to be rushed to the hospital.

The wake lasted through the night and all the next day. Everybody went—all Grandma's relatives, everyone in the neighborhood, all her friends. People came from as far away as Palma Soriano to look their last upon her, from Santiago de Cuba, from San Germán, from every place where she had friends. And she'd made so many friends in so many places! Two people stood at the head and foot of her coffin as an honor guard, and everybody sang the Cuban national anthem for her.

They say children shouldn't be allowed to see the dead, but I caught a glimpse of Grandma's face through the glass pane on the coffin lid. *Ay,* how sad I felt, seeing her like that! They told us, "Your Grandma has gone to sleep."

All the grownups followed the coffin on foot for the two leagues to the graveyard while we children stayed at home. When I saw them taking the box out, I asked, "Violeta, where are they taking her?"

"*Ay,* my child," she wailed, "don't ask where they're taking her—my own mother!" I didn't understand why she cried. I wasn't like kids nowadays, who are born knowing what death is.

The truth is that Grandma's going made a great and permanent change in our family. With that one part gone, everything collapsed. She'd always been the one who showed us the way and encouraged us to go on. It's like a house raised above the ground on strong wooden posts. Take one post away and the whole house falls. That's exactly what happened to us. We lost control of ourselves.

The months following Grandma's death were terrible ones for us children because *mamá* became so overcareful of us that she wouldn't even let us play or do anything at all. It was as though *mamá* was afraid we'd die too. She wanted us to sleep right next to her, and would get up three or four times a night to check on us. She was so afraid to let us out of her sight she stopped sending us to fetch water. During those months *papá* ran all the errands himself.

There was nothing we could do about it. *Mamá* mourned her mother. It was as if a big piece of her heart had been cut out. At night she'd heat water for our baths, bathe us, and tuck us in. After we were in bed—all five of us slept in one big bed—we consoled ourselves by playing games. It was our only chance to play at all. Christmas passed, the New Year, the Day of the Three Kings—we suffered through all the holidays behind closed doors.

Seeing *mamá* so nervous, I got scared. I had nightmares. I saw my grandma and felt as if I were dying. I'd wake up screaming. Many times I called out to her, believing she was really and truly alive!

One day when I was quite a big girl, my sister and I were going to the river to do the wash and *mamá* was all alone in the house. We were about halfway down the hill when I heard a scream, "Camelia Tabares!" It was *mamá*'s voice, full of sorrow, trying to call Grandmother back to life. We hurried back home and found *mamá* in tears. "*Ay, mami*, why do you weep so?" I asked her.

"*Ay*, let me weep," she answered. "My child, your grandmother died and she'll never again return to us." And so little by little we were undeceived and got used to the idea.

Grandpa lived all alone in the house next door. He couldn't get used to living without his wife. For him she was still lying in bed sick. We children were terrified of him because *mamá* had warned us, "Stay away from your grandpa. He's crazy and might hurt you." But after the violent phase, he became very sluggish and just lay there all day long. He had to be propped up to eat. Every day *mamá* would bring him his food and medicines and quite often she'd take us to see him.

About two years later, Grandpa got it into his head to sell his house and leave. He went to join some relatives in the Sierra. Uncle Héctor and his family went with him; they still live there.

After three or four years, Grandpa hitched up with another woman, Señora Zoila Martínez Guerra. She never bore him any children—both of them were too old for that. He's very old now, almost blind, with hair as white as a puff of cotton.

It's twenty-three years since Grandma died, but *mamá* still remembers her and weeps. We have a framed picture of her on the wall and *mamá* puts flowers before it on Grandma's birthday, saint's day, and the anniversary of her death. On those days she weeps disconsolately, remembering such a mother.

The very year of Grandma's death, my sister Estelita, the eldest of us all, died. Estelita was born sickly; it was her bile, the doctor said. When she had her attacks, even her eyes got yellow, and every single hair on her skin was like a dripping water pipe. Her blood turned to water, they said. It was a very strange disease.

Estelita never became a señorita and her breasts never filled out. Her body simply didn't develop into that of a grown woman. She was tiny and very slender, the prettiest of us girls, I think. *Papá* was crazy about her and he spoiled that girl to death. She never had to work, because she wasn't strong enough. We had to help her walk and often carried her piggyback to Uncle Héctor's and Grandma's farms.

Everybody in town knew and loved Estela because she'd been so sickly. She could knit and embroider, and everybody brought her blouses and handkerchiefs to embroider.

Before Grandma's death, Estelita's health had improved greatly. She no longer had to be carried and there was color in her cheeks. But when Grandma died Estelita went into a decline. Every *centavo papá* earned at that time was spent on her. Nothing did any good. The burden of sixteen years of anguish was too much for her.

Papá took her to the doctor at the Miranda *central*. "Look, Rojas," the doctor said, "I'll give it to you straight. There's no hope for your daughter. Let her die at home with her folks around her." So *papá* took her back home, where she lived three more days.

I remember one time before Estelita died, we were talking about death.

My little brother asked, "Does one live again afterward?"

"No, we have to die and that's that," I told him. Then I said to Estelita, "I wonder what it's like to die. What happens to make one die?"

"It must hurt an awful lot," Estelita answered. "That ox that died, do you remember how he bellowed? I'll never forget it."

"*Ay*, dear God," I said in a panic, "don't ever let me feel such pain!"

I don't believe in God, but in my family there are many who do. When they have a problem, they cry out, "Oh my God, oh my God!" That means they believe, doesn't it? I've heard that there is a God, but how do I know? I hear people say "God exists," but I've never seen him. I don't know what to think about it.

Besides Estelita, I have five sisters—Agustina, Carolina, Lupe, Marcelina, and Amanda Luz—and five brothers—Fabiano, Bernardo, David, Pancho, and Virgilio. I also had a friend, Gloria, to whom I always told everything. We grew up like sisters because her *mamá* died and my parents raised her. First an aunt of hers took her, but *papá* wanted to raise her because Gloria was such a pretty girl. I was about five years old at the time and I remember as in a dream *papá* coming home with Gloria in his arms. Oh, she was so lovely—fair-skinned, blue-eyed, just like a doll! We all adored her and outdid each other trying to do things for her. She was a good little girl, quiet, never interfering with anybody. She was a good playmate, too.

I was rough and playful with my brothers and sisters. I loved to play tricks on them. For instance, once when I was undressing to take a bath and wearing very torn bloomers, I noticed my brothers Fabio and Bernardo sitting in the parlor. I knew how Fabio hated that sort of thing, so just to annoy him, I went out into the parlor wearing nothing but my torn bloomers and a brassiere. I was a big girl—about eleven or twelve. Bernardo didn't mind, but when Fabio saw me, my God! What a fuss he kicked up! He yelled, "*Papá, papá,* come see what Sarita is doing! She's doing it on purpose!" *Papá* didn't approve of such games either, but he practically died laughing that day.

I never saw either of my parents naked or any of my brothers either. In our family the children didn't sleep all piled into one bed, no indeed! We had two bedrooms with two beds in each, not counting the cribs of the smaller ones. The girls slept in one room and the boys in the other.

We children believed that babies were brought by the stork. We didn't know about women having to go to a maternity hospital or anything. At the age of ten or eleven we never talked about such things. We talked about school, about helping our parents when we grew up, about wanting to be a teacher, about how much I liked to sew. But we never talked about having sweethearts because none of us had one.

Almost every Sunday we had a picnic. A whole bunch of us cousins, nieces, nephews, and friends would get candy, cookies, and a jar of water and go way up to the top of the highest hill to sit and eat. It was a real party for us. All the girls would wear makeup that day, and we'd gather leaves to make wreaths for our hair. It embarrassed me to paint my face. I'd walk out of the house hanging my head and never raise it until we were quite a distance away.

Everything looked so pretty from the hilltop. You could see the farthest places—the cane fields, the little towns—and the air was so cool. We'd sit and talk until we felt the cool of the evening. At 5:00 or 6:00 we'd go back down to bathe and change our clothes. We never missed a Sunday picnic on the hill unless there was something more important to do, like going to a party.

Before the Revolution we lacked many things, especially those of us who were the eldest. We all went to school, but not often. Things were not the way they are now, with rural schools everywhere. Ours was quite a distance from our house. It was a ramshackle wooden building, practically falling down, with only one large classroom and two little rooms for all the grades up to sixth.

I loved going to school. I had such a longing to learn. The work was easy—simple sums, learning the vowels and such. But how could we get ahead when we stayed away more often than we went? To go to school at 7:00, we rose at 4:00 in the morning to take the animals to pasture. Even then it was impossible for us to go every day. During the rainy season the river often was impassable. Or sometimes we'd go only to find that the teacher herself was absent because of illness. That made *papá* very angry, but we were sent even if it meant we couldn't do our chores at home.

After I was in school for about a year, when I was about nine, Agustina about twelve, and Fabio seven, *papá* said to us, "You kids can't go to school anymore, it's too far away." Then he explained that all the parents in the neighborhood were going to get together to build a house and see if they could raise the money to pay a teacher for the children of the barrio. They made the shack and hired a man they all knew who had a fair amount of schooling.

Practically all the barrio children went there—my cousins, my brothers Pancho, Bernardo, and David, my sisters Lupe and Marcelina. Many of them completed the fourth, fifth, or sixth grade, because that man was a good teacher. But Agustina, Fabio, and I had to stay home because there was always so much work to do. *Mamá* was recovering from a miscarriage and was under treatment for a full year. The teacher would send us school tasks to do at home and we'd send them back with my brother. I often cried to see the others going to school while I had to remain ignorant.

While I was in school I learned about Maceo,[62] who was a patriot, and about Martí, who fought for our country. Our teacher used to tell us about the places Martí had been. When I heard talk about Havana, the capital city, I'd think, "That must be a beautiful place. I'll have to go see it before I die." But the fare from Oriente to Havana, plus the expense of staying there, was more than any poor person could afford.

My grandfather's second wife, Zoila, could read beautifully and tell you what the big words meant. What a beautiful mind that woman had! Whenever she came, she'd read to us from one or another of my

62. General Antonio Maceo Grajales (1848–96), a famous black Cuban nationalist and a principal military leader (along with Máximo Gómez) in the War of Independence (1895). Maceo and his brother José were commanders of the *mambises,* the army of volunteers who fought against the Spanish. Mariana Grajales, the mother of the Maceo brothers, is also honored as a great Cuban patriot and revolutionary.

grandmother's novels. My grandmother had been in Bayamo and left us the magazines and books of stories and great thick novels she'd brought from there.

I'd also seen TV and the movies, because we were only an hour away, on foot, from Miranda *central* and Bayate. Bayate was not a town but rather like a big *batey* with thirty or forty buildings, all of them shops. A few friends we had owned the stores we went to. We bought on credit and *papá* paid every two weeks when he got his wages. At the *central* there were doctors, a hospital, a dentist, a pharmacy, a warehouse, two or three small cafés, a movie theater, and a ball park. There I could watch TV, go to the movies, and watch ball games.

I once spent a week in Miranda when I was thirteen. I had an attack of appendicitis and *papá* carried me on horseback to the *central*. After the operation I stayed there with *papá*'s sister.

My very first party was Uncle Héctor's saint's day. He was still living on the farm with us then. For a saint's day celebration we always built a bower of palm leaves where we gathered to eat and drink. Many friends came to the fiesta. Uncle Héctor had spread the word around that all his friends were welcome to come and have a good time. He slaughtered a great big hog he'd bought just for the occasion.

Mamá had been working on a dress for me to wear on March 15, which was a holiday under the dictatorship. Every year they had a public celebration with a big band at Mangos de Baragua, where there was a monument. People gathered around it and sang patriotic songs. Lots of war veterans, including my great-grandfather, Pedro Tabares, who'd been a prisoner of war at Cueta, went all decked out with their medals. We were always eager to go because that day they set up stands selling soft drinks, turnovers, sandwiches, and oranges. That's what we kids went for—the food.

Ay, mi vida, what a fiesta! How deliciously juicy the pork was, how crisp the skin, how cool the drinks! My cousin Leda played the guitar and all of us little girls danced with one another. We always did that, even when we were older. It was quite usual for the women to dance together because we outnumbered the men. I was a good dancer and knew all the *guarjiro* dances. My sisters and I were popular with everybody. We weren't shy and we taught our younger cousins to dance. Listen, we *made* the parties there! People would say, "If Inocencio's daughters don't come, we just won't have a party."

I asked for just one tiny drink, but *mamá* wouldn't allow it. I watched her, *papá,* Grandfather, Uncle Héctor, and everybody drink glass after glass. Every time somebody passed out, those still sober would pick him up and put him to bed. *Papá* got drunk and they laid him on my sister's cot. Liquor always upset him. Usually, when he drank, he'd toss our dolls down and throw dishes, but this time he was fine—he just quietly passed out.

At 10:00 the next morning the party was still going strong, with everybody eating roast pig. We children had gotten tired hours before, of course, and had been put to sleep on two big beds. We sure had good times in our youth!

The first time I danced with boys was at one of my great-grandfather's baptismal fiestas, when I was thirteen or fourteen years old. Both my parents went and so did all my brothers and sisters. I was dressed up in high heels and a terrific outfit. It was an occasion to be proud of. I'd never danced with boys before—it was out of this world! The first boy who asked me for a dance was a cousin, then one of my uncles, then a boy who played the bass in the combo. None of the boys got fresh with me. I guess they didn't dare, with all the old people around.

It was the usual thing to baptize children in my barrio, and it was my great-grandfather's custom to bring a priest over once a year to do it. It was easier than going to church. The baptismal parties were always held in my great-grandfather's house because it was the best place for a fiesta. He was better off than any of the rest—he had his little farm and didn't have to work outside like the rest of the men. He threw those parties to get customers for his stand, where he sold beer, ground pork turnovers, soft drinks, and lots of other things. He'd invite whole crowds of kids.

Anybody who wanted to have his baby baptized and could afford to pay the priest his 3 *pesos* was welcome to have the baptism at my great-grandfather's. The godparents had to pay for the refreshments and for their godchild's clothes. These parties usually started on the day before Easter, Saturday of Glory, and would sometimes last two or three days. People we'd never seen before would come and everybody would have a fine time playing music, dancing, eating, and drinking.

It was unheard of for a young girl to go traipsing off to a party all by herself. We had to go with somebody like *papá* or one of our uncles, who could stand up for us in case of trouble. If a girl had some young fellow courting her, the old folks would let her go if he took her and saw her home.

Ours was a very united barrio and we were all very respectful, honest people. I never heard of any bad people there, not since I was old enough to notice. Perhaps it was because everybody there was a cousin to everybody else, but the fact is that from childhood, we all got along with one another and there never was any trouble. For instance, I've heard of prostitutes, but as for seeing one—never in my life! Goodness no! No such woman ever came to our barrio. I'd like to see one of them try, that's all. She wouldn't be allowed to. We have a very different kind of mentality.

When a girl gets to be thirteen or fourteen, the young fellows start looking upon her as a señorita and treat her accordingly. Her parents have to be more careful. Girls are kept close to their mothers, but boys can go anywhere they like and do pretty much as they please.

When a boy was given entry to a girl's house—that is, had her parents' permission to visit her—he never tried anything bad. He had to toe the line, because if he didn't, out he went! Sweethearts could sit in the parlor and talk, but kissing and putting their arms around each other was strictly forbidden! I might kiss a sweetheart, sure, but as for going to bed with him ... goodness, no! From the very first day of their courtship, the man had to respect the woman and she had to respect him. You couldn't put anything over on the old folks back home. If they had a hunch there was something between you and some boy, you'd never see the outside of your house after that. Not even to get water from the well.

It was up to a girl to get herself a sweetheart to suit her own taste; parents had nothing to do with it. Whoever heard of a father picking a sweetheart for his daughter? Not in our barrio at any rate. Our parents found out we were in love when the boy went to ask for the daughter's hand in marriage and permission to visit as her official fiancé. Girls may have several sweethearts before they finally marry. Nobody looks down on you for leaving a sweetheart. When a girl and boy break up, they go on being friends.

Many of the young people fell in love with boys or girls who moved there from strange barrios. Often they weren't relatives, or else were distant relatives. Some boys married a girl because she had more land, and some girls took that into account, too, because that way they wouldn't have to worry about the future. Nobody blamed a boy or girl who married someone richer, but many got together who didn't have one bit of property between them.

A husband was head of his house from the very first. He gave the orders and his wife obeyed. That was her duty. A man who didn't rule his own home was respected even less than a woman. It's up to a man to lay down the law in his own home. A woman who tries to rule the roost is called a *macho*. A man must rule everything! If not, he's called a good-for-nothing.

In my barrio all the women were docile from the very first moment they had a sweetheart. The boy would tell his girl, "Remember, I'm *macho* in everything. I expect to be the one to rule. If I consult you you may give your opinion, but don't try to give orders. You give the orders in the kitchen and in the house as long as it's about things you understand." When a husband gives his wife an order, the wife should never answer, "No, I won't!" Not unless she wants to find herself out in the street.

As for the children, both parents have authority. Suppose a friend says to me, "Sara, may I take your daughter to the movies?" Well, I can say yes without waiting to ask my husband—if he's not here. But suppose they invited her to make a trip to Oriente? I'd certainly ask my husband first, and what he says goes, whether it's yes or no. In those things the man rules absolutely. In little trifling things the mother may use her own judgment. That's the way it is in my barrio.

Agustina was the first one of us girls to get married. Her husband, Juan Francisco Chávez, cut cane on our farm. They saw a lot of each other that way. I guess it's how they fell in love. *Papá* fixed up the little room next to the kitchen and for one year they lived with us.

I was about thirteen when Agusta bore her baby. In those days when a woman was pregnant, two large jars of a drink called *aliñado* were buried in the ground and kept there until the birth, when it was drunk in celebration. *Aliñado* is just rum, but they put anise in it and a whole heap of stuff.

When my sister bore a daughter, people brought so much food that the table was heaped with tins of crackers, boxes of spaghetti, bottles of beer and *maltina*. Everybody was bustling about without paying any attention to my brother-in-law and me while we sampled the *aliñado*. I didn't realize I was getting high until I heard *mamá* say she thought I was going to pass out. I felt as if I'd been turned upside down. That was the first time in my life I ever got drunk. All of a sudden I felt nauseated and threw up. *Mamá* bathed me and put me to bed. At noon *papá* carried me to the kitchen and they gave me a bowl of chicken soup to sober me up. After that, everybody insisted that I take "just one more little drink," but I said no and stuck to it.

I wasn't the only one drunk that day, not by any means. There were ten or twelve people lying on the floor drunk. *Papá* went around with a pail sprinkling them with cool water so they'd sober up enough to sit up and drink some more. *Mamá* was the only person who didn't drink with the rest of us. After everybody was back on their feet and walking around normally, she said, "Now it's my turn." *Mamá* always did enjoy her liquor. It took her a long time to get drunk, but once she did, nobody could make her lie down. She'd go all around the barrio, glass in hand, insisting everybody she met take a sip. When somebody refused, she'd get mad and tell them, "If you won't drink with me, you're no friend of mine!" That's the way the drink affected her that day. She got drunk as a grape, but she stayed on her feet. *Mamá* was strong, stout, and red-cheeked.

"Don't anybody dare say a word against my drinking today. I took good care of my daughter," she announced, "and today is my day." *Ay*, with so few boys in the barrio, Agustina was the only married daughter she had as yet. Besides, the baby weighed 9 pounds at birth. All in all, it was a great occasion.

Agustina and her husband have been happy in their love. I haven't seen her in ten years, but we keep in touch through letters.

My sister Carolina was real fresh and very strong-minded. She was fifteen when she went off with Niceto, but they never did get along very well. *Papá* had always opposed that match, I don't know why. They separated when Carolina was pregnant with her little girl. When the child was about a year old, my sister married José Raventos, a first cousin of ours who lived in *chucho* 9. They have eight children so far. After the triumph of the Revolution, he was a military guard for about three years. Now he's a farm laborer.

The lively one is my sister Lupe, who's had three husbands. She broke up with Rodríguez Arango, the first one, following *papá*'s advice. The fact is, those people have relatives from Jamaica. *Papá* is colored but he's a bit of a racist all the same. He said that instead of improving our breed, my sister was setting it back, because Jamaicans are black, black, black, with very bad hair. Lupe left Rodríguez Arango and married Huberto Mora, whose hair is so-so, coarse but not kinky. But as it turned out, unknown to Lupe, that little *compañero* already had a wife, who turned up and claimed him. So Lupe was left husbandless. And they'd been so fond of each other, too!

Then she married Sebastian, who's a first cousin, and now they have four children. They live in *chucho* 9 too. Sebastian is a brother of José Raventos, Carolina's husband, and of Ignacio Raventos, who's married to my sister Marcelina. So three of my sisters are married to three of the Raventos brothers, who are our cousins. They're a big family—the parents live right close by.

I love all my brothers and sisters equally and treat them all the same. But Bernardo is the brother I've lived with longest in the same house, because I lived with him and his wife when they had the apartment upstairs in this building. Bernardo and Ana Teresa were married by law, but they've been separated several times because they were forever quarreling. Now Bernardo is living with his second wife, Catalina, at *papá*'s farm.

My brother Pancho worked in the FAR and lived here with me for a while. He has the most schooling of any of us—about the third year of secondary school. He got that far because he was in electronics.

Then there's my brother Virgilio, who's single. I don't know much about his life because I've been living away from home so long. He was a *columnista* [63] and is now working a forklift.

---

63. A member of the Centennial Youth Column. Organized in 1968 to celebrate 100 years of the Cuban Revolution (dating from the beginning of the War of Independence in 1868), the Youth Column was composed of young people between the ages of seventeen and twenty-seven recruited to work in agricultural production. The *columnistas* received room and board, clothing, and a monthly allowance, and in addition were considered to

What I like most about my family is the closeness and love that we share among us. We give freely to each other with no thought of repayment. *Mamá* had eleven children and she gave her love to all equally. If she ever showed any preference for one over the others I never noticed it. She always kept us beside her and gave us the warmth of her love. Always, to all of us, she was a loving and indulgent mother. Even now that we're grown men and women we say with great pride, "Look, this is our family!"

Last July when I went to visit my parents, I hadn't seen my younger brothers for four years. One of my brothers said, "Before our sister leaves, we'll have to see the day in, dancing." And so we did. We all love parties and lots of good food, and my parents always gave wonderful parties. All my sisters and their husbands and all our friends in the barrio came to say goodbye to me. They slaughtered an enormous hog and had a lot of liquor, and at 2:00 in the morning they killed a goat because all the hog meat was gone.

My brothers have a combo that plays for the National Council of Culture. My brother Panchito has such a voice! And my youngest sister, Amanda Luz, helps out in the chorus. Every time the band struck up one of those *sones,* I was inspired. I know every dance step there is, and when the music comes out smooth and you've had a bit to drink . . . *ay!* Listen, we saw the day in. It was 9:00 in the morning and we were still dancing!

My parents didn't approve of the first boy who came courting me, so I dropped him before we even became sweethearts. I was still a child at that time. I hadn't had my first period yet; in fact, I didn't even know there was such a thing.

I had my first period at thirteen. It was March 15 and I felt sad, awfully sad, because I didn't know what it was all about. When I saw the blood I was scared to death. I lost my appetite. I had such great respect for my mother that I was embarrassed to explain to her what was happening to me. I kept worrying, "What if I die of this?" I finally told Gloria, and she explained to me, "It means that you're now a señorita." She told me I had to use some cloths which should be washed afterward to be used again. I lay down on a hammock and stayed there all day long.

After I started menstruating, *mamá* explained to me about the things I could and couldn't do. She told me I could bathe every day during my period as long as I used warm water. You couldn't buy cotton at the store in those days, so when the cotton trees on our farm were in bloom, *mamá* would gather the little puffs and make pads for us. When there weren't any, we used old rags. *Mamá* would never let us go out in the rain or eat

---

have fulfilled their military obligation. In 1973 the Youth Column was merged with other paramilitary labor groups to form the Army of Working Youth, under the Ministry of the Revolutionary Armed Forces.

acid foods or chop firewood while we were menstruating. She explained that if one did, the period would stop and that could make a woman sick. I don't know whether that's true or if it's just what she herself was taught when she was young. In any case, we heeded her warnings. Nowadays people don't pay attention to any of those rules, though I still do.

As soon as the three eldest of us girls were big enough to take over, *mamá* took a rest from washing, ironing, and cooking. We divided the work among us: one would head for the kitchen, another would go do the wash, and the third would clean the house. But *mamá* still directed our work. It was the same in all the houses in the barrio.

I was about fourteen when I fell in love. *Mamá* didn't say anything to me about such things because of the respect between us, but my little friends told me a lot about what you do when you fall in love. I and my sisters and my cousins would talk about it, and we decided, "Well, it's kind of scary, but one has to go through with it."

Casimiro Marichal, my first husband and the father of my five eldest children, wasn't from Monte dos Leguas. He came there from San Luis for the cane harvest. That was his trade—cane-cutter. He was twenty-five years old when we met in my house. We knew his sister. She visited us often, and when he came to Monte dos Leguas she brought him over to call on us. *Papá* told me to prepare some coffee for him, and I did, but I didn't even look him in the face. I simply wasn't interested.

Two or three days later he came back. Nobody was home but me, my sister, and my little brother. My parents were away for a month visiting my grandfather in the Sierra. We chatted for a while and then he left. Two days later I got a note from him saying that he liked my ways and that if I agreed to marry him he'd ask my parents right away. I passed the note to my sister. When she'd read it she said, "Listen, send this note back to that fellow and tell him never to darken our door again. If *papá* finds out, he'll scold all of us who are alone in the house here." So I returned the letter to Casimiro's brother and said, "Take that letter back to your brother and tell him I'm just a little girl, much too young to fall in love."

After my parents returned, Casimiro came calling again. He told them he'd visited our house because he was in love with me and I was in his thoughts day and night. "I don't know you," *papá* answered, "and neither does my daughter, so there's no reason why she should pay any attention to you."

Time passed and Casimiro kept on visiting our home. Practically every evening after work he'd drop in. One day while we were in the kitchen making supper, he stood there talking to me and I suddenly made up my mind to love him. I don't know what got into me, but *bang!* like that I was in love with him. Right away he asked *papá* for my hand.

"Well, if you and she are of one mind about this and you think you can make her happy, you may come inside my house to talk with her," *papá* said. Once a fellow is admitted like that, one can always find out his faults just by talking with him. You try to trip him up to see what his weaknesses are, and you can also figure out whether he really has marriage in mind.

Well, Casimiro made all the proper promises and began to make arrangements. He even gave one of my cousins bedsheets to embroider for us and bought a bed and all the stuff for the kitchen. One afternoon he told me, "Sara, let's you and me just take off together." I didn't want any legal ceremony myself. I explained it to *papá:* "I don't want to sign papers and stuff, *papá*. That way I won't have to bother about a divorce later on."

At first my parents wouldn't agree. They argued I'd never be happy with him that way and that we'd never make old bones together. "Besides," *papá* said, "he'll be taking you from your own home and you're still a virgin."

Gloria opposed my marriage too. She said that Casimiro could never make me happy. "Why don't you try to get yourself another man?" she said. "Maybe I'm mistaken, but I've got a hunch that Casimiro isn't the right one for you."

"Well, I'll try," I answered to all her objections. "Maybe it will work out." And I did try. For ten whole years. I wouldn't listen to any advice from my family.

The first night is never any good, and that's a fact, because if a girl's still a virgin it hurts an awful lot. I didn't cry. I bore it as best I could but I kept thinking, "Oh my, so this is what it's like." All sorts of silly things kept going through my head. I didn't enjoy it in the least, although Casimiro was very affectionate those first few days.

Casimiro was a loving husband. He bought me everything—dresses, shoes, bloomers, brassieres. He handed them to me with these words, "When you go to visit your parents, I want you to wear everything new and not go back with what you brought."

My mother-in-law was as nice to me as if I'd been her own daughter. Casimiro wasn't home most of the time because he worked quite far away, so I talked a lot more with his old lady than with him. But kind as Casimiro and his mother were to me, I was sad all the same. I'd never slept away from home like that, and I missed the old folks. I couldn't help thinking all the time, "I shouldn't have gotten married. Why didn't I stay home with my own folks?"

Papá hurried over to see me just a few days after I'd left with my man. "Gloria is crying her eyes out," *papá* said. "I think you'll have to go back home. It's pitiful to see how much she cries and how much she misses you." We were like sisters, you know. I went right away. Somebody caught sight of me and said, "Here comes *la negra*," and Gloria was the first one to rush out and hug me.

Three months later *papá* came to see me again. When he left I went off all by myself to weep. "If only I'd stayed home," I thought, "nobody could come around bothering me. I'll try to persuade Casimiro to build a house on *papá*'s farm. I'll be happier that way. And he'd better not say no, because if he does, I won't stay long with him." Not that he'd given me any reason to leave him. I simply didn't feel romantic about Casimiro. I don't know why it was, I just couldn't.

So then they made a little house for me, and when two of the walls were covered and nothing was left to do but make the roof, I returned home. I felt real proud going back to my old folks. I felt as if I were a single girl again. My sister said to me, "I guess it won't be long before you have a baby."

"Why?" I asked. I still thought babies were brought by the stork. Then my sister explained to me how it was and I burst out, "*Ay*, Jesus Christ! If I'd known *that*, I never would have married!"

Mamá said to me, "You always look so sad, my child. I hope you won't go getting yourself a belly now. If you stay home living like a señorita with no children, some day another man will come courting you, somebody you can really love. Make a decision before it's too late."

I was ashamed because my husband was so sweet to me. The house he built for me right below my parents' was a lovely little house of cedar wood. It had one bedroom, a parlor, a dining room, a kitchen, and a garden, which we filled with plants. It was the cutest little house! About four months after moving there, my daughter Concha was born. I kept that baby as neat and pretty as a little cup of gold. My little sisters and my parents were crazy about her, so she was over at their place most of the time. "Oh *mami*, I feel so happy to be a mother!" I told her.

"Now look, why make two or three more bellies when you feel as you do?" she objected. "You aren't happy. Leave that fellow before it's too late. Your *papá* is very happy with your baby girl."

One day Casimiro and I quarreled. He'd told me, "Don't go away from the house today. We have several brooding hens just about ready to hatch out their eggs, and if you aren't around to look after them, ants will get into the nests and kill the chicks." I paid no attention to him. I went to *papá*'s house and stayed overnight.

Casimiro got home before I did. I could see by his face that he was displeased, so I said, "All right, if you don't like it you can lump it. *I* like it." After I bathed and fed the baby, I went over to *papá*'s house and sat on the big rocker on the porch, singing a lullaby. My little brothers and sisters clustered around, kissing and petting the baby. All of a sudden *papá* said, "I'd like some soup for dinner tonight."

"*Ay, papi*, so would I!" I put in. "Let's have some good strong broth made from an old hen." Then I laughed and said, "I've moved back with you, you see."

That night I slept there. When Casimiro realized that I wasn't going back that day, he packed up and went off to his *mamá*'s house. About two months later he came to see *papá*. "Look, Inocencio," he said, "I went back to my old folks because your daughter simply walked out on me that night. She up and left without even bothering to fix my supper." *Papá* couldn't think of any good excuse to make for me. The truth is that there *was* no excuse for what I'd done. So I went back and soon I had a big belly again—that was Gerardo, the one who's a *columnista* now.

Casimiro told me that two visits to my old folks' house, one in the morning and one in the afternoon, were plenty. But after I'd done all my chores at home, I always took the baby and went to visit them. I was accustomed to it. He wanted me to take on my responsibilities as a married woman, but instead of looking after him and talking with him, I'd go to my parents. I'd ask Casimiro to go along, but he'd say he was busy. It was my lack of experience that made me act that way.

Then one day Casimiro said to *papá*, "Your daughter isn't the way she used to be when she was a señorita. You people have spoiled her. She simply can't go on acting like this now that she has a married woman's duties."

"You're quite right," *papá* agreed. Then he gave me some good advice and I took it. After that, if I asked Casimiro's permission to go to *papá's* house and he said, "No, don't go; stay here and make me some coffee," I'd say, "All right," and I'd stay and make the coffee or whatever he wanted.

Every year my parents threw a party to celebrate their wedding anniversary. *Papá,* Grandpa, and my aunt went over to fetch me for the occasion. I told Casimiro, "I'm going over to papá's to stay awhile. Today is their wedding anniversary."

"I told you you couldn't go anywhere," he snapped. Then *papá* and Grandfather invited him too, but he refused. "All right, don't go," said I. "But I'm going. It isn't that I want to go but that I have to. It's my duty to go."

He expected me to stay home all day long behind closed doors. He wanted to make a hermit out of me. That kind of life will do for a woman without relatives, a woman who's alone, but with so many relatives coming to call on me, I couldn't lead that kind of life. If he'd spent all his free time at home, then he'd have had a right to talk. But he hadn't. He was always going to visit this friend or that.

I simply couldn't see things from Casimiro's point of view. I didn't understand him, that's all. I never knew what his ideas were or his opinions about anything. He was too rude; he had a very aggressive personality. Sometimes I wouldn't talk to him because it was too upsetting. And I didn't enjoy having sex with him; many times I did it against my will. I'd ask my friends, "When your husband makes a pass at you, do you always feel like doing it?"

"Yes indeed, because I love him," they all answered. So then I figured it out: "I know what's wrong—I don't love Casimiro. That must be the reason why I get pregnant so often, because I do it against my will." By that time I'd borne Casimiro two more children—Violeta and Hilario.

I'd never heard anybody in the barrio talk about birth control, and I didn't know how to go about it. Casimiro did because he was older, but I was too embarrassed to talk about it. Maybe he did it on purpose, but the fact is that I had one pregnancy after another. When I got pregnant with Estela I tried to get an abortion, but the doctor refused to do it because I'd waited too long—four months. The truth is, my eyes opened too late. If I'd analyzed his character better, I wouldn't have stayed with him that long.

In my barrio people didn't know much about birth control, and the problem was that some of the women would get pregnant every two or three years. When the state began to help pregnant women, oh my! Didn't a whole bunch of women there start growing bellies right away! Some women get pregnant again right after having a baby, others have a longer wait between pregnancies. I don't know if it just happens or if they do something to make it that way.

After all our five children were born, Casimiro got awfully quarrelsome, and lazy to boot. It was fight, fight, fight all the time, and he didn't want to work. Everybody was amazed at the change for the worse in him. I said, "Look, Casimiro, I used to be the one who didn't pull her weight around here, but now it's you. I'm more experienced now and I know that having a family, we've got to struggle to get ahead. You've got to face up to things and find a way of supporting these little ones." Before, I didn't need you as a husband because I led a perfectly happy life with my parents."

A day came when there was no food for the kids and that's the truth—there was *nothing*. *Mamá* called them over and fed them at her house so they wouldn't have to go to bed with empty stomachs. "Look, Casimiro," I said that day, "do you think it's fair that our kids should have to be fed at *papá*'s house? *Papá* and *mamá* raised their children without ever having to send them to this or that house to ask for so much as a glass of sugar water. Nobody has ever been heard to call *papá* a bad father, and moreover, he never showed up drunk in front of *mamá*. It hurts and humiliates me that my children should have to be fed at my parents' house. If I leave you, *then* I won't mind, because if I'm alone and don't have a job, it's only right and natural that my parents should help me out. But as long as you're here, it's up to you."

But I was the one who had to get the food for the kids. Casimiro would go eat at his *comadre*'s house every night. I hid the food and cooked only for the children. Not one cup of coffee did Casimiro get from me from then on. If I could have given him poison, I would have—but food, no!

And then, on top of everything, he started mistreating the kids. Once, when Concha was five, he bashed her on the head with a stick and cut her scalp open. Another time he struck her so hard with his belt that he cut the flesh. I defended them tooth and nail. Then Casimiro and I would have a hot battle of words. He never hit me—he wouldn't have dared. *Papá* had threatened to get him jailed if he ever did. If Casimiro had stayed with me, he might have ended up killing the kids.

Casimiro tried to play a dirty trick on me. He wanted *papá* to turn over to me, legally, the part of the farm belonging to me. "Don't you do it, *papá*," I said, "not for anything in the world. Casimiro thinks the minute I have the deed of gift in my hand, he could have it put in his name by some crooked lawyer." Such tricks were common at that time. But I told him that my father's farm was too good for him and that the way he didn't respect other people's property was just plain shameless.

In those days I was just skin and bones. I couldn't eat or drink or sleep in the midst of so much quarreling and insanity. I was afraid to leave him because he'd threatened to cut my head off if I did. One night he came home with several drinks in him and tried to lie down beside me. I said to him, "You'll sleep alone from now on. I'm not going to risk your making me another big belly. I've lost all hope of finding my life's happiness with you." After that, he never dared sleep with me again.

My one wish was to make Casimiro go away, and finally he did. When I couldn't stand it any longer I said to him, "This is the last day I put up with you." So then he left. He returned one night and started rattling the door. I was all alone, but I was careful not to say so because anybody might have taken the opportunity to play some sort of dirty trick on me. I struck a match and lit the lamp, and there was that man, machete in hand!

"Either you come back to me or I'll chop you to pieces!" he threatened.

"You may chop me into a hundred pieces," says I, "but I'll still say no, and I'll keep on saying no until the last handful of earth is dropped on my grave."

"Look, Sara, I'm going to work for my children," he promised.

"If it's your children you want, take them. But as for me, I don't ever want to see even your picture again."

He moved his machete at me but I wasn't afraid of it or of anything else in the world. I don't know what was protecting me, but I felt no fear at all, alone as I was. I managed to calm him down. At about 2:00 in the morning he cleared out and has never bothered me since. If I'd gotten scared and backed down, I'd still be with him, going through a thousand troubles.

When the kids told *papá* about it the next day, he got real mad and said I had to come back and live at his house. My brother got a handcart and started bringing all my stuff down and loading it on the cart. The chickens, the pigs, the goats—they moved everything. So I moved out of that house and never returned again.

Getting rid of that little old *compañero* of mine was like winning top prize in the lottery without ever having bought a ticket. I felt happy and relaxed. I tell you, the ten years I spent with him were years of ax and machete. I've never seen hide nor hair of him since.

During the Revolution we were Fidelistas. I felt a thrill of joy every time I saw a Fidelista. They looked so handsome with their long hair and beards. I think young boys look real cute with their long hair the way it's worn nowadays. It reminds me of when the *barbudos*[64] used to come down from the Sierra to our home in Monte dos Leguas. Many of them had relatives around there and they'd slip in at night and see them every time they had a chance. We'd hide the Rebels, and when the enemy showed up nearby, we'd send a warning message to the Sierra.

Those who hadn't gone off to join the revolutionaries had to live on the alert to evade the police. The police didn't allow anybody to enter or leave the barrio. We had no way to get food, we couldn't come and go, and we had no money either. We were almost on the point of going hungry. All of us in the barrio lived on our wages, and if we couldn't go out to get work, how were we going to eat? Until Cuba was free we couldn't get jobs, because everybody had to watch out and protect himself from the police.

The people in Oriente rebelled—thousands upon thousands of the young people went to the Sierra. Many of my cousins left while the Rebels were still fighting in the hills, but my brothers never had an opportunity to go. The only camp near enough would have been the one Raúl set up on his way to the Sierra del Cristal, but that only lasted a short time. So even though my brothers were sympathizers from the first, they didn't start working for the Revolution until after the Triumph. Fabiano, Virgilio, David, Bernardo, and Pancho have each served three years in the FAR.

From the minute everybody began to rise against Batista, I was all for the Revolution. I hoped they'd win because we suffered a great deal from the henchmen of the dictatorship. They browbeat us, the children as well as the grownups. One day I took my little boy out to get some oranges because he was sick, and two *casquitos* grabbed my horse by the bridle, pulled it back, and asked me, "Where are you going, Señora?"

"To get remedies for my little boy," I explained.

Then one of them slapped the horse twice, "So as not to slap you," he told me. "No, *chico*, leave her alone," the other one said. "She's going for medicines for her little boy." But listen, I looked up and down and around me and God only knows what color I turned, because the truth is I was dying of fear.

64. The "bearded ones," a term used for members of Castro's Rebel Army.

The problem was that the people in our barrio were on their list of those to be shot for being involved with the Rebels. Some stool pigeon had talked and the *casquitos* had caught a *compañera* of mine with a box of armbands we'd made for the Rebels in the Sierra. She tried to make up some sort of story to explain them but they were black-and-red Twenty-sixth of July armbands commemorating the first attack on Moncada. We really were nervous that day! There were rumors that Sosa Blanco[65] was approaching, burning and destroying everything on his way, and I thought, "Now we're in for it!" We were digging up sweet potatoes and a plane bombarded us. There wasn't a tree or a bush big enough to hide behind when that big bug flew over spewing bullets. We had one heck of a scare.

That night such a wind rose that you could hear nothing for its howling. And all the dogs barked as if they were ready to eat you alive; they must have sensed the movement of people nearby. Next day they told us that Raúl's troops had marched past in the night on their way to the Sierra del Cristal.

I saw nothing else, but my sister Agustina was right in the midst of the Revolution. She saw a lot and has been nervous ever since. For nine months we had no news of her. It was impossible to send her a letter because we were isolated. People told us there was a lot of fighting in the Sierra, that things looked bad, and all the time we didn't know whether Agustina was dead or alive.

There was a cave near my sister's house, and every time an airplane went over shooting, they'd all make a dash for it. That cave was a lifesaver. Nothing could happen to them as long as they stayed there. Often they spent a whole day in it without eating. It was like being in a different world, she says.

One day the police went after my brother-in-law because they said he was spying for the Rebels. They shot at him, but the bullet went through the back of a chair instead. As they were taking him to the police station, he hit one of the policemen and knocked him out. He ran away and hid in the cave, but he could hear the cops shouting outside.

Agustina had a big she-goat so pregnant that when she walked, her udders dragged along the ground. When she heard the cry, "Everybody hide!" that goat was the very first one to reach the cave. She even gave birth to two kids right there.

They also had a sow tied up with a chain. When that animal heard the first shots, she broke the chain in her fear and ran away, abandoning her litter. As long as the Revolution lasted that sow never returned. My sister was sure she'd been killed and eaten by somebody. Well, two or three

65. Jesús Sosa Blanco, an officer in Batista's Army accused of crimes against the people of Oriente Province, was tried and sentenced to death in the first public war trial under the Castro government (January, 1959).

days after the Revolution triumphed, that sow came back home. It was as if she knew what was happening and said, "Well, now that Fidel has won, I can go back home." Honestly, those two animals were human!

When the Rebels took the Miranda police station, we felt as if the sky had opened up for us. If the Rebels hadn't taken it, we would have been deep down in a hole, all of us. Later, the other police station gave up without a fight. On January 1, when Fidel won and we were able to walk into the police station, we could see the graves and the holes they'd dug. That's all we saw. We didn't see either the fighting or the corpses.

After the triumph of the Revolution, my folks came to Havana every time Fidel held a mass meeting in the Plaza Cívica. The country people would flock to all those meetings, no matter where they were. They went on a special railroad train and the fare was free. *Papá* is very fond of Fidel. He's known him since Fidel was a child. *Papá* and Uncle Euquerio were day laborers on the farm of Fidel's father. Old man Castro was a nice guy who hired a lot of people living round about.[66]

During the Literacy Campaign,[67] the *brigadista* assigned to our house was Luciano, a plump twelve-year-old boy from San Luis. He turned out to be a real nice kid. He called me "Auntie" and was so fond of my baby that I felt as if he were my own son. After the Campaign, he came back two or three times to visit me and the kids. He was a big help as long as he stayed with us. In the daytime he kept hard at work fetching water and firewood, tending the animals, and running errands. At noon he gave us classes for half an hour, and at night he'd teach us until 11:00. He also read the newspaper to us every day.

Papá, who was already in his sixties, made tremendous progress. Luciano also taught my sisters Lupe and Marcelina. I didn't study because I told them, "I can read and write a little. I completed the first grade." They said, "Well, this is only for illiterates who can't read or write at all."

Everybody in the barrio had a *brigadista;* at night all the houses were lit up during the three-hour class. I think the *brigadistas* stayed with the families there and in the Sierra for about a year or perhaps a bit longer.

66. Fidel Castro's father, Angel, owned a *colonia* of about 10,000 acres that employed 500 people. The main crop was sugar, which was sold to the Miranda *central*. (Thomas, *Cuba: The Pursuit of Freedom*, p. 805.)

67. The year 1961, declared by Castro as the Year of Education, saw a massive campaign to eradicate illiteracy in Cuba. Schools were closed in April and 100,000 students from junior high through college level were mobilized as *brigadistas*, trained and sent into rural areas to teach reading and writing. Teachers called *alfabetizadores* taught illiterates in the cities. The Campaign was reported successful in reducing the illiteracy rate from 23 percent to 3 percent. (Lockwood, *Castro's Cuba, Cuba's Fidel*, p. 126.) A Cuban government publication set the illiteracy rate at 3.9 percent in the mid-1960s, stating this figure included 25,000 Haitian residents who did not speak Spanish and people who were mentally retarded or "too old to learn to read and write." This pamphlet estimated the total number of volunteer teachers during the Campaign at 271,000. (*Cuba: A Giant School* (Havana: Ministry of Foreign Affairs, n.d.))

The *brigadistas* really gave the Cuban people a big push forward. We country people owe them a lot of gratitude. Those kids in the Sierra Maestra worked hard, rain or shine, cleaning up, removing stones, clearing fields of weeds, in order to teach people to read and write. They even got spectacles for those with poor eyesight. Why listen, I saw a photograph in the magazine *Bohemia* of an old, old woman with a white kerchief tied around her head who learned to read and write!

The Revolution has helped my sister Agustina by giving her clothes, shoes, food, and schooling for her children under the plan they have for the Sierra. We don't have that here in Havana. That's the way she keeps her ten children clothed. And four of her kids are studying on scholarships at Caney de la Mercedes.[68] Agustina herself only went about as far as third grade.

When we least expected it, someone from the government came to our house especially to fetch my sister Marcelina. The government paid all her expenses—the fare to school, clothes, shoes, food—and took her to Havana for six months to study. She made good use of those six months and came out as a teacher of dressmaking. Fidel gave her a sewing machine.

They went to fetch my son Gerardo, but he didn't like the scholarship they gave him to study seafaring and fishing. Then they came to fetch him again and he joined the Youth Column and stayed in it. There are lots of country boys in it. They're taught to read and write and are given their meals, shoes, and clothes free, besides being paid wages. When they have to cut cane or do any other kind of productive work, they do it. They render their service and are allowed to study whatever they choose. My son likes it in the Column. All the boys are very happy there.

No new houses have been built in my barrio since the Revolution, but there's a CDR and a Women's Federation and the farmers' organization, which resolves any problem country people may have. There's also a school which Raúl had built in Mayarí.

When I got together with Eduardo I had five kids, but I wasn't old— only twenty-five. He was twenty-one. He was a very affectionate boy but not a bit talkative. You practically had to pull the words out of his mouth. He was a good, quiet man and I loved him pretty well. I saw in him a man one could live in peace with because he never interfered with anybody. He was well liked in the barrio.

Everybody said I was the first girl Eduardo had ever courted. I've never heard that he'd had so much as a childhood sweetheart before. He courted me by letter, because we were both so busy we didn't have much chance for talk. I was always doing housework or shopping for food or

68. Site of the Camilo Cienfuegos School City, which opened to students in 1960. It is a boarding school founded to accommodate peasant children who live in the mountains and are unable (for reasons of distance) to attend the regular day schools.

something, and he worked hard at his job too. Eduardo has always been a real worker. He'd write little notes and ask the kids to give them to me. He said he was in love with me and would make me happy and all that stuff. Then I'd write back and he'd write me another note, and so on.

In all that time we were never able to have a word alone together. He'd visit me at home, but our house was always full of people in the evening. Eduardo and I simply sat there and talked with everybody, so I never knew how he kissed or anything. I knew he was quite fond of me though. He kept after me like that for quite a while until I finally gave in and said I loved him.

What I most like about Eduardo is that he took me knowing I had five children by another man, and he's always been very fond of those kids. Not once in all these years has he said to me, "Those are not my children." Never. He raised them just as if they were his own.

I tell my children, the older ones anyway, "When I need you, be sure to take good care of me without begrudging it, because I've been a mother to you. If I'd been a bad mother, I'd have gone off with another man and left you abandoned God knows where. But when I took another *macho,* the first thing I did was grab you all and bring you with me. And I promised you that if the *macho* didn't turn out right, I'd leave him and take you with me, because you're my children and a woman who walks out on her children doesn't deserve the name of mother."

After the Revolution Eduardo and I got a piece of land in *chucho* 9 from the government. It was on a large farm and the man in charge of it was *papá*'s cousin Eulalio. He was the one who allotted the pieces of land there to people who asked for it, and gave them wood to build a house. He didn't have to give us any though, because we used the palm wood and palm leaves of the house I'd lived in with Casimiro. We took it over to *chucho* 9 in a cart drawn by two oxen. Eduardo and I, *papá,* and Uncle Euquerio all worked on building the house. It had one bedroom and a parlor and was built on a low hill, right beside the river. I hated the place because when the river rose, I was afraid one of the kids might fall in.

Just after we built the house in *chucho* 9 Eduardo went to Santiago de Cuba to join the Army. When he was transferred to Havana to take a battery course, I was left alone with the children. Then one day I got a telegram from him: "Sara, come here. I'll be waiting for you at Managua. I want to see if you like it here." So I came to Havana with the baby, Amanda María. That was in 1961.

It was after I moved to the city that I began having trouble with Eduardo. One day my brother-in-law Abelino came to see me. He's very fond of me; I can confide in him and trust him to keep my secrets. He said, "I've got something to tell you, Sara. I came to tell you that I think Eduardo has a sweetheart, a very young girl."

"Ah," I said, "that's nice." That day I didn't make any noise about it. I didn't get angry or anything because I thought, "Well, a man in the street is a man and sometimes he has to prove it." That's what I thought with the little experience I had. "And after all," I told Abelino, "we get along well."

Abelino didn't tell me the girl's name, but about a week later I found a letter when I was going through the pockets of Eduardo's olive-green pants. It was signed "Pomposa." I read it, and that night I took it out and showed it to Eduardo, saying, "Take this jewel, comrade. You left it in your pants pocket."

Eduardo turned pale from shock.

"Go on, take it," I urged him. "It's yours." He still didn't reach for it, so I laid it on his knees, saying, "Here. I don't need it anymore. I already wrote down the address. I think I may have some news for her."

The following Friday I showed up at the girl's house with my daughters, Amandita and Faustina. I was ever so polite and proper—I don't know how I got so much decency! When the girl's mother opened the door, I asked, "Does Eduardo Rojas's fiancé live here?"

"Yes indeed, *hombre*. Come right in. Here she is."

"That's all I wanted to know," I said. "Did he ever happen to tell you that he's got a wife and two children?"

You could have knocked that woman over with a feather. "How could he do such a thing!" she exclaimed. "My Pomposa is only fourteen years old. How dare he get engaged to her when he already has a wife and children? How could he treat a young girl in such a way?"

She fussed around me and begged me to take a cup of coffee with her, but I answered, "No, *compañera*, I won't drink coffee with you. I came here to find out the truth, not to pay a social call."

A comrade of Eduardo's told him he'd seen me on such-and-such a bus with the two girls and right away Eduardo figured it out and said, "I bet she went to Pomposa's house." The next morning when he got home, he asked Amandita, "Child, where did you go yesterday?"

"We went real far, me and Faustina," the child answered.

"Go ahead, Amandita, tell him we went to pay a call on his sweetheart," I put in. Then I said to him, "From the minute you take off with her, remember not to set foot in this house again. Just keep on sending the money for the kids and call it quits."

My friend Olga advised me not to move out of my home or even consider abandoning my children. She said, "Look after them, give them a good example day after day, and wait. He may be merely passing the time with that girl—he's still young and thoughtless." So I decided to take Olga's advice and stay home.

I went through a terrible time with that man while we were living in Marianao and when we first moved here to Miramar. We lived like cat and dog. I simply couldn't put up with the idea of his getting all lovey-dovey with another woman, but the worst of it was that I loved that son-of-a-bitch. To me, losing him was to lose the whole world and everything in it.

From the time I was very young I'd thought, "I'm going to be a failure—it's my fate. It's written that I'll fail and that in the end I'll have to marry a man who's already married to someone else." I'd known Eduardo from the very first day of his birth. I thought I knew him well and yet he turned out to be false. I never imagined he'd do what he did to me.

Well, we hadn't lived in Miramar more than a few days when that brat Pomposa finally forced Eduardo to take off with her. She wrote him a letter addressed to his unit, saying that if he didn't take off with her, he wasn't a man. Then Pomposa's mother forced him to marry the girl. I'd lived with Eduardo such a long time and borne him two children and he never even spoke of marrying me. Then he went and granted marriage to that woman.

Imagine how I felt! To think that I'd given myself to him unconditionally and then he goes and marries another woman legally! I couldn't eat. I lost so much weight I practically wasted away to a skeleton. If I'd had a gun, I would have killed him like a dog. If ever there was a madwoman, it was me. I was out of my mind. Eduardo was my life, my world. I felt that even if I never lived with him again, I couldn't possibly love another man, so great was the ache in my heart.

I left the apartment in Miramar and went to Oriente, because *papá* said, "Stay here with us for a time, until you can get a bit stronger; then you can go back to Havana." In Oriente I'd wash and iron clothes, weed cane fields, plant cane or harvest it ... I did forty thousand different things over at the Julio Antonio Mella *central*. After working in Oriente a couple of months, I'd come back to Havana to pay the rent or deal with some other problem. I kept on paying rent because Bernardo asked me to. Sometimes I'd bring all the kids with me, and sometimes I'd come alone and leave them there to go on with the work. I kept coming and going, coming and going.

Once I stayed on in Havana with two of my brothers for about two months, but I missed the kids, especially at night. Bernardo was working on the vegetable trucks in the marketplace and would go to work at 8:00 in the morning and come home at 8:00 at night, and then he often had to stand guard all night long. David, who was working at La Cabaña, was only here on Saturday, and my brother Panchito was in Oriente. I'd go anywhere I felt like going with Lala or some other friend, because I had nobody at home waiting for me. I didn't go to the movies once in all that time, but I'd visit around and go shopping with Leticia and so forth. I'd go to the beach and bathe in the sea. I had a good time.

In Oriente I had lots of suitors, but I didn't want another husband. Many men wanted to marry me. Yes, I had lots of chances to remarry, but I rejected them all, saying, "I'm perfectly happy as I am."

In spite of what Eduardo had done, I wanted him and no one else. I guess I must have still been in love with him. Besides, I wasn't an innocent young girl but an experienced woman by that time and I wasn't about to trust any man blindly. I'd think, "Sure, I'm pretty now. I've grown healthy and plump, I feel strong. How do I know he doesn't simply want to grab what he can and then drop me?" But you know what really held me back? Shame, that's what. It's something that's always bothered me—the fact that I had one husband who made me five kids, then another one who made me two. What would people say if I hitched up for the third time and made three or four more bellies? It embarrassed me terribly; that kind of thing isn't well thought of in Oriente, and that's a fact. But perhaps it's different in Havana.

Eduardo gave me to understand that Pomposa opposed his sending me money for the children's support but that he wouldn't give in to her in that respect. For six or seven months he sent the money to me, but then he started to come with it every fifteen days. He didn't fail even once to give it. He'd bring some 30 to 40 pesos each time. He couldn't commit himself to a fixed sum because his earnings were irregular. Sometimes, when he earned enough, he'd bring 50 or 60 pesos, or even 75.

If one of the kids got sick, Eduardo would come and take her to the doctor. So we saw each other quite often, and I never refused to speak to him. When he came, I'd always offer him coffee if there was any, or prepare his lunch. He never stayed to sleep though; he'd just sit there for a while and then leave.

The girls would watch for him, and when he was still far off would run to tell me, "Here comes pipo." Then they'd run out to meet him. The girls were so affectionate with him whenever they saw him that it probably made him feel guilty. One day Amanda asked Eduardo, "Pipo, why are you going?"

"I have to go to work, baby," he answered. He didn't want to let the kids know that he went because I didn't want him in the house. He'd come often, even if he only stayed a little while, so that the little ones wouldn't catch on.

Eduardo's wife respected me enough never to show her face around me. Frankly, I'd have liked to meet her alone, but there must have been somebody who warned her, "Here comes Sara." She was pretty scared of me and that's a fact. If she hadn't known Eduardo had family duties before he ever met her, I wouldn't have blamed her. But she did know. She made him marry her to get my goat and I wanted my revenge.

Although I never had the chance to talk to Pomposa alone, I did manage to run into her once. Eduardo and I had been separated about three years. We were both visiting our old folks in Oriente then, and I'd volunteered to go plant sugar cane with the group from the Women's Federation because I thought it would be my chance to meet Pomposa face to face. One day, after a meeting of the Federation, I stopped by the home of Eduardo's *mamá*. As I was going in, who should come out but Pomposa!

"So now I've finally caught you!" I said. That woman flung an insult at me and vanished into the bedroom. I was raving mad because of what she'd said. I wanted to catch her—nothing else mattered to me. But she'd locked herself up in the bedroom and I didn't know whether she'd hid under the bed, jumped out the window, or what. All I know is that when she saw me, she looked as if she'd seen death itself, although I had nothing in my hands except my work gloves. It was the gloves that kept me from getting a good hold on her, they were so hard and slippery. I barely managed to grab a lock of her hair, but she easily slipped out of my grasp.

I talked to her through the bedroom door, saying, "When a woman does what you've done she's neither a mother nor a real woman. I wouldn't blame you if you hadn't known Eduardo had other ties. But you've known from the first that the bread you're eating belongs to another. If I'd wanted to keep him, you could never have taken him away from me. He's mine, mine, not yours! And any time I want him back, he'll come back to me, understand? You say you're a woman. Well, prove it! Come out and fight!"

I wasn't going to let her think I was scared of her. I wanted to show her I was a real woman. I've never in my life gotten into a fight with anybody. If anybody so much as raised his voice to say three or four words, I'd slip away and hurry back home. That was the first and last time in my life I ever got into a fight and had to act like a woman.

The scene upset my mother-in-law terribly. She hugged me and said again and again, "Enough, my child, enough! Don't create any more problems. That's all over and done with now. You know that Eduardo is yours and nobody else will ever take him away from you. I invited you in for a cup of coffee because you've always been a very good woman." So I sat down and drank my coffee while she gave me advice.

When Eduardo got back he asked his mother what had happened. Then he turned to me and said, "Stop looking for trouble. I've already made up my mind to leave that woman because I'm not going to abandon my children. I don't trust her. She told me she'd take off with me even if I had 100 children by another woman. And just as she took off with me, she's likely to take off with another man someday. She and I have already broken up."

Eduardo had a talk with *papá*, who said it was up to me to decide. "If he's going to do again what he already did, I don't want him back," I said.

"I'll never do that again," he assured me. "I don't want my children to have a hard time or to pass into another man's hands."

Well, Eduardo and I got together again. I went off with him to his *papá*'s house. *Ay,* Uncle Euquerio was so happy when he saw me! Right away he called the old lady and asked her to give me a cup of coffee. Then, well, we were together that night. About 8:oo in the morning we got up. The old man had made coffee—and brought us ours to drink in bed.

I was happy to be back with Eduardo because he promised he'd never make things hard for me again by returning to that woman and I don't know what all. He told me, "You and I are going to raise the children together and you'll have a calm, peaceful life from now on. Now let's go back."

I thought my parents would get terribly offended when I went back to Eduardo after all he'd made me go through. I was scared to tell them because I respect those old parents of mine a lot. They were pleased with me, though. Well, if they disapproved they didn't show it—perhaps because they could tell I felt rather sad. They told me, "Well, he's the father of your children, what else could you do? Now the two of you must try to make your marriage work and avoid more problems."

Papá took me back to Eduardo's old folks on his horse that night, but I returned to *papá*'s the next day and sewed there for two days. I'm not sure whether I was embarrassed or what. I felt as if Eduardo had taken off with me from my parents' home all over again. He got a telegram ordering him to report to work and he went back in a hurry, but I stayed in Oriente a couple of months longer because I wasn't feeling well.

It's been three years since Eduardo and I got together again, but the love I used to feel for him is dead. What I feel for him now is very different. The great trust in him I used to have is gone. He tells me I should feel sure of him and he promises to always be good to me, but how can I believe him after what he's made me go through? He notices it and says to me, "Sara, you aren't as you used to be."

When Eduardo tells me, "I'm going to the movies," I immediately think, "He's taking some girl along for sure." It's like that all the time. I live in a state of anxiety and distrust. That's not what I call happiness. I always search like a thief for his wallet, but he no longer leaves it under his pillow or in his pocket as he used to. Now he hides it from me, perhaps because he doesn't want to make me suffer.

We've been together for ten years already and we know each other through and through. By now I know what he likes and doesn't like, and he knows my likes and dislikes too. Perhaps after a time he'll be disillusioned with me and decide I'm not the right woman for him, though I don't believe it. Then again, sometimes I'm convinced that since he betrayed me once, he's bound to do it again. Most men are bachelors at heart, as I well know from experience. No man considers himself truly married. A few men belong to one woman alone, but most belong to whatever number of women will put themselves in their paths. You know how women act in the street nowadays. Damn shameless, that's how! They no longer wait for a man to come courting, they court him themselves. But I'm not one of them. Goodness, perhaps if I were a bad woman I'd have gotten a beauty for a husband.

I wish I were a happy woman, one whose husband never gave her any reason to be unhappy, but I never got a man like that. I don't know whether I'm selfish in love or what, but from the minute I see a man making up to another woman, that man is nothing to me. I want my man's love all to myself. A man who's attracted to another woman when he has a wife of his own is no man at all. Not to me he isn't. That's why I can't love Eduardo as I once did. And if someday we break up again, it won't mean a thing to me.

Ever since we got back together, Eduardo has been behaving himself. I'm satisfied with the way he's acted so far. He's even good about sharing fairly what little money we have. I've no reason to complain about him on that score, so I take good care of him in return. As long as I'm living with him, he gives me everything for my children. If I left him they'd suffer. I'm an old woman and should think of nothing but my children's upbringing. After I've raised them and they all have houses of their own and good jobs, if I'm not around anymore I won't be missed.

I'm simply waiting for my chance. The minute he makes a slip I'll say, "Well, Eduardo, this is the end of the line for us." And if he says I can't keep the children, what the hell! I have too heavy a load on my mind—housing problems, the problem of keeping the kids in this situation—I'm in no condition to bear up under a man's unfaithfulness on top of everything else. I'm sorry, I simply can't.

Ever since I started living with Eduardo I've been separated from my folks. I wish I were with them. When I brew coffee, I wish the first two cups could be for those two little people, the way it was when I lived with them. And when I cook, I'd like to be able to say, "I'm serving these two plates of food to *mamá* and *papá*. My greatest concern is to be at their bedside when they die. If I'm here in Havana I won't be able to reach them in time. When the lives of those two little old people fall away from me, I won't care to live one hour longer. I say that from the bottom of my heart. As far back as I can remember, I've felt that way. I often brood about it.

According to Eduardo, my problem is that I'm overly fond of my parents and can't live without them. He says it's very wrong to put one's parents ahead of one's children. But you see I've adapted to my parents' ways.

If my father sends me a telegram, "Come at once, I need you," I set off without giving a thought to my husband or anything else. Death is the only thing that could stop me from going to my father's side. No husband, no child of mine means anything to me compared to him. Never in my life will I be able to find another man such as my father. If I died and were born ten times over, I could still never find his equal. Another like him will never be born.

I want a man to be like my father—serious, respectful, hardworking. I love the nobility of his character, his affectionate ways, his kind manner of treating people. He shares his food and his house with others. Whatever he has, he offers with all his heart. He's a sincere man, completely sincere, as round as a *peseta*.[69] Never in my life have I seen my father show one kind of personality today and another one tomorrow. He's always the same. His hopes were all concentrated on his children—that we should be good, that we should study. He only studied the first grade, not even that. He approves of the many schools we have nowadays and hopes his children will study for careers, now that it's so easy to get schooling.

My father is a whole man because he's so loving and decent, because he . . . I can't put it into words. You've got to know him to understand what I mean. When we've been apart for a time, his eyes fill with tears the minute he catches sight of me. Again and again he's urged me, "Come live with me, Sara. You're having such a hard time in Havana. Don't stay there. Come home to your *papá* who loves you. You know you wouldn't be a trouble to me, you who have always been the delight of my home! But now you may turn out to be the greatest tragedy of my life, because the day I hear that man of yours has beaten you will be my last day on earth."

When Eduardo walked out on me, *papá* went to his house and told him off. "You have no right to abandon Sara for any other woman in the whole world," he said. "She's a good woman." *Papá* won't allow anybody to criticize me in front of him. If anybody does, he hates them forever. But if they say, "I love this *negra*, I love her as if she were my own little hoard of gold," then they've won him over.

I went to sleep on *papá*'s lap even when I was ten years old. Until he rocked me in a big rocking chair we had, I couldn't go to sleep. The minute he sat down, I'd go and lie down across his knees. "You're a grown woman now, my child," he'd say. "You already sweep the house and wash the dishes. How much longer must I go on rocking you to sleep?"

"Until I decide to give up sleeping, I guess. I can't fall asleep unless you rock me first."

69. A coin worth one fifth of a *peso*.

When he returned from work, I'd run out to meet him, shouting, "*Papi,* here comes *papi!*" And I'd hug and kiss him, all sweaty as he was. There will never be born another man who's as good a father as my *papá.* He never spanked or scolded us. Whatever pleasure he could afford, he gave us. He didn't like to see us barefoot or ill-dressed. Whenever I had a problem, I'd talk it over with him. Doesn't such a father deserve the best treatment from his children?

If it weren't for my *mamá* and *papá* I wouldn't be in this world, and they raised me in a way no other parents here in Cuba will ever equal. They love their children, worry about us all, and give us moral support. Of course we were good children, too. I've been a good daughter. I've always been obedient and done whatever they ordered me to do. The only worry I've ever brought upon my parents is the fact that I'm unlucky in love.

People say it's children who make the happiness of a married couple. Well, I don't agree. I have eight children and I'm bringing them up—I can't neglect them, they're mine, I already bore them and the worst of it is over and done with—but let me tell you, there's nothing that ages a woman so much as raising kids. And there's nothing worse than being pregnant. It's a horrible feeling, like something coming up, and you simply feel like dying. When I see a woman in such a state, I help her even if I'm not up to it myself because I know how terrible she feels. Sometimes she doesn't feel like doing housework. She lies down and sleeps, and then when her husband gets home, nothing is done. Men realize that a pregnant woman isn't in a normal state and that being pregnant is no laughing matter, and they respect it. At least I've never heard anybody complain of such things or laugh at a pregnant woman for not being her usual self.

No sooner do I conceive than every kind of food becomes repulsive to me and upsets my stomach. The first things I give up are coffee and cigarettes. All I can stand are guavas, green mangoes, and juices. I buy two or three boxes of bicarbonate of soda at one time, but two boxes don't last me one full day. I eat the stuff!

With my last pregnancy I got a craving for cigarette ashes. Every time Eduardo lit a cigarette I'd put a saucer beside him, saying, "Now remember to drop all the ashes in here; I want to eat them." He did as I said and made no objections because he knew it was because of my belly.

During my very first pregnancy, my delight was to eat a small cake of soap every day. That was my breakfast, and how delicious it tasted! It was for that reason that I had a very bad belly, even though when I'm carrying a girl I have no trouble at all.

All the babies I've miscarried have been boys, and they all gave me a horribly bad belly. When I was pregnant with the boy I lost after the exchange, I hated everybody. My brother Bernardo couldn't turn on a light without my eating him up alive. I felt like killing my husband and tearing the kids to pieces when they were naughty. If I could have chewed them up I'd have done it. Eduardo kept telling them, "Leave her in peace, for goodness' sake!"

When he'd get into bed I'd say, "Look here, *chico,* can't you sleep in one of those other beds? You know I don't want you here." Imagine saying that to a man who gets home all tired out from work! I'd be sorry for him after I said it. When he put an arm or leg over me in his sleep, I'd push him away. He always ended up moving to one of the kids' beds because he couldn't get any sleep lying beside me.

As for having relations with me when I'm pregnant, I'd be capable of putting a rope around his neck and strangling him. A man who tries to have sex with a pregnant woman is an inconsiderate beast! The baby can't stand the weight of his body and I feel as if my belly will burst.

I'd been living here in the garage about two months when my baby was stillborn. That day, as soon as Eduardo went off to work, I started washing clothes. I was busy at my tub when Leticia passed by and I said to her, "You know, Leti, I feel sick." She found someone to drive me to Maternity, and at 2:00 o'clock that afternoon the baby was born dead.

When I didn't hear him cry or anything, I wondered what was wrong, but they didn't tell me anything at first. Then I got angry because all the babies but mine had been taken to their mothers. The woman doctor told me, "Don't worry, my child. You lost your baby, but just be quiet and rest so you can get well. You already have plenty of children anyway and they need you." Later the doctor explained to me that a blood clot had gotten into the baby's windpipe and robbed him of the right to be born.

A nurse brought my dead baby for me to see; she'd dressed him and everything. The doctor scolded her for it and told her it was against the rules. The baby's image remained fixed in my eyes. He was so exactly like Eduardo!

I was so unhappy, but I couldn't cry of course. They say you shouldn't weep for a stillborn baby. But no matter what anybody says, when you've carried a child in your womb and gone through labor, the greatest pain a mother ever has to go through.... I'd like to have seen to his burial myself.

The doctors, a man and a woman, kept working on me for eight days, giving me one shot after another, before I was allowed to go home. And then they told me I had to rest one more month after I got home. When the children saw I wasn't bringing a baby home with me, they burst into tears. *Ay,* it cut me to the heart. They kept on asking, "*Mami,* where's the baby?" Eduardo told them we'd left it at the hospital, trying to hide the truth from them. But they already knew because they'd heard the grownups talking. Then Leticia said, "Stop deceiving those kids. Tell them the baby was stillborn."

About two months later I got pregnant with Elsa. She was born in the same hospital. I bore six of my children at home and two in the hospital. It's more or less the same thing, but I like it better at home because I'm more used to it. And at home I can make myself more comfortable and do as I please, not as the doctor tells me. Having one leg here and another there, that's what scared me.

In some ways it's nice being a mother, and in other ways it isn't. It's hard on a woman, for instance, when her children marry and go far away. Every mother would like to keep her children close to her all the time. Take my son Gerardo—I haven't heard from him in six months. That's why I say it's not good to be a mother because you suffer a great deal. Even so, every woman wants to be a mother and know what it's like. A couple without children are all alone.

There's a big difference between having children and having none. Your own personality changes. Before you become a mother, it makes no difference to you whether you sit down and take a nap or go out. Now I'm no longer free to come and go as I will. That's the way it is. Once a woman has children, her life is filled with care.

I didn't want to have any children at all. That must be the reason why I have so many. I didn't like kids; that is, I like other folks' kids all right, but to have them myself . . . well, one or two maybe. I don't want to have any more, but Eduardo says that if he only had a bigger place to live, he'd want more, because he doesn't have any boys by me. He just has the two boys by Pomposa and we've had three girls. You know how it is, you don't want to but your husband does. If I'd never had either a husband or children I could have done so much!

There used to be lots of women in my barrio who induced abortions, but I don't know how they did it. *Mamá* miscarried, but always from natural causes like falling down or something. I've heard stories about how some women abort by taking things, but it's only lately that one knows about the ring. Before, there was nothing, and one wasn't allowed to have an abortion either.

Not long ago I was hospitalized for loss of blood. It turned out I'd been two and a half months pregnant and the loss of blood was a miscarriage. When they told me that, I wanted to have a ring inserted, but they said it couldn't be done at that time. They told me, "If you always menstruate so heavily, the ring would be washed out every time. You simply can't use a ring, it wouldn't work for you."

"All right, then tie my tubes," I said.

"No, no. We can't tie your tubes when your womb is perfectly healthy. That could do you a lot of harm."[70]

"Well then, what are you going to do for me?"

70. According to Elizabeth Sutherland, at that time a woman could have a tubal ligation only if she were over thirty-eight and had had five children. (*The Youngest Revolution,* p. 178.) Sara was not old enough to qualify.

"We'll put you under treatment, then see what can be done," the doctor said.

"And meanwhile I keep on having more and more children?" I protested. "I only wish you could see how we live! I *can't* have any more children."

"It would be worse if we tied your tubes and you died of it," he told me. I don't know what it is they see in my insides that makes them say that. But then he said if I followed his course of treatment, they'd try a ring later. They'll have to do something!

I love all my children equally. I play no favorites. When they get sick, I take each one wherever he needs to be taken to get well. But in my heart, I feel somehow closer to Estela than to the others because she and I are so alike.

Estela has been living with my parents since she was six months old, but she's always known that I'm her mother. I saw her every day because we lived right next to *papá* and *mamá*. When I moved to Marianao, I kept her about fifteen days, but she couldn't adapt so I sent her back. She was a fairly big girl then, five or six years old. Of course I missed her and asked if she wanted to come back to Havana with me. But she said, "No, I'm staying here with Grandma." Now that she's bigger, the young lady says she's coming to live here. She keeps crying, "I want to be with *mamá*, I want to be with *mamá*." So even though she never lived with me, I haven't lost my daughter. If I had, would she be wanting to live with me now?

The last time Violeta visited my parents, she brought Estela back to Havana with her. They simply decided to come on the impulse of the moment and set off without giving it a second thought. The truth is I was very surprised when Estela showed up.

Estelita is in the fifth grade, and while she was here she was out of school for fifteen days. I talked to the school director and she said she'd admit Estelita, but only to the first grade. The reason was that Estela had no papers to prove she'd ever been in school. They must have an official statement of the tests she's passed in school—her school record—before they can admit her to any grade but the first. The director said it would be best for her to go back to the country and continue the fifth grade there. Then, after she finished fifth grade, I could get a release and transfer her to a school here.

When I told Estelita she took it hard. She burst into tears when I sent her back to Oriente. You could hear the screams a mile away. "You see? She doesn't love me," she told the other kids.

"But child," said I, "you aren't going to stay there forever. You're coming back home. I'm going to get you myself." I think perhaps she doesn't trust me to go and get her. You see, I'd told her the same thing before and then didn't go. But I did explain, "Look, my child, I didn't go to get you because I couldn't."

I don't know what's the matter with Estelita. I've got it into my skull that maybe she wants a career, and that's one thing she can't get out in the country. She told me she wants to study, but she didn't say what. The way she put it is, "Say, *mami*, I wish I had a career. Give me a boost, will you? If you'd only let me stay with you in Havana, the people at the school would fill in the blanks for me so I could go on to secondary school." Well, looked at from that angle, she's got something there, I don't deny it.

They teach differently out in the country; here in Havana the kids learn a lot more. Here there are classes morning and afternoon, but out there school is open only in the morning. The school she goes to is quite near my parents' home. It has all the elementary grades, and according to the children they've had good teachers and middling teachers there. The latest was a young girl with no more than a second- or third-grade education—the kids knew more than she did. There are no regular teachers now because they all have to do agricultural work. I thought the children were lying, but the director of the school here said, "Yes, it's true. That happens in a lot of rural schools—the teachers have to stay away because of all the work there is to be done outside." Heck, I couldn't believe it!

What am I going to do if Estela doesn't get a release from the school? She won't be able to go to school here or in Oriente. I'm taking all the steps to go to Oriente and get her as soon as the summer vacation starts in July. The important thing is to resolve the girl's problem. I told Eduardo that if by any chance I couldn't take all the kids along with me, he'd have to get leave from work to stay home with them. He agreed to do it.

I treat both Estela and Violeta just the same, but I'm sorry for Estela because she looks so depressed. She doesn't seem to get any joy out of life; there's nothing gay or happy about her. Violeta is different—she's always happy. I'm very affectionate with her, and she and I always have a lot to talk about. We have long conversations, wondering how her sisters and brothers are doing and things like that.

I don't know what makes Violeta fight so with her younger brothers and sisters. It's not jealousy or anything, not any more at least. I guess they provoke her, but she sure hits them a lot and gets mad if they cry. Then I spank her, but if you so much as lay a finger on her she yells bloody murder.

There's a lot of good in that kid though. When I'm sick, she gets all generous and noble-hearted. She scurries around, sweeping, cooking the meals, and doing whatever has to be done, quiet as a mouse. And she'll warn the others not to make any noise.

When Violeta was thirteen or fourteen, I took her to stay with her grandparents and she went to the same school as Estelita. Naturally she's fallen behind, but even before that she was behind, because they didn't teach her anything in that country school and she lost an awful lot of time. When she came back to Havana, the school here gave her a test and she flunked it, so they put her back.

Violeta has been out of school for most of the last two years. A teacher at Hilario's school was going to help me get her into a night school, but then the teacher was transferred someplace else and I lost her address. So I haven't been able to do anything about it. Then I talked with some other people and they told me she was too young to get a job, too.

I think Violeta is intelligent, and as soon as she starts working and studying I know she'll make progress fast. She was a good student and always got good marks. She got a lot out of school as long as she was there.

All my children are doing well in school. Amanda María will soon be ten and is in the second grade, Faustina is seven and in the first grade, and Hilario is thirteen and in the fourth grade. He could have been in the sixth grade by now, but he was a very sickly child and had to spend most of his time in the hospital. He wants to get a scholarship for the school of the Camilitos, a very good military school that Fidel has for the sons of soldiers. But he'll have to complete the sixth grade first.

I had fewer problems with the kids when we lived in the second-floor apartment. Up there they were model children. With plenty of room to play, they never bothered anybody. It was easy to keep them clean, too, because the house was clean. They could lie down wherever they wanted and didn't have to play in the dirt. But what clean place is there for them to play in this garage? There are days when I've cleaned the place out four times with bucketfuls of water, and they still get so grimy it's pitiful. And yet, every single day, from Monday on, I wash clothes.

When parents tell you they never hit their children, you may be sure they're lying. Any child will sometimes be naughty, and then you have to spank him or punish him some way. I never punish my children harshly, no sir, not me! Usually I spank them with my hand or pull their ears, that's all. I've never struck them hard. I'd rather tie them up than do that. I keep a rope expressly for that purpose.

The children behave better when Eduardo is here. I find it harder to look after them when he's away because they don't mind me. He says it's all my fault because I don't punish them enough. I defend myself from that accusation. "Listen, Eduardo, if I punished these kids any oftener than I do, they'd all be dead by now."

I don't know what's in my children's minds—whether they want to take advantage of their upbringing or sink into a life of crime. Kids here are practically raised in the street, and you've got to tell them to look sharp because this is the city. But they pay no attention to me. It isn't that they're intentionally bad, but they don't have the good sense we have. There's no point in explaining to them why they shouldn't do things, they simply won't understand. This new bunch are all alike.

Sometimes I'm bursting with rage against all of them. I'd like to eat them up, kill them—that's the truth. Maybe I feel that way because I wasn't raised like them. There were eleven of us kids at home, but we never in our lives gave our *mamá* any trouble. She'll tell you that we were eleven noble-hearted boys and girls. But as for my kids, ever since we've lived in the garage it's been hell.

From the very moment your child is born, you must teach him and explain to him that you're his mother. You must tell your children how you carried them in your womb for a long time and fed them with milk from your breasts, and all the trouble you've taken for them. And yet, there are many children who never make their mother a proper return for the trouble and grief of bringing them up, or for the nine months they grew in her womb, or the pain she had bearing them. Oh yes indeed, there are many ungrateful children in this world!

Look, maybe I'm wrong, but I'd rather die myself than lose one of my children. If any of them died before I did, I don't know what would happen to me. I'd go crazy, I think, or kill myself, or God knows what. I can't help crying when I think about such things. I don't know why such thoughts come into my head at all. I just hope that when my children are all grown men and women, I'll die a peaceful death before I have to see any of them die.

Eduardo Rojas

I was born in December, 1939, at home on the Miranda *central*. The place we lived in was called a *chucho*—that's where they have a crane for unloading the cut cane. They put up a few rows of houses there and a barracks, because they employed a lot of people. When the Revolution came, all that was torn down and everybody got a house—there are sixty or seventy houses there now. I knew everybody living in the *chucho* and several of the families were relatives of ours. Sara's father never lived in our *chucho*, but he used to come to work in the cane and he borrowed the *colonia*'s oxen to plow his farm. They lived about a kilometer and a half away.

I don't know how many *chuchos* there were on the Miranda *central*. There was a no. 1 and a no. 44, but there are more than that. During the *zafra*,[71] people came from all over to cut cane. And when it was over, they all went away and only the people who lived in the *chucho* were left.

Our *chucho* had a store that sold clothing and shoes and a grocery store with food and liquor and such. The grocery store also had a counter, and there was a very small lunch stand. We had a cockfighting arena too, but that was outside the *chucho* itself.

There was another *chucho* about half a kilometer away, but it belonged to an American. We got along well with the people there. The only difference between the two was that they had a better work situation, better opportunities. The American kept them on, giving them odd jobs during the dead season, which was the hard time of year. Our company didn't do that. When the working season was over, that was it.

I was the first child my *mamá* and *papá* had together. Of my six older brothers and sisters, five were my father's children and one was born to *mamá* before she came to live with my *papá*. My father's name is Euquerio Rojas Quiñones, and my mother's name is Dinorah Raventos López. They separated when I was about ten years old. I don't know why. It made me very unhappy.

71. Sugar-cane harvest, approximately six months between January and July.

My *mamá* left us and remarried right away—to Laertes Navarro, who's the uncle of Sara's sister-in-law, Ana Teresa. They're still living together and have four boys and two girls. I don't know most of them by their real names, only by their nicknames.

I can't tell you much about my mother and how she'd have treated me, because she didn't bring me up. I can't put the blame on her or anybody. There's nothing to say. She might have liked to have me with her, but she just didn't mix with the old man and his habits.

If you only knew how hard life was for us, living with my old man. After my sister Jacinta married, my brother Amadeo and I were left alone in the house. We were still little kids but we had to cook and take care of the house. My brother Luis was still too young to help. Then my father got another woman. Luisa Escobar had children and a husband, but my father took her away from the other guy. It didn't last long, because when my father saw that she didn't treat us very well, they separated.

The truth is, I practically brought myself up, with only my *papá* to look after me. I still loved my mother even after she left us, but I'll be frank with you, I love my *papá* more. He's the one who's gone through all the troubles with us.

I still sought out my mother and I used to visit her when I was a child. After all, she only lived four or five blocks from us. She was always glad to see me, but then she went to live on a farm in the Sierra and I didn't see her for about two years. I've never deserted her. In fact when they were in the Sierra I did a lot for her. Her husband has always been a roughneck, and he and one of his brothers got into a row in the Sierra and killed a man. While they were both in prison I went up there to take care of my mother. I worked and gave her all I earned. She had three or four children by then.

My old man was a thousand times harder on me than I am on my children. If I did anything he didn't like, he'd beat me with a new ox whip made of rope. Sometimes he'd wait until I was in bed, then he'd grab me, tie me up, and beat me with a rope while I writhed around stark naked. He was likely to punch you, or kick you, or anything—he was a real brute! My old man has sons of forty-odd years who have ten children of their own, but they don't dare say one dirty word to him because he'd bash their heads in. Those old people in Oriente were like that. Nowadays you see kids who'll say anything to their parents.

Papá didn't even know how to read or write. During the Literacy Campaign a teacher came and he took classes, but he didn't learn a thing. All he likes are fighting cocks; he's raised them from the time he was a boy. He had a brace of roosters, too. I got knocked around a lot for forgetting to give them water or letting one get loose.

The last time I got into a fight I was cutting cane as a volunteer. Townspeople everywhere hate the cane-cutters, I don't know why. It's true that we cane-cutters are bastards, going around getting drunk and starting rows, ruining parties for everybody.

This fight was in a social club. A whole gang jumped a cane worker from our contingent. They knocked him to the floor and formed a circle around him. When I saw them all swinging at him, I went to break up the fight and they began to beat on me too. Someone socked me in the eye, but later I told people that a stalk of cane hit me, because I felt too ashamed to tell the truth about it. I took out my gun but couldn't go after him because the others fell on me. It's just as well because I was so excited I might have wounded the guy.

I had on regular civilian work clothes, but I always carry my revolver with me and I had it in my hand when the police came. They took me to the station but didn't hold me more than five minutes. I didn't have to show my identification card; they didn't even ask me for my name. They told me to hand over my pistol but they gave it back to me when I left. What they wanted to know was why I'd taken it out.

"Well," I said, "this fellow is from our contingent of cane-cutters and seven men ganged up on him. When I saw such a mob scene I took out my revolver, that's all."

The only thing they said to me was, "Comrade, that isn't the right way to go about it."

I slept with my first woman in Oriente. She was one of those low women that men used to bring around on payday during the sugar-cane harvest. They didn't have houses or anything. The fellow would root around and find some old sacking and throw it down on the ground right in the field. Of course it had to be far away from the mill, because if we'd been caught, or had gotten a disease off one of those women, the procurer would have been in a spot.

I knew the guy, that first time, but he didn't say anything to me. He'd just come to the *batey* and call out, "This way!"—something like that— and the men and the big boys would come up and he'd tell them where to go. Then he'd stand outside with his big knife and collect the *pesos*. Guys like him were called *chulos*. The men who paid to go to the prostitutes were called *puntos*.

I was still barefooted when I first went. It had been raining a lot and my feet were all muddy. I paid the guy my *peso* and he said, "Go in over there."

The place he chose was like a pathway through the cane field. He'd stand in front of the row of cane to take the money. When I went behind the cane the girl was standing there, stark naked. I knew her because I'd seen her around before. She was almost a little girl, only thirteen. When she saw me she lay down. She didn't say a word. I already knew what I had to do; that is, I knew where to put my thing. I think we're born knowing that. I was only there a few minutes. It was just a kid's idea of it.

Up and down a couple of times and that was it. Then I got up and left without saying anything. What was there to say?

I liked it all right and it became a habit with me after that. I went a lot in Santiago, while I was in the Army studying at the school there. We all went to the same girl, whether it was one of us or twenty, and one right after the other. They had water and towels there so we could wash afterward.

I had girl friends before Sara but I don't remember their names. One had a husband and broke up with him on account of me, even though she never slept with me. She went away to the Sierra Maestra and I never went after her.

I've known Sara ever since I was a boy, not more than ten. She was married and living with her first husband then, but they got along worse and worse until they finally separated. I began to court her in 1959.

I used to go to Sara's brother's house and I got to know her when I played dominoes there. We kept getting more and more interested in each other, but I didn't try to talk with her there because her sister-in-law and my nephew were around. I went to her own house. At first I'd just drop in and we'd chat. Later, when we were *novios,* I'd take her things to eat. I didn't bring her any presents because times were pretty bad then.

I worked on the *colonia,* hoeing and such. I wasn't paid by the day but by the hour. I didn't have any regular working hours, it depended on the work. We'd start at 6:00 in the morning and leave off for lunch at noon, then work from 2:00 o'clock until 4:00 or 5:00. I ate the midday meal at my sister's and visited Sara at night or late in the afternoon, and on Sundays.

Sara's personality was the same as it is now. I don't know how others feel but I think she has a good disposition. At least she's serious-minded and doesn't go flirting around. Of course, now she's settled and doesn't go in for any of that nonsense. Most of the time she's cheerful, too. It depends though; she can get annoyed or angry, but she's not a sour type of person. She's never bad-tempered, except maybe when we have a quarrel, but that isn't very often. She's happiest when some relative comes to visit, either my family or her own, it doesn't matter. Even when she's just doing housework she has days when she's really happy.

When I began courting Sara I told her, "I'm in love with you and I'm offering myself." She didn't say anything except to ask me whether I was just playing with her, because I was practically a boy and she had five children. I told her no, that wasn't what I planned to do, that my being in love with her meant I wanted to take care of her. Otherwise I wouldn't call it love. At first Sara said no, because she had the children. "If that's the way you feel about it, all right," I said. But finally she said yes. We were *novios* only about four or five months.

When we got married my father didn't have anything to say, but Sara's did. People say he told her she didn't know what she was doing, that I was just a boy and so forth. And other members of her family told her to look before she leaped. I took her off to my grandparents' to get her away from them. Also I thought that it looked worse for me to stay there with her than to take her away. If it's just an affair, that's different. Or if you marry legally, you can stay on in a house like that, but not if you live common-law. In the country most couples do what we did.

When I took Sara away, the children stayed behind with their grandparents. Then the next day I came back alone and talked with Sara's family and they said we could live in the little house Sara had been living in. Sara came later that afternoon to pick up the children and we went home.

The house we lived in was made of wood and palm thatching, with an earth floor. It had a bedroom, a living room, and a kitchen. I didn't have to buy furniture because Sara had everything we needed. The privy was a little outhouse with a palm-thatch roof.

We bathed in the house or in the river nearby. When it was very cold we'd heat water and bathe behind the house or in the bedroom, whichever we liked. We didn't have a bathtub there. We had to go down the hill to the well and then carry the water pails back up to the house.

Shortly after I married Sara, I joined the Army with several of her brothers. I was sent to Santiago for basic training, but Sara stayed behind in Monte dos Leguas. When I came home on leave, Sara and I moved our house to *chucho* 9, where my family lived. My uncle gave me a little piece of land and I set the house up there. My father and I did it together, using the materials from the house we'd torn down. At the *colonia* I borrowed a wagon and a yoke of oxen to move all our furniture and household things.

The amount of time needed to dismantle a house and put it up again depends on how many hands you have. My father and I took down our house in two days, and it took the two of us about five to rebuild it. The re-roofing was the toughest job. Our new house was just like the other.

In both our houses Sara cooked on a wooden stove. It's an oblong box with a wooden bottom and sides, about 80 centimeters high. The stove itself doesn't burn up because you fill it with earth, put bricks on top of the earth, and the firewood on top of that. We used kerosene lamps for light because there was no electricity in *chucho* 9 at that time. About half the houses in the *chucho* have electricity now. We didn't pipe water in but the river passed near the house. And we didn't have to walk so far to the grocery there.

In Monte dos Leguas we kept pigs, chickens, and goats. I had a filly of my own there, too. We fed the animals cooked vegetable peelings and sugar cane. We had a lot of chickens in Monte dos Leguas but even more at *chucho* 9, at least twenty hens, and six or seven roosters also. That spring our sow dropped a litter of six, the young mare foaled, and two of the goats were carrying young. We also got two pairs of rabbits for Amanda.

We kept the animals for our own use. We'd slaughter an animal when we needed it. Sometimes if you needed money you'd sell them, but we never had to do that, although I did sell the mare. And once Sara gave a hog in exchange for a sewing machine. We were more interested in barter than in selling outright. The truth is, once I got outside work we didn't want for anything. I got my 40 *pesos* regularly and we were doing all right. We spent the money on food, rice and such things, and on clothes. We shopped in *chucho* 9 and also *chucho* 10.

I don't think we lived especially well. Today everybody has what we had then, animals and all. My old man still keeps animals there. And they have corn, squash, and sweet potatoes planted. The plot isn't very large, not even a block long or wide, but it's enough.

When we came to Havana we left the house to my sister. We wanted to have it there in case we didn't get anything here and had to go back. My sister has moved since and lives near the new *batey*, but when I go back for a visit I can stay at my relative's house there, and Sara can too.

My basic training course was held at one of the Santiago beaches and lasted about five or six months. After that I was stationed in a lot of different places. From the school I was sent to Palma Mocha, then to the Guantánamo base, San Pedrito, El Castillo, and finally to another spot whose name I can't remember. My unit was working at the Santiago fair, too. In all those places we stayed in dugouts. I didn't like the work but I had no choice. My starting pay was 40 *pesos* a month.

When we were ordered to Havana they didn't tell us where we were going. They just told us to turn in our arms so they could be taken to the train. Then we went to the station at Santiago de Cuba and boarded the train, each man with his own company. But I didn't know where I was off to. In the Army they just said, "Get on board," and you went wherever the train took you. That's just the way it is. So I didn't have time to let anybody know I was leaving, and I was here nine months without seeing anybody in the family. They had news from me because I sent them letters.

I couldn't read a word then, so when a letter came for me, I had to take it to a comrade to read, and then one of them had to write my answer. This embarrassed me a lot. I said to myself, "This is too much. I've just got to learn to read and write." At that time we were living in dugouts, all covered over except for the entrance. I took a bottle and made myself a lamp with a wick from a kerosene lamp, and I'd work in the dugout, putting letters together to make words. I already knew the alphabet but I didn't know how to join the letters. One of my comrades was in a little field house nearby, and when I didn't understand something I'd go ask him. One day he said he'd teach me. He began giving me lessons, but it was just a little bit from time to time. Later I went to the school in Regla, but I didn't learn very much there either. Then they gave me classes in the unit. Little by little I learned, though I still don't know much.

Lately I've been taking classes in the Ministry, but right now they're suspended for the sugar-harvest mobilization. When they start up again I have to go because it's obligatory. I'm only at the fourth-grade level, if that, but I plan to finish at least the sixth grade. To this day reading is an effort for me. I'd rather listen to Fidel's speeches than read them, because when I hear something it stays in my mind better.

I stayed in Havana until I was given a pass, then I went to Oriente. The first time I went back, things were so changed! Man, it was like a different world! Sara gave me a great welcome. But her little girl didn't even know who I was, can you beat that? She said I wasn't her *papá*. She thought her *papá* was my father, whom she saw every day, but she'd never set eyes on me. Everybody was happy that day. I'd brought a machine gun and I let off a few rounds to celebrate. I could only stay a few days before I had to go back.

My unit was stationed at Camp Managua then and I lived in the barracks. When I went out, I rode the bus right to the end of the line and all the way around back to where I started, never getting off. I was afraid to get off because I didn't know the city at all. "No sir," I said to myself, "I'm not getting stranded here."

One time I got off in Marianao, and as I was standing there in a big park waiting for the next bus, two bombs went off in a building nearby. That was in the early years, when people were getting killed by those bombs all the time. It wasn't too close, maybe half a block away, but I was so startled I just stood there and didn't even go to see what had happened. When the bus came I didn't get on; I was too flabbergasted.

Another thing that bothered me was you couldn't drink water or coffee or buy sweets in lots of places because you might get poisoned. In fact, at the beginning, soldiers and police were forbidden to eat and drink things on the street. There were *gusanos* all over the place then, and there are still a lot of bad people around. I never had any comrades who were poisoned that way, but we knew of a lot of cases. And not only the military but just ordinary people. When the scholarship program began, some of the students were killed. I guess nobody wants to talk about that, but it's true. They found a scholarship student dead right there under the Marianao bridge. Somebody had thrown him off the bridge. There were a lot of such cases.[72]

72. Although several student teachers in the Literacy Campaign were murdered, we are unable to verify this report of the murder of scholarship students in Havana.

Later I started going out with my comrades from Havana and got to know my way around. Some of them would take one of us out someplace or maybe to their homes. One of the first places I went to was the Hippodrome. At that time they still had horse races there.

I went back to Oriente about five months after my first visit. And a few months after I got back to Havana I found out where my uncles and other relatives lived, so I sent a telegram asking Sara to come here. She came with Amanda, who was just a little tot then. The other children stayed behind with my *papá*.

When I saw Sara I went running over to hug and kiss her. After that we got on the bus and went to my uncle's house. He was very happy to see Sara. Anyway, I told my uncle that she'd come to stay for good and he said, "That's all right, son, no problem." He was in the Army and slept at the barracks like me. His wife lived alone with her mother, a little old lady. They all adored Amanda.

Some country people are afraid of everything in the city, but Sara used to go to the supermarket near the house. She's a bright woman and knows how to get along. By now she can go anywhere herself. And to think that at the beginning I was afraid to get off the bus because I thought I might get lost! I'm not going to say I know the entire city now, but I know a lot of it, and the countryside outside of Havana, too, especially the small towns.

The worst problem I had with Sara was when I took another wife. Sara is my common-law wife, but I'm legally married to Pomposa Padilla. We have two sons. The older one is named Francisco Rojas Padilla and the younger . . . it's slipped my mind. Oh yes, Liborio, that's his name. I named the older and she chose the name for the younger. She wanted a little girl but I like boys better. I lived with Pomposa for a little over two years but right now we're on the outs. I haven't abandoned her though. I give her 30 *pesos* a month and visit the boys often.

I met Pomposa late in 1963, or maybe the beginning of 1964. There was this young girl walking down the street and I fell in love with her. My unit's CDR was across the street from her house and a lot of people in it were from Oriente. So I'd drop around there from time to time and I'd see her, but I never got a chance to talk with her or anything. Then one day I did speak to her and wanted to have a conversation. She didn't answer me, so I told her I was going to send her a letter. At that time I was just learning to read and write and I had a comrade write it for me. He didn't know I was already living with Sara.

I don't know what was in the letter. He put whatever he thought was best in it. But she answered, saying she was very new at all this and that she was studying. I wrote her another letter and told her it didn't matter, that I was willing to wait. And she answered yes.

She was just fourteen and in the second or third grade then. We kept regular company for about four or five months. Once I told her I had a wife and children but she didn't believe me and kept seeing me. After we became sweethearts I told her again, in case she wanted to change her mind, but she didn't pay any attention.

I'd already told Sara I had a girl friend, because her brother Fabiano lived near there, and Bernardo knew too, and since she was their sister they were sure to tell her. Sara was mad and refused to go to bed with me. She told me to go sleep with the other one. This lasted a couple of months. But I came home every day and coaxed and petted her. And I gave her a little extra money. After a while she was happy again. It was easy. I told her, "Look, I'm not going to leave you for anybody else. I'm not going to abandon you, but I want you to stay quiet here at home. If you go over to Pomposa's house, we'll have a fight." And she said all right, that she had no reason to go there. It wasn't long, though, before Sara turned up at Pomposa's house. Somebody took her there, I don't know who. Anyway she went and told Pomposa's mother that she, Sara, was my wife and so forth.

I learned about it that same day while I was still at work. "Oh Lord," I said, "things have certainly gone bad." I had a lot of my things at Pomposa's house but I didn't want to pick them up, because I was afraid the old folks would say something to me since I'd told them I was single.

I went to Sara's first and I was mad. "Look," I said, "I made it very clear that there would be trouble between us if you went there. Well, you did it and you can take the consequences." That's all I said. Then I got my things together and took them all over to the barracks. On the way I passed by Pomposa's. They were all in bed and she was crying. What a mess! I thought everything between us was over. So I said to Pomposa, "Get my things together because I'm going to take them with me." I was carrying an army knapsack for my belongings.

I called for her mother but she wouldn't see me. All the time I was putting my things in the knapsack, Pomposa was tugging at it and crying. "Listen," I said, "please don't cry. Nothing's happened." And I left.

I didn't go back until about a week later, because I was off cutting cane at the Hershey *central*. All that time I couldn't get the thing out of my mind.

I came back to Havana with my brother Luis. When I got to Pomposa's house, everybody was sleeping. There I was, standing outside the house, and I decided that if Pomposa still cared for me, I'd take her with me. The house was a run-down wooden shack and I knew where Pomposa's room was. So I got a long thin stick and shoved it through a crack so that it disturbed her mosquito netting. She got up, peeped through the crack, and saw me. I made a sign for her to get up. When she did I said to myself, "If the chick's getting up, she must still go for me."

After we'd talked a little I said, "If it's true that you still go for me, I'll take you with me." She said yes, she'd go. So that very night I took her to a comrade's house several kilometers from Regla, because I had to go back to the cane. I didn't go to bed with her then.

The next day I went back to her parents' house early in the morning. One of her brothers—she has four of them and two sisters—was outside in the yard and I told him I wanted to talk with the old lady. But the stepfather came and said she had nothing to say to me. So I just called out, loud enough for them all to hear, "I just came to do you the favor of letting you know I'm the one who took Pomposa away."

It seems the stepfather was against my taking Pomposa, and he told the mother not to speak with me. When Pomposa went home to pick up her things, her parents lodged a charge against me with the police. I received a court summons and appeared there. They asked me if I planned to marry her and I said yes, I did. We were married in Regla several months later. That was in 1964.

During all that time, Sara was in Oriente. She must have told my *mamá* what was going on between Pomposa and me because *mamá* knew about it. I have no idea whose side my mother was on because I never spoke to her about it and she never said anything either, except that she was always giving me advice to look before I leaped and things like that.

After we were married, Pomposa's mother told us we could come to live at their house. Imagine, she broke up with her husband over this. I get along fine with Pomposa's brothers and we go out together sometimes, or one of them may drop around to see me at work. But it was hard to get any privacy in that house. All of us slept in the same room, though Pomposa and I had our own bed.

One of the brothers, Cheo, had poliomyelitis and slept with the mother even though he was almost grown. He must have been eleven or twelve then, but he has this trouble with his legs. He's always falling down and he's a little soft in the head, not very bright, though he talks all right. The other two brothers slept in another bed, and the sister, Ida, on a mattress on the floor. She was living there because she'd divorced her husband, but she didn't have her two children with her because he took them.

When Pomposa and I did get a chance to sleep together, nobody spied on us or woke up or anything. And they didn't make jokes about sex or pass remarks the next day. But our bed always made noise. It wouldn't have been any better sleeping on the floor because there were so many mosquitoes and we needed the mosquito netting for the baby. There wasn't even any point in buying a crib for him because it wouldn't fit into the room.

When it was time to sleep we had to move out the furniture—two or three straight chairs, the table, a couple of easy chairs, the ironing board, and a few other odds and ends—to make room for the beds. Two of the beds stayed in the living room during the day but the old lady's bed had to be taken up, and we stored the sister's mattress on a shelf made by the crossbeams. Later on her brother and I hunted up some boards at the warehouse and made a tiny room up in a corner of the rafters. The old lady was very happy about that. You can imagine what it meant to her.

Shortly after we got married I took Pomposa to Oriente. We stayed at my father's house while I worked a sugar harvest there. During the harvest they always give cultural programs and parties. I went to one with Pomposa, and Sara went too, because she had brothers in the harvest. Even though Sara didn't tell me she was coming to Oriente then, I already knew about it through someone else. But I wasn't worried, because she hadn't seen or talked with Pomposa since that time she went to see her at home.

While I was up front taking part in the program, it seems that Sara came along and tried to pick a quarrel with Pomposa. One of my little brothers came up to me and said, "Look over there, Eduardo, Sara wants to beat up Pomposa." So I went over and saw that Sara was threatening the girl. Sara is always the tough one. She was doing all the talking. Pomposa wasn't saying anything.

It was all words, just passing words. Neither one of them was crying. But Pomposa was afraid. She was nothing but a girl and never had to deal with any problems.

I stepped between them. "You've got it all wrong," I said. "As long as I'm around, you don't touch this girl. You're crazy if you lift a finger to her. I'm the only family she has here." And I said to Pomposa, "Let's get out of here and go home." Sara didn't say anything.

During the time I lived there with Pomposa I didn't have any feeling for Sara and I didn't help support her. I don't know exactly how she managed to get along. But she had her brothers, Panchito and David, and it seems to me Nardo was there too. Probably they took care of her. Later when I came back to Havana and began working I was able to give her money for my children again.

While I was living in Regla with Pomposa, Sara was in the big house in Miramar. I used to come around every once in a while then. I even stayed overnight and so forth. I started by chatting with her and telling her we should go back together again. I don't think she was really too angry, because after all that had happened she used to give me everything—coffee, meals, and all—even when she was living alone in the big house and I was only visiting. At first she'd say to me, "Look here, you're with that woman out there," but in the end she accepted me. To convince her, I just petted and caressed her. I guess Sara suffered over what happened, but not as much as she made out. You know how women are.

During that time I'd spend a week or so with Pomposa and then come back over to Miramar to see the children. Then when Sara got over her fit of jealousy, I stayed over here because we were in that moving mess.

The reason Pomposa and I parted is that our economic situation was very bad. At that time my job didn't pay enough and her mother's house was worse than our garage. It was just an old wooden hut with a cardboard roof. There were eight persons living there: her mother, three brothers, a sister, ourselves and the baby, our older boy.

I had friends around there and I was ashamed to have them drop in and visit me. So I said to her, "Look, let's leave; this isn't the place for us. We're too short of money." I told her that if she wanted we could go to Oriente, where I could build us a house or fix one up or else stay with my family there. But she wanted to stay with her mother, so I went off to Oriente alone. I was fed up. A woman of mine has to be where I am. If it's otherwise and her family rules her, let her stay with her family.

While I was in Oriente, Sara came and we were together for a while. When I returned to Havana, I came back here to the big house; I started working again and sent for Sara.

If Pomposa had gone to Oriente with me there wouldn't have been any trouble with Sara. I'd have left her in the big house, where she was living then. But since Pomposa didn't want to leave, I just went without her. And she's been mad at me ever since. I think she considers me the one who broke things off because I left. It's been almost three years now.

Even though we're separated, Pomposa hasn't divorced me. I don't sleep with her now, but she doesn't have anyone else so far. If she wants to look for another husband I'm not stopping her. It's nothing to me.

Once I talked to the old lady about the children's future and offered to take Pomposa and the children because I had enough to bring them up, so they wouldn't want for anything. She told me she'd talked to Pomposa and told her she'd do better to come back with me than to take another man and give the children a stepfather. But Pomposa was stubborn and still mad at me. I've told her myself that if she takes another man she'll have to give up the children. I'll come and get them and bring them here to the house.

My children Faustina and Amanda know that I have others because I brought them to the house. And Sara treated them fine. Of course it may have been only on the surface, but she was nice to them. I think she'd take good care of them. She's very fond of them because, after all, they're my children, and if she doesn't care for them she doesn't care for me either. See how fond I've become of her children—the ones that aren't mine—and give them everything? That's the rule here. She has to be the same as me. The truth is, Sara would rather have the children here instead of my having to give the money to support them there.

I don't use anything to keep from having more children and neither does Sara. She's never gone to the doctor to ask him for anything. But if you don't want to have children, that's easy. You just have to control yourself and not let the thing go while you're inside. The woman doesn't have to worry. You just pull the critter out in time. I always do it that way. I told Pomposa that I can do it for her, too, but she doesn't believe me. She thinks if I go to bed with her we'll have another child, and she isn't having any. She's never asked me to come live with her again. When I take the money she just says hello and that's about all. Quite a few times I've sounded her out, but what the heck, no interest at all.

Sara doesn't know about this. Although I've told her, "You know, I've been trying to get to Pomposa, but she isn't interested." All Sara does is laugh. Maybe it irritates her that I say these things, but she doesn't let on. She's just happy the other doesn't want to. Sara knows very well that if Pomposa wanted, I'd lay her quick as a flash. I'd be there with bells on.

When I think of the two families, Sara's and Pomposa's, there's no comparison. Pomposa's family is half crazy—no, I don't mean that exactly—not very bright is more like it. The one with polio works once in a while, but he's not up to much and all he earns is peanuts. One brother is strong and healthy and has a wife and two children and her mother living with them. But he loves to drink. That guy drinks and drinks and is always leaving his jobs.

Almost a year ago a hurricane flooded Pomposa's home. When the government saw what had happened they gave the old lady a new house, mostly because of the two little children. If there hadn't been babies in the family, the government might not have done it. It's a private house, a really good one made of masonry. Whoever used to live there left the country. It's a large, roomy house with four bedrooms, two baths, a kitchen, a living room, and a porch.

Nobody in Pomposa's house is working now. I don't know how they're going to manage. They're trying to make do with the money I give for the children. And they have to pay for the house and furniture and all. A broken family is an awful tangle.

Even though I've offered to go back to Pomposa, I don't think I'd accept that now. Sure I'll go to bed with her if I get the chance, and I'll keep paying the expenses. But I can't take charge of two households anymore. I'll be frank—Pomposa attracts me more, but Sara is the better wife from my point of view. The only edge Pomposa has is that she's stronger and fresher, that's all. Sara's more affectionate and sweeter and wants to be closer to me. She really is a homebody. I have three children with Sara now and I don't want to make a change. Pomposa can go her way and I'll go mine.

It used to be easier for men to have a wife and also another little woman in a separate house. Before the Revolution any man might have two or three women, and some had even more. The custom is on its way out now. It began to lose popularity when the Party was organized, because anyone who belongs to the Party isn't supposed to do that kind of thing. It's all right for the man on the street, but even there things have changed a lot.

I'm not bucking for Party membership. The truth is, I don't ask for anything. I just work and try to do the best I can. But since it's no longer the thing to do, I'm not going to have two women. A casual thing, yes, if I don't have to give anything for their support. I'll have as many as I can, as long as I don't have to keep them. Right now I don't have any women. Well, I do visit Pomposa, but that's because I'm giving money for the children.

Not speaking of Pomposa or Sara in particular, these are the qualities I look for in a woman. I don't care for a gadabout. My woman should look after me and the house and not be running around. She should know what it means to be a housewife. Of course I like our going out together, and I wouldn't prevent her from going out either, but this business of a woman spending all her time in a neighbor's house or some other place is something I don't care for. Then, of course she shouldn't do me dirty. I'm not looking for horns.

I like a woman who's affectionate with the children and takes good care of them, but she's got to be wide-awake too. You've got to be on the ball with children. A mother who goes about wool-gathering is likely to find that the kids have gone off and she has no idea where. A child can go out on the street and be killed. I think a mother should punish children but not beat them. A child just gets worse when you beat him, and then you have to beat him some more. I want my wife to be loving and to behave herself, and, as I said, she shouldn't fail me.

Sexually my women shouldn't be too backward. The ones I call backward are the ones who don't make a move unless you get on top of them first. She shouldn't lie down, roll over, and go off to sleep. Women who lie there like mummies don't appeal to me. If she's sick or feels bad or something, that's different. But when a woman is strong and healthy, she should be loving and bring the man around. What I really like is for her to make the first move and get the man interested in having relations. That really excites me.

The woman who satisfied me most was Pomposa. I've had some really good ones too, more passionate than she is, but my other relationships usually only lasted about a month. I don't know whether Pomposa satisfied me most because I took her from her home when she was still a virgin or because I was in love with her.

At times Sara argues with me over things, but not very hard. I don't know whether she thinks she has more ability or what, but sometimes she'll say, "No, it should be this way." When she starts to kick up a fuss I just say, "You shut up" or "What's the matter with you?" But I've never raised a finger to her.

I don't think it makes any difference in a marriage if the woman has studied more than the man. Sometimes the husband knows more and sometimes the wife. At times you see a marriage where one partner is illiterate. I don't think it affects the marriage, because if people really want to marry they won't care whether one has finished this grade and the other that.

The most important thing in a marriage is that the man live up to his responsibility. After all, you can't take on a woman and not work to support her. When you take it on, you have to be committed to it. Whenever Sara asks for money I give it to her if I have it, and if not, I borrow it somewhere. I usually give her 40 or 50 *pesos* a month and keep the rest, but it all ends up going to the family.

Sara has been washing some uniforms for a young fellow from Oriente who's a friend of ours, but she's doing it on her own. Even though the money comes in handy, I don't like her to take in washing. I've told her again and again not to do any more outside washing. It's only a matter of 2 or 3 *pesos* and doesn't make any great difference in my finances, so why should she do it? She says she does it because he's from home and she feels embarrassed not to, because the boy has gotten attached to us and keeps on bringing his laundry here. I'm not sure, but I don't think he's the only one. I think she also does laundry for two young fellows who live around here, but it's only a few odds and ends, two or three pairs of trousers, things like that.

I spend about 10 *pesos* a month on myself, if that. Once in a while I may spend 3 or 4 *pesos* in a pizza place, and for cigarettes and the bus, but that's all. I don't drink on the street or spend money on women or any of that. Sara and I almost never go out. Once in a while we do, but always with the children, never alone. It has to be for some necessary errand to the doctor or something special for us to go out alone.

I don't think it's enough just to give money to a woman and expect her to train the children, clothe them, and take care of their health. She can't do everything. There are errands about the house for the man to do too. When one of the children gets sick and I'm at home, I go for the medicine myself, no matter where. If my wife's very busy, I do the grocery shopping. I cook, too, when there's cooking to be done. I don't think cooking lowers a man. It depends on the situation. If the wife is just sitting there, of course he isn't going to do any of those things. But if she's doing something else or is sick, I'll put my hand to anything around the house.

I think I treat my children differently from the way my father treated me. A person should treat his children well. When they deserve a reward I try to get them one. If they're bad I sometimes say to them, "Nothing for you this year!" The end of the year is gift time. We try to give them something for their birthdays also, but right now where can you get anything for a present? Sometimes if you get right in there, you find something. I spent a whole day at the store to get a cake for Faustina. We weren't able to get cold drinks and other things for a party because you have to speak for them ahead of time. The custom is to give a little birthday party for a child, with a cake and all, but we've never done it.

Sara never tries to give the children penalties. She just pitches in and beats them with a strap or something. I don't know which of us is harder on them, but at times I defend the children against Sara. There's one thing I don't like. When Faustina, who's just a little kid and doesn't know anything yet, does some silly little thing, Sara hauls off and hits her. But suppose Sara says to Violeta, "I want you to do this." Violeta says, "Oh no, I'm not doing it and that's all," and Sara doesn't touch her at all. That's when I object. I tell her, "Look here, why do you let the ones who don't obey and answer back go free, and then give it to the youngest one of all?"

I don't think you have to punish girls as much as you do boys. I don't do anything to the boy children and not much to the little ones. They can do hundreds of things and I don't do anything to them, but sometimes I may say to Faustina and Amanda, "Go to bed now. You can't go out anywhere." After a while, though, I feel sorry for them, closed up in there, and tell them to get dressed and go out.

I try to give the children as much affection as I can. I kiss and pet them all but I think I pet Elsa more than the others because she's the littlest. I love Hilario and Violeta about as much as the other children. Hilario has lived with me since he was little. The problem with Violeta is that she's big now and at times she wants her own way. That doesn't suit me.

Sometimes we put the older children in charge of the little ones. For example, when they go around the neighborhood, Violeta is responsible for the whole group. Hilario looks after them on the way to school to see that they get across the streets all right and that some older boy doesn't give them a sock. The children get along well with each other, but at times, of course, they fight. I don't think their being half-brothers and -sisters has any effect on that. But one thing is true: the big ones sometimes mistreat the little ones just for the fun of it. I've had to tell Violeta not to hit the little kids. Every once in a while Faustina comes to me with a cut lip or forehead or a bloody nose. Violeta comes up with an excuse but she doesn't even turn a hair or shed a tear. I've told Sara that I don't want to catch Violeta hurting the children anymore.

I ask the children to do things, like take care of the house, and I tell them I don't want any more complaints from the school, that they should behave themselves there. Whenever there's a problem at school, the teacher sends me a note right away. I've gotten these notes about three or four times. It used to be for Hilario, but I don't remember what he did. Just lately I got one for Faustina, because she gets into fights with the other kids. Never for Amanda—she's a little angel and never gets into trouble with anybody.

Sara and I share the job of seeing to our children's education. They have to be sick before they can stay home from school, or there has to be some good reason. They can't stay home just because they feel like it. When I'm home I make sure they get up on time, or their mother does. But usually they have their own schedule and wake up by themselves. All of them made good grades when they passed last year.

Hilario is a lot slower than the others. He's been in school for years and he's still only in the third grade. Faustina started in kindergarten and now she's in the first grade. She entered at the right time, when she was five. Amanda didn't start school until she was seven. For a while both the girls were semi-boarding students, that is, they got their lunch at school and had to stay on until later in the afternoon, but that was only for a couple of months.

In 1963 Amanda was in a *círculo*, but that meant she spent the whole week there and we took her home on the weekends. They took good care of her there and she got her meals and medicines and everything. She was just a little tot then, about two and a half, but we had her there because we didn't have any regular housing. She was there only about three months because I couldn't go to see her except when I had a pass. Sara was the one who usually went because my passes didn't often coincide with the days we had to pick her up. Once when I came to visit her, she cried when I left. I didn't want that so I took her out.

I'd like my children to be scholarship students. Those kids are the little angels of the Revolution. They don't have to bring a thing from home. They get shoes, clothes, underwear, I don't know what all. The government delivers everything to their school door—meat, chicken, everything. They live better than anybody and they get it all free. They have enough to spare, and yet if they see somebody with a loaf of bread, right off they're looking for some.

What I don't understand is that some of those scholarship kids around here are real fresh. A lot of them think nothing of stealing fruit and things from private homes. We've never lost anything, but they've gone into the homes of some of my relatives and taken little things without asking. Since I'm a member of the police, part of my job is to catch kids when they do such things. I've found kids stealing fruit and turned them over to their housemothers, and I've also caught quite a few playing hooky and have taken them back to school.

Some of the boys play tricks or pester older people. On our street, for example, they've thrown rocks at the garage door, and once they even threw one in the house, just missing the baby. That's why I don't dare keep the door open, even in hot weather. I threatened to take them to the housemothers, but they're not much better than the kids themselves.

The youngsters don't respect them at all. I'm not saying the students are all alike—after all, I'd like my children to get scholarships—but they have their share of bad kids and rude brats.

We haven't made any effort to get Violeta to go to school. What would be the use? She could only go at night and there aren't any night schools near here. If there were, Sara and I would let her attend.

I don't care what my children decide to become when they grow up, as long as they learn some trade so they can support themselves and aren't the way I was. My father never demanded I go to school and it was wrong of him. I never learned anything. I'd like them to do a lot of things, but they'll be the ones to decide what they'll study and what they'll do.

Leticia Manzanares

I have only vague memories of my childhood. We lived in Limón, a barrio on the outskirts of Morón, Camaguey, and I'd say we were pretty well off. We had everything we needed, but of course my parents had to work for it. Considering we were poor people, we did all right. We lived in a large concrete building where several other families lived, each in their own apartment around a big patio that everyone shared.

When my parents were single, they both moved from their hometown in Las Villas to Limón, but I don't know why. Probably because they believed they'd be better off there. In those days moving was easier, since all you had to do was find a house and rent it.

Morón was a nice town with a small beach called Laguna de la Leche. The seaport, Nuevitas, isn't very far away. Some people in Morón worked on the docks at Nuevitas and Punta Alegre. Morón was a busy trading center then, and had what were called "commercial stores"—warehouses—and the country people would go there to buy. Anybody who wanted to could get a job shining shoes, working in the stores, or any number of other things. Sugar-cane growers often came there looking for men to hoe their land.

Papá was a farmhand. He never worked in Limón but always found a job of some sort elsewhere. He was probably paid by the day, because before the Revolution work in the country was usually paid by the day or by the hour. He'd travel far and wide to get work. I remember him being away most of the time when I was little, often for months on end.

Mamá was a hardworking woman. If she had to take in laundry, she did. If she had to take a job as cook or maid in somebody's house, she'd go right ahead and do it. When she worked, she always left us little ones at home.

I kind of think my parents never got married but just took off and lived together. They had nine children—three daughters and six sons. My brothers are much older than I am. I'm one of the youngest. Erasto, the eldest, is pushing fifty. He's exactly like *mamá*, with a real thin nose and better hair than we have. The rest of us, from Nicolás on down, look pretty much alike. Some have flatter noses than others, that's all. Tomás and Nicolás have the coarsest features of all.

Mamá was strict with the boys. Out in the street they'd get into mischief, fighting and throwing stones and everything, but at home they behaved themselves because *mamá* would hit them like crazy, with a stick. But she was always kidding, just like me. I felt more at ease with *mamá* and respected her less than *papá*. I addressed her as *tú* and him as *usted*. We were always close to her, you see. *Papá* was serious and reserved, not unpleasant or unfriendly, just reserved.

When Tomás was about five or six years old, my brother-in-law asked *mamá* if Tomás could go live with his family and she said yes. They were people of good position. Tomás stayed with them until he was a grown man. My sister Nerina and I used to visit them on their farm. Those people lived in plenty—they had everything. Just imagine, every two months they'd slaughter two hogs, fry the meat, and put it up in lard. Then on Sundays, which they spent in their house in town, we'd get into the tin of meat and really stuff ourselves. We'd eat those delicious fried pork chops with the lard still clinging to them. After the Revolution the government didn't take the whole farm; they still have a part of it. *Ay!* life was really wonderful there! If that way of living ever comes back, I'll go live in the country.

My eldest brother Erasto was raised by my mother's mother. He lived with her until she died. Except for Erasto and Tomás, we children grew up together. We were all in the same boat—what little we had was shared equally. When *mamá* bought something for one, she bought something for all.

It was a sad thing for us when *papá* left *mamá*. I don't remember his exact words since I was only five or six years old, but he said he was going because he couldn't keep on living with *mamá*. I was too little to know much about it. Besides, I thought that when people quarreled they didn't really mean the things they said. *Papá* took another wife but that was only a short time ago. He never had any children with any woman except *mamá*.

Mamá suffered a great deal because we were still young children and she had to bring us up all by herself. But she was as good as bread to us. She helped us and struggled for our sake as long as we were small. She'd get so upset if anything happened to any of us!

After separating from *papá*, *mamá* married Constancio and we moved to a house she built on a bit of land the government gave her. There she bore Constancio a son, who's now twenty-two years old. We got along fine with my stepfather. He was the one who raised us from the time we were little. He has a steady job now—everybody has nowadays—but at that time he didn't. He's a mason and he used to be hired when a building was going up, but as soon as it was finished his job was over. If he couldn't find work in town as a mason, he'd work as a farmhand out in the country, so he always had something to live on.

Around 1958, just before the Revolution, Constancio came to Havana looking for work because things were getting really bad in the country. The Rural Guard[73] were on a rampage and they'd just up and kill anybody. He'd been to Havana before and knew it well. At first he worked in the marketplace and sold fruit up and down the street. After the triumph of the Revolution, when he got a steady job in construction, he brought *mamá* to Havana. They separated but he visited us once or twice a month and always gave us money. He still does even now that we're married.

In the old days the public schools were open to everybody through the fifth grade, but education wasn't obligatory the way it is now. There were also many boarding or semi-boarding schools. You had to have influence to get a child into one of these. Nowadays anybody can get their children into boarding school, and if the mother goes to work, the children are given scholarships.

I was real bad when I was in school, always fighting with the other kids and taking their snacks away from them. I did it out of sheer mischief. They sold soft drinks and everything at school, and I could have bought whatever I wanted. But I fought and stole snacks from the time I was in the second grade until the fifth. God, was I bad! Kids are bad and that's all there is to it.

After the sixth grade the students went on to the Institute, where they had to pay for their own textbooks. *Mamá* was too poor to send me so I never went beyond fifth grade. My brothers continued studying, though. Two of them put themselves through school by shining shoes, and Primo was helped by his godfather, who bought his books. All three of them became mechanics before the Revolution and are now heads of workshops. My godmother helped me through school by buying my shoes and clothing and by taking me home with her from time to time. She had a little money because she was a medical midwife, which is practically the same as being a doctor. She'd charge as much as 40 or 50 *pesos* for a private case.

After leaving school I worked as a housemaid. I was twelve years old then. I washed clothes, cleaned house, and so on. I got along fine with the lady of the house. They were good people. They owned farms and had lots of money, and they lived in an enormous house. I don't know whether they stayed here or went North after the Revolution.

I earned 10 *pesos* a month on my first job. I'd give *mamá* a few *pesos* now and then. It wasn't much but in those times it went a long way. I really

73. During the second Batista presidency (1952–59), the *Guardia Rural* (or *guardia*) was a separate branch of the national police stationed in the rural areas and under the command of the army chief of staff.

worked to pay for my own clothes. I had lots of pretty dresses to wear to dances. Cloth wasn't expensive then, nor were shoes. In those days you could buy good material for 40 to 99 *centavos* a yard.

I stayed on that job about a year, then I took another job where they paid the same but there was less work. We'd find out about jobs by word of mouth, from other girls who worked. The second family I was with owned a printing shop where they prepared invitations and cards of all sorts. They also printed *bolita* numbers. They earned a lot of money and had a good social position. They treated me well, otherwise I wouldn't have stayed with them for four years. I left because I got married.

I met my husband, Domingo, in the country. We're both from Camaguey and were practically raised together. We weren't next-door neighbors, but we grew up in the same barrio. We started kidding around and wound up together for good. I very much wanted to marry him and my family never opposed us, so we were married a year and a half later. We've been together fifteen years now.

Our families get along well with each other. I've stayed with Domingo's family for months on end. In fact I lived with them before I moved here. It's easy to get along well with them now because we live so far apart. Nobody knows what's going on at each other's home. When we happen to meet, we're like "new relatives" as the saying goes.

Nowadays when people get married they have a big family party. As for Domingo and me, we were married by a justice of the peace and then we went home. It was as simple as bread and water. Only very rich people got married in church. It was a luxury the poor couldn't afford. *Mamá, papá,* and my brothers were at our wedding, but most of my relatives weren't because they were already living in Havana. Domingo's *papá* also went to our wedding.

We started our married life living by ourselves in Limón. We had a single room but it was large and was built partly of cement, partly of wood. It was only four or five blocks from *mamá*'s and I visited her every day. I wasn't working so I had plenty of time.

When I got married my life changed. I became more talkative— people teach one to be talkative, you know, and one gets to meet all sorts of different people after marriage. I got over my shyness. As a child I hardly ever opened my mouth. I sucked my two middle fingers until I was fourteen and now they're shaped differently from the rest. I'd put my fingers in my mouth and fall asleep whenever I sat down. I don't know just exactly when I stopped sucking my thumb, but when my brothers come to visit me from the country they still say, "Well, and how's everything, Thumbsucker?"

After we were married Domingo and I kept going to parties. We both love them and go as often as we can. Domingo isn't a jealous husband

and he enjoys dancing as much as I do. The dances in my time weren't all pushing, pulling, and jumping like the ones nowadays. There was an orchestra in Morón, but at private parties people mostly had a combo or danced to records. The bigger bands played at the Sociedad dances.

My family belonged to the Sociedad and so did Domingo's. The Sociedad had dances about once a month and also on special occasions, such as the Fiesta of the Flowers on May 20, when everybody dressed in white. As long as you were a member of the Sociedad and had the proper clothes, it wasn't expensive to go to those dances. The dues weren't high, though I think you had to pay an extra 3 *pesos* when they had an orchestra. I loved to have a good time so I went to every dance I could.

My family also belonged to the Unión, which is the colored people's club. Only the people who had the necessary qualities could belong. You didn't have to be rich or have a good social position, but you were required to be a moral person. A girl who ran around in the streets couldn't be admitted. No girl ever showed up alone at the Unión parties. If your *mamá* couldn't go, the president was responsible for taking you to the party and then back home. If a member took off with his sweetheart, they were dropped—not that anybody held it against them, but those were the rules. In those times it was very common for couples—white as well as black—to simply take off together instead of getting married. It's only now that most people get married. But even back then you had to marry by the law or by the Church if you wanted to keep on going to the Unión.

My sisters and I often went to the Unión activities. You could go there to listen to the radio and to the gatherings they held. They also had meetings to criticize members who'd done something wrong. I liked the Unión. I don't think it's right, the way young girls are let out loose in the streets nowadays and don't respect anybody. I don't like it at all. Poor as we were, we were brought up not to go out alone late at night.

When we first married, Domingo was working in a warehouse loading heavy crates. He earned about 3 *pesos* a day. He was a good worker and never complained about having to work. He was used to it because he began when he was very young. They sold groceries and hardware and everything at the warehouse, so we always had what we needed. When we wanted cash to pay the rent or anything, we'd ask Domingo's boss for 30, 40, or even 50 *pesos*. At the end of the year they'd settle accounts, but Domingo was never in debt to them because he worked extra hours to make more money.

Domingo worked at the warehouse until we came to Havana in 1957. We stayed with his sister in Regla because Domingo didn't have a job.

In Regla there were a number of people who were revolutionaries, but we only found out about them after the Triumph. Why, we didn't even know that the fellow next door to my mother-in-law was a revolutionary until they arrested him. He was taken away and beaten by Batista's men because they found an olive-green uniform and a pistol in his house. After a week they let him go, saying that on January 6 they were going to hang him and a lot of other revolutionaries in front of their own houses, as a Three Kings' Day gift to their families. Then came the Triumph, so the revolutionaries were saved. The boy next door put on his uniform and so did many others.

Before, it was as dangerous to talk about the Revolution as it would be now to talk about making a counterrevolution. *Mamá* didn't like to have anybody bring up that subject—she was too scared. You couldn't so much as mention Fidel's name. If you did and the police heard about it, they'd cart you off to jail. That's how come I never heard talk about Fidel before the Triumph. I knew there was a Twenty-sixth of July Movement, but nobody talked openly about it. I knew only that they painted proclamations on walls at night, asking the Cuban people to rise up. But I never read any of those proclamations because as soon as people saw them, they'd start erasing them before the police came.

The day Batista left Cuba I went to work the same as ever. I was working in Luyanó then and nobody there had heard the news, so everything was normal. But after the word spread around, people gathered in the streets and there was a lot of noise and shouting.

Was it ever hard for me to get home that day! All Cuba knew we had a new government and you can imagine. . . ! It was terrible! I couldn't get a car to take me and the buses weren't running. Traffic was stopped, just as if there'd been a strike. *Ay,* dear God, there was shooting all over, and I had to walk through open country with no buildings or anything to protect me. I started walking at about 3:00 in the afternoon, alone and trembling with fear. I walked and walked, thinking that the blessed hour when I would see my sister-in-law's house would never come! Night fell and I was still on my way. I walked through empty roads with not a soul in sight, not one little house or anything, only a car speeding by now and then. "Suppose one of those cars stops me?" I kept worrying but nothing happened to me. My heart was in my mouth until I got home. Never in my life have I been so scared as I was that day!

I arrived after nightfall with my tongue hanging out. When I got home they said, "My goodness, we thought something had happened to you! We couldn't go to fetch you because there were no cars." When I told my story they were amazed. Never in my life have I walked as I did that time! It was quite an adventure!

After Batista left, his government fell and all the people who live in those big houses in Vedado ran away, leaving them open and full of stuff. Lots of people got into those houses and took whatever they wanted. The police were kept busy trying to catch them.

When Fidel entered Havana, we went with a lot of people from the *reparto* to watch him march in with the Rebels. Everybody was out in the streets that day. People were happy to see the *barbudos*. I was happy too, because I thought, "Well, let's see what it's like." By the time we got to the highway Fidel had already passed, but there was still a whole caravan of people going down the road. They came on horseback, bringing everything they'd had up in the Sierras—the jeeps, the mortars, and all their arms.

Five days after Batista's flight the buses started running again and I went back to work in Luyanó, the same job I'd had when I first came to Havana. Everything was normal here until they gave us ration books for food. Before that, you could walk into a store and buy clothes or anything you pleased. The change came when the interventions started, and food-rationing and so on.

Since the Revolution Regla has been very different. It used to be a happy place. I loved it because I love gaiety and parties. Sometimes people got into arguments or quarreled in public but not usually. Everybody knew everybody else because it was a small *reparto*.

There used to be bars and parties all over the place. The bars had jukeboxes and you could go there to drink beer or soft drinks and listen to records. We'd go to the bar across the street because the jukebox was always on. Now there isn't anyplace in Regla where you can hear music unless you have a radio at home. People were so accustomed to having those bars nearby that they griped when the government closed them down.[74] It's just like when they rationed liquor—those who liked to drink practically went crazy at first but they got used to it.

There was no way of telling whether the people of Regla were happy with the change or what they expected to happen. I guess they felt kind of strange because they were used to the old system. But by now they've adapted to the new one.

Morón has also changed since the Revolution. There used to be lots of hotels, but most of them have been closed. Now people have to stand in line for the ones that are left. The government tears things down so they can build them differently, but then they leave the job half done and tear down something else.

At least some of the people in Morón are better off than before. Everybody has a job now. Before, you had to keep your eyes open if you wanted to find work. Things have improved a lot as far as jobs for

74. Nightclubs and bars were closed in 1967 during the official period of mourning for Che Guevara. In April, 1968, they were nationalized as part of the revolutionary offensive announced the previous month. Since the Christmas holidays of 1968, some nightclubs have been open several nights a week, but the bars, which the government regards as hangouts for loafers, have remained closed. (Booth, "Neighbourhood Committees and Popular Courts," p. 94.)

women are concerned. Lots of women are working in factories, drugstores, nursery schools, and so on.

I've heard that Batista's government was imperialist. That means everybody tried to grab more than everybody else. At least I think I've heard somebody say that's what capitalism is all about. All the big landowners before the Revolution were capitalists. But they're gone now because they couldn't adapt to the new system. I've also heard that true socialism—or communism—means everybody shall study and work. And, well, as I see it, the Revolution is mainly to help poor people and have them improve themselves. Domingo knows a lot about politics because he's been in the Army and he's a man and has been around all sorts of people. He could explain all those things but I can't. I don't even listen to Fidel's speeches because I don't remember what he says. I simply don't pay attention to politics.

Before the Revolution Domingo didn't have any problems with the Army. He never volunteered and they didn't draft him because he had a steady job. But after the Revolution, practically all the men at his work center joined. I didn't miss Domingo when he was in the Army because I was used to having him away most of the time. He'd set off for work in the morning and come home at night. When he was out in the country, he was even away all night.

When Domingo went to Algeria I had no idea where he was, but I knew he wasn't in Cuba. He didn't tell me himself, someone from the High Command did. He said Domingo was going out of Cuba, but didn't tell me where or what he was doing, or how long he'd be away. They weren't allowed to give that information. I was worried but I had no idea he was fighting or anything. I thought maybe he'd been sent abroad to study on a scholarship, because at that time they were sending lots of people.

Domingo wrote to me but still couldn't tell me where he was. His letters took a long time to get here. He sent me one where he told me in *jeringonza* where he was. That's like a secret language he knows. He asked me to show that part of the letter to my brother who knew *jeringonza*. But it looked like Russian letters so I thought he was somewhere in Russia. I showed the letter to a Russian teacher and he said, "*Ay*, my child, the truth is I haven't the slightest idea what this means. This isn't Russian, Czech, or any of those languages."

I never showed the letter to my brother because I thought, "If even the Russian teacher doesn't understand it, what's the point of showing it to anyone else?" If I'd given it to my brother, he could have figured it out at once.

I got pregnant with Lina right after my marriage; she was born fourteen years ago. Two years after her birth I bore Bárbara, and two years later Andrea. Lina was born at home according to the custom at that time, with the help of my godmother, who acted as midwife. She'd also attended my mother when I was born. My godmother acted as my midwife for Bárbara too, but she didn't attend me when Andrea was born, because here in Havana it's customary to go to a hospital when you have a baby.

I've borne five children and never had a difficult labor. I did have a few bad symptoms when I was pregnant with my son, because Tomás was unusually big and made my hips open up too much. Besides, when you're carrying a boy you get a strong pain in the back, but that was all.

The day Tomás was born, Domingo was due at headquarters. He had to go because anybody who stayed away was punished. My labor pains started before he left but I'd had pains all along with that belly, so I didn't think a thing of it and didn't tell him. My sister took me to the Calixto García Hospital and we got there just in the nick of time.

When they told me "It's a boy," I said, "I don't believe it!" Then they brought me that big baby boy with such fat little arms! Imagine, after having had three girls in a row! He weighed 8½ pounds and was squirming and yelling at the top of his lungs because he was born hungry. What a joy he was to me! The only boy, and born so strong and sturdy!

Our youngest child, Ana Luz, is Domingo's pride and joy. He's even fonder of her than of Tomás. You know how it is—the youngest is always the pet whether it's a boy or a girl.

I don't do anything to keep from getting pregnant. My brother's wife, Clarisa, has a whole bunch of children and had her tubes tied. My sister Nerina had a ring inserted after she had four children. Febe has five already and suffers from high blood pressure so she had her tubes tied. She'll do all sorts of fool things. Once when she was four months pregnant she decided to have an abortion. As for me, if I have another baby—well, we'll manage somehow or other, what the hell! I'm still nursing Ana Luz but that's got nothing to do with my not getting pregnant, because I'm having my periods.

I think it's a good thing to have sons but I don't want more than one. Girls don't bring you headaches the way boys do. On the 31st of last month Tomás decided he didn't want to go to school, so he up and told me school was closed that day. He's home one minute and out in the street the next and who's to say no to him? No matter how much he respects you, a boy will go his own way. He'll tell you he's going to the movies but later something will catch his interest and he'll go somewhere else. I've always liked girls better and that's the truth. Naturally it's good to have at least one boy to take care of you in the future, but one is enough—and maybe a bit more than enough—for me anyway.

Tomás is the only one of my children who hasn't been baptized yet. His godmother lives out in the country, in Camaguey. Last time I went there, she was in Varadero because her husband had won the trip for outstanding volunteer work. I've thought of twenty friends who could act as godmother to Tomás, but I hate to take him away from her because she asked to christen him way back when I was pregnant. I've got to get him baptized soon, because if I let it go much longer he might say he doesn't want to. We tell him that he's a Jew if he isn't baptized.

The baptismal ceremony is still the same as it was before the Revolution, but I know it won't be long before baptism is forbidden altogether. The new system is against religion, but as long as it's possible to baptize children I'm going to have mine baptized. All my brothers and sisters, except one, are Catholic. *Mamá,* especially, was very devout. *Papá* isn't a believer, but he always approved of baptizing children, and we were brought up to believe in it too.

Erasto is the only one of my brothers who's not interested in Catholicism and doesn't go to church. He's the kind who neither dyes nor gives off color, which is to say he's neither Catholic nor communist. He was baptized just like the rest of us, so I guess it was after he grew up that he got to like communism, or at least politics. As a child I often heard *mamá* say that Erasto was a communist, that he was sympathetic with communism and liked to talk about it. I didn't know anything about political systems then so I wasn't much interested in those conversations.

Some Catholics don't go to church anymore because they're afraid to. They're Party members and they can't afford to be seen at Mass or in processions, but we aren't like that. Domingo and I don't go regularly, but there's a church in Old Havana where we go when we feel like it. When Domingo was working, they told him they were considering him as a candidate for Party membership, but he said no, he was a Catholic and couldn't renounce his religion. They told my brother Fermín the same thing and he also said no, because he was a believer, a Catholic.

Mamá died eight years ago, before Domingo went to Algeria. She was in Camaguey and I was here in Havana. She got an embolism, what's called a cerebral hemmorrhage, which is a real killer. When you get that once you don't get it twice, because it kills you right away. They sent a telegram to my sister's house asking her to go to Limón immediately because *mamá* was seriously ill.

Fermín, my sister, and I went together on the bus. It was already full but we showed the driver our telegram and he gave us seats at once. We didn't arrive until noon the next day, and *mamá* died before we got there. The bus drove us straight to the funeral parlor. *Papá* and the rest of the family were there when we arrived.

Mamá was buried at 5:00 that afternoon in an enormous graveyard on the outskirts of Morón. I don't want to remember that day. I usually don't go haywire but I don't know what happened to me then. My sisters both have nerve trouble. They're high-strung, especially the eldest, because of her high blood pressure. Both of them had hysterical fits; Febe had to have injections and everything.

There are times when I can't believe *mamá* is dead. Even now I begin remembering, and it seems to me that she's still in Limón expecting me. She was in perfect health when she said goodbye to us in Havana less than a month before she died. She was going to be fifty-six on October 26 that year. It was so unexpected ... but, as the saying has it, "To die you need only one thing: to be alive."

All my brothers and sisters are middling well off. By my standards, Odeberto and Nicolás live well, but I guess perhaps Tomás is better off than the rest of us. He was raised by people of means and he's had good jobs and someone to help him along. Constancio, the youngest, is a screwball. He's in the service in Oriente. He's about twenty-two and he's had more problems than the rest of us. He took off with some girl, they had a baby, then he left her. I only met her once. But all I can say is any woman who'd hitch up with him is even crazier than he is. Why did she marry him when he didn't even have a job to support her?

There are five of us living here in Havana now. Primo and Fermín were here lately to visit me, though Febe, Odeberto, and Nicolás are the ones who visit me most often. Sometimes all three of them come to see me the same month. I'm the one they visit most. I don't see much of my eldest brother, Erasto, because he hardly ever leaves home. He's an old bachelor; he's not lively like the rest of us. He's working in a factory now and says he can't take time off.

Ours is a united family—anyone can see how close Fermín and Primo and I are. The only one who's a bit distant from the rest of us, even though she lives here in Havana, is my sister Nerina.

Marriage is important to me. I've been lucky because Domingo and I have always been together except when he was in the Army. Then we were apart for two months while he took a course, and again for six months while he was in Algeria.

We always got along well with each other. I'm the quarrelsome one, the one who starts nagging him, though I know his illness makes him act the way he does. I simply can't help myself. But we have no real conflicts. I get mad, but the next moment I'm cracking jokes. We laugh and kid each other most of the time.

I never ask Domingo to do anything, because he's such a slowpoke he drives me clear out of my mind. I simply don't have the patience to wait for him, so I just up and do it myself. If I weren't quick and active I could never get through all the work I've got. I can't spend even one day in idleness. But I'm used to bustling about and keeping busy all the time. I have to do all the housework—cleaning, cooking, shopping for food, waiting in a queue when there are clothes to be bought, doing the laundry—everything falls upon my shoulders in this family and there are no two ways about it.

Domingo's illness is my worst problem. He never had any health problems until about five or six years ago when he got his allergy. The first time it happened was after we'd been living in Havana about a year. The back of his head got inflamed and hurt so bad he couldn't stand it. He was crazy with pain. The doctor says the glands there swell up because of the allergy. He was sent to the Naval Hospital in East Havana, a lovely hospital which was a military one at the time. I was scared when the doctor said he had to be hospitalized immediately. What a sight Domingo was! He looked lopsided, as if one side of his head had been pushed in and the other side puffed out. And he was in such pain he couldn't even turn his head without screaming. I was sure he had a malignant tumor or something of the kind. What a relief when he came out of the hospital. He was much better and at least he didn't have to go back to the hospital for quite a while afterward.

As far as I remember, Domingo got his allergy after they operated on his spine. That was eleven years ago, and he's been ill ever since. After his operation I began to notice how, little by little, his illness came on. While he was in Algeria he got better, but as soon as he came back he got worse again. Now it's worse than ever. He hasn't been able to work for almost two months. You don't know what it's like to have someone sick at home and to do this and that for him, yet still he can't get well. The medicines work one day and the next day they don't so he has to take different ones. The doctor is always prescribing new medicines for him.

The problem is that Domingo is allergic to most kinds of food so he can eat only a very few things, but they won't include a diet allowance in his ration book. They say that those special diet allowances are for people with illnesses like cancer or tuberculosis. Domingo went through all kinds of tests to find out what he can and can't eat. About three years ago the doctor gave him a song and dance about how he couldn't eat anything that had flour or sugar in it, and only a very little coffee. He followed the diet for about fifteen days but couldn't keep it up. Right now it's been over a month since there have been any vegetables on the market and he's got to eat something.

Perhaps if he'd stop eating the food that's been forbidden he'd get better. But look, those are the only things we can get. The stores have no potatoes or tubers. If we could get vegetables I'd let him have our ration and the rest of us could eat whatever else was available. Right now the stores have *malanga* but our allowance was only 4 pounds—enough for two meals—and what's he to eat the rest of the week? They don't give us any chicken for the kids, and the beans they're selling now are terrible. I buy beans and we hardly touch them; it's a waste. You might say that we're living on the bit of meat we get every week. We're having a hard time and that's a fact.

If Domingo doesn't eat any of the things the doctor has forbidden him and can't get special items for his diet included in his ration book, then what's he going to eat? What the rest of us eat, that's what. He can't let himself starve to death. This isn't child's play, it's a bad problem.

Last year they hospitalized him again because of the itch. It was scratch, scratch, scratch all day long. I thought, "Now they'll be sure to make some more tests." But they didn't do any such thing. The doctor didn't put any medication on the rash and didn't give him a diet plan either. He came home just as sick as when he left. The skin on his back has changed color and his arms are covered with the rash. He used to be real hairy and now he doesn't have one single hair on his arms. But, after all, Domingo's illness is our only problem.

I don't have much schooling but I've got a good mind. When I set myself to learn something, I find that it's more or less like what I've always thought anyway. I take notice of things and know what's what. I've got a well-developed mind. It isn't easy to deceive me. Heck no! I'm one of those people who lets others talk, but I keep my eyes and ears open. Later on, when I'm alone, I turn everything they've said over in my mind and more or less figure out what they meant. I've always been like that, ever since I was a child.

Physically, I think I'm all right too, mainly because I'm healthy and never get sick. I only go to the doctor when I'm pregnant and then only because one is supposed to, not because I get ill. I'm perfectly satisfied with the looks God gave me. I think my features are pretty good, considering my color. People tell me I have a fine-featured face.

Taking one thing with another, I'm satisfied with being as I am. I don't think I'm perfect but I'm not bad either—just about average, I guess. Others may think I'm wrong to be that way but that's my system. Otherwise I'd have to be worse than I am!

The truth is I've never heard that anybody has spoken ill of me, so I can only hope that whatever people say is good. I'm a sociable person who gets along well with everyone. I kid around with everybody. When I can help somebody, I do; when I can't, well, that's their tough luck.

Domingo Labrada

Ours is a very large family—some of us are light and some dark. *Mamá* is just a little bit darker than me, and my sisters Laura and Avelina are lighter than Coloma, Dámaso, and me. My half-brother Andrés is lighter-skinned than all of us, like his father. My *papá* is a real Moor, dark with Caucasian features. And yet, as time goes on he's been changing physically, because he used to work as a stoker, shoveling coal, and the heat made his eyes red.

I don't remember *mamá*'s father any too well. I know he was colored, but if I told you he was black black, I'd be telling you a lie because I don't really remember. I believe that *mamá*'s mother was quite advanced; I mean, she was a quite light-skinned mulatto like *papá*'s mother.

I have lots of relatives I've never met and don't especially want to meet. It isn't that any of them have ever snubbed me personally. I haven't given them the chance because I've never tried to get in touch with them. Some of my relatives, though, have taken the trouble to get acquainted and gotten snubbed for their pains. Know why? Because they visited others who were very advanced, like the children of my mother's sister Avelina. She was a mulatto and must have married a light-skinned man because her children are white, white, white. One day my cousin Imelda, who's as black as ebony, went to visit them in Matanzas. But when she knocked at their door, they denied being related to her. In order to pass for white, they couldn't admit to having black cousins, could they?

Generally speaking, I'd say that in my family we don't take color into account. Most of us, black and white, are on good terms with one another. We were on good terms with Aunt Coloma and her daughters, white though they were, whiter even than the cousins in Matanzas. Aunt Coloma was quite advanced, a *mulata* who married a white man and that's how come the daughters are white. But they didn't deny their relatives in order to pass as whites.

In my family, we all have friends of every color. Like right here in this building, if a white family offered me hospitality while a colored family didn't, I'd have to offer hospitality to the whites in return, no? Because for us color doesn't exist. Any time you come to my house you may find white friends or black, or both at the same time.

Papá tells me that he and his parents had to live through slavery.[75] His mother was a big strong woman who worked in the cane fields. She must have been some woman, that grandmother of mine! I never met her though. She died years before I was born and so did my grandfather. *Papá* was the eldest of the family. He was born in the country, in Pinar del Río, in 1800-and-something. He doesn't know his age but we've figured out from stories he's told us that he's ninety-four.

Papá's full name is Fernando Labrada Pompa, but I call him Nando for short. His two brothers both died in the war of 1895. One sister is still alive, the other two died not long ago. There were schools in *papá*'s time, but very few, so he never studied. He was taught to sign his name, that's all. But after the triumph of the Revolution he learned to read and write.

Papá left home at seventeen and went to Havana, where he got a job as houseboy for a family who owned two sugar *centrales* in Camaguey. *Papá* soon left that job to go cut cane in Matanzas. He tells me he set out with a suitcase full of white clothes, and after the fields had been burned over, he'd show up to cut cane in a stiff-collar white shirt and tie. So people nicknamed him "El Loco."

Mamá is from Colón, in the province of Matanzas, and that's where *papá* met her. He was working there as a mechanic in a sugar *central*. *Mamá* is sixty-seven and easily young enough to be *papá*'s daughter. Neither of them has ever told us whether they were legally married; we think they simply got together.

My parents must have been living in the Vitoria *central* when my eldest sister was born because they named her Vitoria. A few years later my sister Laura was born. She's had a temper ever since she was a little girl. Even now she's the most domineering of us all. Avelina came next, and as a child she was as good as bread. Any little thing used to make her cry. After a time Coloma was born. She and I were always as close as fingernail and flesh. After Coloma came Dámaso, and finally me. I was born in 1929, in Limón, a barrio on the outskirts of Morón. *Mamá* had a midwife to assist in the birth.

We brothers and sisters always got along very well with one another. *Mamá* would go out to work and leave us with the older girls. They were like little mothers to us. But since Vitoria was the eldest and I the youngest, she carried me around most of all. I remember how angry

75. Domingo's father was born around 1876, four years before Cuba passed a law providing for the gradual abolition of slavery through a period of "tutelage" known as the *patronato*. Slavery was officially abolished in 1886 by a royal decree from Spain.

Coloma would get. She'd cry, "No, no, no! He isn't yours, I'm yours!" But Vitoria always picked me up. That's why I've never forgotten her, even though I was very small when she died.

I remember well how Vitoria got sick in Limón. At that time if you got appendicitis it was very difficult to arrange for an operation. My Uncle Rodrigo and *mamá* brought Vitoria to the Calixto García Hospital in Havana, but it was too late. We were eating when the telegram announcing her death arrived. Kids will do whatever the people around them are doing; I saw the others cry so I burst into tears too, but I didn't know what it was all about. I remember my sister scolded me because I went on eating. At first I kept asking my mother when Vita was coming back. "Vita died, my child, she'll never come back again," *mamá* would tell me, and after a time I understood what she meant.

I was only three or four when my parents separated, so I can't say I really knew *papá*. I got to know him later on, when he'd come to visit us. I never saw them quarrel; the reason for their separation is their secret. We children never dared ask them about it, or about any other personal matters the way children do now. God no! We were expected to be always respectful to our elders. We had to greet them formally if we wanted to talk with them.

One of my sisters once asked my mother why she and *papá* had separated, and *mamá* said, "Let the subject drop. Why in the world do you want to know? It isn't any of your business." But she didn't get mad or anything.

The way I figure it from conversations I've heard, *papá* didn't want to let *mamá* go out in the street for fear she'd find out about his affairs with other women. He was such a philanderer, you see. Even now, when he's over ninety, my old man can't see a woman without making a pass at her.

When *papá* went away, he left the house to *mamá* and Uncle Rodrigo, *mamá*'s brother, who was real crotchety. All of us kids stayed with them. When I was five, *mamá* went to work as a cook in the home of Floriano Moreno, a rich *colono*.[76] Moreno also owned the branch rail line from the sugar mill to the main track, and they got all the money from the fares between those two points.

The Moreno family had an enormous house, with so many rooms some were never occupied. All along one side were rooms for the workers, and on the other side, behind a large kitchen–dining room, were the owners' living quarters.

We lived in the room off the kitchen. My brother and I slept in a sturdy little folding bed and *mamá* and my sisters slept on the other two beds. I was the only one who ate with the Moreno family, because the

76. A sugar-cane farmer; refers to all cane growers whether they owned or rented their farms.

father was fond of me. I was an obsession with him. When he went out to eat or to other places, he'd take me with him. I called him Moreno and he called me "son." He liked to pick me up and carry me around.

Sometimes when he sent for me, I refused to go. Often he'd say to me, "Come on, my *negro*, show me how to handle my knife and fork. I don't know how to do it." Because, you see, I've known how to handle my knife, fork, and spoon ever since I was a tiny little thing. Listen, I had a horribly strict unbringing! If I held my spoon wrong, *pam!* they'd slap my hand. All my folks have good table manners. They haven't been brought up any which way, let me tell you!

Moreno's only fault was that he drank too much. When he got drunk he'd kid *mamá* and tease her. He was apt to be rude then, but he never got fresh with *mamá.* Child as I was, I understood that he was a swell guy when he was sober. I've come to the conclusion that it isn't only poor people with problems who drink too much.

I started school when I was about seven years old. The late Moreno paid for our education at the same private school his youngest went to. The school was run by a colored man. Now there was a real teacher! When he gave us a lesson to study, we weren't allowed to go home until we knew it perfectly. Otherwise he'd keep us until nightfall, when our parents would come to fetch us.

Moreno gave us 1 *peso* every day to buy a snack at school. We never spent the whole *peso.* In those times you could get plenty with just a *medio.*[77] We'd spend 15 or 20 *kilos* at school and give the rest of the money to the old lady. In fact, I figured out later that's how *mamá* paid for all the trips to Morón. There was a whole battalion of us kids so the round-trip fares amounted to quite a bit of money. Some months we went to Morón as often as three times. We'd always leave in the afternoon, stay in Morón the whole next day, and come back on the third day. We'd all go with *mamá;* she never left a one of us behind. We had a big apartment with two bedrooms there. It was one of a compound of apartments built around a common courtyard, the kind of setup we call *cuartería* in Morón, or *solar* in Havana.

On one of our trips from the *central* to Morón, when I was seven, we went to see *papá.* My parents always spoke politely to each other so I thought *papá* only stayed away because of his work. On this trip *papá* went to *mamá* to say that he wanted to keep us children with him so we could go to school. The old lady said we were already going to school and that she wouldn't let us go to live with him. Finally *mamá* said we could visit him for short periods. On every trip to Morón we children would visit *papá* early in the afternoon and run back to *mamá* by evening. Sometimes *papá* would make us stay with him for weeks at a time, but I

77. Five *centavos.*

never wanted to. It was then that it became clear to me that my parents were separated.

You probably won't believe this, but as a little boy I was happier hanging on to *mamá*'s skirts than playing. And yet, she tells me I wasn't a crybaby or anything of the kind. Why, some of the neighbors who visited the house didn't even know there was a little boy there, that's how quiet I was. Of course, after I grew a bit older I'd romp and play outside. But whenever I got into trouble, I'd run and hide behind *mamá*. It wasn't because of fear but simply because I was so attached to her. I've never in my life been afraid. Never! On the contrary, I like to see new things and try them out.

For poor kids we dressed well. *Mamá* couldn't possibly have earned enough to buy all our clothes and shoes. I figure that's the reason why Uncle Rodrigo used to take us to stay with him in the country now and then.

He lived in a great big barracks on a *colonia* with all the workers who were away from their families. They'd buy the food, cook it themselves, and eat together, there in the barracks. My uncle, being the eldest, had a corner all to himself. He lived alone because his wife had died several years before. He had no children, only a godson who worked in the company workshops at Morón.

When my brother Dámaso was only eight, he liked to play tricks on people and beat up the other kids. On his way home from school he'd punch every boy he met. *Mamá* would get all sorts of complaints about him, then she'd spank him and take off all his clothes so he couldn't go out. So one time Uncle Rodrigo took him to the *colonia* to help him hoe cane.

I missed Dámaso terribly—after all, he was only one year older than me and we'd always been very attached to each other, almost like twins. Two years later, when my uncle brought Dámaso back, I told him I wanted to go to the *colonia* too. I went when I was about nine. There my uncle said to me, "I'm going to make a hoe especially for you, so you can earn money to take home to your *mamá*."

You should have seen me, standing in the middle of a patch of weeds, hacking away with my little hoe. I've worked ever since I was a little kid, and I liked it. My uncle paid me by feeding me. Often he'd go to work in the morning and leave me asleep in the barracks. Sometimes I'd spend a whole day at the house of a Jamaican woman, Lucerne, who was a friend of his. That's how I lived until *papá* took me away.

My father was a mechanic who went from one *central* to another working, and he happened to pass by on a trip one day. He didn't like the idea of my being out in the country with my uncle. He wanted to take me back to town because he knew I'd be better off there, going to school and learning something instead of hoeing and lugging sugar cane. But *papá* lived alone in a single room and spent most of his time away from home.

He really wasn't in a situation where he could take charge of me. So he said to me, "I'm going to get me a woman so I can take you kids home to live with me."

Although *papá* was a lot better off than my old lady, he never sent her money for us. I don't know whether or not he ever offered to. As for *mamá*, she never wanted to go to court to ask for support money for her children or anything. Both she and her brother worked to support us, *mamá* slaving over a laundry tub and an ironing board. When *papá* kept insisting that we children live with him permanently, it was Uncle Rodrigo who gave in, see? He said to *mamá*, "Let the kids go with him!" He argued and argued with her about it. He's *mamá*'s godfather and she has a lot of respect for his opinion. The point was that with *papá* we'd have a better standard of living than with *mamá*. I was too little to understand that, but it's true that with *mamá* we were all crowded into one little room.

I'm pretty fond of the old lady. She's as good as bread. I can't find fault in the way she raised us or her grandchildren and great-grandchildren. I've even become a bit jealous of her affection, I admit. You see, when I was a little kid she was fonder of me than later. She was raising one of her granddaughters and I got the idea she loved that girl better than she loved me. It wasn't so, I realized later, but I was jealous for a time, because whatever that niece of mine happened to ask for, *mamá* would go out of her way to get for her.

This went on until one day I came right out and told *mamá* how I felt. "You sure have changed, old lady," I said.

"That isn't true," she protested. "I've always been the same." That's the only answer she ever gives me: "I've always been the same."

I lived with my old lady until I was nine, and after that I moved to my father's house. *Mamá* stayed on at her job with the Moreno family. When I lived with *papá* I'd spend seven or eight months at a stretch with him, always longing for *mamá*, then I'd go and stay with her for a time. When I returned to my father's house, sometimes he'd be away working. At that time I loved *mamá* a lot more than *papá*. But *papá* was very affectionate with me and little by little he won me over.

Mamá seldom spanked me but I got plenty of blows from *papá*. My upbringing was a harsh one. I never tagged along after him. He beat me for any little thing, and his friends did too, even more than he did. Suppose I was out in the street throwing stones and a friend of *papá*'s saw me. He'd call, "Domingo, come here!" and I'd have to go. Then he'd ask me, "Is it right to throw stones?"

"No sir," I'd answer. Then he'd cuff and slap me right there in the street and say, "Now run along home and don't let me see you around here again!" Later *papá* would find out about it and scold me again. That's how strictly we were brought up.

When I first went under *papá*'s wing, he arranged for me to stay with a

friend of his, a lady called Vivian, since he was away working most of the
time. Vivian was very, very strict. She never spanked me but she
punished me plenty. She was a little old lady, a widow of fifty-five or
sixty at the very least. Her son Nero also lived there, and her mother,
Claudia.

Vivian was very demanding. We all had to do housework there because she said it was as much a man's duty as a woman's to learn how to
do household tasks properly. I had to shake out the bedding, make the
beds, and empty all the ashtrays before sweeping the floor. Then I
dusted the furniture. If I did anything in the wrong order, she'd call me
over and say, "Domingo, what did I tell you about housecleaning? What's
the first thing one does?" At meals she did the same thing. If she saw me
holding the fork wrong she'd ask me, "How did I tell you to hold the
fork? Are you shoveling earth or taking food?"

In the afternoons she'd tell me, "Domingo, run outside and play for a
while." So I'd stand out in front of the house and spin my toy top. After a
while she'd say to me, "Time to take a bath and change into clean
clothes." After my bath I wasn't allowed to play anymore. I'd sit on the
porch until I was called in to dinner. After dinner I had to sit at the table,
or in the parlor when there was company, until bedtime.

I went to the public school that was right across the street from
Vivian's house. I'd run across to school in the morning and run right
back home as soon as school was out. When I started they put me in the
first grade, then, at 10:00 o'clock on the very first morning, they sent me
on to the second grade. The next day they promoted me to the third,
and at the end of the school year, when I was about ten, I was put in the
fourth grade.

During the year I stayed with Vivian I missed my folks and my
brothers and sisters. But I learned right off that it was better not to
complain to *papá* about anything Vivian did. Once I told him she'd
pinched me and he spanked me. So I soon learned to keep my troubles
to myself, and in time I got used to living there.

I was brought up alone, in a manner of speaking. For two or three
years I played without playmates. As a child I lived the life of an adult.
Naturally, as long as I was living in a stranger's house I had to act like a
model child. When I played they watched me. I never had the warmth
that, for instance, my children have and will someday remember. Still,
I'm very grateful to Vivian. The time I spent at her house was the best
training in respect I've ever had. She taught me how to do all sorts of
things well and thoroughly.

I used to think that the things she made me do were women's work,
but I've come to understand that it isn't so. Sometimes when I'm alone
here or when my wife has to go out shopping, I cook our dinner, iron
our clothes, and clean the house. I grab a pail of water and scrub the
floor and don't wait for somebody else to do it.

After *papá* had talked it over with his woman, my brother Dámaso and I moved in with him, in a large wooden house he'd rented. Before that, *papá* had kept the front room for himself and had rented out the other six to different people. When my brother and I went to live with him he took the back room for us, so then we had two.

When *papá* was away, a man called Sancho would come over to cook for us. He worked with *papá* at the Adelaida *central* but had been laid off. Before he was called back to work he taught us to cook, wash our own clothes, and clean house, and then Dámaso and I had to do all that for ourselves. By the time I was ten I was such a good cook that when *papá* had guests to dinner they were delighted with the food.

One of *papá*'s close friends, who lived on the next street, was an awful drunkard. One day when I was about eleven, I found him drunk in the street and helped him home. After that, whenever he had a chance, he'd go to my house and ask permission to take me out. We'd go to a place where they served liquor in small coffee cups and he'd say, "Bring me two cups of coffee." When they brought them he'd say, "Well, *negro*, go ahead and drink!" I did and I liked it and that's how I learned to drink. *Papá* never caught on because I didn't get drunk.

At last, after more than a year in *papá*'s house, he brought home the woman who was to be our stepmother. She'd already been with him, if you know what I mean. I remember that day very clearly. It was almost 6:00 o'clock in the evening when he showed up with her and told us, "Look, boys, this is Miriam González, the lady who's going to look after you from now on." He took two more rooms for the four of us—he, his wife, Dámaso, and I. And finally he took over the whole house.

At first our stepmother was nice—the first days were heavenly—but after that things got very bad. Everything changed for us. It was all on account of her daughter María Julia, who was about my age. When she got to be about twelve and began to get interested in dressing well and so on, our stepmother grabbed everything she could for her. I still remember the quantities of clothes and shoes she bought for that girl, while we had practically nothing to wear. We quarreled about that often. When she finally got around to buying us shoes, she'd get rough, thick-soled work shoes, the kind we call "knock-you-downs."

And yet, in spite of everything, we played with the little girl and got along fine with her. The trouble was that every time the kid cried because of some trifling thing, her *mamá* would rush out asking what had happened. If María Julia said that Dámaso or I had done something to her, our stepmother spanked us plenty, but she never spanked her own daughter. If I should ever have to give my children a stepmother, I wouldn't pick a woman who already had children of her own. Not after the experience I've had!

Papá has always been happy and good-humored. He was truly affectionate to us, but he was sixty or more when he got together with that woman, who was only twenty-eight or twenty-nine at most. You know— the story of the old man who married the young girl. No matter what she said, he believed her and ignored us. And what that meant was blows for us. She'd spank us, and when she made any complaint against us, our old man would whip us with a whole bunch of electric-light cords. Now look, I'm not denying that blows can be helpful in some ways, but not when people whip you just for the hell of it, understand?

Our stepmother treated us like intruders in our own home. If Dámaso and I were sitting out on the porch when she served dinner, she wouldn't call us in to eat. She'd serve herself and *papá*, and my brother and I would have to go to the kitchen and fill our own plates.

One time *papá* was so furious he foamed at the mouth. He went so far as to put a rope around Dámaso's throat to strangle him. And it was all that woman's fault. That day she told *papá* a lot of stories, as usual. She threatened to leave him, saying we were intolerable, that she couldn't stand us any longer, and all that sort of thing. Our next-door neighbor had to break the fence between the two yards and run into the house to keep *papá* from choking Dámaso.

In cold weather—I'll never forget—our stepmother would tell her daughter, "Hurry up and take your bath now, while the day is still warm." But she wouldn't remind Dámaso and me, and we were too interested in our play to remember our bath. Boys will be boys, you know. When evening came and it got really cold, I'd say to Dámaso, "I'm not going to take a bath today, it's too cold."

"I'm not either," he'd answer.

Our stepmother made no objections, but when *papá* came she'd tell him, "The boys went to bed without having bathed." *Papá* would cuff us awake at 1:00 or 2:00 in the morning and say, "Go take your baths in the tub that's out in the yard!" And we'd get up and bathe in that freezing water. And it really was freezing, because she'd fill a tub full to the top and set it out in the cold night air with the midnight dew falling into it.

One day she made me kneel down with two flatirons on the palms of my hands. When I couldn't hold them up any longer, I hurled the irons away and screamed, "That's enough! No more punishments, ever! Not one more! I won't take it!" I spoke violently with my eyes starting out of their sockets.

That scared her. "Domingo, you're insane!" she whined, and then she shut up for the moment. But when *papá* came home she told him the whole story, and as you can imagine, he nearly killed me. But at least she never again dared to punish me herself.

Not long afterward I went to see my old lady and simply stayed on with her. A month later, *papá* went there to fetch me and I went back with him. What else could I do? I had to obey.

Every time my old lady came to Morón, my old man would send us to visit her. "Let's go with *mamá*," we'd say. But most of the time she sent us right back to *papá*.

Papá never took us out to the park or anywhere. Of course I understand he was usually tired, and besides, he didn't feel exactly free, if you know what I mean. Just imagine! A house where what a woman told him carried more weight than anything his sons could say!

In spite of everything, I've never stopped having warm loving feelings and great respect for my father. Respect, yes, because as a boy I had a lot of sense in a way. I felt misunderstood, but it was all my stepmother's fault. As time went on we got more and more used to her ways, and in the end we won. Yes, she didn't win, we did. One day the old man said something to her—I don't know what—and she up and left him. In spite of the way she made life a misery to me, I bear her no grudge. I even go to visit her sometimes.

As we got older once in a while *papá* allowed me and my brother to go out as far as the corner of our block in the evening, but we had to be back by 9:00. One night, when I was fourteen, I was standing with a group of friends in front of a grocery store puffing at a cigarette when *papá* sneaked up behind me and snuffed out the lighted cigarette right in my mouth. I turned around to see who'd done it and he slapped my face. I ran away but he called me back and said, "Do you earn money to pay for your cigarettes? Don't let me catch you smoking ever again as long as you live."

But I kept on smoking on the sly because I already had the habit. It's only lately that I've begun to smoke in front of *papá*. Even after I was married and had children, I didn't dare light a cigarette in his presence.

Nobody can imagine how bitterly hard my childhood was. I suffered, really suffered. That's why I don't like to spank my children. I suffered so much that when I was only nine a patch of my hair turned gray, and a few years later all my hair turned white. I never told *mamá* the troubles I had at *papá*'s house—not until I was a grown man anyhow. She'd ask me, "Is your stepmother nice to you boys?" And I'd always answer, "Yes, she's nice to us." I figured that telling her the truth would simply make things worse.

It would have been much nicer for me to be brought up by *mamá* and *papá* together. I'll tell you why: I wanted to study. Now my brain has become dull and numb and I can no longer grasp what I read unless it's quite short, but as a child, even though I'd get respiratory trouble whenever I read anything, I could engrave it on my mind. A school inspector who heard me recite my lessons said I was one of the most promising students in the school.

But no one seemed to care to help me. My stepmother got her daughter private lessons and afterward sent her to preparatory school, while I, who was such a promising student, wasn't given that kind of help. I decided, "Very well then, I won't study anymore." I stayed out of school every day until the teacher sent for *papá*, who beat me up in front of everybody. He pinched me in the belly again and again. Back home he said to me, "All right, either you go to school or you get a job."

"I'll get a job," said I. So one day I went to see Cayo, a man who lived around the corner from us and worked on a beer truck. I asked Cayo for a job helping him load and unload. "All right," said he, "come tomorrow at 4:00 in the morning." I started working with him, as a helper. At the end of my first trip, he gave me 1 *peso*. I went home happily and gave the money to my old man. When *papá* was away, I put my wages into a tin can he'd made into a bank by locking it with a padlock.

I was as skinny as a strand of dry spaghetti at the time and not nearly strong enough to load and unload a case of beer. But when I was fifteen, after working a year, I unloaded a *casilla* that held 300 cases of beer. When a cargo of beer was expected at the warehouse, I was always there to unload it, but when no beer came there was no work for me. Business was best during the sugar-cane harvest, when the grocery stores of all the *centrales* and *colonias* ordered the most beer. Then I earned good money.

In Morón there were large warehouses that had everything—a place to toast coffee, a bakery, bottles of Canada Dry, hardware. They sold wholesale, and aside from that they had a grocery store where they carried on retail trade. Many stores, especially country stores, bought their supplies from those warehouses. Practically all the grocery stores on the sugar-cane plantations were stocked by them.

The warehouse we delivered beer for was owned by a Spaniard from Galicia, Rosendo Garrido. When beer sales were slow, he'd employ me to stack sacks of salt or sugar and sometimes to clerk in the store. He always had some kind of job to offer me. On days when no corn arrived at the warehouse something else did, so there was always work to be done. I'd earn 2 *pesos* a day in the store over and above what I earned loading and unloading beer. It all added up to quite a tidy sum.

Nowadays I don't have the cockfighting fever I once had, but when I was young, I always went around with a bantam cock under my arm. Near my home they raised fighting cocks, and there I learned how to take care of them. One day, when I was sixteen or so, I visited Angel's cockfight place, "El Circo," and Angelito asked me to stay on and work. When I refused he approached *papá*, who forced me to. You see, I wasn't master of my own person, you might say, until a relatively short time ago. So as long as I was living with *papá*, I was under his orders and had to obey him.

Angelito exploited me. He paid me only 6 *pesos* a month, and he'd kid me along, saying, "I'll pay you more when you learn the job." But he didn't do a lick of work; I was the one who did everything.

I lost very few of my own cocks because I was lucky. A Haitian gave me one that I had in six different fights. That bird was quite an expense, I'm telling you! I'd go for days without food so I'd have enough money to care for it. When the cockfighting season was over I'd go back to loading and unloading beer.

Mamá moved to Havana and rented a room in El Vedado. She lived there with Coloma and Andrés, who must have been about five or six years old at the time. Andrés is my half-brother.

I can't tell you much about Andrés's *papá*. *Mamá* had relations with him but they never had a house or anything together because he had a wife, so I don't know how he treated *mamá,* how long their relationship lasted, or whether they even saw much of each other. As far as I know, *mamá* had no other man except him after she broke up with *papá*. We kids had no idea what was going on; *mamá* never gave us the slightest reason to suspect she was having a relationship with a man.

My sister Avelina came to Havana too, with her husband and daughters. All my sisters and my mother worked as housemaids there. My brother Dámaso left his first wife and his two small daughters in Camaguey and came to Havana. Meanwhile Laura's husband had died, and Coloma had hitched up with someone. They all lived together in Havana but I stayed with *papá* in Morón, working on the beer truck.

Finally, when there were eighteen or more relatives and friends living with *mamá* in Havana, they all moved to a larger place in Regla. Not that it was all that big—it was a tiny wooden house—but at least it was better than living in a single room. It had three small bedrooms, a parlor, the dining room and kitchen together, and one bathroom. It was a puzzle sometimes to figure out who was going to sleep in what room and on which bed. You can imagine how crowded they were! Those who couldn't find a place in bed would hunt for a bit of space on the floor. If you got up at night after everyone was in bed and all the lights were out, you had to feel your way around carefully to make sure you wouldn't step on anybody.

Where I worked there were trucks that often made trips to Havana to buy merchandise, and I'd ride along so I could visit my family. Other times I'd come by bus. I loved to make that trip to Havana. I'd get on the bus without even a spare shirt. Sometimes I'd be out near the terminal with my friends and catch sight of the bus and *pam!* I'd hop on and go to Havana just as I was. By 6:30 in the morning I'd be there. The fare cost a bit over 8 *pesos*.

When I went to visit *mamá* I'd go in one door and out another, so to speak, because I didn't like Havana. I went to visit her because she's as good as bread and I love her dearly, but I didn't have any intention of living there. *Mamá* used to call me "our man on the road" because I'd often arrive in Havana in the morning and *pam!* I'd leave that very night.

A couple of days later I'd receive a letter from *mamá*: "*Muchacho*, here I was thinking you were still in Havana and you'd already left!"

It wasn't that I was scared of Havana—I'm not afraid of anything—but I was used to living in Morón, where I was welcome to go here, there, all over the neighborhood. In those days you couldn't do that in Havana. You could barely greet your next-door neighbors. I found city life oppressive and unpleasant. That's changed a great deal nowadays. At least there's more solidarity between neighbor and neighbor than before. *Coño*, Havana isn't a shadow of what it used to be!

It was horribly difficult to get a job in Havana, though I managed to work there now and then. But there were lots of jobs to be had in Morón, and I went back to the agency where I'd worked before, loading trucks. They went wild with joy, even if I say so myself. I was the favorite there. "Hey, are we ever glad to see you! There's a terrific rush today." It was Christmas Eve, see? So I got busy right away and simply stayed on working there.

There was a lot of competition among the three most popular beers—Polar, Cristal, and Hatuey, in that order. The company I worked for asked me if I'd be willing to go out at night to help sell their beer. So after work I'd take a bath, change my clothes, and go to a bar. I'd go in and say, "Pepe, give me a beer, and while you're about it, serve everybody. The treat's on me." It wouldn't cost me 1 *centavo* out of my own pocket because the company would give me money and pay for the trip. I'd order as many as 200 or 300 beers a night and then sign a slip for them. I got used to being sociable and having a good time. I always felt happy doing that job. Before I knew it, my personality changed. My brother Dámaso always smiles when he's having a good time and I do too. I'm happy even when I'm not smiling.

At that time the other beer companies kept trying to get me to work with them because I did such a good job. When I work, I get a lot done and even stimulate the others to work harder. I was promoted step by step until I almost reached the rank of head of the warehouse. I got a lot of consideration from the owner of the warehouse. For instance, it was against the rules to drink on the job but I was authorized to do it.

Let me tell you one thing. I never drank because of any problem. Drinking won't rid you of your problems, no matter how drunk you get. See what I mean? It's a fact that anybody who drinks to forget his problems isn't going to do anything except make them worse.

I worked for the beer company as a temporary worker. There were too many men rather than too few; there wasn't always enough work to go around. Then only those with seniority, like me, were given jobs. The time came when I'd been employed there the longest, though I couldn't prove it. That was my problem—I didn't appear in their books as an employee. There were several others in the same boat. They were all considered substitutes—temporary workers—who worked for the company for stretches of time but weren't down in the books as regular workers.

I never had fixed wages. Some months I'd get 100 *pesos*, others 200 or 300. The minimum one could earn in one month was 60 *pesos,* which were the wages they paid—2 *pesos* a day. But during carnival time I got paid 2 *pesos* a day whether or not I showed up for work. I worked steadily then, unloading beer night and day, and didn't get home to sleep until 2:00, 3:00, or 4:00 in the morning. If I was too tired to work the next day, I wouldn't show up but I was paid anyway.

Before the Revolution I often participated in carnivals in Morón, but I haven't been to one since. They used to last one month, and later on fourteen more days were added. They were really something! There were many *comparsas.*[78] Every institution formed one: the Unión Fraternal, the Sociedad del Liceo, the Colonia Española, the Sociedad Asociación Canaria, and so on. There were also private *comparsas* formed by groups of young people who didn't belong to any of the clubs. We formed one made up of people living in the same *reparto.* I myself organized it and taught them the dance steps. I love to dance, especially when I'm out front directing and organizing. The company I worked for partly financed our costumes because it was good publicity for them. Our *comparsa* got first prize for dancing, and two other *comparsas,* a colored people's club and a whites' club, got prizes for the best costumes.

When I was young I was a member of the Sociedad Fraternal, a colored people's club in Morón. I never had any trouble getting in, but there were people who didn't qualify for membership. Being poor was no bar to membership as long as you were decent. You couldn't belong if you dressed in rags or went about dirty, or used dirty words in front of the women. Every December 7, the anniversary of Antonio Maceo's death, the club brought orators from other towns to speak about Maceo's life and everybody was invited.

The Sociedad existed mainly to hold dances, but they didn't have them often enough to suit me, so I dropped my membership and went dancing in Velazco or some other town. That was expensive in those times. You had to pay 4.50 or 5 *pesos* to get in, but here in Havana poor people could dance at La Tropical or La Polar for only 49 *kilos* a night.

78. A group of costumed, masked dancers. In Cuba the *comparsas* traditionally took part in the processional festivities of the annual carnival on Epiphany (January 6, the Day of the Three Kings). The *comparsas* date back to the nineteenth century, when it was the policy of the Spanish colonial government to receive in procession official delegations of the *cabildos de nación,* mutual-benefit associations of native Africans. The *comparsas* were banned at the time of the War of Independence and re-emerged in the twentieth century in the carnivals of Havana and Santiago. In Cuba today, this form of African expression takes place largely in the *Conjunto Folklórico Nacional* under the National Council of Culture. (Booth, "Neighbourhood Committees and Popular Courts," pp. 240, 241, 259.)

I began to go to fiestas and wakes for the santos[79] only after I was seventeen or so and was free to do as I pleased. Now I'm a santero myself and have an altar at home. I'm a devotee, or, as we say, a son of St. Lazarus. I adore all the other saints, but his image is the largest one on my altar. Those whose devotion is for St. Barbara or the Virgen de la Caridad del Cobre honor their favorite saint in the same way. The saint that you put at the forefront of your altar is the one you most adore.

I don't know an awful lot about santería, even though I'm a santero myself. It's true that I've gone to fiestas de santo; papá did too, but not mainly for the sake of the saints, though he does believe in them. No, he went for much the same reason I go—to see the women there. Mamá believes in santería and spiritism but she never taught us about them. Not mamá. As far as I can figure it out, there are those who are santeros because they made a ceremony to get a guardian spirit, and others who are santeros because the spirit descended unasked and crowned them.

The first time I visited a brothel I wasn't yet fifteen, but I was well grown and muscular because of the heavy work I did. There wasn't anything to do at night in a small town except go to the movies, unless there happened to be a street dance or a fair. I liked the brothel and it was so easy to say to a friend, "Hey, compadre, let's go there." We went often and I made more and more friends there, until finally we wound up going almost every night papá was away. When papá was home, I'd stay home too and go to bed early.

I had to keep my visits to women from papá. It was hard to carry on a secret affair. I'd leave home in the morning already dressed up and go to work that way. After work, I'd go to the girl's house and get home all out of breath around 6:00 the next morning. Papá would be up and he'd ask me, "Hey, what's this? Didn't you come home to sleep last night?"

"I stayed up all night at the wake of a friend's father," I'd tell him. I sure killed off a lot of my friends' relatives that way! Sometimes, to vary my stories a bit, I'd tell him it was a wake for some saint. I always had a story ready.

I had more than one sweetheart before I got married. The first one—her name was Coleta—burned to death. Frankly, I didn't court her, she courted me. She worked in a club and they gave a dance every week. I knew from the very first that she wasn't a virgin; in fact, she was a woman of the life. And the things she said! Being a man, I had to play a man's part, right?

The very first night, Coleta took me to her house. I didn't live with her long, though. I had my job and helped her out, but she kept on working. I was young and didn't have enough evil in me to lead the life of a pimp.

79. In santería, the word santo embodies both the Roman Catholic concept of saint and the Yoruban concept of orisha or spirit.

I never took money from her—at first. Later on I found it easy to, and *pam!* I found myself falling into a life of evil. Any man who lives with a prostitute and claims he doesn't live off her is lying.

I soon realized I'd taken the wrong path. I didn't have the courage to tell *papá* what I was up to, though. Then things began to take a turn I hadn't counted on. Coleta wanted me to move all my clothes over to her house. I decided not to because I'd only get in deeper with her. Finally one day I told *papá* everything. He said that in a way it wasn't important, but it might be very bad for me to get too involved with that woman; it might ruin me as a person. So I broke with her.

Ever since I was a boy, *papá* has told me stories about people and explained what life is like. He's taught me many things and I'm grateful to him for it. I've always consulted him when I've had a problem. Even now, if I find myself blocked in figuring out something, I ask for my parents' opinion. I tell *mima* some things but I tell *papá* everything.

After Coleta, I'd go into any bar in Morón and all the women would fuss over me and call me "darling"—*alma mía*. Not because I was handsome or anything but because at the time there weren't many men making 4 *pesos* a day. Besides, my job allowed me to spend all kinds of money on beer. Coleta started living with another man, but one day she set herself on fire. No one ever knew why she committed suicide.

I felt bad about Coleta, but after all, I had to leave her. I didn't want to get in trouble with the law. I'd been accused of stealing before. I'd taken an examination for a job as a lineman for the railroads and for a time was employed to relieve the workers on the trains. Well, after I'd been working there about two weeks, they discovered that an iron bar about 7 feet long was missing and they blamed me.

Papá went to Camaguey to talk to the police and of course they called me in to the Morón office for questioning. One of the policemen lied and said he'd seen me take it. "Why would I have stolen it?" I argued. "What would I use it for?" But they canceled my job and I went back to the beer company, where I earned more money anyway. About two months later they found the iron bar, but I already had a police record.

I had some other trouble with the law in 1949 or '50. I was on my way to work when a cop arrested me for stealing. He took me to the police station, where a little old white woman took one look at me and said, "Yes, he's the one." I had to go on trial and everything. The judge asked her, "Well, ma'am, what do you have to say?"

"Well, Your Honor," she answered, "I'm not accusing this man. Frankly, all black men look alike to me."

Then the judge said, "The defendant may speak now. And may I inform you, ma'am, that if he wishes to, he has every legal right to sue you for slander." He went on and on and I was declared innocent. I had the lawyer from my work center backing me, and everybody was in court that day, even Rosendo, the owner of the warehouse, but I didn't choose to bring charges against her. I wasn't born into this world for the purpose of harming anybody. The only thing I asked was that she repay me for the two days' work I'd lost.

You know, sometimes I still look at Leticia with a kind of amazement that she's my wife, in spite of my having been married to her for so many years. We've known each other since we were kids. I was about fourteen when I first saw her, which means that she was about four because I'm ten years older. If anybody asked me when I first began to fall in love with her, I couldn't say because I honestly don't know. *Ay,* imagine trying to remember a romance that took place fifteen and a half years ago!

Leticia's family lived near *papá,* and one of her elder brothers was my playmate. We were great friends and his *mamá* was like a mother to me. She was affectionate and had a gay, happy temperament. She was a lot of fun. It's eight years since she died, and when I look at that picture of her on the wall, I feel she's still alive.

When Leticia was a girl I went around with her but we weren't sweethearts, though everybody took it for granted that we were. It was odd because we liked each other a lot, yet neither of us expected to fall in love. She was a very, very affectionate girl. I had nobody at home to do my laundry, so she washed my clothes and that gradually won me over. Before I woke up to the fact, she'd gained a lot of ground in my affections. She was a very capable girl and I was quite conquered by her. Well, I simply decided to be her sweetheart.

I wanted to have a talk with Leticia's *mamá* and tell her we were engaged, but somehow it was very difficult to do. I was afraid her *mamá* might feel I'd shown her disrespect and taken advantage of the family's friendship to woo her daughter. So the day I went to tell her, I was about twelve steps under water, as we Cubans say. I'd taken a heap of drinks. But even then, if Leticia hadn't pushed me, I think I might never have had the courage to talk to her *mamá.*

I needn't have worried. When I finally managed to get out that I wanted to marry Leticia, her *mamá* answered, "And who better?"

We got married by a judge in April, 1954. I was twenty-five and Leticia almost sixteen. Naturally I wore a *guayavera,*[80] and Leticia had on a dress of some sort but it wasn't a wedding dress. A few of her relatives attended the ceremony, but none of my family was there and we didn't throw a big party or invite this or that person. No indeed, nothing like that.

One usually has to pay the notary, but it didn't cost me 1 *centavo,* because the beer company sent whole cases of beer, free, to the notary and even to the chief of police. So I could relax as far as that was concerned, because the notary didn't charge me anything.

80. A pleated shirt-jacket popular among Cuban men.

I didn't get nervous—that only happens to a kid of seventeen or eighteen—because as a grown man I thought that getting married was the right thing to do. I mean, I had some experience of the world and I thought, "I'm going to get married so I can calm down and stop running around with lots of women and settle down in a home of my own." My brain accepted what I was doing as something positive, legal, and useful.

After we were married, we went straight from the judge's office to our new home. We didn't get it really fixed up until the next day. The bed had been set up but the mattress was standing end up against the wall and everything else was still packed. The room was in a house belonging to the owner of the warehouse. The place was what used to be called a *cuartería*, but we were the only tenants because Rosendo had made everybody move out long before and used the rooms to store salt. He needed to have someone living there, see, because otherwise people could break in and steal things. So you might say I was there as a kind of night watchman. He turned the whole *cuartería* over to me. We spent two or three months in one room, then I had the room next to it painted and moved my stuff into it, bedroom set and all. The furniture was made for me by a carpenter friend of mine. Everything else I could buy at the warehouse and pay them back with work.

I had no cause to complain about my boss. When a 300-pound sack of sugar smashed my toe, Rosendo rushed me to the clinic. I was there for nineteen days and he arranged for the insurance company to pay.

After that, I went to Havana and was operated on for hemorrhoids at the Calixto García. It was a public hospital, so I didn't have to pay anything there either. I was paid my full wages during the whole of my stay in the hospital, both in Morón and in Havana. I asked Rosendo for 150 *pesos* for the trip, and a week later I sent for 50 more, which I didn't really need.

In 1955 there was a change in the warehouse personnel. They fired Torcuato, the manager, because he was embezzling from the food section. That guy was like a knife, slicing away at the profits. They appointed a Spaniard, Diego Sánchez Barbudo, who'd come to Cuba to escape from Spain.

Under Diego I assumed a new responsibility. I was, you might say, almost head of the beer warehouse. I looked out for sales and had the authority to put the other men to work. Diego also put me in charge of the grocery store at the Colonia Margarita, a *colonia* belonging to Benigno Rosales. He was Spanish and one of the richest landowners around. The Colonia Margarita wasn't awfully big and the cane was ground at a sugar mill near Morón.

During the entire sugar harvest of 1956—from January to April—I was the one who ran the grocery store, out there in the country. If we were running short of rice or anything, I'd make an order for whatever it was, say ten sacks of rice, five of sugar, ten cases of *aguardiente*,[81] ten cases of cognac, and so forth. Then at night I'd leave a note, and in the morning, *pam!* they'd bring the merchandise from the warehouse.

It was Diego's job as steward of the *colonia* to keep the accounts of the cane-cutter's wages. He added up the total number of *arrobas* they cut so that when payday came he knew how much each one got. The steward also kept track of what each worker bought on credit from the store, and the cash advances he got. Then, on the 1st and 15th of the month, when the workers got paid, Diego knew how much to deduct from their wages.

Diego was very harsh with practically all the workers under him. Frankly, I never had any cause to complain until the very last, but he was a despot with the others, the kind of man who wouldn't say a polite word to a *machetero*. And in those days, a cane-cutter didn't earn enough to feed himself. I should know—I had to keep a special record of their wages. On paydays we'd set up a table and Diego would sit down with a bookkeeper and me to hand out the pay.

There were over 150 Haitians and Jamaicans in that *colonia* and I was ready to be of service to them. Some spoke Spanish and others spoke Congolese, more or less. I mean their speech was more blurred. Most of them were bachelors and lived in the two big barracks about 150 meters beyond the grocery store. One or two of the Haitians or Jamaicans might have a brother or cousin working in Cuba, but only very rarely would you find one with a wife and children. The same thing was true of the Chinese. The men came here to see the world and then got used to the place and stayed on. Cuban workers also lived in the barracks, because when a Cuban goes to cut cane he leaves his family behind.

Most of the barracks where the workers lived were filthy sties and didn't even have a stove to cook on. The workers would make a wood fire and set their cookpots on three large stones or on two rows of stones on the floor. It was real crude. Some *colonias* had mess halls where a cane-cutter could have his name put down on the eating list for about 1.50 *pesos* a day, I think. Every fifteen days, when he got paid, he had 25 *pesos* for his meals deducted from his wages. They also deducted whatever he spent on tobacco, matches, bread, and any such trifles that he'd charged at the store.

At the *colonia* where I was, the workers had to buy food from the grocery store and cook their own meals. The *colonia* owners never gave anyone anything except a job. The Cuban workers slept in their own hammocks made out of sugar sacks, and they even had to buy rope for their hammocks at the *colonia* store. Some store owners charged for the sacks too.

The Haitians slept in a kind of bed they call *canapé*, made mainly with banana straw and palm leaves. First they make the crib frame, then the

81. An alcoholic drink, in Cuba made from sugar cane.

rope network with dry banana leaves. They place the palm leaves underneath and cover them with sacks. The insides must be changed now and then, though, because the leaves rot. Sometimes the barracks stank horribly of rotting leaves.

Some of the Haitians went from place to place like swallows, from the first tobacco harvest in Pinar del Río, to the sugar harvest in Camaguey and Las Villas, and finally to pick coffee in Oriente. Some would go back to Haiti after the coffee harvest but not all of them. I know because I heard them talking about it.

Now that we're in the revolutionary process, cane is cultivated differently. In the old times there used to be men who planted cane and nothing else, and others who watered it and nothing else. After the harvest some men did nothing but rake dead leaves, for very low wages.

During the dead season when there was no work, the owner of the *colonia* would keep on three or four of the neediest workers full time. He'd also hire a few others who worked on their own and were paid by the job. Say there was a cane field and you agreed to hoe it for 15 *pesos*. If you were working for the company, you got paid at the rate of 1.50 or 2 *pesos* a day, which were the rates then. Low wages, eh? And some worked for even less, depending on the man's quality, you might say. That was one thing about the Haitians—many owners of small sugar-cane farms exploited them. Imagine a man earning 1.25 *pesos* a day! How much of that would he spend on food? But a fellow who worked on his own got better terms. He could say, "I charge 8 *pesos* for hoeing that plot of land." Then the bargain was struck and he got the work done in two or three days.

The dead time was really dead because very few people remained in the *colonia*. The grocery store closed down and you had to go as far as Morón or Punta Alegre to buy food.

After I began working for Diego, I found that the store wasn't doing any business. There were stores in the other *colonias* too. Each *colonia* employed hundreds of workers, and the cane-cutters could buy on credit only at their *colonia* store. None of the men working in Diego's *colonia* wanted to buy there because of all the abuses—the dirty tricks and rude treatment—that had been committed against them before I came. But while I was manager, I gave credit to numbers of workers from other *colonias*, and I got them, and even the customers of other stores, to buy from me. Some of my credit customers were people who made a long trip to buy at my store because they knew they'd be well treated there.

In those days most shopkeepers would give a customer 2 ounces less than he paid for, if they could get away with it. The Haitians used to walk 10 leagues to reweigh their purchases in other shops to make sure they hadn't been cheated. But when I weighed the goods, they never doubted me. The workers would come to me from the cane fields and say, "Labrada, give me a shot of *aguardiente*."

I'd say, "Easy, boys. First of all, I want you to have a drink on me." Then I could hear them murmur, "Labrada is a good guy. Labrada buys us drinks." It only cost the store 35 *centavos* for the whole bottle, and every customer who drank a shot of it would buy something. I'd give them an ounce and a half less of this, that, and the other, and by the time I added up the total, they'd be paying for 10 or 12 ounces more than they'd bought. Which means that I got full value for every shot of liquor I gave away, but the client never knew it. He was grateful for the drinks, and since they trusted me, they never, never re-weighed the stuff. That's the way I worked it, see?

The following year the store at the El Glorioso *colonia* was reopened for the *zafra,* and they asked me whether I wanted to take charge of it. I refused. I was fed up with the country and wanted to move back to town. But I want you to know one thing—I got along fine with everybody there. Listen, once someone tried to rob me. I fired a shot, and all the Haitians flocked to the store to see what was the matter. Another time I got there at 4:00 in the morning and they were all there, surrounding the store to protect it because they knew I was away. And when my wife was pregnant with Bárbara, they dumped a pile of trussed-up chickens in the barracks for me to take to her.

Toward the last of my stay on the job in the store, I brought my little brother-in-law Fermín to help me. We slept right there and he learned to wait on customers and everything. At first I'd stay in the store seven or eight days at a time, see? Then I'd go home and take 20 *pesos* to my wife and write down the amount. I kept strict accounts of the wages due me and of what my wife spent. But the Twenty-sixth of July Movement was very active then and Batista's government was killing a lot of people, so at times I didn't go home for about twenty-five days. That made my wife kind of distant with me. Of course, it's understandable. As she said, I was working near home and had no work at night, so why didn't I come home? Especially when I had helpers looking after the shop when I was away.

That was years ago, when Leticia and I hadn't been living together very long. She got jealous and brooded over it, until she finally wrote a letter to Diego. I don't know what the letter actually said, but according to Diego, she wrote that I was going around with other women because I never went home to sleep or anything. It was some kind of crazy story people had put into Leticia's head. They also told Diego that I left the store every night to go play dominoes with the Haitians, and so forth.

I didn't quarrel with Leticia or anything. I simply asked her, "If I were doing what you suspect, would I have your brother with me?"

As chance would have it, the one day I really did leave the store, Diego happened to go there to make a delivery! I went to Morón, and when I got back, there he was. He told me he'd heard I hardly ever was in the store because I spent all my time going around with women. "*Caray,* what goings-on!" Diego said. He spoke so rudely to me that I told him, "Look, kid, there are two ways you can go about this—either you take over the store or I keep on managing it, so there's nothing more to be said."

Diego turned his back on me and walked away. He's the kind of a guy you simply can't explain things to. "Ask the cane-cutters and all the neighbors here," I told him. "I often go to visit the Haitians and play dominoes with them until 11:00 at night or so, but whoever told you the other stories about me lied."

I took care to get along with everybody—my fellow workers, the customers, the owner. I always made friends easily and many of those friendships have lasted. It's been a long time—years in fact—since I managed that store. Yet when I go back, I get along fine with the people I knew because I'm always nice to people. Manners make the man, you know.

Everything was going fine until Diego heard those stories. After that he changed toward me. I stayed on at the store a little longer. But things weren't going so well anymore. They didn't treat me the way they used to. I'd sold piles and piles of stuff—I'd really helped that business—so at the end of my last fifteen-day period there, I said, "Gosh, Diego, I need 100 *pesos* for my brother, who's going to Havana." I didn't really need them, but I know how to go about things. There's no point being good in this world. That's life.

He answered in these words, "We'll try to find a way to arrange this, Domingo, but I don't think you've got 100 *pesos* coming to you here."

After the harvest, Diego manipulated the accounts to show that he didn't owe me anything. Since that store didn't pay for a license, we were outside the law, see? So if I thought I should be paid a commission, what law could I appeal to? How could I win if I sued? Diego knew what he was doing—that guy's a genius—so I resigned myself. I mean, what the hell, I was born with nothing, wasn't I? I told them to get someone else to run the store for the rest of the *zafra,* and I went back to work at the warehouse.

That same year *papá* was in a train collision. The machinist was killed, and *papá,* who was working as a stoker, fell underneath the train and his leg was crushed. They were going to chop it off, but he escaped from the hospital, broken leg and all. In those days they'd amputate a leg or an arm for anything like that. Well, the bone knit again—the doctors could hardly believe it—but his leg was lame.

Papá retired after that and was in Morón all by himself. So when Leticia decided she wanted to move to Havana in 1957, I thought it would be best to take *papá* with us. I said to him, "You're old. If you should get sick and have to be hospitalized, you'll be better off in Havana, where we can all go to visit you. Here you don't even have anybody to take you to the doctor." So we all moved to Havana and I brought *papá* to live at *mamá*'s house in Regla. The only thing *mamá* said to him was, "Well, have you finally settled down?" He stayed with her for a while and they got along very well. But the grandchildren made a lot of noise and he likes to nap in the afternoon, so he moved to a little room down the block.

One day *papá* got to helping a girl carry bricks and one of them hit him on the bad leg. The blow hurt the bone and made all the splinters come loose again. They started to rot and he got boils, so I took him to the hospital. "*Chico,*" the doctor told me, "the only way to cure him is to amputate that leg."

I told him, "Look, doctor, I'd rather he kept his leg even if it meant he'd die in three days and if cutting it off added ten years to his life. And another thing—I'm going to take him home and take care of him there. I'll bring him to you every week for a checkup."

At home I started plucking out the bone splinters from *papá*'s leg with a pair of tweezers. It must have hurt but he never cried out. He only made a face. I can't even tell you how many splinters I pulled out. I collected a whole jar full. Now all he has left of his illness is a kind of hollow in his leg.

Leticia and I were staying at my sister's house, also in Regla. To look for a job I'd get up at 4:00 or 4:30 practically every morning and walk all the way from Regla to Havana. I had to get to the construction sites before 7:00, when the foreman arrived, but often there was nothing. That's the way I lived for several months.

Later I decided to go back to the country because I couldn't make a living. I had to leave my wife in Havana. Hard up though I was, I didn't want Leticia to take a job. I've never liked that—I'm the one who should work. But after I went to Morón, I think my old lady got her a job, because when I came back Leticia was working.

I stayed in Morón about four months, asking around for a job. That was near the end of 1958, see, and by then people weren't taking on new employees because of the Revolution. My kind of job was closed. Why? Because one couldn't go anywhere. They'd blown up the bridges and there was no way for the trucks to get in or out. You could always earn a couple of *pesetas* helping to unload merchandise, and if it was a sugar truck you could earn 8 or 10 *pesos*. But now all the transportation circuits were cut off. Everything was stopped—construction, everything.

There was a lot of vice at that time—gambling houses all over the place and thousands of people living like parasites, spending all their days at those joints. They lived on their winnings. But I couldn't even do that. What was I to gamble with when I could hardly afford to eat? There I was right in my hometown, yet I went hungry. Yes, I went hungry!

My wife's family was still living outside Morón, and I went to visit them. I often slept at their small house but I never took so much as one single plate of food from them. They'd ask me, "Have you already eaten?" and I'd always say yes, even if I hadn't had a bite all day long. I simply didn't know how to act, because such a thing had never happened to me before. More than once I went to bed at night without having eaten all day long. But "Forward," I said to myself, "Forward!"

I talked to Rosendo and he gave me a three-day job in the store I'd formerly run. Sometimes I had to go to him for 2 or 3 *pesos* because I had nothing to eat. "Well, Rosendo," I'd say, "I've sure knocked around all over the place, but here I am again." And it seems he understood the situation I was in.

If I should tell anyone I had even a faint idea of what the Revolution was, I'd be deceiving him. I wasn't connected with it in any way. I had many close friends who were involved in the Twenty-sixth of July Movement—I really did—but in spite of that, I can't fill my mouth with boasts and say, "Yes indeed, I was involved and did thus-and-so for the Movement."

At that time I was ignorant of everything that was going on. There was talk about the attack on the Moncada and all that, but the first time I remember hearing Fidel mentioned was one day when some American newspapermen went to the Sierra to interview him.[82] I couldn't explain why Fidel was in the Sierra; I slowly learned about his ideals after the transformation.

Diego was involved in the Movement and he used to ask me to go along with him, and I'd go, quite innocently. He'd park the car in front of some place and I'd sit outside waiting for him. He never explained what it was about. Seeing as how we were such close friends, if he didn't tell me what was going on, why should I ask him? He didn't look to me to join and we weren't so close that he dared trust me with that kind of a secret. But he and the others would kid me and say, "This *negro* is going to be a lieutenant one of these days." But I had no idea what they meant by it. It was only at the very last that I found out what was in their program.

The Revolution wasn't really out in the open until the *casquitos* came to Morón. The *casquitos* were young boys in Batista's military service, but if you so much as looked them in the face they'd beat you up, right there in the street. It was then that I woke up to what was going on. My opinion that things were bad was based on what I myself saw.

There were people who tried to make you talk to find out what you really thought. I didn't dare speak about anything because I didn't know who was to be trusted. Often at midnight they'd knock on this or that

82. Herbert Matthews of the *New York Times* interviewed Castro in the Sierra Maestra in February, 1957.

guy's door and take him away. So I simply didn't talk about anything that could get me into any kind of trouble.

The Batista regime had a long list of people to be killed as a "gift" on the Day of the Three Kings in 1959, and if the Revolution hadn't triumphed they'd all be dead by now. I can't swear that my name was on that list, but a guy I know told me it was. And it could be. Do you know why? When Comandante Oligario of Batista's police force came to Morón from Ciego de Avila, he tried to get men to join the police. I told Rosendo I didn't want to join because I wouldn't make a good cop and didn't like the idea of being one. He said not to worry because there was a lot of work at the warehouses and he needed every man he had. In the end, Rosendo didn't agree to let any of his workers join the force.

Comandante Oligario was well known to everybody in Cuba during Batista's regime. He was terrible. He had three big mulattoes as body-guards. When he passed by somebody he disliked, all he had to do was nod his head slightly and walk on—his bodyguards would take care of the guy. Oligario was a good-looking fellow, over 6 feet tall, always very well dressed. When he fell for a girl he'd keep after her. He'd go to her parents' house and tell them, "I've come here because I'm a man who respects others. I'm in love with your daughter and I'm not the kind who'd stand out in the street and pay compliments to a girl as she goes by."

Then, suppose the parents said, "But look, Señor, my daughter is engaged to a man she loves."

"Do you know who I am?" he'd answer. "I'm Comandante Oligario." And from that day forward the girl's parents would live in fear and trembling. Why? Because the man was a murderer. Of course I didn't see any of those things with my own eyes; I've only heard about them.

Then the parents would say, "Look, my child, this man has honorable intentions. Accept him." So he'd start courting the girl, and in a few days he'd take her to live with him. After a while he'd say to her, "I've got to go away now. I'll leave you in charge of a business I have that I won't be able to attend to myself." So he'd make her cashier at his club. In a week or so he'd have laid another girl, so he'd demote the first one to waitress and make the other one cashier. Every one of the women working in his club got there that way.

The club occupied the whole building. It was a big, big place, a kind of cabaret with bedrooms, and he had lots of women there. Vulgarly speaking, he had rooms to rent out in the back, like a *posada,*[83] and when a man went there he had plenty of women to choose from. Now there's a school where the club used to be.

I didn't know about the triumph of the Revolution right away. On that night I happened to be home and was about to go to bed when my

83. A lodging house where rooms are rented by the hour.

brother-in-law showed up. He'd just won a pile of *pesos* at a gambling joint and wanted me to go out and have a drink with him. So we went from bar to bar until we were both drunk and staggering down the middle of the street. We were in the part of town where the bad women were when he started yelling, "Long live Fidel Castro!"

We came to our block still shouting. A woman we'd known since we were kids opened the door and called, "Are you fellows crazy? Shut up before you get arrested and killed too!"

"Nuts!" says I. "Nobody can kill us!"

That very night the militia was organized to keep watch over the town, but we didn't know a thing about it. We didn't even know Batista was gone. Things looked perfectly normal. Why there were even lots of Batista's *casquitos* out in the streets!

The next morning we got the news. Everybody was talking about it. People were running around outside and everything was upside down. Somebody would close down the shops and in a few minutes a new group would come by and open them to take what they wanted. People were carrying out the electric fans and adding machines from gambling joints and destroying the gaming tables. That's what it was like. I had one hell of a hangover but I saw all that.

In a little while the word went round that the *guardia* was in the army headquarters. "I'm going there to see what's going on," I said. Several people had Twenty-sixth of July flags and even I went around with a flag on a stick—right out on the street! People were saying that the *barbudos* were coming to town and that we should be prepared to fight the *guardia*.

When the Rebels came down from the Florencia hills, the whole town went out to meet them. The Rebels marched down the street to army headquarters. They sent a commission in and the soldiers handed over their arms. Then other Rebels moved out of the crowd of townspeople and joined them. The *guardia* surrendered without a stone thrown or a shot fired! There was fighting only under Camilo, in Yaguajay and Santa Clara.

When I saw such a transformation take place, naturally I was happy, even though I had no idea at all what was going to happen next. I felt emotion because of the abuses that had been committed. Why look, before, you couldn't even laugh!

During all this time I was trapped in Morón. I couldn't even get word to my family in Havana. I'd write letters and post them and they'd stay right there in the mailbox. I wasn't able to get to Havana until January. There I found that some of my friends had put out flower wreaths for me, thinking I was dead.

Naturally in Havana I was out of a job. A nationwide strike began on January 1 and all the businesses were closed. Several comrades of mine were in the police force, but I said, "I'd rather work with a pick and shovel than be a policeman." Nobody looked kindly on policemen here because they'd beat people a hell of a lot. Also many who joined the police after the Triumph weren't revolutionaries; some had never shot one little bullet for the Revolution. Why, there were nobodies who even had the rank of captain. I didn't want to get involved with anything like that. But later on, when there was a real need, I rose to the occasion and joined the Army.

It wasn't until 1960 that a job came my way, when the work on the East Havana housing project started. After Fidel laid the cornerstone, I went to talk with a man who was in charge of hiring personnel and told him I could work as a carpenter, as an assistant, or as a common laborer. "Whatever work there is to be done, I'm willing to do it," I said. About twenty of us comrades got together and decided to go to Fidel's office. That day there were sixty or more men waiting for jobs. Five of us went up to speak to Fidel for the group and one of his secretaries gave us a note. The next day when we showed up at the project, the place was like a seedbed of workers, but we were all given jobs.

About a year later, in January, 1961, when we were expecting an American landing in our country, the workers were asked to volunteer to defend the fatherland. At that time the armed forces didn't have half the men they have now. So a number of trucks were sent to the construction site and many of my comrades at work scrambled aboard. As they were taking off they called, "Domingo, come on, *chico*, come along with us."

"No, no, not me," I answered, but all of a sudden I said, "I'm going!" And I jumped into the nearest truck.

We were driven over to the FAR, and at midnight we marched in formation to the Naval Hospital. From there we were sent to the coast in trucks, to work with picks and shovels for twenty-six days. Before I left, I sent word home twice with a fellow who worked with me, though we weren't supposed to tell our families where we were.

I was put to the proof for those twenty-six days out in the field. It was a kind of test, but many of the guys there didn't catch on to that. We camped out in the open—it so happened that during that month of January it rained every night and we had to take shelter under the trees—and there were days when no lunch or dinner arrived and we went hungry all day long.

The man we elected as our group sergeant quit when the food problem came up. He said, "I don't want any more trouble." Then I said, "Don't be silly, gentlemen. Anyone can go one day without eating."

"Very well, then you be the sergeant," they told me.

"All right. From now on, I'm the sergeant," I agreed. The very next day a jeep arrived at our camp. It had broken down and that's why they hadn't gotten food to us.

After twenty-six days we were transferred to the tower of *Radio Progreso*, under the orders of Comandante Universo Sánchez and Captain Núñez Jiménez.[84] On our third day in the tower, Núñez Jiménez arrived by helicopter and talked with us. He's a very open, hearty sort of man. I told him a number of comrades had cuts on their feet from walking barefoot out on the coast and he got shoes for them right away.

Some nights later we were all given passes to go home until early Monday morning. But on Monday very few men returned. In fact, all of the men on the East Havana construction went back to work. So at 3:00 that afternoon several trucks came and all of the workers were ordered to get in. Some of the fellows didn't do it, but as for me, *pam!* I jumped into one and went back to the camp.

There Núñez Jiménez spoke to us. He said we'd all be like sons of his. "Comrade Núñez Jiménez wishes to congratulate all of you," they announced, "and soon he'll enroll you in a program to train as sappers, because there are very few of them in Cuba. When you finish, you'll be prepared to teach it to others." The course lasted five and a half months, and 135 of us took it.

All that time we were on alert, like during the October crisis, when we were expecting something to happen from one minute to the next. Sometimes when we were about to go out on a pass, everybody would suddenly be ordered back to camp. When it was time to go to sleep we were locked in, with no idea why we were being confined to the barracks. Then, around midnight, when we were quietly sleeping, the sirens would sound. We'd jump out of our beds, half out of our minds because we didn't know whether this was simply a practice alarm or the real thing.

At first it took us eight or nine minutes to get ready during an alert, but later we did it in six and a quarter minutes. We really worked fast. I'd pick up my rifle first thing, not to show off but to protect myself. I'd keep it by me whether or not I was on guard duty.

We never received diplomas or graduated as sappers because Playa Girón was attacked just as the course was ending. We'd planned a hike to Havana that day, but instead we had to join Fidel's First Column at Playa Girón. Everybody wanted to go. When it comes to fighting, Cubans aren't cowards! But they said to us, "Well, gentlemen, we don't have enough equipment for the whole column and that means we can't all

---

84. Universo Sánchez, among the survivors of the *Granma* landing of December, 1956, is still an officer in the Cuban Army. Antonio Núñez Jiménez, an eminent Cuban geographer, joined Guevara's column at Santa Clara near the end of the campaign against Batista. He was a principal author of the first Agrarian Reform Law and served as the first director of the National Institute of Agrarian Reform until his dismissal in January, 1961. He has since served as president of the Academy of Sciences, ambassador to Peru (1974–75), and in 1976 was elected deputy from Placetas to the National Assembly.

go." So we drew lots and only six men of my platoon got to go. I had to stay behind.

After Girón was over, we were incorporated by platoons into different military units and the platoons were scattered. My platoon worked with explosives. In our new unit we had to load boxes of explosives as big as armchairs. We also made a shooting field for the tanks and were responsible for all the odd jobs around the unit. We even had a painter who was varnishing the *comandante*'s office. He got the paint all muddy-looking and the *comandante* called me in to oversee the work and I ended up by doing it myself. Heck, I don't know anything—I'm a jack-of-all-trades and master of none, but for all of that, I fixed the *comandante*'s office. I've got an ideal about work that's pretty progressive. I mean, heck, I've got brains.

One day, while we were working on a parking lot, the siren sounded and we all jumped on trucks and my group was taken back to camp and locked up under guard. About a week later, *pam!* my brother Dámaso and my friend Eladio showed up as part of the same group. Dámaso had joined the Army about two or three days after me, but we were separated when my group was confined. I said to him, "We've been locked up because we're about to be sent on I don't know what mission!"

"Ah, you don't know anything! From what I've heard, both of us are going to be sent overseas."

"All right," says I. "I'll go anywhere."

I was happy to go, especially with Dámaso and Eladio there. I've had only one real friend in all my life and that's Eladio Mazarredo. We grew up together, we've known each other all our lives. I feel great affection for him, even more than for Dámaso. Yes, yes, even more than for my brother. And as it turned out, we were all to go to Algeria together.

I knew about the Revolution in Algeria and Morocco and had discussed them with Lieutenant Fuentes. We'd read the newspapers together and he loved to discuss what he'd read. So much so that later they made him a teacher. I remembered that he'd said, "You know, Cuba will probably have to send reinforcements to Algeria."

"Well, *compadre*, if that happens, I won't miss the chance to take that trip," said I. When I said it, I had no idea I was really going.

There were 720 men selected from different sectors to be sent to Algeria. A friend of mine begged to go—he even knelt—but they wouldn't accept him. Three days later, after we received our orders, our group was taken to a military school. We stayed there two days doing sentry duty.

The first day Lieutenant Zayas was talking over the problem of hours and how the sentinel duty was going to be assigned, when I put in, "No, *chico*, it's easier to figure out the turns if we calculate the hours in minutes."

Well, he liked my attitude and said, "Yes, you're perfectly right."

On our second day there, Raúl Castro came to speak. There were over 300 of us waiting for him in a classroom. He began his discussion with the hardships we'd have to endure, and a number of fellows quit right then and there! Then he said, "If any of you has a problem, let him raise his hand." A heap of hands shot up right away. "Comandante, look, I can't go because my *mamá* is in the hospital and I...." Well, everyone went on like that, telling their problems.

"Comandante," I said when it was my turn, "I'm willing to go, not only to Algeria, but to any other place in the world, as long as you resolve my problem. I don't have a home of my own. My wife and kids and I live with relatives. We're overcrowded and we live in such-and-such conditions. Something has got to be done about it."

"Don't worry," said Raúl. "Anybody with that kind of a problem can go to Algeria and trust me to resolve it."

After they'd eliminated those men who were no good—kind of filtered out the impurities—Raúl spoke to us about what it was like in Algeria and explained what we were going to do. He said religion there was so strong that to root it out you'd have to kill every last Algerian, and we'd have to respect that. He told us how the women go around with veils over their faces and how the men are very jealous. "You should be very careful to respect the women," he said. Heck, you know what Cubans are like after they've been cooped up!

"You won't be able to go out in the street every day or anything like that," Raúl warned us. "You're going to be confined to camp most of the time. If any of you gets a pass, don't go to any bad places—that's my advice to you fellows. Why not? you ask. Because of the rottenness—the VD—understand? There's a lot of it there." The man told us everything.

After that meeting with Raúl, we filed out to the waiting buses, which took us straight to the docks. We took along cooks and everything we needed. We also took all sorts of armaments, tanks, antiaircraft batteries, the works, because those people had no weapons to defend themselves. They'd made a Revolution with their bare hands!

Well, I'd read about the Foreign Legion in *Selecciones*[85] and I'd said, "That's a bunch of lies! How can an army exist independently in a country, doing just what it pleases and yet being respected by the whole world?" Then I went to Algeria and found it was all true. I was right there, in the same place as the Foreign Legion, see? That was an important fact for me.

In Algeria we were directly under Comandante Efigenio Ameijeiras,[86] and he got his orders from Cuba. There isn't another guy like him in the

85. Spanish-language *Readers' Digest.*
86. See Part I, n. 22.

whole world, and I'm not kidding. He's a man with a hell of a lot of character. Why, he'd go around in the terrible cold of Algeria in nothing but a thin little sweater and play baseball. "Let's play ball now," he'd say. And we'd form into teams.

Ameijeiras went back to Cuba once while we were there, and while he was gone the Moroccans crossed the frontier. Ameijeiras's second-in-command wanted us Cubans to form a cordon there to keep the enemy out. They'd sounded the alarm and everything. There I was, ready to march to the frontier, when Ameijeiras suddenly showed up. When they told him what was going on, he said, "No! How can I take my men to the frontier to be killed in cold blood? No, my men aren't going, but if we ever do we won't stop there, we'll march on to Casablanca and to Spain if necessary." If it hadn't been for Ameijeiras, a heap of us Cubans would have been killed.

Over in Algeria we'd play checkers or something in the afternoon until dinner time. Then we'd eat and afterward we'd go back to our games. Some of the guys would make hot chocolate for everybody because it was so cold. Brrr, how I suffered from the cold there! I even froze my foot marching in a parade. It was a ceremony to hand over the weapons we brought from Cuba. The parade was on January 1, because whenever there was a parade in Cuba, there had to be one in Algeria too.

We were in formation on the road by 6:00 in the morning because nobody knew exactly at what hour Ben Bella[87] would pass by. It was snowing and raining at the same time, and there we stood, shivering in the cold. I'm telling you... ! Finally, at 11:00 in the morning, after five hours of waiting for the man, he showed up!

At the end of the parade we stood right in front of the reviewing stand. I was there, standing firm, and little by little my feet sank into the mud, until I was standing in a hole. When we finally got the word to march, I was limping. My foot swelled up, big as a ham. As soon as I got back to the barracks, I put it into the live flame and didn't even feel it. My foot was completely frozen and I limped for fourteen days. Luckily my brother Dámaso got me some tennis shoes, but even so I couldn't walk straight. Finally I got rid of the limp, but my foot still hurt. After I returned to Cuba, the warm climate here cured me completely.

Our families were well looked after while we were in Algeria. If *mamá* so much as said *"Ay!"* someone from the Party would come and say, "Let's go to the doctor." And they'd take her whether she wanted to go or not. Leticia was lucky enough not to get sick while I was away, but she didn't have to worry about me or Dámaso not being there. No, no, on the contrary—she had better attention with us two away than she ever had when we were there. I'm extremely grateful for that.

87. President of Algeria 1963–65.

We were allowed to receive letters, so after two months I wrote to Cuba asking for a snapshot of my daughter Andrea, who was a tiny little thing then, and they sent it to me. And of course they kept their promise to get my family a place to live.

Even before we returned from Algeria, my old lady was already having her house built. Dámaso had asked them to do that for her instead of finding him a place, because he was all alone then, without a wife or children. Although I've never mentioned it and never will, most of the material used to build the new house belonged to me, so they didn't have to spend anything on that. I was planning to build a new house, see, and I'd gotten over 1,000 cement blocks, as well as cement and about 12 meters of sand.

When I returned, the foundation had already been laid. I don't know who made the plans; the house is strongly built and all that, but far too small for the number of people who live in it. If they'd at least made a few rooms big enough to set up a couple of beds, that would have been plenty. Instead, it has two tiny bedrooms, each with space for only one bed, a small parlor, a tiny dining room, and a tiny kitchen. Just about big enough for a married couple living alone. But *mamá* has fifteen people living with her!

A new house was needed, of course, I'm not denying that. The old one I'd built for *mamá* was of wood, for one thing, and the roof leaked, so when it rained we had to move the beds and put buckets under the leaks. And of course there's no room for Dámaso, so, as it is, he has nothing.

All in all, I'm glad things worked out the way they did. And let me tell you something—the Revolution is very important to me because it gave me the opportunity to make that trip to Algeria. Still, I was glad to get back to Cuba. After six months overseas, my very first words when I got back home were, "Give me something to drink, I'm thirsty!"

My wife had saved a bottle of Bacardi rum to celebrate my return. I reached for it and they said, "No, *caballero*, no!" But I grabbed it and *pam!* emptied it in three swallows. It gave me the chills but I'd been wild to get home and have a drink.

I requested my discharge from the Army in June, 1964, and got it because the military situation at that time allowed it. There's a military committee whose function is to find jobs for men who leave the service. But in a year and a half, the only job they got me was in some public-works project. On my first day the foreman told me I had to work with a pick and shovel, so I quit. That wasn't the kind of job I was looking for—not by a long shot.

I began looking for a job on my own, and got one here in Havana driving a taxi. Of all the jobs I've ever had, that's the one I most liked because there was a lot of social contact. I made lots of friends there, both among the bosses and among my comrades, because I'm the kind of guy who makes people like him right away.

For the past two years, though, I haven't been able to work right, because of a skin problem. I've been suffering from it since 1965. There isn't a thing I can say to explain my illness—if the doctors can't, how the hell can I? All I can say is that it began when I first cut cane and it itches like hell. I've been hospitalized three times already. I spent a whole month in the hospital in 1968. They formed a committee of doctors to study my case and prescribed compresses to cover my whole body. They'd wrap me up from head to foot in cotton soaked with some cold stuff and keep me that way for half an hour at a time. They did their very best to cure me, but I left the hospital itching worse than ever.

The last thing they prescribed for it was a series of intravenous calcium injections, but that treatment only made me itch more. The doctors keep changing and changing the prescriptions; if they really knew what was wrong they'd prescribe the same thing every time. That's the reason I've given up going to doctors. What's the point? I know by now that none of them can cure me.

The itch is bad in cold as well as hot weather, but it's worst when I sweat. I used to get under the shower at any hour of the day and night and I'd get out feeling a lot better. But as soon as I dried off, I'd feel worse than ever, because bathing so many times a day dries the skin and makes the itch worse. The worst time is at night, after I go to bed. Sometimes it gets really fierce and I lie in bed scratching for several hours until I finally manage to fall asleep.

My wife and children are affectionate and worry about me, but sometimes Leticia starts nagging, "Don't scratch so much!"

"*Chica,* get out of the room and let me scratch in peace!" I tell her.

She thinks I scratch because I want to, but the fact is, I can't help it. I feel as if something is boring right into me and I have to scratch to get rid of it. My skin looks raw and burned, and my scalp is covered with pimples. Well, whatever my illness may be, at least it isn't contagious. I've kept on sleeping with my wife right through and she hasn't caught it.

The only thing that worries me about this is that I'm beginning to think it's going to be the death of me. I've been living in torture and nothing helps. I know the day will come when I lose my head for a minute and decide to . . . well, you know. "Bear up," people tell me. Well, talk is easy. If they had the same trouble themselves, they'd sing a different tune. Why, I look ten years older than my brother Dámaso, and he's two years older than me.

I never get nervous when Leticia is going to have a baby. Heck, she's borne five babies and come out fine every time. Naturally, as a husband I must feel my wife's pain, or rather the reflection of her pain, but listen,

Leticia's the kind of woman who could be sitting right next to you when labor pains start and she wouldn't even mention it. You'll find her washing clothes only a few hours before having a baby. She washes, irons, shampoos, and combs her hair the very day she's due to give birth.

My two eldest children were born at home. Our second child, Bárbara, was born in the midst of a terrific rainstorm while Leticia's mother and me, soaked to the skin, ran here and there fetching things. I was so wet and chilled, I drank a whole bottle of Bacardi while waiting for the kid to be born. When it was all over, the minute Leticia saw me she said, "Take off those wet clothes, old boy."

Our other three children, Andrea, Tomás, and Ana Luz, were born in hospitals here in Havana. In the case of Ana Luz, Leticia had already been admitted to the Naval Hospital and been prepared for the labor room when they made her get up and transfer to the Workers' Maternity Hospital because they found out I was no longer in the Army. It's a miracle that Ana Luz wasn't born dead because she was already "crowning" when they moved Leticia. After having attended her all through her pregnancy, they shouldn't have sent her away just when she'd started labor. Somehow or other, there was influence used in that case.

After our fourth child I said to Leticia, "All right, let's close down the factory." But in spite of everything, we had a fifth child. Now I often say to her, "We should load up the ship again. We need a baby in this house." She gets terribly upset when I say that. She doesn't want any more children; but as for me, I'd like fourteen instead of just five.

My children can make me suffer more than my wife ever could because I'm far fonder of them than I am of Leticia. Yes I am, that's a fact. For example, if I ask one of my children to do something and he doesn't do it, I feel very unhappy about it. But as a matter of fact, none of my children gives me any real trouble.

Lina is now fourteen and every bit of advice that girl has ever had has come from me, not from her mother. Heck, I've always told her what's right. I've taught her to cook, I've taught her table manners, I've taught her everything. If she wants to go to the movies, I take her. If I have to accompany her to Coney Island or to the zoo, I do.

Lina is at the age where she's beginning to like boys. I talk to her a lot about the kind of problems men can bring. Gradually I'm opening her eyes. She's such a young girl, with no evil or malice in her, and she might have the bad luck to fall in love with, say, a married man with children. If sometime in the future she should make a mistake, it will be because she wants to, not for lack of a good upbringing.

I give my children all sorts of advice about everything there ever was or will be. I tell them, "If you want another kid to talk your problems over with, I want you to think of me as that kid and tell me whatever is troubling you. And if you feel you need a grown person to confide in, well, I'm that grown person, too. When you tell me your secrets, it will give me great satisfaction because I'm the one best able to advise you. And I won't spank or even scold you."

Sometimes I'll tell my kids, "We're having a meeting today." We all get together and I talk with them as if they were grown men and women. For instance, I'll tell them, "Listen, kids, I've noticed something that's wrong in this family. When your *mamá* tells you not to do such-and-such, I want you to understand that it's bad for this-and-that reason." You should see how they say at once, "Yes, you're right, *papá!*"

Their mother says to me sometimes, "Hey, lately you never leave the kids in peace. Let them be, now and then, let them be!"

You know, my own parents never went to such lengths in my upbringing, but even so, *papá* still likes to be consulted about any kind of problem. But my brother Dámaso has two grown children and he can't get close to them the way I can to mine. He never knows what his kids are up to or how they feel.

When my eldest daughter goes out, she's got to ask permission first. I'm not so strict with the little ones; they go in and out pretty much as they please, because you can't pressure little kids too much. Lina goes downstairs almost every night but she always asks permission first. Her *mamá* usually makes objections and wants to get her busy doing one thing or another, but I say, "Never mind all that, my child. You may go downstairs as long as you sit on the fence and don't go wandering anywhere." That's the reason why Leticia says that I'm the children's advocate.

As long as we've been married, Leticia and I have never quarreled. We get annoyed at each other sometimes, sure. What married couple doesn't? Like when a fellow tells his wife, "Don't go to such-and-such a place" or "Don't wear such-and-such a dress," and next thing he knows she's done it. But those are trifles, right?

A friend's wife once said that my wife was the man of the house—imagine! And do you know why? Because, as she explained, the only voice that could ever be heard by the neighbors in this building was Leticia's. Well, I like to talk in a low voice. I never raise my voice and I don't like people yelling in my ear. And I don't argue with my wife—I hate to argue with women. In fact, I've never gotten into an argument with anybody in all my life. I'm a tactful man.

My wife's got her own way of loving. As the saying has it, "If you aren't jealous, you aren't in love." The time I really ran around was before I got engaged. I used to go to a lot of parties in other towns. Yessir! I had my fun first, but after I got engaged to Leticia, I stopped doing all that.

A man's love problems are the same as a woman's because a man loves as deeply as a woman does. I know a bit about that kind of problem and I never make a mistake about it—never. A person may have studied for years and made a great career for himself and still not know much about married life. As for that, experience counts. Every person is a world unto himself, and let me tell you, I'm completely different from other men. But completely!

Now that I find myself living in a home of my own with my wife and children, all I ask of life is to be able to go on living with them, to come straight home from work and stay there until it's time to go to work again. All I need to be that kind of man is to have more comforts at home. For instance, if I had a TV set my children would stay home more and I could instruct them. They wouldn't be forever running to some neighbor's place and I myself would stay home more.

Justa Díaz

During the eight-month period the Hernández family were part of this study, interviewers were unsuccessful in getting Justa Díaz to discuss her childhood. We know that she was one of eleven children and had been raised in the countryside near Guantánamo. Her father was a dispossessed farmer who worked as a day laborer. Justa married at fifteen and was barely out of her teens (although already the mother of three children and pregnant with a fourth) when she joined Gerardo in dangerous underground activities for the Twenty-sixth of July Movement. Justa was profoundly affected by the many stories (some true and some apocryphal) that she heard about terror and torture by Batista's forces. She lived in fear for her life and for the lives of her husband and many of their relatives. Nevertheless, according to her account, Justa followed Gerardo and his brothers into the Movement without understanding its objectives, and therefore without understanding the cause for which she was risking her life.

Justa herself could be counted among the casualties of the Revolution. She claims to have suffered from a "nerve sickness" since that day in 1958 when, while visiting a Rebel encampment, she survived a bombardment by Batista's air force. She has experienced speech loss and hysterical paralysis, for which she has been hospitalized at least once. According to her daughter Genoveva, Justa was under a doctor's care in 1969–70. Despite her illness, Justa had four more children during the decade after the Triumph. The Hernández household, which seemed to lack any organization or routine, reflected Justa's frenetic state. Field workers, who visited the home regularly and engaged in informal conversations with Justa and the children, observed, for example, that the children often ran around while taking their meals. Justa's elder daughters were both ill—one had been recommended for psychiatric care—and her younger daughters were poor students and one had discipline problems in school.

In 1970, at age thirty-five and still barely literate, Justa continued to be obsessed with stories of torture during the Batista era and was fearful of being attacked by the United States. Despite her rhetorical fervor, Justa was not politically active, did not participate in any of the mass organizations, and was generally unable to discuss coherently any of the Revolution's major objectives. She was, essentially, a woman who lived for and through her husband and children, and she rarely left her home except to do some household errand.

A small, wiry woman with missing front teeth, Justa talked rapidly and often in a loud voice which the neighbors could hear. When she talked to interviewers, however, she used little of the threatening language or street vocabulary for which she had gained such a bad reputation among her neighbors. The interview that follows is not a sketch of Justa's life but a series of vignettes about her life immediately before and after the Triumph.

We were living in Glorieta when my husband and his comrades began doing their revolutionary work in our house. I didn't realize what was going on. After all, one doesn't pay much attention to what the menfolk talk about when they get together. I'd see the comrades come in—Captain Salvador, who's now a *comandante*, Javier, a good friend of ours, another one called "El Zarzo," and many others who are now very big people in the Revolution. Often I'd see letters from Efigenio,[88] who was their chief at the Second Front. They'd even store leaflets there, saying things like, "Tonight, the Twenty-sixth of July Movement will take such-and-such a town." I still didn't know what was happening. My husband never let on to me, he's that reserved.

Once when they had a big meeting at our house, my husband played a trick on me to get me out of the house and out of town for a while. He said to me, "The baby has a sore throat. You must take her to your mother's house in Guantánamo."

Without suspecting a thing, I said, "All right. I'll start out tomorrow morning." The next day I took the bus to Guantánamo. My mother-in-law lived only three blocks from my *mamá*, and I decided to go visit her. I wanted to say hello and ask if she'd heard from my husband. As I got near her house, I saw the street was full of people. I was wondering what was going on when I realized they were standing right in front of her place. "*Ay,* what can have happened?" I walked up to the crowd. "What is it?" I said. A man who was standing near asked, "Are you going to Felicia Nadal's house?"

"Yes, she's my mother-in-law."

"Don't. Go to her sister's house."

"May you thrive," said I, and ran as fast as I could. When I got there, I found my husband's aunt down on her knees, sobbing and screaming. "What happened?" I asked her.

"They've been shooting at my sister's house and my son was hiding there too!"

There were seventeen Rebels hidden in my mother-in-law's house and a neighbor woman had turned stool pigeon. When the police found out, they started shooting right into the house, but the seventeen Rebels and my mother-in-law managed to escape through a neighbor's yard. They

88. Efigenio Ameijeiras.

only wounded one, my husband's cousin, Eusebio Castillo Hernández, but he got away. And now he's a captain.

I was still feeling the shock. If it hadn't been for that man's warning, the dictatorship would have killed me right then and there. Before they left, they shot up the roof of my mother-in-law's house. Everything was destroyed or taken away—all the glass-fronted cabinets, all the china, all the clothes. And then they set fire to the house. The whole family had to leave town.

I was still in my husband's aunt's house when a man there said, "There's a job to be done. We must get those men out. They're in different houses around here."

"But how?"

"We'll have to find a way," he answered. "We'll have to get them out in disguise." Then he says to me, "Are you brave?"

"Yes," says I. "Just tell me what I have to do." Then they explained to me what it was all about.

In broad daylight, at 3:00 in the afternoon, I went to get Juan Manuel Hernández where he was hiding. In the midst of the shooting, with no disguise except a big umbrella, I put my arm around his waist and lit a cigarette. I'd never smoked before; that was the day I got started. The police were looking all over the place for him and the others, but I told him, "Just keep on walking with me, don't look back." There were two other *compañeras* doing the same thing, and we got them all out that way. The guards didn't recognize anyone because each of us made just a few trips, taking a different route each time. We disguised the men by switching their clothes. We took them to a place outside of town and that night a car from the Twenty-sixth of July picked them up and took them to Loma de la Piña. There the comrades were already in contact with the Rebels of Camp Aguacate and they were sent on to the Sierra. That happened in 1958, when everything got really hot.

When I went back to *mamá*'s, she was scared because she'd been told what I'd been up to. I said to her, "Don't worry, I won't get you in trouble."

I was afraid because I had no way of getting in touch with my husband. "How is he?" I wondered. "How is he getting along, all by himself in the house?" Actually, he'd gone to the Sierra but I didn't know it. On the eighth day I decided to leave.

"Where are you going?" *mamá* asked.

"Home," said I.

"But that's 6 leagues from here and the road is lined with police. Not even the men dare travel that road!"

"You must be crazy," *papá* chimed in.

"I've got to go. I must find out how my husband is." I'm very determined, you know. So I set out with Genoveva, Gabriela, Florinda, and my big belly.

A man, going the same way, asked me, "But woman, where are you going?"

"Home," said I. "I don't care how late we get to Glorieta."

Then he said, "But don't you know? Aren't you Hernández's wife? Didn't you know that all those people had to leave because the police were looking for them?"

"Looking for them? Why?"

"Because they all belong to the Twenty-sixth of July Movement."

I felt so afraid, so sad. I said to him, "Where is it they had to go?"

"To fight for Cuba."

"What do you mean, to fight for Cuba?" All the way to Glorieta he explained things to me. I knew nothing about the Movement and had never had anything to do with it. He himself was involved and he told me about the Revolution and why Cubans must fight against the dictatorship and how imperialism had exploited us all our lives. He told me it was time we freed ourselves. It was then that I began to see it all and to understand what my husband and his comrades were doing, what those meetings in my home were all about. How reserved my husband was! He told me later that he'd kept it all secret because once women get to talking they're apt to let something slip and people's lives depended on their comrades' discretion. "It wasn't only my life," he said, "but the lives of many." At that time a glance would have been excuse enough for them to tear your head off your neck.

When we got near Caimanera all hell broke loose. Batista's soldiers, the *casquitos*, were blocking the road with tanks. They suspected the comrade who'd been traveling with me. He was carrying a sackful of groceries—rice, condensed milk, and so on—for the Rebels, but he told them it was for his children. They surrounded us, right there on the road, see, and one of them asks me, "Señora, where are you going?"

"Home," I said. "I was in another town when the strike began. You know there are no cars or anything and I'm desperate to get home because all my family is in Glorieta."

"*Ay*, Señora," says he, "I wish I could drive you home in one of these cars. But we can't, more's the pity." And all the time I was dying of fear! "Be careful, Señora, there's a bunch of madmen loose, and they're killing everybody they come across." He says that to me, the wife of a Rebel!

When I got back to Glorieta all the neighbors came out to meet me, crying, because they thought I didn't know my husband was gone. They were just as involved as we were; their husbands and brothers were active and they put me in contact with the Twenty-sixth of July right away.

From the very beginning, the Movement knew my husband was married and how many children he had, so he could be assured we'd be taken care of when he went to the Sierra. When he left, his comrades paid for the children's milk and all their food and medicines, and the rent on our house. We had a doctor, we had everything! Hernández had made all the necessary arrangements for our comfort before leaving, just as he does now. He makes sure we'll have no problems while he's away. He even arranges for me to have someone to talk to if necessary.

After I returned from Guantánamo, I started working for the Movement. I'd help by taking parcels of things they needed—clothes, food, cigarettes—from Glorieta to a place called Yuraguanay, up in the mountains. We'd just walk out as if we had nothing to hide. We had contacts in different towns, so we went back and forth at all hours of the night. I made those trips, pregnant as I was.

I went back to Guantánamo even though they could have identified me through my husband's photos, which they'd taken when they attacked his mother's house. It was different in Glorieta. Most of the men in the Navy were on the side of the Revolution and more or less knew that the Twenty-sixth of July people went in and out of town whenever they pleased. And the men at the old police station never fired a shot, and they never tortured people the way the others did. They knew what was being done but they had to stay at their posts till the triumph of the Revolution. Many of them are working here now.

The first general strike[89] caught me there in Guantánamo. I was at *mamá*'s and was about to go back to Glorieta, but in the morning everything was closed and there was shooting all over town. People were out in the street; police cars were driving around. "*Mamá*, what's going on?" I asked.

"It's a general strike, child. We can't stay out." So we ran back home and remained there during the seven days the strike lasted. There was no traffic of any kind, and all communication was interrupted. Every town in Cuba cooperated, but Havana failed the Revolution—that's why there were so many dead and so much trouble. We've feared and distrusted Havana ever since. That's why Fidel has to live here, you know.

The only time I got scared was later, when I went with a *compañera* called Sabina. She asked me to take a parcel to Los Caños, to Jorge, one of my *compadres*, who was a Rebel. "*Ay no, chica,*" said I, "not that far! What about my children?"

"They'll be all right with your neighbor. Come on, we've got to bring Jorge some underwear, cigarettes, bullets, and Twenty-sixth of July uniforms." I'd never seen their uniforms before. In order to hand the parcel over to him at Los Caños, we had to board a launch near army headquarters. A man was waiting for us and signaled the boat to come

---

89. The general strike of April 9, 1958, was called by the Twenty-sixth of July Movement and the Havana Civic Resistance. The communists and the labor unions did not observe the strike and it failed badly. Thomas estimates that in addition to civilian and police deaths, perhaps eighty revolutionaries were shot in Havana and another thirty in Santiago de Cuba. (*Cuba: The Pursuit of Freedom*, p. 990.)

pick us up. Batista's guards were on the dock with gasoline tanks and such, because they were mobilizing their troops to go after the Rebels. The guards and the sailors knew me so they didn't pay any attention.

I'd never been in a boat before. We traveled by sea to the place where we met Jorge. We arrived at midnight and I was overjoyed to see him, but was startled by his shaggy beard.

The very evening I returned to Glorieta, I gave birth to my son. Just think, he's the same age as the Revolution! He'll soon be eleven. The Twenty-sixth of July gave me his whole layette and all my food. When the boy was only thirty-five days old I took him to Camp Aguacate, where my husband was. I wanted him to see his new son.

I went with a lady called Pucha, who was going alone to the Rebel camp to see her boy. I still lacked five of the forty days of rest after giving birth,[90] but I said to Pucha, "All right, if you need someone to keep you company, I'll go."

"You're crazy!" she exclaimed. "In this rain, with the planes dropping bombs and with policemen all over the place? Suppose they kill you and your baby?"

In those days, you see, the Rebels were getting ready to take the towns. Fidel had said towns were to be taken no matter what the cost. "If they kill me with the baby, it won't matter," I said. "At least my husband won't die without ever having seen his son."

I got ready. The neighbors cried and said they'd probably never see me again. "I can take care of myself," I told them. We'd all worked together as *milicianas* in the Resistance, which was a dangerous thing. We lived among the people, not in the mountains like the Rebels, and we had to risk our lives all the time. Lots of things had to be carried up to the Rebels—hammocks, bullets, cigarettes, food, and all sorts of stuff they needed, and it had to be done in secret.

Pucha and I went by car from Glorieta to the Esperanza sugar mill, which was as near to the mountains as we could drive. After that, we still had several leagues to walk. When we got up in the mountains, I went past the first and second camps and there, at the third camp, was my husband. I really got scared when I found myself in the midst of all those bearded men. Besides, planes were bombing everywhere and I'd never been in a bombardment before. A *compañera* said to me, "Throw yourself down on the ground." I set the baby down and flopped to the ground beside him. The plane flew low and killed one of the comrades. I'd never seen anything like it and I began to lose control of my nerves. I've had the nerve sickness ever since.

Raúl Castro held a meeting at Camp Alto de la Victoria and that's the first time I saw him. He went there to meet with the peasants, to ask for

90. Traditional forty-day period of confinement for a mother and newborn child.

the use of a piece of land for the camp. They told the peasants that the Rebels had no intention of taking any land that was legally the peasants' and that they hadn't come there to kill peasants but to fight for the liberation of Cuba. Many farmers hadn't understood what it was all about before he talked to them, but afterward they were on our side. This meeting took place the very day I arrived at the camp. Later, when I went to Aguacate, I met Vilma Espín—Raúl hadn't married her yet at that time—and Che's wife, who's a very nice person. That was in late 1958, just before the triumph of the Revolution.

My first cousin, Modesto Montáñez Castillo, was a combatant and one of the first to join the Rebels. He's in Mazorra[91] now because he was tortured. The police of the dictatorship caught him in 1958. He was only eighteen at the time. They beat him brutally and burned his flesh with red-hot irons. They cut off his sexual parts by looping a piece of wire around them and tying the other end to his feet. Finally they left him for dead—they couldn't believe anybody would survive such torture, I guess, and a group of Rebels went down to get him and carried him up to the camp.

I was there at the time and I heard a comrade say to Captain Fulgencio, "That wounded boy is Modesto Montáñez Castillo."

"He's my cousin!" I cried. "His father is Modestito Montáñez, who lives on a farm on the Isabel *central*." And I gave them the address of the farm. "He works in the sugar mill."

"Yes, that's his father all right," the comrade said. I thought I'd die. He was in a terrible state—nobody thought he'd live. He'd lost his memory completely and for years he didn't recognize anybody. He was attended by several well-known doctors—there were lots of doctors among the Rebels. They told us, "He may live, but if he does, he'll be insane." My cousin was never again able to fight.

When the Revolution triumphed, they sent him to Mazorra, where he got a lot better. He's been treated by Soviet doctors, who've done him a lot of good. He got so he could recognize his father and all his relatives. The Soviet physician warned us that he might be six months or a year like that, but that he definitely wouldn't retain the improvement he'd shown. Two years ago they gave his relatives permission to take him for a visit to our hometown. He recognized the town all right, but after five days it seems he began to remember what they'd done to him there and the shock of it drove him right out of his mind again.

The psychiatrist says there's no chance now that he'll ever be cured. When he gets upset, they give him an injection. But never, never, never again will they let him leave the hospital. The dictatorship de-

91. A mental institution in a small suburb of Havana.

stroyed him completely, mentally and physically. And he isn't the only one; there are thousands like him in Mazorra. Look, those people—I don't know what to call them—what can you call somebody who had the heart to do such things to a person?

Delmira Toledo, a neighbor of ours, also went crazy because of what they did. She had four sons, none of them in the Revolution; they were only schoolboys. Well, one day those kids, Delmira's sons, were sitting there reading comic books, when Aguero, a Negro in league with the devil so people said, happened to drive by in his jeep. He saw the children and said, "Aha, you kids are just what I need." Their mother heard him and came out to ask what it was all about. "Don't worry, Señora," Aguero assured her, "I'll bring them right back."

Only minutes later some people came to tell Delmira that her four sons' bodies were lying on the road to Glorieta, riddled with machine-gun bullets. That's the way Aguero was—he killed for pleasure. Delmira lost her mind and has never recovered. Aguero was sent before a firing squad after the Revolution and do you know what he said before he died? He said, "My only regret in dying is that I won't be able to kill any more people."

When the Revolution triumphed, we went into the army headquarters in Caimanera—my kid brothers used to shine shoes there—and we found a small room with a kind of well in the middle, filled with some kind of liquid. Their own soldiers would be put in there if they refused to go out and fight against the revolutionaries. They sewed up their lips with wire and killed them slowly with that liquid and with hammers and nails. And that isn't all we saw. We saw big irons, the kind in Chinese laundries, with pieces of human flesh still sticking to them. In Guantánamo, near the Lion's Club, we found paper bags full of people's fingernails. Fidel has all of those things now.

It was the most terrible and shocking thing that ever happened in my town. It was our own townspeople who were tortured—the way people in Vietnam are now tortured. Everyone saw it; the Rebels made it public so we'd know what life was like under the dictatorship. If Fidel hadn't pushed ahead as fast as he did, by the time the Revolution triumphed there wouldn't have been a living soul in Cuba.

I met Comandante Camilo when he led Armando Castro's troops into Caimanera, where I was visiting relatives. That was in 1958, when the Revolution was taking all the smaller towns.[92] The police started shoot-

92. Camilo Cienfuegos was not with the Second Front forces that took Caimanera, so it is very unlikely that Justa saw him there at that time. Armando Castro (no relation to Fidel and Raúl) was an officer in the Frank País Second Front, but Cienfuegos was commander of the Northern Zone of the Las Villas Front. He and Guevara, who was commander of the Southern and Central zones of the Las Villas Front, took over Havana in January, 1959.

ing and he announced, "I'm Camilo Cienfuegos, come to take this town, and I'm not afraid of bullets." I'll never forget those words.

Not one single shot more was fired. The policemen just stood there staring at him. Everybody crowded up to shake Camilo's hand while he kept on talking. "We're brothers," he told the townspeople, "and we should understand one another. There's no reason why we should kill one another." And then he talked about the dictatorship. Such a lovely speech! The whole town flocked after him. He always acted natural with everybody, even with children. He picked up every child that came within reach and kissed him. We were very impressed.

When I saw Camilo, I said, "Dear God, he's a Christ!" He really did look exactly like Christ. Just compare his face with a picture of Christ and you'll see.

After the triumph of the Revolution, when the Rebels were in Havana, we heard his second speech—one of the very few he ever made, because he wasn't fond of making speeches. I was living here in Havana when he disappeared and the search for him was going on.[93] I was listening to a serial on the radio when all of a sudden it was interrupted by a news bulletin saying that Comandante Camilo's plane had disappeared and it might have fallen into the sea. After that every radio and TV station kept commenting on that bulletin. Two days after his disappearance I was in the yard hanging out the wash when the woman in charge of the building called, "Justa, Justa!"

"What is it, Ema?"

"They say they've found Camilo! There's a man lying in a mangrove swamp and they say he's Camilo."

Everybody was overjoyed at the news. Flags were raised again to the top of the staff. But half an hour later they retracted. The man in the mangrove was somebody who'd been fishing and apparently had gotten hit by something and passed out. When that news was broadcast, I said, "See, Ema? Didn't I tell you that Camilo wouldn't be found?"

I was watching television when Fidel let the people know the truth, that Camilo had fallen into the sea and had disappeared forever. While telling us there was no hope, Fidel himself wept, because Camilo was his *compañero* and his guide. Whenever he went anywhere he'd always ask, "Am I headed in the right direction, Camilo?"

When I heard that we'd lost Camilo forever I tried to get up from my chair, but I was gasping for breath. It was my nerves, I guess. Ema called a comrade of ours, Celeste, and when Celeste saw me she said, "But my goodness, what's wrong with her?"

"It looks as if the shock was too much for her," Ema said. They got real scared and took me to the Military Hospital right away. I was in a hospi-

93. October, 1959.

tal for fifteen whole days. They even had to spoon-feed water to me because I couldn't move my hands. The shock was so great I was temporarily paralyzed by it. I even lost the power of speech.

When I came to, I felt like a zero. I started looking around and little by little I started remembering. Then I saw my husband and asked him, "Ricardo, what's this?"

"Oh, nothing, nothing," he said.

"Has Camilo been found?" I asked.

"Relax, don't talk," the doctor said quickly. Then I fell asleep and about three or four days later I was released from the hospital and told to get a lot of rest. Even now, whenever I feel the least bit upset or scared, I lose my voice right away.

We've never forgotten Camilo or El Che, not for one moment.[94] Their deaths were very hard to take. The entire Cuban people were very saddened. Not a year goes by that we don't mourn the anniversaries of their deaths. We still go down to the sea in memory of Camilo.

I was in Glorieta when the Revolution finally triumphed. The following day my husband's column set out for Havana, but I wasn't able to meet him there. I had other revolutionary work to tend to right there in Glorieta. The Revolution had triumphed, but we didn't know what would be the reaction of imperialism. We had to expect the worst so we couldn't abandon our posts. We had to be ready to run with the equipment, the sick and wounded, the arms—everything. I was in the reserve and I had to stick to it. I am Hernández's wife, but I'm conscious of the Revolution, too.

It was four months after the Triumph that my husband wrote and I joined him in Havana. Before we were given a home of our own, we lived in Almendares, where we were surrounded by people who disagreed with the government. Because I've been part of the Revolution myself, I can more or less tell when somebody is engaged in espionage. We had our countersigns, but the counterrevolutionaries aren't as skillful at this kind of thing. Once I saw a suspicious group of people acting as if they meant to attack a police station or something, so I climbed over a wall and went to the militia and told them, "Comrades, near my home, at such-and-such a place, a number of people are gathering together and they look awfully suspicious to me. I'm the wife of a soldier and I don't know where he is now. I'm afraid those people may kill me and my children."

"You may go home in peace," they assured me. "We'll take care of the problem."

94. Guevara was killed after his capture by government troops in Bolivia in October, 1967.

"Don't say I was the one who accused them," I said.

The militia surrounded my building and arrested all those people. They turned out to have weapons, papers, bombs, hand grenades—the works. They were ready and waiting for an uprising because they'd been in touch with the CIA. Those people had even taken the precaution of telling their relatives to clear out of the building because they were going to burn it. The militia found papers with instructions for each person in the group, you see. They planned to eliminate all the Rebels.

Among their papers was a leaflet saying that not one communist would be allowed to live after they took over. I saw those leaflets—the counterrevolutionaries scattered them all over the streets. Even an American plane dropped leaflets on us saying, "The day we land in Cuba, not one Cuban will be left, because they're all running away from communism." That's the kind of provocation we've had to put up with from the Yankees and the CIA people who've infiltrated Cuba.

The day of the attack on the FAR[95] we were all busy with housework. I happened to be ironing. The window was open and I could see an airplane. I said to my neighbor, Pura, "Ay, Pura, that plane up there scares me. It looks as if it's dropping bombs."

"Why, so it is, chica," she answered.

I was terrified. I threw my arms around the children and burst into tears. Then I locked them up in the bathroom and shut all the windows and locked the doors. It was a crazy thing to do but I simply lost my head. "This is war!" I thought, with all my nerves on edge.

"Control yourself, control yourself," Pura kept saying. But imagine what it feels like just waiting to have a bomb drop on you. There was no time to get us out of there to a safer place.

The neighbors came to keep me company and without thinking I went out to the grocery store to buy ice and soft drinks. At such a moment!

Everybody was outside watching the plane drop bombs. Other American planes bombed Havana that day. The sharpshooters had already taken up positions all over; there were some right in our building. Trucks were driving all over the streets with people in them shooting antiaircraft guns to keep them away from the buildings. Then shots from the FAR reached the plane and set it on fire. We could see it burning.

I stood and stared at the FAR because in my desperation all I wanted to do was to go there. I could see the plane throwing bombs and people scattering and running . . . no, no, no! That day one of the comrades they killed wrote the name of Fidel with his own blood as he lay dying.[96] That was a tragedy! My mind filled with dark thoughts and I felt re-

95. See n. 2.
96. Eduardo García Delgado, a militiaman, now a national hero.

jected and humiliated because nobody came.... Oh well, they knew I couldn't leave the house, and it all happened so suddenly....

Fidel spoke over the radio and announced that those were American planes bombing the FAR. He asked the Cuban people to keep calm. But I couldn't think straight. I was out of my mind; all I wanted to do was to get out and fight. I looked toward my bed and had a very strong impression of a Rebel lying there. I cried out, "Oh my God, they must have killed somebody! Pura, I've just seen a dead Rebel on my bed. Could it be my husband?"

People tell me it couldn't have happened but I did see it. It was over in a flash. In my opinion, it must have happened at the very moment they started to fight at Playa Girón. I don't know what happened after that, because I passed out.

Pura said, "Oh my goodness, this girl has had a nervous fit!" The doctor was called and gave me a shot. For many days afterward I was like a lump, with no wish to talk or move.

My husband, his brother Felipe, and his first cousin, Captain Eusebio Castillo, were all fighting in Girón, but we had no news of them. They and all of Ameijeiras's police force were among the first to be called because Fidel trusted them the most. Only the first to be trained got to fight that time.

The day of the attack, Felipe and another man were injured and two other comrades were killed in a truck accident. Perhaps the driver was nervous; after all, we were at war. Felipe went on to fight, but when the battle cooled down he began to feel pain. He was attended to at once and kept under observation all the time, because an injury to the spine is dangerous. He kept on working and everything in spite of the pain. But his condition got so much worse they finally did have to operate, because his legs were becoming paralyzed. He was in the hospital for a long time and still is not perfectly well.

Just when the dictatorship had been crushed and we thought we could begin to live in peace at last, the Americans began sabotaging us. Things are quieter now—or seem to be. We'd rather not fight but we know that imperialism is going to attack us sooner or later, and we wish the Americans would make up their minds—the sooner the better—to get it over with. Time is running out for imperialism. It isn't that we're fanatics—we aren't the only ones, it's the whole world. Many countries have suffered from imperialism. It's done much, much harm—many, many bad things.

Ricardo Hernández

I was born north of Guantánamo in Oriente on January 8, 1933. There were nine of us, seven boys and two girls. I was next to the youngest. According to *mamá* I was my father's favorite. She said he'd take me everywhere he went. His brothers had a vegetable farm quite a distance from us, and we used to go visit them now and then. *Mamá*'s family was from Guantánamo, but I don't know what town my father came from. I never knew any of my grandparents but they all lived in Oriente.

Our economic position was about average. We didn't always have what we wanted, but we never went hungry. *Papá* was a machinist in a sugar mill, but I can't remember much about him because he was killed in an accident at work when I was five. After his death my old lady received some kind of compensation, which she decided to invest in a house in Guantánamo. It was the first house she'd ever owned. It had four bedrooms and was built partly of wood and partly of cement. At that time my brothers supported the family. They were construction workers— one was a mason, one a carpenter, and so on.

Just before we moved to the new house, some politicians started going around telling people they had to give up their voting cards if they wanted to keep their children in the public school. *Mamá* and my older brothers and sisters refused to give up their cards for that racket, so I was taken out of school in the second grade. One of my sisters gave me lessons whenever she could and I learned quite a bit that way. But it didn't last long because she got married.

When I was about thirteen, I decided to go to work for my brother Sergio, who had a grocery store. About that time I also started playing baseball with the school team. I wasn't in school but they put me on the team when they were going to Havana to play for the championship, because I'd been a good ball player since I was a little kid. They let me play on the team but they wouldn't allow me to go to school!

When I was about sixteen or seventeen, a North American came to Guantánamo to sign up ball players. I was offered a chance to go to Havana to play ball for 100 *pesos* a season, but I never looked on baseball as a way of earning a living. What was I to do when the baseball season was over? Starve, that's what! The season lasted for only three or four months and I'd have been out of a job for the rest of the year. Besides, they'd sign up players for a certain amount of money—say 500 *pesos* a season—but when the season was over, the player got 100 *pesos* and the man who signed him up got 400. That's a form of exploitation, and I've always been against every kind of exploitation.

I met Justa when a cousin of hers who played baseball with me brought her to watch a game. She gave me her address and I called on her often, until we fell in love and got engaged. Justa's family and mine liked each other from the first, but they didn't see each other often because they lived quite far apart. It all happened very fast; we got married four or five months after getting engaged. Justa was fifteen.

At first we lived in *mamá*'s house and I continued to work for my brother until our first child, Genoveva, was born. Then I needed more money, so I got a job in the brick factory where Justa's father worked. I didn't know anything about that kind of work, but he talked to the people there and they hired me.

Justa's father had owned a small farm, but it was taken away from him before the Revolution. His farm was next to that of a wealthy man who wanted the land and pulled many strings to get it. As happened so often in those times, they took the farm from the poor man and gave it to the rich man. And that's how Justa's father lost the little farm that he had depended on to eke out a living.

I worked in the factory with my father-in-law for several months but I didn't much like the work. We were supposed to be paid every two weeks, but sometimes a whole month would go by and then they'd pay us only half of what they owed. I was earning a little over 1 *peso* a day, which was more than I'd been earning in the store, but at least my brother paid me punctually every week. Then we all lost our jobs because the factory owed rent money or something and the Army came and took it over.

Sometime after I lost my job at the factory, my brother Sergio talked Nilo Riera into giving me a store in Glorieta to manage. Riera was one of the richest men in Guantánamo—practically all the farmland around there belonged to him. Running a store in those days was tough. If you made a profit, the wholesalers would raise their prices, and if you weren't able to pay the bills, they took the store away from you. Since I was a rookie in the business, that happened to me several times. For a while I went to work at the American naval base, laying pipes for the plumbing, but there was a work shortage and I got fired. I had two children by then so I went back to the grocery business.

I was living in Glorieta with Justa and our two daughters when I joined the Twenty-sixth of July Movement. It became clearer and clearer to me that the situation of the Cuban people was going from bad to worse. The streets were full of barefoot kids who should have been in school. The citizens who came to the store usually had no more than a couple of *pesetas* to spend on a whole day's food for their families. Some citizens even asked us for the scraps we saved for the dogs—and that's what they fed to their children. It was plain things couldn't go on like that forever. So I decided, "Well, the best thing anyone can do is fight against this and try to change things so people will have what they need. We Cubans can't go on living like this, with no jobs and no schooling."

A comrade who's now a captain was the one who told me about the Rebels and the Twenty-sixth of July Movement, about what Comandante Fidel Castro was doing, and about the assault on the Moncada and everything. My talks with him made a lot of things clear to me. Finally, in 1956, I joined the Twenty-sixth of July Movement.

I was assigned to making subversive proclamations and preparing homemade bombs. I made the bombs at home but even my wife didn't know about it. I'd send her to visit her mother, and while she was out of the house I did my work. After I prepared the Molotov cocktails, I hid them in what we called a "kitchen," a secret deposit of weapons. Mine was in a washtub buried beneath some floorboards. It was well hidden but easy to get at when needed.

Time passed and things kept getting worse. Then the dictatorship killed my brother Juan. He wasn't working for the underground; he never interfered with anybody. He was a hardworking construction worker, that's all. When he died he left a wife and about five children. We don't know why they did it except that they killed just about anybody whenever it took their fancy.

The dictatorship had a group called "El Cien," "the One Hundred," who used to go out at night in a car called "the Toad." The car was nicknamed "Get in and ask no questions" because that's what they'd bark at you when they drove up. Whoever they took was done for.

My brother Juan went out for a few drinks one night and "El Cien" killed him in the street. They left his corpse in a half-built house. The next day some friends of his came to tell us. His body was full of bruises and swellings and broken by the blows they'd given him. A man called Abreu, who at that time pretended to share our revolutionary ideals, made the funeral speech. Only a few months later Abreu was bribed by Batista; he was given a post in a government ministry and he turned against us. He's been in Miami or one of those places ever since he ran away.

Mamá was a revolutionary from the first. Her brother, my Uncle Juan, fought for Batista, and when he was killed by our soldiers, *mamá* said, "I'm sorry he got killed because he's my brother, but after all, why did he refuse to join you in a just cause?"

Uncle Juan was ambushed in a jeep with several others. I wasn't in the ambush and knew nothing of my uncle's death until later, but my aunts bear me a grudge because he died fighting against our side. His son Cheo is practically a brother to me though. Whenever I go to Oriente, I see him and he treats me just as he always did. I get along well with his sisters, too. If they bear me any kind of grudge, that's their problem. My brothers and I sent plenty of letters to Uncle Juan asking him to join us in fighting against Batista.

When we were completely involved with the Twenty-sixth of July, a stool pigeon told of a meeting the Movement was having in my old lady's house. So they attacked the house with *mamá* and one of my sisters-in-law and her month-old baby in it. Two of my brothers, a cousin, and several comrades who are still with the Revolution took part in that shooting match, but I wasn't there that day. They couldn't catch anybody because they all managed to escape through the back. *Mamá* had to remain in hiding with me for several months. After everybody escaped, Batista's men broke in and discovered our hidden weapons and a batch of Twenty-sixth of July uniforms, all of which they took. Our family snapshots were there and they took those too, to identify us. Then they threw a grenade into the house.

The *guardia* went to Glorieta with the photos to arrest me and my brother Sergio. I managed to escape but they got Sergio. They beat him up but Nilo Riera got him out, because Sergio was a good worker and brought him a lot of business. Riera was the one who gave the orders around Guantánamo. When he said, "Do this," people did it and that was that. So they let Sergio out and then they went to get me.

The *guardia* went around to all the grocery stores asking for me. I was forewarned because of my brother's arrest, so when they got to my place I gave them a false name. When they left I slipped out, leaving the shop open, and from that day to this I've never set foot in that shop again. That was early in 1958.

I hid out until dark in a house by the beach. That night the Twenty-sixth of July Movement sent a girl to help me escape. They took me to an island—I forget which, but it was close to Glorieta. A cousin of mine was already there and we stayed on that island for a week. We couldn't have survived much longer because we were living on crackers and sardines and drinking seawater. We were swollen and half dead when they got us out of there. My cousin went one way and I another. They took me to the farm of Judge García in Glorieta, where I stayed until further orders. Then I joined a group with orders to take Caimanera. That was my first time in combat. We took Caimanera and held it for two hours, but reinforcements from Guantánamo didn't arrive and we had to abandon the town.[97] Before we could leave, we had to fight the *guardias* again at the edge of town.

---

97. The Rebels first attacked the naval barracks at Caimanera, south of Guantánamo, in April, 1958. Just prior to the Caimanera attack, Efigenio Ameijeiras and others led an attack on the barracks at Jamaica, and Raúl Castro attacked the barracks at Soledad *central*. Both were unsuccessful, but eight months later Raúl's Second Front forces returned to capture all three sites.

While our troops were still in Caimanera, the comrades with families near there were given leave to go home for short visits. I had no chance though, because just as I was leaving, they came to tell me we had to clear out. So I called a comrade who lived nearby and gave him three bullets, saying, "Take these to my wife and tell her I'm alive." The bullets were thirty-eights and I marked every one of them with three scratches made with the point of a dagger. I'd invented that countersign when I first left to join the Rebels. Justa knew my bullets; they'd prove that the comrade was telling her the truth.

Justa had come to see me at the judge's farm several weeks before the attack on Caimanera. I hadn't seen her for about a month, and when it was time for her to leave she started to cry. "Don't cry," I told her. "This is something we've got to do. If I get killed, that's my tough luck, but we've got to make Cuba free." It was then that I told her I'd send her a marked bullet if I couldn't go to her. That was all I said to her at the time. It was impossible to talk with her except to urge her not to cry. She was in such a state!

After the attack at Caimanera, Raúl Castro sent word to us to join him in the Sierra del Cristal, so we did.[98] That was in April, 1958. Over 100 men from Glorieta, Guantánamo, Caimanera, Jamaica, and other small towns joined Raúl. Two of my brothers were in the same group I was, but later we were scattered. Another brother was at a different camp. When we got to the Sierra, Raúl himself congratulated us for taking Caimanera. He shook hands with every one of us and hugged us and congratulated us. I talked to him personally.

Just after we got to the Sierra, the hunger crisis and a lot of other troubles started. Batista's air force began to bomb us and all we had to eat were the mules killed by the bombs. We got orders from Comandante Tomassevich[99] that only those who had courage and staying power could stick with the Rebels, because the war might last one year or twenty-five or thirty or fifty. "Any of you with the guts to take it, step forward," he said. We were in formation at the time. I stepped forward with most of the men. Only a few, a very very few, failed to take the step forward. And even those joined up again in the Sierra, because it was impossible for them to live in town, where everybody knew they'd been with the Rebels. Those who returned to town were killed. Some of the corpses were found with nails driven into their heads. Those tyrants would do anything!

98. At this time Raúl Castro was organizing the many small groups of Rebels who were working in the Guantánamo area and incorporating them into the Rebel Army's Frank País Second Front.

99. Raúl Menéndez Tomassevich, who in 1958 was commander of Company A of Raúl Castro's Second Front command, became commander of the FAR's Eastern Army and is now a deputy from Santiago de Cuba to the National Assembly.

The next stage of the war had begun—to capture army posts and fight our way to the plain. I participated in about five or six battles and any number of skirmishes. I was still in the Sierra del Cristal when I took part in the famous battle of Victoria, which lasted seventeen days. It was the longest battle I fought.

The enemy's aim was to cross over and reach Comandante Raúl.[100] Our objective was to keep them from crossing. At one point in the fighting there were only fourteen of us at the front. Some of the others ran out of bullets or had been hit and some simply fell back, so there were only the fourteen of us keeping three thousand *guardias* at bay. We were on higher ground, taking advantage of the gullies that served as natural trenches, though the place had been cleaned out by mortar shells and bombs and there weren't any trees or anything in front. We fought them until they realized they couldn't carry out their mission and fell back. That's when they began to throw jelly firebombs. It was the only battle they firebombed us, I think.

There was fighting each of those seventeen days, and our forces were bombarded daily from the air. Batista sent B-26s and jet planes against us. The last night we practically didn't go down to fight because we couldn't use any artificial light. To light our way we gathered fireflies and scouted around at night trying to find something to eat. I only remember eating once during those seventeen days. They brought us a big tin container of spoiled, wormy meat, which we ate because that's all the food we had. We boiled it first and ate it without salt or anything.

At the beginning of that battle we lost three comrades, which I felt deeply. One of them, Comandante Díaz's cook, fell beside me. He was shot through the head. Another comrade fell and I carried his body in a hammock down to the plain. We buried him there and went back up.

Our enemies hardly ever fought us face to face. Since they had so many weapons, they'd creep up inside our territory and start shooting until they got tired. At night they'd retreat. Then, the following morning, the planes would fly over again and bomb us. That's the way we lived for seventeen days—caught between two fires, the troops below and the planes above. Then one morning at daybreak, their fire swept through our ranks again, but instead of advancing, their shots sounded fainter and fainter with every volley. We realized they were retreating and firing simply to prevent us from going after them.

After the battle was over, with the place cleared of enemy forces, we had a few quiet days there. Even the bombardment of the camp eased up a bit, because a group of our soldiers some distance away had captured a busload of North Americans at gunpoint and driven it up to the

100. Raúl Castro's headquarters were in Mayarí Arriba.

Sierra.[101] Since the Americans were Batista's allies, his air force didn't dare drop any bombs on us as long as we kept them. After we let the Americans go, the bombardment started up again. When the North Americans returned home they said they had a very good impression of the Rebels in the Sierra and the fighting up there, and so on.

After I reached the Sierra I didn't see my family until after Reinaldito was born. My wife brought him to the Sierra to show him to me before the forty days were over. She was allowed to pass because some of the fellows knew her and escorted her up to camp. She stayed a week.

Then came the battle of Soledad.[102] We captured Soledad, and stayed in the plain all night. I'd been drinking and was a bit high, so I asked the High Command for a pass to spend New Year's Eve with my family. The High Command gave it to me and I was home by December 31.

The triumph of the Revolution caught me in Glorieta. I'd just crossed a long stretch of country, risking everything to go see my family. When I got there, I learned that our forces had taken Caimanera again, this time decisively.[103] I'd only been with my wife a little while when the jeep drove up to get me. By the time we got back, the Revolution was victorious. Some comrades gave us the news when we arrived. "Listen, Batista took off and he stole I don't know what all and they're turning the tanks over to us." Everybody whooped and yelled and ran all over the place like crazy.

From there we entered Guantánamo and every nearby town until we got word that Raúl was expecting us at the airport. So we gathered there and set off in a caravan to Havana. We made the trip in trucks and we looked like a gang of invaders. From Oriente we went to Camaguey, and it was there that we came to a halt because we couldn't take it any longer. We got to Havana after we'd been seven days on the road without food or water.

101. In July, 1958, Raúl Castro's troops kidnapped seventeen U.S. and three Canadian businessmen and, in a separate action, thirty U.S. sailors and marines returning by bus to the U.S. naval base at Guantánamo. The hostages were taken to Rebel camps in the Sierra del Cristal (Fidel was in the Sierra Maestra), and during the time the foreigners were held, bombing and strafing of the camps by Batista's air force was stopped. In return for the release of the prisoners, Raúl asked for a U.S. guarantee that it would stop sending arms to Batista and stop refueling Cuban government planes at the Guantánamo base. The United States said it was not sending arms to Batista at that time, and the U.S. ambassador stated in writing that Cuban military aircraft had not been and would not be refueled or serviced at the naval base. The hostages, who were released a few at a time, were generally favorable in their opinion of the Rebels. (See *Life,* July 7, 1958, pp. 20–23, and July 14, 1958, pp. 29–32.)

102. A *central* north of Guantánamo.

103. Caimanera was taken by the Rebels on December 20, 1958.

PART III

Ten Years of Revolution

Eulalia Fontanés

After I married Armando, he talked to me a lot about the Sierra and about the time he spent there. Then I began to join revolutionary organizations. We joined the CDR in 1964; Dora, who was in charge, brought over the blanks for me. She wrote down my name, birthplace, and the organizations I belonged to. She told me I'd be elected organizer for the block because I'd lived here for years and knew everybody. Armando was the block president, but since he was never here, I organized it. My sister Fina was in charge of Finances, and Sulema, who lived in the neighborhood, was the secretary. At the sectional level, Fina was in charge of Education and my brother Diego of Vigilance.

There was some trouble because Domingo wanted to run the Committee and so did Horacio. As for me, I didn't want it at all. Domingo kept saying, "I'm going to set up the Committee in my house." As far as I was concerned, he could have set it up wherever he wanted it. But they came directly to Armando and me to set up the Committee at our place. When we called everybody to a meeting, they were surprised. Juan had just come to see us about setting up the Committee and I said to him, "But Juan, the Committee has already been set up and named and everything."

"How come?" he asked.

I explained, "They came to us personally to set up the Committee here and I've been visiting everyone on the block, asking them to join."

Leticia joined the Committee in spite of her anger, and so did Domingo and Leticia's brothers Fermín and Segundo. Nardo and Ana Teresa joined, and Sara too. Eduardo belongs to the Committee now because we urged him to, but he's never helped us with anything.

When we held a meeting, everybody went because we made a point of going from house to house announcing it. Each month we gave out dues stamps, did volunteer work, and stood guard. On Sundays we'd have two people, a man and a woman, standing guard for three hours at a time. Sometimes it would be a married couple, and then one man alone would do it the rest of the time. On holidays like the Twenty-sixth of July, we'd decorate the Committee office. We also took charge of keeping the block clean. Every Sunday, we women would sweep the block—Fina, Leticia, Fina's mother-in-law Sonia, Sulema, and my sister-in-law Patricia. The one who never helped us clean the street or anything was Sara. Now she passes for a very good revolutionary but she never helped in anything. She doesn't even pay for her stamps.

When Armando and I had the Committee in our house we never had problems, but we quit because it was too much work. It's hard to be in charge of a Committee, spending your days out in the street, going to see people to ask them to do volunteer work. I had to leave my kids home while I was out in the street, and I had to keep after the ones who refused to volunteer.

The CDR is working all right, but now that Nicasio is president, nobody wants to volunteer for productive labor. He and I are the only two on this block who work for it, and two aren't enough to do everything. But people simply don't want to work for the Committee. Before, those who had no social consciousness didn't bother to join. Now, everybody in Cuba has to join the CDR and the Federation because the work center requires it. So people join everything, but when they're called upon to work, they beg off.

Everybody should work together or it won't succeed. Like in the case of the newspaper delivery.[1] They used to get to us very late, if at all. A pack of copies was sent to the president's house, and his wife would simply set it down anywhere for their kids to tear to pieces. Then I told the president I'd take charge of distributing the newspaper on this block. I'm not always at home—sometimes I go to the grocery store—so they leave the papers for me at my sister Serafina's house. The papers arrive about 10:30 in the morning and I pick them up and distribute them right away. There are only eight copies, so it takes no time at all to toss one in every subscriber's doorway.

There's nobody to direct the CDRs, that's why they're so disorganized. We're not even standing guard. There's an order to organize the guard again, but so far nothing has been done about it, not even at the sectional level. Nicasio told me that the sectional has been closed for the past month because there's nobody to direct it. I've heard that new people, real workers, are going to be put in every post. That would be fantastic! Maybe then Miramar would change.

I don't want to be president of the Committee or anything else. I don't want any new posts. I'm in charge of Public Health for the Committee, which means I have to vaccinate people every year, and whenever there's some public-health activity, I have to go. Women also have to have the cytological test which we make in the polyclinic, once every two years I think it is. I had one last year.

---

1. *Granma,* the official daily of the Cuban Communist Party.

Dogs are vaccinated too. Notices are posted at the sectional office, in our Minimax, in the Casa Blanca grocery store, and all over the block to inform everybody to go to the sectional to vaccinate their dogs on a certain day.

I'm also the organization and finance secretary for this zone of the Federation of Cuban Women and I have to bill everybody for their Federation dues. We've got seventy-two members in our delegation, so I bill each one every three months. There's an activist on every block who collects the dues and helps the principal delegate of the Federation. I direct them, but without their help I couldn't possibly collect all those dues. If there are no activists on a given block, the dues are simply not collected.

When the activists bring the money, they also hand in an account of the whole operation. Later I analyze the whole thing. I also have to list those people who've dropped out of the Federation because they've moved. The dues depend on how much the woman wants to pay. I pay 50 *centavos* and Fina pays 30. Justa pays 25 *centavos* and so do Leticia, Sara, and Alma. Horacio's wife pays 30 *centavos* and Mercedes pays nothing at all. The total is very little, 8-odd *pesos* in all.

For agricultural work we prefer to volunteer to the Federation instead of the Committee because the Federation has a bus and we all ride comfortably. With the CDR, you have to ride in an open truck and you get wet if it rains. And when we get there, the Federation gives us a snack to eat and sends a soft drink truck, too.

When we work in the country, I outstrip everybody. Only the other day the Party man who was responsible for our group remarked, "Lala must be from the country—no *habanera* could spread fertilizer the way she does." I keep hard at work from the minute I arrive until it's time to leave. We plant cane differently now. We used to dig holes, then we'd cut up the best stalks and put two pieces in a hole. Now we throw whole stalks into furrows and they tell us that this new thin variety of sugar cane yields much more sugar. I don't know what country they brought it from.

The Federation is in a hurry to make goggles for the cane workers.[2] Volunteers can work in a Federation office or in a Committee office from 2:00 to 5:00 in the afternoon and from 8:00 to 11:00 at night. The work goes on all day so that each volunteer can go whenever it's most convenient. We have to work fifty-five days, and it's hard to organize and schedule all the things I have to do outside and at home.

I told Justa's daughters Florinda and Genoveva about the need for volunteers and both of them promised to go help. Leticia said she couldn't go; as usual, she's too busy. I also told Alma about it, but her

2. To reduce the high incidence of eye injuries among cane workers.

kids are sick. As for Mercedes, no matter what you ask her to do she always says she can't. Norma, with a small baby, can't go either. Magda, the wife of the CDR president, has three children. Serafina is going to Pinar del Río tomorrow. Sonia works, so I haven't said anything to her yet, but I will. Justa is pregnant and has small children besides. Sara says she doesn't feel well. I'm going to see Violeta to ask her if she wants to go. I should take at least five people tomorrow. So far I have only Genoveva and Florinda.

I have nothing to do with *Poder Local;* that's up to the Committee president. And I don't know who the Committee has appointed as *Poder Local* delegate for this zone because I haven't been to a meeting of the sectional for a long time. My duties are with the block Committee. But *Poder Local* has done absolutely nothing here to help, not even when the Committee president himself wanted to put up a dividing wall in the garage where he lived. He had to resolve that problem through his work center.

When I joined the Committee, I also started working as an investigator for the Department of State Security. Nobody knew I was an investigator; when any of the directors of the Department visited, people thought they came to see Armando about something concerning the CDR. At first I didn't want the job because my children are so small. But Dora told me I wouldn't have to go out or anything, because the people from the Department would come to see me. So I accepted. I don't like the work because it's too much for just one person.

I'm not supposed to tell anybody what I do for the Department but I must know everything going on on the block, and make a census of all who live in it. When you make an analysis for the Party, you have to include everything from beginning to end. I keep a diary where I write the history of everybody living on this block and their relatives. I write down everybody's surname, place of work, age, and the license number of his car if he has one. My department has nothing to do with the foreigners living on the block; that's under another department.

Sometimes they ask me to watch all the cars that stop at somebody's house. I have to be alert to every detail, to look at everybody who goes in, and write down their height, race, and so on.

Sometimes three or four men from the Department will come here and I've got to sit down and talk to them. Once, one of them stayed so long I finally had to leave him to Armando. He came at 5:00 in the evening and it got to be 8:00 in the evening and he still wouldn't go. He simply sat there asking questions and more questions, and you must pay attention because you can't neglect those people. When they come here, I know they've been sent straight from the Department and I'd be embarrassed to tell them, "I can't see you today, come back tomorrow."

A comrade from the Department spent one whole day here to watch

Horacio's movements.[3] That was a case I was most satisfied with. Horacio had been suspected of stealing, and I was told to watch all the cars that came and to observe everybody who went in or out of his building. About 4:00 in the afternoon the comrade phoned the Department from Mercedes's apartment, asking to have all the cars in place. At that very moment, Horacio boarded a Frozen Zone truck and left without our seeing him.

The cars parked in different places and the men got out, dressed as civilians. Two were on the sidewalk in front of the building. The comrade hiding in my place couldn't make his presence known. In about ten minutes, Horacio returned and I pointed him out to the comrade and he signaled the others. Horacio was with Armando, and when he turned his back, Armando made signs with two fingers to the two men who were standing in front, and they arrested Horacio, walked him to the corner, made him get into a car, and drove away. There was no explanation except that Horacio was engaging in illegal activities. They arrested a lot of others at that time, including the chief of police, Ameijeiras, who'd been involved in some matter having to do with women.

Later, Horacio told us he'd been in the hospital because of a leg pain, but I knew he was lying. Just like the lieutenant in the middle apartment here. He's carried off all the things he has there. After he moved here, he took four tires to his sister in Oriente for her car, but I have to catch him at it before I can accuse him.

How can Mercedes afford to live as she does on what her husband earns? Well, her husband makes his real living at another kind of business: selling machinery parts above the legal price. They already came once to investigate him because something was missing at his place of work. They came from the Department to ask me about him. I reported that he brought in a lot of things with several friends and that many cars drive in there to be fixed out in the back. I was told by the heads of the Federation and the Department for this zone to keep an eye on them and to report any box I saw taken in or carried out, so it could be checked on.

There are some revolutionaries here and some who only pretend to be revolutionaries. Horacio is a good revolutionary and really works hard. Sonia, in no. 407, also is very revolutionary. Wherever the Revolution sends her, she goes. Her children are also revolutionaries, but in their own way. They don't like to be sent to do volunteer work or any of that. Alma and her husband moved in next door about two or three months ago. He's a real revolutionary but Alma is a halfhearted one.

Norma, in no. 419, is not a revolutionary. She didn't belong to the Federation until I made her a member six or seven months ago. When I

3. This took place in 1966.

went to her, I said, "Well, Norma, aren't you going to join up? Now don't tell me you're going to refuse!" Then her husband, Emilio, said, "Yes, make her a member!" She always refused to join the Committee. As long as the old woman she worked for[4] is with her, she has no problems. But now that she sees the old girl going, she's suddenly caught on to the fact that she'd better get organized quick. The first thing they ask you is what organizations you belong to. When the local school refused to accept her son and sent him instead to one farther away, she said very harsh things about the Revolution—really terrible things.

Mercedes is no revolutionary and she doesn't have a social conscience, though her husband, Juan, does. She says the stores don't have anything and you have to fill out twenty questionnaires every time you do anything. We all know that, but what's the point of griping about it? That's the Revolution—everybody has to be organized. Well, lately she joined the Committee.

Neither Leticia nor Domingo are revolutionaries. Domingo says it's because he's a spiritist, and so is Leticia. She criticizes the Revolution terribly, and Domingo doesn't work at all. Leticia says he's too ill with the itch but he's not too ill to drink beer. My goodness, I've got the itch myself. And Armando, who's really sick, is working. So Leticia works hard to support them both. She has a bit of money because her brother Fermín gives her some. He's a mechanic and earns very good money. Segundo used to give her money too, but now he's gone. Her father handed her 50 *pesos* the other day in front of me, and her *compadre* also gives her money when he comes here.

Actually, Domingo doesn't work because they transferred him and he said he wasn't going, so they eliminated him from everything. Now he's got to wait until the Ministry calls him. Domingo isn't sick. There are lots of jobs he could do with no harm to his health, like being a sales clerk for INIT, which isn't tiring, or driving a truck to distribute merchandise. But no, he doesn't want anything. In all the time I've lived here, I haven't seen Domingo put in more than one full month of steady work. He doesn't like to have a steady job, that's all.

Our ration book[5] has the names and ages of every member of our family, plus my brother Diego. At the moment, we're four adults and three children, because Mandito is over seven and counts as an adult. Buying meat and coffee is no problem because that comes to the grocery store every week. They give you a number and you wait in line until your turn comes. When lots of goods arrive at the same time, the Minimax fills up with people. You take your ration book and you say, "Give me everything I'm entitled to get." They write down exactly what things you can buy and in what amounts. You give the paper to a girl, who then gives

4. Carmen Tamayo.
5. See Appendix A.

you some of everything and marks down the amounts in your ration book. Without that slip of paper you aren't allowed to buy anything.

The problems start when you have to stand in different lines for the different products. I stand in one line and wait until someone else comes to stand in back of me, then I tell her, "Wait, I'm going to another line." So I go to the end of another line and wait until someone stands behind me there and do the same thing so I can go save a place in a third line. I mark my place in the three lines at once and keep switching so that I spend a few minutes in each. Of course you lose your turn if the person you asked forgets and leaves before you get back.

One day when Fina and I were in line, a little old man lost his turn and everybody started arguing. Fina and I managed to slip ahead in the line because they were too busy arguing to notice. We got our things and left everybody still arguing. That's illegal and I don't like to do it—or to get into an argument in line, either.

I haven't much hope that the scarcity of food and other goods will be over soon. Of all the shortages we have, the hardest to live with is the food shortage. But now that they've increased the rice ration,[6] our food lasts all right. I get the whole month's rice ration at one time, but my family doesn't like rice much, so I often exchange some of it for something I need more, sometimes for plantains to fry. No cooking oil has come to the store for almost three months, but when it does come, it lasts fine. I'd have enough to fry with if only they'd give me something to fry.

We're entitled to one and a half bars of bath soap per person per month. They let me have two giant-size tubes of toothpaste whenever it comes to the store. They gave us a cloth for mopping the floor and toilet paper in October and in March, and they haven't given any more since. They aren't putting bread in the ration book, because there's an abundance of it now. We got *malanga* for the kids in the first fifteen days of March and then none at all until the last fifteen days of May.

Cheese we never see. Butter was on sale in August and September of last year, but there hasn't been any since. Meat comes pre-packed, so you don't get a choice. When you open the package, if you're in luck it's good; if you aren't it isn't, and that's that. Fish comes every week too, and veal whenever it's in season.

We always save a bit of meat each week to be sure to have enough to last till the end of the month, when the food situation is always at its worst. Instead of eating meat every day, we eat fish first and then fish again, so we have meat left over that week. But sometimes the only fish is mackerel, and I won't eat that no matter how hungry I am.

They give us flour every month, but there aren't any tomatoes left, nor rum, tinned meat, or sweets. Christmas foods, like Spanish nougats, guava, rum, oil, hard cider, peaches, and pork, won't come until July

6. In 1969 the rice ration was increased from 3 to 4 pounds per person per month, then to 6 pounds in 1970.

next year, eighteen months from last Christmas. Canned fruit is no longer available, which is a pity because my kids are just at the age when they need it most.

Vegetables are very scarce, and we never see fresh fruit in the stores either. I eat fruit when my folks bring me some from the country. The other day *mamá* brought me three enormous mameys, and I made milkshakes for the kids with them. *Mamá* always brings me some pork, too. That's practically all I eat back home. Here in Havana we only get pork at Christmas, and this year we'll have to wait extra long for Christmas.

Coffee lasts all right because I'm not fond of it and I never give it to the kids for breakfast. I prefer milkshakes or dessert, because I love sweets. I'm forever making papaya slices in syrup, bread pudding, and all sorts of desserts. As long as I have something sweet to eat, I don't need anything else.

We must adapt to doing without many things we're used to, like laundry starch. For a time they'd bring yucca to the grocery store and we'd make yucca starch. When I go home, sometimes I bring back some of *mamá*'s yucca starch, or she often sends it. When I was completely out of yucca starch, I used cornstarch. That starch is fine; it gives the clothes a sort of shine and makes them look real pretty. I used to get cornstarch from my folks, or sometimes from the Chilean woman next door. Then, when it got scarce too, I invented bread starch.

To make bread starch, I soak stale bread, or sometimes fresh bread, in water, then I strain it. What comes out is starch. It can also be made from vermicelli. That's what we're using now and it works fine. When something is lacking, one must find a substitute. There's always a way to solve problems.

When Mercedes receives bananas or something, she always brings me some or gives some to my children. Sometimes I'll exchange milk for things she has; for instance, six cans of milk for 4 pounds of rice. We don't exchange regularly, only when I need some extra rice. Mercedes doesn't often exchange things. The other day I needed eggs and she gave me some as a gift. When she runs out of soap I'll let her have it for nothing. Last month she ran out of powdered detergent, so I gave her two boxes full and she gave me 2 pounds of rice. Usually she gives me things for the children instead of exchanging. When she has applesauce, which Eloyitos never eats, she gives it to my kids. The other day Juan brought home lots of candy, so she gave some to my kids. She's always giving me things.

I also exchanged with a Galician woman living nearby. I'd give her oil, detergent, and soap, and she'd give me a handful of plantains in exchange. She gets them from some other *gallegas*[7] in Marianao.

7. A *gallego* or *gallega* is a man or woman from Galicia, Spain, but the terms are used in the vernacular to refer to light-skinned people whether or not they are of Spanish descent.

I hardly ever exchange with Leticia. When she doesn't have something, she asks me for it. Then, when I need something, I ask her. The other day I went to ask her for a can of milk, and later I tried to pay her back, but she wouldn't hear of it. How could she when she asks me for so many things? She often asks for beans because I have more than I need and she always runs out. Sometimes I give her rice in exchange for the milk she gives me.

Justa has never exchanged with anybody in the building. As for Leticia and Mercedes, who never got along together, once they exchanged rice and milk, indirectly through me, as if I were the one who wanted to exchange.

When Sara came back from Oriente, she said she suffered black hunger there, but she had 12 pounds of rice stashed away here, and she got all her meat ration, too. Well, when I went to Oriente I took my whole month's supply of rice along. When I came back, I had the next month's supply waiting for me at the store. Sara doesn't cook for her kids, either. "Feed those poor innocent children of yours, old girl!" I'd say. I don't know what she does with the food she gets. Those people simply don't know how to manage their rations.

Leticia is that way too, but she gives her food to visitors. Only yesterday she had visitors and cooked two enormous chickens that she'd brought from Camaguey. Why not save them to feed her children, eh? She came here and asked me, "Can you let me have a bitter orange for some chicken I'm going to cook?" I thought, "My goodness, don't you have more sense than to cook chicken on a Sunday, when there are bound to be visitors?" I cook chicken on a working day, when nobody is going to show up. I save tender meat and all the good things for my own family, but Leticia doesn't, and Sara is just like her.

One day I asked Sara to sell me three cans of milk, and she said to me, "Oh, I sell milk around here for 1.50 a can." So I said, "All right" and bought them. I don't usually buy them at that price. Sara also sells milk to a little old woman, Dalia, who lives in no. 406 and often comes to visit her. The other day the lady Dalia works for drove Sara home in their little car, and I thought, "Hm, that one's come to get something."

Sara sells far too many things. But Dalia keeps going there to get things. Some people like to sell everything they can lay their hands on. I don't need to sell anything. On the contrary, I'm always looking for things to buy. What do they want money for? I don't care for money. I'd rather you gave me a chicken than 10 *pesos*. What good is it to have 10 *pesos* stashed away in a bureau drawer when my belly is empty? But then, Eduardo's wages aren't enough. He's married to that other woman who bore him two children, and he must send her money. I guess they really need the money they get by selling their rations.

I can't imagine how Mercedes splurges the way she does on what Juan earns. When I filled out the questionnaires for Juan, I found out he had to pay back rent, because for a while they couldn't afford to pay any rent.

Their rent is 26.75 *pesos*. Just before Evidio left, Juan told him he had 8,000 *pesos* in the bank. But that couldn't last long if they keep taking out money without putting any in. I think her mother gives them money; that must be how they manage.

Leticia manages to make quite a bit of money taking in laundry—sometimes over 100 *pesos* a month. She works like crazy and is very clean and neat, too. The lieutenant still earns too little but Justa earns extra money by washing the uniforms of some of Hernández's comrades. Armando earns 160 *pesos* a month, but we pay no rent and only a bit over 2 *pesos* for electricity, and we aren't as many as they are.

If they gave me a choice between a house and a frigidaire, I'd tell them, "Give me the frigidaire and I'll stay on living here." I'd rather have a frigidaire than a television, too. I hate to bother people, and if I had a frigidaire it would solve a lot of problems for me, especially during our hot summers.

The electric iron I have now I bought with Mercedes's mother's ration book. She lent it to me because she already owned an iron. I still had one electric item in my ration book, but at the time the irons were put out for sale, it was Mercedes's mother's turn to buy, not mine, so I made the exchange with her. She told me to save the coupon and get an electric fan. But Armando told me to buy an electric blender if I saw one for sale.

I think our old radio was much better than the one we just got with our ration book. The new one runs on flashlight batteries, which sometimes you can't get. We always used to be able to get big Admiral brand batteries for our old radio. My sister had to stand in line for three days to get the new one. I'm not sure how much it cost. I know that five radios costing 150 *pesos* each came to the store. There were also some record players but a radio was what we wanted.

Nowadays, whoever wants a career can study for it because it doesn't cost a *centavo*. Before, only the rich could study. Out in the country you had to make a lot of sacrifices if you wanted to study a little. Frankly, if it hadn't been for the Revolution Armando would still be a savage in the hills. He'd never have studied, because it's up to one's parents to educate their children. Armando's mother didn't bother. Her nine children are illiterate and she herself can neither read nor write.

I don't intend to go back to live in the country because I can educate the children better in Havana. I want them to be able to study. The public schools used to teach a lot about Cuban history and martyrs of the old times, but now they teach current events as well. My children are getting a better education than I ever had, and now each grade has its own teacher. I can ask my kids anything and they'll explain it. Armando asked Mando why El Che died in Bolivia and Mando answered perfectly, just like a grown person. "And do you think it was right for Che to do what he was doing there?" Armando asked.

"Yes, he was right," Mando answered.

"Why?" Armando insisted.

"Because he was there to liberate Bolivia. Every country should be free," Mando explained. We were never taught things like that.

My youngest, Dieguito, said recently, "*Papi*, I'm the same as El Che."

"Sure you are!" said Germancito. "And where's El Che now? In the graveyard!"

But Dieguito insisted, "No, no, no, I'm just like El Che."

When we were in school they only taught us to read and write. They never taught us to march or how to get into formation at school. We'd run here and there, instead of in perfect marching order, one behind another. We never had Pioneers; I never even heard of the Pioneers until my kids joined. How proud they were! Mando came home bursting with pride because his group was assigned to a military unit which is right near here, and all the military men were there to make them Pioneers. Mando and Juan Pablo were made Pioneers at the same time because all children from the age of seven up are accepted if they behave themselves in school.

When Juan Pablo was in the first grade, he could already read the newspaper. That boy has got a good head on his shoulders. Mando doesn't—he had to repeat the first grade and now he and Juan Pablo are together in the second. None of my children ever was in a *círculo;* they went directly to school.

It isn't only the children who are different. Parents have changed too. Now the teacher says, "Today the child is in school and so are the parents." My sister Isabel was one of those who learned to read and write as an adult.

Mando says he wants a scholarship for the Camilo Cienfuegos School, and so does Juan Pablo. Armando says that as soon as they graduate from the sixth grade, he himself will see to it that they get good scholarships. All he has to do is explain to the Party that he needs scholarships for the boys. When the Party investigates and sees how things are, they'll make a formal request for the scholarships right away. Party members have more rights than anybody else. Those having a greater number of responsible jobs to carry out for the Revolution have the most privileges.

The Camilo Cienfuegos is a military school, so the boys will do their military service at the same time they learn whatever trade they choose. When they graduate they can be transferred to the school in Marianao,[8] which is very good. From there they graduate as officers in the armed forces.

I wouldn't want my kids to have Makarenko scholarships. Those kids are sadly neglected and look pitiful. They're away from their families

8. The Military Technological Institute.

and are very badly looked after, with no one to wash and iron their clothes. They're left to their own devices all day long. Those kids spend their days wandering around the streets, throwing stones and fighting. Children should be either with their own mothers or else on a good scholarship program. If my children can't get a good scholarship, I'd rather keep them home and send them to a school near here. Then let them do their three years of military service afterward.

The neighbors here are protesting the Makarenko situation because those children are left with a bunch of women who don't look after them. Horacio had to intervene once when they were fighting one another with machetes. We've been told they plan to move from here soon. They're building houses for them elsewhere so the boys and the girls can live in separate areas. In the boys' houses they'll have military men in charge.

The food they serve those kids isn't good; that is, they don't watch the kids to make sure they eat a balanced diet, the way a mother does. I make Mando eat whether he wants to or not, but nobody in the scholarship program is going to take such good care of him.

It's important that the Revolution succeed, so one must make sacrifices for the sake of the general good. I've had to live apart from Armando for most of eight years, so I know sacrifice. It's only recently, while he was working for INIT, that we've been together more often. They took him away to do volunteer work with his militia unit for one week or so, but I didn't carry on the way some women do. It only makes life bitter for yourself and your husband too. One must adapt to the situation.

If the Revolution needs men and Armando is involved with communism, I let him make his own decisions, though I'd rather he didn't work in agriculture because his health is bad. He has the beginning of a stomach ulcer and is easily upset. I wish he'd join the Army instead, because then he'd come home to eat. But any Cuban woman must adapt to her husband's situation or he'll divorce her if he's a real revolutionary. She simply must let her husband go where he wants to.

In 1965, just before Armando was admitted to the Communist Youth, he said to me, "Do you know I'm being analyzed as a possible member for the Youth?"

"Oh, grand!" said I. I was glad to hear it. It wasn't more than two years before he was admitted to the Party. I knew he was going to be admitted because the president of the Committee here told me so. Nicasio said, "Know what? They came around to investigate Armando because they mean to promote him to full Party membership." They're not supposed to tell the person involved, because if he was doing something wrong, they wouldn't be able to catch him if he was forewarned. People get wary when they know they're being watched.

When Armando volunteered to go to the Isle of Pines, the Party told him that if any problem came up while he was gone, I should call them and they'd come over immediately to resolve it. If I needed money or a car to drive one of the children to the doctor, or in case of any other emergency, I should call them at any hour of the day or night. So Armando told me what they said and gave me their phone number and street address.

Nobody wanted to go to the Isle because life there is very difficult and people are really driven hard. But those who refuse to go are investigated by the Party. If they're living in comfort and have no legitimate excuse for refusing, the Party sends them elsewhere or takes away their Party cards. Carlos, who lives next door, had his Party card taken away because he refused to go. His excuse was that he lived in a miserable little room.

Armando agreed to go from the very first. He could have stayed here but he was wild to go out to the country where he was really needed. He thinks about his home and his children but believes the Revolution needs him more. The kids are all right, he comes home every time he has a pass, and besides, we won't lack anything. If that's the way he feels, I can't prevent him from going. He's been that way all his life, keeping nothing for himself and doing whatever the Party asks him to. He misses us, and I miss him too, but I'm proud of him. I wouldn't want a man who lived only for himself.

When they asked him whether we had any housing problem he answered, "We live in two rooms which aren't bad, but there's no place to wash clothes and my wife has to lug clothes up and down the stairs, which is hard on her. That's our only difficulty as far as housing is concerned."

They told Armando they'd pay him 80 *pesos* and give me money to pay the bills, but he refused it. He said we had no expenses of that kind except the electric-light and milk bills. Armando told the Party people, "You can go to my house and see for yourselves that we cook with kerosene. As for the rest of the household expenses, they don't amount to much."

I have about 300 *pesos* saved and I don't spend that much. Besides, we have nothing left to buy in the clothing ration book, except one pair of pants and socks for the boys that I'm going to buy when my turn comes. I'm most worried about getting socks for the kids. I've also heard they're selling corduroy and I want to get a few yards to make pants for the boys this winter.

I still wash clothes for the MINFAR scholarship students, who are Leticia's friends. They're taking a course here and also work. They're civilians, not soldiers, though they receive a soldier's pay. If they bring Leticia forty pieces of clothing, she gives me half and keeps half to wash and iron herself. She sets the prices and gets the money from them—50 *centavos* for each shirt and 50 for each pair of pants. On the 20th of the month they pay her for the whole thing, then she pays me for the clothes I've washed. She keeps her accounts and I keep mine.

I've been working with Leticia for about three years. Last month I earned 30 *pesos* with her, and there have been times when I've earned as much as 70 *pesos* in one month. When I'm sick or something, I don't wash. I'm not working now and I didn't from the time I got married until Mando was eight months old, especially when my belly was growing.

I liked the job I used to have, working as a cleaning woman for the Frozen Zone. I felt good when I had a job because I had more friends and acquaintances. I worked in different houses and didn't worry about my own home. I didn't want to quit, but Armando insisted that with two children I shouldn't work outside anymore. Later on, after Juan Pablo's birth, I wanted to sign up for work, but Armando wouldn't hear of it.

Aside from that, I iron for other people, like Mercedes. I charge 10 *centavos* for each of her little boy's shirts, 10 for his pants, 15 for uniforms, and 15 for her little girl's dresses. I don't iron any of her clothes or her husband's. She gives me the clothes already washed and starched.

I don't want a job until I have the boys in boarding school. Besides, Armando argues, "I earn enough for all of us, so why should you kill yourself working? If you got a job, you'd also have to go out to the country to do volunteer work and get involved in all sorts of activities." We have more money than we can spend and we've got savings, too. Anyway, there's nothing to buy, except what's in the ration book. Besides, as Armando says, when he came from the Isle on a six-day pass he'd have to spend his days alone at home if I was out working.

If I were living out on the Isle with him, then I'd work. The women there work as well as the men. That would be different, because we'd be together and would go home together after work.

If I wanted to get a job now, Armando wouldn't really mind. We could place the children in school as semi-boarders, though they'd get only their lunch at school. I'd still have to cook two meals a day. If they were given three meals a day, then it would be easy for me to hold a job.

But how could I abandon my children? No matter how well they fed them in school, they'd never cater to their tastes the way I do. Dieguito is very squeamish about his food, and Mando eats only the things he likes—ripe bananas, fried beef and such. And he won't drink his coffee unless it's strained. And you've got to keep after him to make him eat. I'd end up going to school every day to see that he ate his lunch. Do you think I'd let my son die from lack of nourishment?

If every Cuban was the kind of revolutionary Armando has been since he came down from the Sierra, the Revolution would really be getting ahead. But most people are simple opportunists. Armando isn't the kind of person who craves a big government job—any kind of work will satisfy him. After fourteen months in the Army he could have had an apartment, but he never asked because many people live in much worse places than ours.

In Old Havana there are people living in houses where the roof is about to fall down on them. And when I made the census here I saw people living on top of buildings where they had to jump over a wall to get to the laundry tubs. If they should happen to slip, they'd fall all the way down to the street. I've seen about twenty people living in such places.

Armando and I have both had a hard time and we know all about poverty and hardship. I know what it is to have stayed home from parties because I didn't have a decent dress to wear. Such things are still happening, but some people care only for themselves. And if we all sit on our behinds instead of going to work in the countryside where the things we need come from, well, everything will come tumbling down on top of us.

The worst problem now is the scarcity of food. The clothing shortage is easier to take because you can make yourself a dress out of any scrap. But some people aren't satisfied with that—they want twenty dresses. If it were possible, Fidel would gladly let every Cuban woman have a hundred dresses! We get enough clothes and nobody has had to go naked so far. There are those who go around in dirty clothes, but they do it because they want to. *My* clothes don't stink and *I* don't go barefoot. One can always manage to get something somewhere. Of course, things are in tight supply, but there are weeks when we have a lot. So far, we don't really lack anything we need.

Right now the sugar cane is under water, so they're sending everybody out to clean up the fields to ready them for the harvest of the 10 million in 1970. Fidel has said that after this harvest we'll be able to pay for everything. In the 1970s—that's when we'll be well off here, and we'll keep on making harvests like that, or 15 million tons, or whatever Fidel decides, because the cane has already been planted, and that's the hardest part of the job. You just wait and see. You won't find any of us at home then; we'll all be out in the country harvesting sugar cane. Women, too, will all gradually be called to work. I'll be the first to go, without waiting to be called. As long as I know my children are well taken care of in a school, I'll work on a job all day long.

I approve of the changes in our lives since the Revolution. Things are better than before because now we're free. I'm telling you, Cuba has a bright future. You can see it in the way we're progressing with each day that passes. If things keep up as they've been so far, if nothing happens to stop us, we Cubans will live well in the future. I'll be rather old by then but my children will enjoy all the advantages.

Armando Cárdenas

They first analyzed me as a Communist Youth prospect when I was working at the ice cream parlor. I'd noticed, of course, that lots of fellows became militants in the Youth, but, well, I wasn't particularly interested. As time went on, though, my comrades at work got to know me and saw how I got along with the others. The employees held a small meeting to nominate a young militant who was qualified to be a Vanguard Worker.[9] They told us that to be a Vanguard Worker, a comrade must be committed, involved, revolutionary, get along well with his comrades, and perform his duty in the revolutionary organizations he belongs to. In most units, everyone knows perfectly well how committed everyone else is, because all that is discussed, and besides we had every worker's record.

Some comrades from the Youth had sent me a message saying they were going to meet with me and with delegate Osorio, who was going to be analyzed too. They could have chosen as many as three comrades from our center, but I was the only one selected. If there are others with the qualities required, they must all be accepted. But a small work center hardly ever runs into that particular problem.

9. The Vanguard Worker program was part of a new system of union organization introduced in 1965–66. The union reorganization followed the restructuring of the Communist Party in late 1965 and Party cells were being established in all work centers. Requirements for Vanguard Worker status were similar to those for Party membership, so these workers provided a reservoir of potential Party candidates. The objective of the reform was to remove union bureaucrats and professionals from leadership positions in work centers and bring the workers more into the day-to-day decision-making process. Vanguard Workers met as a body to enforce policy and assume responsibilities for achieving work norms and replaced, to a large extent, the traditional union structure. Assemblies were held at the enterprise level four times a year to nominate Vanguard Workers. These assemblies coincided with four revolutionary holidays (also used to designate emulation periods): the triumph of the Revolution (January), May 1, July 26, and the Day of the Heroic Guerrillas (October 10). (The Vanguard Worker program and union reorganization are discussed by Lionel Martin in the *Guardian* in a series of six articles beginning in the issue of May 10, 1969, and ending on July 5, 1969.) This merger of union and Party functions for Party membership selection was abandoned after 1970, but the Vanguard Worker status has been retained. By replacing union bureaucrats with Party personnel, the program apparently further stifled worker participation instead of enhancing it as the Party had hoped.

I felt very happy about being nominated. Afterward, the first manager, Carlos, met with two comrades from the Youth so he could inform them more fully about me. "Frankly," he said, "I don't know anyone here who deserves the honor of being a Youth and Vanguard Worker as much as this comrade here, because I've observed the kind of person he is and have seen how he works with the comrades."

Above all, I know how to treat my comrades at work. And if any of them tries to take advantage of that, I know how to put him in his place, because I am, first of all, a leader of the Revolution, and I'm a manager.

They called me in again, this time by myself, to explain to me the duties of a militant Youth. They came to my work center in the afternoon, bringing the life-history form, and they started asking questions.

"Do you have any religious beliefs?" they asked me.

"No, none at all."

"To what organizations do you belong?"

"To all of them," I said.

"Were you ever in the army of the tyranny?"

"No."

They asked specific questions about all those things.

Out of the more than 100 candidates nominated that time, only a little over thirty of us were chosen as militants.

The Vanguard types were picked on their work record alone. If you stood out as a good worker in your center, that was all that counted, because at that time people didn't do much volunteer farm work. Vanguard Workers had to be outstanding in the number of extra hours they worked without pay. In analyzing me, they didn't take into account the amount of time I gave to my job as a manager, because a manager doesn't have fixed working hours—he must stay on the job as late as necessary. So working long hours is not considered something special. It's taken for granted.

Vanguard Workers had to make sacrifices and do their best to render good service. They were rewarded with prizes then, not like now. Competition was within the unit and those picked as outstanding were given money prizes. There were even prizes for not being absent from work. Lots of guys put forth their best efforts for the money.

After I was made a Vanguard Worker and admitted to the Youth, I became manager of the Pabellón Martí cafeteria. I belonged to the committee that met at the Hotel Vedado restaurant. We organized study circles and also carried out different assigned tasks, such as volunteer productive labor in the country.

Among the political activities entrusted to me as a militant Youth was serving as a Pioneer leader. I was part of a team of four leaders assigned to a school on Menocal Street. We presented ourselves to the director of the school and she took us around to all the classrooms and introduced us. "These comrades are your Pioneer leaders who have come here so you'll know them." Then the students applauded.

I didn't have a very clear idea of what a Pioneer leader was supposed to do. Somebody should teach us what to do with the kids. But I'd go to the school and ask for information I thought might be useful for whatever a leader was supposed to be. I never learned what my functions were. I simply did whatever came to my head.

To cover the whole school, our team divided the grades among us. I don't remember which grades I visited, but I went during recess, when the children weren't in class, so I could talk with them. We went practically every day because that was our duty. Some days I couldn't go because I had too much work, but I always kept in touch with them. They came freely into my work center and would yell for me. They were badly brought up, as small kids always are.

The Pioneer leader is supposed to take the children to playgrounds, historical landmarks, and so on. One day we planned an outing to the zoo for the first grades. Two or three teachers accompanied us and two or three parents as well. Everybody cooperates in such activities. The children made a lot of noise on the bus because there's always a leader who teaches them songs and leads the singing. Not me. I don't know how to sing or anything like that.

After we took them through the zoo we went to the playground, where they rushed for the swings and the bars. The girls climbed up the jungle gym and the boys stood below, looking up. Children's mentality sure has changed a lot! When I was that age, it would never have entered my mind to try to peek under a girl's skirt. But nowadays! Modern kids know quite a bit more at the age of five than we did—anyone can see that. Before, you'd find boys of thirteen or fourteen who didn't know anything. And a country boy nowadays knows as much as a boy in Havana. I'm not criticizing; it's a sign of progress.

Being a Pioneer leader was fun, but during that month I kept worrying about my work. I explained to them, "A Pioneer leader has to spend four or five hours at a stretch with the children. I'm a manager and I can't spare more than a couple of hours at a time." So they freed me from my duties as a leader.

Luckily, I've never had to deal with any counterrevolutionary at work. There were some boys stealing oranges from the store where I worked, but they can't be called counterrevolutionaries. I don't even blame the boys too much for stealing—it's the parents' fault. If a kid's parents let him run loose in the streets, then you can't blame the kid if he turns out to be a hooligan and a wild beast.

The stealing occurred when I was managing a restaurant. Out back was a run-down old building we used as a warehouse; we hung the banana bunches from the rafters and kept milk, sugar, coconuts, and fruit in there. One day I got a load of oranges and stored them inside the warehouse. The weather was hot so I opened the outer door and closed the door made of iron bars. The orange crates were about 5 meters from the doorway.

Next day when I went to the storehouse, I said to myself, "What the hell happened here? How did that orange crate get next to the bars? What does it all mean?" Then it occurred to me that somebody had solen something.

The next day I sat in the store, watching the warehouse door to see if I could catch the thief. At about 3:00 in the afternoon I saw some little mulattoes pass by and look in at a box of grapefruit I'd placed there. Those boys would have torn down the door if they could, to get at those grapefruit! The blackest one stuck his legs in through the bars as far as they'd go, then poked around with a stick, trying with such eagerness to pull the box toward him.

I cut around behind the building and tried to grab the big boy, but he was real light on his feet and ran off, fast as a deer. The best I could do was run after them and grab the little one. He struggled and jumped like a little goat trying to break loose. I don't think he could have been much more than eleven years old.

Well, I pulled the little one into the office and called the police patrol. A patrolman came by two or three hours later. He claimed the patrol car had set out earlier but hadn't been able to find the place. The kid's mother showed up before they arrived. She came weeping, with another son who was in the military service.

I said to her, "Look, Señora, these things are now in the hands of the state and I simply can't let the kid go. It's up to the police to decide. Frankly, I don't think you have much to worry about. They'll probably give the kid a good scare and let him go. I called the police to prevent your son from growing up to be a thief."

While we waited for the police, the kid cried and cried. I talked to him. "Look here," I said, "don't you go to school?"

"Yes, I do."

"Well, hasn't the teacher there taught you how to be a good boy? Are you a Pioneer? You are? Well then, don't you know what it means to be a Pioneer, eh? You're supposed to set a good example for the other children. Don't you know it's wrong to steal and you're too young to start going wrong? Don't you know anything about the society we live in?"

The kid's brother explained, "He's been out of school for quite a while because our old lady is working in the country."

Well, we took the boy to the police station, where they filed charges. When I signed the accusation, they asked me more or less how many oranges he'd stolen. "Well," I said, "there must have been 50 pounds of oranges in the crate."

"And where are those oranges?" they asked.

"Heck," I said, "how do I know? They took them away. The questions you people ask!"

Then I tried to get the information out of the kid. I said to him, "Look here, where did you kids take those oranges?"

"We sold them to a woman," he said.

"You did, eh? Well look, did that woman run any kind of business?" I wanted to find out because there are people with their own private business who egg the boys on to steal so they can buy cheap from them.

"No," said the kid, "she was a housewife." But I thought, "Even so, she could have her own little business at home, selling fruit juice and so on. Here's my chance to kill two birds with one stone."

The police did a lot of investigating into the boys' families before the trial. They went to the boys' houses to see how their parents lived, whether the father and mother were living together and that sort of thing. They found out that the little kid's father and mother were separated. The father was earning good wages at the docks, but he'd abandoned his wife and child. That's why the mother had to get a job out in the country—she had no choice.

The woman is a nice lady, very easy to get along with. She scolded the boy severely because she realized her son had done wrong, and she agreed that he should be taken to trial for it. The kid's brother, who was in the military service, also gave the kid a good scolding.

I didn't regret having accused the boy and having him brought to trial. I was doing my duty as a manager, because I had to account for the oranges to the officer in charge of business matters at the regional office of INIT.

The trial was finally held about six months after the theft. I was no longer manager of the restaurant by then. At that time, the People's Court was still being organized,[10] so it wasn't conducted by a People's judge. Of course I went to the trial, as did the mothers of both boys. The other boy, the ringleader, wasn't at the trial because he'd already been sent to a work farm for stealing a fountain pen.

First of all, it was necessary to pick the jurors. The judge asked the boy's mother, "Do you recognize any of the members of this jury? If you do and wish to dismiss this jury, you may do so." If she'd recognized somebody there who she thought would twist things around, or who had some kind of a grudge against her or the boy which might affect his opinion, then the jury would have been dismissed. When they asked me, "Do you wish this trial to be suspended?" I answered, "No, comrade. This trial must go on because it involves state property. And this boy should be taught a lesson."

The judge ordered the trial to proceed, and they called other witnesses first, then questioned me. The defendant has the right to have

10. See Part I, n. 34.

somebody speak in his defense, but the kid didn't have anybody. His mother was the only one to speak on his behalf.

The jury went inside to deliberate and stayed a long time. When they came out, they sentenced the boy to six months' house arrest. That meant he had to go straight from his house to school and from school straight back home. The CDR was to be responsible for keeping an eye on the parents and seeing to it that they obeyed the Court orders. The other boy was also sentenced to six months, to be served concurrently with his sentence at the work farm. Besides that, the parents had to pay us 3 *pesos* for the oranges.

The problem wasn't the 3 *pesos;* it was the boys themselves. They had to be saved from a life of crime by making them understand the error of their ways. You still find kids like that in Havana. Suppose you're going down El Prado and you see a boy doing something he shouldn't. If you stop to tell him, "Now look, kid, you can't do that," he'll face right up to you like an adult, talking back and saying all sorts of rude things. It's terrible to see a little child talking like that to a grown man. Kids are running wild and no one can control them. You can't slap them, because hitting a kid is looking for trouble. You just have to sit and watch them be disrespectful to their elders. There isn't a damn thing you can do about it.

I keep up with the news by listening to the radio. I hardly ever read the newspapers. My favorite reading is about historical matters, but I don't read much. In fact, I've never completely read any of Fidel's speeches because my eyes are weak. I'd rather listen to him than read his speeches.

We had study groups at the Youth sectional to discuss Fidel's speeches and all sorts of international problems. The Youth organized the meetings, but they were led by a very capable Party militant who explained whatever we didn't understand. The number in a study group depends on the number of militants in each sectional. There were usually four or five of us militant comrades at those meetings. I didn't always attend because of my work.

Sometimes each militant was asked to tell what he thought about a lecture. Since some people are on a higher cultural level than others, they can explain things better. In fact, a few of the comrades were economists for the regional Committees, which means they're on a very, very high cultural level and know a lot. When they asked for my opinion I said what I felt with my whole heart, not something someone told me to say. No one has ever tried to brainwash me.

For instance, once we had a meeting to discuss the most rapid way to get to power, whether through armed struggle or political discussions. The Venezuelan Communist Party is against a revolution by armed struggle. They believe that by holding meetings and talking, they'll come

to power by political means. Well gosh, if we spend our time talking
things over with the Venezuelan government, how are we ever going to
get anywhere? My own theory is that the best means of taking power is
by force and I said so at the lecture.

Here in Cuba, we kicked out all the old regime's military men as soon
as the Revolution triumphed. Why? Because they were like a needle
pricking our hide, since they were still against the Revolution. And that's
exactly what's going wrong in Venezuela. If you start fooling around
with politics, other people begin to protest. Then you have to start meeting secretly, and if the meeting is discovered, twenty people might be
killed. You'll never get anywhere that way.

That's why Fabricio Ojeda[11] got killed. He was trying to unite the
guerrillas with the Communist Party when they caught him. Besides
Ojeda, Douglas Bravo[12] and a lot of other people believe that the quick-
est way to get to power is by armed struggle. But the Venezuelan Communist Party doesn't support these revolutionaries.

We asked the comrades discussing the problem with us, "When the
revolution triumphs in Venezuela, who should we recognize as the real
communists? Those who grasped their weapons and fought for power or
the ones who went around giving little talks?" I think the real communists are those fighting up in the mountains, whether the Venezuelan
Communist Party likes them or not. We should recognize the people
who acted as liaisons between the guerrillas and the city people. But we
should never grant recognition to those who went around saying they
were communists and at the same time telling people that the Communist Party didn't believe in taking power by force.

Everybody in the study circle agreed with me. That was the only thing
we were unanimous about. It didn't occur to anybody to say the best way
was by means of elections. Hell! All of us were good communists.

It's not often that anybody opposes anything at a meeting. At least I've
never heard anybody get really contrary. One way or another, everybody
agrees in the end. For one thing, the study group meetings aren't very
long, only an hour or an hour and a half. So we have just enough time to
read and discuss the pamphlet we're given.

11. Fabricio Ojeda was president of an independent leftist coalition, *Junta Patriótica*, that
overthrew the Venezuelan dictator Pérez Jiménez in 1958. In 1961 Ojeda resigned from
the coalition government that had replaced Pérez Jiménez and joined the Venezuelan
guerrilla movement. He was captured in 1966 and put in prison, where he was either shot
or tortured to death. (K.S. Karol, *Guerrillas in Power* (New York: Hill and Wang, 1970),
pp. 373–74.)

12. Douglas Bravo was commander in chief of the Venezuelan guerrilla movement. In
1965 Bravo was purged from the Political Bureau and Central Committee of the Venezuelan Communist Party for his opposition to the official Party line of cooperation and
conciliation toward the government of President Leoni. In 1967 he was expelled from the
Party. (*Ibid.*, pp. 373–74, 536n.46.)

I was deeply affected by the death of El Che, though I knew it was bound to happen. If only he'd asked for followers from Havana, he'd have had the biggest movement of people ever seen there. You know how many have left Cuba because they don't like communism? Well, even more people would have followed El Che out of Cuba, wherever he led, to fight for his ideals.

El Che did a lot of traveling after he left Cuba. I've heard he went to Africa, and everybody said he went to Vietnam, too. But I suspect he didn't because he wasn't the kind of guy who liked to work at something somebody else started. At the time of the Santo Domingo crisis, many people claimed Colonel Caamaño[13] said something over the radio about El Che being in Santo Domingo. But in spite of all the rumors, I knew Che couldn't be there, because Santo Domingo isn't yet ready for a revolution.

Very shortly before El Che's death, the newspapers started publishing items about his being in Bolivia and that a price had been put on his head, so I felt pretty certain that's where he was. I knew for sure when Regis Debray, who'd interviewed El Che, was arrested in Bolivia.[14] It stands to reason that Debray wouldn't risk going up those mountains unless El Che was there.

I thought of El Che as a courageous man, a guerrilla fighter. I knew he did all that could be done to escape from the encircling enemy forces. I said, "It would take an unbelievable effort for anyone to be able to take El Che alive." He had his techniques to slip through such traps, so when I heard that he'd been taken alive and killed later, I figured he'd been betrayed by a deserter from the guerrillas.

At the time, I was doing productive work with a work battalion, planting coffee between Ciudad Libertad and Havana. There were 3,000 to 5,000 of us men working together. The day we were demobilized I arrived home from the country with my nerves shot. I knew Fidel was going to speak and I suspected it meant that the rumors about El Che's death were true. That was a bad day for me. I don't know how others reacted, because I wasn't noticing anybody else. I only know what I felt, and I felt terrible.

13. Colonel Francisco Caamaño Deñó, a U.S.-trained army officer in the Dominican Republic who served as provisional president of the rebel government in 1965. In 1973 Caamaño tried, with a handful of supporters, to begin a guerrilla action against the Balaguer government. He was killed by government troops in February, 1973.

14. The French writer and philosopher who, while teaching at Havana University, wrote a controversial though officially endorsed interpretation of the Cuban revolutionary experience: *Révolution dans la Révolution?* (Paris: Librairie François Maspero, 1967). In April, 1967, Debray went as an accredited journalist to Bolivia, where he was arrested and imprisoned at Camiri for alleged assistance to Che Guevara. In late 1970, when the Bolivian government changed hands, there was new pressure from the Bolivian left and from the international intellectual community to free Debray. The new president, Juan José Torres, released him in December, 1970.

Fidel didn't speak in the Plaza but from a television studio. Those who owned a TV set heard him at home; those who didn't, went to a neighbor's house. We went to Sonia's, our neighbor in no. 407. Everybody was there—Sonia, Lala, my kids, Serafina, Sonia's children, Frida, Paz, Guido, Rodolfo—I don't remember who else, but everybody went to hear Fidel speak. I listened because I wanted to know for sure whether El Che was dead and to see how Fidel gave the news, to find out what his state of mind was. I also wanted to know exactly how Che's capture and death had taken place.

I didn't have eyes for anything except the TV screen where Fidel's image appeared. When he started to speak, I already knew what was coming. He came right out and told the truth, and everybody cried out in pain. If ever I saw Fidel unhappy and telling things exactly as they were, that was it. Everybody was shocked and sad, naturally. When he began to show the photographs, my eyes stung because I was close to tears. And it's got to be something pretty damn sad to make me cry.

In fact, Che's death is the unhappiest memory of my life. It affected me deeply, and even now, whenever I talk about it, I feel bad. What most struck me about El Che was his international spirit, the way he went to fight in the Latin American countries. That's what I most liked about him. Che didn't set out to win any advantages for himself, he cared only for his ideals, just like me.

The way I see it, the failure in Bolivia was due to a lack of contacts. Bolivia wasn't ready for revolution. El Che tried to go too fast and that's why his attempt ended in failure. Those Bolivian Indians don't trust anybody. When someone has been deceived as much as they have, it takes time and trouble to win their trust again, and without trust, you can't expect people to fight on your side.

Another problem was the lack of cooperation from the Bolivian Communist Party. They wanted a revolution, sure, but they wanted to command the troops and even El Che himself. But he refused. Still, it's only right that each country should initiate its own revolutionary struggle under the command of its own leaders, though that doesn't mean other countries can't help them. The rural people wouldn't trust a foreigner as much as one of their own, but once they're prepared, it's up to the leader to guide them rather than lay down the law. And he must make the masses understand that it's his superior knowledge that makes him the leader.

El Che has greatly influenced my ideals. I'm all for his international politics. I'd like to win the freedom of other peoples, so they, too, can live. If it should be necessary to give my life for that cause, I tell you from the bottom of my heart, it's as good as given. Here in Cuba we live in a liberated country, free to go anywhere we please, and I think every country should enjoy the same advantages. As far as I know, we haven't sent anybody to fight outside Cuba yet, but I'm ready, willing, and able to fight in any country in this hemisphere. I'd be happy knowing I was doing my duty and helping my brothers.

In my work brigade I had a comrade called Gregorio, who was also a Youth militant. As we worked together and talked, we found we had the same ideals. One day—this was before El Che's death—Gregorio told me he'd talked with a Venezuelan *comandante* when he was in Havana for the OLAS[15] conference, about the ways and means of going to Venezuela. "Look, Armando," he said, "when we finish our work with the brigade, let's go to the Venezuelan Liberation Front and talk the problem over with them."

After Che's death, Gregorio and I went to the Venezuelan National Liberation Front; it's across the street from the Focsa building. We were prompted by the Youth declaration: "El Che is gone, but other voices will call for war, other hands will grasp weapons to defend our countries, and other comrades will move forward to take Che's place." El Che's ideals were with us all the time. I wanted to be one of those who helped to fill Che's place. We'd been planning to go anyway; this simply made us act more quickly.

We talked about our ideals with the *comandante*, and Comrade Gregorio told him we'd decided to go to Venezuela. "And from there we want to go to some other country," he said. Then I said I felt the same way.

The *comandante* explained that it wasn't up to the Venezuelan National Liberation Front to make such a decision. "It's the government who decides such things, and it's a secret," he said to us. "But we'll keep your request in mind, and if anything turns up we'll call you. Meanwhile I'll invite you to our study circles every Saturday, so you'll be prepared in case you're sent to Venezuela."

We agreed to go to the meetings, because when anybody decides to fight in a foreign country, he must be prepared for the conditions he'll face there. He must be a guy who's been proven, who's ready and willing to face death in many forms. He might be killed by a bullet, starve to death, be bitten by a poisonous snake, or fall off a cliff. To face that, he must be an internationalist, willing to fight in any country in the world to fulfill the ideals of El Che.

At the Venezuelan National Liberation Front they gave me a copy of Fabricio Ojeda's book and several pamphlets. They wrote down our address and our work center telephone number, but they didn't call. Then I changed from that work center to another, so I lost track of the Liberation Front.

15. Latin American Solidarity Organization. The conference referred to opened in Havana on August 4, 1967.

Even though we didn't leave our homeland to fight for the cause of freedom, we can still follow El Che's example by working, struggling, and studying as much as our fatherland requires of us. We must struggle against imperialism by all possible means, and if an invasion comes, we must fight to the end. We've warned them again and again. If they want to test our words, let them come! Any foreigner with aggressive intentions who sets foot on our land has as good as signed his own death sentence. We must follow in El Che's footsteps. We won't take one single step backward!

My wife knows very well what my ideals are. If I should die before my children grow up, I know she'd tell them what kind of a man I was, what I did, and why I had to go fight and die away from them. El Che said that if he fell for the cause, his children wouldn't lack anything, and I say so too. If any Cuban goes overseas to fight, his family won't starve, lack medical attention, or anything, because that's precisely what we fought for here in Cuba, and that's what we're working and struggling to build.

In January, 1968, I was assigned the job of managing the coffee shop at the Deauville Hotel in Havana. Comrade Agustín, the director, sent for me and said, "Comrade Armando, we're sending you because that's a place where there are foreigners, and we need a responsible comrade there, a true revolutionary. We need to do political work there. That's why we chose you for that post." So I went.

It was while I was working at the Deauville that I was considered for Party membership. As soon as a Youth militant turns twenty-eight, they automatically analyze him. You don't request it and no one proposes your name; it's automatic. If you have the necessary qualities, you're promoted from the Youth to the Communist Party. If you don't, you stay on as a militant in the Youth. When they begin to analyze you, they call you for an interview. There they fill in your life-history blanks and ask you lots of questions. Of course, being a good communist, I was bound to tell the truth.

I'd had some similar experience, because every so often the regional office of INIT asks us for information, and we ourselves must know all about those who work for us, and the managers and executives we work for. Suppose I arrive as a new man at a certain work unit. If I don't know anybody's degree of commitment, what should I do? The best thing would be to take a notebook and ask them their names, addresses, telephone numbers, and the revolutionary organizations they belong to. The women should belong to the Federation of Cuban Women or to the CDR, the men to the CDR and the militia or some military unit. It's my duty to know all about every single employee in my work unit and who are the comrades I can trust.

I, too, had been given written lists to use in making those investigations. So when they called me for my life history, I caught on right away.

I knew they were going to check up on me. They asked how long I'd been in the Army, where I'd been assigned, and what my attitude was. They even went to Oriente, where I used to live.

I knew they'd also investigate in my neighborhood to find out what my moral attitude was, but I wasn't supposed to know anything about it, see? In the neighborhood, they simply asked the people there, "Do you know Comrade Armando Cárdenas Pardo?" Then they'd visit a member of the CDR or some other responsible person and ask, "What do you think of Comrade Armando Cárdenas Pardo? Do you believe the comrade to be a revolutionary? Does he have good qualities? Has he ever had problems out in the streets, for instance? Or does he go around picking fights? Is he a marijuana smoker?" They asked everybody in the neighborhood about me, except my own family, of course.

Everybody on my block knows me as a hardworking, serious-minded man. They see me returning home from work, going out again to school, and from there returning back home to sleep. And the next morning it's back to work. No misleading information could get to the people who were judging my fitness as a Party militant because the facts they gather are analyzed before they make a decision.

After they analyzed me, they asked me to go to the Party sectional. When I arrived, a *compañera* asked me, "Are you Comrade Armando Cárdenas?"

"Yes, Miss," I said.

"Are you married? Do you have any children?" I said I was married and had four children. "Are they baptized?" she asked. "Yes," I answered. "Now look here," she said, "don't you think that, as a matter of ideological principle, you shouldn't have baptized them?"

"Sure, but the kids were baptized before I became a militant Youth. My wife insisted on it, and since I don't believe in anything, I made no objection. It simply wasn't important to me. Besides, I wasn't even home when she had them baptized. One was baptized while I was in the Army on the Isle of Pines. The other was baptized in Pinar del Río, while I was working here in Havana." At that point she dropped the subject.

Three of my comrades from work, Julio, Maida, and Angel, were called at the same time for their analyses. Julio was made a militant before me. That's when I realized I was sure to be made one too. I'd seen the biographies of about twenty people who'd been made Party militants, and if they made it, it was impossible that I wouldn't.

They had a party for Julio, served drinks, and we all toasted him. I said to a comrade at the regional, "Next week you must come to the granting of my militancy at the center."

The funny thing was that a week after I'd told her I was going to get my membership, I did get it! On July 7, 1968, exactly a week later, the director of the Deauville called an assembly of the coffee shop workers.

I knew why they called the assembly, because the day before, one of the

workers had said to me, "A *compañera* from the Party is coming over
to make some decisions about you." I've always been a nervous, appre-
hensive guy, but what I imagined this time gave me a lot of pleasure.
What revolutionary wouldn't be proud of being made a Party militant? That day they closed the coffee shop from 3:00 to 3:30 so the
assembly could be held there.

At the meeting Comrade César read a list of my merits and told how
I'd earned the privilege of being in the Communist Party. I have so many
merits that even I myself can't remember them all. Then they asked the
women who worked there with me whether anyone had any objections to
make. "No!" they chorused, "Then let's have some applause!" So they all
clapped for me. The director made a speech and then another worker
spoke about me. He asked the hotel administrators and the union local
to give their opinions. My comrades got up one by one and spoke magni-
ficently in my praise. It was terrific! Every one of the workers, from the
janitor to the executives, praised me.

The greatest thing that ever happened in my whole life was being
chosen a militant in the Communist Party. They asked me if I felt proud.
Muchacho, how could I not feel proud! That was the greatest honor I
could have received, and it was my proudest moment.

We couldn't have a party to celebrate because the coffee shop had to
be opened at 3:30. They did plan to have a party for me sometime later,
though, but the plans fell through, because I was responsible for a
brigade working in the country and had to go there. So I said, "Let's not
have any celebration. We already had the ceremony giving me the Party
card, so why do anything else?"

I spent fifteen days filling sacks in the country. When I came back, a
compañera told me that since I was a militant I should prepare myself
by going to a self-improvement school. The project was delayed for
quite a while, long enough for me to go to work in the country and
come back again, but I kept asking about it. When I finally enrolled in
the school, I was assigned to administer the candy and soft drink stand
there during the school games. The athletes for the sixth annual school
games had just arrived and there was a great deal of politics going on. So
they had to have a revolutionary comrade, skilled in politics, to manage
the soft drink stand. That's why they chose me.

Well, I was there for twenty days with two *compañeras* and another
man who'd been chosen just like me. Afterward I went back to my work
center, and to date I haven't been able to go to school.

The way I look at it, communism means we should all be united like
brothers, at work and in the struggle to make the Revolution. And we
must never act hypocritically, no matter what our relative positions may
be. Supposing I were one of the great leaders of the Revolution and I
met you out in the street; well, you should treat me like one more

brother, not like a great leader or a high official. What I mean is that even though I was assigned to be the manager of the coffee shop, I want my workers to regard me as simply one more worker among them, managing the place because the task was assigned to me. That's what communism means to me—a union among workers and leaders. We all belong to the same human mass and we all go forward together.

I'm proud that I'm always friendly and affectionate in my dealings with my comrades at work. The janitor at the coffee shop was a good friend and I went everywhere with him, though I was the manager. When I arrived at work I felt happy right away. It was as if I were with my own brothers and sisters. I joked and laughed with them, and when I went anyplace in the hotel, the women threw their arms around me and hugged me.

Hardly any male managers like to work with women because women are the worst thing to mix with work. But I know how to get along with them, and I know they're satisfied to work for me. I like to have the women at work talk frankly with me, just as they would with another woman. Whenever they have a problem, I want them to tell me what's wrong. And I'm frank with them too. I once worked with eleven *compañeras* and there wasn't one who didn't discuss her problems with me, no matter how serious they were. They'd tell me frankly why they'd been absent, or why they wanted leave.

I had one woman employee who was a youngish brunette and quite well preserved. She was having an affair with a man, but didn't want to live with him because she had children by another marriage. One day she phoned me and spoke to me with complete frankness. "Listen, Armando," she said, "I have a problem. Remember the man I was having an affair with? Today he asked me to go to Matanzas to meet his mother, but you know what the schedules are right now. Could you give me this afternoon off, so I can go with him?" Now, that's what I call being frank!

I was simply overcome with her honesty. How could I say no when she'd been so sincere? So I arranged the work schedules and gave her the day off because she hadn't made up any excuses. Ever since, if I ask her to work overtime or to substitute for a comrade who's absent, she never says no.

One *compañera* at work told me I was too easygoing to be a manager. "Oh," I said, "you'd like me to tighten the screws? I can do it all right, but I won't as long as I don't have to, because I know how to deal with people."

I don't apply the labor law here unless a worker does something really serious, like stealing. Even when my employees quarrel in front of me, I don't step in legally. I just call them to my office to talk it over, because I don't think we should be jumping on workers every minute. We should be constructive, making a comrade realize he's doing something wrong and teaching him how to do it right.

Some managers will make a tremendous fuss if a worker arrives fifteen minutes late to work. Not me. I'm an understanding person. Since I
travel by bus myself, I know that buses sometimes run out of gas, causing
a worker to be late. And when one comrade had to stay home to do the
wash, I said it was all right. And there's a young girl who has such
abundant monthly periods that she can't work during those days. Well, if
she felt enough at ease with me to explain such intimate details, I
couldn't tell her she had to come to work no matter how ill she felt. I
have to take all those problems into account.

I won't stand for somebody staying away from work without warning.
And I won't take his pretending to be sick when he isn't. All I ask is the
truth, not some excuse, like "I had a bellyache" or "I couldn't come
because I hurt my foot." It's no use coming to me with such stories,
because I won't be taken in by lies.

If a comrade is having a love affair and I know about it, I won't object
to his being absent now and then to see his girl. I've no right to find fault
and put obstacles in his way. I'd be overstepping my duties if I interfered, and I'd give him every chance to straighten out. But if the guy
were a militant comrade like me, then I'd intervene. I'd say, "Remember,
you're a militant and can't get involved in this kind of thing." I'm sure a
case like that won't come up, because a militant would do nothing of the
kind. I'm very, very sure of that.

Lala must have felt kind of jealous when she went to the coffee shop
and saw how affectionate the *compañeras* were with me. They hugged
me and said *"mi chino"* and *"ay, papi"* when they talked to me. I felt
affection for all of them, whether they were white, black, or whatever, but there was nothing intimate between us. I'm not saying I'd never
have an affair with an employee, but she'd have to be a very aggressive
woman, one who'd come right out and say, "Armando, I want you to be
mine." And that isn't very likely to happen. From a certain point of
view—following the political line and taking into account you're a
leader—such things shouldn't be.

As a man, I like women. As a militant though, I know I must control
myself. I have a wife and she's the only woman I have a right to have,
period. And I know what my attitude toward her should be. Sometimes
she's jealous of me, but that's her problem. She can feel perfectly sure of
me. I know what stand I'm supposed to take and what line I must follow.

A married man who's at all conscientious knows he can't go around
playing with other women, since he can't take any responsibility for
them. As a citizen of this socialist republic, I should do my best to give no
opportunities for such a situation to arise. Besides, why should I break
up my marriage to live with another woman?

There are many married militants who keep another woman, but they
keep the affair well concealed. What a militant can't do under any circumstances is to keep two households openly. To do that is to flaunt

one's immorality in the face of the Party. Heck, if a militant kept two women, how many women would the non-militants keep? If we militants didn't set a better example, anything could happen, even prostitution.

After I got married, I took up the political line and changed my ways. I simply put such things out of my mind. When I get on a bus, I don't look around at the women or try to flirt. I don't turn around to look at a woman in the street either, no matter how pretty she may be, though I'd notice one showing a lot of leg, because that's a new thing—miniskirts, I mean.

If I see a pretty girl I look at her, like any other man, but I keep my thoughts to myself. I might *think*, "Hell! What a shape! How sexy!" But I wouldn't come right out and say it within hearing distance. Of course, if I'm standing with a friend at a street corner, I might say it to him. I'm a man, after all. But I don't follow girls or whistle at them. No, no, I wouldn't waste my time that way. No more than I'd go out of my way to peek if I saw a woman with one leg up in the air. What would be the point? A man's brain can wear away looking at that.

If I wanted to have a love affair, I could easily find myself a woman. Having a sweetheart on the side is the most commonplace thing in the world here. After all, a man's out in the street all day long, and women are rather provocative nowadays.

In India until very recently a man could have as many as four wives. This was true of many Asian countries. There are also places where women are allowed to have more than one man. In those places they regard such things as normal and people don't get jealous, but I think it would be very, very difficult for us Cubans to accept such a law. For the man, yes! A man can have as many women as he likes. But the woman? No! I'm sure that no socialist country in the world would pass a law allowing a woman to have two men! Hell no! That wouldn't be right.

The Party doesn't have any business interfering in marriage. Everything else we share equally among the people, but not women! I've got my wife, and I want her to be mine and only mine! I wouldn't put up with another man having rights over her, because the relations between a man and his wife are something very intimate. So let each be content with his own.

I'm not a jealous husband. If you're jealous of your wife, it means you don't trust her, and in that case it would be better to leave her. I'm speaking frankly about my feelings. City people may feel differently, but I grew up in the country, and that kind of attitude isn't something we're told to think; it comes from inside the person himself.

Suppose my wife were putting the horns on me, as it's vulgarly said, while I was away working. Well, the Party would soon suspect what she was up to and they'd watch her, because they know that an unfaithful wife would worry a militant comrade and might interfere with his work. When they were sure she was deceiving her husband, they'd present the evidence to him and say, "Look, here you have proof that your wife is deceiving you. You must choose between your wife and the Party. It's your own conscience that must decide." If I ever had to make such a decision, I'd leave my wife, because I could never leave the Party, not for anything in the world.

I have a more developed revolutionary conscience than Lala does. Since she's been under my protection, I've led her toward the revolutionary way, but it isn't something she's felt since childhood as I have. I inspired her. Besides, I'm different from her because I'm a Party leader and she's not. Lala is a leader in the Federation of Cuban Women and would like to be a Party member too, but she doesn't have the merits to be accepted as a militant yet. I wish she were a militant. I'd have no objection at all to her carrying out a militant's duties, even though that means the Party might send her to the Isle of Pines without me for two or three months.

If a man's wife goes to work where her husband is, the Revolution sends their children to a boarding school, where they stay all week. It's a very good arrangement. If only one partner of a married couple is sent away to work—well, that's where one's revolutionary conscience comes in. I'm willing to live separately from my wife not merely for three months but for ten years, if necessary. Whenever the Party tells me, "You must go to such-and-such a place," I'll go. My wife simply has to put up with it. I can't tell the Party, "You must do this and that for me before I agree to go." When they say "Go," I simply ask, "Where? What work has to be done there?"

A communist woman isn't like old-fashioned women, who thought of nothing except doing a little bit of housework and going to parties. Women aren't like that anymore. Under communism, a woman's role is the same as a man's. Nowadays, besides being mates and companions, they feel they must work as a man does. They don't feel inferior to men. They're strong enough to struggle just as we do for a socialist fatherland. Women must be one more root to strengthen the tree that's growing. Women have a really important place in the communist scheme of things.

For six months in 1969 I managed two units of INIT, a coffee shop and a place where they served beer. But there was so little to do that I really wasn't working at all. Half an hour after I arrived, all my day's work would be done. In the morning I drew up the coffee shop accounts. We kept a complete record of the bank slips, and of goods coming in and going out of the warehouse. I had to file the credit slips by number and by name of the user, then I counted the money and added up the total. After that I drew up separate accounts for food, beer, and tobacco. When I finished the bookkeeping, I had to oversee the cleaning and general operation of the shop. Well, frankly, there wasn't as much work as I like.

Idleness makes me uncomfortable. As long as I can keep busy, I have no problem with my nerves. I had lots of time to think about all sorts of foolishness. What a state I got into! I'd get upset every time I couldn't find the merchandise I needed. I simply couldn't let such matters go, so I'd start raging at the commercial supplier, with no tact at all. I said whatever came into my head. That's the way things were, until I went to the sectional to state my problem and ask for a transfer to work permanently in the country.

"I can't stay where I am. There's nothing to do there. I want to go somewhere where there's important work going on and where people are needed," I told them. "You've got to solve my problem, no matter what. You simply have to take me out of there."

"Well, let's wait a bit," they answered. But finally they decided to send me as a *permanente*[16] to do agricultural work on the Isle of Pines.

They told me that according to Resolution no. 20, we'd get paid 80 *pesos* a month, and if we'd been paying rent, they'd pay our rent as well as gas, electricity, and whatever other household bills we owed to the government. At the very end of the application blank it says "Observations," and there's a space to write down whatever you feel concerned about. For instance, if your house is in bad condition and you want it fixed, you write that down. My salary was 138 *pesos*,[17] and I was worried that my family couldn't live on 80 *pesos* a month, so I wrote that down.

When I posed the problem to Lala, she said, "Well, we've already been through that, haven't we? For two years we lived on 80 *pesos* a month and we can do it again. We'll be on a tight budget, but we can do it."

After I wrote down my worries, I felt easy in my mind. We must have faith in our organization. I knew my problem would be resolved, because our Party wants every comrade working in agriculture to be free of family worries. And after all, money problems are small problems. We shouldn't need money at all, and the time will come when we won't.

That day I kissed Lala goodbye and left. Women always get childish when their husbands go away. Lala said she'd miss me, that she didn't know when we'd see each other again, and that time would seem awfully long to her without me, and so on. But she didn't quarrel about my going away or anything. As long as I spend my five days' leave with her every fifty-five days, she's satisfied.

When we arrived at the Isle of Pines, we were first taken on a tour of the whole Isle, then the secretary-organizer of that region came to give

16. A long-term volunteer for agricultural labor.
17. After deductions.

us a talk. He told us we'd continue to be paid our present salary. "Forget Resolution no. 20," he said. "You've been told that here you'll be earning only 80 *pesos* a month. Well, that's what people are told in Havana. But it isn't so. Now that you're here, I can tell you that you'll continue earning whatever you earned before you came here. That will be no problem."

The comrade went on to explain. "Some of you may feel that what you were earning before isn't enough to support your family. If so, tell us about it. We'll discuss your earnings and the expenses your family has, and if you really need a raise, we'll grant it." Most of the men brought up the problem of their kids and asked to have them put on scholarships. The requests were noted and passed on to the province, where they do their best to resolve all of them. I didn't bring up any problems or ask for a raise because my family can more or less manage on what I earn.

The Isle of Pines has changed a lot since I was there with the Army in 1962-63. At that time the place was planted mostly with melon and a few citrus trees. Now there are new products and a lot of new construction. The Isle has a great future.

We were shown a map with a whole bunch of big dams, about five or six. The two dams that are already functioning—Vietnam Heroico and La Fé—plus those that are being built, will supply enough water to irrigate the whole Isle. The La Fé dam is enormous but it's a real problem because many rivers and small streams empty into it, and when it rains too much they have to open the sluices to let some water out. If they made that dam any bigger, though, it would cut into the kaolin factory, which is right on the edge of it.

The Vietnam Heroico dam was made to contain 45 million gallons of water, but during the rainy season it's filled to twice that amount. When we passed it on our way to the fields one day, the water had risen almost as high as the bridge. By nightfall it had overflowed the bridge and had opened a 2-meter hole in the dam. The water ran through the orange groves and flooded the road beyond. That's a real headache for the Party. They had to open the sluices of another dam farther down to let the excess water flow into the sea.

They're going to build a town called El Pueblo de los Communistas near Vietnam Heroico. It will be located in the center of the Isle and will be the capital city. They plan to accommodate about 35,000 inhabitants, but they haven't started yet. There will be a main highway, bisecting the Isle, from Nueva Gerona to Santa Bárbara. That's where the international shipping docks will be for the citrus fruit traffic.

The Isle is going to be one of the biggest producers of citrus fruits. Its citrus farms are called Vietnam–Los Indios, Patria, and Frank País. They grow some lemons, but mostly oranges and grapefruit. They also have plans to build fisheries on the Isle of Pines. Right now the Isle's fishing fleet consists of sixteen boats and they say there are enough fish in the

Vietnam Heroico reservoir to keep the whole fleet busy.[18] They've already built a lobster cannery in Nueva Gerona.

The Sierra Maestra, La Reforma, and La Victoria are the three dairy farms on the Isle. Most of the cows on the Isle are Zebu,[19] and the farm that has the most is La Reforma. They do a lot of the milking by machine on the dairy farms. The Sierra Maestra ranch has two or three dairy farms with milking machines.

In 1962 I was stationed north of Nueva Gerona, and now I'm south of it. Our barracks are built of cement blocks with fiber-glass roofs and cement floors. They're well ventilated, with plenty of doors and windows. The bathroom is very good and has five showers. The toilets are the same style as those at home, but in better condition. Their only defect is that they don't flush. After using one, you fill a pail of water and empty the water into the toilet bowl.

When we arrived, the place wasn't very clean. The men there before were pretty sloppy, but we started setting a good example right away. We noticed that some careless comrades were going to the showers with nothing except a towel wrapped around the waist. The women's barracks were only about 10 meters away and the women could see them clearly. We fixed that situation immediately by building a screening wall between our part of camp and theirs.

Laundry is a problem there. We have to wash our own clothes in two large sinks. My work clothes get very dirty after a week of wear; we can't allow ourselves the luxury of changing our work pants every three or four days. On Sunday we only work in the morning; in the afternoon we wash our clothes. The next time I come to Havana, I'm going to get a paddle to beat clothes with. Just a flat piece of wood with a handle will do. It's a trick I learned from my old lady so you don't have to kill yourself rubbing out the dirt by hand. I bet the fellows will laugh when they see that. They'll think, "Comrade Armando has gone crazy!"

One comrade, who's a militant, has an iron and an ironing board and he offered them to us. "Whenever you need them, just open the closet and take them," he told us. The ironing board was bare so one comrade used his free time on Sunday to pad it. We all helped. Anyone who sees

18. Under the Castro government the fishing industry has undergone tremendous growth, with the construction of more than 6,000 new boats, and two schools for training industry personnel. In 1958 the island's total fish catch was 21,900 tons; the industry exported 2.1 million *pesos'* worth of marine products; and the national consumption rate was 4.8 kilograms per capita. In 1974 the catch was 165,000 tons; exports were valued at 50.1 million *pesos;* and the consumption rate had risen to 10.7 kilograms per capita. (See Castro's report to the First Party Congress, *Granma Weekly Review*, Dec. 28, 1975, p. 6.)

19. The small, hump-backed cows that Castro decided to crossbreed with Holstein bulls to produce dairy cows. In 1969 this crossbreed animal, the F-1, was the subject of a heated public debate between Castro and his British advisors, who believed that Cuban conditions were more suitable for raising beef cattle. (For a discussion of this controversy see Barry Rockford, *Does Fidel Eat More than Your Father?* (New York: Praeger, 1971), pp. 143–61.)

how we cooperate and doesn't admire our morale and comradely attitude must be really unconscious of what's going on around him.

Some of the men have *compañeras* wash their clothes for them, but that takes time. You've got to get acquainted and become friends first, before you can ask a woman to do your wash. So far I don't know any *compañera*. There are very few women working in the furrows. Instead, we work with contingents of scholarship students sent from Havana.

I was amazed to see how many comrades went to school at night. At 8:00 P.M. you'll see a parade of people on their way to school. Comrades come from far away to study at the secondary school, which is at the cattle-breeding center. There's no primary school in our town because they have semi- and full-time boarding schools for the kids.

The Party has set a goal that by July 26, 1970, all the old militants must have completed the sixth grade, if they haven't done so already. Those are the Party's orders. Those of us at the citrus fruit center aren't required to go to the Party's school, because we can easily go to the one in our own center. I finish my day's work at 4:30 and eat at 6:00. So I'm free to go to school at 8:00 in the evening, when classes begin. I haven't started yet, but I can take the sixth grade here without any problem.

Every day, a little before 7:00 in the morning, the truck picks us up to take us to work. Our breakfast and lunch are brought out by truck in thermos containers so the food won't get cold. Then we sit under the pines to eat. So far, the food has been very good.

Occasionally the truck breaks down, because there are only three trucks for all the work on the farm. To prevent that sort of thing they make surprise inspections on the road, checking the truck's motor, oil, the battery, everything, and they arrest the guys who don't keep their trucks in top condition. That's a very effective preventive measure.

At night we have our supper in the cafeteria. They serve from 80 to 100 people, because many comrades from town eat there too. One of the chefs there told me, "The meals are at their worst at the end of the month, because we always run out of spices." I myself have observed that that's true everywhere. But we ate well toward the end of last month, so imagine how good the meals are at the beginning of the month! That's when the new supplies come, seasonings and all.

We arrived at the center during the orange-tree trimming. Two men worked on each tree. The first day each pair consisted of one old and one new comrade, so the more experienced comrades could teach us. I was new but I'd already had experience in that kind of work, because I grew up in the country. Now I'm so expert I can trim an orange tree all by myself.

As soon as our group arrived, production shot up tremendously. They'd been averaging two or three trees a day for each pair, but in our group each pair does from eight to ten trees a day. The comrades who were already there were terrifically impressed with us. They try to be friends and infiltrate our group, because they can see how close the ties among us are. We're Party militants, Communist Youth militants, and non-militants and are really a united bunch. Many comrades think we must have been friends in Havana, long before we were sent to the Isle of Pines, but only three comrades in my group worked for INIT.

Our settlement has about eighty prefabricated houses in two different models. The community also has a pharmacy, a medical center, a clothing store, a consolidated shoe-repair shop, a microwave radiotelephone service where you can call Havana, a hairdresser's salon, a barber shop, an INIT cafeteria, four small but very pretty parks, and a social club where they play checkers, dominoes, chess, and ping-pong. There's a nice ball park and an outdoor movie theater, which has free shows every evening except Monday. We don't live right in the town—we're about 500 meters from the city limits.

Our camp is right across the way from the movie theater, so we can sit and look at the movies for free. We even have open-air shelters, woven out of palm leaves, and palm-leaf seats to watch from.

You can get a haircut, shave, or anything at the barbershop for free, although the hairdresser's salon does charge the women. There are plenty of women on the Isle. Some are housewives who live there with their husbands and children, but most are workers. They're employed in the hairdresser's shop, in the clothing store, and in the neighborhood store, which is large and very well stocked.

There's bus service to and from Nueva Gerona every hour or hour and a half. The trip takes about fifty-five minutes to an hour each way.

It's no problem for me to stay here. My parents are in Oriente and I've been seeing them only about once every three or four years anyhow. I can visit them as often from the Isle as from Havana. If they give me a house, my wife and children can be right here with me. Lala knows about my plans and she's dying to settle on the Isle when they find us a place to live. "Even if it isn't a house but just a single room, I'm willing to go," she says. But finding a place to live takes time, a year at the very least.

There's a very good chance that I can get a house, because there are plans to build lots of them here. Right now our settlement has very few inhabitants, not even 1,000, though they hope to have more. More than ten comrades out of twenty-six in my group have already said they're willing to stay if they get a house to live in with their families. They feel exactly the way I do.

There are some empty houses right now, but they're reserved for the people being brought in from the country to work on the dams that overflowed. If I put up a fight, going here and there to try to solve my problem, I might get a place to live within eight months. Then I could move my family to the Isle right away. But it won't do to pester the comrades there and make them nervous. You must be patient and give them time. They do what they can.[20]

There's a factory on the Isle which makes panels for prefabricated houses, but they're awfully shorthanded. In fact, they have two factories for that purpose, but only one is functioning at the moment. There's plenty of material, it's the manpower that's lacking.

I think that as conscientious militants we should be ready to work toward developing the Isle of Pines. There's still a lack of personnel there and I want to help solve that problem. One of the most important jobs is working with machinery, and for that you need stable, permanent workers, not temporary help.

There should be twenty operators of MCZ tractors, but we have only sixteen. They're planning to fill the four vacancies by bringing in four truck drivers from the mainland. But when those comrades have completed their two years' service, they'll leave the Isle and practice their skills in Oriente, in Havana—anywhere but on the Isle of Pines. That happens all the time, because very few workers have any intention of staying permanently. Now, if they trained me as a machine operator, I'd stay and at least they'd have one permanent worker here.

I'm making this effort toward the development of the Isle because I know that agriculture is important to the fatherland. Our agriculture is backward and we must modernize our techniques and make it more productive. The government is getting ready to appoint new leaders for the Isle. We may be reassigned soon and many of us may be chosen for responsible posts. They'll divide the Party militants among the different units to make sure all units function as they should.

The plans have been made and now it's up to us to make them succeed. If the Party militants didn't volunteer, then who would? We must push forward so others will follow. We must set the example.

The word "communism" comes from "community." That means everybody should live as equals in the community, and share and share alike. It means all of us working together to make our country free and industrialized. And it means we should all live in the same way, as equals, with an equal right to work. I will not have more than you, nor will you have more than me. Take the ration books, for instance. Rationing means that people with money eat the same as those who don't have money. It's fair and equal. Before rationing, people with money could get all sorts of things that were out of reach for those who didn't have money, and poor people like me were wandering from place to place, dying of hunger. The only way I could think of resolving the problem

20. In early 1970, Lala and the four children joined Armando on the Isle of Pines. Their apartment in Miramar was sealed until their return.

was to get rich myself, so I could help the poor. That's why I did my best to help the Revolution go forward in every way, even though I didn't know anything about socialism or communism then.

If anyone spoke of communism before the Revolution, it was in secret. Nobody told us what it was really all about, so after the Revolution the people weren't ready for it. Fidel couldn't tell them about it right away. He had to wait and prepare them before they could understand that this is socialism and that we're becoming a communist country. That's why I knew nothing, absolutely nothing about communism. But it sounded good to me from the beginning.

It's necessary to struggle to obtain full freedom. Before the Revolution, our freedom was in the hands of others. The War of Independence freed us from the Spanish, but then we fell into the clutches of somebody worse. But it was the proletariat that caused the triumph of the Revolution, and that's when things started to change. A lot of the bourgeoisie also took part in the Rebellion, but only to save their own property. After the Triumph they tried to reinstate themselves, and that's when the counterrevolution started and the capitalists turned against our government. They've tried to turn communism upside down and make it into something bad. Even now there are people in high government posts who aren't in favor of the Revolution. Since they're directing things, it's easy for them to mislead people about communism.

Communism means we should help one another like brothers. And we should try to help underdeveloped countries liberate themselves, just as other countries have helped us. When Algeria was liberated, we sent them doctors because they had very few of their own. Some of our comrades are still there. Any small country that wants to liberate itself can count on our help and moral support. We'll encourage them to fight. If they should ever send me to fight in another country that would be the proudest day of my life. I'm not particular—I'd be willing to fight in any country in this hemisphere. And that's what I tell everybody.

If we send men to fight in other countries, it has to be done very discreetly, because it could bring us a lot of trouble. Perhaps we're doing it already, but if we are, we're doing it so secretly we don't even know it. But heck, as Fidel said, "If we give permission to so many Cuban citizens to go away and take refuge in the North, then we can't deny permission to those who want to leave to fight for the liberation of other countries." And he's damn right! After all, they're just as Cuban as those who want to go North.

There's a lot of difference, of course, between them. Those who go North already have permission from a foreign country to live there with their relatives. Those who go to fight in another country will be returning to help Cuba; those who go North won't.

We must struggle for Cuba's future. Some of us are pretty well off already, but some are still poor and deprived. As our greatest leader says in practically all of his speeches, "We must work and struggle together to bring communism to Cuba, so that abundance will come, and a whole people, united, can lift themselves out of their poverty. If we don't rise together, we'll sink together." I hope all of Cuba will prosper by our united efforts.

Our two basic problems right now are food and housing. The situation in both areas is pretty bad at present. I want the time to come when everybody lives in equally good houses. I don't mean we should live in mansions or palaces, but everybody should have a home with enough room to move around in, and everything they need, without having to stand in line so long for food. The only thing that could disappoint me in the Revolution would be seeing those who are badly off now continue to be badly off. I've struggled and intend to keep on struggling to see everybody live as equals. If, after all that, I should see the same inequalities as ever, then I'd be bitterly disappointed in the Revolution. But I'm quite sure that nothing like that will happen.

I believe the American people are honest, really honest, from the bottom of their hearts. That can be clearly seen in their marches for peace, in their mass opposition to the war in Vietnam. Thousands of young American men refuse to let themselves be drafted into the armed forces because they know they'd be sent to kill poor, unhappy people in Vietnam and get killed themselves there. It's pretty big of them to refuse to go because they disapprove of the war. But the men who govern them are lackeys. It isn't the people who are the oppressors, it's their government. And their government has to do such things in order to stay in power.

Another thing that one must admire the Americans for is their voyages into space. They and the Soviet Union have done great work in that area and it means progress for all humanity. Their trip to the moon was very important, even if they are Americans. To me, the most negative aspect of the United States is the way they interfere in the problems of every country in the world instead of letting each country solve its own problems. They oppress all small, underdeveloped countries, and it's the people there who suffer—the workers, not their governments. In fact, the men high up in the governments of those countries live and eat well.

With regard to Cuba, the worst thing the United States has done is the economic blockade.[21] It's wrong to make all the surrounding countries break diplomatic relations with us and not let them send foodstuffs or

21. The United States imposed a partial embargo on trade with Cuba in October, 1960, and a total embargo in April, 1961. Both embargos resulted from a series of actions and counteractions by the two governments, beginning with the approval by the U.S. Congress of an administration-backed bill authorizing President Eisenhower to cut or eliminate the

anything. They want to choke us to death. They think that will make us give in to them. But their plan has failed. They haven't been able to keep all the other countries from selling to us. The Soviet Union put out a helping hand. Through their mediation, other countries have started to re-establish relations with us. If it hadn't been for the Soviet Union's help, we wouldn't have most of the things we have now.

I don't know anything that I can criticize the Soviet Union for. The best thing about them is that whenever a country is trying to free itself from the oppressor's yoke, they try to help. They give any kind of aid the country needs, because the Soviet Union is the foremost communist state in the world.

It seems to me that China and the Soviet Union follow two different lines. Although they have problems of their own, China has helped us quite a bit, and still does. The most admirable thing about the Chinese is that they don't go around threatening, "If you shoot me, I'll shoot you." Or, "Listen, if you hit me, I'll sweep you off the face of the earth." They were sending us rice but they had to stop. Perhaps they had to send it someplace where it was needed more.[22]

China has only one leader as far as I can tell, and people believe he's the only one who can do anything. They think that when Mao dies, China will die. It shouldn't be like that. They should have different kinds of leaders. If Mao dies—well, all right, someone else will take up where he left off. One of his ministers will succeed him and Communist China will go on its way.

We don't think that if Fidel dies, Cuba will collapse. The Socialist Republic of Cuba will live on. We have great leaders here who are quite capable of stepping out front and carrying the Revolution forward. If there's one thing I'm sure of, it's that the Cuban Revolution will not be overthrown and will not fail.

We'll know how to replace Fidel when he dies. The Council of Ministers will meet and decide which comrade has the necessary qualities to be our Prime Minister. They'll run through the whole list until they pick the right one.

Raúl Castro has a lot of good qualities, but there are times when the China matter kind of goes to his head. Sometimes it's the things he

---

quota on sugar imported from Cuba. After this, in June, 1960, Castro nationalized U.S.-owned refineries that refused to refine petroleum from the Soviet Union. In July Eisenhower signed the sugar-quota bill and issued an order refusing purchase of the 700,000 tons of sugar remaining in the 1960 sugar quota. Castro began nationalizing U.S.-owned sugar mills in August; the partial embargo followed in October. In January, 1961, the United States broke off relations with Cuba and three months later imposed the total embargo.

22. Cuba received 250,000 tons of rice from China in 1965, and asked for 285,000 tons in 1966. China promised to deliver only 135,000 tons, citing increased aid to North Vietnam as the principal reason for the decrease.

remembers about fighting in the Sierra that affect him. So it's very possible that our next Prime Minister won't be Raúl. My own personal opinion, however, is that he should take his brother's place. But it could be anybody. It could even be me, Armando Cárdenas Pardo! Life has many strange and wonderful turns.

Mercedes Millán

In 1961, after the Revolution, my husband and I went on a tourist trip to the Soviet Union and Czechoslovakia. Our group consisted of anyone who wanted to go—students, professionals, housewives, young and old. Now only people who are given the trip as a prize can go—laborers or cane workers who distinguish themselves during the harvest, or students and people sent on business. Tourist trips no longer exist. There were only two or three like ours.

I don't know how Juan found out about it. He brought me a prospectus with a list of places to visit, and the cost. He's always liked to travel, and so have I, but I had my doubts about that trip. It meant leaving my daughter for a month and that took some thinking. But Juan was wild to go and kept urging me, "Ah, come on, let's go." He finally convinced me. *Mami* said she'd be glad to keep the child while we were away.

So we began our arrangements. Meetings were held at INIT, the Tourist Institute, to explain the trip to the group. All expenses were prepaid—hotels, food, and travel. We didn't carry any money, but they gave us some crowns in Czechoslovakia and rubles in Russia to buy things for ourselves and for gifts to bring back. I think it was the equivalent of 30 *pesos* in foreign currencies for each of us.

In Russia we went to Moscow, Leningrad, Kiev, and Yalta, then back to Moscow. There we saw the changing of the guard at the Kremlin. They change the guard every hour—it's a very formal ceremony. Just lovely! But at night it gets so cold on Red Square, *ay, mi madre!*

We were there on the day of Tito's return to Moscow. Tito spoke and so did Krushchev, who was then Prime Minister. The Red Square was full of people, thousands upon thousands of them. It was a great demonstration. Our group went out with a Cuban flag and marched to Red Square singing the hymn of the Twenty-sixth of July and chanting, *"Cuba, si, Yankees, no!"* You know what we Cubans are like—there we were, making noise in Red Square in Moscow! The Russians were amazed.

The Russians treated us very well. In Leningrad there were many people at the airport to greet us, even representatives of the Pioneers and other party organizations, though the trip was sponsored by INIT and had nothing to do with the Communist Youth or the Party. But we were the first Cubans to go there, it was the beginning of the Revolution and the whole world's eyes were on Cuba, so they met us, carrying Cuban flags. It was very nice.

In spite of the welcome, I liked Czechoslovakia better. The Czech character is more like ours. Fifteen days is too short a time to know, but it seems to me the Russians are more serious-minded. For instance, they go to parties and enjoy themselves, but they never take alcoholic drinks. Cubans need to drink. Not me, I'm no drinker, but even a sober, respectable man like Juan likes to have a few drinks now and then. In the Soviet Union no liquor was sold after midnight, and there were no cabarets or nightclubs. In Czechoslovakia, yes. Not many, but some, and you could drink there. We'd go anyplace—to the beer halls—and they'd invite us in to have a drink. The Czechs made friends at once, even though there was a language barrier.

When we traveled in 1961, rationing didn't exist in Cuba. You could still buy everything freely. All the best things that were invented or manufactured in the United States found their way to Havana within five minutes. They were all displayed in shop windows, so we were used to seeing pretty things, quality stuff. Nothing I saw for sale abroad interested me. I looked and looked at the yard goods and couldn't find anything I liked. The shoes I thought horrible—terribly old-fashioned. I guess the people there liked them well enough. Ugly or not, that's all they could get when they needed shoes. Frankly, I found the things we had in Cuba much prettier than anything I saw in the stores of Russia and Czechoslovakia. No doubt their taste is different from ours. For instance, all the new buildings in the Soviet Union look exactly the same. I didn't like them. Even if the government builds them all, why can't they at least have some variety?

Now they're more advanced, according to a friend who was there two years ago. People could buy anything they needed, yet they too once had rationing. They had limitations at the beginning of their Revolution. We're only beginning now—we're still unable to buy a pair of shoes, or even food, when we need it—they've progressed beyond that. Their Revolution is at a more advanced stage than ours.

At the time of the landing at Playa Girón, in April, 1961, we were in the midst of moving to our own apartment. Juan had gone to Oriente to get oranges to sell, as he did every fifteen or twenty days. I was still at *mamá*'s house with my daughter.

The first action here was the attack on the military airport. It was very near us, in San Antonio de los Baños, and we were terribly scared. The noise was so loud it sounded as if they were fighting right beside our house. That was about two days before the landing at Girón, I think, so everybody was already scared by the time the landing took place. Besides, there had been the explosion of the ship *Le Coubre*.[23]

Then came the invasion. Naturally, we spent the day close to the radio to hear the news. The invasion was brought under control pretty rapidly, but there were hours of tension. We had some pretty bad moments, I can tell you! Now I feel calmer, though I have a hunch they're still plotting something, perhaps another invasion. In those first years of the Revolution we were always jittery.

At the time of the crisis of October, 1962, I was here at home with my maid and my daughter. The three of us were waiting. As at the time of Girón, everybody was called to arms. Juan didn't have to join the Army because he worked in the market and the flow of supplies couldn't be interrupted. He had to stay at his work center all the time, day and night.

My life went on as usual, looking after the child and supervising the housework. Everyone gets tense in a time of crisis, of course, but goodness, *hombre*, I'm no bundle of nerves! I don't run ahead to meet trouble or start imagining all the terrible things that could happen. I react to things when they actually happen. I don't go around wringing my hands and saying, "Oh my goodness, suppose this happens? Suppose that happens?"

Naturally I worried about what would happen to the Revolution, to Juan, to the child, to my parents, if there should be an invasion. And you don't know where a bomb is going to fall. We might be in as much danger staying home as Juan if he should go out on the battlefield. So I did feel anxious, though I wasn't taking tranquilizers and didn't think I was going crazy. Not me. I listened to the news on the radio, went on living my life, and waited to see how everything would turn out. And in the end, fortunately, nothing did happen.

My life has changed so much! Before, we had everything, now we don't. I stay at home most of the time so it doesn't matter how old my clothes are. I wear the few clothes I have only to go out, so they last a long time. I had so many before that I still have enough. I can say sincerely that I don't worry about myself, but it's different with the children. They're growing, so their clothes don't last very long and their shoes wear out. You can't expect a child's shoes to last as an adult's do.

The worst problem is food. That's what really affects me, not the lack of money. There are so many things that are simply not available. It's worse for the children because adults understand what it's all about and can manage. It really hurts, though, to see that the children can't have what they need. I can't say we've ever gone hungry, but it's annoying to lack some things we really need or would very much like to have. It's a

23. In March, 1960, the French ship *Le Coubre* exploded in port at Havana, causing eighty-one deaths. The Cuban government attributed the incident to CIA-sponsored sabotage.

real worry when one doesn't have something essential. I believe things are bound to improve and that these shortages are temporary. If not, we're in a bad fix.

Meat and milk are the two most important foods in my home. We get 1 liter of fresh milk a day for Eloyitos. He drinks milk for breakfast, lunch, in mid-afternoon, and at dinner. The girl gets six cans of milk a month, and my husband and I get three cans of milk a month each. So we have a total of 1 liter of fresh milk a day and twelve cans of condensed milk a month.

That's not enough. It doesn't matter if I don't have it, but we don't get nearly enough for the children. Some days we've gone without breakfast because there wasn't any milk, and we never drink milk at lunch. We also have bread with butter for breakfast, if we have any, but we haven't seen butter for a long time.

The milk ration for adults is only distributed at the Minimax during one two-week period each month. Sometimes it's the first, sometimes the second half of the month. Twice this year already milk hasn't come. When that happens, we have to get it either by exchanging other things for it—rice, for instance—or buying it from somebody who wants to sell it. I forget exactly how much I've paid for a can of milk, but I think it was about 1.50 *pesos*. It's wrong for people to take advantage, but milk is so essential that even though I know I shouldn't let them overcharge like that, I've got to buy it.

Usually I have some rice left over that I can use to exchange for other things. I try to exchange rice for milk at the rate of 1 pound of rice for six cans of milk. The rice ration is too small for about 99 percent of Cubans, but in my house there's usually quite a bit left over.

I sometimes exchange with Leticia and sometimes with people in *mamá*'s barrio, or with friends in other places. Occasionally I exchange food with people I only know through mutual friends. I've also exchanged with Lala and Justa, but not with Sara. She's no friend of mine.

I manage the best I can with meat and try to stretch the rations so I don't run out of things. We reserve the tender cuts for the children. In fact, we leave practically the whole ration for the children, not only theirs but ours too.

My parents send us their meat ration, although *mamá* needs meat. She has a liver ailment that makes most foods disagree with her. I explain to her again and again that she should keep her meat ration for herself, but she'd rather do without than know the children have no meat. She buys her meat ration regularly and sends it over to me. Counting all our rations, including *mamá*'s and *papá*'s, I have enough meat for the children.

Eloy always has soup made with meat and also gets his beefsteak, usually chopped up in the blender, puréed with his vegetables. I give

Mercedes beefsteak one day and an egg the next, so the meat lasts the week and she has protein every day.

My husband doesn't like to have a heavy meal at night. He likes a beefsteak or something like that, but not rice and beans. Now he eats those things of course, because there's nothing else. But when things were normal, before there was any scarcity, we had dinner at midday and a light supper at night with ham, cheese, bread and butter, and milk. We had meat twice a day. If it was summer, we'd have a milkshake with fruit or chocolate, and in winter we'd have the milk in hot coffee or chocolate with bread or crackers.

At lunch now we have legumes—black beans, peas, or chick-peas, whatever there is—made into a thick soup. Sometimes we have rice, sometimes macaroni. When there are enough tubers, we all eat them. When there's a shortage, Eloy has priority because he's the smallest.

Coffee is one thing I dole out to make it last. The boy doesn't drink coffee, and the girl hardly at all. I don't drink black coffee because I don't have that vice; I only drink it with milk. The only real coffee drinker in the family is my husband. So coffee more or less lasts us as long as it's supposed to.

Cooking fats also last about as long as necessary, and I always have sugar left over, but I don't give it to anybody around here. I send it to my husband's grandmother in Oriente. She uses sugar to make preserves with the fruit that grows in the country.

We get eight soft drinks when they come, more or less every ten days. I space out Merceditas's soft drinks, not to make them last—that's one item I don't care about—but because she's so fat. I limit her to one a day.

I used to have a man fetch the groceries for me, but he couldn't keep on coming because of his job, so I've had nobody for the past five or six months. I find out what things have come to the store and tell Merceditas what I need. She shops and always brings me the correct change. If the groceries are heavy, we borrow Serafina's cart.

It can be a problem sending Merceditas. You know how children are. I'd go myself if I could leave Eloyitos. I never send her to the Minimax more than once a day. If something comes into the store after she's been there, I leave it for the following day. Sometimes her *papá* picks her up in the car after she's gotten the groceries.

I hardly ever ask others for anything except, for instance, I'll ask Lala for sugar if I suddenly run out of it. That rarely happens though. Lala is very generous. If she goes to the country or if one of her relatives comes to visit and brings her some hot peppers or lemons, she offers to share them with me.

I'd also ask Justa if I needed something and knew she had it to spare. She's very obliging too. Things like ice, cumin seed, bay leaves, or any little thing we feel free to ask of one another when we run short. Practically every day Justa asks me for ice because their refrigerator is out of order. Mine broke down too, but we have a freezer, so I put ice trays in it.

To me, the refrigerator is the most important piece of electrical equipment. It must be a serious problem to be without one. Meat is distributed only once a week, so people who can't keep it refrigerated at home and don't have any friend or neighbor who can keep it for them must eat the whole meat ration the same day, or the next, or it will spoil. As for the milk—imagine! Besides, if they have no ice, they have to drink tepid water.

For instance, Lala kept her meat in my refrigerator and got her ice from me too, for about five years—from the time the family she worked for left until Serafina got married. The garage where Serafina lives belongs to Clara Falcón's house, and since Clara has a frigidaire and a freezer and is all alone, Serafina keeps her perishable food there. Lala does too, but she still asks me for ice now and then.

Sometimes we have no food at home, and then we go to a pizzeria. Restaurants are really essential, especially in the present situation when food is scarce. There are different kinds of restaurants and the prices vary according to the kind of food they serve. Even so, they're all rather expensive because prices have gone up. I think they raised the prices because the cheaper it is, the more people will eat out, and they don't want the restaurants to be so crowded.[24]

We've never waited in line to get into a restaurant. My husband is downright allergic to lines, and I agree that it's better to eat any old thing at home rather than queue up to get a better meal. It's so much trouble now to go in the morning to stand in line to get your turn for the restaurant. In the pizzeria it's first come, first served, and at some hours the line is short. There are always people in the pizzerias, especially toward the end of the month when people's rations are gone. It's terrible!

There's a pizzeria fairly near us, in El Tesoro. We can go in the car, but people who don't own a car have to take the bus to get there from here—it's about thirteen blocks. There's nothing really near in Miramar. This *reparto* was simply not built for this system. It was for people with a standard of living very different from anything that exists now in Cuba. Before, you only had to phone and all the stores would deliver what you ordered, and bill you every month or fifteen days. If you needed something in a hurry you could go to El Tesoro, and there was the dime store and so on.

24. Prices for nonessential goods and services were set high to reduce the excess currency in circulation. Due to the scarcity of consumer goods, many Cubans had surplus cash, a sizable portion of which was being spent on the black market.

In Havana it's different. *Mamá* lives about halfway down a block which has food shops on all four corners. On one, the grocery store, on another, the stand where they sell produce when there is any; the third corner has the poultry shop, and the fourth, the butcher shop. She's been buying at the same places for years. So as far as buying food is concerned, she has everything within half a block of her place. If she needs something from a drugstore, there are three or four a few blocks from her. When something comes to the drugstore—cotton, for instance—most of the time I don't even know about it. Where *mami* lives, it's very easy because one neighbor tells another. But here our way of life is very different.

Usually people shopped for clothing in Havana. At the beginning of the summer you'd go shopping and in one day get everything you needed for the whole season. At the beginning of the winter it was the same. But the present system of going to the stores whenever merchandise arrives is very difficult, especially since everything is so far from here.

Mamá used to make all my clothes and my little girl's too, but lately she hasn't because she's been sick. Besides, she has so many things to do, mending clothes and so on, that she really doesn't have the time.

It's difficult to buy clothes in the stores. Sometimes everything is gone by the time you get there, or you can't find your size. When I'm allowed to buy something in the ration book and find it only in *mamá*'s size, I buy it if she needs it. If you buy shoes that don't fit, you've lost your turn to buy another pair later on.

I hardly ever go shopping now. You go one day, and they're all out of what you want. You return another day, and they're still out of it. I can't keep going, because transportation is bad and it's a lot of trouble to have to drag two kids along. It's just too difficult. *Mami* lives near the shops, so I usually leave my ration book with her.

Very few children believe in the Three Kings nowadays. How can they? The toys are out on display and people start queuing up to buy them right away. They even announce over and over on radio and television when the toys for the Day of the Three Kings are going to be put on sale. Children hear all those things, so they know it's their parents or some other relative who gets them. And then, too, the child may ask for something they can't give him because there aren't enough of the best toys to go around.

There are almost enough dolls so every girl can get one, but it may not be the one she wanted. You have to stand in line two or three days and nights, even a week . . . oh, you have to go to all sorts of trouble to get a doll. And then, not everybody is able to get one. The same thing is true of bicycles. The toys that most kids want are the hardest of all to get. You get what's allowed in the ration book—one toy costing more than 3 *pesos* and two costing less—that's all. It isn't the way it was before, when parents could get anything at all for their children. The only limit was the amount of money they had.

Another problem is the dry cleaners. I send the clothes to *mamá*'s house because the cleaners don't have trucks anymore and there's none near here. They used to come by to pick up the clothes, but they discontinued that service about three years ago. Well, of course we have a car, so whenever I go over to *mamá*'s, I take along whatever clothes have to be dry cleaned. Then *papá* and *mamá* take the clothes in and pick them up for me.

I take all my bedclothes to *mamá*'s house too, and the laundry picks them up there. It seems to me that there isn't as long a delay for those things in Havana as there is in Miramar. I'm lucky because I have a car, but somebody who doesn't have a car or a relative in Havana has a hard time. You can't travel by bus with a big bundle of dirty clothes—or clean clothes, either.

Lots of people would probably wash their clothes at home if soap weren't so scarce. Not only that, now it's not easy to find a washwoman, so everybody sends their clothes to a laundry or a dry cleaners and it's impossible for them to give quick service. They take as long as fifteen or twenty days, or even a full month.

My goodness, everything is so difficult nowadays! Right now our TV set needs fixing, and maybe I'll ask my friend Matilde's husband to do it. That set has gone bad five or six times since we got it. At first we called the store where we bought it and they always sent a mechanic right away. Later, of course, it was nationalized. Now, when an electric appliance breaks down, you call the *consolidado*.[25] But you try everything else before that because of the terrible delays. Sometimes you can get it fixed by a friend who's a technician, and if you need a part replaced, there are still people who have some. When the children's air-conditioner broke down, we called the *consolidado*. We exchanged the defective air-conditioner and paid 300 or 400 *pesos* for a new model.

Another problem is getting cooking fuel. At first we were allowed two gas tanks, but three years ago they collected all the tanks and now nobody is allowed more than one. Sometimes you can get a replacement quickly, but the last time I called on the 10th of the month, and they didn't bring it until the 20th. I bought a two-burner electric hot plate—I was lucky because you can't get them anymore—and thanks to that, I can manage when I run out of gas.

Whenever I go out, I leave the yard gate unlocked so the delivery men can have access to the motors and to the gas, if they should happen to

25. A general term of reference for any consolidated enterprise; here it is an abbreviated way of referring to a state-operated repair-service center.

come. Once I left the gate locked, and when I came back I found that the gas men had broken the padlock. That annoyed me. It's disrespectful, just like breaking in the door and entering without permission. I told the man in the gas office, "They broke my padlock."

"Oh no," he said. "They opened it with a key." Then he said he wanted Juan to go over and have a talk with him about that gate. I told him there was nothing to say about it, and anyway from then on I'd leave it open.

For any medical problem we go to the clinic. I used to belong to the Hijas de Galicia, which was a clinic in Luyanó founded by a Spanish association. *Mamá* joined the clinic soon after she arrived from Spain and I was born there. When I was older I joined the association, and both my children were born in the clinic too.

There were many other private clinics belonging to mutual-benefit associations. The members paid monthly dues which covered all medical care and medicines. Now, of course, all those clinics belong to the government and are grouped under what is called *Clínicas Mutualistas*. We still pay monthly dues. I pay 11 *pesos* for the three of us, 3.50 for me and 3.75 for each of the children.[26] Our monthly dues at Hijas de Galicia used to be lower, about 2.75 a month for adults and 1.50 for children. They send my bill to *mami*'s address. If nobody happens to be home when they bring the bill, you have to go to the clinic to pay. This happened to me twice, so now *mami* pays and I reimburse her.

I transferred my daughter and myself to the Clínica Sagrado Corazón in El Vedado when I made my son a member. The Sagrado Corazón has general medicine and pediatrics, but no gynecologists or obstetricians. If I were to have another child, I'd have to go to a different clinic. When Eloyitos was sick, I took him to the Sagrado Corazón and they attended him very well. I have no complaints. They're very polite and efficient—nurses, doctors, all of them.

Before we married, my husband never belonged to any mutual-benefit association. He went to a private clinic, where you paid for the specific services. Then he joined the Benéfica, which was formerly part of the Centro Gallego. One day about eight years ago, Juan had an earache and he went to the Benéfica clinic. Clinics are just like polyclinics—you have to have an appointment, unless it's an emergency or a serious illness.[27] He went without an appointment and the doctor

26. Cuba's massive public-health program is based on the principle that medical health care is a biological right. There are no direct costs for in-patient care, and out-patients pay only for medicine. (Ricardo Leyva, "Health and Revolution in Cuba," in Rolando E. Bonachea and Nelson P. Valdés, eds., *Cuba in Revolution* (New York: Anchor Books, 1972), p. 477 and n. 73.) In 1969 individuals could seek out medical services in addition to those provided by law, as Mercedes and Juan had done.

27. Polyclinics in urban areas are equipped for out-patient treatment, but the mutual-benefit clinics also handle in-patients. Each urban polyclinic is designed to have, in addition to nurses, a gynecologist, dentist, pediatrician, epidemiologist, and internist on duty. Rural polyclinics have broader services, including in-patient treatment. (See *ibid.*, p. 477.)

told him he couldn't see him that day. Juan is quick-tempered and tore up his membership card right there and told the doctor he wasn't going to pay the clinic 1 *centavo* more as long as he could afford to go to a private doctor and that was that.

Recently Juan had some very painful back trouble. The doctor at the work center of the Ministry sent him to the Orthopedic Hospital and they attended him perfectly. They gave him treatment right there, and prescribed injections and pills. It was quite a struggle to find them, but finally he did.

Getting medicine is a problem these days. You used to be able to fill prescriptions in the clinic's pharmacy, but now they seldom have the medicines and you have to buy them at some drugstore. For Eloyitos they prescribed a lot of medicines, but the hospital pharmacy didn't have any of them. I had to go to the public pharmacy, where I got everything, except cough syrup and liver extract. I bought benadryl, which is a good expectorant, but I haven't been able to find the liver extract yet. I haven't started the child on the B-12 shots either, because he's supposed to have them both at the same time.

I think education has deteriorated since 1959. There's a tremendous lack of school discipline now. I'm not sure whether it's the fault of the schools, the teachers, or the children. When I was young, a teacher was sacred and the director even more so. But not now. I've seen children talk back to a teacher or even to the director. Children are given a scolding and they react as if it were nothing at all. Never before have I seen such lack of respect! All the teachers complain of this. I think this generation of children is unbearable.

The schools are housed in good buildings, but there's too much teacher turnover. Perhaps this isn't true of all schools. I've talked with friends who have daughters in the same grade as Merceditas, and some of them have told me that their children have excellent teachers and that there are no problems in their schools. But since kindergarten, Merceditas has not been through a single year with the same teacher. In first grade she had three different teachers, in second grade, three or four. In third grade I lost count. That holds a student back. Each teacher has her own system and gets to know her pupils as time goes on. If she has the same class from the beginning to the end of the school year, she acquires a certain amount of control over her students.

None of Merceditas's teachers has ever been to our home, except one of her fourth-grade teachers, who dropped in for a friendly visit on the girl's birthday. Usually teachers go to a pupil's home only when they have to make a complaint.

I think education is important for everyone. The better educated a person is, the better he'll get along in life. Take me, for instance. So far my marriage has worked out all right, but who knows what the future holds? I hope my daughter also marries and has a happy home, but if it should turn out differently, if she can't depend completely on her husband, it would be much better if she had a career. I hope she chooses to go to the University and get a degree. I'd like her to be a doctor or an engineer or something. I want her to get a better education than I did.

A woman of thirty years ago was by no means the same as a woman now, especially in a socialist country where she's expected to go out and work. The world changes and progresses. With every day that passes, more and more women get an education, stop being housewives, and go out to face life. Juan is perfectly willing to let me get a job. He thinks a woman should get an education and work, but I can't decide to leave my son when he's still so little.

There are *círculos,* of course, but I heard about a nurse at a *círculo* who'd poured boiling water in the tub for the child's bath and then forgot to pour in cold water. The child got serious burns. I don't know whether it's true, but that's the story that went around, and, as they say, "When the river makes sounds, it's dragging stones." I also heard that a certain employee at a *círculo* fed several children with the same spoon. Of course I have no way of telling whether or not that's true. I've been told that they take off the children's clothes and shoes when they go in and only give them back when it's time to leave.

One advantage the children in *círculos* have is the food. They get *malanga* and other vegetables that aren't always available in the stores. They even get chicken, and what they eat there isn't deducted from the family ration book. In any case, there isn't room in the *círculos* for all the children whose parents want to send them, and I prefer to leave my children with someone I can trust entirely, like my mother. But *mamá* is sick and lives too far for me to drop Eloyitos off there. I *should* get a job and I will, too, when he starts school and I can manage better. Of course I will.

The truth is that this apartment is awfully big. If I could get a responsible person to do the housework, I'd get a job now. But the last time I had a maid was four years ago, when Serafina, Lala's sister, worked for me. She cleaned the house and washed the dishes and Merceditas's clothes. I paid her 45 *pesos* a month and we got along well.

My mother-in-law has always had a maid. It's a struggle, but she says she's used to having a maid and can't get along without one. She isn't very well. She found another maid for me when Serafina left, as I was already pregnant with Eloy Tomás. When I came home from the hospital with my new baby there was so much work and so many diapers, it would have been too much for me to do alone. That girl stayed about one month. Another one came from Oriente, from Juan's hometown, and stayed about a year. Then I had two or three who stayed only one or two days each. None of them was any good. I got fed up and decided I'd rather do without help, even if it meant working hard. Today, women will work two weeks, then quit just when you think they've adapted to the job.

It's hard to get a good servant now because there are so many opportunities to work, even for people without much schooling. They can get jobs cooking for scholarship students or taking care of the boarding houses, or doing farm work, or handicrafts . . . there are twenty different kinds of work they can do. Those who are still doing domestic work aren't revolutionary. Revolutionaries usually work for the government.

So, vulgarly speaking, what one gets is the dregs—women who'll insult you for any little thing. I've never in my life spoken rudely to a servant—I know they too are human. I don't think one should look down on somebody just because she's in domestic service. What we eat our servants eat, sitting at the table with us. I've paid as much as 60 *pesos* a month, and I still can't find anyone to work for me. Sixty *pesos* isn't such a terribly high salary, but you have to take into account that they have no expenses because they get their meals and everything. But none of that does any good—the job doesn't "suit" them.

I could be a lot more useful to the Revolution if I taught school because there's such a great need for teachers. I could be doing that instead of cooking and cleaning. I don't have an awful lot of schooling but I used to enjoy studying. I really did. I've become completely illiterate and stupid staying at home, but with such a scarcity of teachers they'll take people who've only completed the sixth grade. I have more education than that, and I believe I could do it little by little.

I think the Revolution is a good thing, but I can't work for it so I'm not a good revolutionary. I don't cooperate with the Revolution because the house and children take up all my time. It seems that women in general aren't doing anything to speak of for the Revolution. I don't even belong to the Women's Federation. For one thing, I have nobody to baby-sit for Eloyitos, so I have to lug him around wherever I go. That's the main problem. If you belong to the Federation, they have meetings and ask you to work for them. It's a sacrifice for me to find time to do anything, even if I left Eloyitos with *mamá*. Besides, I must be home when Merceditas returns from school.

I seldom go out, even to amuse myself. The girl is old enough to take with us, but what about the boy? I don't like to take him to the movies or any other place because he doesn't enjoy it. He likes to go to the park, where he can run and play. When it's that hard just to go out occasionally, imagine how much more difficult it would be to undertake the obligations of belonging to an organization.

Lala's case is different. She and her sister live near one another, so when one goes out, the other can stay with all the children. But who can I leave my children with? I wouldn't bother a neighbor unless it was an emergency.

I belong to the CDR but I don't have time to go to meetings or do anything.[28] At first the Committee was in Lala's house and Armando was the president. But then he said his work didn't leave him enough time for it, so it was moved to the scholarship students' house on the corner. The CDR president lives in the garage and that's where the Committee is.

I know the president, but he isn't a friend of ours. I see him, say hello, and exchange a few words with him. I've talked more with his wife than with him. The Committee cooperates with the Street Plan[29] in making parties for the children. The street is closed and the women bring cake and piñatas. It's been a long time since they had a fiesta—I think the last one was to celebrate the Twenty-sixth of July.

The Committee used to organize guard duty for the block. I stood guard whenever it was my turn, because I could leave the children with Juan at night. Now guard duty isn't organized by blocks but by zones, and that's too far for me. I haven't done guard duty since. I don't think any of the women do. I don't like standing guard anyway. It's frightening to be unarmed in a dark, lonely place. You're supposed to be protecting a lot of people, but if somebody comes and knocks you over the head, who's to protect *you?* At least here on the block there were always two women standing guard together. I didn't mind that, but I don't like going eight, ten, twelve blocks away to a different neighborhood. Those blocks are awfully dark and you stand guard with a stranger. Juan goes on guard duty whenever it's his turn—once a month now. It's all right for a man.

Sometimes the Committee organizes a group to work in the country. I went with Juan to gather cane two or three times when I had only Merceditas, but I haven't gone since Eloyitos was born. The men cut the cane and we women heaped the stalks for the crane to pick up. Not long ago Rodolfo, Serafina's husband, came around asking for volunteers. Juan couldn't because he had to do volunteer work at his work center. I told Rodolfo I couldn't go either, though he didn't ask me.

28. Juan Pérez was in charge of Organization for the block Committee in 1966, but in 1969 he could not remember the name given to his Committee or the names of the current officers. This is not particularly surprising since most of his volunteer work was not done in the neighborhood but through his work center and militia unit.

29. *Plan de la Calle*, a recreational program for school children developed by the National Institute of Sports, Physical Education, and Recreation in cooperation with the CDRs, the Women's Federation, the Young Communists, Pioneer leaders, and school faculties, all of whom assist in its implementation. The *Plan* is initiated at the regional level, then passed down to the sectional or (in rural areas) the *municipio* level, where it is adapted for the local school. The recreational programs (e.g., parties, games, and parades) are not designed for individual schools but rather for groups of schools which employ the grounds, facilities, and neighboring streets of one centrally located school. (*Cuba: El Movimiento Educativo, 1967/68* (Havana: Ministry of Education, 1968), pp. 89–90.)

I don't know what the *Poder Local* does but I think the People's Courts are a good idea. When somebody has committed a fault or been delinquent, these trials in a person's own neighborhood are a lot more effective than court trials. It makes sense to let the people who know the accused impose the sanctions. They know what the person's circumstances are in a way a stranger couldn't possibly know. They can tell whether the person's environment or his parents or some other things influenced him to act as he did. Many times it isn't the person's own fault but a result of his environment. I haven't been present at any of the People's Court trials, so I don't really know.

These aren't good times we're living through, at least for us. Others may have now what they've never had before the Revolution, but not us. Only people who had nothing at all before the Revolution are better off now. We were never rich but we had what we needed. My children lack things I never lacked.

Naturally I know this is a process, a phase, and that we're not the only ones affected. Thousands of people are involved. Some have benefited from the changes, while others, like us, have suffered. There's no point in saying that everybody is gloriously happy—you can't cover the sun with a finger. Happiness would be having all the problems solved, having shoes and all the food you need. My goodness, there are so many things I want!

The idea of leaving Cuba would never enter Juan's mind. He's so integrated in the Revolution. I believe he belongs to every single organization created by the Revolution. He's a member of the Communist Youth and now he's anxiously waiting to be admitted to the Party. That's very important to him. As for me, I don't volunteer any opinions. It means nothing to me. If they admit him, good, if they don't, that's all right too. But if Juan can't conceive of leaving Cuba, then neither can I. Our home comes first. Even if I didn't like the Revolution, even if I disagreed with it, it wouldn't be right to deprive my children of their father. He wouldn't go, there's no doubt about that, and he'd probably refuse to let the children go if I went.

It's all very hard, especially for people with our standard of living. As I said, most people here in Cuba are living better now than before the Revolution, but we aren't. I don't say this merely because of myself—it's my children I'm thinking of. They've occasionally had to do without a coat or a pair of shoes, or even food. It hurts when one's child says, "I'd like to eat such-and-such," and there isn't any. Knowing that we have enough money to buy it makes it worse in a way. I don't ask for luxuries, only for necessities, understand. Well, they say these are years of transition. I certainly hope so.

Juan Carlos Pérez[30]

After the nationalization of the Mercado Unico was completed, Juan Carlos Pérez was appointed to an administrative position in the Ministry of Domestic Trade, to help supervise the nationalization of other markets in Havana Province. In 1964 he left this job because of a disagreement with Manuel Luzardo, then the Minister of Domestic Trade. The dispute was precipitated by a problem in the distribution of pineapples. Due to a planning error, the entire crop was planted at once and therefore had to be picked in a single harvest. Pérez and his boss received far more pineapples than they could distribute and the result was great spoilage and loss of money. Luzardo placed all the blame for the planning errors on Pérez's boss, causing him to lose his job. Pérez quit in protest, claiming that Luzardo's refusal to accept any responsibility was indicative of his shabby treatment of all intermediate-level administrators.

In his work with the Domestic Trade Ministry, Pérez had worked around the clock and had had great responsibilities. When he quit, he transferred to another ministry as a Class A clerk, hoping to find a less demanding job. He worked on a student schedule of six hours a day (8:00–12:00 A.M. and 2:00–4:00 P.M.) while studying a technical program at the University in the evening (7:00–11:00 P.M.). His salary was 185 pesos a month.

According to Pérez, he finally accepted a position of greater responsibility in the Ministry of Foreign Trade in 1965 because his fellow workers "begged" him to do so. In this new position he earned 200 pesos a month. After one year of technical training, he had to give up classes because of a conflict in hours. Transferred to another division in the Ministry, Pérez was officially responsible for buying planes and replacement parts, but he says Fidel made all the decisions on what to buy and Pérez's office merely did the paper work. His official salary was 375 pesos a month, but he continued to receive his old salary of 200 pesos a month because of a wage freeze.

During a departmental reorganization in 1966–67, Pérez was transferred to another ministry and made responsible for the import and repair of certain

30. This account of Juan Pérez's work history has been reconstructed from interviewer Claire Siegelbaum's notes, based on untaped conversations with him.

kinds of small machinery, although he claimed only a rudimentary knowledge of mechanics.

In 1969 Pérez was, as previously mentioned, under consideration for Party membership. He had been a member of the Communist Youth for eight years and had served (probably in his sectional) as propaganda officer and as supervisor of culture. At thirty-two Pérez was too old to belong to the Youth; he "didn't want to show his face around there," he said. For him, "it was the Party or nothing."

Sara Rojas

I think the Revolution is trying to make a new kind of people, so I guess it must be a new idea. But as for communism, I don't know a thing about it. I don't know what it is or how it began. I know no more about it than if I lived in China. Somebody is going to have to teach me. What I do know is that before the Revolution we poor people had no money to buy things with and now we may have to stand in line, but at least we have money to buy whatever the stores get. For me that's the greatest thing the Revolution has done.

Since the triumph of the Revolution anybody can get an education for their children whether they're in the city or on the farm. Some little country girls who were brought here to Havana to study are now nurses and schoolteachers. They cleaned our barrio of children, let me tell you. All the kids were sent to Havana or Santiago or someplace else to study. That's one of the most valuable things the Revolution has brought about.

When I was young, my keenest longing was to study and have a career. I wanted to learn a lot so I could get out of that place. I wanted to be a teacher; when I was little I'd get other kids to play school and I'd be their teacher. I'd write down the letters and numbers for them on a piece of cardboard. It was nothing but a dream and I knew it. In those times it wasn't easy to give one's children an education. If I'd ever had the opportunities my children have now, I'd have been . . . *ay*, something great.

It's such a joy to see one's children studying and know that someday they'll have a career. I feel very proud to have a son who's studying.

While we were living in Marianao, Eduardo and I went to Aldita in the Frozen Zone office to see about help for the other children. The people there took down the facts about us and then admitted Amandita to a *círculo*. It was just after Faustina was born, so Amandita was about a year and a half old then. They also wrote down Concha and Hilario for scholarships.

They gave Amandita everything at the *círculo*—medicines and all—and she got just beautiful. But she slept in her crib and was all alone and I didn't like that. We had to get her every Friday; usually Eduardo went to pick her up. The first Friday she didn't want to go to him, and much less to me after they got home. Eduardo held her in his arms and she kept giving me dirty looks over her shoulder. One time I went to get her and the woman there refused to give her to me because she only knew Eduardo, and the baby didn't seem to recognize me either. When that woman asked Amandita, "Is this your mother?" the baby shook her head no.

Finally the woman told me to have Eduardo come and get the child. They're extra careful because once a woman was given the wrong child. But when Eduardo went to get Amandita, she didn't want to go with her *papá* either, and that made me mad. There are so many girls taking care of the babies at that place! They all pick them up and play with them and I guess Amandita found affection there. Children are like dogs—where they find affection, there they stay.

Amandita remained in the *círculo* only five months. Once when Eduardo was going to Oriente, he went to fetch her and they refused to let her go. He took her anyway, and they took the scholarship away from her because of that. Her scholarship was on the same grant as that of the two eldest children, so they took it away from them too. So then none of the three belonged to anything, and I never went back to Aldita.

What I really want for my kids now is a scholarship. I tell the children that if I can get scholarships for them they'll be better off, because at school they'd have nice airy living quarters and they'd get their health back. But they can't see that; they hate the idea of going to boarding school. As long as I'm not given a proper place to live, I'd rather have them all out of the house and that's the truth.

I'm taking steps to get the scholarships. I've got to see Nena Gil[31] in the Ministry of Education; she's the one who handles all the scholarships. I also want to have a talk with Llanusa[32] in Education, if I can find somebody who knows him. If I told him my problem, I think he'd give my kids scholarships right away. If not, damn it, who can one talk to? If I could bring him right here to the garage and say, "Look, Llanusa, you can see what my situation is. I want to ask a favor of you. Could you take steps to have all my children put on a scholarship? There are so many of them!"

I always hear Fidel's speeches over the radio or TV, but I've never seen him personally. I love to listen to him because he never lies to the

31. Elena Gil Izquierdo, head of Special Plans for the Ministry of Education and member of the Central Committee of the Communist Party.

32. José Llanusa Gobel, Minister of Education until 1970, when he was replaced by Belarmino Castilla Mas, who was in turn succeeded by José Ramón Fernández. Llanusa is now director of the Matanzas cattle-breeding project and a deputy to the National Assembly.

people. If there's going to be a food shortage, he tells us about it ahead of time. That's what I like about him—he's conscientious and never tries to deceive us.

The truth of the matter is that with such a large family as I have, if things were still as they used to be, my kids would be sleeping on the floor. The wages my first husband earned cutting cane would simply not have been enough to support eight children. When I was married to him I had only five, and even so they didn't have enough clothes and shoes. That doesn't happen now. When my number comes around, I can go shopping and buy whatever they need because I've got the money.

I have more food now than before the Revolution. Now I can buy my quota of rationed foods every month, but before the Revolution there were times when I didn't have a *peseta* for food. When relatives come to stay without their rations I run out of food sooner, but even so, my children and I have never gone hungry. Toward the end of the month, when I'm short of one thing or another, I send the children to eat at the Club Obrero. I always manage somehow.

I think life is harder here in Havana than in the country. If you run out of something here, you have to wait until the Minimax stocks it. But in the country you can kill a chicken, dig up a bit of yucca, pick a few plantains and a few ears of corn, and make a stew for the kids. You can't do that here. If you don't have meat, you've got to wait until it comes. You can't invent a dish out of thin air. If you don't have the proper ingredients, what are you going to do? Oh well, it doesn't matter if we have to do without, as long as the kids have enough. If it comes, fine, and if it doesn't, it doesn't. I'm not going to change things by talking or by not talking either, so all I can say is "Forward!" like Maceo.

It's a problem to get enough milk for the children. Sometimes the milk truck breaks down and doesn't get around to delivering until about 2:00 in the afternoon. When that happens, we can't have fresh milk for breakfast, but what can I do? At least I get twenty cans of condensed milk a month so the baby can have that every day. When the baby refused her powdered milk formula, I had to get my special infant formula allotment changed to regular condensed milk. The doctor wrote out a prescription which I took to OFICODA. The people there put a slip of paper in my ration book noting the special diet for the baby.

The baby's diet is a problem because all the foods she's supposed to eat are hard to get. But food for grown people is every bit as scarce. It's hard to get eggs, *malanga,* and so on. Strained fruits and vegetables are very scarce—you can only get five jars per child a month.[33] It makes a lot of difference when a child is old enough to eat more solid food, rice and all that.

33. The official ration of baby food for infants was thirty jars per month.

Another problem with the baby's food now is that Elsa can't take her milk warm. She has to drink it very, very cold. If I can put ice in it, that's best of all. When I gave her hot food she'd get sick, and the doctor asked me whether I had a refrigerator to keep the food cold, and I told him I didn't. "Well, that's not right," he said, and wrote a letter marked "Urgent" recommending that I be given a refrigerator. But I never did get one.

Comrade Nery, a young militiawoman who's a good friend of mine, told me I could keep all the baby's milk and fruit in her refrigerator. That solved the problem for a while, but now the comrade says her refrigerator is too full. When she returned my food, she was very embarrassed and apologized for not having room to keep it. Now I keep the milk sweet by boiling it two or three times a day. I put the milk in water to get it cold and then give it to the baby.

Now I have no place to keep meat, either. I'm going to have to cook the whole meat ration when I get it or I'll have to salt it. But I don't always have salt and then I can't do anything to preserve it. Last week when I got my meat ration, I cooked it all at once. Normally it lasts me three days.

Some people get more money than others. They've got better wages or else there are three or four people working in the family. That makes quite a difference. Here we have only Eduardo's pay, and with that we must buy clothes, shoes, food, medicine, and everything. Every time I get money, I set half of it aside. That way, before I know it I have 200 or 300 *pesos*, and—thanks be to God and the Virgin—when something is released for sale I can get my full quota. If our number to buy comes up and my husband hasn't gotten paid yet, I'll ask a friend or comrade to lend me some money until payday. But even then I can't buy all the things I'm allowed to buy.

If I had more money, I could have bought a number of things I need—a tablecloth, a coverlet ... well, no, I'd buy a mattress first, that's what I need most. I'd also buy ready-made clothes. I haven't bought any so far, not for lack of money but because my number for that hadn't come up until this month. But the day I went shopping, the women's-wear departments in all the stores were closed because the clerks were away doing productive work, so I couldn't buy anything. Oh, I did buy a few trifles, but nothing really important.

I keep track of my turn to buy different things by the announcements on the radio. When they announce it's the turn of Group 1 to buy such-and-such a thing on a certain day, I keep track until my number comes up. I'm in Group 4. The Minimax also puts up the number of the group whose turn it is to buy.[34] If you keep track of those things, you can get in line early on the day your turn comes.

34. This purchasing plan does not apply to food items, however.

The first time my turn came around, I bought myself a wristwatch. I tried to get one for Eduardo too, but they'd only released fifteen men's watches for sale at that store and I was thirty-fourth in line. I try never to let my turn go by without buying something, you may be sure of that. I may not get everything I want, but I manage to get hold of something or other. The way I do it is by getting in line early.

After Elsa was born[35] I couldn't get a crib for her. The doctor gave me a letter to take to *Recuperación de Bienes*[36] asking them to give me one. I still have the letter, but I never could get the crib. The place where you have to get them was over at the Malecón. The wind blows so hard there and I had to go stand in line at 2:00 or 3:00 in the morning. I went once and had the money to pay for it, but they were all out of cribs. The girl there told me, "Send your husband or your son next time, but don't come yourself. It's too cold." If I'd been able to go back, they'd have given me not only the crib but also a tub to bathe the baby in, a child's rocking chair, and a potty chair.

Other people could get those things because they had somebody to stand in line for them. But I was alone here with the kids. My brothers Pancho and David were not living with us then and it was too far for Violeta to go. You have to take two buses to get there. Eduardo did go one night, and just as it was his turn, the woman in charge had to leave because her husband was seriously ill. So Eduardo didn't have a chance to get the crib. Leticia went one time too, and stood in line for us. But at that time Domingo was working, so she couldn't stay long as she had no one to leave her baby with. With one thing and another, I couldn't do anything about it.

I had to let Elsa sleep in my bed. We fixed it in such a way that nobody could roll up against her in their sleep. We arranged the mosquito net that came with her layette[37] over her part of the bed and the rest of us slept outside the net. The nights Eduardo slept at home, I had to sit up and let the baby sleep in my arms because I had nowhere to put her.

During the day it was easier. I'd put a pillow beside her so she couldn't roll off the bed. But twice she climbed over it and fell off. The first time she fell, she rolled out the garage door and Concha picked her up outside. *Ay,* what a scare I had! She wasn't hurt though and didn't even cry. The second time she hit herself against the garage door and got a terrible blow.

Eduardo would have gotten angry if he'd known about it. He says I never obey him. He'd just been telling me that if the baby ever fell off the bed, he wasn't answerable for what he'd do. He said, "I don't care if the kids eat up all the bread and milk and all the food we have, but if the

35. December, 1968.
36. The agency for the confiscation of property of emigrants, and the recovery of other property regarded by the state as unjustly gained.
37. See Appendix A.

baby should fall off the bed, I'm going to beat up everybody." Of course he didn't mean it, but after that fall I carried her as much as I could.

Standing in line is such a problem. I had to let my turn go by when my numbers came up for purses and yard goods for tablecloths and slipcovers. But as soon as they announce, "Sewing machines are to be released for sale to Group 4," I swear by *mamá* that if I have to stay in line all night long and sleep there, I will. Lots of people in my group are bound to have sewing machines already, so maybe the queue won't be so long. But long or short, I'll wait, because I need a sewing machine badly. I'd be able to make clothes for the kids out of any odd bits of cloth without having to use somebody else's machine. And when you sew at home, nobody knows you've made your children's clothes out of old rags.

Another thing we need badly is shoes. Eduardo left a comrade to substitute for him at work one day so he could go and buy shoes for Amanda, Faustina, and me. He measured our feet but I guess he measured wrong because the shoes he brought me were too big. Amanda's and Faustina's were a good fit though. When Faustina heard she was going to get new shoes, she tossed her old ones in the trash can. The garbage was picked up before I knew about it, and those old shoes had at least another month's wear in them! Now she has only one pair. I tell you, it's the kind of thing only a crazy person would do, but I can't help laughing now when I remember it.

The one who has no shoes, but really no shoes at all, is Violeta. I can't buy any for her because she's already used up all the shoes in her quota. They're pretty poor quality. I sent her a pair last year when she was staying with my *mamá*. Well, the shoes turned out to be just a bit too big for her and what did she do? She gave them to her sister Estela instead of sending them back so I could exchange them for a smaller pair. Then she showed up here in tennis shoes and I was ashamed to have her go out in the street wearing them.

There's a place in the country where you can barter tennis shoes, clothes, dishes, liquor, and things like that for all kinds of farm products. There's practically nothing they won't barter for. The comrades on the farms don't want to sell their produce and stock, they prefer to barter them for a dress or something like that.

That kind of trade is called "black market." It isn't legal but the people trade that way to get the things they need. The government must know all about it, even if they give no sign of knowing it. It isn't just the people in the area who trade there, but others from as far away as Palma Soriano, San Luis, and even farther.

While I was in Oriente, my folks went there and got some big ripe plantains. They also bought oranges—a kind of orange that was pure honey—and they saved some for me. They bought about six laying hens, too. When they went to trade, they took flashlight batteries, coffee, a pair of tennis shoes, and a few other odds and ends. Considering how little they took, they brought back plenty. By the time the train gets to Oriente, you can't budge because the aisles are so full of sacks of tubers and other farm products.

If I had anything to exchange, I'd go there myself to get a few vegetables, plantains, or chickens. I'm trying to find out whether they sell beds there. But there's a problem because the trains are so crowded, and I wouldn't be able to take the baby.

The last time I was home, they were distributing clothes in my barrio in children's sizes. They were also giving away shoes free to the kids, which is another advantage I find to living in the country. I also noticed that many people were building themselves new houses—the most beautiful little cottages you ever saw. I couldn't take my eyes off them. When I compare those houses with the place I live in. . . ! I've got to have a house of my own before I die, even if it's only a wooden one.

I had a big problem with my ration book after my brother Bernardo and his wife, Ana Teresa, moved out of here. Ana Teresa had bought a lot of items that were assigned to *my* share. When my name was in their book, they put down in my name whatever they bought, all the dishes and everything. She even got a sewing machine, an iron, and an electric blender; she'd taken just about everything.

I took the book to OFICODA and they hunted up the old ration book turned in when we all moved into the apartment upstairs, to see whether I'd bought any of those things before. But my old ration book was blank. All the items assigned to us had been bought by Bernardo and Ana Teresa. OFICODA sent for Ana Teresa but they weren't able to settle anything, so the case was transferred to the sectional. That's where they finally put everything straight. They charged all the items against Ana Teresa's ration book and gave me a blank one. If they hadn't done that, I wouldn't have been able to buy a thing. The minute they handed me a blank ration book I made a beeline for the store and bought lots of things.

I joined the CDR because everybody is supposed to, as well as the Federation of Cuban Women and every other organization we can participate in.[38] When Lala and Armando ran the CDR, I certainly had no reason to complain of them, although they weren't much help to me when the exchange of apartments was going on. They helped me, but

38. Eduardo Rojas also belonged to the CDR, although he had not taken part in any voluntary work, such as cleaning up the neighborhood. He said he would have liked to participate but his work schedule made it difficult. According to Rojas, the volunteer work sessions organized by the CDR were held in the morning and he was on duty at his work center from midnight until noon the following day. He had done volunteer work through his work center.

only a very little. Lala did keep telling me not to allow the exchange to go through. "Just stay put, all of you," she advised. "It's a crime to make that exchange." Yes, she definitely advised me against it.

But she had no authority to stop it, you see. If she'd wanted to take the case to trial before a People's Court, she could have, and so could we, for that matter. I'd like to have done that, but at the time I didn't even know about People's Courts. I didn't know People's trials were being held or how the system worked or anything. I didn't know anything because I had nobody to orient me.

At a meeting of Nicasio's Committee last year—in October, I think— members agreed to stand guard in the neighborhood. Both women and men took turns, usually for two hours at a time. When our turn came around, somebody from the Committee would bring us a slip of paper saying who was to relieve us. Two women are always assigned to stand guard together; when it's a man, only one is assigned to a given turn.

I usually had my turns with Justa or Leticia. We had to go to Fifth Avenue first, and then we'd go back to Seventh. There were guards at every corner, and at intervals we'd walk from one post to the next. It's been a long time since anybody has stood guard here though. I don't know why they stopped.

The Federation of Cuban Women came around getting the facts about women's schooling, and I talked my problem over with them. They asked me if I couldn't attend a cutting and sewing workshop at least two hours a night. Well, since then there hasn't been a night when I've been able to leave home for two hours. After working so hard all day long, I'm exhausted. And even if I don't happen to be tired, I often don't feel well. But if they send my kids away to school and put the baby in a *círculo*, I'll pass the course with no trouble at all and get a job. I'd tote my little notebook and pencil to school and study for two or three hours a day without having to say, "I must hurry back now and cook the kids' supper" or "I have to go wash the baby's diapers."

My children's lives will surely be different from mine because they have opportunities I never had. With their opportunities and my brains, what couldn't I have done! With my intelligence and a good education, the government would surely have sent me to several of our sister countries to study. And how proud I'd have been! It must be wonderful to visit places you've never seen and go from country to country.

I'll soon be thirty-four, but in spite of my age I still have hopes for the future. Here in Cuba people are given opportunities to better themselves no matter how old they are. With a middling amount of luck, perhaps I'll live quite a few years longer and be able to give something. So I'm planning for the next step ahead and I've never lost hope. I'd feel proud, very proud indeed, to work in a cutting and sewing workshop, and have my kids on scholarships where I'd know they're safe. That would be a big step forward for them, too.

I think the Revolution will help me. After all, that's what I'm a revolutionary for. As Fidel says, children are the future. It seems to me, seeing the situation I'm in, and bearing in mind that children are the future, he's just got to help me somehow. He's got to. Just think of what he could make out of these children—maybe four or five teachers, engineers, all sorts of things. That future isn't for me, it's for them.

Leticia Manzanares

As far as I'm concerned, the Revolution hasn't made any changes in my life. I worked before and I work now. I see a better future for my children, though. Right now, the main problem of the Revolution is giving everybody food and keeping the children well nourished. We can make do with the clothing they give us even if it isn't much. Housing is a big problem too—there are many people in great need of a better place to live—but still, to me the gravest problem is the shortage of food.

Before the Revolution I sometimes felt it was unfair that I should have so little when others had so much. Oh well, that's the way things have always been. It's still happening. A lot of Cubans are living off payments for the houses they had before the Revolution. Others still have money from before and live on that without having to work.

There are still rich and poor people in Cuba, no doubt about it. The old man who lives across the street is rich, and another man who lives down the street has money. I don't believe anybody's gotten rich on the Revolution, but some people have improved their situation a lot and have a good position. They aren't exactly rich but they're comfortably well off and living a lot better than they did before. Yes indeed, there are a lot of those. The ones who are best off among the poor are the lieutenants, captains, and *comandantes* in the Army. They may be poor but they get whatever they want, one way or another. I don't know whether you'd call such things injustice or taking advantage or what, but after all, that's life. You've got to expect a bit of trouble.

Considering the short time we've had communism, we're well off; every problem can't be solved right away. Times are better now and people say they're going to get even better. Russia has had communism for I don't know how many years and we have it soft here compared to the way communism started there. Anyhow that's what I've heard, but as I've said before, I don't know about such things.

All of my brothers work for the Revolution, but they aren't interested in politics. None of them plan to go anywhere, so they've become integrated and are working for the government. Since I don't plan on joining the Party or anything, I simply go on believing as before.

My family has never had any trouble with either the past government or this one, and I've never known anybody who did either. Even when I knew for sure that Batista was gone, I didn't care, because the truth is, it made no difference to us. Sure, I used to hear people say that they'd murdered this one and torn the head off another and I don't know what all. But whoever they killed must have done something, no? At least it seems to me that there must have been some reason, but then I don't know about such things.

I didn't know anything about politics then, and I don't know any more now. And when I don't know what's what, I simply keep my mouth shut. My politics is to have a good time and kid around and laugh as often as I get the chance. I'm friendly with everybody and I smile a lot but I don't go around telling everybody what I think. I keep my feelings to myself or I talk them over with my family. With outsiders, I always put a good face on things.

For us Cubans, life has always meant a lot of drinking, music, parties. We've always loved fiestas, but things aren't as they used to be—no indeed! People used to be gayer. Oh sure, there's music still, fiestas at the Tropicana and at Social Circles, but it's not the way it used to be. Before, people would go to parties every day, now one must work. Things are better organized in that sense.

For my part, I'm busy every single minute. My only recreation is waiting in line at the Minimax or in some shop in Havana. The only day I ever go out simply to amuse myself is Sunday.

I work part-time doing laundry and it helps me make ends meet. Domingo didn't want me to take in laundry, but I just had to have more money. I've bought lots of things for my apartment with that money. Besides, here I am, home all day, how can I just sit down and do nothing? Why shouldn't I work? We don't exactly live in abundance.

Lala feels just the way I do about it. Armando doesn't want her to work and actually she doesn't need the money right now. She has plenty with what he gives her, and he just got paid for accumulated leave and everything. She's got enough, but I haven't.

Whether Domingo has money or not, I've gotten used to having a bit of my own to spend as I please. It's money I earn with my own sweat and it's extra, over and above the household expenses. Mostly I use it to buy more things from my clothes-ration book, because I have Domingo's money to pay for the food, as well as the money my brother sends me. Or I use it for any extras that come to the stores, like a bicycle for the kids or an electric blender.

I have *papá*'s ration book—there's a room set aside for him here, that's why—and he lets me buy the things that are of no use to him, like the saucepan he wasn't interested in. What I most wanted was sheets, but he'd already bought those. He's going to let me have the pressure cooker and the sewing machine too, if the stores get them. I can't get a sewing machine on my ration book because I used that coupon to buy an iron long ago when it was classified as "Basic Equipment." What I do have a right to buy is an additional iron or a radio, but I already have a radio. I'll get an iron the next time my turn comes.

There isn't much left to buy in *papá*'s ration book. If only I could get a refrigerator! That would be wonderful! That's really necessary. I keep my meat at a friend's house in El Vedado and have to take the bus to go get it.

If I wanted a steady job I could get one through the Women's Federation. But I don't want to have a regular job right now, because a woman with a job has to leave her children alone and doesn't have time to do the housework right. So I take in clothes to iron, mostly from the scholarship students.

When my children are old enough, I wouldn't mind getting a job. I'll have to take anything the Federation gives me because I don't know any trade. I've never had a skilled job, but there are lots of factories where one can get a job without any special training.

After the Revolution I enrolled in night school. My sister-in-law had enrolled and I decided to go too, because I had nothing to do at night. I'd completed fifth grade in school so I was placed in a high level there. They taught us all sorts of things, arithmetic and so on, and also about the Revolution. Of all the classes, the one I enjoyed most was typing. Many of the women there got scholarships to learn how to drive so they could drive cars for hire. You know those little cars that went along the same routes as the buses? It was the women who drove them. But I got scared so I quit.

I enjoyed studying and never got bored, because the classes lasted only a few hours. But I quit when my *mamá* died, seven and a half years ago. Then I got pregnant with Tomás and never went back.

I joined the Women's Federation and the Committee when I lived in Regla, and I still belong because I intend to live in Cuba until I die. If I stay here it means I feel revolutionary and am in favor of the government, and even though we didn't fight for the Revolution we're cooperating with it.

The Women's Federation is a good organization. When women are needed to work somewhere they call a meeting and ask for volunteers. The only problem is, you've got to participate. They also call a meeting when the sectional sends information about classes for women who haven't graduated from the sixth grade, or for those who are interested in taking a course in cutting and sewing.

The CDR here doesn't do a thing. They don't hold meetings and they haven't even been around to get the dues this month. Our Committee president, Nicasio Bolanos, hasn't called a meeting of the members for a long time, I don't know why. Perhaps he hasn't received any orientation from the sectional or maybe he's too busy. It's also been a long time since our Committee got people organized to stand guard. You see, when they tried it some people showed up and some didn't. I don't think that's right.

We need a better block Committee. The CDRs are supposed to look out for the Revolution, to organize volunteer work, to gather raw materials, and to deal with any wrongdoing in the block. The block Committees have the authority to do all those things, and they should, because that's what they're for. When you have a problem, the Committee is supposed to tell you who to see about it. For instance, a tile in my kitchen broke and the Committee told me to go to *Poder Local* about it.

I heard that they were going to hold a meeting to see who wanted to take over the Committee, because Nicasio doesn't have the time for it. But I don't know . . . as far as I'm concerned, I don't want to take on any more responsibilities. I simply can't. All I want is to see it functioning the way other Committees do, because I think all CDRs should be the same. Some of the block Committees in the neighborhood are much better than ours. They often hold meetings to discuss different problems, they stand guard every single night, they go around picking up things to be recycled, they do volunteer work at the Minimax, and all sorts of things. I like to do those things when I'm able to.

Lala and I are the only people here who get out and work when something must be done in the Committee. I used to be in charge of keeping the street clean, but not any more. I clean it whenever I want to—I don't need the Committee to tell me when. Not long ago Lala and I cleaned up the whole block. We did it on our own because the street was so dirty, not because the Committee told us to.

My family does volunteer work through the Federation too—cleaning streets, gathering bottles and cardboard, and going to work in the country whenever we can. For a time I went every Sunday, and I still go whenever I can. On a day when I can't go, I send my girls instead. I've gone only on Sundays because I can't go for long stretches. When you go for as long as one week at a time, they pay you, but I can't leave the children alone that long. When I go on Sunday, Domingo always stays home to look after the baby.

I like to do volunteer work; it's a lot of fun because they drive you there in a bus and you talk and crack jokes along the way and look at this and that. We've gone to dig up potatoes, to plant sugar cane, and to weed in cornfields. The last time I did volunteer work I went with Lala—it must be about three months ago.

I think volunteer work is a good thing. You can learn a lot and get to know the country. I've learned to plant potatoes and to do hard farm work. One's body needs that exercise; it's real good. And besides, I like the country. I've also done lots of volunteer work at the Minimax, like cleaning up or putting stuff into containers or any kind of work that needs to be done.

The best thing we Cubans can do if we have nothing against all this is to join the Committee and the Federation. You know how it is: if a Cuban citizen doesn't belong to any organization people think he isn't with the Revolution. Then if he has to go to the law about anything, both the Committee and the Federation investigate him, and if they find he doesn't belong to either, nobody will back him up even if he hasn't done anything wrong.[39]

If you belong to the Committee it stands up for you, so to speak. I mean, it's a kind of guarantee that you're revolutionary. And if the Committee speaks well of you, that's the biggest recommendation you can get. It's really of great value to a person to belong to the Committee.

I'd like to have my children belong to the Communist Youth someday, because under this government to belong to the Youth means that you've got a social conscience and are recognized in the Revolution. You're a person with whom nobody could find fault. One of the best things about the Revolution is that the people who join the Party are chosen for their good behavior and conscience. Take Lala's husband, Armando; he's a Party member. He works hard, and if he sees anything that's being done wrong in regard to the Revolution, he attacks it. Even when he's sick, he goes to work and does a good job. He's just gone to the Isle for a two-year stretch, and maybe when he comes back they'll do something to improve his situation. They might give him another place to live, for instance, because the truth is he needs it. They show a lot of consideration to people like him because he really makes an effort.

Juan and Mercedes are the best off in our building. They say they used to be rich, and they do have more than the rest of us. Their apartment is very well furnished with the kind of things rich people used to have before the Revolution. I don't believe the lieutenant and his family live better than we do, because they must earn just about the same amount of money, give or take a few *pesos*. But it's easier for them to get things than it is for us. I don't know whether Party members have any advantage over the rest of us, but it seems to me that they're rewarded with better living conditions.

Racial prejudice has changed since the Revolution. Now everybody can go to the same clubs and beaches. In that we're all truly equal now. But for me there's been no change that way, because all my life I've

---

39. Under Article III of the Law of Penal Procedures, the Vigilance officers of the CDRs are aides in juridical work and must do what is requested of them by the prosecutor, the court, or others in charge of a case. (*Granma Weekly Review*, Feb. 17, 1974, p. 3.) Probably the most frequent kind of assistance given to the courts by the local Committees are the depositions they are required to submit on the character (e.g., work and social habits, political history) of any resident of their block who becomes a party to a court case.

moved among both blacks and whites and had both as friends. The only difference is that before the Revolution the blacks and whites each had their own separate social clubs. For instance, in Morón there were three separate social clubs, the Colonia Española for the wealthiest whites—doctors, lawyers, and so on—the Liceo for white people who weren't so high up, and the Unión Fraternal for the colored people. And there was a fourth club, the Unión de los Ingleses, for the colored people who came from Jamaica and Haiti. There were many of them in the countryside working as farmhands and cane-cutters.

Even though whites and blacks had separate clubs and amusements, I wouldn't say there was ever any serious racial prejudice here in Cuba, either before the Revolution or after. Even before the Revolution there was nothing to prevent a white person from marrying a black. People were free to choose their own husbands and wives. There are more mixed marriages now than before the Revolution, that's true. That's because the colored men who go abroad usually marry foreign girls and bring them to Cuba.

Nowadays colored people have better work opportunities, because they can study more. Before the Revolution only rich white people had a chance to study. None of the poor, black or white, could afford to stay in school long enough. Now everyone can go as far as they want in school and everybody has the opportunity to work.

Only yesterday the school director sent for me to tell me my two girls have the ability and the vocation for teaching. She wants them to get scholarships to study education. It would take four years, just like basic secondary school. If they get a diploma for teaching and later want to study something else, they can go to the University for four more years. I told the teacher I'd agree if the girls liked the idea.

Last year Lina applied for a scholarship to study education, but they didn't call her up. The director said there'd been a slipup by the people in charge but she'd see that it didn't happen again. My second eldest daughter, Bárbara, told me she likes dancing and if they recommended her for ballet she'd request a scholarship for that. They go to the schools looking for young people who want to study ballet and who have the ability.

As for my future, perhaps I'll be happy and comfortable in my old age, because my son Tomás says he's going to work and give me the money he earns. I don't know about the rest of my children, but at least that's what Tomás says. He's kind of spoiled, but tenderhearted in spite of everything. I sure wouldn't like Tomás to get involved in things like guerrilla fighting. I wouldn't want him to die like El Che! He'd no longer even be a son to me because he couldn't be by my side.

If I go on as I am, I have nothing in particular to worry about as far as my future is concerned. My own life is already made and shaped, so all my hopes for the future concern my children. If they get to do something worthwhile, I can be at peace. I hope they take advantage of their opportunities to study and be whatever they like so they can be happy and secure. Nowadays it doesn't matter whether you're black or white, rich or poor—you can pick the career you want. You can be a doctor, a nurse, or anything else you like. That's one very good thing this government has done, and after all, it's one of the most basic things. As for the rest, one can always manage.

Domingo Labrada

The improvement in my housing conditions was one of the most important changes that the coming of socialism brought to my life. Under imperialism, I lived in a house where the rain would blow in through the kitchen and sweep through the house. Now I'm living in a very good apartment in a residential section—Miramar, no less. That's because the government kept its word to the families of the men who went to Algeria. I don't know whether any of the comrades who went to Algeria failed to get a house or an apartment. One fellow I knew had to argue with the High Command several times because he was sharing a place with another family and wanted one of his own. But that was a completely different problem. It had nothing to do with what we'd been offered when we went to Algeria.

We had absolutely no cause for complaint. Raúl himself must have said, "The families of the men who went to Algeria must be taken care of." Three or four times a week they visited each family to see if they had any problems or if anybody was ill or needed anything. My gratitude goes out to the Revolution, not to the comrade who went around to see my family. After all, he came because he was sent, eh?

Sometimes I suffer discomfort from the scarcity of this and that, but it's like the story of the sheep and the climate. The shorn sheep adapts to the climate and we adapt to the system, especially when one is living in a system which, compared to the one we had before, has truth in it. There are certain things that have to be taken into account and analyzed to understand the shortages.

Our mattress is all torn, for instance. I stood in line for twenty-two days to buy a mattress at El Tesoro, and when I finally reached the counter I found that the mattresses hadn't arrived yet. That was a couple of months ago and they still haven't come. Or take undershirts. They're made right here in Cuba but there are certain things that make it impossible to produce as many undershirts as they used to. So if I don't get undershirts, I adapt myself to not wearing them. That kind of thing doesn't depress me. I don't start worrying about where all the undershirts go. I'm a very understanding guy in regard to such things.

One of the things I most feel the lack of nowadays is a refrigerator. I have to bother my neighbors all the time. I used to salt the meat to preserve it, but even so it would stink after a few days and I'd make Leticia throw it away. So that's the only thing I hanker for—a refrigerator.[40] Aside from that, I don't want anything I don't already have.

Salaries were very low under capitalism. A cane-cutter under the old system didn't earn enough to feed himself. Nowadays, if a guy earns 10 *pesos* a day working for the dairy industry and volunteers to go work in the sugar-cane fields, he's paid exactly as much as he earned in his regular job. My salary used to be about 2 *pesos* a day, and I had to look around for odd jobs to supplement it. Now, under socialism, doing a different kind of work, I earn 160 *pesos* a month instead of 60, though I still don't have a bank account. I've been out of work for several months on account of my illness, but I receive half-salary. That's why I haven't been able to save. Under capitalism, if I'd been an employee in a factory my boss would have kicked me out months ago, right? He'd have said, "Well, enough is enough!"

It was all the fault of the personnel office at my place of work that I'm on half-pay and classified as "partially incapacitated." They assigned me to the Camilo Cienfuegos drainage project behind the Hershey Canal. You should see that place—clouds of gnats and mosquitoes all over. Imagine me there with this skin condition! How could I be expected to work there with those infernal insects stinging me? I explained this to the comrade in the personnel office and asked for a transfer, but he said, "You've got to go back to the Cienfuegos drainage works. They're asking for more personnel and I can't send you anywhere else unless you bring me a medical certificate."

I got a medical certificate but they refused to transfer me. Instead, they classified me as "partially incapacitated," which means pretty damn useless. I didn't want to sink to that level. I tried to argue the Ministry of Labor out of it, because my medical certificate didn't say I couldn't work, only that I should be transferred. The Ministry promised to find me a job that wouldn't affect my health, but I've been waiting six months and they haven't found it yet.

The Ministry sent me to a school for unemployed drainage workers, but twenty days later they sent me to ESA[41] for a four-month course in automotive repair. I studied the theory and practice of the management of auto parts from capitalist countries, as well as Hungarian and German spare parts. I didn't like the treatment I got at ESA. They took away my day of rest, and once when I was absent, they refused to accept the

40. In 1970 Domingo Labrada's brother Dámaso moved in with the family, bringing with him a refrigerator.
41. *Empresa de Servicios Automovilísticos* (Automobile Services Enterprise).

medical certificate I took them. When I don't like a job I quit it, so I quit at ESA.

After that I did volunteer work a few times on coffee plantings and so on. Now I have a job as a truck driver, but I'm still classified as "partially incapacitated." I like my work except that I'm still sent to work sites that are harmful to my health.

I asked to be returned to my old job as a taxi driver, but the Ministry of Labor said that unless a request was made to them for my services, they couldn't do a thing about placing me there. I just want to work, that's all, and to be removed from the "part-time" classification.

Before the Revolution I was working on my own, and if I didn't work one day, that was my business. I'd work when I found a job, and when there was none to be found I didn't work. There was no problem of absenteeism; if somebody was absent from his job, he got fired and that was that, unless he worked on his own, like me. Nowadays anybody who stays away from work without a damn good excuse is called an irresponsible parasite.[42]

The government sets somebody to work who for years and years has been used to working only two days a week. His body is adapted to that routine; it's hard on him to work full-time, week after week. So he works for two days, as he's used to doing, but on the third day he can't even drag himself up out of bed, much less go to work. So he's absent two days from work. If you analyze the problem, that's what you'll find at the bottom of many cases of chronic absenteeism. When I worked for the taxi company, there were many comrades who worked five days a week with Saturdays and Sundays off. But honestly, I can't do such a thing. Still, I can say I've worked places where there were three or four Party members, and I worked every bit as hard as they did. You don't have to be a Party member to be a good worker. If you're conscientious, you do your work well, and if you aren't, you don't. That's all there is to it.

The half-salary they pay me isn't enough to support my family. Frankly, what I earn nowadays all goes for food. But at least we can afford to keep our complete food ration for our own use. We don't have

42. After a long campaign against absenteeism and vagrancy, the government passed an anti-loafing law on March 15, 1971 (more than a year after Labrada's interview). Under this law, all men between the ages of seventeen and sixty, and all women seventeen to fifty-five who are physically and mentally able, must work. Those who do not work are considered to live "parasitically" and are guilty of "anti-social behavior." Persons absent from work for fifteen days or longer without due cause, and persons who have been reported by their work centers to their Labor Council two or more times, are subject to sanctions under the law. This can take the form of internment in a rehabilitation institution doing productive work, or a period of home arrest coupled with supervised work at the former work center. Sentences can be suspended if the individual shows improvement. (For the text and discussion of the law see *Granma Weekly Review*, Mar. 28, 1971, p. 2; also Lowry Nelson, *Cuba: The Measure of a Revolution* (Minneapolis: University of Minnesota Press, 1972), pp. 121–26.)

to sell half of what we get as some people do. I've managed all these long months by sheer luck. Leticia takes in laundry to make a bit of money for household expenses. My father-in-law has been coming to see us since I've been sick, and every time he comes, he gives us 50 *pesos*. My wife's brothers also help, especially Fermín, because he lives with us. And when my brothers-in-law come from Camaguey they bring vegetables, and that's a big help because what we get with the ration book isn't enough to feed me, let alone my whole family.

In the old days I used my money to have a good time with my friends. As long as my old man worked, he gave me everything I needed. Even after I was married and had children, you might say he still supported me. Now if I need 5 *pesos,* I don't try to borrow it from a friend, I still go straight to *papá.* I'd rather ask him for money than borrow from somebody who's nothing to me. If you borrow and say you'll pay back tomorrow, what happens if, when tomorrow comes, you can't pay? It would be damn embarrassing. Instead of taking such a risk, I go to my old man.

To me, socialism is something that brings about the unity of people with one another. It brings about a feeling of fraternity. Socialism means that the community is for everybody. It's sharing equally among the masses, something like splitting an orange in two equal halves. Imperialism means that everybody is out for himself, that everything is for only one person, right? The stores are full of all sorts of stuff, and that's fine for people who earn a lot of money, but it's a different story for those who are poor. Under capitalism there's exploitation. If I owned an enterprise—a store, a warehouse, a cement factory—all the profits from that enterprise would be mine, mine alone. But under socialism, everything goes to the government and is shared by everybody.

Frankly, I've never liked politics. I can argue some points, sure. I was in the armed forces for a time, and I like to learn. If somebody from the political committee gives a talk, I always make notes and try to refute him, because that way I learn more. But I don't lose my head over politics or anything like that. It simply doesn't interest me. I have a certain amount of knowledge, and if I should go in for politics, I know I'd hit the nail on the head. But, well, my interests just don't run that way.

I never studied life in Russia under communism, or communism in Cuba, for that matter. I'm out of touch with that kind of thing. If I said I agreed or didn't agree, I'd be deceiving you. The plain truth is that I simply don't know what Fidel said about communism. I'll tell you why not. My brain tends to other things. And in the conditions I'm living in, I simply don't have the comfort for reading when I get into bed at night. With this and that, my mind isn't alert enough to read a book. I mean, there may be certain things that impede a fellow from learning about communism, although it's a very interesting subject.

To me, Fidel is a great man, a very great man indeed. He has a great brain and a great heart. I truly admire him. As for my revolutionary integration, I belong only to the block Committee. My wife belongs to the Committee and to the Federation of Cuban Women, and whenever she's called to a meeting, she goes. And whenever she's asked to go to the country to do productive work, she goes, unless there's a very good reason. In fact, she's always gone wherever she's called by the Revolution.

I feel as revolutionary as Fidel himself. I do, I do! It isn't simply that I say so, my mission as a revolutionary has been recognized by the armed forces. I'm no longer in the Army, but I still feel revolutionary. Hell, the most important moment in my life was the triumph of the Revolution!

Justa Díaz

All you have to do is compare things as they used to be with the way they are now. Before the Revolution, I never had 40 or 50 pounds of rice in my house as I do now. And if I needed to I could buy more above the legal price. I've got more than enough money to do it. But we manage with what there is and I have rice left over at the end of the month in spite of all the visitors who eat here.

Nowadays you can buy what you please from anybody willing to sell because people have plenty of money. You hear people say, "Sure there's money, but you can't get this or that." They simply don't analyze. The same person who says that probably couldn't afford to buy before, when the stores stocked everything.

The other day in the Minimax I overheard three colored women talking about the "good old times." When I hear a person of my own class shooting off her mouth like that, I get plenty annoyed, but when it's a colored person, it burns me up! I simply don't get along with colored people; they're apt to say such fool things. One colored woman was saying that anybody who didn't want to live well was a fool. "We used to be really well off in the old days," she was telling her friends. "At home we bought a sackful of rice every four or five days."

Liar! No drag-in-the-mud white could afford to buy that much rice at one time, let alone a drag-in-the-mud black! Only a person with a lot of money and connections could. But who had money? Half the people didn't have 1 *centavo* to their names. To work in the government at that time, or even to mop floors in a clothing store for 10 or 11 *pesos* a month, you had to know somebody.

I'd been sitting there with my shopping bag all the time listening to the colored woman talk. I took a good look at her and knew she was a drag-in-the-mud. After she left, one of her companions commented, "Her husband abandoned her, so the government gave her a job, put her daughter in a *círculo,* and got her a decent place to live. She's earning good money." And to talk like that after the government has done so much for her! It burns me up!

Under Fidel Castro, opponents speak up with complete liberty any-where, even in a crowded bus, out in the street, and we allow it, no matter who hears them. But during the dictatorship, if they so much as suspected you, they'd come get you and kill and bury you.

People suffered hardship during the Revolution, but you have to compare the way they lived before and the way they live now. During the dictatorship, the rent on a tiny apartment like the one we shared in Havana with Ricardo's brother and sister-in-law was 100 or 200 *pesos* and you had to work your head off, because if you didn't have the rent money one month they wouldn't wait. They'd drag your furniture out and throw it in the street. Why, there were those who lived seven and eight to a tiny room, paying 50 to 80 *pesos* a month for it, with everybody scrubbing floors or doing whatever work they could get. And now with frigidaires, TV sets, and everything, they complain! Nowadays people pay a certain percentage of what they earn for rent. Even if only *one* person in the family is working, they still pay only a percentage of his earnings. And if you don't have furniture, the government gives you whatever you need.

Fidel says that by 1970 nobody in Cuba will have to pay rent, but I don't begrudge what I'm paying now.[43] After all, we pay rent to the government, and whatever the government gets is spent on us, so it's our money anyhow. We're paying 19.50 *pesos* a month for this apartment and the place isn't half bad. Now I can afford things I've always wanted, like fine glassware. I had to make a lot of sacrifices to buy it, but it was something I needed. I know I must take good care of it because it belongs to me. I don't mind paying the government for it. It cost the Prime Minister money to import it, didn't it? Well, I can't expect to go to the government and say, "Hey, I want some glassware. Will you give it to me?" I'm happy to be able to buy it at all. It's more than I could do in the old days. In fact, I couldn't even go into the shops where they sold that kind of thing.

Before the Revolution only the rich had gas or electric stoves. Until I moved to Havana eleven years ago, I used a kerosene stove. When I was last in Oriente, eight years ago, most people were still cooking with charcoal or wood or one of those little kerosene stoves that you pump. But there must have been a lot of changes since then. Now everyone in Havana cooks on electric or gas stoves. That's one of the big differences. Some people don't notice, but we poor people do.

The same thing holds true for washing machines. Who had washing machines before the Revolution? Only the rich or the Americans. I never could afford even the kind of washing machine that cost only 15 *pesos*. It

43. Rent payments were continued beyond 1970; the high amount of currency in circulation was given as the principal reason for the continuation (see n. 24).

wasn't that I didn't have 15 *pesos,* but if I'd used both a washing machine and an iron, what I earned taking in laundry wouldn't have paid for the electricity. One doesn't have to be a revolutionary to analyze such things.

And in those days only somebody very prominent could get gas delivered within fifteen days. Some people had three tanks full, but if I'd called for some they'd just as likely not have brought it, because I wasn't anybody in particular. Now we're getting better service on gas delivery. Until recently there was a fifteen-day delay in filling orders, and once Mercedes had to wait twenty days. But lately they send my order four days after I've phoned in, and there have been times when I've placed an order in the morning and had it delivered that afternoon.

One thing that must be taken into account about the service now is that most of their personnel is away cutting sugar cane, and they have only one or two people working there. They told me so at the gas *consolidado.* "Comrade," they said, "there's a delay in filling orders because there's only one person working in the office, so we can't deliver your gas today and we want you to know why. But if it's an emergency case, we'll make the sacrifice and send it over today." If you have a cripple in the family, or children, or if you don't have a hot plate, they send the gas right away.

My husband earned 89 *pesos* when he first became a policeman, and we managed just as we do now because I've always worked too. All my life long I've liked to help my husband. When two comrades get along well, like us, and are poor, like us, it's a good thing they help each other. Besides, the children aren't just *his* children, they're *our* children.

I don't have fixed wages. The state pays me every week according to how much laundry they send me to do. Suppose they send me ten shirts at the rate of 50 *centavos* per shirt, I get paid 5 *pesos.* I get 25 *centavos* a tablecloth and 10 *centavos* a towel. As soon as I hand them back the clothes, they pay. That's one good thing about them.

What I earn helps, but it's Ricardo who really pays for everything here. He hands me his paycheck and I hand him mine. Sometimes he'll give me 100 *pesos* a month and sometimes 200. We don't keep accounts. There are some *compañeras* who—would you believe it?—ask their husbands how they spend every *peso.*

Ricardo went to a school for two years and graduated as a lieutenant. While he was in school he came to visit me every two weeks if he could, but sometimes he stayed away longer. That's why I'm getting used to his always being away from home. He's a patrol chief, but recently he went to cut cane for his work center. I've never gone to any of the places where he works, not unless the state calls me. I'm not like some *compañeras* who are always going to see their husbands on the job. I'm not in the habit of pestering my husband with questions; I don't meddle in men's affairs. I trust him, and anyway I always know more or less what he's doing.

My husband joined the Party four years ago. I can be sure of him—all wives of militants can be sure of their husbands. I'm not in the least worried about him that way because he's always been faithful. If he ever did anything like that, he's never told me about it. But I'm sure he hasn't. Yes, that's one thing I'm sure of. He's a very serious man who respects his wife and marriage. He and I are well adapted to each other by now. Whenever the Revolution calls, he goes.

Our baby girl[44] was born last year while Hernández was away doing farm work. He came to see her when she was twenty-one days old. A lot of Party comrades came with him to visit me because he'd told them it was a boy. We only have one boy, you see, one lone boy. We both wanted another boy this time. Well, when they found out it was a girl, they sure kidded him about it. He looked awfully put out but he told them, "All right, it turned out to be a girl. So what? She's my child and I'm just as proud of my daughter as I would have been of a son!"

Some people claim they're revolutionaries, but there are many different kinds of revolutionaries. Not everybody who wears an olive-green uniform is one. You've got to dig deeper and try to find out more about him, to see if he has a revolutionary conscience. I can tell you my husband and I are revolutionary and you can go to Guantánamo and ask whether it's true, or ask Fidel and Celia if you want to. Everybody knows Fidel and Celia are revolutionaries, but as for the rest, all I can say is, "Perhaps; I don't know."

Here in the building, where I more or less know everybody, I don't see many who act like revolutionaries. For instance, I haven't seen Leticia make any progress, but that's mainly because of her husband. He's a sick man who for three years has kept his wife home all the time. Lala and Mercedes have remarked on it. Ask Leticia, "What's the matter with your husband? Why does he sacrifice you, making a sick woman like you rush about!" My husband suffers from an ulcer, heart problems, and nerves. He needs rest and yet look where he is! A good revolutionary recognizes such things. And look at me. I'm sick and yet I say, "My husband is involved with the Revolution, so whatever I can do. . . . I'm both the man and the woman of the house and I resolve any problems that come up at home."

And Lala's husband, Armando, has bad nerves. He has to be hospitalized often, but see how hard he works. Juan's just the same—he lives and dies working. Ever since I've lived here, he's spent more time in the fields than at home. Hernández and I have talked about him and I say, "There's a man who can't be accused of not being a revolutionary." A

44. Their seventh child, also named Justa. At the time of the interview Justa Díaz was pregnant with their eighth child.

man who goes ahead and works, no matter what, is a true communist.

There are people who say, "I don't want to have anything to do with communism because of the limitations it imposes upon us." And yet these men do their duty and work hard so this country can get ahead. Our neighbor Horacio, for instance, has no book-learning, knows nothing, yet he's a better communist than most. This kind of thing has been discussed by the Party leaders. Since he's a man who never talks, who sacrifices himself, who doesn't abandon his country, who never annoys or offends anybody, and who does his work, we say that he's a revolutionary. A good revolutionary is a man who works, sometimes twenty-four hours a day, and who can stay away for days and months without seeking the comfort of his wife and children.

But as for Leticia's husband, Domingo, I see nothing in him to make him deserve to be called a revolutionary. He doesn't work but gets a salary from the government. He spends twenty-four hours of the day at home, but while Leticia is running around washing and ironing, he can't even go out to pick up the groceries. If there's a problem at school, she's the one who goes there to deal with it. I wouldn't keep a man like that in my home. What's he good for? I wouldn't be a bit surprised if he turned out to be counterrevolutionary. From such a man you can expect the worst. What can one think of a man who does nothing to make his country progress to insure his children's future? Being sick is no excuse. Everybody's sick. But it's our task to work, not for our sakes but for the future of our children.

I have no idea if Mercedes is a revolutionary, but she's never criticized the government. Not only that, I've heard her say that she'd like to place her children on a scholarship so she can work as a teacher. I think her dearest wish is to get a job. She can't go to work now because of the children, especially the youngest, Eloyitos, who spends so much time in the hospital.

Lately the boy hasn't been sick so often, but just wait until Juan goes to work in agriculture. We've analyzed that. When Juan goes away, the boy gets so sick he has to be hospitalized. I myself have told Juan he shouldn't go away anymore. When he was on the Isle of Pines for about three months, that child was in the hospital more than two of those months! They had to send somebody to ask Juan to come back. I kept calling from here to the farm where Juan was, and Mercedes practically went out of her head. After that he went to work on a citrus farm—I don't know where—and again they had to hospitalize the kid. He went to Camaguey for the sugar harvest and the same thing happened.

Now, according to what I've heard, Juan is going to work in the cane fields again for three or four months. He's just like Hernández that way. No one can deny that he does his share. And every single time he goes away, his little son gets deathly ill. Mercedes lives in fear for that child. "You tell me whether I can go to work and leave that boy!" she says. Her *mamá* has heart trouble and has thousands of problems so she can't count on her for more than a day or two.

My husband left again yesterday to do volunteer agricultural work. Just as he was leaving he blurted out, "I'll be gone until 1970." He didn't say *when* in 1970. He's like that. His motto is, "I know when I'm going away but not when I'm coming back." Well . . . anything for the Revolution.

Still, when your husband just ups and says he's going to be away about eight months . . . well, one can't help feeling something. Ricardo is dry, but I'm kind of sentimental in some ways. I start wondering whether he's all right, so far from me. And if it starts to rain here, I wonder if it's raining where he is too, and if he's getting wet.

Ricardo has always been the same, ever since we were sweethearts, but since the Revolution he's been more reserved than ever. I know about things that happen to him only because I see them happen, not because he tells me.

The kids miss him when he isn't home, but not the way they miss me. The older ones are used to their father being away all the time, but not the littlest ones. He was here for a whole year when Antonita was smaller. They call for him, Justa most of all. I tell her *papi* is out working in the cane, but she soon forgets and starts calling for him again.

I didn't sleep last night and neither did Florinda. We were both feeling nervous. It was raining and I said, "*Ay*, Florinda, think of all those trucks in this rain!" Then she started praying, and every little while she'd interrupt herself to say, "*Ay, mami*, suppose one of those trucks skids and overturns!" It happens many times, in fact. We stayed awake until 3:00 in the morning, and by 5:00 I was up again.

I feel even sadder when I'm alone. At least I have the children with me now, but Florinda is leaving for school tomorrow and then the boy will go soon and I'll be left alone with the little ones. Then I'll lock up the house and go about my work as usual, but I won't be happy.

I know Hernández is well and that he's working, but it simply isn't the same. It'll be many days before I get used to his being away again, but I know all the comrades' wives are going through the same thing. A woman who loves the Revolution and loves her husband has got to adapt to these things.

Ricardo Hernández

When I first arrived in Havana in 1959—I was twenty-six then—I started working in the police command. While attending officers' school I decided to be a militant, and then, straight off, I became a Party member without ever having been in the Communist Youth. My war record, my behavior after the triumph of the Revolution, my work, and everything else, all contributed to my being granted militant status. You have to give them a complete account of those things. They asked about my work here in Havana and my behavior on the job, whether I'd made any mistakes—they ask you about everything in detail.

At the graduation exercises of the officers' school at the end of 1965, they informed me that I'd been accepted in the Party. I felt wonderful. The greatest ambition of every revolutionary is to belong to the Party. Anybody who isn't interested in becoming a Party member can't be a true revolutionary. Ever since I learned what communism really is, I longed to be accepted into the Party. I said I didn't care for military rank or anything except belonging to the Party. That was my one ambition.

I never knew what communism was until after the Triumph. Before that, we'd been taught that communism was a wild beast, a monstrous thing. One got that impression everywhere, but it turned out to be just the opposite. To me, communism is the greatest thing in the world. I've seen how it works here in Cuba, how it's bringing tranquility and well-being to all of humanity. I compare the situation of my family before the Revolution with what we have now.

Before the Revolution my problem was simply to find a way to feed my family. I lived in anguish because there was no work. Even before I got married I noticed the problem. You couldn't get a job until you gave your voter's card to someone in power. You couldn't even hospitalize a sick child until you did that. This never happened to me personally but it happened to many of my relatives. For instance, my brothers had to peddle their votes and those of their families before they could get a job working with a pick and shovel. To get even the hardest, worst-paid job, you had to sell your vote. Practically every Cuban election has been this way. After Batista's coup, things got tougher than ever.

I've seen things change since the triumph of the Revolution, as Cuba became socialist and communist. World communism would help all countries get along with one another by creating brotherhood among workers and bringing well-being to the entire world. Anybody can see that's what the world needs.

PART IV

The Children

Introduction

The opportunity to improve the miserable lot of tens of thousands of children was one of the great joys in victory for many Cuban revolutionaries. "Children are the future" and "Children are the Revolution" have been bywords of the Castro government. However, Cuba was traditionally not a child-oriented culture. Under Title V of the 1940 Constitution parents were "obligated to support, aid, train and educate their children," and childhood and youth were protected "against exploitation and moral and material abandonment," but the Constitution was not enforced and was virtually worthless as a working document. Children had almost no rights with respect to their parents; they were expected to defer to their elders in all things, including submitting to them for corporal punishment. Children were seen as giving legitimacy to sex and fulfillment to women, and as reproductions, even possessions, of their parents, but rarely as individuals with independent needs and aspirations.

Poor children, especially those in urban slums, were rushed through childhood to bear heavy responsibilities at home or to help support the family by taking a job. For girls this often meant leaving home at twelve or thirteen to become a domestic, or marrying very young and moving out of the home. For both boys and girls, attending school was almost always secondary to fulfilling family obligations.

Among the urban and rural poor, children seldom received gifts, nor were they subjects of special celebrations and parties. The experiences of middle- and upper-class children—having toys and pretty clothes, parties for saints' days and birthdays (especially the fifteenth birthday party for girls), gifts on the Day of the Three Kings, and no real responsibilities—were the privileges of a minority.

I

In 1969 the majority of children lived very differently from the way their parents had lived. With employment available to all who wanted to work, and with rationing and public-health programs, material insecurities were disappearing, and through compulsory education and state penetration into the home (largely through mass organizations), parental domination was gradually diminishing. New social pressures gave children increased protection from physical abuse and neglect. Sympathetic neighbors might go over the parents' heads to the neighborhood CDR, which in turn might refer cases to the People's Courts or send someone to talk with the parents.

To extend to every child the opportunity to celebrate his or her birthday, a cake and party foods were made available for each child in the family ration book. Many parents did not take advantage of this, but group birthday celebrations were often held in the schools. For Three Kings' Day the government substituted a national Children's Day on July 6, at which time toys were distributed for sale to stores across the island. A toy allotment for each child was included in the family ration book.

While the state has been busy on one hand trying to ensure a childhood for every child, it has on the other hand been trying to impress upon children a new order of priorities. Along with a new sense of security, children have been given a new and heavy responsibility. Speaking at a Pioneer celebration in 1974, Fidel Castro told a group of young children: "Somebody once said that children are born to be happy. And that is so; everybody should be born to be happy. But you are also born to struggle, to work, to study, to build the future, to carry society forward, to cooperate with your teachers and to help your parents."[1]

In this same speech to the Pioneers, Castro explained that the government was moving Children's Day to a date later in the month because July 6 coincided with the last week of school and consequently with final examinations. The holiday atmosphere was believed to have had a negative effect on children's test results, and the change of date was considered a necessity. It is a good example of the hierarchy of responsibilities for children in the new order.

The problem now confronting the government is how to go about making revolutionaries out of these well-fed, clothed, housed, educated, and medically cared-for children. In 1971, when the National Congress of Education and Culture was convened in Havana, political socialization was a topic of primary concern. The Congress expressed a special interest in the role of the family in the formation of political values and the influence of teachers, as well as parents, as role models. It recommended programs of continuing education for both groups. The Declaration of the Congress proposed some programs for immediate adoption, but placed great stress on the importance of long-term research and observation of children.[2]

1. *Granma Weekly Review*, July 14, 1974, p. 6. The first line is a quote from the great Cuban nationalist, José Martí.
2. The text of the Declaration appeared in *Granma Weekly Review*, May 9, 1971, pp. 3-6.

One month after the Congress, a Children's Institute was established under the supervision of the Federation of Cuban Women, in collaboration with the Academy of Sciences and the universities. The Institute was to oversee training of all personnel working with children and to do research on the growth and development of "children in our environment."[3] One of the Institute's first projects was a survey in Havana to investigate the relationship between parents' values and their children's education.[4] To get parents involved in the educational process, a mass campaign was initiated by the FMC and CDR Education fronts to recruit brigades of "Militant Mothers for Education" and periodically to select "Exemplary Parents" from each block. In some areas, Parents' Schools were established to "stimulate the interest parents should have to continue in the home the patient work of forming the new man, bolstering the habits the day-care center teaches the children."[5]

The 1971 Congress called for rewriting of textbooks, creation of a new body of children's literature, and the retraining of school and day-care personnel. The Congress endorsed the policy of maintaining a cumulative file on each student from preschool to university "to show characteristics and changes which are noticed in the process of development of the student in all aspects."[6] The Congress also stated the need for policy coordination and cooperation between parents, teachers, administrators, and community leaders for the achievement of unity in the process of socialist formation. "If the process of formation through education must exist from childhood to the postgraduate level through a permanent process of study and work, personality development, integration and communication with society and other factors, it is clear that, as was expressed in the Congress, there must be coordination and great educational unity."[7]

The Congress further recommended that outside the classroom children take part in activities that "create a sense of responsibility toward the care and upkeep of collective property." To achieve this, children were to be brought into contact with state and community at the earliest possible age and to maintain that contact through a lifetime of memberships in organizations sponsored by the state. Castro outlined this progression to a group of Young Pioneers.

> As you know, we're all organized. First of all, there's our Party; then there's the youth organization; and then, the . . . mass organizations. Our workers are organized in their trade unions; Cuban women are organized in the Federation of Cuban Women; neighbors are organized in Committees for the Defense of the Revolution; farmers are organized in the National Association of Small Farmers; students are organized in the FEEM [Federation

3. *Ibid.*, June 13, 1971, p. 10.
4. *Ibid.*, Aug. 29, 1971, p. 5.
5. *Ibid.*, July 4, 1971, p. 8.
6. *Ibid.*, May 9, 1971, p. 3.
7. *Ibid.*

of Students of Intermediate Education] and the FEU [Federation of University Students] and children are organized in the Pioneers, the UPC. And the Union of Pioneers of Cuba is like a great school in which you are preparing yourselves for the future.[8]

While the state was restructuring schools, curricula, and the form and content of extracurricular activities, it was also establishing guidelines to transform family life. In 1975 a new Family Code replaced Title V ("Family and Culture") of the 1959 Fundamental Law, which had been incorporated almost verbatim from the 1940 Constitution. Among the main objectives of the new code were: to contribute to "the most effective fulfillment by parents of their obligations regarding the protection, moral upbringing and education of their children so they can develop fully in every field as worthy citizens of a socialist society," and to "the absolute fulfillment of the principle of equality of all children."[9] To that end all legal distinctions between "legitimate" and "illegitimate" births have been eliminated. The Code also regulates adoption and tutelage, defines the conditions under which children can be removed from their parents' care, and sets down the obligations of children to parents and of parents (single, divorced, or married) to children.

Cuba is certainly not the first state to try to influence all aspects of child development, but there is something astonishing about seeing the policy set down in print. The following lengthy excerpt is from Chapter II, section 1, of the Family Code: "Relationship between Parents and Children: *Patria Potestas* and Its Exercise."

ARTICLE 82.—Minors are under the *patria potestas* of their parents.

ARTICLE 83.—The exercise of *patria potestas* corresponds jointly to both parents.

It will correspond solely to one of them as a result of the death of the other or as a result of suspension or deprivation of its exercise.

ARTICLE 84.—The children are obliged to respect, show consideration for and help their parents and to obey them while under their *patria potestas*.

ARTICLE 85.—*Patria potestas* entails the following rights and duties of the parents:

1) keeping the children under their guardianship and care; making every possible effort to provide them with a stable home and adequate nourishment; caring for their health and personal hygiene; providing them with the means of recreation fitting their age which are within their possibilities; giving them the proper protection; seeing to their good behavior and cooperating with the authorities in order to overcome any situation or environmental factor that may have an unfavorable effect on their training and development;

2) seeing to the education of their children; inculcating them with the love for learning; seeing to it that they attend school; seeing to their adequate technical, scientific and cultural improvement in keeping with their

8. *Ibid.*, July 14, 1974, p. 6.
9. The full text of the English translation of the Family Code appeared in *Granma Weekly Review*, Mar. 16, 1975, pp. 7–9.

aptitude and vocation and the demands posed by the country's development; and collaborating with the educational authorities in school programs and activities;

3) training their children to be useful citizens; inculcating them with the
love for their country, respect for the country's symbols and their country's values, the spirit of internationalism, the standards of coexistence
and socialist morality; respect for social property and the property and
personal rights of others; arousing the respect of their children by
their attitude toward them; and teaching them to respect the authorities,
their teachers and every other person;

4) administering and caring for their children's property; seeing to it that
their children use and enjoy in a proper manner whatever property
they have; and not to sell, exchange or give any such property except in
the interest of the children and pursuant to the requisites of this Code;

5) representing their children in every judicial action or arrangement in
which they are involved; giving their authorization in those cases where
full capacity for taking action is required; and taking action opportunely
and in due fashion to defend their children's interests and property.

ARTICLE 86.—The parents are invested with the authority to reprimand and
set straight adequately and moderately those children under their *patria
potestas.*

The final sentence of this excerpt, "The parents are invested with the
authority . . . ," is especially significant as a reminder that the investor of
all authority is the state, which entrusts parents to raise their children to
serve the needs of the larger society.

It is young people, Guevara said, who are the "malleable clay" from
which would come "the new generations . . . free of the original sin."[10]
This belief, combined with the public attention and the priority given to
the welfare, happiness, and education of children, as well as the youth-
fulness of the leadership itself, fostered a kind of youth cult in Cuba
after 1959. The state did not officially discourage the old pattern of child
deference to elders, but the changing power relationship between parent
and child has considerably altered it. Because the ways of their parents
are often part of the "old life," children may find themselves feeling
superior to their elders, instructing them in the new ways, and encouraging them to return to school.

This type of generational conflict arose not only between conservative
parents and revolutionary children, but between first- and second-
generation revolutionaries as well. The young people often had great
admiration for their parents' heroism, as well as guilt feelings about their
great sacrifices, and perhaps some envy of that aura of romanticism that
surrounded the Rebellion. Yet they knew that the older generation had
been irreparably molded by the old system and could never belong to the
generation of "new men."

As the language of the Revolution has changed, communications be-

10. George Lavan, ed., *Che Guevara Speaks: Selected Speeches and Writings* (New York:
Merit, 1967), pp. 134–35.

tween the generations have deteriorated. Many older revolutionaries with backgrounds of tremendous material deprivation find their children discussing poverty and colonialism from textbook lessons instead of firsthand experience. Veterans of the eclectic Twenty-sixth of July Movement who had joined in a flush of idealism are confronted by young people who argue narrow points of dogma and compete for membership in a Party of ideologues.

As the government institutionalizes the Revolution, it must reach a compromise between the two generations by bringing older revolutionaries from their tradition of opposition and extralegality to respect for new laws and political institutions, while getting younger Cubans to see beyond institutions and dogma. Although it may be impossible to maintain the intensity of any revolutionary experience, the government has tried to keep it alive by saturating the mass media with retellings of the Rebellion and by re-enactments of crucial events in the Revolution. The Revolution's leaders challenge the younger generation to bring the same sense of urgency and level of commitment to the development of Cuba that their parents brought to the rebellion against Batista.

II

In their behavior toward one another the twenty-three children[11] in *Neighbors* reflected the relationships between their parents. Although these children all lived in the same building, they generally did not intermingle; they did not come together as a group for play in the street, for instance. Children whose parents were on cordial terms tended to play together, while those whose parents were not friendly generally avoided one another or engaged only in casual conversation. The children in most frequent contact with one another were Merceditas Pérez and Engracia and Gabriela Hernández. Genoveva and Florinda Hernández also visited the Pérez home occasionally to watch television or to bring their younger sister Antonia to play with Eloy Tomás.

Mercedes Millán was not on friendly terms with her black neighbors, and according to her daughter did not allow her children to play with the Rojas children, although Merceditas did occasionally play with Andrea Labrada. The children of the two black families played most frequently with one another. The strongest relationship was between Amanda and Faustina Rojas and Bárbara and Andrea Labrada; their brothers also played together. The two older girls of these families, Lina and Violeta, were friendly but their activities and interests rarely brought them together. Although the adults in the Rojas and Hernández

11. Does not include the three children from Sara Rojas's first marriage who were not living with her.

families were not on speaking terms, their children did greet and talk with one another. This contact was limited, however, since the three eldest Hernández children boarded away during the week.

The Cárdenas boys were generally quite shy and reserved and did not spend much time with the other children in the building. They were always neat and clean in appearance, had a fairly strict schedule, were kept indoors much of the time, and were not allowed to run as freely as the others. When they did play with the neighbor children it was usually with Eloy Tomás Pérez and Tomás Labrada.

In general, boys played with boys and girls with girls (with the exception of Eloy Tomás and Antonita, both under four); their play included traditional games such as shooting marbles, playing house and baseball, and skipping rope. For the most part, the children's games and play, unlike their school activities, were free of ideological content. An exception to this was a card game the Labrada children cut and assembled from a children's magazine. It was a variation on Old Maid with paired cards having pictures of Pioneers, teachers, schools, and camps instead of animals or fairy-tale characters. In place of the Old Maid card there was "the Absentee," a caricature of an extremely ugly old man. (Absenteeism was a serious problem in Cuba at that time and a long campaign was being waged against it, culminating in the anti-loafing law of 1971.) It is possible that the Labrada children, whose father was a chronic absentee, did not connect the message with their father, but it would have been difficult for them to have missed the association made between absenteeism, ugliness, and undesirability.

All the children in the building had some store-bought toys, but the Pérezes had by far the greatest number. They had a bicycle (the Labradas were the only other family to have one), several large toys such as a pedal car, and, in their backyard, a swing, slide, and teeter-totter. The use of these toys by the other children was very limited since the backyard was fenced in and the neighbors only entered when invited. The Pérez children also had many small toys; Merceditas had a collection of costume dolls and also received gifts, usually small, mailable items such as paper dolls, from her godmother in the United States.

The Pérezes and the Hernándezes were the only families in the building who owned television sets, but the Hernándezes' set was broken; their children and, less frequently, the Cárdenas boys watched television at the Pérez house.

One or more of the children in each of the families except the Rojases had had a party in honor of a baptism, a birthday, or a saint's day, to which other children and their parents had been invited, again depending on the relationships among the adults. The Rojas and Labrada families were excluded from parties given by the Pérezes. These parties marked the few occasions when whole families came together, but there was not a single occasion when all five families, parents and children, participated in a common celebration.

It was unusual for all members of a single family to participate in any common activity. Sometimes children went with their mothers to the doctor, or on a trip or errand, but it was the exception for children to go out accompanied by both parents. The Pérezes went out more frequently than any of the other four families, perhaps because having a car made it easier for them. They also had the most extra cash and the fewest children to manage. They went out together to eat (usually to a pizzeria), to parties, to movies, and to visit relatives. They also went to Varadero beach on vacation trips that were arranged by Juan Carlos through a friend who worked in INIT.

The only other family to go on outings together were the Labradas, who sometimes took their children to the zoo or to Coney Island as a reward for good behavior or for achievements in school. In the other three families the fathers were rarely at home and participated in very few activities, or even conversations, with their children.

Of the twenty-three children, sixteen were of school age. Of these, one was not attending school, three were scholarship students in boarding schools outside of Havana, one went to a local high school, and eleven were enrolled in two neighborhood primary schools two blocks from their home. None of the seven pre-school children attended nursery school; all were kept at home and cared for by their mothers.

Violeta Rojas, fifteen, the one school-age child who was not enrolled in school, was not a deliberate dropout. She and her parents wanted her education to continue but were apathetic about taking the necessary steps to place her in the appropriate school. Violeta had frequently moved back and forth between Havana and Oriente and had been out of school more often than in. She was at the fourth-grade level when she stopped attending school in Oriente and was too old to enroll in a regular primary school when she settled in Havana. She might have enrolled in a neighborhood night school for adults but had not brought the required transfer papers from Oriente. Violeta was also unemployed, and she spent most of the time at home helping her mother with the chores.

The three students on scholarships were Genoveva, Florinda, and Reinaldo Hernández. Genoveva, seventeen, and Florinda, fifteen, attended the Makarenko Pedagogical Institute at Tarará, and their brother Reinaldo, eleven, was a fifth-grade student in a school not far from Havana. All three children lived at school during the week and came home by bus for the weekends.

We have no teachers' assessments of these students' work; however, in her interview Genoveva characterized her performance in school as very poor. She said she would have failed her courses if it had not been for special tutoring from the teachers. According to Genoveva, her sister Florinda was a better student, but both girls had to leave school temporarily in late 1969 because of illness. Genoveva was hospitalized for a nervous disorder and was advised by her doctor to seek psychiatric help. Florinda suffered from asthma and related circulatory problems and was also undergoing tests for kidney disease.

Lina Labrada, fourteen, had graduated from the sixth grade of the local primary school in 1969 and was attending a basic secondary school six blocks from her home. She had been an excellent student and her sixth-grade teacher had recommended that her parents apply for a scholarship for her to attend a teacher-training institute. They did so, but Lina did not receive the scholarship, even though she was among the top students in her school.

The eleven remaining children attended the two local primary schools, the Mártires de Girón, which offered pre-school classes through second grade, and the Abel Santamaría, which offered grades three through six. Both schools were in vacated private houses that had been converted to classroom use. In addition to the house, the Abel Santamaría school used an adjoining two-story garage, with one classroom on each floor. In the fall of 1969 the school was expanding into a third home on the block, to end the school's practice of doubling up teachers and grades in some classrooms.

The two schools had a total enrollment of 645 students, including about twenty foreign students from the United States, Poland, Chile, Spain, and Hungary. The director of Abel Santamaría reported an average daily attendance of from 95 to 98 percent. She said although the school worked hard to maintain good attendance, including encouraging competition between classrooms, it was not a real problem. "There are teachers who say that environment plays an important role, and here in Miramar . . . the conditions are very good. Children see their friends going to school every day so the pattern or habit has already been established in this neighborhood."

School Programs and Activities

Classes at Abel Santamaría and Mártires de Girón began at 8:30 A.M. and broke for lunch at 12:30. They resumed between 2:00 and 2:15 P.M., ending for the day at 4:30 or 4:45 P.M. Only qualified children could enroll in the school's lunch program; these students, referred to as *semi-internados*, ate a hot lunch at school and afterward participated in organized play or interest circles until the other students returned for classes.

The *semi-internado* program was begun in the Abel Santamaría/Girón schools in 1965 for the children of working mothers, originally on an

ability-to-pay basis. By 1967 it was offered free not only to children of
working mothers, but also to children from families with economic,
health, or other problems. Each school was allotted a quota of students
for inclusion in the program, but the quotas apparently were not strictly
observed. At Abel Santamaría/Girón 226 were enrolled in 1969, although the quota was 200. Recommendations for participation were
sought from the block CDR, but the school also made a study of each
student's family to determine which ones should be included. Only
rarely was a child admitted to the program through a direct request
from the parent to the school.

The food was brought in thermal containers from a central kitchen
and two employees at the school did the serving. A group of older
girl students ran the dining room: distribution of milk, clean-up, etc.
with teacher supervision.

Among the children of the five families Engracia and Gabriela Hernández were the only two who were *semi-internados;* the other children
walked to their homes for lunch. Three of the Rojas children—Amanda,
Faustina, and Hilario—had been enrolled in the program for a short
time in 1968, but after a disagreement with Amanda's teacher, Sara
Rojas decided that her children should eat at home. The director of
Abel Santamaría, quoting the girls' teachers, said that Amanda and
Faustina came to school "half asleep, as if they might be suffering
from malnutrition." Amanda's teacher continued to give her extra milk
occasionally.

The schools planned a number of extracurricular activities, many in
conjunction with the Union of Young Pioneers (UPC). Membership in
the Pioneers, an adjunct of the Union of Young Communists (UJC), is
open to all children between the ages of seven and fourteen. There was
90 percent membership at Abel Santamaría and 75 percent membership
at Mártires de Girón (difference due to ineligibility of the preschoolers).
All eleven eligible children from the five families were members.[12]

A general outline for Pioneer activities was given to the schools by the
UJC, although other in-class activities were planned by the teachers.
Because many Pioneer activities were integrated into the regular
classroom schedule, even non-members participated in them. The UJC-
recommended activities included patrol duty, studying revolutionary
heroes and martyrs, attending cultural events, going on recreational and
educational expeditions, and, especially for fifth- and sixth-graders,
doing agricultural work on weekends, usually Sundays.

These extracurricular activities were supervised by *guías,* volunteer
leaders, most of whom were Vanguard Workers and members of the
UJC or Party. The leaders for Abel Santamaría/Girón were men at-

12. Reinaldo Hernández also belonged to a Pioneer delegation at his boarding school;
Florinda and Genoveva belonged to the block CDR and the Federation and Genoveva was
also an aspirant to membership in the UJC.

tached to a nearby militia unit. They were advised "to instruct the children in revolutionary goals: to study; to learn to love people; to be healthy and strong; to defend the socialist revolution by all means, even reporting deviations by friends; and to hate imperialism."[13]

The director of Abel Santamaría said the parents of children who are not members are contacted and asked why their children have not joined. They tell the parents that the Pioneers "is an organization in line with our system of government. We convince them and later we set aside a specific day for a general initiation for all those newly won over." The school held its initiation ceremonies at the sponsoring militia unit's headquarters or in the school. The leaders took responsibility for planning the ceremonies and handing out the Pioneer kerchiefs.

"The advantage a child has [in belonging to the Pioneers]," the director said, "is that he feels part of an organization and we can follow his formation from the beginning. . . . It's the discipline of the system—the educational system—that's good for them." She also explained that when there was a tie for an award, or in the evaluation of grades, and all other things were equal, "the decision goes to the Pioneer, because he's the one who has adapted to the system of our country and is part of an organization."

In addition to Pioneer activities, the older students had the opportunity to participate in interest circles, most of which were led by volunteers who shared their special skills with the students. In 1969 the schools had interest circles in guitar, sewing and knitting, coffee and sugar cultivation, carpentry, teaching, and architectural sketching. A circle for military training was to get under way as soon as a volunteer leader could be found.

Parental Involvement in the Schools

Once each month there was a school advisory meeting when parents had the opportunity to meet with teachers and discuss school activities and hear reports on the progress of their children. From 50 to 60 percent of the Abel Santamaría/Girón parents attended these monthly meetings. The teachers also participated with the parents in a number of volunteer activities such as standing guard at the school from 6:00 P.M. to midnight. There were fifty or sixty parents who alternated with the teachers to do the patrols. Other projects for parents included putting protective covers on textbooks and monitoring school attendance. Each volunteer monitor was asked to check one classroom daily and to visit the parents of children absent from school.

None of our informants participated in volunteer parent-teacher activities, although Lala Fontanés had once volunteered to be a classroom

13. *Area Handbook for Cuba*, p. 102.

delegate. The teachers had met Sara Rojas and also Lala Fontanés and Mercedes Millán, both of whom had attended the first school advisory meeting of 1969. Teachers of the Labrada and Hernández children said the older children in the families had come once or twice to check on the progress of the younger ones, but the mothers did not respond when notes were sent home inviting them to visit the school. The director of Abel Santamaría was the only teacher to have met any of the children's fathers. Ricardo Hernández and Justa Díaz were called to the school in 1968 to discuss their daughter Gabriela's truancy problems.

Some of the parents showed interest in their children's education by supervising homework. However, all the children except Merceditas Pérez have or will have surpassed their parents' educational level when they complete the first six grades. Sara and Eduardo Rojas were barely literate, but a few of the other parents had taken advantage of adult-education programs; Ricardo Hernández had attended officer-training school for several years, and Armando Cárdenas irregularly attended both night classes and Party schools. The Party required its members to finish at least the sixth-grade level.

The Cárdenas boys and Merceditas Pérez had time set aside in late afternoon or early evening for homework, and in the case of Merceditas, close attention was paid to her work. When her grades fell, Merceditas's parents threatened sanctions, such as loss of vacation trips. In the Labrada family, the older children's work was supervised by the parents or by Leticia's brother. The younger children were assisted in their work by their older sisters. The Rojas children did their homework independently of one another and without parental assistance. The three Hernández children who boarded at school did not have the opportunity for daily parental involvement in their school work, but Genoveva and Florinda apparently consulted with their father on occasion. According to Genoveva, the children in her family were under great pressure to perform well in school and to pursue career studies. This was due, in part, to the fact that the three eldest children were on full scholarships, and also because it was considered one's revolutionary and patriotic duty to pursue an education to the highest level his or her abilities allowed.

Teacher Evaluations of the Children

Evaluations of the children's progress in school, obtained from their teachers, are included here with some reluctance since we have so little material from the children themselves or other information about them. We present the evaluations as nothing more or less than the teachers' opinions of the children as students.[14]

14. The majority of the teachers at the two schools were normal school graduates, several had studied specialized subjects at the university level, and one was a student from

According to their teachers, the most outstanding students among the eleven children were Merceditas Pérez and the three Labrada children. Merceditas, ten, was in the fifth grade and was characterized by her teacher as studious and well-organized, very sociable with many friends, but careless about her appearance. In the fourth grade Merceditas had been a *vanguardista,* that is, among the first in her class.

Bárbara Labrada, twelve, received a glowing evaluation from her sixth-grade teacher: "a wonderful girl, magnificent conduct, very organized for everything, one of the best in the classroom . . . a superior student." Both Bárbara and her sister Andrea, ten, were on the school's honors list.[15] Andrea had been at the top of her class for two years and was one of the few children in her third-grade class to have grades consistently above 9. She was "an interested student, had good handwriting, read well, was quiet . . . a magnificent child."

Tomás, seven, was also an excellent student according to his second-grade teacher: "Tomás is a very good child, very happy, lovable, learns well, clean, very intelligent, one of the first in mathematics, very sweet, gets along with everyone, well-disciplined and well-behaved."

The remaining seven primary-school children received poorer evaluations from their teachers, for a variety of reasons. Armandito Cárdenas, eight, was in the second grade after having repeated the first. He wrote well, according to his teacher, but could only read by syllables. His behavior was considered "normal" but his school work very poor. His brother Juan Pablo, seven, was also in the second grade and was described as "well-behaved" and as "a slow learner who is making normal progress."

The Rojas children were from one to four years behind their grade levels. Hilario, at thirteen, was only in the third grade; his sister Amanda, nine, was repeating second grade; and Faustina, seven, was in first grade. Hilario's teacher said he behaved well and played normally, although he was somewhat introverted. She believed this shyness was related to a speech defect caused by an orthodontic problem (later corrected). He did his work well, she said, was punctual, and seemed to be interested in studying. Amanda was reported to be doing well, and Faustina's teacher described her as an average student who got along well with others. She believed Faustina's untidiness and variations in behavior were related to her "family situation" and her periodic preoccupation with it. Some days Faustina came to school, she said, as if "floating on a cloud," and then it was necessary to shout to get a response from her.

---

the third year of basic secondary school. None belonged to the Communist Youth or to the Party. The teacher-student ratio was about 1:25.

15. To qualify for the honors list a student was required to have good attendance, be punctual, be neatly dressed in uniform, and, most important, to have notebooks correctly completed and have made good grades (scoring over 9 points on exams).

Included among the poorer group of students were Gabriela Hernández and her sister Engracia, both in the fifth grade although in different
classrooms. Gabriela, fourteen, was described as a mediocre student with
a poor attitude toward her studies. She had an absentee problem, sometimes because her mother kept her home to care for the younger children, and sometimes because she played truant, once taking her sister
with her to the beach. Gabriela had also talked back to one of her
teachers, and as a result was transferred to a different classroom. She got
along well with other students, but her teacher considered her young for
her age, lacking in maturity and responsibility. To help her overcome
these problems, she had been assigned extra responsibilities, including
supervision of the classroom library and assisting in the lunchroom.

Engracia's teacher also considered her immature for her age, citing as
evidence her "need to play, especially with dolls." She was also reported
to be "disorganized and restless, but not a conduct problem." She got
along well with others, but did not like to study and had "poor manners."

Activities at Home

In addition to school and homework, some of the children had regularly assigned household chores. In all families the older children assumed some responsibility for the supervision of the younger children,
especially at play. Merceditas Pérez had the rather large responsibility,
for a girl of ten, of doing the family's marketing. Her mother gave her a
shopping list, but Merceditas used her own judgment in making many of
the purchases. She had no other regularly assigned household chores,
although she helped with small cleaning jobs from time to time.

Violeta Rojas helped her mother with daily household chores, but
these were not assigned to her in any systematic way. She and Hilario
helped care for the younger children, ran errands, and helped with the
shopping, especially for items that required standing in line. Hilario had
the additional responsibility of carrying dinner to his stepfather at his
work center, which was thirty-five minutes away by bus.

Lina and Bárbara Labrada were alternately assigned housecleaning
and babysitting responsibilities. The three eldest girls were in charge of
washing the clothes of the younger children, and Tomás, the next to
youngest, had as his only responsibility washing the dishes.

The two eldest Hernández girls were away during the week, but on
weekends they helped with the younger children and with housework.

Children's Interviews

In 1969-70 the eldest child of each family, with the exception of
eight-year-old Armandito Cárdenas, was interviewed; these four were

Merceditas Pérez Millán, Violeta Rojas Tabares, Lina Labrada Manzanares, and Genoveva Hernández Díaz. All but Lina's interview are presented in this section. Lina was very shy and looked to the interviewer for
cues, responding to questions with a simple yes, no, or don't know, or by
restating the question in a declaratory sentence. Her interview therefore
was of insufficient value to be included. Florinda, the second eldest of
the Hernández children, was also interviewed, but the tape and tran-
script have been lost.

In the following three brief interviews, the influence of parents, home,
and family on the socialization of the child is very evident. Indeed, if all
names and identifying references were removed from their interviews,
the children could be easily recognized by their resemblance to their
parents. Merceditas, for example, reflecting the values of her middle-
class parents, wanted to marry an architect or doctor and live in a "simple house" in Havana or El Vedado. "I would be happy," she said, "with
a bath, two bedrooms, a dining room, living room, and kitchen."
Genoveva, whose father had fought in the Sierra and whose mother had
collaborated with the Twenty-sixth of July underground, unequivocally
admired her parents' sacrifices; their courage during the Batista era
bound her to them and helped her accept their views and authority.
Following in their path she was an ardent revolutionary and a candidate
for membership in the Communist Youth.

Violeta was, like her mother, torn between staying in Havana or returning to relatives in rural Oriente. Her mother and stepfather, up-
rooted by a Revolution they sympathized with but did not understand,
were unable to integrate into either urban or revolutionary life. An
unemployed school dropout, Violeta spent most of the time with her
family, where she was almost out of reach of peer pressures and the
political socialization process. She had acquired some of the rhetoric of
aspiration, but had little understanding of what it meant; hence she
spoke in the same breath of wanting to become either a seamstress or a
doctor. Given her parents' inability to resolve the problem of her schooling, and not knowing where to turn for outside help, Violeta remained
at home in a kind of limbo, without much sense of direction. As might be
expected, she showed less generational change than the other two girls.

Although there were pronounced similarities in the attitudes of Merceditas and Genoveva and their parents, there were also some significant
differences between them. Merceditas may have shared her parents'
material values, but by attending school she was more in touch with the
mainstream of thinking in Cuba, and it was against these standards that
her performance in school and her worth as a person were judged by her
teachers and peers. She evidently had some appreciation of the discrep-
ancy between her mother's behavior and what was expected of an integrated woman. Her mother not only chose not to take a job, despite her

high school education, but also depended upon her daughter in small ways to help run the household. Perhaps because of Merceditas's greater acceptance of the Revolution and her responsibilities at home, she felt at times superior to her mother. Interviewers noted that in conversations between the two, Merceditas frequently "talked down" to her mother.

Genoveva was eager to please her parents and to serve the Revolution, but she tended to break down under pressure. Wanting to find a slower pace more suited to her personality and abilities, she reacted negatively to her parents' demands upon her to finish school. Genoveva was more flexible than were her parents in her attitudes on sex roles and on the right to freedom of personal expression—in dress and music, for instance. She was, however, quite rigid in her political conceptualizations and was impatient with her mother's lack of familiarity with the new dogma. To Genoveva the textbook distinctions between a communist and a socialist, for example, were all-important, while to her mother a communist or socialist was simply anyone who supported the Revolution and opposed poverty and injustice. In a comment typical of generation-gap frustration, Genoveva's mother said that her daughter may have had a lot of "book-learning" but that she still didn't know a thing.

Merceditas Pérez Millán, Age Ten

I worry a lot about myself because I'm very fat. I want to be a thin girl. I have a friend Gladys who is thin and wants to be fat. That's the way it is in Cuba.

I take after my father's family, especially my father's mother. I'm practically identical to her. She's fat and walks with her feet pointing out, the same as me. They keep giving me orthopedic shoes because I walk knock-kneed. It's natural for me to walk with my feet pointing out and that hasn't changed with orthopedic shoes. But if I want to make an effort, I can walk straight.

My personality is just like my grandmother's, too. She's very nervous and gets upset easily, and she has a bad temper just like mine. She's always saying that I'm her all over again. *Papá* is also that way, very quick-tempered.

My mother says I have many faults. When I'm being difficult, she calls me Amalita. For instance, sometimes she says to me, "Merceditas, go to the Minimax!" But if I don't want to go, she'll yell "Amalita!" She was mad at me just today because I was going to the Minimax and only wanted to get meat and crackers. She made a list with eggs and bread and other things, but I began to protest because I don't like to carry so much. And that caused a mess. She said to me, "Okay, I'll go, but I don't want to see you anymore!" So I turned on the television and watched a movie.

I think that sometimes I behave badly and other times about average, but really, really good, no. Like when I take a bath, I leave my things all over the place. I'm very lazy and don't like to pick up after myself. *Mamá* doesn't like that, and says a thousand things to me.

I don't like to be punished; I always start to cry. Neither *mamá* nor *papá* makes me do anything like kneeling, but *mamá* hits me with her hand sometimes. That doesn't hurt, but when she picks up something like her apron and hits me, that sure hurts. Sometimes my father punishes me, but he never spanks me. He'll sit me down on the terrace and I have to stay there until *mamá* calls me.

I really don't know what my mother thinks of me. She can't have a really good opinion because at times she gets so mad at me. Well . . . she could think *some* good. The other day she went to the parent-teachers meeting and they told her I was behaving well. *Papá* shares the same opinion as *mamá*. My grandparents think highly of me, but all grandparents think well of a grandchild.

I was six years old when my brother was born. I remember the day my mother went to the hospital—a Saturday at 7:00 in the morning. I felt good when my brother was born, even though I wanted a girl more. I wanted to hold him, but *mamá* didn't let me because he was like a little ant. And did he take milk! Like a glutton, up to half a bottle. If they didn't give him more, he'd cry and cry. Now he hardly eats.

While the baby was still small, the cyclone came.[16] Then the gas was off in my house and there was no water or lights either. That was hellish! We stayed at my grandmother's house from October to July and I finished second grade while I was there. Afterward, on July 25, 1967, to be exact, we went to Varadero for a while.

I've been told that I was a little devil, but that my brother is worse. In my whole life I broke one little knicknack of my mother's and nothing more, and it was an accident. My brother has broken a lot of things. He broke a crystal cat, a music box that played a song about Moscow, and other things. I get very upset when Eloyitos breaks something of mine. I don't like him even to touch my things because I'm afraid he'll break them.

Eloy is very fresh and thinks he's a professor already. He thinks he's the one who rules in this house. The other day I left some little notebooks on the table, and he came and took them and scribbled all over them. My friend Teresa said to me, "Let's go outside and get away from him."

Eloy is three years old, and even though I'm older, my father always takes Eloy with him. For example, when *papá* goes out and can take only one of us, he'll take Eloy instead of me, because he's a boy. As for *mamá*, it's always Eloy, because he's the smallest. That's why they have more things for him.

Before Eloy was born, I used to go all over and spend the whole day with *papá*. We'd go out to a friend's house and I'd play with the children and have fun while *papá* was having a conversation. Now I see *papá* in the morning, if he comes for lunch, and sometimes when he comes home at night. At times he'll ask me about different things, and other times he just asks me what I saw on television.

Our house has four rooms aside from the living room, dining room, and kitchen. One is for our toys, another is empty, another had an

16. Hurricane Inés, September, 1966.

air-conditioner in it until it broke, and the fourth is our bedroom. There's a big bed and two small ones—one for me and one for Eloy. The four of us used to sleep there. But *papá* has fixed the air-conditioner and now they sleep in their own room and Eloy and I in ours.

To get to school on time I have to get up about 7:00 or 7:15. For breakfast I have coffee with lots of milk, and sometimes I have bread too, if I want. After breakfast I go right to school.

I always wear a uniform to school. I have four blouses and four skirts, counting the new uniform. They give us one skirt and one blouse every year; we used to get two, but now it's one. I don't like my uniform this year because it's heavy gabardine and makes me perspire. I wear my blouses for two days, but I can't stand to wear them for a third day. Last year it was better because it was a very light linen.

This year my subjects in school are biology, language, geography, history, and mathematics. My favorite subject is animal biology. I've had bad teachers in other years, but this year I have a good teacher. She explains the subjects well and she's been our teacher all year. In fourth grade we were changing teachers all the time—we had fourteen or fifteen in that one year. They'd come and go because the classroom was so bad they just couldn't bear the kids. The students haven't changed a bit—they lack respect and are badly brought up. They can't be quiet for half a second.

I go home for lunch at 12:30. I almost always eat beefsteak with plantain or something else. Sometimes they send food from my grandma's house when she has things left over.

I did farm work in the third grade during the Victory Week celebrating Girón.[17] One morning we went to the park on 24th Street and they gave us little black nylon bags which we filled with dirt. I filled thirty-two. These bags were distributed all over Havana and little coffee plants were put in them. After the plants began to grow, they were taken from the bags and planted in the ground.

Besides going to the Minimax, I don't have any other duties around the house. Sometimes I do the wash for my mother if she has to go out in a hurry, or sometimes I'll clean the terrace. But I don't do any cleaning in the apartment.

I like to go to the Minimax just for the walk, but I have an even better time when I go with the girl from upstairs, Engracia Hernández. She's very good and helps me a lot. I don't like to go alone because there used to be a time—and it might still be going on—when some people would kidnap children. There was a little Russian girl living here in Miramar who left school with some people who said her father had sent them for her, and they killed her. I don't know what those people are called, but

17. Children's Victory Week is part of the national celebration of Cuba's victory at Playa Girón (Bay of Pigs), April 17-19, 1961.

they cut up children and big people too, for their flesh, then they throw the remains in the bushes.

There also was a very fresh man with a moustache who was hanging around here. Some female relative of Normita's—Normita lives on the corner, is very good, and sometimes gives my brother injections when he's sick—well, some female relative of hers was sitting on a fence in front of her house and this man said to her, "Looky what you have underneath here," and he lifted her dress. Then that bold fellow started running. He sure was daring. Now there are motorcycle patrols and police cars out in the streets and they seem to know who the people are who commit those crimes.

I spend most of my vacation playing, usually with Engracia. When I'm at my grandma's house, I play with my friend Gladys. This year we went to Varadero twice, once for a day and the other time we spent a whole week. Varadero has a very pretty beach. We went bathing and ate lunch in a restaurant. We slept in one of those guest houses where there's a room for every person. There are other guest houses with maybe four dormitory rooms, each large enough for ten people. Some people have their very own houses in Varadero or another beach resort.

In this building I get along with Justa's children, Engracia and Gabriela, and we play together. Gabriela is older—she's fourteen—but she's behind in school. She's in the fifth grade but she should be in the second or third year of basic secondary school. Two of their sisters, one fifteen and one seventeen, are already studying to be teachers.

Gabriela is tall and thin and has short hair and is as difficult as I am. She's a liar and invents all sorts of things to tell you. I don't like to go to the Minimax with her because she gets involved in a lot of messes.

Sometimes Engracia and I play house and sometimes we play dolls, but we share all our little things. We don't like for one of us to have more than the other because when we do we start saying twenty thousand things to each other.

Leticia has two girls who are educated and well brought up even though they're colored. They're very good. Andrea is the one who plays with me sometimes. She has a lot of little pots and pans and other things we play with.

I don't play much with Lala's children since they're all boys. I don't play with Sara's daughters even though I know them. I don't know why *mamá* doesn't let me play with them, but I think it's because they sometimes play at things they shouldn't, like sweethearts' quarrels and all that. There are also two girls in my classroom who are involved in these things with the scholarship boys. One of Sara's daughters is eleven years old and in the sixth grade because she repeated the third. The other girl says she's eleven, but one day she brought her birth certificate to school, and according to that she's fourteen. You learn a lot of this type of thing going on and that's why *mamá* doesn't like me to play with them.

My other little girl friend that I play with is Felicidad, Sonia's granddaughter. She's very good.

My favorite toys are dolls and I like to have a lot of clothes for them. I have a special shelf in my room with twelve dolls, but they're just for decoration. I don't play with them. Before 1966 my favorite doll, which is now my second favorite, was a very delicate bride doll. If you drop her, she'll break. She's pretty but her dress is stained and *mamá* hasn't bothered to wash it because she has a lot of things to do. My favorite doll now is one they introduced in 1966 called "the Blonde from Pello" because she has white hair and there's this singer of Mozambique music who also has white hair. I played with her for a while but then *mamá* said no, that I should put her on the shelf too, so I did. The other doll I like is a Spanish one they named Marina. They don't feature certain dolls anymore like they used to do.

Once we went out on the day to buy toys, and by the time we got to the store we couldn't get a turn. There were no more toys. This year my father and I went shopping with a friend of ours who's an administrator of a store. She helped us look for pretty things in the store. They bought me a doll called Lilita, and a cat with a parasol that was very cute, and a little bird, but they all broke except the doll. Eloyitos got a beautiful battery-run machine gun—the last one they had—a ball, and a circus truck with three little elephants. He also got an erector set and we played a lot with it. Anyhow, he destroyed the whole thing. He always destroys his toys. He doesn't take care of anything. He has a bicycle that they gave him on Three Kings' Day. It was mine but a friend gave *papá* some bicycle parts and my parents fixed it up for him, and now it's always broken. They sent the pedals to be soldered but they broke again.

Toys were always bought in December and given to children on January 6, the Day of the Three Kings. But not now. I don't know if the Kings will go on existing. It's January and it's still 1969. This year has eighteen months because Comandante Fidel Castro has made it that way. I don't know why exactly. When he gave his speech on January 2, 1969, which was the tenth anniversary of the triumph of the Revolution, he declared the change in the year. Anyway, I didn't hear the explanation. Now Christmas isn't in December, it's in July. The Christmas almond nougat is to be given out in July. But instead of being called 1970, it will still be 1969.

I like to go to movies. I saw *New in This Plaza* four times. I go with my parents or with a girl friend, or sometimes my class at school goes. Once I saw a movie called *Marked Fingers*. The picture wasn't true life; it was about a crazy man's imagination. The man wasn't crazy to begin with, but he became crazy. His left hand was cut off and his right hand couldn't move. He kept the left hand in a strongbox, like the kind they keep money in. Then he saw the hand playing the piano and walking. When I left the movie I didn't understand it, but later my *papá* explained it.

Then he went out for guard duty and I don't know how long he was gone, but when he came back he began to tease me. He turned off the light and came pulling me and touching me and he made me very upset until finally they took me to their bed, and I slept with them that night.

My favorite television programs are "Revolutionary Heroes," "The Great Admiral," which is all about Christopher Columbus, and the children's programs. I also like "Household Hints" on Channel 40, and "Horizons."

The last party we had at our house was the wedding of some friends of ours, Matilde and Leocadio, and that was a terrible uproar. I wasn't at the party; my friends and I were in another room. The bride had taken off her tiara and left it on the bed and we were all putting it on and grabbing the purses lying there. The record player in the other room was loud so we heard the music and were dancing. We were all girls and we had a lot of fun.

We don't celebrate birthdays every year. They celebrated my second and fifth birthdays with big fiestas but my seventh and ninth birthdays were just small parties. I remember my second birthday celebration. They bought me a piñata, a pin-the-tail-on-the-donkey set, candy, cake, beer, and so on. The guests were *papá*'s friends, our relatives, *mamá*'s friends, and people from the neighborhood. Lala's children weren't born yet. They celebrated Eloy's third birthday but that was another big uproar.

I like living in Havana but there are a lot of scholarship students here and I don't like that, because if you're walking along and whether you're fat, skinny, or whatever, they begin to call names and say bad words and twenty thousand things. If you answer them, they only come back with forty thousand things. And all the scholarship students have lice. One of the girls, Miranda, is full of lice. I don't want to be a scholarship student—never!—because I like to see my parents often and because they have everything hygienic, and the classmates I would have there wouldn't be clean. Even at vacation time they don't let scholarship students go home. I know a girl who's a scholarship student. One day during vacation we went to see a woman in an office around here, I don't remember the name of it, but it's where they control the whole zone. The student asked for a pass and they wouldn't give it to her. They told her that the passes were only for farm work.

I don't have a boyfriend, but when I'm bigger I want to marry. My husband would have to be a hardworking man, because if he's lazy that would be unthinkable. I like architects, but if he's not an architect he'll be a doctor. I'd like to live in downtown Havana or in Vedado, not in a big house but in a simple one. I'd be happy with a bath, two bedrooms, a living room, a dining room, and a kitchen.

I want to be a doctor ... well, that's what my parents want and all my relatives. My mother finished high school, but then she married my father so she didn't study for a career. That's why she wants me to study and to learn to drive. She really hopes I'll be a pediatrician when I'm grown up. Eloyitos is very sickly and *mamá* wants me to attend to his children when we're both grownups. She wants her grandchildren to have a doctor who would tell them the truth. There are doctors who deceive in order not to upset people. I'd like to be a doctor, and I'm almost always the doctor when I play with Engracia, but I don't like to study. If it were up to me, I'd be playing the whole day long.

Violeta Rojas Tabares, Age Fifteen

There's nobody in my family that I want to be like. I don't mean they're bad—they're all good, but I simply don't want to be like them. I don't want to be like anybody I know. Not like my friends either. I want to be like me.

I wouldn't want to resemble my father. Grandma told me about him, and *mamá,* too, often told us how bad he was. He's a criminal and has a bad temper. He was haughty—that's what they call someone who throws his weight around and says bad words and all that. *Papá* was a *jabao;* he was light-skinned, but instead of hair he had wool. People say my brother Gerardo looks like him. But I don't know whether that's true because I don't remember what *papá* looked like.

At first *papá* worked weeding cane fields, and he bought us whatever we needed. But later he said he wouldn't work even if someone tried to drive him to it with a stick. *Mamá* says he wanted her father's farm for himself—he went in as a hanger-on and wanted to come out as the master. They sold coffee and *papá* wanted all the money for himself. Well, it couldn't be, that's all.

Mamá had no trouble feeding us well. She had lots of farm animals and my grandparents had lots of vegetables growing on their farm. And *mamá* was free to take whatever she needed. *Papá* would eat at his parents' house. He had no right to eat at home when he didn't work, so we didn't save any food for him.

Papá mistreated *mamá.* He called her something that nobody should ever call a woman: a whore. He'd provoke Grandma on purpose—shouting insults at her which had nothing to do with the case. *Papá* treated all women that way. He would have killed every woman in the world if he'd had his way. He told *mamá* and Grandma right to their faces that someday he was going to cut their heads off. But *papá* never beat *mamá* because Grandpa told him that if he ever lifted a hand against her, he'd land in jail. I guess that scared *papá* plenty because he never hit her. Grandpa and my uncle say that if *mamá* hadn't left him when she did, they'd probably be in jail now for having killed him.

Papá was the kind of father who was always beating his children, just for the heck of it. *Mamá* says that if she hadn't left him in time, that man would have ended up killing all of us kids—that's how bad he was. Once when Concha was washing dishes in the river two saucers drifted away in the current. When *papá* found out he whipped her with a strap so hard he left raw places on her flesh and they turned into sores. He was always hitting her over the head. She still isn't quite right in the head. Another time *papá* hit Gerardo on the head with a heavy steel file, the kind that's used to sharpen machetes, and cut his scalp with the blow.

Mamá's trouble turned her bitter. She was so unhappy she got as skinny as my little finger. What was *mamá* to do with such a man? I'm telling you, the best thing she could have done was to leave him.

Really, *mamá* didn't leave *papá*, *papá* left *mamá*. I remember the day he walked out on us and never came back. We were eating our supper at the time. *Mamá* and *papá* had a terrible quarrel that day. It all started because of my sister Concha. She was playing with an empty bottle and she said to *mamá*, "Here, *mami*, drink some rum."

"Go give the rum to your father," *mamá* answered, because *papá* drank a lot of rum. Just because of that he got mad and he and *mamá* quarreled about it. That very night *papá* and *mamá* broke up. She simply told him she'd taken as much as she could take from him and she couldn't stand it anymore. After *papá* left, *mamá* took us to Grandma's. When he came back to fetch us kids, Grandma told him, "No matter how often you come around trying to get these children, I won't let you have them. They're staying here with me."

After *papá* left us, he went to Marcané and married a woman who already had five children. Estela, my youngest sister, was only five months old then. She's twelve now and in all those years he's never come back to see us.

I don't know many of *papá*'s relatives, only his brother Delfin, and Ernesto, who's either his brother or his uncle. Both of them treat us well. They don't have my father's evil instincts. I see them whenever I go to Oriente because they live near Grandma. I ask for their blessing and they don't say anything to me about my father. *Papá* must know about me because my uncle sees him often and tells him about us. But he doesn't want to have anything to do with us. Not long ago my cousin saw *papá* and asked him if he ever went to see his children and *papá* punched him. I guess that after not even trying to see us for so many years, maybe he's ashamed to ask about us.

When *mamá* moved to Havana, we stayed with Grandma and Grandpa. They wanted me to stay with them because they think I'm a very good girl. They really love me, a lot more than *mamá* does.

Whenever I stay with Grandma she caresses me and gives me things. When I grow up I'd like to be like my grandmother. She isn't a bit like *mamá*. She never hits us, but she's very strict and doesn't like to play with children or anything. I don't much like to play with kids either.

My grandparents' youngest daughter, Amanda Luz, lives with them. She's only thirteen and they never spank her or anything. She sure leads a happy life! Also, my youngest sister, Estela, lives with them. She's twelve years old but Grandpa picks her up and carries her around in his arms like a baby. Both he and Grandma love her.

That grandmother of mine was a real mischief-maker when she was a kid. We all die laughing when she tells us stories about her childhood. She still likes to have her little jokes. Me too, especially when I'm out in the country.

Everyone in my family likes to play practical jokes. Uncle Virgilio, for instance, would watch to see where we put our rag dolls; then, when we weren't looking, he'd take them out, put nooses around their necks, and string them up in a tree, playing he was hanging them. Every time he hanged our dolls, we cried our hearts out.

One day Aunt Lupe really played a mean trick on me. She shitted on an old plate I'd been playing with, then covered it up with a piece of paper. *Ay, mi madre*—did I ever get mad when I lifted up the paper! What a loathing I have for that stuff! I started to vomit and did she ever laugh! Oh, the tricks those relatives of mine play on people! They were mischievous kids, and now that they're old they're just as mischievous.

I love to play practical jokes on Grandpa. Sometimes I'll pull him by the legs until I make him fall out of bed, and all he does is laugh. He never punishes me for it. When I tease Grandpa, Uncle Virgilio says to him, "You spoil those kids to death, *papá*. They sure will miss you when you're dead!"

I play practical jokes on *mamá*, too. I grab her from behind, start shaking her, turn her around, and do all sorts of things. She always pushes me away and tells me to quit bothering her. But she can't help laughing and it doesn't make her mad.

I started school when I was five years old. I don't remember much about it except that I didn't want to go because I had no shoes. *Mamá* made me go anyhow, and I'd cry all the way there because I was ashamed of my bare feet, even though a lot of the other kids went barefoot. Later on, the revolutionary government called the parents to a meeting in the schoolhouse and decided to give shoes to all the children. They gave us shoes all right, but such big ones! I tried to wear them but they blistered my feet. Finally they took the shoes over to the CDR and exchanged them for a smaller pair, so then I wore shoes to school.

I had lots of bad teachers when I was little. My first-grade teacher was really mean. She slapped us plenty and pulled our ears, too. If you didn't know the answers, she'd hit you. She didn't have any pets; she hit everybody. One day she hit me over the head with a stick because I'd added some numbers wrong. I failed the first grade and had to repeat it. It was the teacher's fault, *mamá* says, because the teachers out in the country are absent a lot.

I think parents and teachers are always right. Every child has two mothers: his real mother, who's the main one, and his teacher. What's most important for children and young people is to obey them. Lots of parents don't like to have the teacher spank their children, but I think they should when we're naughty. It's for the kids' own good, see, because nobody loves a nasty child.

Of all the teachers I've ever had, the one I liked best was Ferro, my second-grade teacher. She was very strict; she really made the kids respect her, and she explained things well in class. I was awfully fond of her because she seemed to like me a lot. Ferro didn't have any children of her own so she'd always take one of the little kids from school home with her. I spent a heap of time at her house. She wanted me to stay with her for keeps but *mamá* said no.

My Uncle Pancho brought me here to Havana when I was eleven or twelve. When I first came I got lost in that big apartment. I slept in the same room with my aunt and uncle but I had a cot all to myself. Once I went into a closet in my room and locked the door and then I didn't know how to get out. I called for help and Nardo came and opened the door for me. Another time I got lost at night when I stooped down looking for a way out of the bedroom and crawled under the bed by mistake. I started to cry and yell that I was scared until Nardo came and turned on the light. I can't help laughing now, but at the time I was scared to death.

Leticia is the most helpful of our neighbors in Havana. Whenever we need something she lets us have it. Lala is nice too. She's done favors for us and we've done favors for her. Hilario shines her children's shoes and her husband Armando's, too. I've fetched things for her from the Minimax and helped her wash the dishes.

I've only done one favor for Justa: to get some spaghetti from the Minimax for her. *Mamá* and Justa were still friends then. I wasn't in Havana when they quarreled, so I'm not sure what it was about. It had something to do with Gabriela and Concha. Gabriela said something or other to Concha and Concha called her a "hunk of dried-out codfish." Then Justa called *mamá,* and I don't know what they said but when I came back from Oriente they weren't speaking to each other. As long as they were friends, Justa was real nice. I don't have any complaints against her. I was real fond of her. She treats me the same as she always did and so do her daughters.

I don't think we've ever asked anything of Mercedes, except once *mamá* asked her to start the motor of the water pump because we didn't have any water in our place. I myself have never been in Mercedes's house. Well, I did go once in a while when the girls called me to study there at night. Mercedes is very pleasant. I have no complaint against her. She's never said anything disagreeable to me or to *mamá* and neither has Juan Carlos. They're good neighbors because they don't interfere with anybody.

Most of the time I'd rather live in Havana, where one can go to the movies and watch TV. All I ever did in the country was help my grandma wash dishes and sweep the house and yard. For fun we'd climb a mango tree and throw down the fruit. But in Havana we never go out anywhere at night. *Mamá* won't let us. There are bad men, called *coquís*, who grab women and rough them up. I've heard that they're all young kids, about fifteen to eighteen years old. They do a lot of mischief. Whenever the *coquís* see a girl out in the street, they try to . . . you know. I've never seen any of the *coquís*, except the guys who came over to the students' residence across the street. I know about them though, because people tell *mamá* the things they've done and *mamá* tells me to scare me so I won't go out at night. If they caught me, I think they'd kill me.

The last time I visited Oriente, I went to get Amanda's, Faustina's, and Estela's school registration papers, and *mamá* went to get Hilario's. I didn't get my papers because we didn't have the number and they had to hunt through the files for it. *Mamá* didn't want to waste any more time, but if she'd waited a little longer we could have gotten them all. There used to be a charge but now they're free. All you have to do is go and get them. We're still missing three—Gerardo's, Concha's, and mine. When I go back I'm going to get them.

Getting all those kids ready to go somewhere is the most impossible task there is. For the trip back to Havana Grandma packed food for us. They butchered a goat and she also made rice with black beans and boiled some yucca. With all that, the bag *mamá* had to carry was full.

The railway station is a really long walk from my grandparents'. There is transportation, but if we'd waited for it, we'd have missed the train. The train arrived at midnight, and when we finally got on we didn't have a place to sit. It was absolutely packed all the way to Havana. We were suffocating from the heat and could hardly bear it because we didn't have any water. The bag with the water bottle in it fell on the floor and broke. There were also some clothes and diapers in the bag and I lost my blouse. It was a disaster.

I finally got a seat in Ciago and *mamá* gave me Elsa to hold. I hadn't slept for one whole day and night and I finally fell asleep just as we arrived in Havana. *Mamá* woke me up, pulling me by the hair, asking me where in the world Elsa was. She was scared to death because she thought Elsa had fallen out the window, but I found her sprawled out under the seat, crying, poor thing. When we arrived it was so crowded at the terminal we had to push and shove our way through the crowd to catch a bus. I don't know if I'll ever be able to sit or stand again. It's a terrible ride. You really need courage to travel like that.

I'm not important in my family and I don't want to be, either. I know I'm not because *mamá* says so. She's nicer to the little ones than she is to me. I think she prefers the other kids to me, imagine that! It makes me so sad I cry every time I think of it.

I love *mamá* a lot—as much as her own mother loves her, that's how much. I'm happy to be with her. I've seen kids who forget their mother when they're away from her, but I can't be like them. I was staying with an uncle of mine in Managua and *mamá* was here in Havana and I couldn't bear to be away from her. I couldn't even eat, that's how much I missed her. I'd get so unhappy I'd burst into tears all of a sudden. They had to bring me back here right away.

I'm good to *mamá* and I'm affectionate with her, but she never caresses me or anything. She caresses Amanda, Hilario, and Faustina though. She used to caress my eldest sister all the time, but not me. She always gives my sister whatever she asks for, but she never gives me what I ask for. I think she doesn't love me.

Mamá says she wants me to be happy, but I've never seen her do anything to make me happy. Maybe she does, I don't know. . . . She does take a lot of interest in me. She makes me clothes, and if they have to be altered she does it. And when I don't have any shoes she buys me some. She worries about me. She doesn't want me to go out alone or anything like that. She takes care of me like a good mother should. I think she's very right in that, because a mother who doesn't take care of her daughter isn't a good mother.

I guess I don't behave any better than my brothers and sisters, but *mamá* is always telling me that I'm the worst of all. If she says so it must be true, but I don't know why because I don't misbehave. I take the kids out and everything. They're twenty times worse than I am. They really mortify *mamá*.

I don't give an awful lot of thought to whether or not I've done something bad. What would be the point? I know I don't do anything terribly bad. It's easy to be good because then everybody loves you. If you're bad they hate you. *Mamá* says it's important to be good and also to act in such a way that other people know you're good. She says that what people think about you is important because everybody loves a good girl.

Of course if you ask *mamá*, she'll tell you that I'm bad and lazy and everything. It isn't true that I'm lazy. When *mamá* goes out I make the beds and do everything else that has to be done, including the ironing.

Mamá keeps saying I never do anything. She'd like me to do the housework all by myself. Well, why should I? I don't have a husband to work for. It's her duty to do the housework, not mine. When she asks me to do those things, right away I think she's trying to shuffle off her obligations on me.

The garage is always a mess. But how can it be kept nice when as soon as someone straightens the place up, someone else comes in and undoes all the work? For instance, as soon as someone finishes washing the dishes the kids start using them and get everything dirty just for the heck of it. I get tired of cleaning up only to have those kids undo all my work. Now I don't bother to straighten up—one gets tired, you know.

When I'm bad, *mamá* spanks me with a shoe or a belt. She also punishes me by not letting me go anywhere or by taking something away from me. Sometimes she punishes me just for the heck of it if I say something or pull Faustina's hair. I don't think it's fair that they should spank me. They never spank Faustina. And if I hit Faustina, it makes *mamá* mad at me even though I only hit her when she deserves it. *Mamá* herself has told me that younger children should respect their elder brothers and sisters and that when they're naughty I should spank them.

Mamá sure hits hard, hard enough to leave bruises afterward. Once she hit me so hard it left a permanent scar. We were living out in the country at the time. Hilario and I were carrying water from the river when all of a sudden he stopped in his tracks and wouldn't budge. That made me so mad I pushed him into the river, pail and all. Naturally he yelled his head off. When *mamá* heard him crying, she rushed down to see what was the matter. I took to my heels but she ran after me. The faster I went, the harder she ran. She looked furious and kept yelling that when she caught me she'd make me pay for what I'd done. She sure did, too! She whaled the daylights out of me with her belt until Grandma pulled me out of her hands. I was about seven then but I still remember it. It was so funny, the way I ran and jumped over the brook with *mamá* jumping after me. Once in a while I remind *mamá* of it and we both die laughing.

Mamá got real mad at me just recently. It started when I began to make up the bed because it was time to go to sleep, and Faustina and Amanda started playing on the bed. Well, I hit Amanda. Then *mamá* hit me over the ear with a shoe and scolded me. She said I wasn't worth a shit, I was just a degenerate and the only thing I knew how to do was to hit the kids. I don't feel anything when she calls me names. But I kept my mouth shut, because if I talk back she hits me. That night I couldn't sleep because my ear still hurt. Grandma says *mamá* shouldn't hit us on the ears, especially me because I've suffered from earaches ever since I was little.

When *mamá* hits me, I cry and cry. She doesn't tell me to shut up or anything, she simply lets me cry. I think a lot of things while I'm crying. I say to myself that one of these days she's going to beat me to death. But I don't tell her that. When I get real mad, I feel like hurting my own body. Sometimes I think about killing myself by taking poison or something.

I never call *mamá* names or curse her or say dirty words to her. When *mamá* curses me and says she wishes a bolt of lightning would split me or that a car would run over me and kill me, it hurts my feelings and I answer, "I wish that bolt of lightning would really split me." It makes me cry when I hear her say those things.

I wish *mamá* was as nice to me as I am to her. Listen, if somebody gives me a piece of candy, I bring it home and give it to *mamá*, that's how nice I am to her. I don't eat anyplace unless I can bring some of the food home to *mamá*. If I go to a restaurant and buy a sandwich I bring it to *mamá* instead of eating it myself. When I bring *mamá* something, it puts her in a good humor and that makes me feel proud. If only she were that way all the time.

If you asked Eduardo, I bet he'd say I'm good, because I go stand in line at the stores for him whenever he asks me to. One day when they were selling sponge cake, Eduardo sent me to stand in line, and he said to *mamá*, "See? You're always complaining about Violeta, but you came back and she stayed in line, waiting." I'm always the one who stands in line.

I try to win Eduardo's goodwill because he's my stepfather, and if I don't try to please him he'll hate me right away. A stepfather isn't like a real father. For instance, I wouldn't dare ask Eduardo for anything—I'd be embarrassed to. My brothers and sisters call Eduardo *papá*, but sometimes I call him Eduardo. I can hardly bring myself to call him *papá* anymore. I don't feel like it, that's all. In a way, he really isn't our *papá* at all—we've been raised more by Grandma than by *mamá*, that's the reason why we're fonder of Grandma than of Eduardo. After all, we were already pretty big when we came to live with him.

I don't get along very well with my little sisters, because when their *papá* comes home they start showing off, and that makes me uncomfortable. They'll do anything as long as Eduardo is here because they know I don't dare hit them in front of him. He gets angry if I do. As long as he's around, all I can do is cry.

Faustina is Eduardo's pet. He's real fond of that kid, I don't know why. *Mamá* is awfully fond of Elsa and Faustina. My aunts say that *mamá* loves those kids of Eduardo better than she loves us. I used to cry an awful lot and Grandma would say to me, "Don't cry. We love you even if she doesn't."

I get along fine with my brothers and sisters except I quarrel with Hilario and Gerardo because they like to slap people. I play with Hilario because he keeps after me, but he's a pest and I hate a kid who's a pest. He hits me and then I get mad and hit him back. Lots of brothers slap their sisters, but I won't stand for it. I slap them right back.

In Oriente we used to fight with our fists. When Grandma saw us fighting she'd start pouring water over us. The more water she threw, the harder we fought. Now when I stay at Grandma's house I'm real good. I don't hurt anybody or pinch little kids or anything.

We do everything for the little kids. *Mamá* washes their things. Sometimes I fry eggs for them and give them their milk. Amanda María washes Elsa's diapers and *papá*'s socks. *Mamá* gives her the small things to iron. Faustina doesn't know anything. Sometimes she takes the broom, whisks it around the floor a couple of times, and thinks she's swept, but she leaves all the trash lying around.

All the little kids ever do is play. Usually they play together; they don't get along very well with the other children in this building. Leticia's kids get along fine with one another, but when Faustina plays with Bárbara, pretty soon she hits her and Bárbara cries. That happens all the time. They don't fight with Justa's kids because they hardly ever play with them. They only come down to play on Saturday and Sunday. We've nicknamed Hilario, Amanda María, and Faustina "the Wild Beasts," because as soon as they arrive from school they quarrel, kick, pull each other's hair, bite one another . . . *ay, mi madre!*

I think Concha is the most agreeable of all of us children. Everybody says so, even Grandma and *mamá,* but Grandma doesn't say it quite as often as *mamá* does. *Mamá* claims that Concha is the best daughter she has. Concha and I never fight with each other now, but we did when we were little.

Concha can't write at all because she's left-handed. She can't even sign her own name. But nobody can beat her when it comes to sewing. She doesn't have a sewing machine of her own so she borrows a neighbor's or sews by hand. She's made blouses and all sorts of things for Estela. Cute as can be and well-made, too. Nothing that my sister sews ever turns out bad—she's a swell seamstress.

Concha is prettier than me. I know because everybody says so. Maybe it's because of her hair or her nose. But then, everybody says Concha and I look alike so I don't know what to think. Really I don't look like anybody. I'm ugly.

I'm real fond of Concha and I'm sorry I couldn't go to her wedding. She got married in Oriente and I was here in Havana at the time. I didn't even know she had a sweetheart—she never spoke to me about him. That was three years ago when Concha was fifteen. She's eighteen now. My folks know Concha's husband, Manolo, because his grandfather, Silvestre Tabares, is *mamá*'s uncle. Their house was very near Grandma's, so we were always together. We used to play with Manolo and the rest of our cousins all the time, but I never noticed that Manolo and Concha were in love.

As far as I can see, Concha and her husband get along fine. They built a house near Manolo's parents. To get the land and the materials for the house, Manolo had a talk with the man who's in charge of giving land to people without a place to live. He took Manolo to the Committee and they gave him some land and wood and sent a man to climb up the palm trees and chop down leaves for him. The house is made of cedar with a roof of palm leaves. It has a living room, dining room, kitchen, and two bedrooms.

Out in the country when a roof is being put on, they have a thatching party and a big dinner. They roast a pig and make fricassee and all sorts of good things to eat, then invite enough people to get the job done. Some of Manolo's guests had to come on foot from quite far away, so they got there pretty late. But the ones who lived nearby arrived around 7:00 in the morning and got right to work. Breakfast was served at about 10:00, after a bit of the thatching had already been done. Concha served fried bananas, fried pig cracklings, *café con leche,* and crackers.

The house has forked sticks to hold up the walls. The sticks make a kind of bend on the roof that looks round from below, and thatch is laid over the framework of sticks. Before the guests arrived, a heap of palm leaves had been set out ready to be used. First they were tied in bundles, then those of us down below handed up the bundles to the ones on the roof whenever they needed them. They placed the bundles beside each other until the whole roof was covered and watertight.

I went just to eat so I didn't get there until noon. The guests sat around two long tables because one wasn't enough for the crowd. Each table was big enough for six or seven people. Concha and Manolo used their own table and all their stools and borrowed Grandma's dining-room set.

By 2:00 o'clock they'd thatched the whole roof and everybody went home. The roof looked real pretty—men out in the country know how to do a good job of thatching. After the other guests had left, the relatives who lived nearby helped clean up. The whole yard had to be swept up because the palm leaves are covered with little hairs which fall off when you touch them. We threw all the trash down a ravine into a stream which carries everything away when it rains. With everybody helping the work was soon done. Then we washed our hands and went home.

Concha was very happy. She didn't say anything but you could tell she was happy because she laughed and sang all day long. She was already pregnant then but I don't know how many months. Her little girl, Aidita, is a year old now.

Concha was the only one who ever talked to me about becoming a señorita. One day when we were both alone in the apartment, I asked her, "Concha, what happens when one becomes a señorita?" She explained to me that the very first thing I should do when I became a señorita was to tell *mamá* about it so that *mamá* could explain what I had to do.

The first time I menstruated I was scared to death. I remember as if it were today. It happened when I was thirteen, on January 6. I was awfully embarrassed about even *mamá's* knowing it. As for other people—imagine! I thought everybody who came to the house would discover my secret.

There are a lot of things you shouldn't do when you have your period. You shouldn't wash things with Ace[18] or touch the floor with your bare feet or do a lot of other things. When I'm menstruating I bathe every single day, sometimes as often as three times a day, because I feel so uncomfortable I can hardly bear it. All the time I have my period I keep spitting up. Looking at food, especially meat, takes away my appetite. One time I couldn't even eat beefsteak! It seemed to me that when I ate the meat I was eating my own blood. I simply couldn't swallow it.

I've had asthma since I was five. Once when I was little I had such a bad attack I looked dead. So they took me to the doctor and he made me stay in the hospital several days. After that *mamá* took me to a lady named Chita Valverde, who can cure any ailment. She tied a square red leather pouch around my neck and told us that if the pouch got lost we shouldn't look for it, but if we happened to find it without looking we should take it back to her. Well, one day I lost it. My aunt found it and opened it up and found a bit of *majá* skin inside. *Majá* is a kind of snake. That was what Chita Valverde used to cure me. I felt a tightness in my chest for one day but after that I've never had asthma again, or at least I don't have it as bad as I used to.

I love parties because no matter who gives them they always serve roast pork. Last Christmas we went to a party where they killed three pigs and a goat. My uncle took me along because his combo was playing there. The government sent a truck to pick up the combo so the whole family was able to go. My uncles called their combo "Los Brillantes." They started it in 1967. The National Council of Culture gave them a letter so they could get all the instruments they needed. I love to listen to them. They've been playing lots of modern songs ever since they were real young. Nobody taught them to play; they learned by ear.

My family likes to drink a lot. When there's a party, *mamá* always counts on having a little shot. I remember once we were celebrating my uncle's saint's day and *mamá* drank until she couldn't anymore. Did she ever get drunk! My grandfather just laughs when he gets drunk. He doesn't get obnoxious like some people.

I've only gone to one wedding fiesta. It was at my cousin Nereida's and they served beer and roast pork. My cousin Clemente, who's eleven, drank so much beer he almost got sick. He started dancing alone and didn't know what he was doing. We had to take him home. It was terrible. I drank plenty too. My aunt and I helped ourselves to a drink

18. A popular detergent.

whenever we felt like it. We drank floods of beer that day. But I didn't get drunk like Clemente.

There wasn't a kid there who didn't like his liquor, and no wonder, because Grandpa and Grandma love their liquor too. They give us kids wine or whatever drink they have on hand. Just try offering one of the kids in my family a soft drink! They'll tell you that soft drinks don't do a thing for them—liquor, that's what they like. Faustina can outdrink her *papá* any time. When she drinks with Eduardo he gets drunk before she does!

I think Nereida got married in the church in Santiago. They wanted me to come to church with them but I didn't want to. Grandma told me not to go to church, I don't know why.

Catalina, my uncle's wife, took me to the San Fernando church once. They were going to say a Mass for her mother or something like that. But I'm scared of such things. I don't know why it is, but when I see the saints in church I'm afraid they'll grab me and I won't be able to get away. I've heard a lot of talk about the saints. Some of those dead people rise up out of their graves and I don't know what all.

My grandma told me that when a relative of a *santero* dies, they hold a Mass right in their own home. They take a long table and cover it with a white cloth. Then they line up the saints near the edge of the table and place a wreath of flowers on it. After that they light as many candles as they can get, and stay up all night long praying loudly and calling to the spirits. In the morning they throw out the flowers and put away the rest of the stuff they've been using, then everybody goes home.

Uncle David doesn't like such things. If you mention them, he's apt to shit on your mother. He says that's old-fashioned stuff and nobody believes it anymore. And my Uncle Fabio isn't allowed to believe any of those things because he's a Party member.

I'm especially scared of St. Lazarus. In front of his altar there's a little jar that they keep chock full of *kilos*, *medios*, and *pesetas*. But if you take any, he'll punish you with a headache. On the day of St. Lazarus they have a party. All the children are invited and they serve cookies with meat or jam. I've gone there but I don't go into the room. I stand at the door to get my cookies. And I don't kneel down, either. I tell them they can give me the food if they want to, but I won't kneel down. They know I'm scared so they give me the food anyway. Then they light the candles and begin to sing and move their hands. They can't get real candles anymore, so they make their own out of beeswax. All my mother's relatives like that kind of thing. They beat on their drums while they sing. Some of them are a bit old, and it's funny to see them singing and dancing.

Sometimes while the people are dancing for St. Lazarus, they catch the spirits. Denisa, one of my cousins, raises St. Lazarus by dancing on one foot. You should see her! She jumps and tears up her clothes. Denisa is

Manolo's sister but I'm pretty sure he isn't a *santero* because he belongs to the Youth and they'd kick him out in a minute if he got mixed up with such things. His mother and father are *santeros* though, because they're older people who have a lot of faith and all that.

I hate to be alone. It makes me feel restless and uncomfortable. But I don't much like being with friends because they're apt to try and put something over on you. I don't much trust some of my friends, but of course they aren't all the same.

My friends don't take any interest in my doings. How can they? They aren't living at home with me. I'm not interested in their doings either, because I don't know what they do at home or anything like that.

I make friends more easily than my sisters do. I guess that's because I'm the kind of person who doesn't like to harm anybody. I make friends all over the place. When I have to stand in line at a shop or something, I get to talking with other girls and then they invite me to go to their houses and all that.

I'll give away every last thing I own if somebody asks me for it, even if it means I'll have to go barefoot and naked. That's the kind of person I am. *Mamá* says I'm too kindhearted for my own good and that one can't be all that kind nowadays. Well, even if it makes *mamá* mad at me, I can't bear to see anybody having to do without something they need.

Mamá was furious because I gave my sister a pair of brand-new shoes I had, but the shoes were too big for me and I wasn't going to wear them anyway. My sister had a pair of new tennis shoes that didn't fit her, so I exchanged my shoes for hers. What's wrong with making an exchange between sisters? It was all in the family, wasn't it? I did a good deed for my sister, didn't I? She's much too big to go around in her bare feet. But *mamá* got furious at me for giving away my shoes. I didn't have any shoes then but I didn't mind. That's the way I am—I never bear a grudge against anybody.

I dreamed that they made a law making military service required for girls. What a funny thing to dream! I have to laugh when I think of it. I ran and ran but they ran faster and finally they grabbed me. I clung to *mamá* but they said, "Come on, you've got to go too." They made me get into a car and took me away.

Another girl said to me, "Don't cry. They aren't going to kill you or anything. It's only to do your stint with the armed forces." Gosh, it was funny! I'm not really afraid, see, but in the dream I was kind of taken by surprise and that's how come I got scared.

What I really get scared about sometimes is being caught out in the street and scolded for not going to school. The other day a soldier told me I couldn't go out in the street during school hours because I was still of school age. I explained to him why I wasn't in school right now and he said I should do whatever had to be done to be admitted to school because I simply couldn't stay out.

I've been out for one whole year now and I'm worried. They told *mamá* if she kept me out of school, she was going to have an unpleasant surprise one of these days. If the government catches me they'll send me to a *granja*.[19] It scares me to think of it but it doesn't worry *mamá*.

I'm kind of disgusted about not being able to go to school, but it isn't my fault that *mamá* brought me to Havana, not one bit. It bothers me when I see all the other kids in this building studying and getting ahead. Besides, I'd like going to school in Havana better. Here they serve you snacks every day; in the country they don't give you anything, not even a piece of candy. All you get there are lessons.

I can't keep on like this, without studying. I want to go back to school as soon as *mamá* arranges it. After I finish sixth grade I mean to keep on studying until I have a career. Maybe I'll be a doctor. Grandma told me that's a very good career. I'd also like to be a seamstress, but the trouble is I don't like to use a sewing machine.

If I turn out to be a failure it's going to be my fault, not *mami*'s, because she's always given me plenty of good advice. She tells me I should grow up to be a good girl and not get in trouble by trusting men too much. When I have a sweetheart I should bring him to the house and tell her, "Look, *mamá*, this fellow is courting me." She never talks to me about getting a job, but she tells me I should learn how to cook and wash and do all kinds of housework. She says a woman is a failure if her husband walks out on her because she isn't handy around the house.

19. A state farm; in this context, a prison farm.

Genoveva Hernández Díaz,
Age Seventeen

After *papi* left to join the Rebels, *mami* had to take in laundry to make a living because all doors were closed to us. I wasn't admitted to school and nobody would give my aunt a job. Batista's henchmen went looking for our relatives because they were conspiring with *papi*. We were being watched all the time. They figured that sooner or later he'd come down to see his family. They said they were going to catch "that revolutionary dog" someday and kill him.

The most frightening incident of my life happened when I was staying with my grandmother. *Mamá* had sent me there because I was real skinny and suffered from fits. Batista's air force bombed the salt pits near there and all the houses round about. *Mamá* got so nervous she didn't know what to do, so she began piling mattresses on top of my sister and me and I felt as if I were suffocating under them.

Meanwhile, outside, a Chinese laundryman was hanging up sheets to dry, singing as he worked. I couldn't help laughing to see him working and singing, calm as you please, with the bombs falling all around. Inside, *mamá* was crying and a bunch of women were praying. You know how it is: some people cling to such old customs and believe in God and that's something you can't take away from them. The whole scene struck me as the funniest thing I'd ever seen.

A neighbor woman took us all to her house and prepared some linden-flower tea for *mami* to soothe her nerves. But the nervous fit didn't pass. Then all of a sudden, some men flung the body of the neighbors' son right outside her door. His eyes were torn out of the sockets and he was so horribly mutilated he could be identified only by a birthmark on his foot. The mother lost her mind and she's still insane. That was the most frightening day of my life. After such experiences, it's no wonder *mamá*'s nerves are bad.

I didn't see *papá* for a long, long time, not until the triumph of the Revolution. Even then I didn't see him right away because the Rebel

Army went to Havana. He sent for us from there and we found him living in a room they'd given him. We were so happy to see our *papi* again. It had been almost a year and a half.

Now that the Rebellion is over and the Revolution victorious, I'm happier than I ever was before. The Revolution has meant a great deal to me personally. I have advantages I've never had before. I have something for the future. I've been able to go to new schools, even though it hasn't worked out, and I have a scholarship, which is something I'd dreamed of since I was in the fourth grade. The Triumph brought *papá* back home to me, and *mamá* is happy. She's under medical treatment she couldn't afford before. We have enough to eat. We have peace. We've been very happy since the victory.

I can think and talk freely now about ideals I've always had to keep to myself. Now I'm free to think as I wish without anybody saying, "No, this can't be." I don't mean that people are free to do bad things, like plotting counterrevolution. Naturally, if people do that, the government has to intervene. But as long as your ideas are revolutionary and good, you're free to think as you please without anybody getting annoyed with you.

I feel that the Communist Party is like a great mass of people come to represent us. What we have now represents a new kind of future, new ideals for today's youth. *Papi* is a Party member and so are practically all his brothers, except for Sergio, who's a grocer in Oriente.

My *mamá*'s brother, Mateo Díaz, has all the qualities to be a Party member. I always say that of all the family he's the one who does most for the fatherland. He lives on the Isle of Pines and is married, but his wife's family is against the Revolution. Not that they're counter-revolutionaries who'd set off bombs or anything like that. She wasn't a revolutionary, but she's such a good woman that he fell in love and married her anyway. He told her, "Now you must forget all your old ideals and accept mine. And I expect you to become integrated in every way."

Shortly after they were married, my uncle won a telephone because of his excellent qualities. Well, when the men went to his house to connect it, they told him, "We came to install a telephone here because you've earned the right to have one. You deserve it."

"Thank you very much," he said, "I'm grateful, but I want to tell you something. My wife is not a revolutionary. She's a *gusana* and she doesn't deserve to have a telephone. When she gives up her reactionary ideas and becomes a revolutionary, then she'll deserve not only a telephone but a TV set, a refrigerator, and anything I can get her. But as long as she's a *gusana*, I won't allow her to get anything from the Revolution."

Mateo told his wife, "You must become a revolutionary because you sincerely feel it, not because I order you to. When you really feel it, then come to me and say, 'Mateo, I want to be a revolutionary,' and then I'll integrate you. That's the way to win my love. The more revolutionary you are, the more I'll love you. And as for my daughter, she'll be a revolutionary through and through."

I think Party members are wonderful men. If they weren't so wonderful they wouldn't have been accepted in the first place, because you have to win the right to be a Party member. I don't say that just because *papi*'s a Party member, but I'm very proud of him all the same, for that and other reasons. He was chosen from out of the masses to become a Party member. He's earned officer rank—lieutenant—and he's studying to be promoted again. I'm very proud of the rest of my relatives too.

I plan to become a member of the Communist Party but that can't be for a few years yet. Even my Uncle Mateo Díaz, who's such a splendid revolutionary, doesn't qualify for Party membership yet because he's too young. I plan to develop all the qualities needed to be a member by the time I'm old enough to join. I'm an aspirant to the Union of Young Communists and have done many different kinds of work at the sectional in connection with the Young Pioneers.

The UJC is quite different from the Party, although it's a good thing too. They follow the good path and lead others who have the right feelings about the Revolution. The old Young Communists Union, created by Julio Antonio Mella,[20] was different because those young people lived under an enemy regime and really had to make sacrifices. They were good, tough, energetic representatives. Now we have to be even better representatives of the UJC because our young people also deserve the very best kind of representation. And that's just what we're giving them.

When I'm a Party member I'll influence other young people to do as I did. I'll teach them to have the same ideas I have. And I plan to get my family more involved—I think we'll have to organize a PCC unit in our house. The greatest advantage of being a Party member is that you can be a much more effective educator. And that's the advantage Party membership would bring me—the opportunity to help others, to guide those who come seeking strength in me and be able to say, "How satisfied I am with the work I've done!"

People say that PCC members have advantages over the rest of the Cuban people—that they eat better, for instance—but I don't believe it. My father lives a life of sacrifice. I don't regard him as privileged. He's better off now than he used to be, but so is everybody else. If he were really granted the privileges Party members are said to get, we'd be

---

20. Julio Antonio Mella (1905–29), a leader of the university student movement in the twenties, helped found the old Cuban Communist Party (in 1925) and was a member of its first Central Committee. In 1927 Mella went into exile in Mexico, where he became involved in the international communist movement. He was assassinated there in 1929, probably on orders from Cuban President Machado.

better off than other people, wouldn't we? Besides, it was the communists who fought and worked so that everybody could have the same things, wasn't it? They fought precisely to end privileges and inequalities, so it would be impossible for them to accept privileges now. And no matter what people say, I don't believe they do.

People can be corrupted by growing up in a family with the wrong kind of ideals or by frequenting groups of wrong-thinking people. Suppose my parents were integrated in the Revolution but I had different ideals and was friendly with a family who disagreed with the Revolution. Being in constant contact with them, I'd hear a lot of subversive things and I'd become quite confused between the ideals of my parents and those of other people. And then suppose I got quite friendly with a group of girls my age who shared the ideals of the counterrevolutionary family. I'd hear them talk and I'd talk too. I'd be hearing all sorts of different opinions in different places, see? That's why one must choose one's company with great care—because it's so easy to get confused. As for me, I'm in no danger of getting confused. I'm too strong-minded for that. Besides, I'm too old and too experienced in revolutionary matters to make that kind of mistake. But I understand how anybody might fall into error.

I've seen this kind of confusion among some of my comrades. There's a girl I know whose father wasn't a revolutionary and whose mother is only interested in her home and family. She believes a woman can be quite happy just being a housewife. That woman never gives a thought to the Revolution. She has no ideals at all. When my friend was seventeen, she met a boy who's a revolutionary, as are both his parents. When she went back home she felt different, confused. . . . At that time, some forms were handed out in school to be filled out by those who wished to join the Young Communists, the Federation, or the CDR. She put down her name, and when she told her parents, her father practically ate her alive. Her mother said, "Get out of this house! We want no revolutionaries here!"

"All right," says the girl, "I'll go. If there are no ideals in my home, I know where I can find them. There's always a place for a revolutionary. I can stay a little while here, a little while there. I'm going to get married and I know only good can come from my decision."

Next day at school she asked our opinion. We told her that as long as she was in school, she should join us. "If your father refuses to let you stay at home," I advised, "go visit him and your mother anyway. And meanwhile, you can eat and sleep one day in my house and one day in another girl's house and so on. You can even stay at your fiancé's house until you make your arrangements. Why not?" They got married and are very happy together. Her father refuses to see her and is going to leave Cuba soon. Her mother visits her but never mentions the Revolution. The rest of the family are all *gusanos*.

I usually don't pass judgment on my parents. I try to understand them according to the standards of the past. But there are some things I never discuss with *papá* or *mamá* because they belong to an era when children were raised differently. Things weren't all that wonderful in their time—they had family problems too.

In our family I don't feel that I'm of the least importance. I honestly believe that *mamá* thinks of us all as newborn babies. She'll remind me, "Genoveva, you must remember that you're not a little girl any longer but a grown señorita." And two minutes later she'll be saying, "Genoveva, don't do it that way, do it *this* way." I feel she's treating me like a tiny tot and I don't know what to do.

"When will I ever do something right?" I exclaim.

"When you get some sense in your head," she answers.

"And when will that be?" I ask.

"When God steps in and works a miracle!" she says.

She's been very strict with me ever since I told her Rodney was my sweetheart and I wanted to drop out of school. "What are you afraid of when I'm here and he's so far away?" I ask her.

"Because any day he may get on a boat and come here," she answers.

"Oh, sure! Leave his work simply to come and see me for a few hours! If you want to keep me a prisoner just tell me so and I'll go to my room so you can lock me in and never in my life let me out again!"

Now she's got it into her head that my wanting to drop out of school is all Rodney's fault. She argued with his family. His parents have nothing to do with our being in love and she's got no right to say the things she said to them. *Mamá* says I can't marry the boy. She says I can't and I can't and I can't. I'm too exhausted to fight her. I'll simply have to obey.

This is the very first time I've been denied anything I really wanted. Sometimes I think, "*Mamá* didn't fall in love with *papá* the same way I love my sweetheart." *Papá* had to take off with her because her mother disapproved of the match. Well, I'm not going to do that, because I'm the eldest of the children and I wouldn't want to give my sisters such a bad example.

I don't deny that it's a young person's first duty to obey his or her parents. I know parents try to lead their children along the right path. But sometimes they're so blind! They say, "It's always been that way" or "That's what everybody does."

Papá and *mamá* don't play favorites. As far as I can see they love us all the same. Oh, they spoil the little ones more, but that's natural. So far I haven't seen *mamá* idolize any of us. My parents have never told me that I'm better at anything than my sisters. We're just the same so they treat us the same. In my family we do everything together. For instance, if someone tells me, "Genoveva, you're invited to a party," I tell the others at once. If it's a children's birthday party, I'll say, "I'll take the little ones. Of course if the party is at night, we aren't allowed to go.

Sometimes I quarrel with my brother and sisters and say harsh things, but I really get along very well with them, especially my little sisters, Antonia and Justa. I'm a very strange person though, because it isn't easy for me to show affection.

Florinda is a lot friendlier and more affectionate than I am. I'm reserved, she's very outgoing. No matter what you say to her, she turns it into a joke. That's why everybody says she gets along better with people. Well, older people are crazy about her, but she isn't as popular as I am with kids her own age. I always go out of my way to be pleasant. I find a way to talk with people. I make friends with everybody, even with those little old men one sees out in the street.

Sometimes I say to *mamá*, "All my sisters are pretty. I'm the only homely one in the family. Even my brother is better-looking than me. You know how much everyone admires Reinaldito's beautiful eyes."

"How can you say that," she protests. "You're fishing for compliments. Wouldn't I look foolish standing here and telling you right to your face that you're pretty?"

"*Ay, mima*, let me say it!"

"All right, my duckling," she says laughing. "You're perfectly right. Ricardo, look, here's the ugly duckling." That's when she quarrels with me. Afterward she says, "What a silly child you are!"

Mamá scolds me all the time so I can't help thinking, "I must be the worst-behaved one of the lot." She says I'm feather-brained because I'm always jumping around and dashing here and there, chattering about having bought this record and borrowed that one and now I'm going to put it on and listen to it. *Mamá* says Florinda isn't so wild and foolish. She's more apt to think things over. But I say, "Phooey, people who sit and think about doing things never get around to doing them."

Mamá says, "Modern young girls are crack-brained. Having a sweetheart at the age of seventeen—imagine! Besides, you don't even know how to choose the right type of boy; none of you do!"

"*Ay, mima*," I answer, "I guess I'd better go get myself a rich man. Then you'll be satisfied!"

"Who said anything about rich? I don't want my daughters to marry rich men, I want them to marry communists."

"Tough luck. I can't imagine a communist falling in love with me," I answer.

"*Ay*, that's a terrible thing to say! People are going to think you're a *gusana!*"

"But *mima*, who is a communist anyway? El Che was one, Fidel is one, but I'm merely a socialist. I'm all for the Revolution, but what have I done to deserve the name of communist? When I fight and struggle for this Revolution, when I spill a little blood, then I'll deserve to be called communist, as *papi* deserves it. I'm a revolutionary because I love my fatherland, but that doesn't make me a communist."

"If you aren't a communist, you're a *gusana*," she answers.

"Oh, all right, *mima*," I say. What's the use, she doesn't get the point at all. "Communism and socialism are two different things," I tell her.

"You've got a lot of book-learning but you don't know anything," she retorts.

"All right, all right, have it your own way, but I know I'm not a communist."

"*Ay*, what a terrible thing to say!" she repeats.

Mamá shows more concern for my behavior than for my happiness. She doesn't understand me and I don't understand her. She doesn't like my boyfriend, but since I love him she should have the generosity to say, "Well, if she loves him... I'll wait and see. Later on I can find out whether he's good or bad." But does she react that way? Not at all! I sometimes think she doesn't love me. If she did, she wouldn't do this to me. But I keep my doubts to myself. If I should come right out and tell her so, imagine what our home life would be like!

Mamá worries about all sorts of things and it's all in her head. I tell her, "*Mima*, let other people think as they please and let me make my own decisions. If I give up something that's important to me simply to please others, are they going to make it up to me? You're going to lose me and have nothing left but other people."

"Genoveva," she threatens, "say that once again and you'll have to leave this house!" And then she says, "Just you wait till your father comes—I'm going to tell him everything."

But she's never said a word about it to *papá*. He's never home anyway; she's the one who deals with us.

Mamá's concern for me sometimes pleases me but often it's annoying. She's very domineering with all her children. But she's never out of sorts or grouchy. As far back as I can remember, she's always been happy and laughing. She's a loving mother to all of us. She'll ask me, "Genoveva, did you like that dress we saw? How about those shoes?" If I say yes, she buys them. I think to myself, "That's the only way *mamá* knows to show affection because she was never given any love herself."

Mamá's had a difficult life, and sometimes she says to me, "How I wish I were your age now, Genoveva!" It makes me sad to know that she never had the things that young people have nowadays. She never had any love or any childhood or any youth. She's been old all her life. That's influenced her character a great deal. That's why I never think badly of her or belittle her or... or anything like that. And if she wants to give me something, I let her. Why should I deprive her of that pleasure? *Mamá* doesn't try to dominate *papi* because he's just as strong-minded as she is. That's why they get along so well together—they're exactly the same.

We all have a tremendous respect for *papi*. I've never given him any reason to scold me but he's always telling me, "This can't be done. That can't be done." I just keep my mouth shut; we all do. *Papá* sometimes helps me with my school work when I have any special difficulty. Not often, though, because I'm very shy and don't dare ask him. I've never had a real conversation with *papá*, sitting down with him and chatting about anything that comes into my head. I trust him—I'm not afraid to talk with him, though neither of us has ever started a real conversation with the other. But Florinda talks with him a lot.

I'm rather isolated from my friends because I'm not allowed to go most of the places they go. They're always going to parties at night and I'm not allowed to go anywhere after dark. My parents can't take me out because *mamá* has to stay home with the little ones and *papá* never goes out. I simply have to stay home, that's all. My friends no longer invite me anywhere because they know it's useless. But some of them have come to visit me at home and sometimes they go to the beach with me. *Mamá* never criticizes my friends or interferes because she sees they're all good girls. They're all kids on scholarships with me.

There are twelve girls in our group and we always try to dress alike. If we're given tennis shoes in school, all twelve of us choose the same color. Last time they distributed pajamas we ripped them up and made them into housecoats. One of the girls knits and crochets beautifully and made twelve identical pocket handkerchiefs for us. She taught the rest of us to knit, and we each knitted our own socks so we had twelve identical pairs.

I love to be fashionably dressed and I always am. I like to make a good impression. If short skirts are in fashion, that's what I wear. If it should become fashionable to have fringes on all your clothes, I'd be among the first to wear them. One day I'll wear slacks and a pullover, and the next a skirt and blouse. I don't like beads and earrings and all that stuff. Simple but modish, that's the way I dress.

One thing I've always wanted but don't have yet is a pair of boots. *Papi* says he's doing his best to get me a pair but they're hard to find. I wanted sunglasses and now I have them; one of my uncles gave them to me for my birthday. I've been longing for a nylon blouse and it seems I'm going to get one soon. Whatever I want very much I eventually get. Dressing well has never been a problem for me or any of my *compañeras* either. In fact, most of the girls I know dress better than I do. One of them dresses beautifully. We don't like each other very much but among the comrades we're always polite and friendly. I do all right but there isn't much chance of anybody in my family dressing with tremendous elegance because there are so many of us kids and only one wage-earner. My parents do very well to be able to clothe seven kids on *papá*'s salary.

Shoes are a problem for me. I wear mine out fast and they're hard to get. Right now those I have are worn out so I'm managing with a pair of sandals. But I never complain the way some of my *compañeras* do.

I like to see men fashionably dressed—fashion isn't exclusively for women—but I don't like exaggerated fashions, like the hippies who used to dress in a really outlandish way. *Ay*, that hair down to here looks awful on a boy! Those hippie fashions were American propaganda, introduced in Cuba by the CIA. But I don't care; if they want to dress sloppily, let them. I don't think it's that important. After all, fashions come and go. People have worn all sorts of things and I don't see that it's ever made such a great difference. But a few people, especially old women, are always criticizing the young and saying that some fashion is going to corrupt them. How silly! Fashions can't corrupt anybody.

Before the Revolution, women didn't have nearly as many opportunities as they do now. If they weren't prostitutes, or mistresses to military men, if they didn't sell themselves to some boss or some dictator, they didn't have a chance. You may be sure the only other opportunity was to be a servant, scrubbing floors or taking in laundry. But now women are independent, free. A woman can work in the daytime, and if she wants to study, she can go to night school. Who ever studied before the Revolution? What money did they have to study with? What facilities for study were there?

Now a woman chooses her own goals and works toward them in her own way, and she no longer allows herself to be dominated by men. I mean, *I* don't let myself be dominated, and as far as I can see nobody else does either. If I'm about to do something that's right and good and some man says no, I go ahead and do it. Before, if a man said no to a woman, she had to obey. Now the woman says, "You go your way and I'll go mine." If you tell her, "There are many different kinds of work," she says, "Sure, brother. I'll pick mine and you pick yours."

Women are integrated in the working force now instead of being raised as parasites, and they're giving Cuba a new generation of healthy youthful people. I believe that women should work just as men do. That's a new way to help the Revolution. I used to hear married men talk about it and for many of them it was a kind of bogey. They were absolutely against it. "What, women work? Not *my* wife!"

That was kind of dumb of them because we women are doing almost as much as the men now, and the same kind of work, too. Now that the men are out cutting cane, women are substituting for them at their regular jobs. People used to say that men were stronger and more industrious, but now we're seeing that women can work twice as hard as men. I think people must have gotten those ideas because women used to do nothing but housework, sewing, and so on.

There are a lot of old women—I don't mean to say anything against old women, but there are many who think women's liberation is terrible because women go around in the street like men and do men's work. But when *they* were young they sat in a chair all day doing embroidery or playing the piano or taking classes on this and that subject or stuffing themselves with food while waiting for their sweethearts to come and visit them in the parlor. Those women never learned anything useful to themselves or to the Revolution. They've simply sunk themselves, all alone. They regard liberation as a kind of hell. I, on the contrary, think it's a good thing because now women are equal to men.

As for myself, I've been free since I was a little girl. My grandmother allowed me to go here and there. But that changed when I was thirteen or fourteen. My grandmother—"May God have her in Heaven," as *mamá* says—decided that it was time for me to "settle down." She said to me, "You must study in a different kind of school, something quiet. Young girls have become too free; you must be different."

"*Ay*, Grandma, why must I be different?" I said. "I want to be like other girls."

"*Ay*, Genoveva, you're as stubborn as your father," she complained. "He decided to do something and off he went and did it. I'm afraid that's exactly what you'll do."

"Yes indeed, Grandma, that's exactly what I intend to do!"

All she wanted was to see me on my fifteenth birthday, beautifully dressed for the party. But when I went back to school she said, "How mistaken I was when I said modern women were lost! Why, today's women are better off than we ever were. Now women don't have to put up with everything their husbands do. If they aren't happy they can say, 'Go on, beat it!' or 'Stay if you like, and *I* can go. I have my degree. So goodbye, kid!'"

"Granny, how you've changed!" I told her. "You didn't used to think like that."

"No indeed, child, so I didn't. I was a thick-headed fool."

It was my hope to be able someday to help the Revolution by being a good teacher. I'd like to help raise the new generation, the generation of the twenty-first century, to be technicians, doctors, teachers, so they can complete our Revolution and be integrated to the maximum. That's the generation Fidel says must be like El Che. I myself want to become more integrated. But I really don't like teaching. I chose that career because I knew that teachers were needed to help the Revolution. When my sister Florinda chose to be a teacher, I said, "That's what I want to do too," because I've never been separated from her.

She got the forms and we both filled them out and signed them. I got very involved and was always talking about when I'd be a teacher. To hear me talk you'd have thought I was going to be a great teacher and such a gift to the Revolution! Me, I was going to be the greatest! After that, how could I draw back? I wasn't going to make such a fool of myself. Not me! So I submitted my application and thought, "Let things turn out as they will." Until the very last day of school, I intended to study hard and struggle on and triumph. But I got sick and now I simply don't have the strength.

Up to now I haven't had any problems with my scholarship. I've had my ups and downs but I've been a good student. I was preparing for the future. Only I can't keep it up any longer. I can't, I can't, I can't.

My scholarship studies are very difficult for me. I'm bored at school. I'm fed up with studying. I do my lessons but I get desperate doing the same things day after day, night after night. Lots of the other kids at the scholarship students' residence are there because they have a vocation for it, and they don't feel as I do. My sister likes being there. It's what she's wanted all her life. Leave teaching to her, it's not for me. I'm different. My nerves act up, perhaps because of studying too hard—I don't know. So now my parents say I'm bad and that I don't realize what an effort they've made to give me an education.

If I give up the scholarship, I can enroll in the nearest polyclinic for six weeks and train to be a nurse's aide; then I can work and go on studying. I can train to be a nurse and keep on studying but live at home instead of in the house for scholarship students. That way I'll have the freedom to come and go and I'll have everything I need. I'll go on studying, slowly, without pressure, until I get to be a medical doctor. Even after I'm a doctor, I'll take laboratory courses or something.

The thing is, once I have a nursing job, I'll feel calmer and I'll be able to study better. I'd be coming and going from home, not shut in all the time as I am now. If I have to live this shut-in life much longer, I'll go mad. I feel restless and uneasy. Perhaps it's because of all the noise and movement around here.

I say to *mamá,* "Mima, please let me study to be a nurse's aide. In six weeks I'd be earning money and I could help you out."

"So you're trying to bribe me!" says she.

Mamá is too dumb to understand. I'm through trying to explain any-thing to her. She always thought I'd study to be a teacher. Now that I've told her I don't want to, I can see she's worried. I've explained to her, *"Mamá,* I don't like teaching. I can't learn the stuff because it bores me. I simply can't keep on with it." I tell her, "Listen, it's a five-year course, which means that I'll be stuck in school for ten or fifteen years, because I know I'll flunk every year and have to repeat it at least once. Finally the teachers will give up on me and say, 'Get out, Genoveva. Beat it!'"

I haven't flunked yet, but I passed this year only because the teachers gave me fifteen days of special tutoring before the final exams. They helped me because of my good conduct record. I can't study by myself. I try awfully hard but I can't get those things into my head. Something's wrong with me, that's all.

When I went to the school doctor recently he asked me if I'd ever had fits when I was little. I said yes. He looked at me for a minute without saying anything, then he suggested that I go see the doctor at the polyclinic with *mamá*. I said I would, but I haven't. What's the point of going anyway? They all say the same things.

I'm not saying that we don't have good medical service—I think it's very good. But sometimes I think that the best thing the doctors could do would be to call *mima* and say to her, "Señora, you should send this girl away to some lonely place and lock her up there with the animals. Then go away." *Ay,* that's all I want—to go someplace where I'd be left in peace! I feel better, happier, calmer, and more self-confident when I'm by myself. I don't know what it is, but I feel best in the country, where I can be active but alone.

I don't want to go back to the doctor because I know if I do, they'll hospitalize me again. The last time they sent me to the hospital, the school authorities didn't tell me ahead of time. I told the doctor, "I hope you'll call my *papá* and *mamá*." But when days passed and nobody came I said, "All right, I'm going to send word to *mamá* myself."

I asked a cleaning woman at the hospital to let my *mamá* know where I was and how I was. She said she would, but that afternoon I was released.

The teacher who drove me home asked me, "Who sent word to your *mamá*?"

"I did. Why should I deny it?"

"And why did you do that?"

"Because *mamá* didn't even know I was in the hospital. Suppose I'd died there?"

"Look, Genoveva," she said, "next time let us know you've done it, because the hospital employee could have told your *mamá* something completely inaccurate and alarming and your *mamá* would have rushed over here to ask why *we* hadn't let her know."

I thought a minute, and I said, "Well, I was sick in the hospital and it was someone's duty to send my mother a telegram or phone her to tell her so." Then I turned around and went in the house without another word.

Before I left the hospital, the doctor told me I should undergo psychiatric treatment. She said, "I wouldn't interfere with you for the world and I can't tell you what to do. All I can say is that if I had the problem you have, I wouldn't accept a scholarship."

"What do you mean?"

"I mean that you seem to have some sort of mental disequilibrium that affects even your physical development. I'm pretty sure the illness that brought you here was caused by your nerves."

I told the doctor I'd talk to my mother. I did explain everything to *mamá* as well as I could, but she still insists that I get my scholarship again and go back to school.

Sometimes I say to *mamá*, "I'm stifling to death here because nobody understands anybody else. I'm fed up. I'm getting out of this house."

But that's something I just couldn't do. When I say such things it isn't me that's talking. I pack up all my things, but then I think, "Where can I go?"

There's a difference between "rebellion" and "revolution." In school they've explained to us that the Rebellion was the armed struggle of our people: "rebellion"—force of arms; "revolution"—force of machinery and production. The Revolution is the process we're undergoing now in our economy.

I'd say there's less scarcity now compared to what there was before the Revolution. There was a lot of stuff on the market before, but where did it come from? The United States mostly, and no one had the money to buy anything. If somebody got sick, everyone in that family might have to go hungry to buy medicines. I used to get fits and had to be hospitalized, which was a financial drain on my parents. Illness was a luxury *mami* couldn't afford. So what did she do? She gathered all the relatives together and asked them to help pay my expenses, because in those times you could consult a doctor only with money in your hand. For medicines, too, you needed cash. The men of the resistance came and gave *mami* money to help. But it wasn't much and we went hungry, without a bit of food, many, many days. That's what was bad about that old government.

Nowadays we always have something to fill our stomachs. And above all, now we're free and have peace and those are the two most important things.

I don't believe the food shortages will last much longer anyway. I say that because of the productive work I've done. Usually we do productive work on Sundays, and this year the students from my school also spent the month of July on a farm working hard weeding *malanga* and harvesting other tubers. When we finished, we didn't get a pass to go home because it was our turn to work at the state farm.

We spent fifteen days working at Niña Bonita. There they have large stretches of pastureland, lots of honey, and quantities of cattle and milk. They had very good enthusiastic workers, too. I believe that all the *malanga* and grain that have been harvested and all the milch cows and cattle we have right now are enough to put an end to scarcity. The ICAIC[21] newsreels tell us how much food there is and how there's enough rice and eggs and poultry.

21. *Instituto Cubano del Arte e Industria Cinematográfica* (Cuban Institute of Cinema Art and Industry), established in 1959.

The scholarship girls in my group are good workers, too. We have a motto—"This is a matter of *patria o muerte*."[22] It refers to the dedication and enthusiasm with which one carries out an activity or works toward a goal. When there's something to be done they always ask, "Where's the *patria o muerte* group?" And my friends and I are always there ready to work.

Of course things are going to be just a little bit scarcer now, because all the workers are spending so much time on the 1970 sugar-cane harvest, and on industry, too, so we can finally stop being an underdeveloped country and strike yet another blow against imperialism. We're determined that Cuba shall remain sovereign and free, that never again shall a traitor trample it underfoot. My fatherland comes first with me. I'd rather die than see it under the imperialist yoke.

I think a lot about the future. Nothing is impossible now, so whatever I propose to do, I can do. I intend to achieve a great deal; but then, who doesn't? Writing is my vocation. I'd like to be an excellent teacher but I also want to be an outstanding writer. My ambition is to write something that's good for our fatherland, perhaps about our Revolution, so that future generations will know how we lived. Someday I'll be one of its representative people. That's my dream and I know that someday I'll wake up and find it's come true.

22. "Fatherland or death."

Afterword

We began this series with the general objective of showing the impact of a Revolution-in-progress on the daily lives of the Cuban people. That, we think, has been done, particularly with respect to the poorest segment of the Cuban population.[1] By looking at the Revolution through the eyes of people who are living through it, and by juxtaposing their childhoods with their present lives, particularly their levels of integration in the Revolution, we hope to have shown something of the power of the past in determining the speed at which individuals and whole cultures can be transformed. The rapidity of political, economic, and legal change, so pronounced when the Revolution is observed from the top down, is put in clearer perspective when contrasted with the slowness of change in individual attitudes on sex roles, class, status, race, and religion. By providing such a contrast, the life stories illustrate one of the major dilemmas of social planning, namely, the time lag between institutional and cultural change and between behavioral and attitudinal change.

1. One of the objectives of this research was to examine the fate of Cubans raised in the culture of poverty and the extent to which a socialist system had been able to eliminate culture of poverty traits. We have not dealt with this question in these three volumes, however, because only one of the informants—Nicolás Salazar—could truly be said to have possessed these traits. Most of the informants were poor, and a number of them had been raised in urban or rural slums, but the culture of poverty concept was never meant to be used synonymously with slum life and certainly not with poverty in general.

The part of the research designed to examine this question—the Buena Ventura community study (an examination of 100 families relocated from a Havana shantytown to a new housing development)—has yet to be published. An analysis of life-story materials, shorter interviews, questionnaire data, studies of mass organizations and community services is now in preparation for publication. In general it was found, as Ruth Lewis wrote in the Foreword to *Four Men,* that although the majority of Buena Ventura residents were not integrated in the Revolution, "nowhere did we observe the degree of alienation, isolation, despair, or marginality we had seen among the very poor in other countries."

Oscar Lewis had not evaluated the Buena Ventura material as a whole before his death, although in September, 1969, while the research was still under way, he wrote to a colleague: "... it is ... clear that many of the traits of the culture of poverty persist in [the Buena Ventura] housing project. I believe I was overly optimistic in some of my earlier evaluations about the disappearance of the culture of poverty under socialism. However, there seems to me no doubt that the Cuban Revolution has abolished the conditions which gave rise to the culture of poverty."

As one can see from the relationships between the neighbors in this volume, between whites, blacks, and mulattoes, between men and women, parents and children, and between those who were in positions of authority and those who were not, Cuba has a long way to go before achieving that "higher form of social relationship" that is theoretically indicative of a communist society.[2] The Revolution has not been able to destroy racist, sexist, and classist attitudes as rapidly as it did the laws and institutions which gave them sanction. Almost no one, including the revolutionary leadership, expected such goals to be met in a single generation, although at times Castro has been too sanguine about the abolition of old attitudes. In a socialist system, as in any other, policy decisions filter down through layers of bureaucracy and are administered and enforced by thousands of people possessing wide-ranging social and political orientations. Cuban leaders, too, sometimes seem in their official statements to have been pushed to the left, by ideological stance and by international events, faster than they could divest themselves of their own cultural values.

Guevara warned that the new system would have to "compete fiercely with the past,"[3] and the more than 100 families interviewed during the course of the Cuba project do impress upon us the limitations on change within any one generation. In discussing the different ways in which the Revolution affected their lives and how they were changing in response to it, the informants suggest the variety of adaptations to socialism made by Cubans. Their disparate reactions—from the wholehearted support of Armando Cárdenas to the indifference of Leticia Manzanares and the quiet antagonism of Mercedes Millán, are part of the "living reality" Cuban leaders say they cannot ignore.[4]

I

It is not an easy task to make generalizations about the wide variety of experiences under the revolutionary government of the thirty-three informants presented in this series. Nowhere is it more difficult to generalize than in evaluating the impact of the Revolution on family life. Some change in family life was inevitable given the economic and legal transformation that had occurred in Cuba by 1970—the availability of jobs and educational opportunities, rationing, new divorce laws, the enforcement of child-support payments, new housing, and guaranteed health care. Although the majority of Cubans supported these changes

2. Fidel Castro, "To Create Wealth with Social Conscience," in Bertram Silverman, ed., *Man and Socialism* (New York: Atheneum, 1971), p. 372.

3. Lavan, ed., *Che Guevara Speaks*, p. 125.

4. Blas Roca, in a speech reprinted in *Granma Weekly Review*, Oct. 20, 1974, p. 4. In this talk on the work of the Law Study commissions, Blas Roca quoted Castro as saying that new institutions must be adapted to fit reality, and not reality to fit the institutions.

and the new socioeconomic system, they had not given much thought to
its ramifications for personal relationships, nor had they anticipated
anything as extensive as the 1975 Family Code.

Among our informants, some individuals have found in the new social
order the opportunity and strength to change unacceptable personal
situations, while others have used their homes and families as refuges to
retreat from demands which they could only partially accommodate.
The adjustments of Juan Pérez and Armando Cárdenas, for example,
both militant revolutionaries in their public stance, and both decidedly
traditional in their private lives, are examples of the multi-layered responses of Cubans to the Revolution. Some of our female informants
were ready and able to alter their life-styles in accord with their new
opportunities and legal status. For instance, Inocencia Acosta (*Four
Women*) obtained the divorce she had wanted for many years, and Pilar
López left prostitution to become a full-time student and pursue a career
while raising two children. However, in 1970 most of the women informants were not sufficiently politicized nor psychologically prepared to
utilize their potential, and most of the men were not ready to accept it.
The life stories, then, give a clearer understanding not only of the tremendous gains made by Cubans since the Revolution, but also of the
areas of greatest resistance to social change.

In this third volume there is not much doubt that insofar as power
relationships within the family were concerned, the ten adult informants
had expected the Revolution to stop at their front doors. At the time of
our study the division of labor and authority in the five homes followed
basically traditional patterns—the women spending most of their time at
home doing household chores and taking primary responsibility for
child care, the men having final authority in all important household
and family matters. None of the women had made a sustained effort to
take advantage of the educational and job opportunities available to
them, nor were they encouraged to do so by their husbands. Three of
the women were nominal members of mass organizations, and a fourth
was actively involved, but all five women, including Lala Fontanés, the
most integrated in the Revolution, were quick to assert their husbands'
greater competence to discuss political and governmental affairs.

In these five families, all the men except for Domingo Labrada, who
was partially disabled, were the principal wage-earners and were rarely
at home. None was doing the same work he had done before the Revolution, and, with the exception of Juan Pérez, their real incomes had risen
substantially. Through their jobs, voluntary labor, army or militia duties,
Communist Youth and Party activities, the five men were more integrated than the women. Although the men's lives had changed more
than the women's, their attitudes on sex roles and family life had, like
those of the women, changed very little. They retained their image of

women as wives and mothers, and *machismo* persisted as much in avowed revolutionaries like Cárdenas, Hernández, and Pérez as in the less politicized Rojas and Labrada.

Although the division of labor and authority in many homes had not been fundamentally altered as of 1970, other aspects of family life, such as daily household routines, had certainly changed. With the introduction of rationing, household management became more complex and time-consuming, and in most homes each member of the family, except for the smallest children, helped to shop for food and clothing. Nevertheless, with increased work demands, men spent less time than ever in their homes and with their children. Women, too, were gone from home more frequently; although by 1970 less than 18 percent of all women had joined the labor force, tens of thousands were doing voluntary productive labor and serving as active members or full-time cadre in mass organizations. Children spent less time under parental care primarily because of enforced compulsory education (through the sixth-grade level), but also because of the growing number of day-care centers[5] and boarding schools, and the wide variety of state-sponsored extracurricular activities.

For the fully integrated revolutionary, the hectic pace of life, including repeated and sustained absences from home by husband, wife, or both, and the new status of women, undoubtedly contributed to changing family life and to the increase in the divorce rate from 8.5 per 100 marriages in 1959 to 20.3 in 1966–67.[6] Even in cases where couples did not divorce, family life often disintegrated, as happened in the marriages of Mónica Ramos and her sister Renée (*Four Women*).

Well before the Castro government began dismantling the old socioeconomic structure, many families were deeply divided by conflicting political loyalties. Differences in degree of sympathy with the Revolution and the emigration of more than half a million Cubans diminished the unity and stability of thousands of families. Among those who remained, conflicts arose between the early non-ideological followers of the Twenty-sixth of July Movement and the new generation of socialists.

Whatever disintegration of family life occurred as a by-product of the revolutionary life-style was almost certainly not foreseen or intended by the leadership. The Revolution has never directly attacked the concept of the nuclear family, nor has it advocated or promoted alternatives to it as the basic unit of social organization; certainly there has not been any official advocacy (or even any public discussion that we know of) of

5. In 1970 there were spaces for about 50,000 children in the day-care system, not nearly enough to accommodate demands for the service.

6. Nelson, *Cuba: The Measure of a Revolution*, p. 154. The divorce rate fell to 18.1 per 100 marriages in 1968.

communal living, for instance. On the contrary, most of the leaders were profoundly middle-class and Latin in their concept of the family, particularly so in their view on motherhood. Day-care centers and boarding schools notwithstanding, the state has not tried to counteract the traditionally reverent attitude toward motherhood. Cubans continue to view women generally as inherently more nurturant than men, and the state has almost exclusively recruited women to staff the day-care centers that are run under the auspices of the Federation of Cuban Women.

The Castro government has tried to discourage certain patterns of family life common among the urban and rural poor (the widespread incidence of consensual unions, for instance) in favor of a more middle-class tradition. On child-rearing practices, the government has tried to reach a middle ground between the extremes of pampering and indulgence among the children of the upper classes and the hardships, even cruelties, of life for children of the poor. The government's ambition has been to provide all children with stable, economically secure homes where they might experience the common joys of childhood while learning a sense of social responsibility.

Since 1970 the Castro government has placed special emphasis on the restoration and strengthening of family life. The current official view on the family's role in socialist society (as stated in the Family Code) closely resembles that of the Soviet educator Anton Semenovich Makarenko (1888–1939), for whom the Cubans have named one of their major pedagogical institutes. The new code reflects Makarenko's view of the family as "the natural primary cell of society," where parental authority is "based not only on the delegated power of society but on the whole strength of public morality...."[7] According to Makarenko: "The decisive factor in successful family upbringing lies in the constant, active, and conscious fulfillment by parents of their civic duty toward society."[8]

While endorsing the nuclear family structure, the Family Code attempts to destroy the old power relationships between family members by itemizing the rights and obligations of wives, husbands, and children and attempting to put all on a more equal footing. It outlines the responsibilities of men and women in marriage, stressing their equal rights and duties in the education and upbringing of their children and, where both parents are working, in the management of the home as well. It extends to both men and women the right to work and states that it is the duty of each to help the other make this possible. It encourages civil marriages and stable homes for the rearing of children, and to this end it makes divorce obtainable only by judicial decree.

7. Anton Semenovich Makarenko, *The Collective Family: A Handbook for Russian Parents* (New York: Anchor Books, 1967), pp. 27–28.
8. *Ibid.*, p. 14.

The government recognizes that large segments of the code are unenforceable and consist, in effect, of a set of guidelines and a statement of long-range objectives. However, the code does provide the statutory groundwork that will govern legal proceedings for adoption, tutelage, marriage, divorce (including child custody, property settlements, and alimony), and paternity cases, and will probably also provide standards for deciding cases of child neglect and abuse. The code is particularly interesting as a reflection of the belief that correct political thinking and scientific know-how together can produce the desired result, even when the product is human. It is an expression of faith in the force of environmental over genetic factors and of the belief in human ability to control environmental conditions at all levels of the socialization process.

II

A second major purpose of the Cuba project was to give some idea of the range of behavior, personality, and family type within socialist Cuba, an objective we think especially important because of the tendency in many studies of Marxist systems to stress uniformity imposed from the top, thereby emphasizing social homogeneity while understating cultural diversity. We believe that the autobiographies give some idea of how the multiformity of personality, family type, and cultural background have affected the implementation and success of the Revolution's major programs by showing that in some families more than in others the skills learned, the traditions passed on, and the attitudes acquired better prepared their members for adapting to the new system.

The five families in *Neighbors* serve to illustrate how different levels of receptivity to and preparedness for functioning under the revolutionary system create some of the difficulties the government has had in effecting a more just distribution of goods, services, and social-welfare benefits. Among the families the most striking case of unpreparedness for the changes brought by the Revolution was the family of Sara and Eduardo Rojas. Sara Rojas was raised in a poor, tightly knit rural family by loving, indulgent, and protective parents. The numerous relatives who made up her extended family (and populated the village she lived in) were largely closed off from the outside world, providing for almost all their material and emotional needs within the family group. The Rojases rarely went in to the city, or to hospitals or doctors, had no contact with local government, probably paid no taxes, certainly did not vote, did not send their sons to the Army, and had few cash dealings and no experience with banks. They had only the briefest exposure to schools, usually one-room shacks with teachers who had at most an elementary education. They had no contact with professional teachers, administrators, or auxiliary parent organizations. The Church, but not religion, was marginal to their lives. Theirs was a highly personal world and they prepared their children only for staying within that world. They gave each other such training as they needed to manage home and farm; they grew their own food, delivered their own babies, provided marriage partners, cared for each other in illness and old age, and provided their own entertainment. Religion and medicine were learned largely from folk practice and belief.[9]

Family played an important role throughout the lives of middle-class people like Juan Pérez and Mercedes Millán, but family life was not by any means their whole world. One retreated completely into the family only when one failed. Middle-class children were introduced early to the major social, economic, and political institutions, and in general saw the progression of their lives in relation to these institutions. It was the middle class who ran the bureaucracy, staffed the schools and hospitals, held public offices, and so forth; the secular world was their domain. Unlike poor, rural Cubans such as the Rojases, who were bewildered by the new skills required in a highly organized and secular society, a man like Juan Pérez was able to use his familiarity with secular institutions to help solve his family's problems under the new government. He and his wife, who before the Revolution had everything they needed and more, continued to get the best of what was available after 1959. Pérez understood the workings of the bureaucracy and knew how to exploit the system of *socioismo*, the practice of developing personal contacts and using them to get what one wanted. On the other hand, the Rojases, the family with the fewest amenities and the one making the least use of the opportunities and services available to them, knew the least about how to go about improving their position. Even with directions and advice they soon gave up, lost in a sea of strangers and red tape.

In their adaptation to life under the Castro government, the Rojases were not typical of other poor rural families in this study. Leticia Manzanares and Domingo Labrada, for instance, came from broken homes and both had been separated from their families at an early age. They remained close to their parents and to their brothers and sisters, but the broken and scattered family units did not give them any economic security to fall back on. Unlike the Rojas family, who worked the land, Leticia and Domingo were wage-earners and far less self-sufficient. Having gone out in early adolescence to support themselves, Leticia and Domingo had acquired some ability to operate in a money economy and in an urban, secular atmosphere. This work experience, coupled with a sense of pragmatism, helped them adapt after 1959; even though they were at best indifferent to politics and to the ideology of the Revolution,

9. Similar patterns were common among informants from the urban slums, although in their case the primary group was not the extended family but the residents of their barrios.

they were willing and able to take advantage of any new opportunity that came their way.

Lala Fontanés is an example of yet a different adjustment by a rural Cuban. Her father, as a small *colono* who sold his cane to a nearby sugar mill, had some concept of the national economy and of being part of it. Señor Fontanés had also been allied with a political party and had served as a town councilman. The Fontanéses believed in education, respectability, and getting ahead. They were Roman Catholics who had only a marginal relationship to the Church but who were not (uncharacteristically for poor Cubans) anticlerical. Discipline was strong in the home and Lala learned respect not just for parental authority but for the Church and secular authority as well. Lala made a fairly easy transition to the new order; even though she was unfamiliar with the Twenty-sixth of July Movement and its objectives, she did underground work on orders from her employers, just as she acceded to almost every demand made on her by the government after the Triumph. With her appreciation of education as a necessary means for advancement, she was dedicated to the schooling of her own children, oversaw their homework, and never let them play truant. She also helped and encouraged her husband to become literate and to continue his education, in part as a means to improve the family's economic position, but also so that Armando might appear more refined and respectable.

Armando, on the other hand, saw his education primarily as a means to help him fulfill his responsibilities more adequately. He viewed work as an activity to promote the common good, but also as an end in itself. He had little motivation to exploit his position and contacts for personal advancement, and, unlike Lala, he was an idealist who respected the authority of the Revolution less than the principles behind it. If the Cárdenases' housing conditions and their standard of living are to be improved, it will probably be Lala, with her respect for status and her middle-class ambitions, who will provide the initiative.

The desire to get ahead and to make the best of every opportunity was also a characteristic of the Hernández family. Justa Díaz, the daughter of a dispossessed farmer and poor laborer, was barely literate and unaccustomed to operating in an impersonal world. But the style and pace of life in their family was set by her husband, Ricardo, who was the son of a small-town skilled worker; his brothers were tradesmen and shopkeepers and Ricardo himself had been a grocer. Very ambitious, he was always alert to any opportunity to improve his family's standard of living. Justa, likewise, took in laundry to buy furnishings and extras for their home. As a Party member Ricardo was well informed and always among the first in line for any available goods and services.

It was somewhat surprising to find that in a system so highly organized and politicized, where the mass media and the educational system were controlled by the state, there existed such variations in familiarity with revolutionary laws and programs. The Rojases were oblivious to, or simply ignored or avoided, certain services and opportunities because they were too unfamiliar with the procedures or because the benefits were too little valued by them. To get Violeta Rojas enrolled in school, for example, would take the initiative of someone outside the family to do the necessary paper and leg work, and it will be a long time before Sara Rojas, a native healer who distrusted doctors and hospitals, is willing to incorporate regular medical and dental checkups into her normal routine. Which is to say that the state cannot make everyone want to attend school or go to a doctor in the same length of time it takes to build hospitals, clinics, and schools. It is not surprising, then, that the state has had some of its greatest successes in health care, for example, in those areas of practice (preventive techniques such as immunization and cytological testing) which were taken directly to the people in their homes.

The fact that more than a decade after the Triumph the Rojases were still relatively isolated from the larger society and unfamiliar with new institutions and with urban life was in part an organizational failure of the Revolution, but in larger measure it resulted from a contradiction between personality and family type on the one hand and the nature of the political system on the other.

III

One aspect of the community studies planned for the Cuba project was the observation of mass organizations as they functioned at the neighborhood level. For all Cubans employed outside their homes, joining at least one or two of the mass organizations was inevitable; usually this meant membership in the Committees for Defense of the Revolution and in the Central Organization of Cuban Trade Unions, and for women, the Federation of Cuban Women as well. The other principal mass organizations were the militia, the Federation of University Students, the Federation of Intermediate Students, and the Pioneers.[10] Whatever their personal attitudes toward these organizations, every Cuban understood the importance of being integrated—the wheels of the bureaucracy do not turn for the unintegrated person. If Cubans want promotions in their work, scholarships or places in day-care centers for their children, admission to a university, the resolution of a housing or any other problem, the bottom line for qualification is to be organized.

10. The Federation of Cuban Women is discussed in the Introduction to *Four Women;* Pioneer activities are briefly discussed in Part IV of this volume. In the autobiographical materials we have only scant information on the militia (see Pilar López's description of her training) and unions (see Armando Cárdenas's discussion of his duties as union representative and member of a Labor Council).

The Committees for Defense of the Revolution were the largest, most active, and most visible of the mass organizations and of key importance as a liaison between the people and the government.[11] Almost everyone interviewed belonged to their local CDRs, but their attitudes ranged from total involvement to complete indifference. It was not at all uncommon for CDR members to be unable to name the officers of their block Committee. Among the CDRs observed in 1969–70 there was a tendency—much like the assignment of committee work in almost any kind of volunteer organization in the United States—to recognize a few people on each block as willing workers and to consistently turn over most duties to them. The election of officers was a rather casual process; after discussion a consensus was reached among those attending a meeting on who was willing and able to serve, and after a show of hands, positions were then assigned to those persons.

A majority of those interviewed saw the CDR's activities (although not necessarily membership in it) as truly voluntary; if they did not want to participate in a particular activity, they refused. We observed no real pressure to make them change their minds about any particular decision. Some members (Mercedes Millán, Sara Rojas, Alfredo Barrera, to name a few among our informants) did not even bother to attend meetings, while others willing to accept responsibility (Lala Fontanés, Lázaro Benedí, and Inocencia Acosta, for example) were burdened with one task after another.

Despite the organizational breakdown in 1969–70, differences in participation at the block level, and the unevenness of performance of CDRs from neighborhood to neighborhood, the Committees' accomplishments were many. They recruited members to stand guard against theft and vandalism as well as against sabotage, and to do agricultural labor and participate in the government's many national campaigns (such as glass collection). *Cederistas* also helped the government implement the rationing program, carrying out a large part of the initial canvassing of households. One of their most significant accomplishments was in the area of public health: *cederistas* were responsible for vaccinating many Cubans and for giving injections prescribed by doctors. The latter service ensured better follow-up of a recommended course of treatment, saved the patient the inconvenience of waiting for a turn in a polyclinic, and lightened the clinic patient load. CDR public-health officers often supervised block clean-up, fix-up campaigns, and reported untreated health problems and violations of the Public Health Code.

We also believe, although it is a difficult claim to document, that the

11. Initial work on the CDRs was done in five Havana *repartos*, and detailed observations were made on the Committees in Buena Ventura. It is necessary to restate that the CDRs were not observed outside Havana; this is important because the organizational base of the rural CDRs is different, and it undoubtedly influenced the kinds of problems they dealt with as well as their effectiveness.

CDRs made an important contribution by giving many Cubans a sense of belonging, of being useful and needed, and even perhaps some sense of efficacy, that is, of being able to have some effect, however small, on the future of the country. For politically and socially marginal people such as Nicolás Salazar, who suffered from very low self-esteem and had no sense of belonging outside his barrio, to be asked to serve as an officer of the CDR was an important accomplishment. With a new home, a job, and a leadership position in the community, Salazar felt more worthy and more important than ever before in his life. However, for those Cubans such as Mónica Ramos and Juan Pérez who were already well integrated and politically active, CDR membership was at best a secondary activity.

The CDRs were responsible for recruiting into the volunteer ranks many women, particularly housewives who had never worked outside their homes and who often thought that civic work and political involvement were for men only. During the early years of the CDR, housewives were especially important to the organization and running of the neighborhood Committees because their husbands tended to volunteer their spare time to CDRs in their work centers (abolished in the mid-1960s), and to the militia or other non-neighborhood-based organizations. As early as 1963, housewives made up more than 17 percent of the CDR cadre.[12] Men apparently objected least to their wives doing this kind of work because it usually did not take them far from their homes.

By giving women the opportunity to employ their talents and energy and to feel useful outside their homes, CDR work provided a first important step toward the integration of women in the Revolution. In this sense, the Committees were probably more important to the integration of women than was the Federation of Cuban Women. In the early years, the Federation recruited women into traditionally feminine activities such as PTA-type work, the study of homemaking, sewing, and child care, and for at least the first decade of the Revolution, the Federation magazine, *Mujer,* promoted the stereotypical image of the middle-class woman. CDR work, on the other hand, often took women into more traditionally masculine activities such as guard duty and political education. Most important, in the CDRs men and women worked side by side, and women competed with men for office and were often in a position of supervising male workers (although there was little order-giving in the local CDRs).

In 1970 the energies of most Cubans interested in doing volunteer work was all but consumed by the effort to fulfill the government's goal of harvesting 10 million tons of sugar. All organizations in Cuba suf-

---

12. Richard R. Fagen, *The Transformation of Political Culture in Cuba* (Stanford, Calif.: Stanford University Press, 1969), p. 83.

fered for it, but the CDRs seem to have been especially hard hit. Undoubtedly the Central Committee of the Communist Party, to which the National Directorate of the CDR is directly responsible, had little time to devote to the CDR's organizational problems, and many of the full-time cadre at the intermediary and higher levels of the CDR must themselves have left their posts to do long-term work in the harvest. Certainly there was a labor drain at the base levels of the Committees.

All the Committees observed by project field workers had special difficulties. The Cristal Street CDR, as discussed in the Introduction to this volume, had a weak membership base because of the number of students and foreigners who lived on the block. It was functioning poorly in 1970, holding no regular meetings, organizing street patrols and block projects only erratically, and was often unable to carry out directives from above. A few dedicated workers, such as Lala Fontanés, did manage to carry on some of the Committee's most important work, especially public-health activities and recruiting volunteers for productive labor.

In the Buena Ventura housing development, however, the CDRs were in a state of total disarray. Only a few of the members and officers had any organizational or political experience, and most were just barely able to read and write. Such CDRs needed constant attention and supervision from cadre at the zone and sectional levels, but in 1970 they were receiving little if any assistance. Because of the special problems of these CDRs they cannot be taken as representative, although it is true that in 1970 there was an organizational failure in the CDRs across the island. From available information on post-1970 Committee organization and activities, it appears that following a 1971 reorganization they have been revitalized and are stronger than at any time in the past.

IV

Another of the basic objectives of this research was to evaluate the extent to which the Castro government had been able to achieve the major goals of the Revolution. Despite many policy failures, Castro has shown a genuine commitment to the original six objectives of the Twenty-sixth of July Movement: land reform, industrialization, housing, education, unemployment, and health care.[13] However, as the whole world knows, Castro has changed his mind about the best means for achieving those goals since he first outlined them in 1953.

Among the most impressive of the Revolution's many achievements are those in health care, education, and employment. Advances in these areas we believe are well documented in the life stories. As one example of this we offer the much improved infant-mortality rate and the re-

13. Fidel Castro, *History Will Absolve Me* (Havana: Book Institute, 1967), pp. 69–73.

duced incidence of childhood disease. Among the families of our *Four Men* informants, three of Alfredo Barerra's siblings, seven of Nicolás Salazar's, and one of Gabriel Capote's died at birth or in early infancy.[14] Among the *Neighbors* families, Armando Cárdenas's cousin and Sara Rojas's sister died of tuberculosis in early adolescence; Lala Fontanés's sister died of intestinal parasites; and Eduardo Rojas's brother-in-law was crippled from poliomyelitis. Armando Cárdenas himself suffered from parasites and collapsed on the job from malnutrition, yet he never saw a doctor until he joined the Rebel Army. Among the forty children born after 1959 to the informants presented in this series, not one suffered from any of these afflictions or from any other major diseases. Only one informant, Sara Rojas, reported an infant death: her eighth child was stillborn in 1968.

According to government statistics, the infant-mortality rate in Cuba dropped from 60 per 1,000 births in the pre-revolutionary period to 28.9 in 1974, and there have been comparable improvements in the mortality rate of preschool (1.2/1,000 inhabitants) and school-age children (0.5/1,000), as well as of women in childbirth (0.5/1,000).[15] Poliomyelitis was reportedly eradicated in 1963, malaria in 1968, diphtheria in 1971; deaths from gastroenteritis (80 percent of which were children under one year of age) dropped from 4,157 in 1962 to 761 in 1974. Similar reductions were reported in the incidence of tetanus, tuberculosis, and other infectious diseases.

Public-health expenditures increased twentyfold between 1958 and 1975 (from 20 to 400 million *pesos*). The construction of hundreds of hospitals and polyclinics (including 56 hospitals and 118 dispensaries in the countryside) has greatly improved facilities and delivery capabilities in the rural areas. Although Cuba lost half of its 6,000 physicians through emigration, the country now claims 10,000 doctors and a doctor-patient ratio (1:1,000) equal to that of 1959, and is aiming at a ratio of 1:750. To end the concentration of medical personnel in Havana that was characteristic of the pre-revolutionary years (and which has persisted to a lesser extent since), it is now (officially) mandatory for all doctors to serve in rural areas for three years after graduation from medical school. All changes in public-health policies are predicated on the belief that health care is a basic human right and that it should therefore be available to all people at no direct cost.

Among Cuba's most serious health-care problems in 1970 were the shortages of senior medical personnel, sophisticated diagnostic equipment, pharmaceuticals, and certain kinds of foods prescribed for patients

14. Ten of Lázaro Benedí's and three of Inocencia Acosta's siblings also died at birth or in infancy, but these deaths occurred in the early 1900s.

15. Except where indicated, all statistics quoted in this section were prepared by the Cuban government and were cited in Castro's report to the First Party Congress, *Granma Weekly Review*, Jan. 4, 1976.

on restricted diets. Several of our informants—the mother of Mercedes Millán, for example, who was a diabetic, Domingo Labrada, who had a skin disease, and Armando Cárdenas, who had a stomach disorder— were on doctor-prescribed diets and were unable to obtain in sufficient quantities the foods required by their restricted diets. Labrada's case also illustrates a serious deficiency in the diagnostic capabilities of Cuba's health services as of 1970. Another serious problem in 1970 was in the area of dental care, especially preventive care, which had not kept pace with the overall improvements in general health care.[16]

Medical and health care are evidently part of the reason for Castro's renewed interest in reopening trade relations with the United States. Cuba is reportedly interested in purchasing sophisticated diagnostic equipment, such as brain scanners, and also perhaps pharmaceutical products.

Since 1959 public expenditures on education are reported to have increased elevenfold; illiteracy to have been reduced from 23.6 percent (for Cubans over age ten) to about 3 percent, and school enrollment for children between the ages of six and fourteen years to have increased from about 55 percent to almost 100 percent. Education is tuition-free through the university level, and over 600,000 children receive additional assistance, more than half of these through scholarships that provide room and board, uniforms, and transportation to and from home on weekends and vacations. The vast expansion of educational facilities includes a new system of teacher-training institutes, schools for special education, and an adult-education program with half a million enrollees.

Because of the rapid increase in educational opportunities and the opening of hundreds of new schools, throughout the 1960s Cuba suffered from a shortage of adequately trained teachers. Some elementary-school teachers were themselves still students in basic secondary and normal school, and some instructors for the primary grades in adult-education schools had graduated only from elementary schools. Most teachers followed curricula plans drawn up by the Ministry of Education and relied heavily on the practice of rote learning. Children spent a good deal of time repeating lessons out loud and copying into

16. Other weaknesses in health-care services were observed during the course of the project, but we do not know whether they were widespread or isolated cases. One example was that of an elderly man who for two years had been unable to get batteries for his antiquated hearing aid. Another was the continued use of an outmoded penicillin inhalant treatment for certain respiratory illnesses. Although at least two of our informants had been under psychiatric care and had received electroshock treatments, we learned very little in general about the care of the mentally and emotionally ill. There were some discouraging examples of the government's treatment of the physically handicapped. The brother-in-law of Eduardo Rojas, who was crippled by polio, and the brother of Gabriel Capote, who suffered from epilepsy, received no rehabilitation or job training but rather were pensioned off and not allowed to work.

notebooks; stress was on accuracy and neatness rather than on creativity or critical thinking.

At the university level, the introduction of political criteria for evaluating the work of faculty and students brought temporary chaos to campuses in the mid-1960s, and the quality of education undoubtedly suffered for it. As can be seen in the story of Mónica Ramos, there were periods when more time was spent on disputes between rival political factions than on attending classes and studying (this was the modus vivendi for the Federation of University Students before the Revolution), but once the new Communist Party stabilized its organization in the universities after 1965, political activities apparently occupied less of the students' time.

Cuba guarantees the right to work to all men and women and claims full employment of the male labor force. Government statistics show a 58.5 percent growth in the size of the labor force during the first decade of the Revolution and an average annual growth rate in employment of 3.6 percent during the first seventeen years. During the same period the population increased at an average annual rate of 2.1 percent. The Revolution claims to have created 1,400,000 new jobs, 500,000 of them between 1970 and 1974, with male employment increasing during the latter period by 23 percent and female employment by 40 percent. Women comprised about 25 percent of the labor force in 1976.

Castro reported in 1976 that 50 percent of all homes had one working member, 30 percent had two incomes, 12 percent three incomes, and 8 percent four or more. The average monthly salary was reported to be 136 *pesos,* up 21 percent from 1970, and average monthly family income to be 203 *pesos.* For the five families in *Neighbors,* the estimated average monthly family income in 1969–70 was 163.20 *pesos,* while the average annual per capita income was 297 *pesos* (see Appendix B); this compares to an average annual per capita income of 213 *pesos* for the period 1950–57.[17] In terms of real income the gap is far greater than 84 *pesos,* since prices are now fixed and there are rent controls, retirement and vacation benefits, and no direct cost for health care or education. In addition, some jobs provide a clothing allowance, and prior to 1970 there were sometimes one or two free or low-cost meals served each day in work centers.

In 1970 Cuba was still struggling to conquer the problems of absenteeism and vagrancy. Thousands of Cubans, particularly agricultural laborers who had been habitually underemployed, had acquired work habits that were not easily adjusted to the discipline of full-time year-

17. Philip S. Foner, *A History of Cuba and Its Relations with the United States,* I (1492–1845) (New York: International Publishers, 1962), p. 8. For other figures on income in the pre-revolutionary period see Leyva, "Health and Revolution in Cuba," in Bonachea and Valdés, eds., *Cuba in Revolution,* p. 458.

round employment (see especially the story of Domingo Labrada). This was also a problem for urban slum dwellers (see Nicolás Salazar) accustomed to being hired by the day, or to self-employment in small business (such as street vending or the collecting and selling of bottles), or who were resigned to permanent unemployment. The pre-revolutionary unemployment rate—which ranged from 25 to 33 percent—suggests the extensiveness of the problem of poor work habits. In 1971, after more than a decade of relative tolerance and a public education campaign against vagrancy and absenteeism, the government began to take strong sanctions against those who were chronically absent from work or who refused to take jobs.[18]

Another serious problem facing the revolutionary government in the area of employment was the relatively small pool of highly skilled labor on which the state could draw. The new leadership had to cope with the legacy of an inadequate, corrupt, and nonegalitarian educational system that had left 23 percent of the population illiterate and many more barely literate. This situation was compounded by the exodus of foreigners and emigration of a large percentage of Cuba's managerial and professional classes. Partly out of necessity and partly out of naiveté, the government assigned people to vacated positions in management and the bureaucracy on the basis of their revolutionary fervor. Therefore, in the confusion of the early years, people were being shifted in and out of positions for which they were wholly unprepared. Juan Pérez, for example, having spent half his work life in the growing, transporting, and selling of food, was assigned a job overseeing the import and distribution of machine parts—and this at a time when Cuba's system for distributing food, especially fresh produce, was in serious trouble.

This inefficient use of labor also occurred at lower skill levels. Some soldiers followed the Rebel Army to the city and settled there; others, hoping to find a better job, or any job at all, migrated to Havana to take up the labor slack left by the emigrants. None of the five men in the *Neighbors* study was doing the kind of work he had done before the Revolution. After moving to the city Eduardo Rojas, an experienced cane-cutter, became an unskilled security guard. Armando Cárdenas, who had a great deal of experience in agriculture and who, after his education, might have been appointed to a managerial position on a state farm, was made a manager of cafeterias in the city. Wanting very much to do whatever the Revolution asked of him, and performing admirably on the job, Armando nevertheless did not adapt easily to indoor work, city life, or managerial responsibility. He suffered from tension, an ulcer, and had anxiety dreams so severe that he required psychiatric counseling.

18. The anti-loafing law of 1971 (see Part III, n. 32). The government's difficulties in recruiting women into the labor force and the prospects for sexual equality on the job are discussed in the Introduction to *Four Women*.

As late as 1969 the government was assigning inadequately trained revolutionary militants to positions that required considerable expertise. In fact, one of the reasons given by Castro for the failure of the 1970 harvest was the number of unskilled (in some cases barely literate) people in key positions in the sugar industry.

The availability and quality of housing remained a serious problem in Cuba as of 1970, but the state had done much to maximize its available resources. Some of the vacated, confiscated housing of emigrants was used to accommodate army and government leaders, but much of it was reassigned to some of Havana's most needy families, as well as to migrants to the city. Cuba's worst slums were razed and new housing was built for their residents. Under the Urban Reform laws over 268,000 people received title to houses and apartments they had been renting; a ceiling on rent was set for all others, and payments counted toward the purchase price of the house or apartment. But Cuba was unable during the 1960s to build enough new housing to keep pace with population growth, and the country also suffered from a shortage of supplies for repair and maintenance of old structures.

In 1976 Castro estimated that for every Cuban to live decently one million more new units were needed, and that it could take as long as fifteen years for supply to catch up to demand. An intensive effort has been made to recruit people, especially women, into the construction industry. Under the "work plus" program, men and women who are already employed are organized into construction brigades to build multiple-family dwellings which, when completed, are turned over to their work centers to be assigned on the basis of need and merit.

Because our informants were largely from the poorer segments of the population, many had received new housing (which in some cases they had helped build and were paying off in low monthly installments) or title to houses and apartments they had been renting for many years. Although almost everyone was pleased with the rent ceiling, with the no-eviction-of-tenants clause of the reform law, and with the opportunity to buy their homes, others complained about having to wait for years for promised housing. Among our informants' experiences there were some cases of bureaucractic failures and one of abuse of position to obtain housing, but the principal problem was simply a shortage of adequate structures. The revolutionary government began its reform facing such extreme deficiencies in housing and in equipment, skilled labor, material, and supplies that it could not possibly have satisfied every need for new housing.

Informants related a number of stories of persons of high military rank, or with contacts in one of the housing offices, who received preferential treatment in the assignment of available housing. The only documented case of such abuse that appears in these volumes is that of the housing exchange between the Rojas and Hernández families. Lieutenant Hernández may have been technically within the law, arranging the exchange through the Frozen Zone's Housing office, but he took advantage of barely literate rural people who were completely unfamiliar with the system. Using an old army buddy as his contact in the Housing office, Hernández obtained the necessary legal papers and then, when Bernardo Rojas balked at going through with the exchange, invoked the authority of the police and the Revolution.

Other families in the building, except for the Pérezes, agreed with Eduardo Rojas that the lieutenant "had made use of his rank" to move into the building. And even though Sara and Eduardo were left homeless, the exchange was allowed to stand. The Rojases' plight was no bureaucratic oversight; over a two-year period the family had unsuccessfully made appeals to several government agencies and officials.

The Rojas case raises problems other than the misuse of rank and the failure of housing officials to defend the Rojases' legal rights. It illustrates a certain lack of foresight on the part of housing officials, however good their intentions, in the assignment of housing. In its rush to fulfill its promises, the government did not have adequate time or resources to prepare relocated Cubans to live in their new homes and neighborhoods. Many of these people, as they explain in their stories, were completely disoriented in the city; some had never seen a house with ceilings, let alone indoor plumbing and electricity. Many were intimidated by tall buildings, traffic, and public transportation, and were afraid to go out alone to do errands. But once they had arrived in the city, these people were generally on their own, with little or no instruction or preparation in how to adapt to an urban environment or how to care for their new apartments and their modern equipment.

In assigning housing in Miramar to the Rojas family the government was, of course, making use of available housing, but it may also have been deliberately trying to integrate, both economically and racially, the formerly wealthy white neighborhoods. While it is easy to understand why the state did not care what the upper classes might feel about living among the poor, it is harder to explain the lack of consideration for the effects on the poor of living in a strange and sometimes hostile environment. The Rojas family was ridiculed and even ostracized by some of their neighbors, and they seemed unable and (understandably) unwilling to adjust their life-style to conform to their neighbors' demands. The move to Havana upset and destabilized the family, and in the short run at least, lowered the quality of their lives.

Two cases in which housing requests seem to have been lost in the bureaucratic shuffle were those of the Cárdenas and Capote families. Lala Fontanés and Armando Cárdenas turned over to the state the large furnished apartment that had been left Lala by her employers. In return, they requested a smaller home more suitable for their needs. This they said was promised them, but after four children and nine years of living in two small rooms, the family was still waiting for a larger home.

Another more pressing housing problem was that of Gabriel Capote (*Four Men*), who, just after he married, had been assigned a single room in an old Havana hotel. In 1970 Gabriel, his wife, and four children were still living in this room, which had no kitchen and only one cold-water tap; they shared a toilet with eight other families and had no bathing facilities. When the children had to be left alone, Gabriel and his wife were in the habit of tying them to the furniture to prevent them from falling out the windows or running downstairs and out into the street. The older children suffered from nervous disorders and learning disabilities and had been recommended for psychiatric care. Despite the severity of the problem and after repeated requests, Gabriel, a dedicated revolutionary, had been unable to get better housing. In disgust and anger, he resigned his membership in the Communist Youth; when he finally received a hearing to air his grievances he refused to attend.

It is hard to explain such bureaucratic callousness in the face of deprivation as severe as that suffered by the Rojas and Capote families; certainly other Cubans with less pressing needs did receive new housing, and some foreign guests (particularly those who were famous specialists in fields related to Cuba's development) and diplomatic personnel were housed in relatively luxurious—in a few cases even opulent—conditions. Nevertheless, the examples of the Rojases and Capotes are not indicative of what the Revolution has been able to accomplish in housing since 1959. More representative of changing housing conditions for the urban poor are the 100 Las Yaguas families relocated from slum dwellings to new homes in Buena Ventura. However, until the government's construction program can catch up with the demand for housing, and until the old generation of the formerly wealthy die and their properties revert to the state, great inequities will continue to exist.

Although it is true that the objective underlying all of the Revolution's principal goals has been to achieve the most egalitarian distribution of goods and services feasible, this has obviously not meant an absolute leveling of standards of living or wages. In fact, the Revolution's attempts at class leveling seem quite moderate when compared to the radical and violent programs for redistribution of wealth in countries such as Cambodia, for instance, where in 1975 whole cities were evacuated and members of the white-collar and upper classes were executed en masse or made to live and work in the countryside. In Cuba rather startling inequities in the standard of living were not uncommon in middle-class neighborhoods such as Miramar. Thus in 1970 we found the Rojas family living in a garage with no plumbing only several doors away from an elderly woman occupying a nine-bedroom, six-bathroom house.

Under the Urban Reform laws private residences occupied by owners were not confiscated, although most vacation homes and all rental properties did revert to the state. In the latter case there was often restitution to the owners who remained in Cuba; some of those interviewed in Miramar were living on compensatory payments from the state. Families retained all their personal possessions, including furnishings, cars, clothing, etc. Cubans were also allowed to keep up to 10,000 *pesos* in savings, although access to their accounts was controlled by a ceiling set on monthly withdrawals.

Rationing of food, clothing, and consumer goods has probably been the greatest leveler, although members of the middle and upper classes have been better able to supplement their rations because they have greater reserves of clothing, and more money (from savings and higher-paid jobs) to spend on the black market. Other leveling factors have been the rationing of gasoline, the scarcity of spare parts for cars and appliances, and the shortages of supplies and services for home maintenance.

In 1970 there were four graded wage scales for the various sectors of the Cuban economy, ranging from a low of 65 *pesos* a month to a high of 833.[19] The pay scale was based on a recognition of the historical wage, so most professionals and white-collar workers continue to out-earn peasants and blue-collar workers. Ironically, cane-cutters, the backbone of Cuba's principal industry, were near the bottom of the pay scale. There was some cynicism among Cubans (see the story of Alfredo Barrera) about the practice of sending relatively high-paid urban workers to work in the cane fields while continuing to draw their regular salaries. This meant that during the harvest season bureaucrats, professionals, and others who were relatively unskilled cane-cutters, and in some cases complete novices, were earning as much as 200 to 400 *pesos* a month working in the fields, while the highly skilled *macheteros* were earning as little as 90.

Cubas' approach to the redistribution of wealth, then, depends in part on a gradual withering away of the historical middle and upper classes, and while it may be true that as this happens the standard-of-living gap will continue to narrow, in 1970 the middle and upper classes were still far better off materially than the majority of Cubans.

V

It is impossible to evaluate the success of any undertaking without an accounting of the costs incurred. Cubans have paid dearly for their new homes, schools, hospitals, and clinics, for new factories, full employment

19. Mesa-Lago, ed., *Revolutionary Change in Cuba*, p. 228. There are conflicting reports on the current wage scale, but the gap has apparently narrowed somewhat from 80 or 85 *pesos* to 750 (approximately $100 to $938).

with retirement and vacation benefits, increased agricultural production, and a new position for their country in the world community. Part of the price has been paid in long work hours (many of them in unpaid voluntary overtime), forced savings, wages fixed by the state, scarcity of consumer goods, a restricted if adequate diet, limitations on physical mobility (both internal and external travel) and professional mobility, adjustments in life-styles and the conduct of personal relationships, and more limited channels for personal, political, professional, and artistic expression.[20] There were, in addition, the staggering personal costs of the insurrection itself, including thousands of casualties and the political division and permanent separation of families and friends (and the loss of human resources to the country) through the emigration of more than half a million Cubans.

Restrictions on personal freedom and civil liberties would be placed among the highest costs of the Revolution by some people; among them, however, would probably be few from the majority of Cubans economically oppressed under the old political system. At any rate, Cuba's past governments do not have a history of respect for civil liberties, especially not for the lower classes or for oppositionist members of the middle and upper classes.

From the informants' interviews the reader can see that in 1969–70 most of them felt little compunction about criticizing government policies, either among themselves or to foreigners. With only a few exceptions they were not fearful of government reaction.[21] Cuba is a small country with a highly personalized style of government; Castro is constantly going to the people to talk about government policy, and they in turn are quick to offer their opinions. For Cubans, in general, having opinions and giving them, with little inhibition—to a friend, a foreigner, or to Fidel himself if the chance arose—was more common than not.

20. Under the new Constitution, "artistic creativity is free as long as its content is not contrary to the Revolution ... creation and investigation in science are free. The state encourages and facilitates investigations and gives priority to that which is aimed at solving the problems related to the interests of society and the well-being of the people ..." (IV, 38). In general the Constitution guarantees civil liberties only when they are exercised in such a way as not to oppose the Revolution. Therefore, "Citizens have freedom of speech and of the press in keeping with the objectives of socialist society. Material conditions for the exercise of that right are provided for by the fact that the press, radio, television, movies and other organs of the mass media are state or social property and can never be private property" (VI, 52). The rights to assembly, demonstration, and association are guaranteed, but apparently only when exercised through the mass organizations, "in which the members have full freedom of speech and opinion based on the unlimited right of initiative and criticism" (VI, 53). (The full text of the Constitution was reprinted in *Granma Weekly Review* Mar. 7, 1976.)

21. Three exceptions were Señor X, whose case is discussed in the Foreword to *Four Men;* Juan Pérez, an administrator and candidate for Party membership who had once helped bug the office of his boss and was wary of tape recorders; and Lieutenant Hernández, a policeman and Party member, who was trying to conceal a housing exchange of questionable ethics and legality.

The range of freedom one had to criticize or to defy certain laws, however, depended in part on one's socioeconomic background. The people of Buena Ventura, for example, all former slum dwellers, were allowed a good deal of breathing room; life in that *reparto,* and in Bolívar, included gambling, truancy, absenteeism, black-marketeering, rowdiness and violence, small-scale prostitution, and, according to some, the sale and use of marijuana. The government wrote off much of this behavior as inevitable, given the socioeconomic background of the individuals involved. In any case, the residents of Buena Ventura were not employed in sensitive or security-related work, nor were they in positions of influence or privilege; most worked very hard at unskilled jobs for fairly low wages. Complaining and criticizing were a kind of safety valve on discontent.

The government appeared to be less lenient with dissenters from the middle class, especially those who held jobs in universities, the professions, or the bureaucracy, all of which were relatively well-paid positions that sometimes involved privileges not available to blue-collar workers. To illustrate this, we might compare the state's tolerance of the criticisms and illegal acts of Alfredo Barrera, for instance, or of his neighbors in Buena Ventura, with its lack of tolerance for the behavior of Señor X. Señor X was not well integrated and had a long history of criticism of government policies; he was rather openly sympathetic to the U.S. government (as opposed to the American people), but to our knowledge he had not broken any law. Señor X was, however, a scientist who had family connections with high government officials. His desire to make his criticisms known through a published account of his life apparently tipped the balance against him and led to his imprisonment in a work camp. This treatment was quite different from that received by those employed in less strategic work and without highly placed friends or relatives.

This differential treatment of critics of the Revolution was also applicable to active opponents of the government. Many of the peasants who fought in the counterrevolutionary guerrilla actions in the Escambray were sent to work camps for a period of several years of agricultural labor and political indoctrination, while the highly placed opponents such as Comandante Matos—who opposed communist influence in the government and refused an order to surrender his command, but who never took up arms against Castro—is serving a twenty-year sentence in La Cabaña.

Castro told Lee Lockwood in 1968 that much of the counterrevolutionary behavior of peasants was "predetermined by circumstances"[22]—in other words, that it could be accounted for by their past economic condition and social environment. That can be construed as a rather simplis-

22. Lockwood, *Castro's Cuba, Cuba's Fidel,* p. 172.

tic, patronizing way of explaining away opposition, but at the same time
it does explain the government's greater leniency for counterrevolutionaries from peasant backgrounds and for ex-slum dwellers
guilty of what was labeled "antisocial behavior."

In the interview with Lockwood, Castro estimated the number of political prisoners in Cuba at 20,000, based on the number of sentences
handed down by Revolutionary Tribunals, the only courts that try political offenses. This number included counterrevolutionary offenders,
those guilty of crimes "against the people" during the Batista era, and a
number of cases involving theft, embezzlement, or assault which had
nothing to do directly with the political beliefs of the individuals.[23] For
the same period, the Cuban Commission on Human Rights, an exile
group, estimated that there were 100,000 political prisoners in Cuba,
70,000 in prisons and 30,000 on prison farms and in "concentration
camps."[24]

Prison farms or work camps were part of the penal system and therefore common knowledge in Cuba. The term "concentration camp" was
never used by our informants, and even though rumors and gossip
abound in such a small country, there were no stories of torture in the
jails or on prison farms, or of the existence of a separate system of labor
camps. Almost all of our informants had a friend or relative or knew of
someone who had been arrested and incarcerated, although these ar-
rests were in almost all cases for nonpolitical offenses—theft, illegal
slaughter of animals, moral offenses such as rape, etc. With few exceptions the individuals convicted were sentenced to do agricultural labor
on prison farms rather than to serve time in jails or prisons. There were
regularly scheduled visiting days for relatives of inmates and, from the
accounts of visitors, prisoners were humanely treated,[25] although the
work was very hard and conditions austere. Prisoners were paid for their
labor, usually in the form of stipends sent to their dependents.

Imprisoned in these camps might be found vagrants, criminal offenders, and counterrevolutionaries, as well as religious dissenters and, at
least prior to 1970, homosexuals, although the latter were often sent to
the paramilitary UMAP agricultural labor camps (as were some ablebodied

23. *Ibid.*, p. 230.
24. Figures prepared by Dr. Miguel A. Olba Beníto, secretary of the Cuban Commission
on Human Rights, which circulated the information.
25. One case that could be counted as an exception was that of Yara Benedí; according
to his mother, Digna Deveaux, after Yara's arrest in 1964, at age sixteen, for allegedly
slaughtering an animal illegally, he was held in jail without trial for two years and nine
months. After his case was called to trial and the judge was informed of his imprisonment,
Yara was released for time served. Another exception was a soldier from Buena Ventura
who had been sentenced to one year in jail for being AWOL. He reported very poor living
conditions in La Cabaña prison, and harsh and arbitrary punishment by guards in a UMAP
camp where he served the last part of his sentence.

Cubans awaiting exit visas). Other political prisoners (presumably those considered most dangerous) as well as saboteurs, CIA operatives, and foreign agents were evidently kept apart from ordinary prisoners, in prisons such as La Cabaña, where security was greater than on the farms. Castro has commuted the death sentences of some of these prisoners who were formerly sympathetic to the Revolution or who are related to revolutionaries. Of these prisoners we learned nothing.

The whole question of political prisoners is a difficult one for the obvious reason of definition. Who gets classified as a political prisoner is often determined in large part by one's own political viewpoint. If we define as political prisoners only those people who have been imprisoned for making known in nonviolent ways opposing or dissenting views in conversation, correspondence, professional or scientific work and writing, through religious practice or artistic expression—in other words if we exclude the would-be assassins, armed counterrevolutionaries, and saboteurs who would be regarded as criminals in any country—the most clear-cut case of a political prisoner that we learned of during the course of this research was that of the Señor X mentioned above.

Another more ambiguous example was that of Efrén Noriega,[26] a Jehovah's Witness who, after being drafted into the Army under the compulsory military service law, refused to salute the flag, wear a uniform, or carry out any order that violated his religious principles. Until the time of his induction he was allowed to practice (although not to proselytize) his religion, as were all of his Jehovah's Witnesses relatives.[27] In most countries with standing armies, refusal to obey military orders after induction would be a punishable crime, but Noriega had no choice about his induction because Cuba does not grant conscientious objector status and draft-age men were not allowed to emigrate. Noriega was sentenced to serve ten years; he was released after three years and later granted a visa to the United States.

In general, religious activities which do not conflict with the goals of the Revolution or the fulfillment of revolutionary duties have been allowed to continue. A large percentage of the clergy and of the church-going public emigrated, and a number of Roman Catholic churches

26. The nephew of Inocencia Acosta Felipe; she discusses this case in her story, but Noriega's interview is unpublished.

27. On freedom of religion the new Constitution says that the state "recognizes and guarantees freedom of conscience and the right of everyone to profess any religious belief and to practice, within the framework of respect for the law, the belief of his preference.

"The law regulates the activities of religious institutions.

"It is illegal and punishable by law to oppose one's faith or religious belief to the Revolution; to education; or to the fulfillment of one's duty to work, defend the homeland with arms, show reverence for its symbols and fulfill other duties established by the Constitution" (VI, 54).

closed down. (Some apparently open for special days on the religious calendar, especially those saints' days most important to Cubans). Mass is said regularly, and weddings and baptisms are performed for those who want them.[28] It is important to remember that regular church attendance was a predominately middle-class activity in Cuba; many poor Cubans could not afford fees charged for baptisms, weddings, and funerals, and many were anticlerical.

The government regulates the activities of churches and religious organizations, most notably by not allowing them to proselytize. For religious education Cubans must go to the Church; the Church cannot go to them.[29] The sects which probably find it most difficult to practice their religious beliefs in all their aspects are those such as Jehovah's Witnesses or Seventh-Day Adventists, whose taboos on military service and working on the Sabbath, for example, could bring members into direct conflict with the government.

There are a number of devout Protestants and Roman Catholics among Cuba's dedicated revolutionaries (among our informants see Inocencia Acosta), and some of them are apparently still regular churchgoers. A certain segment of the clergy has always been active in Cuba's revolutionary movements, and a few were among the first volunteers to join the Rebel Army. Although these individuals apparently see no conflict between their religious and political beliefs, they know that so long as they publicly profess such beliefs they will be barred from membership in the Communist Youth and the Party.

For other Catholics, such as Gracia Rivera, a former nun, there was a conflict between the practice of their religious beliefs and the demands made upon them as citizens. Gracia was an active lay worker and was resentful of restrictions that effectively confined her work to the church building itself; she believed that she and other lay teachers were in competition with the state for the minds of Cuban children. But Gracia and her family had never been persecuted because of her religious work; on the contrary, Gracia said it was the economic security her family achieved after the Revolution that freed her for this work full time.

Among the informants who identified themselves as Roman Catholics, a few of the most revolutionary did admit modifying their religious activities after 1959 to accommodate to the new order. Inocencia Acosta, for example, stopped attending Mass and Confession on a regular basis, and Lala Fontanés did not have the youngest of her children baptized, in part because of the objections of her husband, a Party member. Neither

28. Religious weddings have not been recognized as legally valid since 1940.

29. For a review of Church and religious activities in Cuba since 1959 see *Cuba Review*, Sept., 1975, and *Cuba Resource Center Newsletter*, Apr., 1973. The latter publication reported that all of Havana's five synagogues were in regular use for Sabbath and holy-day worship services.

they nor other informants, however, reported any lessening of religious convictions. There was also a tendency to be very discreet about the display of religious pictures or icons or the possession of articles such as rosaries.[30]

In 1970 the major Afro-Cuban religious sects were flourishing. The government's official position was to embrace the sects as part of Cuba's cultural history, to promote their study by ethnologists, and to relegate their artifacts to museums. As with all Cubans who professed religious beliefs, membership in the Party or Youth was denied to sect members. But they were able to get the materials they needed to make special clothing, jewelry, and emblems, as well as the animals (often ritually killed) used in their religious ceremonies, even though the government controls virtually all commercial activity. Sect members openly discussed their religious activities and wore the distinctive clothing and jewelry that identified them with the particular saints of their devotion.

It was difficult for the government to curtail the activities of the sects because the overwhelming majority of practitioners were blacks, and attacking so salient a feature of black life and culture put the government in a very awkward position. Cuban leaders were very sensitive about charges of lingering racism and about the small number of blacks in high leadership positions. Also, the cults have no churches or professional clergy or laity whose activities can easily be regulated. They have always been secret or semi-secret societies and their rituals are usually performed in members' homes.

In 1970 Cuba was not a police state in any simple sense of that term—the streets were not filled with armed soldiers or police—nor in any absolute sense—the state, whatever its ambitions, did not control all aspects of social, economic, and political life, as the style of life in Buena Ventura, in particular, clearly illustrates. The government was highly visible (through the presence of mass organizations, not armed guards), and it did have agents for State Security on each block, albeit in name only in some cases, and although it must have had a good sense of the range of behavior within every barrio, it was not willing and/or able to act in all instances of illegal or antisocial behavior. The state was not yet able to deal decisively with the fairly widespread problems of black-

30. Four of the five *Neighbors* families kept religious pictures or objects in their homes. The Labradas had pictures of three saints hanging on their living-room wall, and the Pérezes had a statue of the Virgin Mary in their bedroom. In the home of Lieutenant Hernández, a Party member, a picture of St. Lazarus was hung behind the front door. Armando Cárdenas, also a Party member, was most adamant about banning religious artifacts from his home; he ordered his wife to dispose of a statue of the *Virgen del Cobre* given to her by her mother. When project field workers conducting a material-culture study of the Cárdenas household found a rosary among Lala's personal possessions, Lala immediately hid it in her dress and later gave it to her mother.

marketeering, theft, truancy, school dropouts, absenteeism, and vagrancy, for example.

Undoubtedly some people's image of justice in Cuba has been permanently colored by the televised trials of soldiers, policemen, and officials of the Batista government conducted in a Havana stadium shortly after the Triumph. By allowing thousands of Cubans to participate vicariously in the sentencing of these men, the revolutionary leadership invited the criticism they received from around the world. But the government effectively made its point about the fate—death by firing squad, or long-term imprisonment—of men who collectively shared in responsibility for thousands of heinous crimes against the Cuban people.

Whatever one's impressions of the 1959 Revolutionary Tribunals, they were not then and are not now indicative of the system of justice for the average Cuban.[31] While it is fair to say that within the prevailing political and legal values in Cuba there is not a single standard of justice for criminal or political offenders, the adjudication process is more standardized and less arbitrary than under the Batista government. It is also fair to say that the penal system has been improved in the sense that a prisoner does not have to expect inhumane treatment as a matter of course, any more than he can expect to buy his way out by bribing a guard. Now when such actions occur, they are more the exception than the rule. Based on the cases reported by our informants, it would appear that the ordinary prisoner (criminal offender) incarcerated in a work camp can expect austere living conditions, hard labor, political indoctrination, but also an adequate diet and health care, visiting time for family, financial assistance for dependents, and released time for good behavior.

During this research in 1969–70, project field workers observed six trials held by the People's Courts.[32] Although People's Courts were relatively new in 1969 and had been operating on a nationwide basis for only a few years, the majority of informants were familiar with them and had either witnessed a neighborhood trial or knew someone involved in one. These informants were generally supportive of the Courts.

The Courts dealt with many misdemeanor-type offenses, especially those involving family quarrels and disorderly conduct, petty theft, and

31. According to the Constitution, Cubans cannot be "tried or sentenced except by the competent tribunal by virtue of laws which existed prior to the crime and with the formalities and guarantees that the laws establish." The accused is guaranteed the right to a defense, and any statements taken from him under pressure or by force are to be considered null and void by the court. "Penal laws are retroactive when they benefit the accused or person who has been sentenced" (VI, 58).

32. Two case studies are to be published in the Buena Ventura community study. The study of the People's Courts also included a round-table discussion with court officials and interviews with eleven judges. Field workers did not observe any trials held by the Revolutionary Tribunals and therefore did not witness the trial of any Cuban accused of a political offense.

minor criminal offenses, substantially reducing the case load of higher courts. More important, the Courts brought cases before a panel of lay judges who were from the same general residential area as the defendant and/or plaintiff. Prior to the trials, judges were expected to go into the neighborhoods to familiarize themselves with the backgrounds of the litigants and with the circumstances surrounding a case. (This practice has since been suspended to insure greater objectivity.)[33] Trials were heard before an audience of neighbors and peers who were invited to offer spontaneous testimony.

CDR Vigilance officers cooperated with the People's Courts by reporting offenses and, more often, by writing depositions on the characters of the plaintiff and the defendant for use in the trials. The work of the People's Courts, combined with that of the CDR Vigilance Fronts, brought a large portion of the law-enforcement and adjudication functions down to the neighborhood level. This decentralization expedited both functions and also provided another means of bringing Cubans into the system as active participants. One might argue that such localization of law enforcement and adjudication has the potential for exploitation of the Courts to pursue personal vendettas, especially by the CDR Vigilance officers. We found no evidence of this, and the fact that the maximum sentence the Courts can impose is 180 days and that the cases are heard by a panel of judges militates against their abuse for reasons of revenge. In addition, a defendant has the right to appeal and the right, prior to trial, to reject a judge he feels is not impartial. Before the People's Courts were reorganized in 1973, members of the audience could also protest the outcome of a trial to Ministry of Justice officials who supervise the Courts and request an appeal of the decision.

The presence on each block of a Vigilance officer and an agent for State Security might, however, contribute to guarded behavior among neighbors who police one another. There was some evidence of this in the Miramar apartment building, but the effect probably varied widely depending on how rigorously the security contact exercised his or her function. In Buena Ventura, where all CDR duties were lax, there seemed to be few inhibitions about behaving in ways considered antisocial. Although the Vigilance officers and the People's Courts did help to maintain order and hasten the resolution of cases, they had not, as of

33. Lay judges attended brief training courses before beginning their duties with the Courts. Political education was part of their training and political criteria are used in the trying of cases, in part through character statements prepared by the CDR. The trials and sentences were looked upon as educational and rehabilitative in function: their explicit purpose was to politically educate and better integrate defendants into the revolutionary system. Politicization of the Courts is further enhanced by the fact that the judiciary is not an independent branch of government. The Supreme Court is subordinate to the National Assembly of *Poder Popular* and its officers and justices are elected by that body. The Municipal Assemblies now elect judges for the People's Courts in their jurisdiction.

1970, entirely eliminated disorderly conduct, theft, or other crimes from the residential areas.

VI

The Year of Decisive Effort, during which time the Cuba project was carried out, was a turning point in the Cuban Revolution. It marked the end of an era of massive experimentation as the provisional, ad hoc quality of the Party and the state gave way to permanent institutions. In reporting on the work of the Law Study commissions, which drafted the new laws for the rebuilding of the state apparatus, their president, Blas Roca Calderío, said: "A society cannot change its economic base and its property relations in a revolutionary manner without radically changing at the same time its entire superstructure, the law, and the judicial institutions administering it."[34] This has meant since 1970 a reorganization of the judicial system, revision of the Civil, Penal, and Family codes, the introduction of a system of popularly elected administrative-legislative assemblies (*Poder Popular*), and the adoption of a new Constitution.

Accompanying the process of restructuring Cuba's legal system was a revitalization of the political apparatus, including reorganization of the CDRs, the Communist Youth, and the trade unions, culminating in December, 1975, in the long-postponed First Congress of the Cuban Communist Party.

The Constitution went into effect in 1976, after receiving the overwhelming endorsement of Cuban voters (97.7 percent) in a national referendum. Based on the 1974 trial elections in Matanzas Province, *Poder Popular* was reorganized and introduced across the country. For this purpose Cuba's six provinces were subdivided into smaller politico-administrative units; there are now fourteen provinces (plus the Isle of Pines) comprising 169 *municipios*. In October and November of 1976 the first Municipal Assemblies and the first National Assembly were elected by secret ballot. The National Assembly (with Blas Roca as president) in turn chose a Council of State (from the membership of the Assembly) and a Council of Ministers.

The Party has elected to name this year, 1977, the Year of Institutionalization. Although the institutions are new, the leadership remains the same. All of the Party's leading members were elected delegates to the National Assembly (from their hometown *municipios*) and/or were appointed to the Council of State or Council of Ministers.[35] Fidel

34. *Granma Weekly Review*, Oct. 20, 1974, p. 5.
35. Of the 481 delegates to the National Assembly, 96.7 percent are either Party militants, aspirants to membership, or members of the Communist Youth; 55.5 percent are members of Municipal Assemblies, 12.3 percent hold national leadership positions, 22.2 percent are women, and 7.3 percent are members of the FAR. For an occupational breakdown of the membership see *Granma Weekly Review*, Dec. 12, 1976, p. 4.

Castro was elected president of both bodies, thus ending the practice of separate leadership for state and Party (Castro was elected First Secretary of the Party in December, 1975). The former President of the Republic, Osvaldo Dorticós, now serves as a vice-president of the Council of Ministers and as a member of the Council of State. Of the changes that have occurred, perhaps the most important will prove to be the introduction of regularly scheduled secret-ballot suffrage (although the Constitution empowers the National Assembly to delay scheduled elections) and the decentralization of provincial and local government functions.

Cuba's economic policy has also changed since 1970. Such experiments as Guevara's plan for rapid industrialization and Castro's attempts to mobilize a largely unskilled volunteer labor force to work in the sugar industry were abandoned in favor of more orthodox economic planning. The government is now counting less on quick, spectacular successes that involve great political and economic risks and more on long-range planning for the gradual achievement of its objectives. In 1974 Cuba began preparing its first Five Year Plan (1976–80), keeping in mind, as then President Dorticós told an assembly of workers from the sugar industry, that "the Cuban economy, because of the structure it inherited, the size of the country, the population and the limited natural resources, can never be self-sufficient nor even semi-self-sufficient."[36]

In this same speech Dorticós spoke of the "basic strategic role" of the sugar industry in the overall development of the country, and reminded his audience of the necessity of increasing the levels of exports, sugar in particular, to offset the high cost on the world market of goods essential to Cuba's development. However, the emphasis was on mechanization of the industry and the training of technicians and skilled workers. Use of volunteer labor, especially experienced cane-cutters, is still important, but its significance will probably be increasingly more political than economic.

Sugar is, of course, the principal commodity Cuba uses to pay for the import of capital goods essential to its continued economic development. Due to the wide variations in sugar production (from 3.8 million tons in 1963, when Hurricane Flora destroyed much of the crop, to 8.5 million tons in 1970) and the wild fluctuations in the price of sugar on the world market (from about 3 cents a pound in the first years of the Revolution, to 11 cents in 1970, to over 60 cents on the London Exchange in 1974, and down to 10 cents in 1976), serious restraints must exist on Cuba's long-range planning capabilities. This is partially mitigated by the fact

36. This and the following quotes from Osvaldo Dorticós are from a 1974 speech reprinted in *Granma Weekly Review*, Oct. 20, 1974, pp. 2–3.

that Cuba sells three-quarters of its sugar through multi-year agreements in which the price is prearranged.[37]

Cuba also depends on what Dorticós optimistically termed the "inevitable rise in per capita sugar consumption." It is possible, however, that per capita consumption will fall, given the increasing concern over the nutritional value of foods and the widespread use of artificial sweeteners and beet and corn sugar, the latter being less expensive to produce than cane sugar. Nevertheless, Cuba continues to rely heavily on the sugar industry for the simple reason that it (reportedly) brings in far greater revenue per hectare than any other crop.[38]

The 1970 harvest, when measured against the 10-million-ton objective, was not a disastrous failure; the mass-mobilization campaign achieved a record harvest of 8½ million tons (compared to the previous year's 4½ million and to a pre-revolutionary high of 7 million). This record harvest made it possible for Cuba to meet its domestic needs, quotas assigned under the International Sugar Agreement, commitments to the Soviet Union and to other socialist countries, as well as to sell on the international market.

When viewed against the political and economic investments the country had made, however, the harvest was a great failure. The life stories in this series illustrate not only the tremendous effort made by the labor force but also the enormous psychological investment of the Cuban people in the harvest campaign. Their hopes for Cuba and for their own immediate futures, especially for relief from the austerity they experienced in 1969–70, were closely tied to the harvest's success.

Harvesting the 10 million in 1970 might have been a great political victory in the short run, but it is not likely that it could have been an economic success in any long-range sense, and certainly not on a level that could have satisfied all the expectations of the Cuban people or all the promises made to them.[39] Cubans sacrificed a great deal to help Castro vindicate his economic policies and to score a political victory in

37. Having such a large portion of its crop committed through prearranged deals can prevent Cuba from taking advantage of upward fluctuations in the world price. In 1974, for example, when the price reached an all-time record of 65 cents and the average price per pound was something over 30 cents, Cuba was selling to the Soviet Union at 11 cents (the set price for the period 1973–80). It is also true that the Soviet Union, some years earlier, was buying at 7 cents a pound when the market price was several cents lower. At any rate, 80 percent of the sugar shipped to the Soviet Union is paid for in Soviet goods; Cuba depends on sales on the world market to pay for imports from Western countries. (Lynn Darrell Bender, "Cuba, the United States, and Sugar," *Caribbean Studies*, Apr., 1974, pp. 156–57.)

38. "We ran tests on corn, rice, coffee, and other crops and found we could get $400 a hectare from them. Sugar brings us $7,000 a hectare. So we will continue to sell sugar and to buy other things we need on the world market." (Fidel Castro quoted by Fred Ward, "Inside Cuba Today," *National Geographic*, Jan., 1977, p. 67.)

39. Assuming an artificial situation in which Cuba could have sold the additional 1½ million tons on the world market (it is unlikely that Cuba could have found a market in the West to barter it) at an average 1970 price of 11 cents a pound, it might have meant

the international arena; had the plan succeeded and life not improved for them, the victory might have proved worse than the defeat.

Recognizing their sacrifices, Castro, in his 1970 report on the harvest, spoke of the pending debt to the Cuban people. To fulfill some of his promises and to stabilize the national economy, Castro has had to rely on continued aid from the Soviet Union, reportedly between $1.5 and $4 million a day. With this aid and the discontinuance of the practice of subordinating other sectors of the economy to the sugar industry, the standard of living has improved somewhat, and the pressures of work have decreased in the period since 1970. Food apparently is available in greater abundance, especially those unrationed, seasonal items that were not being efficiently harvested or distributed during the 1969-70 labor crunch. Delivery of services—sanitation, utilities, maintenance, for example—has also improved, and more consumer goods are available— television sets, refrigerators, and small appliances such as blenders and pressure cookers, for example. Recent visitors to Cuba reported more merchandise in the stores, and the opening of a greater number of stores as well. Better services, greater efficiency in the rationing system, more consumer goods, and the greater availability of housing (perhaps the greatest single improvement since 1970) have all contributed to making life generally more convenient, less pressured, and somewhat more comfortable than six years ago.

Although we know little about what has happened to the majority of our informants in the years since 1970, we have received news about the five *Neighbors* families, all of whom were visited in 1975 by Rafael Rodríguez and Olivia Hernández, who had interviewed the families in 1969.

The neighborhood where the families lived had changed somewhat, but the apartment building was much as it had been, with all families living in the same units they had occupied in 1970. The buildings that had housed the Ana Betancourt School and served as dormitories for scholarship students had been converted to residences for foreign consultants and technicians, most of them Russian. The school and the students had moved to newly built facilities.

---

additional revenue of $220 a ton or $330 million total. This is a highly optimistic appraisal, since the additional 1½ million tons on a world market of only 10 or 11 million tons would almost certainly have deflated the price. (Seventy-five percent of all the world's sugar is sold within the producing countries, and about 12 percent is marketed under bi- and multilateral agreements, leaving only about 12 percent to be sold at world market prices. Bender, "Cuba, the United States, and Sugar," p. 157.) Discounting production costs (an average of 4 cents a pound or about $120 million) and the cost of the campaign to other sectors of the economy, almost none of which were able to meet their quotas because of the diversion of their labor forces to the sugar industry, it is unlikely that there would have been any gain really worthy of the investment.

There had been one death among the families—Domingo Labrada, who in 1970 suffered from a skin disease and was partially disabled, died in a Havana hospital in 1974. After the death of his father, to whom he had been very close, Labrada had a relapse from which he never recovered. His wife, Leticia Manzanares, who had been doing laundry in her home, took a full-time job in a factory and also received a pension from the state. Her younger children, all excellent students, were still attending day school and living at home; Lina, the eldest, had graduated from basic secondary and was teaching primary school.

Eulalia Fontanés and Armando Cárdenas spent 1970–71 on the Isle of Pines, where they had their fifth child, a daughter. After their return to Havana, Lala began attending a secondary school for adults and working in a nursery school, taking her youngest child with her. Cárdenas returned to his job managing cafeterias for INIT, the tourist ministry. Their four sons were all in day school and living at home. Through her work center Lala had been able to buy a refrigerator (which they had been saving for since 1969) and a television set, and she was also expecting a new housing assignment in the near future.

For Sara and Eduardo Rojas, conditions in the garage had improved somewhat through a number of small repairs and some new furnishings and appliances. They had finally obtained a refrigerator, and also a new bed and a better chifforobe. Violeta never had returned to school; she had married Fermín Manzanares, Leticia's youngest brother, who had been a frequent visitor at his sister's home. Violeta and Fermín were living in Havana and had had one child. Hilario Rojas had received a scholarship to a boarding school and was no longer living at home. Sara had given birth to two more children, however, so the same number of people were living in the garage. Eduardo was still working as a security guard and had also joined a construction brigade at his work center to help build a new apartment complex. When the building is finished and turned over to his work center, Eduardo expects his family to receive one of the new units. Sara reportedly was much happier than at the time of the study.

Justa Díaz was also reported to be less nervous, in better health, and more relaxed in conversation and behavior. Her husband had changed jobs and was home more often on weekends and in the evenings. They had had another child, their ninth. The younger children were all attending the neighborhood day school, but Reinaldo was still away in boarding school. Florinda had graduated from the Makarenko Institute and was teaching primary school while continuing her education. Genoveva, on the other hand, had not returned to school; she had married the boyfriend mentioned in her interview and they were living in Havana. She had recovered from the nervous disorder that caused her to drop out of school in 1970.

Perhaps the most significant change among the families had occurred in the Pérez home. Mercedes Millán was no longer a housewife but had a full-time job teaching English in a technical institute, and also, since it is a prerequisite, must have joined the Women's Federation. In 1970, just as this study was being completed, Juan Carlos changed jobs, returning to work in food purchasing and distribution after having worked for several years at jobs for which he was not adequately prepared.

Merceditas was doing what she said she never wanted to do—attending a school for scholarship students. By going to a university-preparatory school, however, she was following along the expected path toward a career. Merceditas had the fifteenth birthday party, complete with fancy dress, that she had been anticipating since age ten (although she did not lose the weight her father had stipulated as a condition for having the party). Her little brother, Eloy Tomás, was attending the local day school.

The year 1970 was as much a benchmark for Mercedes Millán as it was for the country as a whole. In 1970 Mercedes's back was against the wall; her way of life was an anachronism and she was becoming increasingly isolated. Her friends had gone North, her sister had emigrated, and her parents were aging. It would still have been possible for Mercedes to have left the country legally, but she would have had to do so alone: Juan would never have allowed her to take the children, and her parents were not interested in starting over. She could have gone to her sister in Spain but they had never been very close. Mercedes had no experience at being independent and no disposition toward becoming so, and even if she could have adjusted to being parted from her children as individuals, she probably could never have unburdened herself from the feeling of having abandoned them.

Mercedes's involvement in the Church, her refusal to take a job outside their home, and her reputation for bourgeois living and for criticizing the government may well have been factors in Juan's failure to be accepted into the Party in 1969. It is possible that Mercedes's decision to integrate was a reflection of her ambition for Juan and the family rather than a change of heart about the economic policies of the government. On the basis of her past it is safer to speculate that Mercedes was less converted than resigned to the Revolution.

Members of the other families also reflected this trend toward settling in. The changes in the lives of most of our informants probably peaked in the 1960s—especially so for the poorer ones. Armando Cárdenas, for example, an illiterate, itinerate farm worker who had never traveled outside his native province, became a manager of a cafeteria in the capital city and was able to read and write, keep account books, supervise other employees, and assist in their political education. From having had no direct contact with the state, perhaps even no conception of it in his childhood and adolescence, Armando became a Vanguard Worker, a dedicated volunteer, a Party member, and a true believer in the eco-

nomic aims of socialism. However, his upward mobility and his transformation from marginal to integrated man were probably relatively
complete by the end of the first decade of the Revolution. It is unlikely
that he will move up in the management levels of INIT or become a
full-time Party cadre. His attitudes may change and his outlook broaden,
particularly in relation to women and their role in the home and in
society, but by 1970 he had probably gone about as far in his work as he
was able. The most significant change that might come in his work would
be if he were to tire again of city life (as he had when he went to the Isle
of Pines in 1970) and return to agricultural labor. Any other significant
change in the family's economic or personal situation would very likely
come through the efforts of Lala, who was altogether more intelligent,
aggressive, and ambitious than her husband.

For many Cubans, as for Lala and Armando, life in the 1960s seemed
far less constricted than in the past: the Revolution promised job and
educational opportunities undreamed of by the majority of Cubans. But
life did not open up in all areas; the direction opportunity took was
controlled from the top, which is to say that it broadened only in ways
that would ultimately advance the Revolution. (That is, after all, the purpose of Cuba's planned economy and the concomitant restraints it places
on almost all aspects of society.) Certain occupations became obsolete,
while new fields essential to Cuba's economic development opened up,
but with quotas set on university enrollments. There is a certain amount
of fatalism, as well as patriotism, in the now stock answer given by Cuban
children to questions about their futures: that they want to serve the
Revolution wherever it needs them.

Restrictions were also placed on certain forms of personal
expression—art and music for recreational purposes, for example (art
supplies were controlled by the state, and some kinds of music, such as
rock and roll, were officially regarded as unacceptable)—and on other
recreational outlets such as nightclubs, bars, and social clubs, as well as
the marathon fiestas for which Cubans were so famous. In place of these
more fleeting and superficial joys, Cubans should substitute, argue the
utopian revolutionaries, the deeper, more enduring inner satisfaction of
working for the collectivity.

It would be impossible, of course, to sustain the fervor of the Revolution's early years; after a time even the revolutionary life-style settles
into routine, and with that often comes a lessening of idealism and a
growing cynicism.[40] In 1970 there was already some evidence of this;

40. We are not referring here to those who were hardened cynics from the beginning
and whose minds were never really open to the Revolution except for reasons of personal
gain. Alfredo Barrera, for instance, who assiduously avoided integration, said of the revolutionary life-style: "The state makes its demands and the needy one invents his tricks."

Gabriel Capote, angry and disgusted over his housing conditions, spoke of the past, "when I raised my hand for everything. . . ." And Nicolás Salazar, so proud of his work in the CDR, was disgusted with the lack of direction from CDR cadre and said that officials came down to the barrio only when they wanted something from the people. Another aspect of this phenomenon was the accommodation of revolutionary institutions to old procedures. "Without *compañeros,*" Juan Pérez said of the new bureaucracy, "nothing would ever get done." In all these instances, however, it cannot be overstated that the skepticism of the informants did not diminish their belief in the goals of the Revolution.

It is a measure of the faith the Cuban people had in the government that the Revolution survived and prospered after the experiment in mass mobilization for the 1970 sugar harvest. Although complaining about rationing and shortages of food and consumer goods was almost a way of life among the Cubans interviewed, they also had some perspective on and some sense of humor about the difficulties the country was experiencing. If we were to construct a composite view of our informants' attitudes toward the shortages and inconveniences they were experiencing in 1970 it would be, "Sure, we have problems, but it's more fair than it was before, and anyway it won't be forever." If not overwhelmingly enthusiastic about every change, our informants were overwhelmingly accepting.

After seventeen years of the Revolution and the setbacks of Guevara's industrialization program and Castro's plan for the sugar industry, the leadership still gives an impression of remarkable resilience and unending energy. It is one of Castro's great strengths as a political leader that he does not cover up discontent or try to discount public opinion. He projects an image—however authoritarian or paternalistic it may be viewed here—of one who takes the people into his confidence, who admits mistakes and appeals for understanding and patience. This gives the people a sense of power (i.e., to give or withhold approval) and a feeling of participating in and of responsibility for the country's successes and failures. At the same time, we believe, Castro has a real feeling of responsibility and of accountability to the Cuban people.

Do Cubans think the Revolution has been worth the cost? Among our informants the response was decidedly affirmative. They, along with millions of other Cubans, and not always those who gained the most from the Revolution, have made countless sacrifices, willingly and in some cases enthusiastically. But no matter how willing one was, many of the demands made by the government, especially those that have upset the most fundamental things in life, have been threatening and destabilizing. This is particularly true of the Revolution's attempts to affect power relationships within the family and the role of women in society, and especially so in the period since 1970, when the emphasis shifted from placing the sole burden on women to enter the labor force to making demands on men to assume a more equal responsibility for home management and child-rearing.

The Revolution's celebration of the people, its absolute need of their labor and support to succeed, its genuine belief in the wisdom of humble people and in their inalienable right to the basic material necessities of life, curtailed, at least temporarily, the degradation of human life endemic to the economic and political oppression of Cuba's past dictatorships. Some may doubt the methods of a socialist economy, but it is difficult not to accept the sincerity of the Revolution's intent to improve the material life of the majority of Cubans. The question is, what will become of life's other, more intangible aspects? When the exhilaration of the Triumph has faded and when the future no longer seems to promise unlimited opportunity, will that gray patina that seems to have settled over all life in Eastern European socialist countries, masking the richness and complexities of their cultures and the individuality of their citizens, form over Cuban society and culture as well? And will Cuba—which seems to be inheriting all of the characteristic weaknesses of the Soviet system of distribution and the shortcomings of Soviet science and technology along with its expertise—with its own growing bureaucracy and concentration of power at the top, also give rise to a new class? If so, when the memory of hunger and of gross material inequities, fraudulent elections, and corrupt dictators begins to disappear, will the victory still seem worthy of the costs? It is the people who live the Revolution day to day and share in all its consequences—those who have made it everything it is—who have the most right to answer.

SMR

Appendix A
Rationing

Rationing was introduced in Cuba in 1962, and by 1969 most basic food and household items were rationed. Ration books (*libretas*) were issued by household for a calendar year beginning in August. Changes in residence and any additions to or deletions from the household ration book had to be reported to OFICODA, the Office for Control of Food Distribution.

At the time of our study in 1969, there were some regional variations in certain rations. For example, egg and meat rations were higher in Havana than in rural areas because rural residents were able to supplement their food allotments with home-grown products. There were also variations in individual rations in accord with age and state of health; infants up to age two, for instance, were entitled to additional rations, including baby food, powdered chocolate, cereal, and fresh milk. Persons with illnesses such as diabetes or ulcers were allotted extra rations of meat, poultry, milk, and tubers. In practice, however, some items, such as poultry and tubers, were often not available even to those who qualified for special diets.

There were several different methods of distributing foodstuffs, depending upon the type of food. The staples or basic items of the diet—rice, milk, sugar, meat, coffee, eggs, salt—were distributed to the stores from central warehouses in a fixed quantity for a fixed period of time. These basic necessities were almost always available in the amount designated for each household. Another group of foodstuffs, including root and other vegetables, wheat flour, mayonnaise, and wine, were distributed in fixed quotas but with no set distribution period. In practice, these foods were often distributed in amounts greater or less than the assigned quotas, depending on the quantities available. A third category of foodstuffs, which included, for example, butter, vanilla, raisins, meat spreads, olives, and canned fruits, had neither an established quota nor a fixed time of distribution. As they became available these foods were divided up among the people registered at each store. This is also the system used to distribute sweets and delicacies during the time of national holidays.

In practice, this system of distribution meant that most Cubans had to make almost daily trips to the grocery stores. Some foods, such as rice, were available for purchase in their full monthly quota on the first day of the month, while others such as meat, a perishable food, came to the stores on a set day of each week, and still other foods, such as fruit, yogurt, root and other vegetables, came irregularly. It would have been impossible, therefore, for a family to buy all of one month's rations in several trips to the store, even if they had had enough money available, a means of transporting a large quantity of food to their home, and a refrigerator to keep perishables. The necessity of standing in line to purchase some items such as meat added to the time required for food shopping. Since it was also necessary to stand in line to buy manufactured goods, shopping for an entire household was far too time-consuming for any one person to do alone. Most families members shared these responsibilities and also devised different ways to share them with their neighbors, thus greatly reducing the shopping time spent by any one person.

Much has been said and written about food shortages in Cuba and about the alleged inability of the Castro government to feed the people. In 1969 there were shortages of some foods, especially meat, poultry, and fruit, and some of the Cubans' favorite foods, such as coffee, root vegetables, and certain sweets. But all the people received a share of these items, and almost everyone received food in excess of a subsistence diet. Cubans did have to work hard at food management, especially to keep variety and nutritional balance in their meals throughout the month. Running out of food before the end of the month was a special problem for those Cubans who in the past had rarely had money to shop for more than one day's food at a time. Lack of experience in food planning made it difficult for them to acquire shopping habits compatible with the rationing system. It was also a problem for some rural Cubans, such as the Rojas family, who were accustomed to raising almost all their food at home.

Cubans who faced the greatest food difficulties were those with special dietary restrictions (especially those on high-protein, low-starch diets) and those on pensions and living alone. A small number of pensioners had fixed incomes as low as 20 *pesos* a month; if they purchased all the food they were entitled to, they would not have had enough money for rent, clothing, and other necessities.[1]

---

1. A 1971 ruling made it possible for all households with monthly incomes of 25 *pesos* or less to apply to the Ministry of Labor's Department of Social Security for exemption from all rent payments. The only condition to granting such requests was that the petitioners have no record of "parasitism" in their backgrounds.

We were not able to obtain a ration book since each household was required to turn in its expired book in order to be issued a new one. The information reprinted below was copied from the *libreta* of the Cárdenas family, and although the itemization is not complete, we hope it gives the reader some idea of the availability and price of certain basic foods in Cuba in 1969. It does not, however, give an accurate picture of a household's total food consumption. For instance, the *libreta* does not adequately reflect the variations from month to month in the number and amounts of non-staple food items that were available. In addition to the items listed here, shoppers might have been buying onions, tomatoes, yucca, watercress, green peppers, cucumbers, radishes, or whatever else happened to be in season and on hand in the stores. Certain rationed items that are not part of the basic diet, such as soft drinks, do not appear in this list copied from the Cárdenas ration book.

Most families also supplemented their rationed purchases in one or more ways: (1) with food from relatives who lived in the country, (2) with vegetables from home gardens or meat from small animals or fowl raised at home (e.g. pigeons, chickens, rabbits), (3) with items purchased from or exchanged with friends and neighbors, (4) with items obtained on the black market. A large number of families also received rations for a greater number of persons than actually ate in the household. Some families had children in boarding school or in *círculos* or who were semi-boarders (ate lunch at school). Often husbands or wives ate one or more meals at work or were gone for long periods of productive labor. All of these individuals remained registered in the household *libretas* and their rations could be purchased for use by the family. Among the five families, the Hernándezes had two children who were semi-boarders and three who were on scholarships and ate at home only on weekends.

Cárdenas Household: Ration Book for Provisions

This was copied in March, 1969; at that time Lala Fontanés's brother Diego was registered with the household although he did not always eat there. This put the household size at seven persons. To facilitate the correct distribution of goods from the central warehouse to the individual stores, it was necessary for the state to know the exact number of people who would shop at each store. Therefore each household was required to register at one store of its choosing, where all food shopping had to be done. In front of the ration book were stamped the numbers of the district, sector, and block of OFICODA in which their store was located, as well as the number assigned to the store itself.

Item prices were given by Lala Fontanés and have been checked against information given by other informants. There were discrepancies on certain items, but they are minor. The figures here are a fair representation of the cost of food in 1969.

Article	Quantity	Price
Fresh milk	1 liter daily per child under 7 years	.25
Condensed milk	3 cans every 34 days for adults and 6 cans monthly for children over 7 years	.20/can
Butter	1/8 lb. per person [only for children; was not available between Sept., 1968, and Mar., 1969]	.95/½ lb.
Rice	3 lbs. monthly per person [increased to 4 lbs. later in 1969, and to 6 lbs. in 1970]	.19/lb.
Peas	1 pkg. monthly per household of 7 people or less	.23 & .45
Chick Peas	1 pkg. monthly per household of 7 people or less	.27
Black Beans	1 pkg. monthly per household of 7 people or less	.27
Lard	1½ lbs. monthly per household	.23/lb.
Oil	1-lb. can monthly per person	.27
Bath soap	1½ bars monthly per person	.16
Laundry soap	1 bar monthly per person	.15
Detergent	1 box monthly per person [when available]	.16/box
Toothpaste	2 large tubes monthly for 7 people or 1 small tube per person	.50
Toilet paper	1 roll monthly per person	.10
Yogurt	1 jar per person [when available]	.20
Crackers	20 per person weekly	2 for .01
White flour	[quota determined by supply]	.15/lb.
Corn flour	[quota determined by supply]	.08/lb.

Article	Quantity	Price
Cornstarch	1 box monthly per person [when available]	.31/box
Dry white cooking wine	1 bottle monthly [when available]	.45
Vinegar	1 bottle monthly [when available]	.45
Noodles	2 pkgs. monthly per person [at times available unrationed in quantitites not exceeding 2 pkgs. a day]	.20/pkg.
Macaroni	2 pkgs. monthly	.45/pkg.
Tomato paste	2 cans monthly	.25/can
Tomato sauce	3 cans monthly [when available]	.16/can
Russian canned meat	[rarely available]	
Sweets	1 bar guava paste monthly [when available]	.15/bar
Sugar	6 lbs. monthly per person	.06/lb.
Coffee	10½ ozs. weekly for 7 people [1½ ozs. per person]	.09/oz.
Produce (misc.)	3 times a week [when available]	
Potatoes	[no quota when available]	.07/lb.
Malanga	2 lbs. per child under 6 years [when available]	.07/lb.
Oranges	[quota determined by supply]	.08/ea.
Eggs	3 weekly per person	.08/ea.
Poultry	[quota determined by supply]	—
Fish	[quota determined by supply]	—
Meat: beefsteak second-grade meat soup meat	3/4 pound weekly per person	.49/lb. .35/lb. .28/lb.
Scrub rag	1 monthly [when available]	.55
Rum	1 bottle [when available]	[varied with quality]

In addition to food, also rationed were clothing, yard goods, household items, toiletries, and all other manufactured items. These could be purchased by Cubans at any store of their choice except those restricted to foreigners and diplomatic personnel. Each household was assigned a number and was entitled to buy only on certain days of the month when that number came up. Number groups and the designated days for shopping were posted in stores and announced over the radio. Upon making a purchase the buyer had to present the ration coupon for the particular item.

Each individual received specific rations for certain manufactured goods—shoes and articles of clothing,[2] for instance—while other manufactured goods were divided into categories, such as small appliances (electric irons, blenders, and so on), with each household entitled to buy a certain number from each category, if and when the items became available. A shopper was not guaranteed, as he was with his food ration, to receive the items to which his ration book entitled him. A store could (and often did) run out of some items before everyone with the proper coupons was able to make his or her purchase; in that case, the shopper could try another store, but he might just have to do without the item.

Children were entitled to extra clothing, usually school uniforms. In addition, family ration books allowed the yearly purchase of three toys (one priced at 3 *pesos* or above and two priced at 2 *pesos* or less) for each child. Infants received a free layette (itemized below) at birth.

15 meters gauze	1 pr. shoes
6 diapers	1 box talcum
4 kimono combinations	1 bottle cologne
2 long kimonos	1 blanket
3 meters kimono material	3 crib sheets
2 bars baby soap	4 pillow cases or mattress pads
2 prs. socks	1 mosquito net

2. Although all items of clothing were rationed, many of the Cubans interviewed had more clothing than one would expect from looking at the ration book (one dress and one skirt and blouse per year for women and one pair of slacks and one dress shirt per year for men, for example). Many adults received special work clothing or uniforms (green fatigues) without ration books through their work centers or militia units. Also, every household received a cloth ration (the full ration was rarely available), and many women made articles of clothing for members of their families. Every Cuban was entitled to buy one regular pair of shoes and one pair of tennis shoes per year, but many adults also received work boots off the ration book. Orthopedic shoes could be purchased whenever prescribed. There was also a substantial black-market trade in clothing.

Appendix B
Estimated Household
Expenditures

In lieu of a complete month's record of income and expenditures for any one of the five families, we have tried to reconstruct their major expenditures from information given in their interviews and from preliminary work done on family budgets. We have done this with full realization that the information is very tenuous.

Food expenditures were calculated from prices provided by Lala Fontanés, from data collected in the other studies, from the project's itemized grocery bills, and from OFICODA. Although these prices were fairly constant during 1969–70, there was variation from month to month in the items available in the store and therefore in how much a family could spend on food each month. We have tried to estimate for each family how much would have been spent if all the items they were entitled to had been purchased, and in addition we have added amounts for items not listed in the Cárdenas ration book. There were also, however, a number of items purchased unrationed.

The single figure we were most interested in was food expenditures as percentage of family income, but this determination was made additionally difficult by variations in income. Salaries of the men showed only minor variations from month to month, but there were significant fluctuations in the women's earnings. Their work was remunerated on a per-item basis, which resulted in month-to-month wage differences of as much as 30 *pesos*.

The amount of money remaining for each family after food and rent expenditures was:

> Pérez—$98.57
> Cárdenas—$80
> Hernández—$76.50
> Labrada—$55.79
> Rojas—$40 (after child-support payments)

Food and Rent Expenditures as Percent of Income

Family	Household Size	Monthly Income[a]	Per Capita Income	Est. Max. Food Expd.	As Percent of Income	Rent	As Percent of Income
Hernández	9	196	21.78	100[b]	51	19.50	10
Pérez	4	175	43.75	50	30	26.43[c]	15.1
Cárdenas	6	160	26.67	80[d]	50	none	—
Labrada	7	140	20.00	75	54	9.21[e]	6.6
Rojas	7	(145)[f]	(20.71)	75	(51)	none	—
		115	16.43		65		

[a]Combined incomes of husband and wife, with the exception of the Pérezes. The women's incomes are averages; the men's are net, after deductions for retirement, health care, vacations, 2 or 3 percent "voluntary" deductions for aiding disaster victims, financing national campaigns, building monuments, etc., and finally, where applicable, 1 percent for union dues.
[b]Based on a household of nine; the family may not have bought the full amount since three children were in boarding school and two were semi-boarders.
[c]Includes back-rent payment.
[d]The higher food cost for the Cárdenas family of six than for the Labrada and Rojas families of seven is due to the Cárdenases' higher milk bill. They had three children under seven and were buying 3 liters of fresh milk a day. The Rojas and Labrada families each had one child under seven and their milk bills were 11 *pesos* less a month.
[e]The Labradas reportedly stopped paying rent in late 1969. This may have been due to Domingo's illness and reduced salary, or it may have been the end of the amortization period, in which case they had received title to the apartment.
[f]Before child-support payments of 30 *pesos* a month.

It was impossible to estimate clothing costs per family with the limited item prices available to us, but for the Cárdenases, Rojases, and Labradas, families with little or no rent, clothing was the most significant expenditure next to food—if they purchased everything they were entitled to in the ration book. Lala Fontanés was the only informant who reported buying everything in her ration book that was available in the stores. Her family and the Pérezes had the largest number of clothing items per family member. The Rojas family had the fewest.

There were a number of additional expenditures which were common to all families, among them electricity, cooking fuel, transportation, CDR and Federation dues, entertainment, cigarettes, and beer. Electricity bills varied from 2 to 3 *pesos* a month for the Cárdenas and Rojas families to over 10 *pesos* a month, at times, for the Labrada, Pérez, and Hernández families.[1] The cost of gas used by the Pérezes, Labradas, and Hernándezes for cooking was about 2 *pesos* a month; the Rojas and Cárdenas

1. Usually paid in person at the utility office or at the National Bank, which collected for the electric and telephone *consolidados*.

families used kerosene at a cost of approximately 2.50 *pesos* per month (one liter per day at 8 *centavos* a liter). All the families except the Pérez used the bus service, which cost 5 *centavos* a ride; Eduardo Rojas and Armando Cárdenas took the bus to and from work, thus spending a minimum of 2 to 3 *pesos* a month for transportation. (Lieutenant Hernández rode to and from work in a police car.) CDR dues were collected monthly and Federation dues quarterly, on an ability-to-pay basis. CDR dues were reported to be 25 *centavos* per month for each member who held a job, and 5 *centavos* per month for an unemployed member. Lala Fontanés reported that Federation dues in her delegation ranged from 25 to 50 *centavos* per member each quarter.

Entertainment might consist of going out to eat, usually to a pizzeria or ice cream parlor, or to a movie. The Labradas took an occasional trip to the Coney Island amusement park, and the Pérezes sometimes went out to a nightclub. Families also held birthday and saint's day celebrations at home, generally serving ice cream, cake, sandwiches, soft drinks, and beer. Beer cost 60 *centavos* a bottle, although for special occasions like birthdays, several cartons could be purchased at the reduced rate of 40 *centavos*. Other liquor was more strictly rationed and quite expensive when available.

Rationing of cigarettes created a serious black-market problem, and the price and distribution system were changed in 1971.[2] In 1969 they were rationed one pack of *fuertes* (strong cigarettes) per person per week at 20 *centavos* a pack, but they could also be purchased unrationed at a higher price. *Suaves* (mild cigarettes), which were preferred, were rarely available. Most households bought their full ration whether there were smokers or not (Mercedes Millán, Lala Fontanés, and Armando Cárdenas, for example, did not smoke), and either gave them to friends or relatives, used them in exchange for other items, or sold them.

There were no known expenditures for religion except for baptisms, and there had not been one for several years prior to the study. The Labradas, however, almost certainly spent at least small amounts in observance of certain saints' days and perhaps on certain other rituals of *santería*. (For an idea of the cost of some of the ceremonies within the Afro-Cuban religions, see the story of Lázaro Benedí Rodríguez in *Four Men.*)

The Pérezes had the highest non-food expenditures among the five families. In addition to the expenditures discussed above, they paid 8.85 *pesos* monthly for the telephone (as did the Hernándezes), and 11 *pesos* monthly for membership in a private clinic (and an additional 5 *pesos* for every clinic visit and 10 *pesos* for every home visit by the doctor). The

2. For a frank discussion of this problem by Castro, see *Granma Weekly Review*, May 16, 1971, p. 6.

Pérezes also availed themselves of a number of services not used by the other families, for example, laundry and dry cleaning, ironing (done in the home), gasoline and maintenance for their car, a dressmaker, wax-bath treatments for Mercedes, and vacations. The family's annual vacations to the resort area of Varadero in Matanzas were arranged by Juan Carlos through a friend who worked in INIT. (The vacations were normally given, in turns, as rewards to workers who had high production records.)

The Rojas family had the greatest difficulty living on their income. After food expenditures and support payments, they had only 40 *pesos* for all other items, including electricity, kerosene, cigarettes, transportation, and clothing. Their lack of experience in managing a steady income resulted in month-to-month inconsistencies. Sometimes they had enough cash to last through the month, even to eat out, and other times they sold food or borrowed cash from neighbors. If Eduardo had not been making child-support payments, the family would have had enough each month for the basic necessities.

The Labradas had some budget difficulties after Domingo's salary was reduced, but they regularly received money from one of Leticia's brothers or from her father. These relatives occasionally stayed with the family and the money was a gift, not a loan.

To our knowledge, the Rojas, Labrada, and Hernández families had no savings. The Cárdenases reported savings of 300 *pesos,* with which they hoped to purchase a refrigerator, and an additional 50 *pesos* set aside for emergencies. The Pérezes reportedly had savings of 8,000 *pesos* in 1961. In addition, Juan Carlos was awarded compensation (in excess of 15,000 *pesos*) from the state for nationalization of his market stall and trucks. We assume that this was being paid in monthly installments. The Pérezes may have been living above their income and drawing on these savings. Withdrawals from savings accounts were limited to 200 *pesos* a month.

Abbreviations

ANAP   *Asociación Nacional de Agricultores Pequeños* (National Association of Small Farmers)

BANFAIC   *Banco de Fomento Agrícola y Industrial de Cuba* (Agricultural and Industrial Development Bank of Cuba)

CDR   *Comités de Defensa de la Revolución* (Committees for Defense of the Revolution)

D(G)OP   *Dirección (General) de Orden Público* (Department of Public Order)

DSE   *Dirección (General) de Seguridad del Estado* (Department of State Security)

DTI   *Departamento Técnico de Investigaciones* (Department of Technical Investigations)

FAR   *Fuerzas Armadas Revolucionarias* (Revolutionary Armed Forces)

FEU   *Federación Estudiantil Universitaria* (University Student Federation)

FMC   *Federación de Mujeres Cubanas* (Federation of Cuban Women)

ICAIC   *Instituto Cubano del Arte e Industria Cinematográfica* (Cuban Institute of Cinema Art and Industry)

INIT   *Instituto Nacional de la Industria Turística* (National Institute of the Tourist Industry)

INRA   *Instituto Nacional de Reforma Agraria* (National Institute of Agrarian Reform)

JUCEI   *Juntas de Coordinación, Ejecución e Inspección* (Boards of Coordination, Execution and Inspection)

MINCIN   *Ministerio de Comercio Interior* (Ministry of Domestic Trade)

MINCON   *Ministerio de Construcción* (Ministry of Construction)

MINED   *Ministerio de Educación* (Ministry of Education)

MINFAR   *Ministerio de las Fuerzas Armadas Revolucionarias* (Ministry of the Revolutionary Armed Forces)

MININT   *Ministerio del Interior* (Ministry of the Interior)

MSR   *Movimiento Socialista Revolucionaria* (Revolutionary Socialist Movement)

OFICODA   *Oficina de Control para la Distribución de Alimentos* (Office for Control of Food Distribution)

PCC	*Partido Comunista de Cuba* (Communist Party of Cuba)
PMR	*Policía Militar Revolucionaria* (Revolutionary Military Police)
UJC	*Unión de Jóvenes Comunistas* (Union of Young Communists)
UMAP	*Unidades Militares para Ayudar la Producción* (Military Units for Aid to Production)
UPC	*Unión de Pioneros de Cuba* (Union of Pioneers of Cuba)

Glossary

aguardiente	an alcoholic drink, in Cuba made from sugar cane
arroba	twenty-five pounds
bachillerato	five-year university-preparatory program in pre-revolutionary Cuba
barbudos	literally "the bearded ones," a term used for members of Castro's Rebel Army
batey	settlement for workers at a sugar mill or *central*
bolita	illegal lottery
caballería	land measure, approximately 33⅓ acres
casquitos	literally "little caps," a derogatory term of reference for men recruited by Batista to fight the Rebels
central	sugar-mill complex, including the adjoining company-owned farms
chucho	small settlement along a *central*'s rail system
círculo infantil	nursery school
colonia	sugar-cane farm; some were independently owned, others were company-owned but operated by tenant farmers
columnista	member of the Centennial Youth Column, an organization of youths from seventeen to twenty-seven who combined part-time study with full-time agricultural labor
comadre, compadre	terms used by a child's parents and godparents in addressing or referring to each other
consolidado	general term of reference for any consolidated enterprise
curandero (a)	native healer
guajiro (a)	Cuban peasant, sometimes used derogatorily to mean a rustic
guardia	the *Guardia Rural,* a branch of the national police stationed in rural areas in pre-revolutionary Cuba

gusano | literally "worm," used in Cuba to refer to anyone who does not support the Revolution, from passive opponents to active counterrevolutionaries

kilo | a *centavo*

machetero | cane-cutter

malanga | *arum sagitae folium*, a root vegetable favored by Cubans

medio | five *centavos*

peseta | one fifth of a *peso,* or 20 *centavos*

peso | Cuban currency maintained by the Castro government at the pre-1959 rate of 1 *peso* = 1 U.S. dollar until 1974, when the rate was changed to 1.25 *pesos* = 1 U.S. dollar

reparto | a suburb or subdivision of a city

santería | Afro-Cuban saint cult that combines Yoruban and Roman Catholic beliefs and traditions

santero | priest-practitioner of the *santería* cult

santo | saint; in *santería* the Spanish word also embodies the African concept of spirit (*orisha*)

solar | a low-rent multiple-family structure, usually one story high, with one or more rows of single rooms or small apartments opening onto a central patio

zafra | sugar-cane harvest, approximately six months between January and June

Selected Bibliography

BIBLIOGRAPHIC NOTE

In a study such as this, the most important source materials are, of course, the interviews from which the life stories are constructed. However, due to the special nature of the Cuba project and to the peculiarities of doing field work in a socialist system, secondary sources and supplementary field materials took on special importance. Since this latter group of materials is not cited in the bibliography, we want to mention those which were most important in helping us better understand the life stories and write footnotes to the texts. Among supplementary field materials we most relied on were: observations of the CDRs in five *repartos* and interviews with officers and members; a conference with officials and interviews with eleven judges of the People's Courts and reports on six observed trials; a pilot study of the *jardines infantiles* and interviews with the program's directors; interviews with officials of *Poder Local;* interviews with Armando Torres, who led the drive to eliminate organized prostitution in Cuba; and special studies of household budgets and material inventories. Finally, there were the apppoximately 12,000 pages of interview material from informants not included in the three volumes of this series; these interviews verified and elaborated on some of the information provided in the published life stories. All of the above-mentioned sources were of great value in providing details on the mechanics of daily life under Cuban socialism, which, as far as we know, are unavailable in published sources.

The following works from the appended selected bibliography have been of particular value to us. For historical background we relied most heavily on Hugh Thomas's *Cuba: The Pursuit of Freedom,* a study of the island from the English expedition in 1762 through the missile crisis of 1962, with heavy emphasis on the twentieth century. We consulted Philip Foner's two-volume study of Cuba from 1492 to 1895 (part of a projected multivolume series on Cuban-U.S. relations) for additional information on slavery, colonialism, and the War of Independence. Other sources of background information were: the classic study of the sugar and tobacco industries by Fernando Ortíz, one of Cuba's most famous sociologists; *Rural Cuba* (1950) by the North American sociologist Lowry Nelson; and Verena Martínez-Alier's study of Cuban women in the nineteenth century (1974). For understanding the terminology and explaining certain rituals and practices of the Afro-Cuban sects, the works of Lydia Cabrera and Romulo Lachatañere were especially helpful. A good general discussion of education and social-welfare policies in Cuba during the first three decades of this century can be found in *Problems of the New Cuba; Report of the Commission on Cuban Affairs* (1935).

The *Atlas Nacional de Cuba,* a magnificent work compiled by the Cuban and Soviet academies of sciences, was most useful to us, particularly as a source for changing place names. Included among its many maps are graphic summaries of some of the Revolution's major achievements. In 1971 its text was translated from the Spanish and reprinted (without maps) by the U.S. Department of Commerce, Joint Publications Research Service.

For information on the general direction of the Revolution's social and economic policies during the first decade we consulted the following: the speeches, writings, and published interviews of Ernesto Guevara, Minister of Industry during the early 1960s; the firsthand account of this period written by Edward Boorstein, then an economic advisor to the Cuban government; and Theodore Draper's *Castroism: Theory and Practice* for its discussion of the early attempts (under Guevara's direction) at industrialization. The Cuban Economic Research Project (*A Study on Cuba,* 1965) published a concise, yet quite detailed, study of the direction of economic development under the Revolution (including some economic statistics for the period 1959–64) in a larger work that includes an economic history of the colonial and republican periods.

For the period 1959–69, the work of Carmelo Mesa-Lago (including that with Roberto Hernández) and that of Lionel Martin (the *Guardian*'s Cuba correspondent) were invaluable for an understanding of Cuba's labor policies. Richard R. Fagen's study of the CDRs is the most comprehensive single English-language work on that organization for the period 1961–65. For additional and more recent information on the CDRs, as well as the People's Courts (and information on other mass organizations, such as unions) we are indebted to David K. Booth for sending us his excellent unpublished Ph.D. thesis (University of Surrey, 1973), which was based on field work carried out in Cuba in 1969.

In Bonachea and Valdés's *Cuba in Revolution,* Ricardo Leyva's article on health care and Valdés's article on education were especially helpful. Government publications acquired in Cuba in 1969–70—general information bulletins, statistical reports, texts of laws, for example—provided invaluable detail, particularly on education policy. Finally, and most important, were the speeches and writings of Fidel Castro, from 1953 (*History Will Absolve Me,* which contains a comprehensive statement of the Twenty-sixth of July Movement's original objectives) to 1976. Castro's speeches were a principal source of information to us on social and economic policies, for details on the implementation of laws and programs as well as on their successes and failures.

Because this series places great emphasis on daily life under the revolutionary system, we found especially helpful journalistic accounts which re-created the general atmosphere in Havana, and elsewhere in Cuba, during the first ten years and after. The most outstanding single work of this kind is *Castro's Cuba, Cuba's Fidel* by the photo-journalist Lee Lockwood. This very readable and informative book, which is based on Lockwood's lengthy interviews with Castro, serves as a good introduction to revolutionary Cuba. Ruby Hart Phillips, the *New York Times* correspondent in Cuba for almost thirty years, wrote two books describing changes in Havana during the two years after the Triumph. The first of these, *Cuba: Island of Paradox* (1959), an evocative account of the first weeks after the victory, was written before Ms. Phillips became a militant anti-Castroite. Three other notable journalistic treatments of life in Cuba in the mid- and late 1960s are Sutherland's *Youngest Revolution* (1969), Yglesias's *In the Fist of the Revolution* (1969), and Reckford's *Does Fidel Eat More than Your Father?* (1971). Overall, Sutherland's work is enthusiastically sympathetic, but it contains good, quite realistic appraisals of race relations and the women's movement during the Revolution's first eight years.

For the purpose of updating information in the life stories, the single most valuable source was the *Granma Weekly Review* (1971–76), an official compilation of each week's most important speeches and news stories, translated and reprinted from *Granma,* the official daily of the Communist Party. Cubanists who are interested in every nuance in the printed media that might indicate changes in policy or leadership will certainly prefer *Granma,* but the *Weekly Review* does contain the complete text of most major speeches, laws, and declarations, as well as articles on Cuban history (particularly on martyrs and revolutionary battles), coverage of international relations and visiting dignitaries, and sports news. The *Weekly Review* has the obvious disadvantage over the daily paper of being a collection of articles selected especially for foreign audiences, and the minor disadvantage of utilizing often stilted official translations.

BOOKS AND PAMPHLETS

Anuario Estadistico, Curso 1966–67. Havana: Ministry of Education, n.d.
Area Handbook for Cuba. Washington, D.C.: Government Printing Office, 1971.
Atlas Nacional de Cuba. Havana: Academy of Sciences of Cuba and Academy of Sciences of the U.S.S.R., 1970.
Bonachea, Rolando B., and Nelson P. Valdés, eds. *Cuba in Revolution.* New York: Anchor Books, 1972.
Boorstein, Edward. *The Economic Transformation of Cuba.* New York: Monthly Review Press, 1968.
Booth, David K. "Neighbourhood Committees and Popular Courts in the Social Transformation of Cuba." Unpublished Ph.D. thesis, University of Surrey, 1973.
Cabrera, Lydia. *El Monte.* Miami: Rema Press, 1968.
Castro, Fidel. *History Will Absolve Me.* Havana: Book Institute, 1967.
Los CDR en Granjas y Zonas Rurales. Havana: Dirección Nacional de los CDR, 1965.
Chapman, E. E. *A History of the Cuban Republic.* New York: Macmillan, 1927.
Constitución de la República de Cuba. Havana: Compañia Editora de Libros y Folletos, 1940.
Cuba: A Giant School. Havana: Ministry of Foreign Affairs, n.d.
Cuba: El Movimiento Educativo, 1967/68. Havana: Ministry of Education, 1968.
Cuban Economic Research Project. *A Study on Cuba.* Coral Gables: University of Miami Press, 1965.
Debray, Regis. *Revolution in the Revolution?* New York: Monthly Review Press, 1967.
Draper, Theodore. *Castroism: Theory and Practice.* New York: Praeger, 1965.
———. *Castro's Revolution: Myths and Realities.* New York: Praeger, 1962.
Fagen, Richard R. *The Transformation of Political Culture in Cuba.* Stanford, Calif.: Stanford University Press, 1969.
———, Richard A. Brody, and Thomas J. O'Leary. *Cubans in Exile.* Stanford, Calif.: Stanford University Press, 1968.
Ferguson, Erna. *Cuba.* New York: Alfred A. Knopf, 1946.
Foner, Philip S. *A History of Cuba and Its Relations with the United States,* vols. I (1492–1845) and II (1845–95). New York: International Publishers, 1962, 1963.
Fundamental Law of Cuba, 1959. Washington D.C.: Pan American Union, 1959.
La Educación en los Cien Años de Lucha. Havana: Book Institute, 1968.
García Alonso, Aida. *Manuela, la Mexicana.* Havana: Casa de las Americas, 1968.

Gillette, Arthur. *Cuba's Educational Revolution*. London: Fabian Research Series 302, June, 1972.

Halperin, Maurice. *The Rise and Decline of Fidel Castro*. Berkeley, Calif.: University of California Press, 1972.

Horowitz, Irving Louis, ed. *Cuban Communism*. New Brunswick, N.J.: Transaction Books, 1970.

Jahn, Jahnheinz. *Muntu: An Outline of the New African Culture*. New York: Grove Press, 1961.

Karol, K. S. *Guerrillas in Power*. New York: Hill and Wang, 1970.

Kenner, Martin, and James Petras, eds. *Fidel Castro Speaks*. New York: Grove Press, 1969.

Lachatañere, Romulo. *Manual de Santería*. Havana: Editorial Caribe, 1942.

Leiner, Marvin, with Robert Ubell. *Children Are the Revolution: Day Care in Cuba*. New York: Viking Press, 1974.

Ley de Reforma Agraria. Havana, 1959.

Lockwood, Lee. *Castro's Cuba, Cuba's Fidel*. New York: Vintage, 1969.

MacGaffey, Wyatt, and Clifford R. Barnett. *Cuba: Its People, Its Society, Its Culture*. New Haven: HRAF, 1962.

Makarenko, Anton Semenovich. *The Collective Family: A Handbook for Russian Parents* (New York: Anchor Books, 1967).

Martínez-Alier, Verena. *Marriage, Class and Colour in Nineteenth Century Cuba*. Cambridge: Cambridge University Press, 1974.

Matthews, Herbert L. *The Cuban Story*. New York: Braziller, 1961.

———. *Fidel Castro*. New York: Simon and Schuster, 1969.

Memorias de CDR, 1962. Havana: Dirección Nacional de los CDR, 1963.

Memorias de CDR, 1963. Havana: Dirección Nacional de los CDR, 1964.

Mesa-Lago, Carmelo. *Cuba in the Seventies*. Albuquerque: University of New Mexico Press, 1974.

———. *The Labor Force, Employment, Unemployment and Underemployment in Cuba: 1899–1970*. Beverly Hills, Calif.: Sage Publications, International Studies Series, 1972.

———. *The Labor Sector and Socialist Distribution in Cuba*. New York: Praeger, 1968.

———, ed. *Revolutionary Change in Cuba*. Pittsburgh: University of Pittsburgh Press, 1971.

Nelson, Lowry. *Cuba: The Measure of a Revolution*. Minneapolis: University of Minnesota Press, 1972.

———. *Rural Cuba*. Minneapolis: University of Minnesota Press, 1950.

La Ofensiva Revolucionaria: Asamblea de Administradores Populares. Havana: Dirección Nacional de los CDR, 1968.

Ortíz, Fernando. *Cuban Counterpoint: Tobacco and Sugar*. New York: Alfred A. Knopf, 1947.

Phillips, Ruby Hart. *Cuba: Island of Paradox*. New York: MacDowell, Obolensky, 1959.

———. *The Cuban Dilemma*. New York: Ivan Obolensky, 1962.

Plan de la Escuela Semi-internado, El Cangre. Havana: Ministry of Education, n.d.

Problems of the New Cuba; Report of the Commission on Cuban Affairs. New York: Foreign Policy Association, 1935.

Randall, Margaret. *Mujeres en la Revolución: Conversa con Mujeres Cubanas*. Mexico, D.F.: Siglo Veintiuno Editores, 1972.

Reckford, Barry. *Does Fidel Eat More than Your Father?* New York: Praeger, 1971.

Semi-internado de Primaria, Valle del Perú. Havana: Ministry of Education, 1968.

Silverman, Bertram, ed. *Man and Socialism*. New York: Atheneum, 1971.

Suárez, Andrés. *Cuba: Castroism and Communism, 1959–1966.* Cambridge, Mass.: MIT Press, 1967.
Sucklicki, Jaime. *University Students and Revolution in Cuba, 1920–1968.* Coral Gables: University of Miami Press, 1969.
Superación y Recreación para Maestros de Montaña en Varadero. Havana: Ministry of Education, 1968.
Sutherland, Elizabeth. *The Youngest Revolution.* New York: Dial Press, 1969.
Taber, Robert. *M-26: The Biography of a Revolution.* New York: Lyle Stuart, 1961.
Thomas, Hugh. *Cuba: The Pursuit of Freedom.* New York: Harper and Row, 1971.
Valdés, Nelson P. *A Bibliography on Cuban Women in the Twentieth Century* (reprinted from *Cuban Studies Newsletter,* June, 1974).
Yglesias, José. *In the Fist of the Revolution.* New York: Vintage, 1969.
Zeitlin, Maurice. *Revolutionary Politics and the Urban Working Class.* Princeton: Princeton University Press, 1967.

ARTICLES

Bender, Lynn Darrell. "Cuba, the United States, and Sugar," *Caribbean Studies,* Apr., 1974.
Berman, Jesse. "The Cuban Popular Tribunals," *Columbia Law Review,* Dec., 1969.
Butterworth, Douglas. "Grass-Roots Political Organization in Cuba: A Case of the Committees for the Defense of the Revolution," in Wayne A. Cornelius and Felicity Trueblood, eds., *Latin American Urban Research: Anthropological Perspectives on Latin American Urbanization,* vol. IV (Beverly Hills, Calif.: Sage Publications, 1974).
Dumont, René. "The Militarization of Fidelismo," *Dissent,* Sept.–Oct., 1970.
FitzGerald, Frances. "A Reporter at Large (Cuba)," *New Yorker,* Feb. 18, 1974.
Fox, Geoffrey E. "Cuban Workers in Exile," *Transaction,* Sept., 1971.
Leiner, Marvin. "Cuba's Schools, Ten Years Later," *Saturday Review,* Oct. 17, 1970.
Martin, Lionel. A series of articles on the Vanguard Worker program and union reorganization, *Guardian,* May 10–July 5, 1969.
Mesa-Lago, Carmelo. "Availability and Reliability of Statistics in Socialist Cuba," *Latin-American Research Review,* Spring and Summer, 1969.
———. "Economic Significance of Unpaid Labor in Socialist Cuba," *Industrial and Labor Relations Review,* Apr., 1969.
Morgan, Ted. "Cuba," *New York Times Magazine,* Dec. 1, 1974.
Nicholson, Joe, Jr. "Inside Cuba," *Harpers,* Apr., 1973.
Ward, Fred. "Inside Cuba Today," *National Geographic,* Jan., 1977.
Yglesias, José. "Cuba Report: Their Hippies and Their Squares," *New York Times Magazine,* Jan. 12, 1969.

JOURNALS AND PERIODICALS

Bohemia, 1968–70.
Centro de Estudios del Folklore del TNC, 1961.
Cuba Internacional, 1969–70.
Cuba Review, 1974–76 (*Cuba Resource Center Newsletter,* 1972–73).
Cuban Studies Newsletter, 1972–75.
Ediciones CDR, 1969–70.
Etnología y Folklore, 1966–68.
Granma, 1969–70.
Granma Weekly Review, 1971–76.
Obra, 1961.